PARASYTE 3

HITOSHI IWAAKI

TRANSLATED AND ADAPTED BY ANDREW CUNNINGHAM
FOLTZ DESIGN

EL
EY

BALLANTINE BOOKS · NEW YORK

A Del Rey Manga/Kodansha Trade Paperback Original

Parasyte volume 3 copyright © 2003 by Hitoshi Iwaaki
English translation copyright © 2008 by Hitoshi Iwaaki

Published in the United States by Del Rey Books, an imprint of The Random House Publishing Group, a division of Random House, Inc., New York.

DEL REY is a registered trademark and the Del Rey colophon is a trademark of Random House, Inc.

Publication rights arranged through Kodansha Ltd.

First published in Japan in 2003 by Kodansha Ltd., Tokyo

ISBN 978-0-345-49825-0

Printed in the United States of America

www.delreymanga.com

9 8 7 6 5 4 3 2 1

Translator/adapter: Andrew Cunningham
Lettering: Foltz Design

HONORIFICS EXPLAINED

Throughout the Del Rey Manga books, you will find Japanese honorifics left intact in the translations. For those not familiar with how the Japanese use honorifics and, more important, how they differ from American honorifics, we present this brief overview.

Politeness has always been a critical facet of Japanese culture. Ever since the feudal era, when Japan was a highly stratified society, use of honorifics—which can be defined as polite speech that indicates relationship or status—has played an essential role in the Japanese language. When addressing someone in Japanese, an honorific usually takes the form of a suffix attached to one's name (example: "Asuna-san"), is used as a title at the end of one's name, or appears in place of the name itself (example: "Negi-sensei" or simply "Sensei!").

Honorifics can be expressions of respect or endearment. In the context of manga and anime, honorifics give insight into the nature of the relationship between characters. Many English translations leave out these important honorifics and therefore distort the feel of the original Japanese. Because Japanese honorifics contain nuances that English honorifics lack, it is our policy at Del Rey not to translate them. Here, instead, is a guide to some of the honorifics you may encounter in Del Rey Manga.

-san: This is the most common honorific and is equivalent to Mr., Miss, Ms., or Mrs. It is the all-purpose honorific and can be used in any situation where politeness is required.

-sama: This is one level higher than "-san" and is used to confer great respect.

-dono: This comes from the word "tono," which means "lord." It is an even higher level than "-sama" and confers utmost respect.

-kun: This suffix is used at the end of boys' names to express familiarity or endearment. It is also sometimes used by men among friends, or when addressing someone younger or of a lower station.

-chan: This is used to express endearment, mostly toward girls. It is also used for little boys, pets, and even among lovers. It gives a sense of childish cuteness.

Bozu: This is an informal way to refer to a boy, similar to the English terms "kid" and "squirt."

**Sempai/
Senpai:** This title suggests that the addressee is one's senior in a group or organization. It is most often used in a school setting, where underclassmen refer to their upperclassmen as "sempai." It can also be used in the workplace, such as when a newer employee addresses an employee who has seniority in the company.

Kohai: This is the opposite of "-sempai," and is used toward underclassmen in school or newcomers in the workplace. It connotes that the addressee is of a lower station.

Sensei: Literally meaning "one who has come before," this title is used for teachers, doctors, or masters of any profession or art.

-[blank]: This is usually forgotten in these lists, but it is perhaps the most significant difference between Japanese and English. The lack of honorific means that the speaker has permission to address the person in a very intimate way. Usually, only family, spouses, or very close friends have this kind of permission. Known as *yobisute*, it can be gratifying when someone who has earned the intimacy starts to call one by one's name without an honorific. But when that intimacy hasn't been earned, it can be very insulting.

PARASYTE 3

HITOSHI IWAAKI

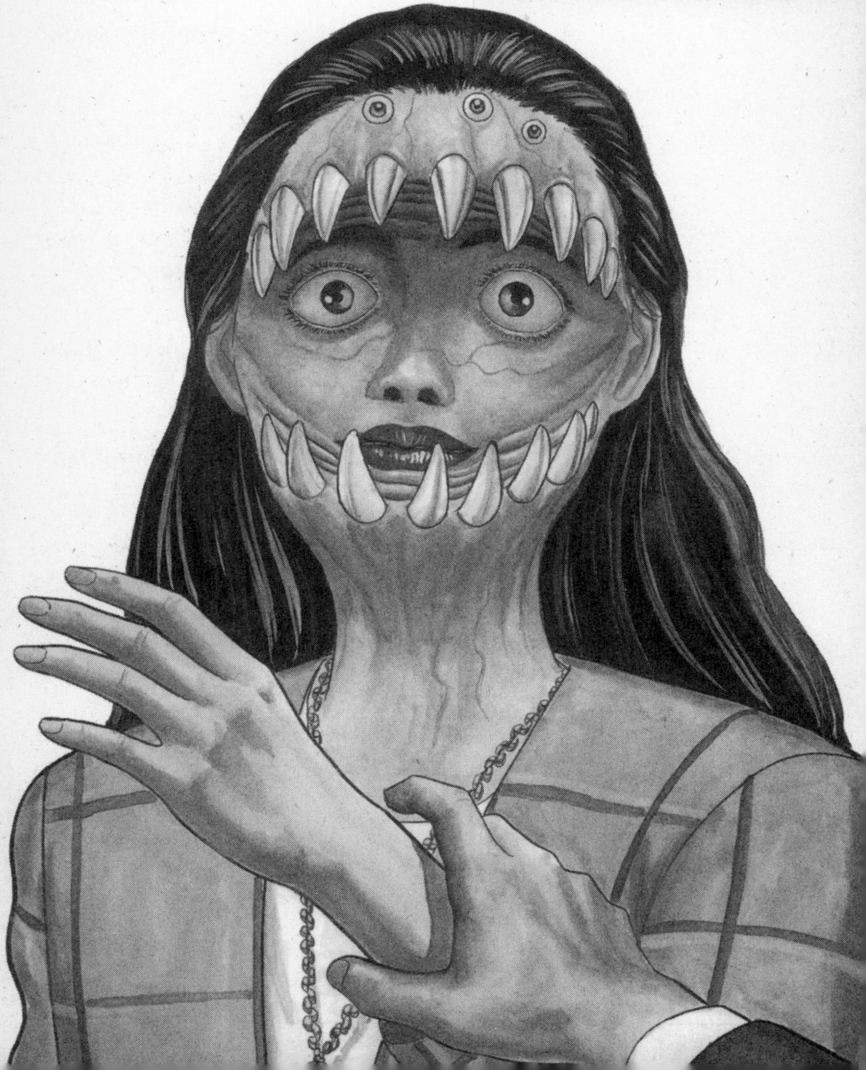

CONTENTS

CHAPTER 18: HUMAN   3

CHAPTER 19: SHIMADA HIDEO   39

CHAPTER 20: SIGNS   75

CHAPTER 21: OBSERVATION   107

CHAPTER 22: FISSURE   143

CHAPTER 23: CONFUSION AND SLAUGHTER   179

CHAPTER 24: ONE BLOW   215

CHAPTER 25: RIPPLES   253

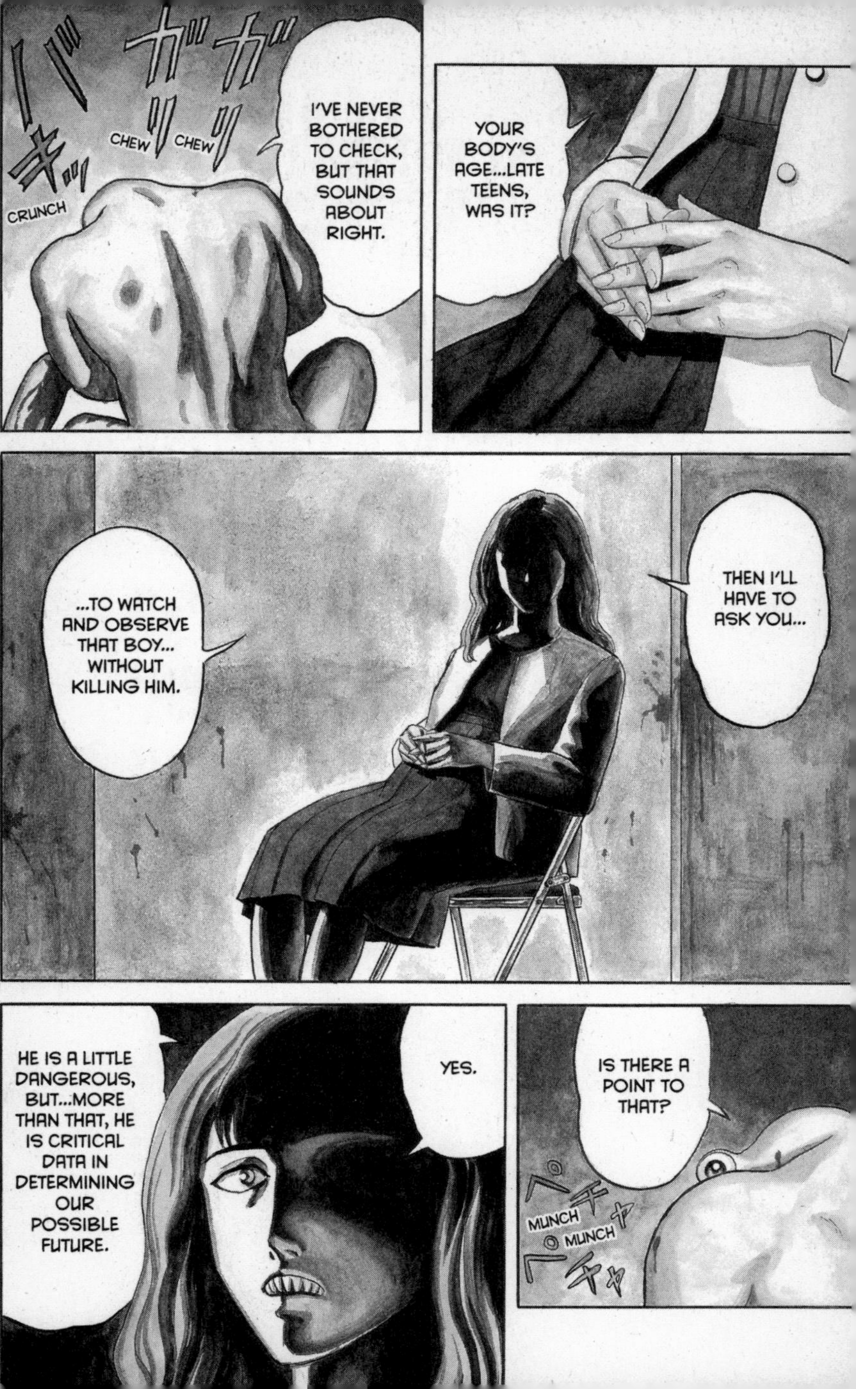
YOUR BODY'S AGE...LATE TEENS, WAS IT?
I'VE NEVER BOTHERED TO CHECK, BUT THAT SOUNDS ABOUT RIGHT.
CHEW
CHEW
CRUNCH
THEN I'LL HAVE TO ASK YOU...
...TO WATCH AND OBSERVE THAT BOY... WITHOUT KILLING HIM.
IS THERE A POINT TO THAT?
MUNCH
MUNCH
YES.
HE IS A LITTLE DANGEROUS, BUT...MORE THAN THAT, HE IS CRITICAL DATA IN DETERMINING OUR POSSIBLE FUTURE.

CHAPTER 18: HUMAN

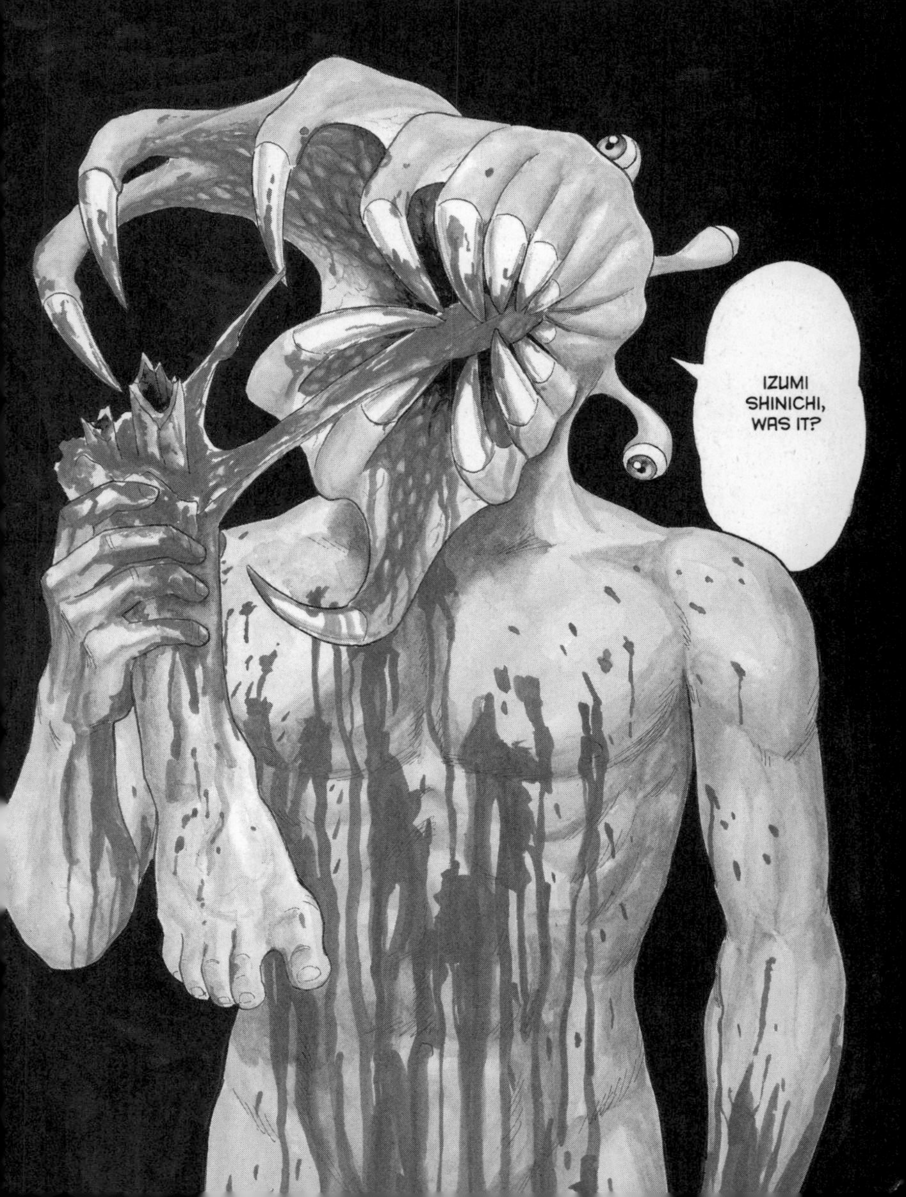
IZUMI SHINICHI, WAS IT?

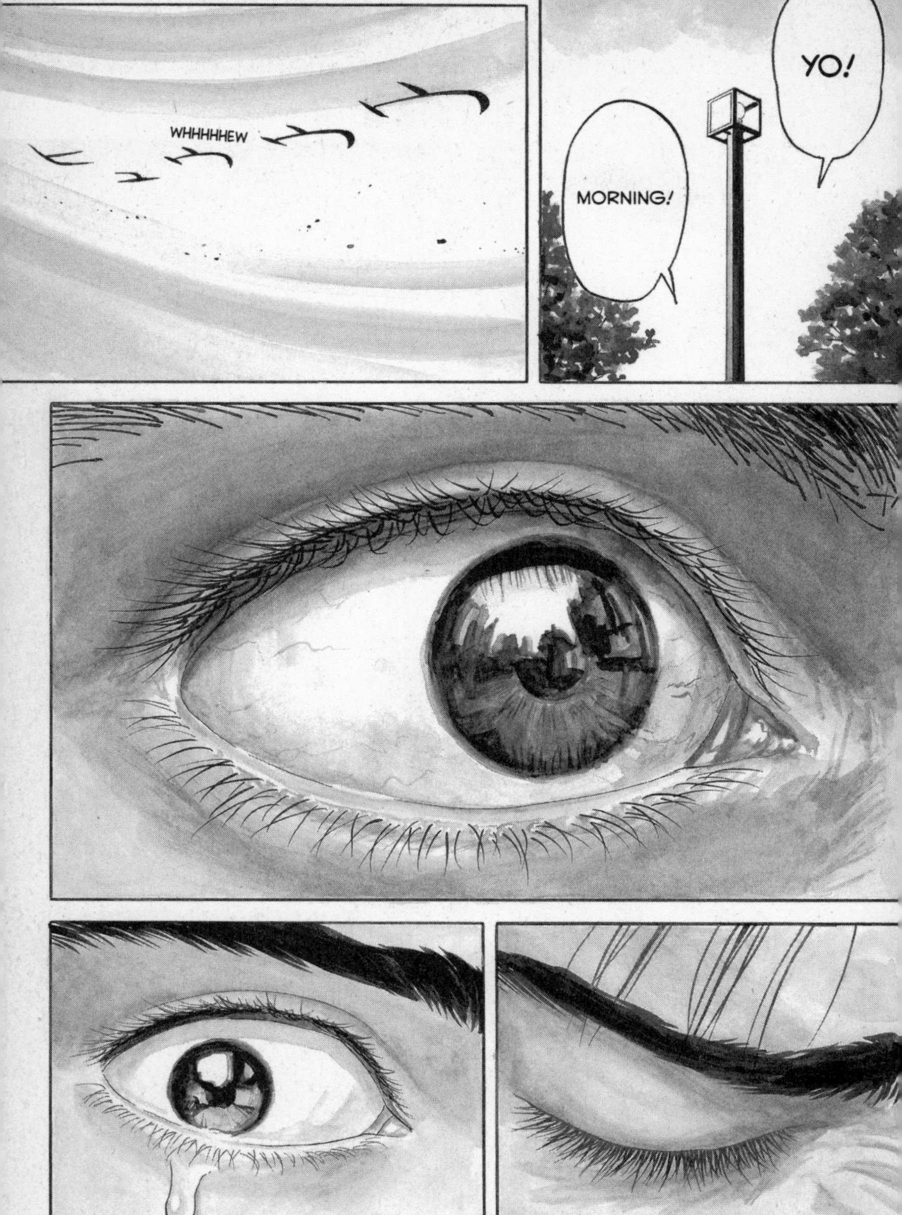
YO!
MORNING!
WHHHHHEW

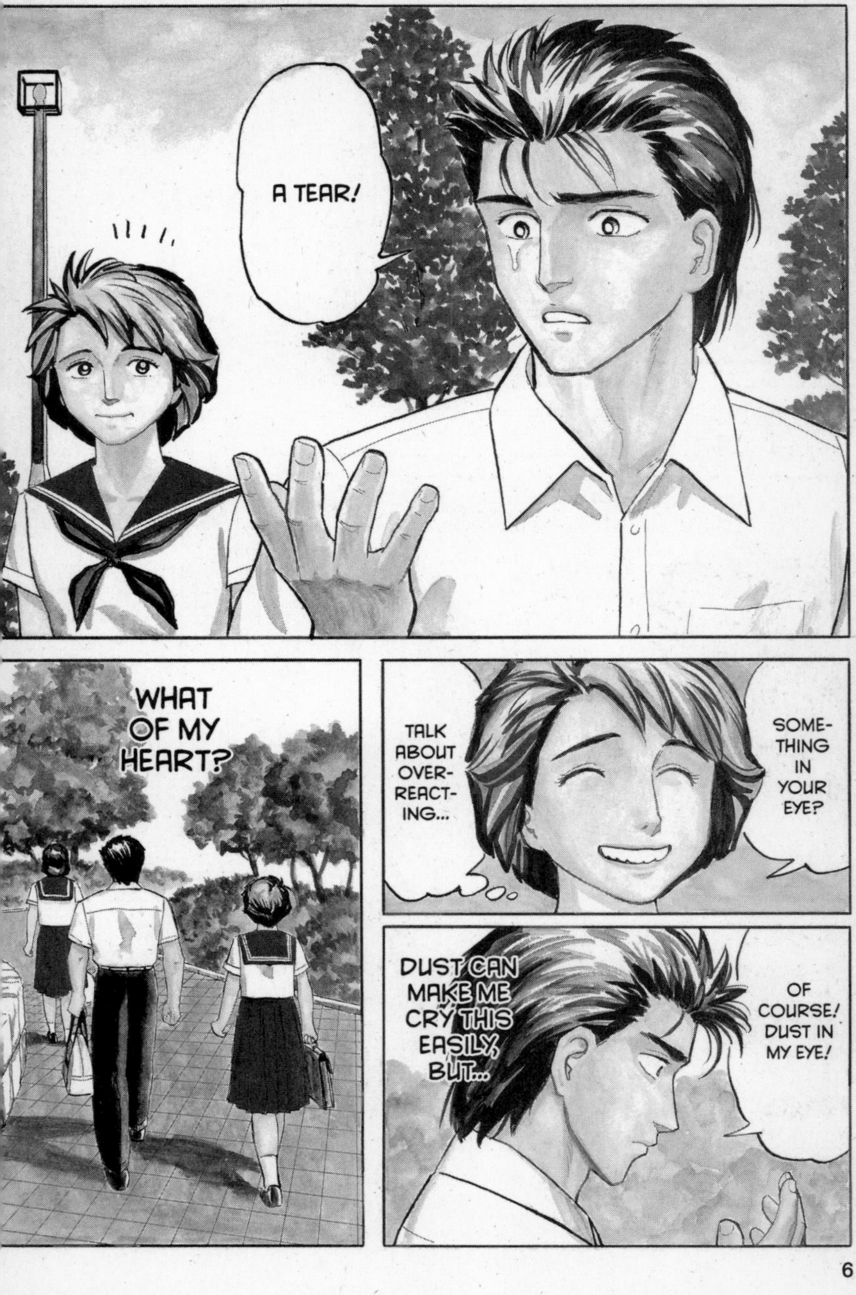
A TEAR!
SOME-THING IN YOUR EYE?
TALK ABOUT OVER-REACT-ING...
OF COURSE! DUST IN MY EYE!
DUST CAN MAKE ME CRY THIS EASILY, BUT...
WHAT OF MY HEART?

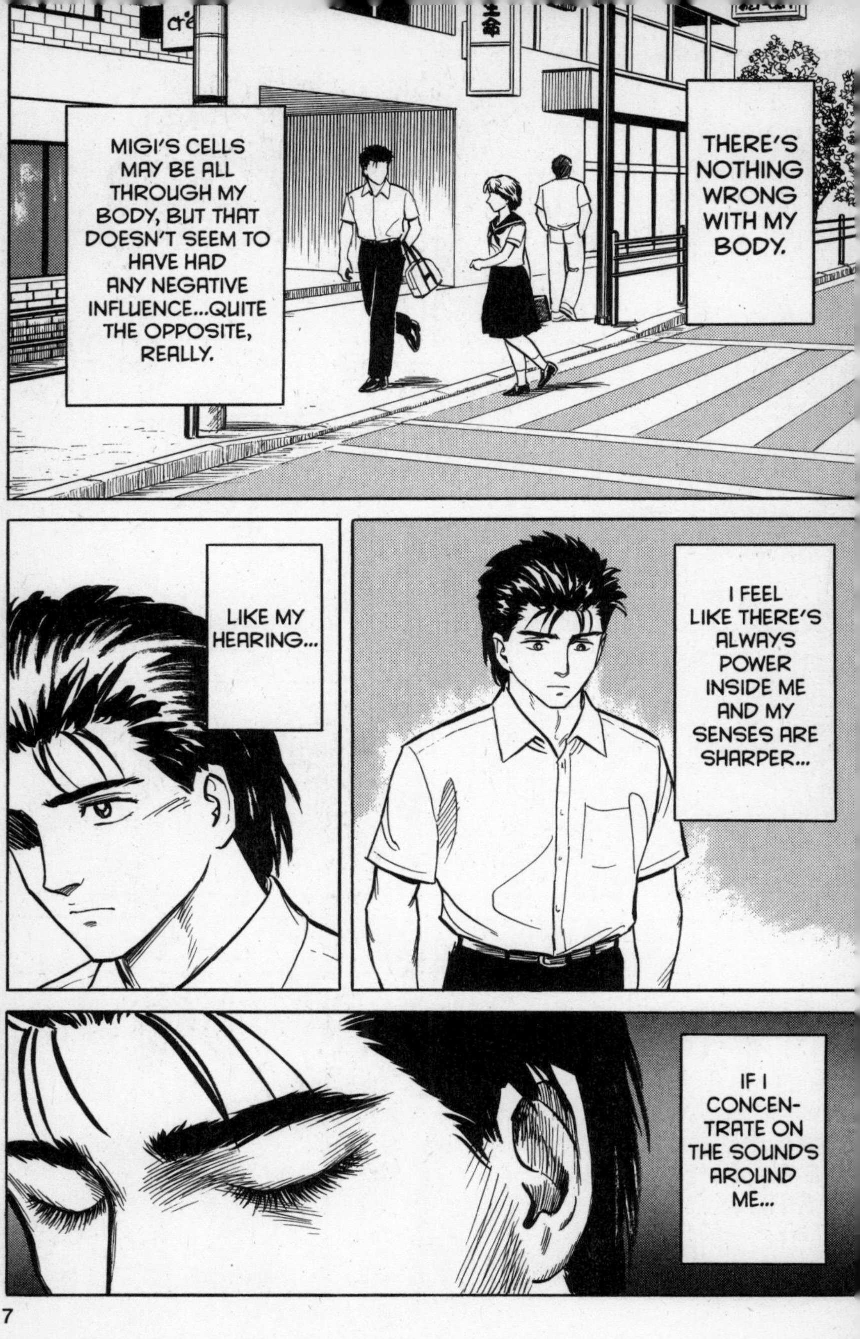
THERE'S NOTHING WRONG WITH MY BODY.
MIGI'S CELLS MAY BE ALL THROUGH MY BODY, BUT THAT DOESN'T SEEM TO HAVE HAD ANY NEGATIVE INFLUENCE...QUITE THE OPPOSITE, REALLY.
I FEEL LIKE THERE'S ALWAYS POWER INSIDE ME AND MY SENSES ARE SHARPER...
LIKE MY HEARING...
IF I CONCEN-TRATE ON THE SOUNDS AROUND ME...

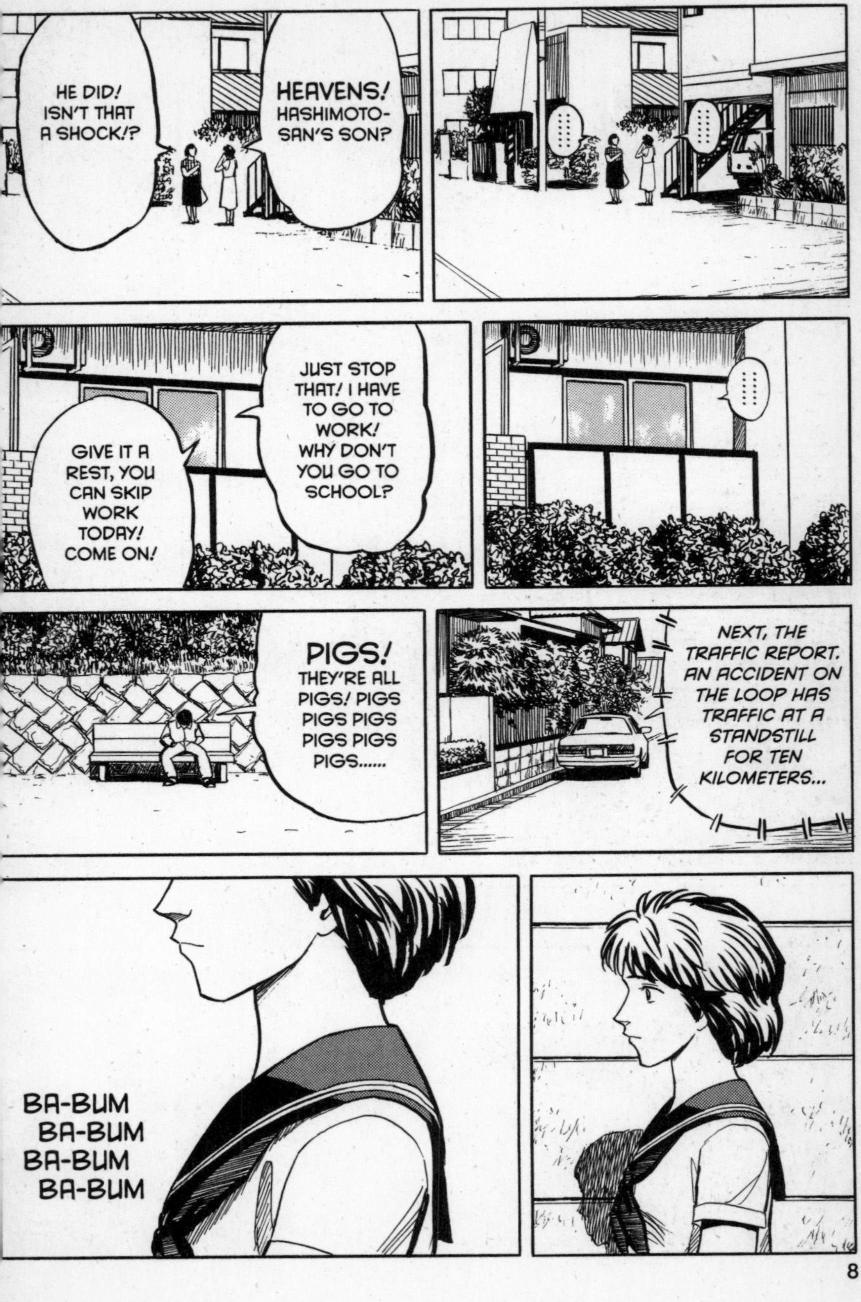
......
......
HEAVENS! HASHIMOTO-SAN'S SON?
HE DID! ISN'T THAT A SHOCK!?
......
JUST STOP THAT! I HAVE TO GO TO WORK! WHY DON'T YOU GO TO SCHOOL?
GIVE IT A REST, YOU CAN SKIP WORK TODAY! COME ON!
NEXT, THE TRAFFIC REPORT. AN ACCIDENT ON THE LOOP HAS TRAFFIC AT A STANDSTILL FOR TEN KILOMETERS...
PIGS! THEY'RE ALL PIGS! PIGS PIGS PIGS PIGS PIGS PIGS......
BA-BUM BA-BUM BA-BUM BA-BUM

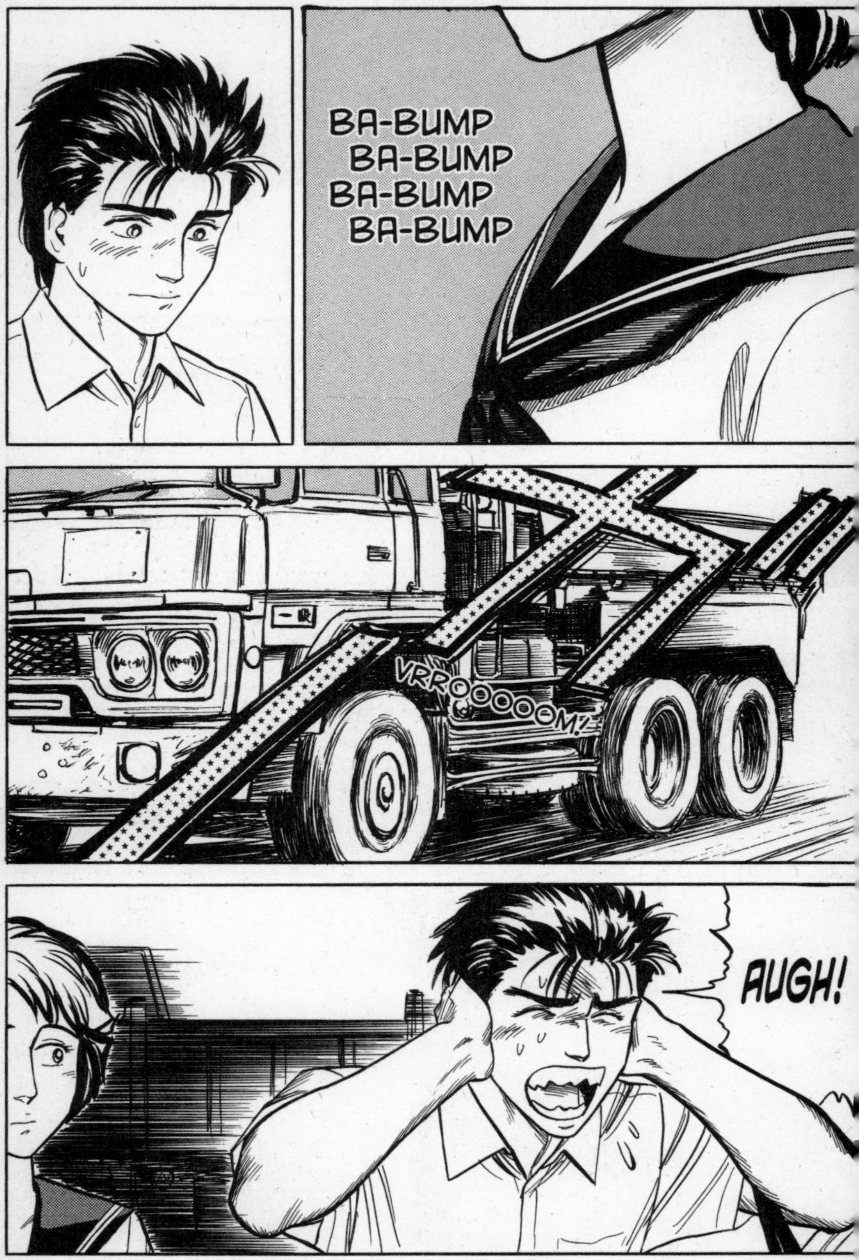
BA-BUMP
BA-BUMP
BA-BUMP
BA-BUMP
VRROOOOOOM!
AUGH!

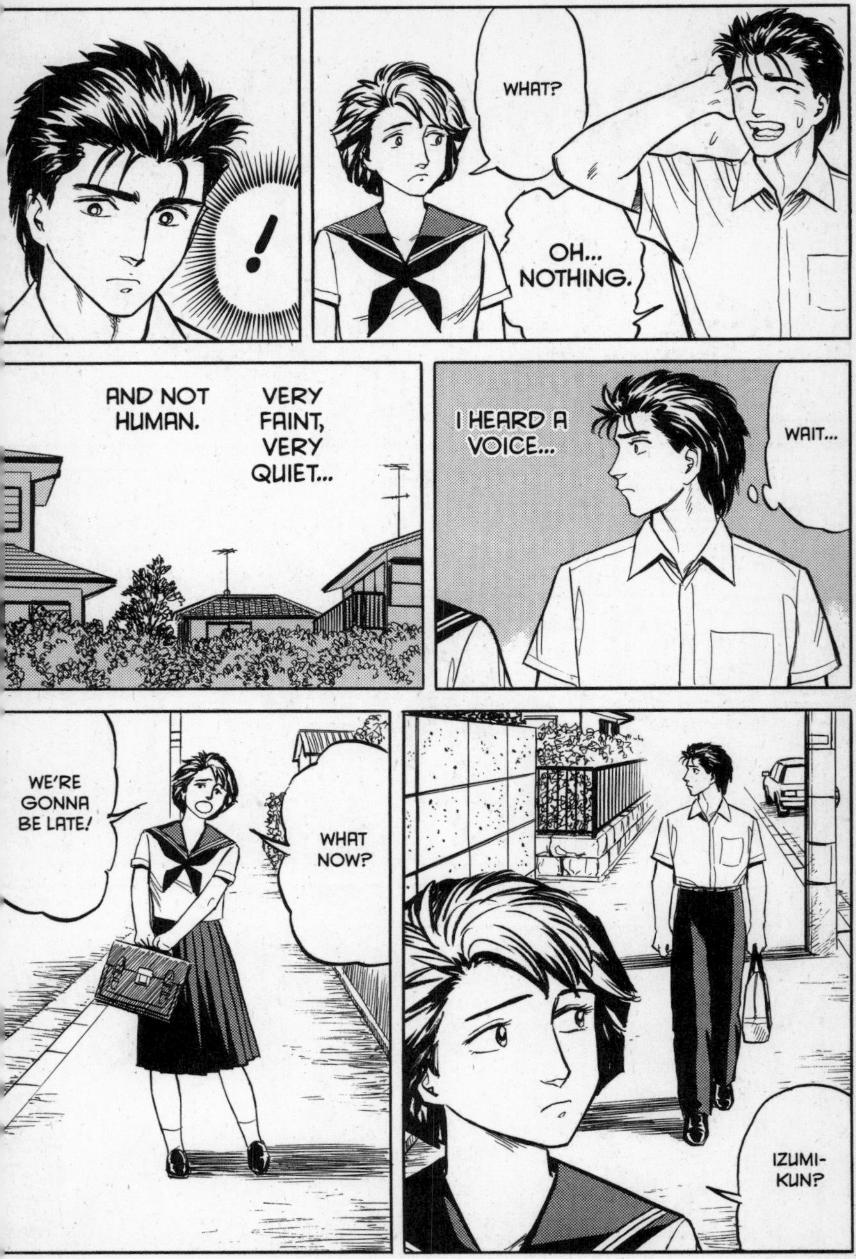
WHAT?
OH... NOTHING.
!
WAIT...
I HEARD A VOICE...
VERY FAINT, VERY QUIET...
AND NOT HUMAN.
IZUMI-KUN?
WHAT NOW?
WE'RE GONNA BE LATE!

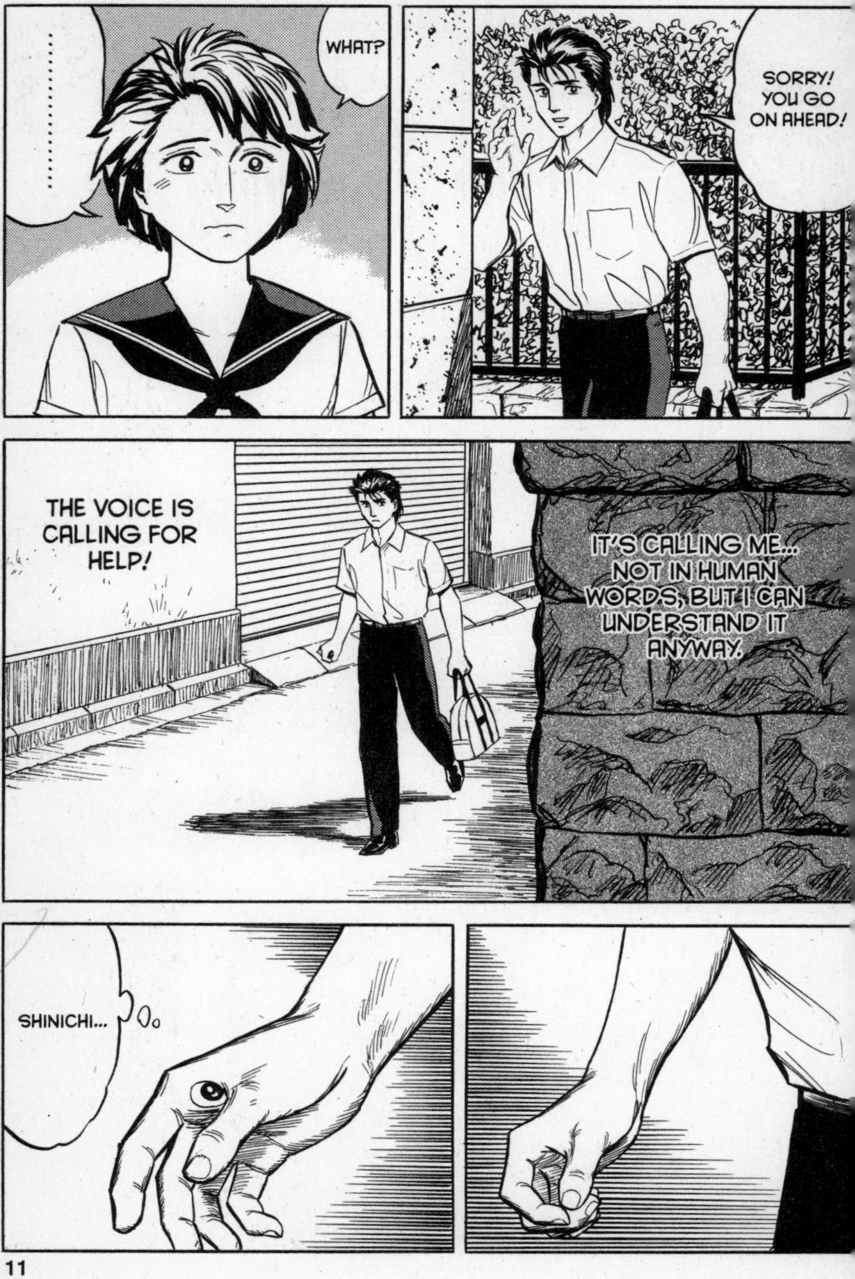
SORRY! YOU GO ON AHEAD!
WHAT?
....
IT'S CALLING ME... NOT IN HUMAN WORDS, BUT I CAN UNDERSTAND IT ANYWAY.
THE VOICE IS CALLING FOR HELP!
SHINICHI...

SHINICHI...

I'M SURE IT WAS AROUND HERE...

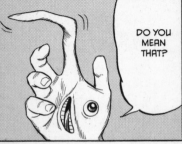

DO YOU MEAN THAT?

YEAH... I GUESS I DID.

!

12

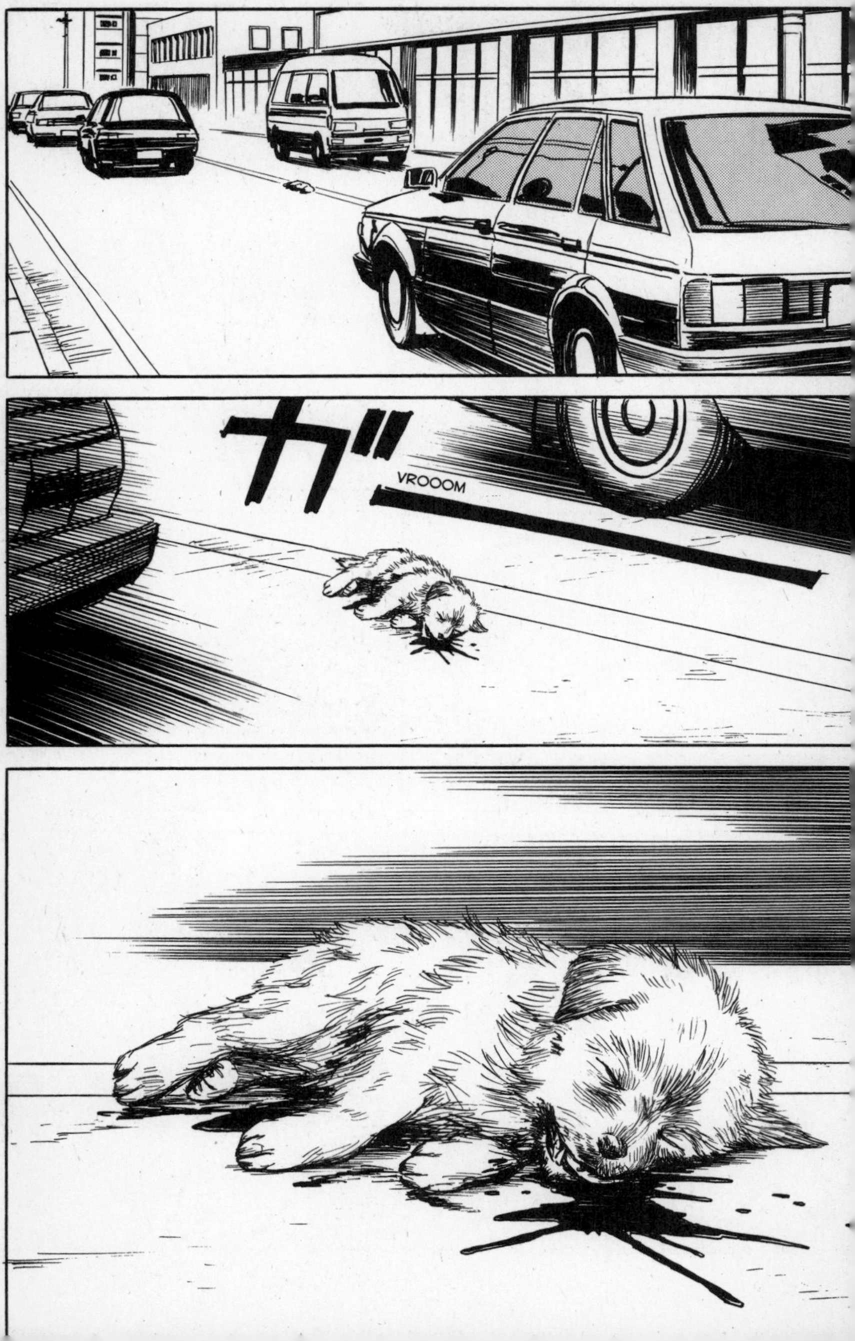
ガ
VROOOM

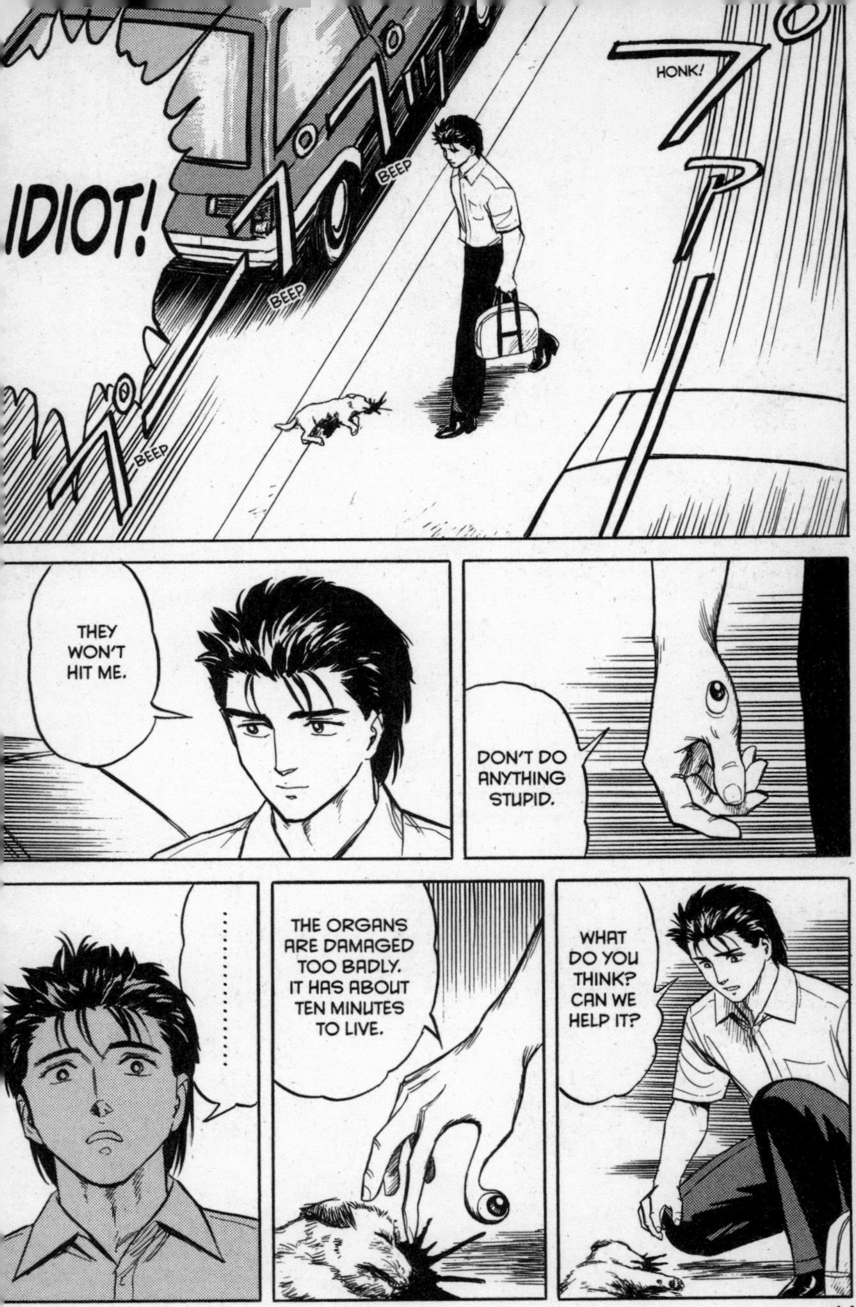
HONK!
IDIOT!
BEEP
BEEP
BEEP
DON'T DO ANYTHING STUPID.
THEY WON'T HIT ME.
WHAT DO YOU THINK? CAN WE HELP IT?
THE ORGANS ARE DAMAGED TOO BADLY. IT HAS ABOUT TEN MINUTES TO LIVE.
......

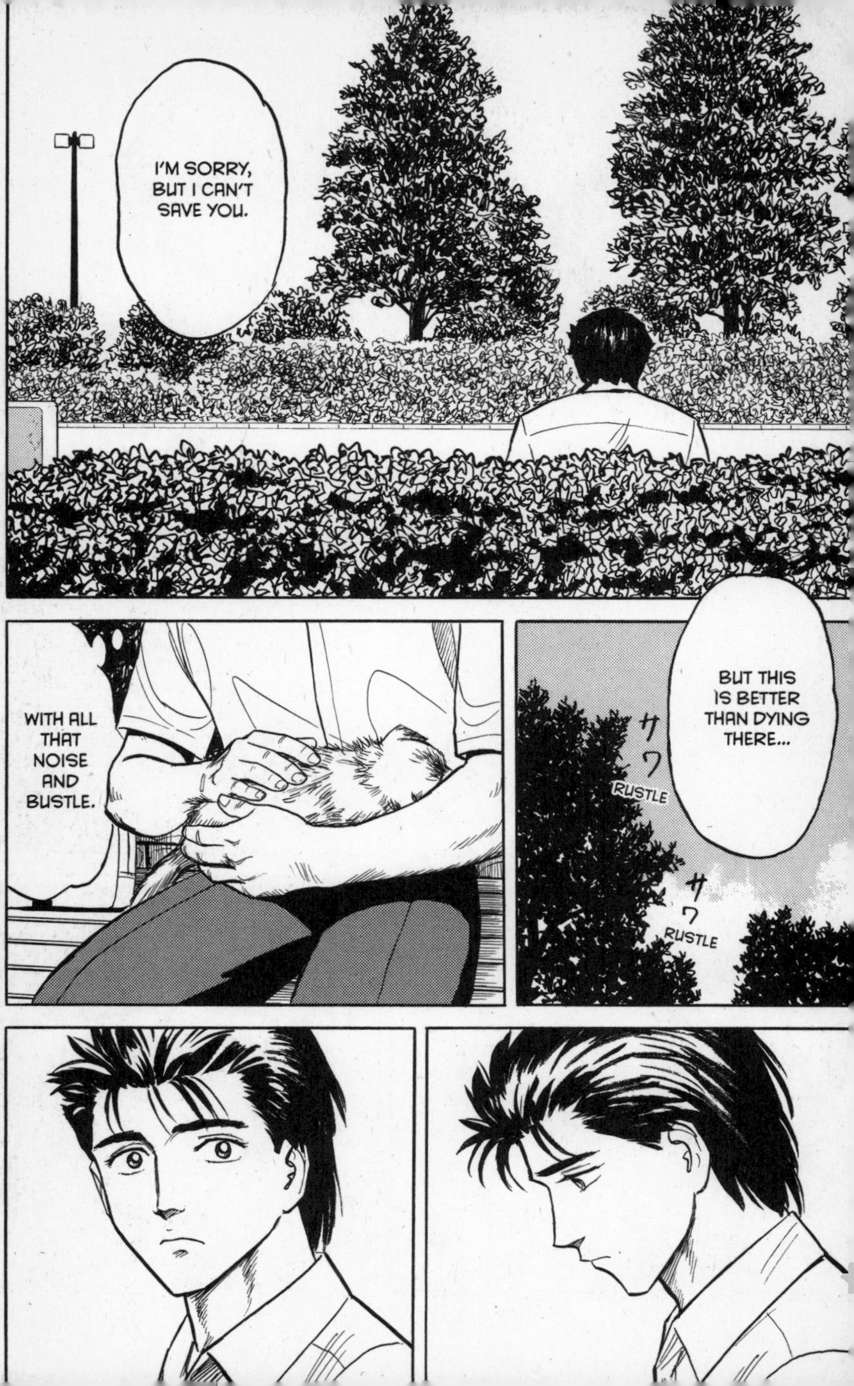
I'M SORRY, BUT I CAN'T SAVE YOU.
BUT THIS IS BETTER THAN DYING THERE...
サワ
RUSTLE
サワ
RUSTLE
WITH ALL THAT NOISE AND BUSTLE.

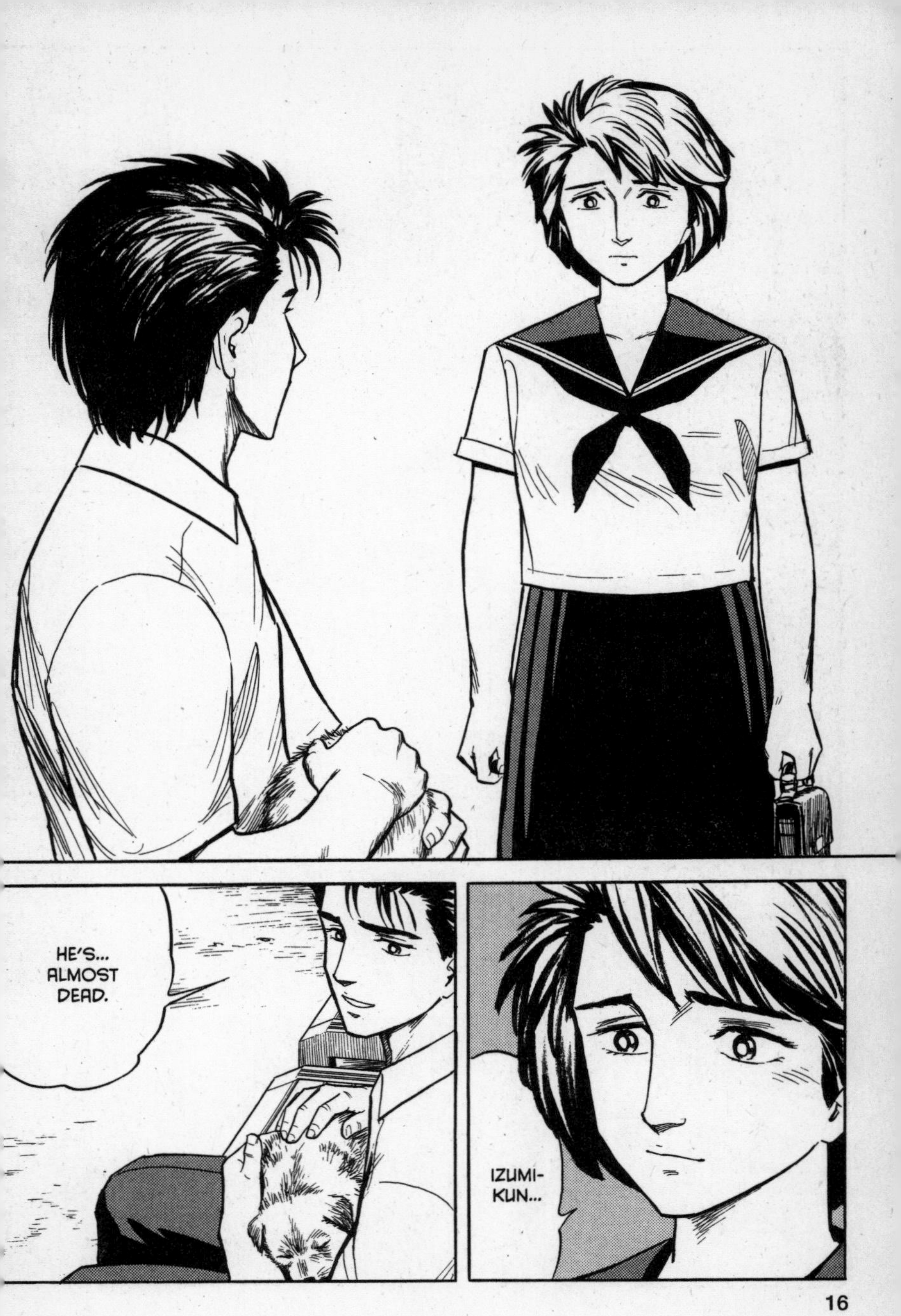
IZUMI-KUN...
HE'S... ALMOST DEAD.

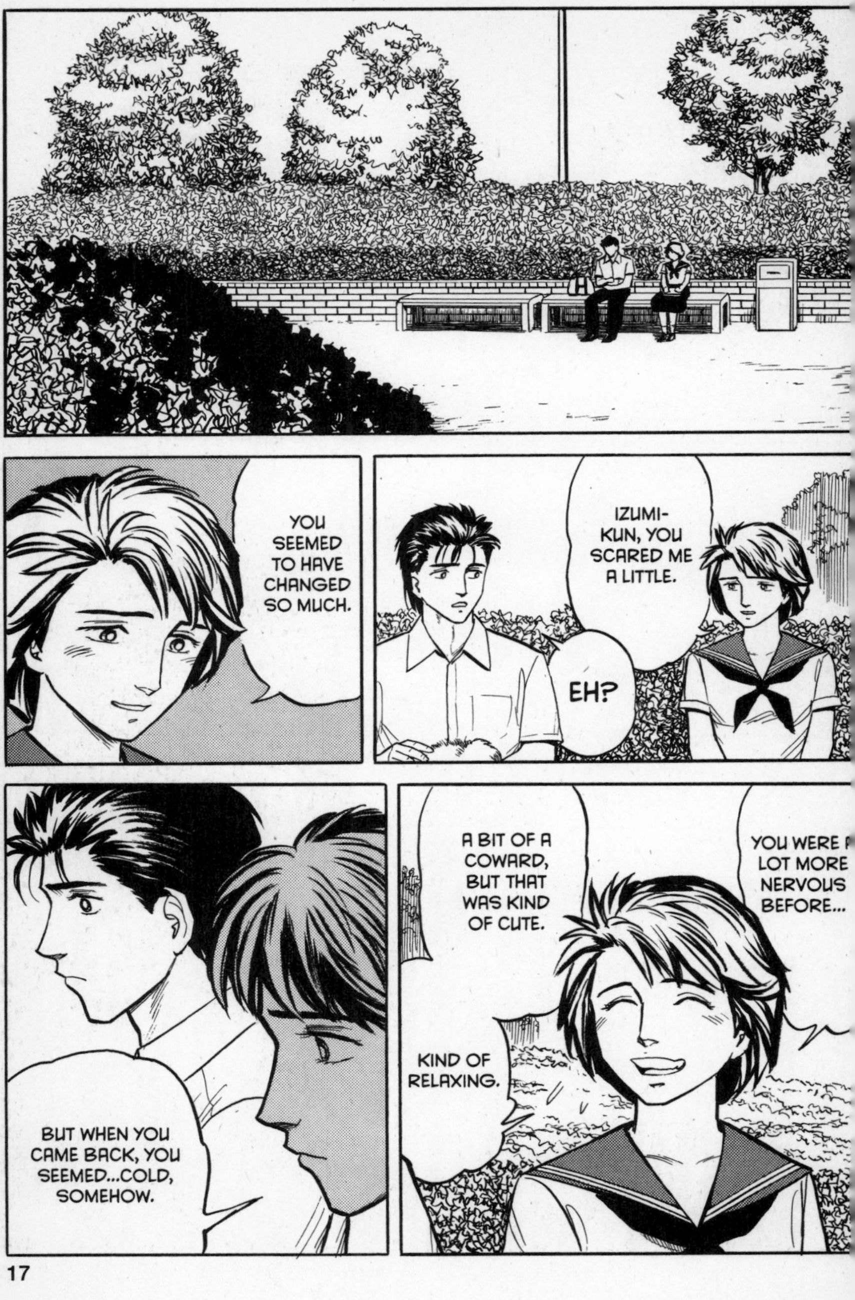
IZUMI-KUN, YOU SCARED ME A LITTLE.
EH?
YOU SEEMED TO HAVE CHANGED SO MUCH.
YOU WERE LOT MORE NERVOUS BEFORE...
A BIT OF A COWARD, BUT THAT WAS KIND OF CUTE.
KIND OF RELAXING.
BUT WHEN YOU CAME BACK, YOU SEEMED...COLD, SOMEHOW.

EH?

IT DIED.

BUT I GUESS IT WAS JUST MY IMAGINATION.

・・・・・・・・

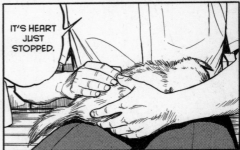

IT'S HEART JUST STOPPED.

LET'S GO... WE'LL BE LATE.

18

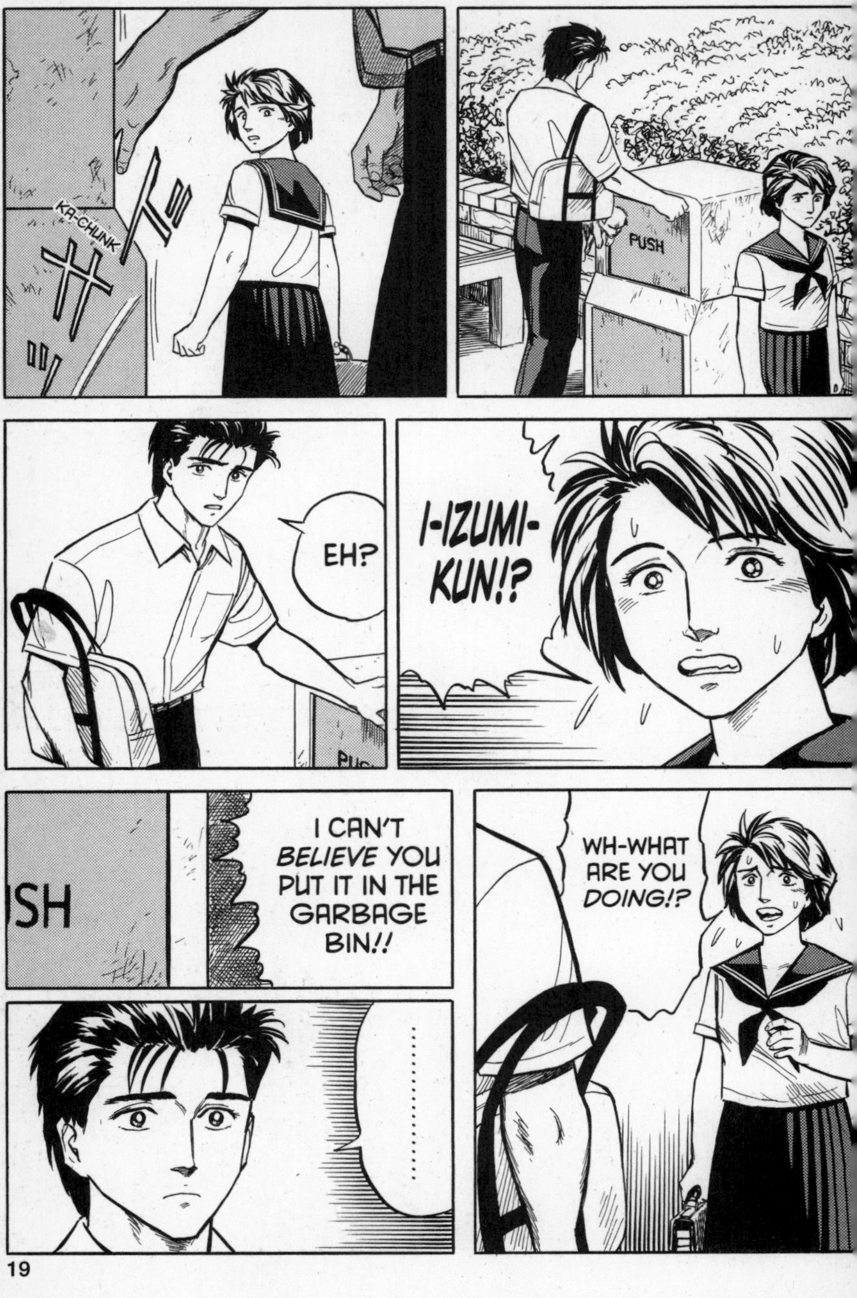
PUSH
KA-CHUNK
I-IZUMI-KUN!?
EH?
WH-WHAT ARE YOU DOING!?
I CAN'T BELIEVE YOU PUT IT IN THE GARBAGE BIN!!
......

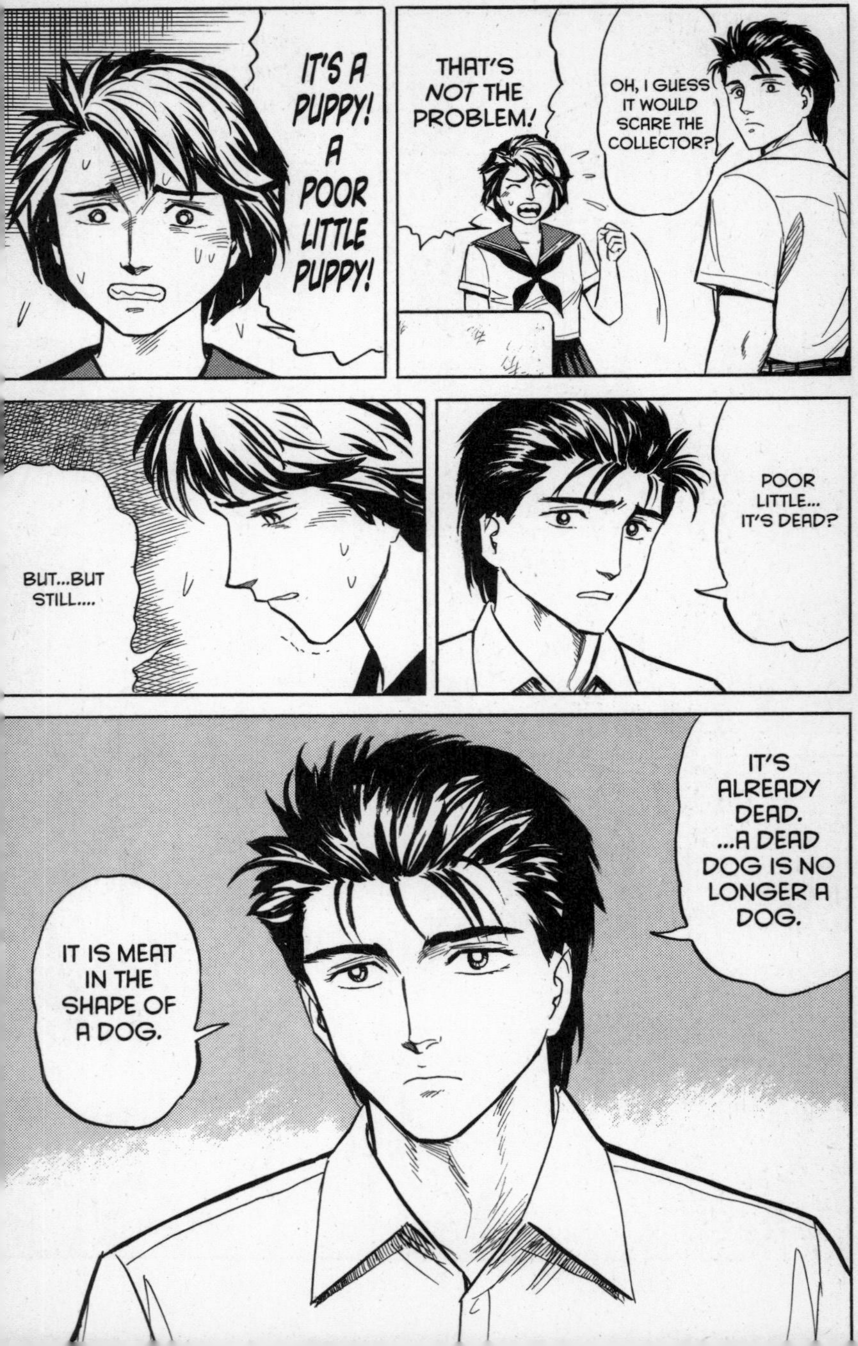

OH, I GUESS IT WOULD SCARE THE COLLECTOR?
THAT'S *NOT* THE PROBLEM!
IT'S A PUPPY! A POOR LITTLE PUPPY!
POOR LITTLE... IT'S DEAD?
BUT...BUT STILL....
IT'S ALREADY DEAD. ...A DEAD DOG IS NO LONGER A DOG.
IT IS MEAT IN THE SHAPE OF A DOG.

...NO.

THAT'S WRONG.

YOU'RE WRONG.

YOU'RE NOT THE IZUMI-KUN I...

MURANO...

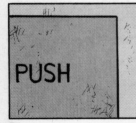
PUSH

WRONG?

H-HEY!

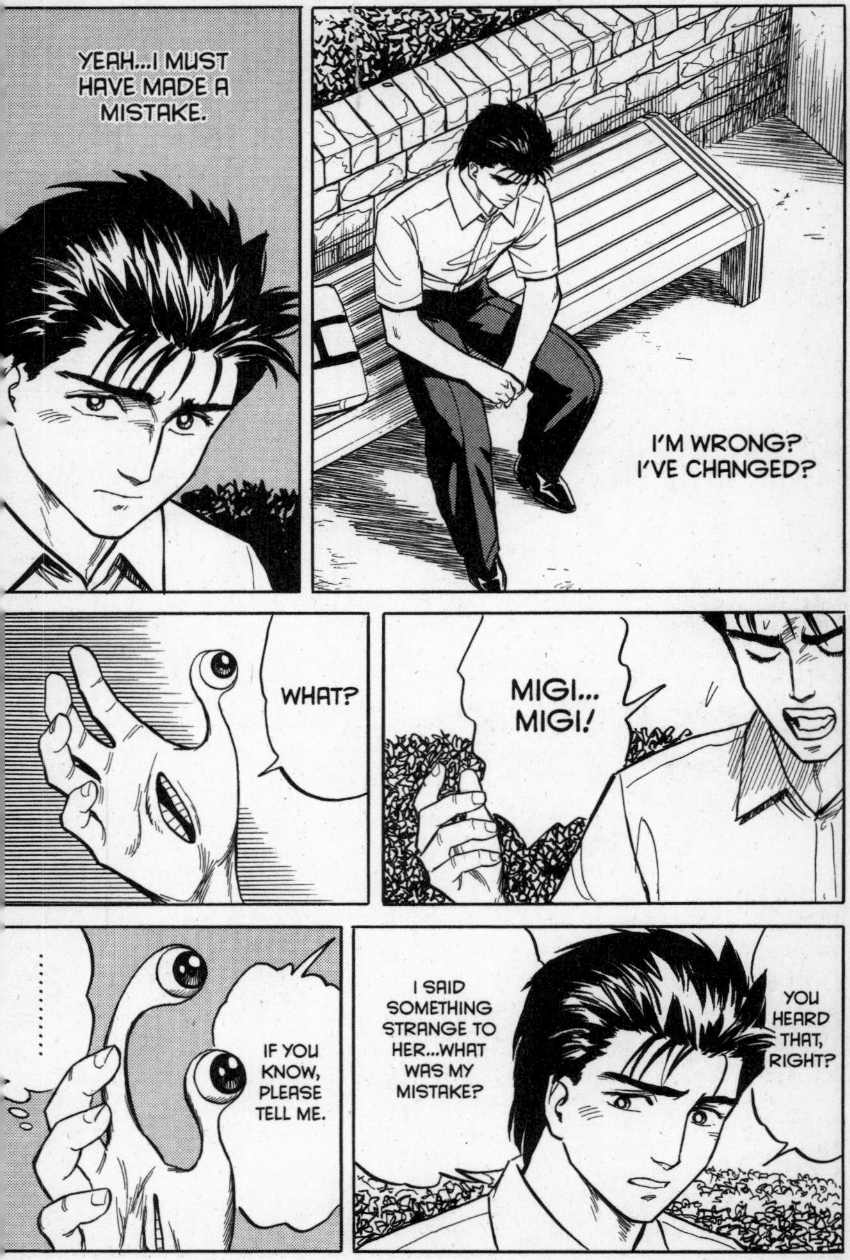

I'M WRONG? I'VE CHANGED?
YEAH...I MUST HAVE MADE A MISTAKE.
MIGI... MIGI!
WHAT?
YOU HEARD THAT, RIGHT?
I SAID SOMETHING STRANGE TO HER...WHAT WAS MY MISTAKE?
IF YOU KNOW, PLEASE TELL ME.
......

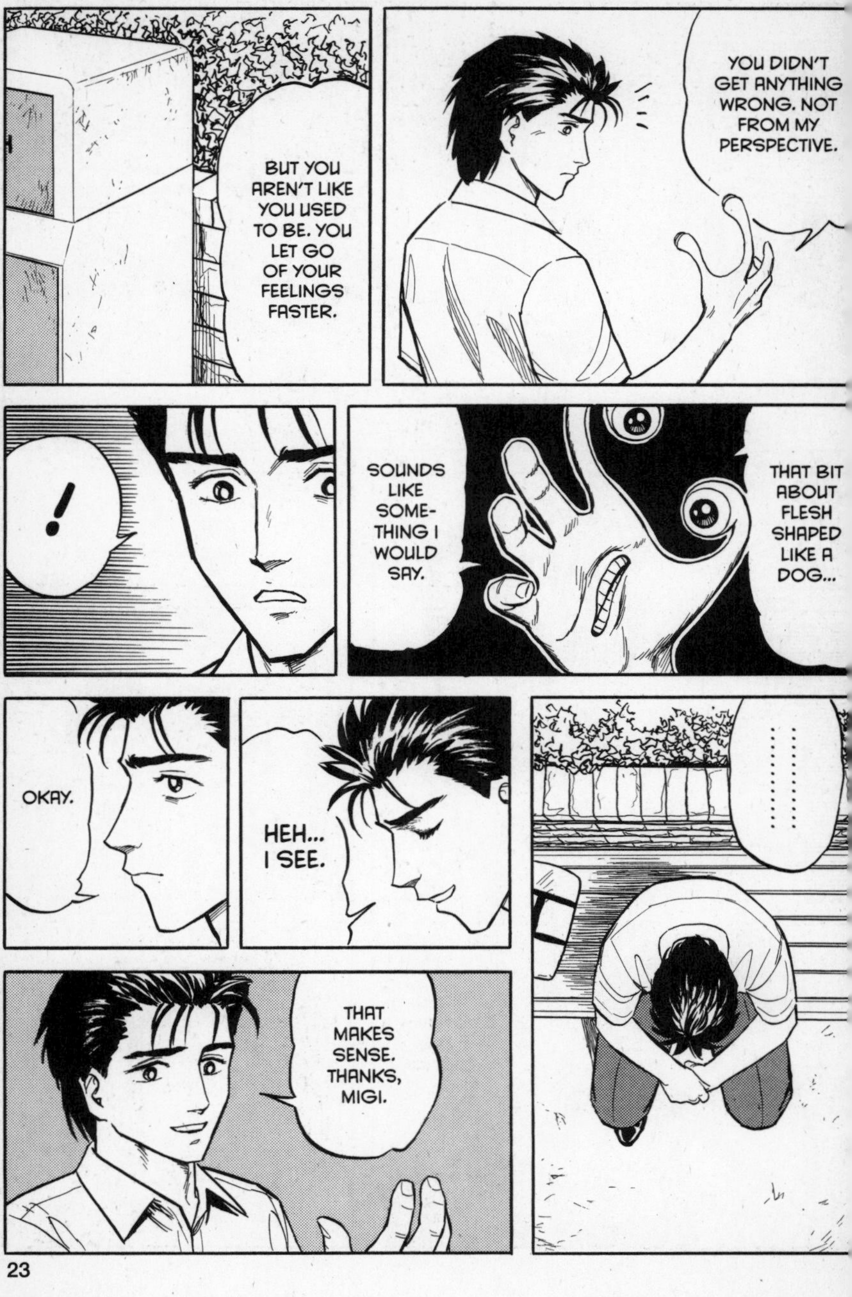
YOU DIDN'T GET ANYTHING WRONG. NOT FROM MY PERSPECTIVE.
BUT YOU AREN'T LIKE YOU USED TO BE. YOU LET GO OF YOUR FEELINGS FASTER.
THAT BIT ABOUT FLESH SHAPED LIKE A DOG...
SOUNDS LIKE SOME-THING I WOULD SAY.
!
......
HEH... I SEE.
OKAY.
THAT MAKES SENSE. THANKS, MIGI.

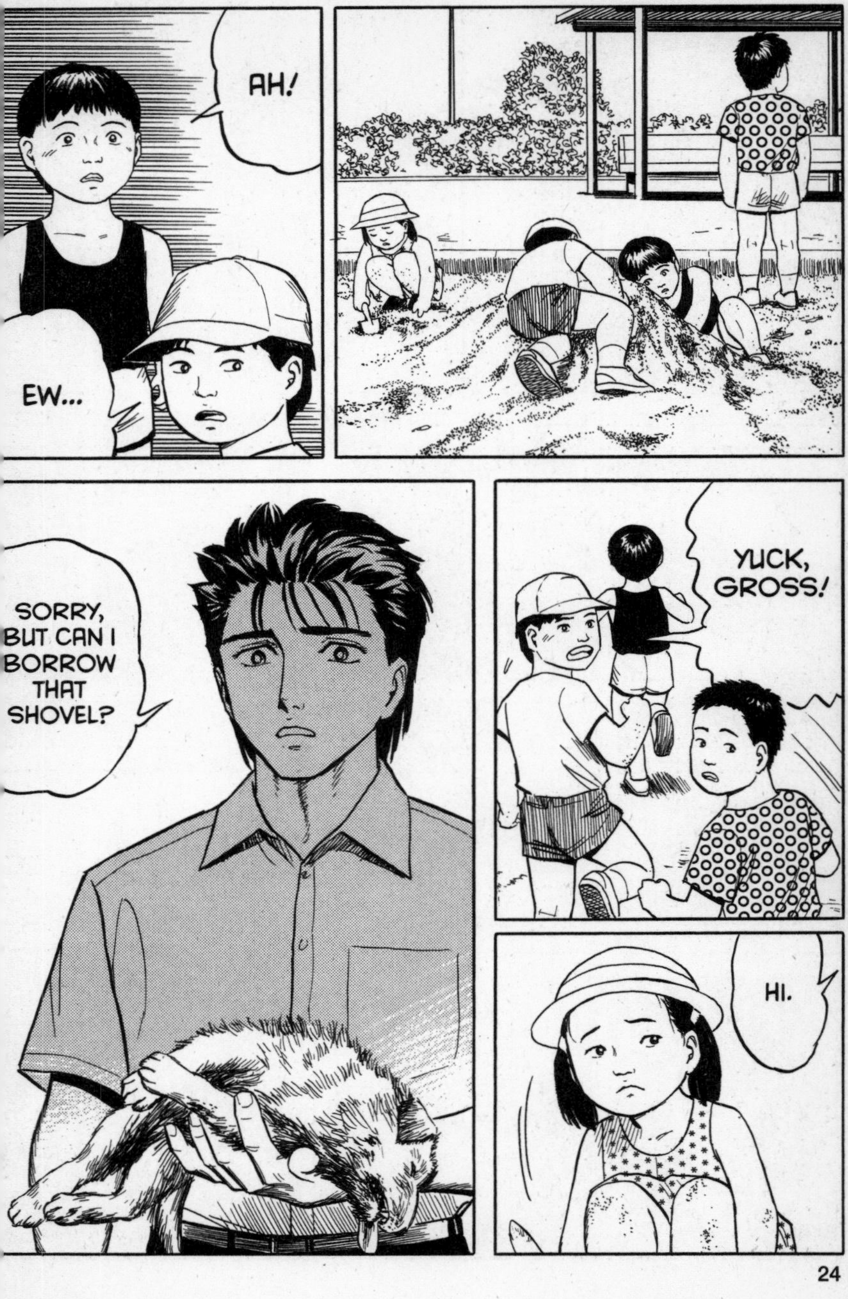
AH!
EW...
YUCK, GROSS!
HI.
SORRY, BUT CAN I BORROW THAT SHOVEL?

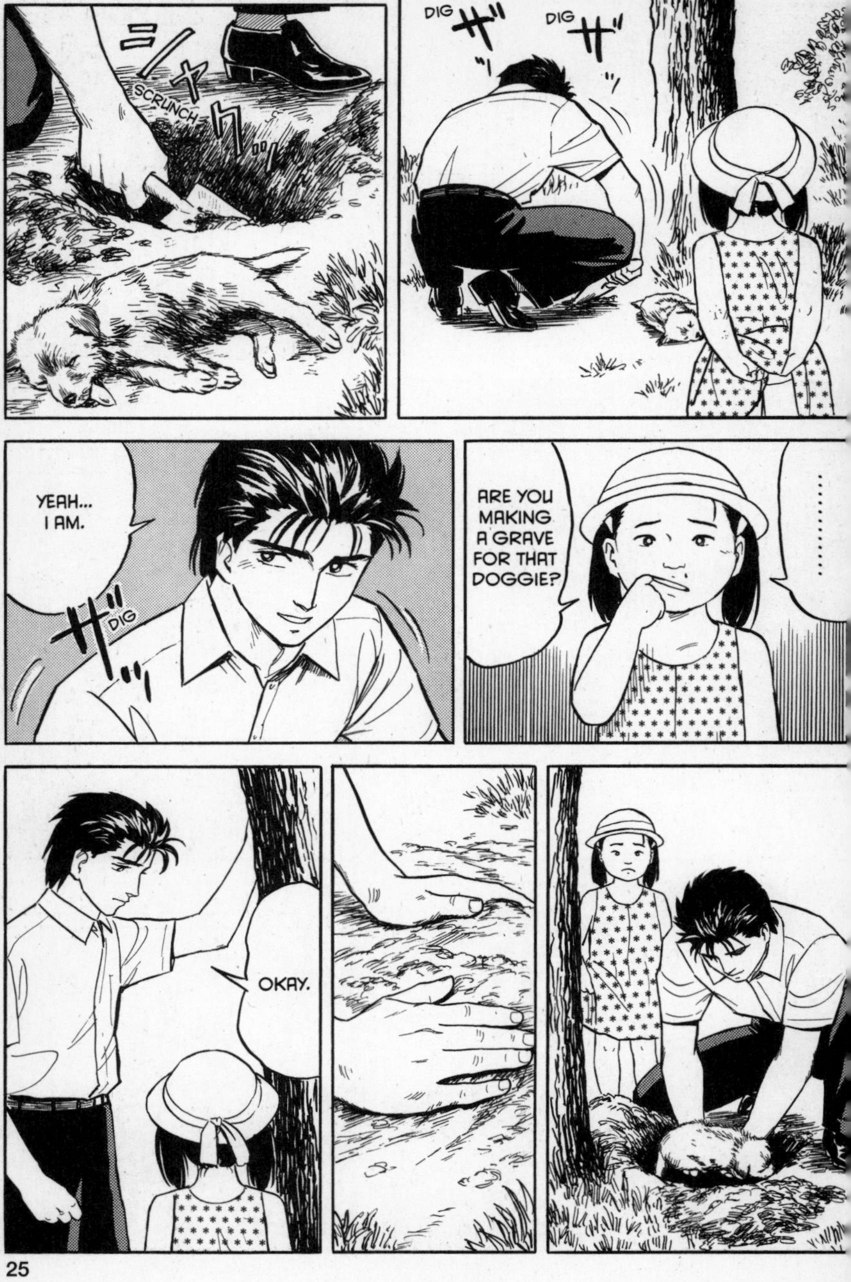
DIG
ザッ
DIG
ザッ
SCRUNCH
ARE YOU MAKING A GRAVE FOR THAT DOGGIE?
......
YEAH... I AM.
ザッ
DIG
OKAY.

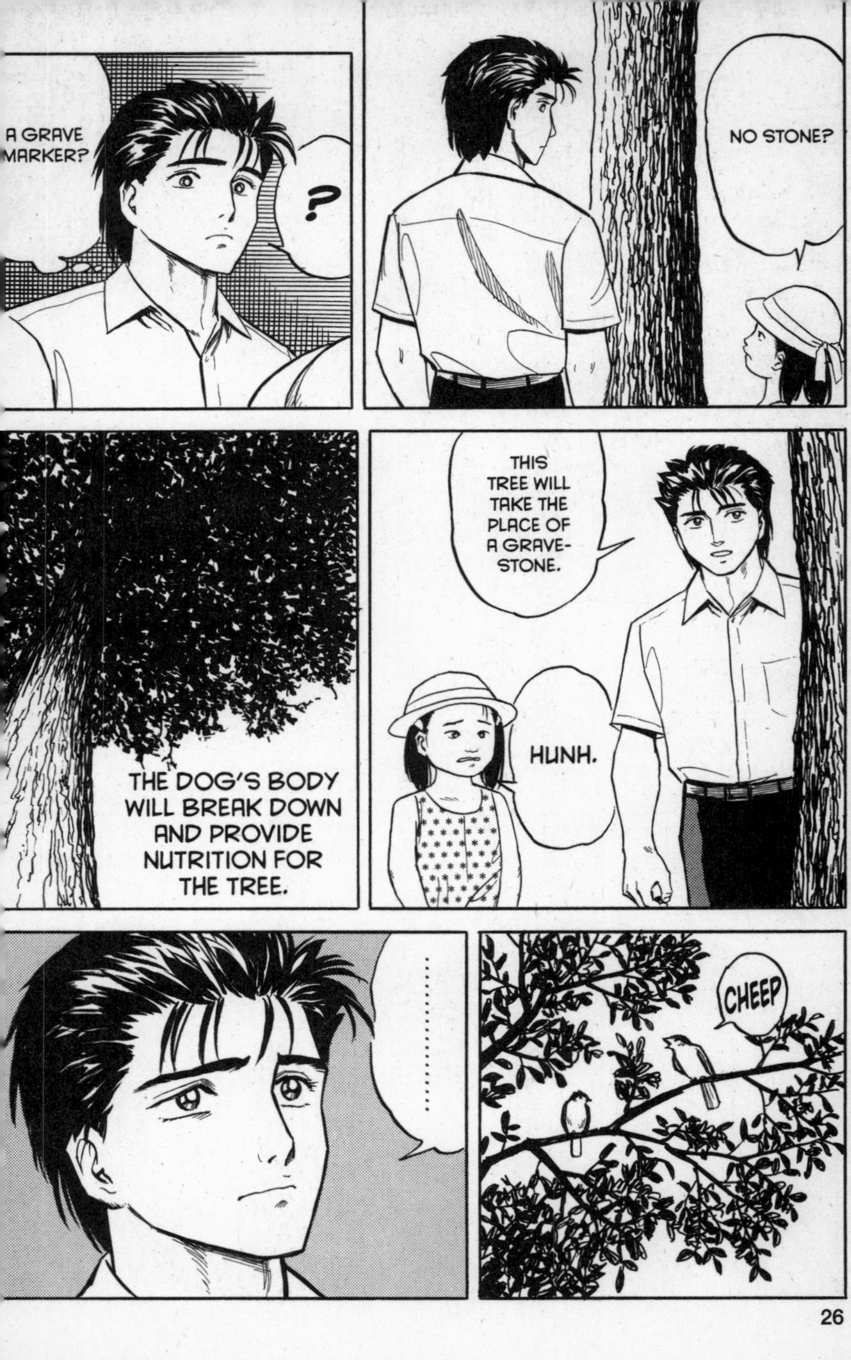
NO STONE?
A GRAVE MARKER?
?
THIS TREE WILL TAKE THE PLACE OF A GRAVE-STONE.
HUNH.
THE DOG'S BODY WILL BREAK DOWN AND PROVIDE NUTRITION FOR THE TREE.
CHEEP
....

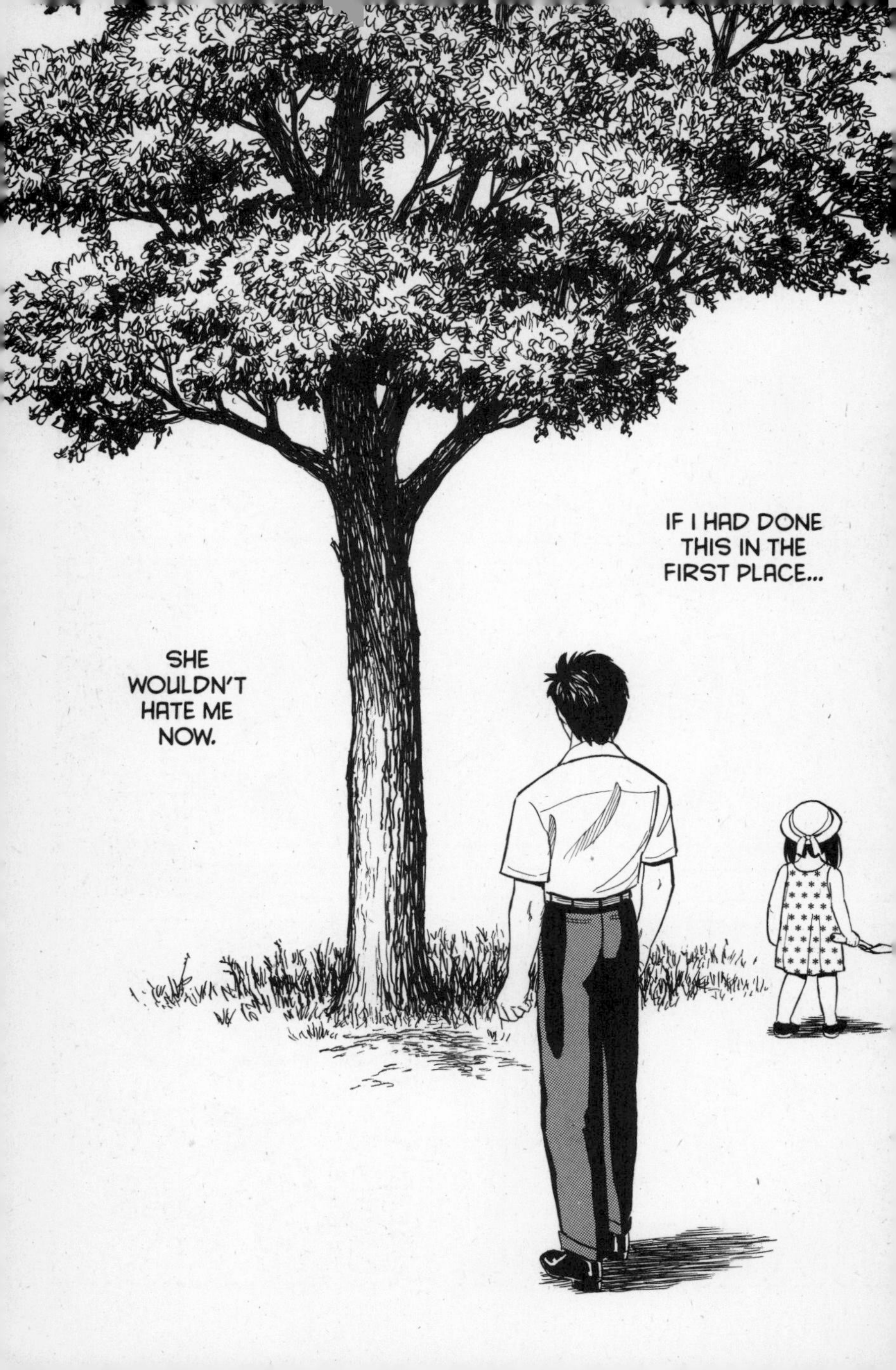
IF I HAD DONE THIS IN THE FIRST PLACE...
SHE WOULDN'T HATE ME NOW.

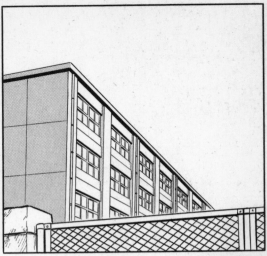

SHE NEEDS MORE TIME.

NOT TODAY.

RUN

AH! HEY...

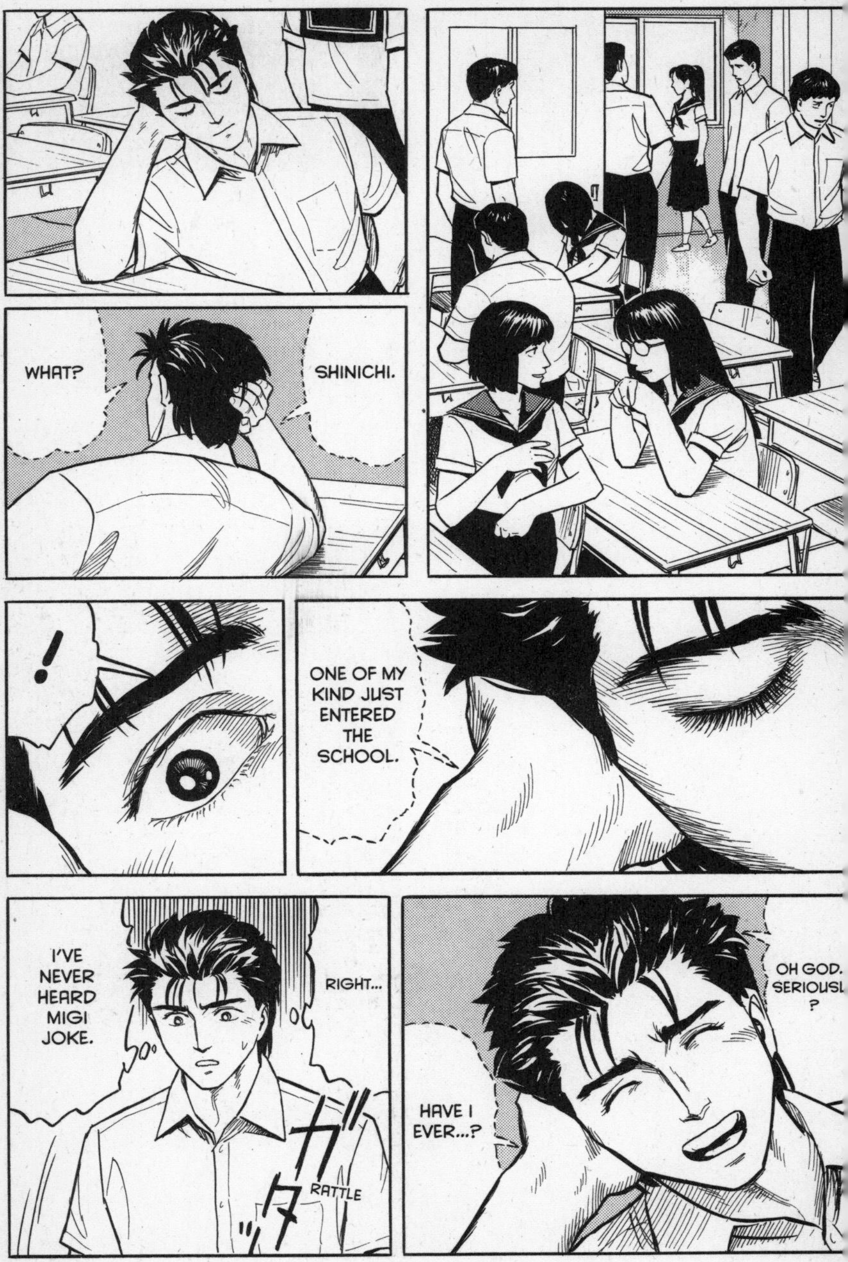
SHINICHI.
WHAT?
ONE OF MY KIND JUST ENTERED THE SCHOOL.
!
OH GOD. SERIOUSL ?
HAVE I EVER...?
RIGHT...
I'VE NEVER HEARD MIGI JOKE.
RATTLE

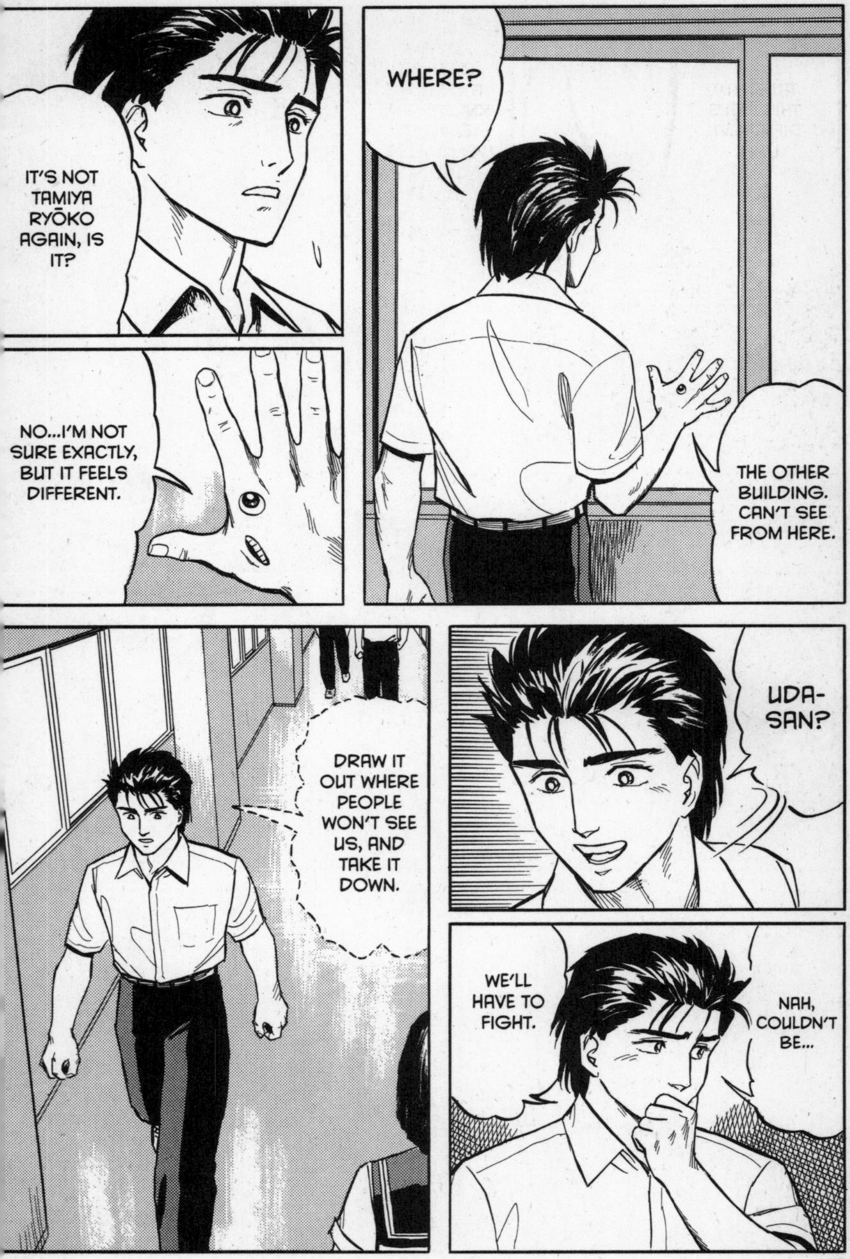
WHERE?
THE OTHER BUILDING. CAN'T SEE FROM HERE.
IT'S NOT TAMIYA RYŌKO AGAIN, IS IT?
NO...I'M NOT SURE EXACTLY, BUT IT FEELS DIFFERENT.
UDA-SAN?
NAH, COULDN'T BE...
WE'LL HAVE TO FIGHT.
DRAW IT OUT WHERE PEOPLE WON'T SEE US, AND TAKE IT DOWN.

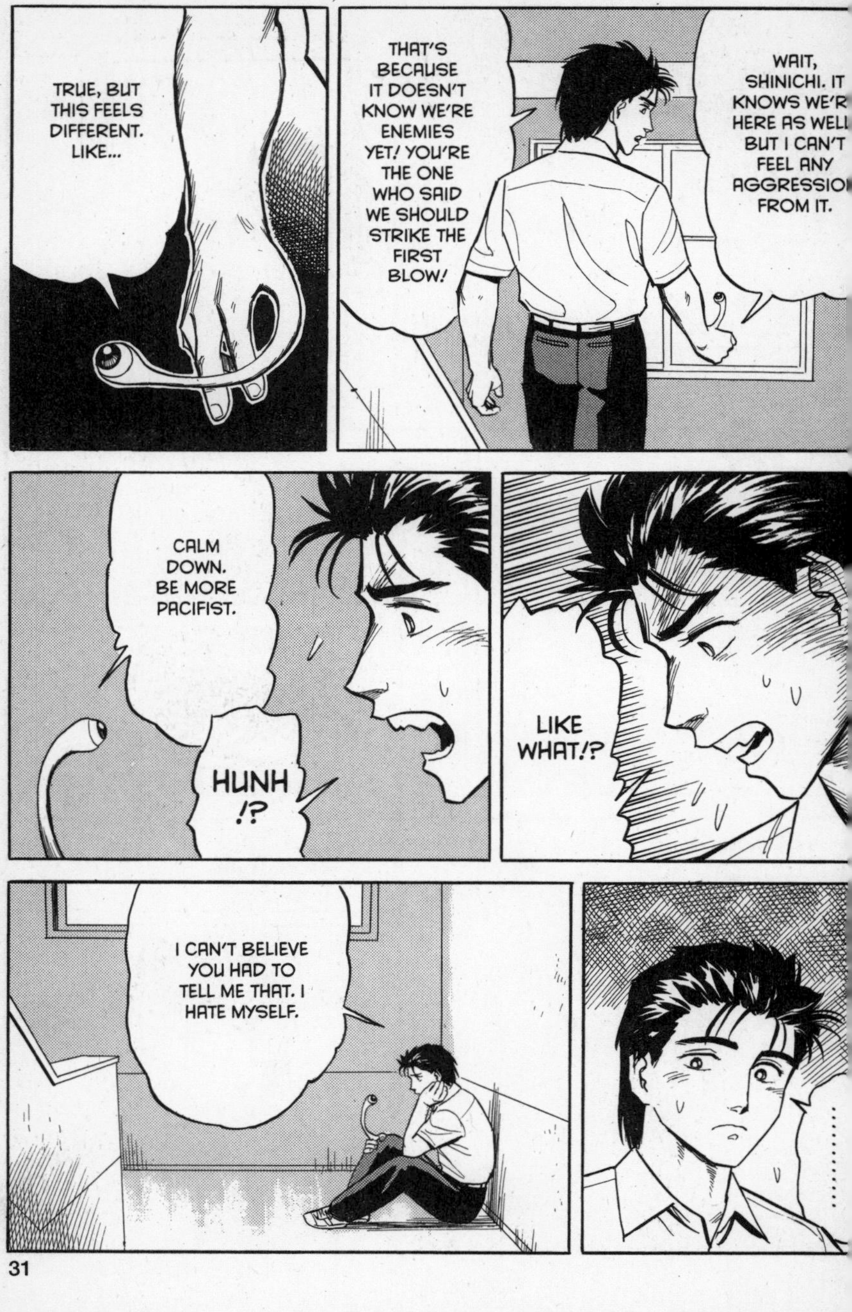
WAIT, SHINICHI. IT KNOWS WE'R HERE AS WELL BUT I CAN'T FEEL ANY AGGRESSIO FROM IT.
THAT'S BECAUSE IT DOESN'T KNOW WE'RE ENEMIES YET! YOU'RE THE ONE WHO SAID WE SHOULD STRIKE THE FIRST BLOW!
TRUE, BUT THIS FEELS DIFFERENT. LIKE...
LIKE WHAT!?
CALM DOWN. BE MORE PACIFIST.
HUNH !?
....
I CAN'T BELIEVE YOU HAD TO TELL ME THAT. I HATE MYSELF.

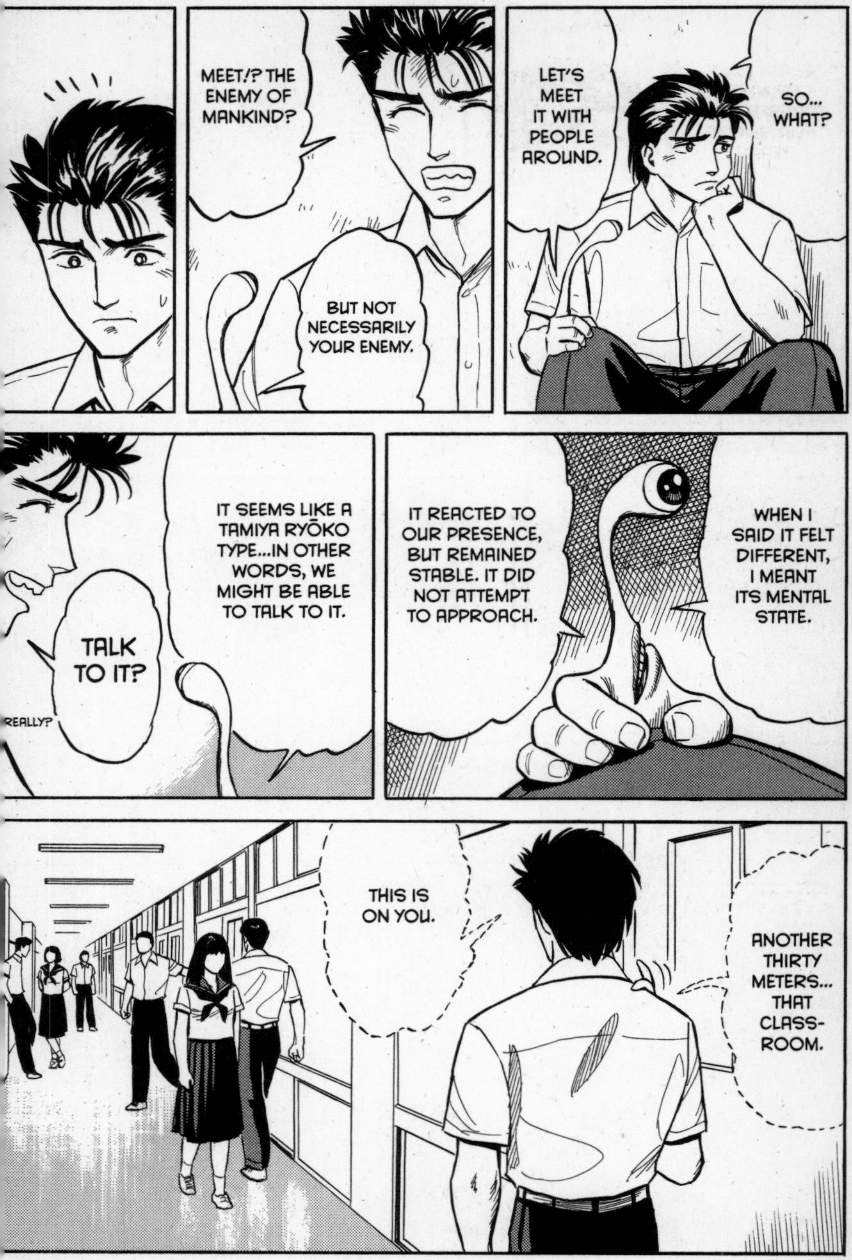

SO... WHAT?
LET'S MEET IT WITH PEOPLE AROUND.
MEET!? THE ENEMY OF MANKIND?
BUT NOT NECESSARILY YOUR ENEMY.
WHEN I SAID IT FELT DIFFERENT, I MEANT ITS MENTAL STATE.
IT REACTED TO OUR PRESENCE, BUT REMAINED STABLE. IT DID NOT ATTEMPT TO APPROACH.
IT SEEMS LIKE A TAMIYA RYŌKO TYPE...IN OTHER WORDS, WE MIGHT BE ABLE TO TALK TO IT.
TALK TO IT?
REALLY?
ANOTHER THIRTY METERS... THAT CLASS-ROOM.
THIS IS ON YOU.

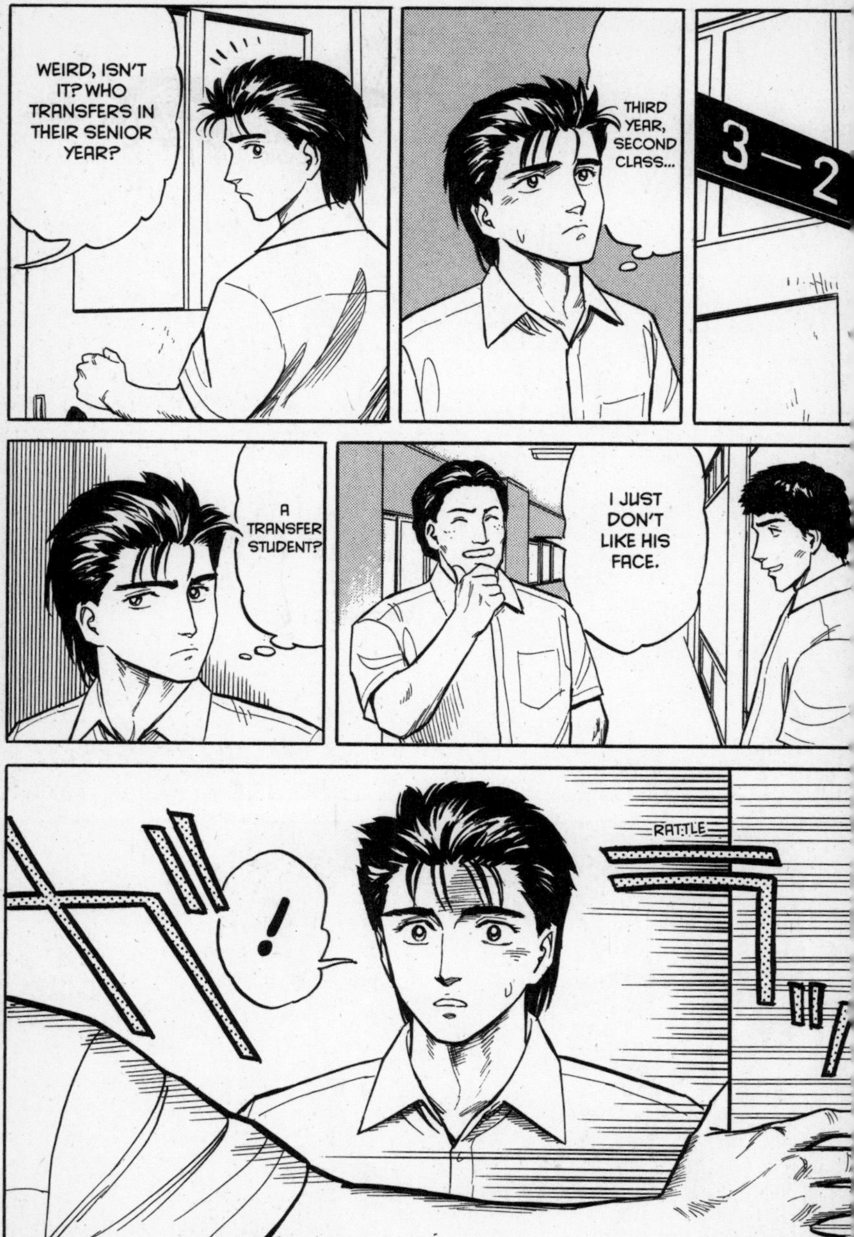
3-2
THIRD YEAR, SECOND CLASS...
WEIRD, ISN'T IT? WHO TRANSFERS IN THEIR SENIOR YEAR?
I JUST DON'T LIKE HIS FACE.
A TRANSFER STUDENT?
RATTLE
!

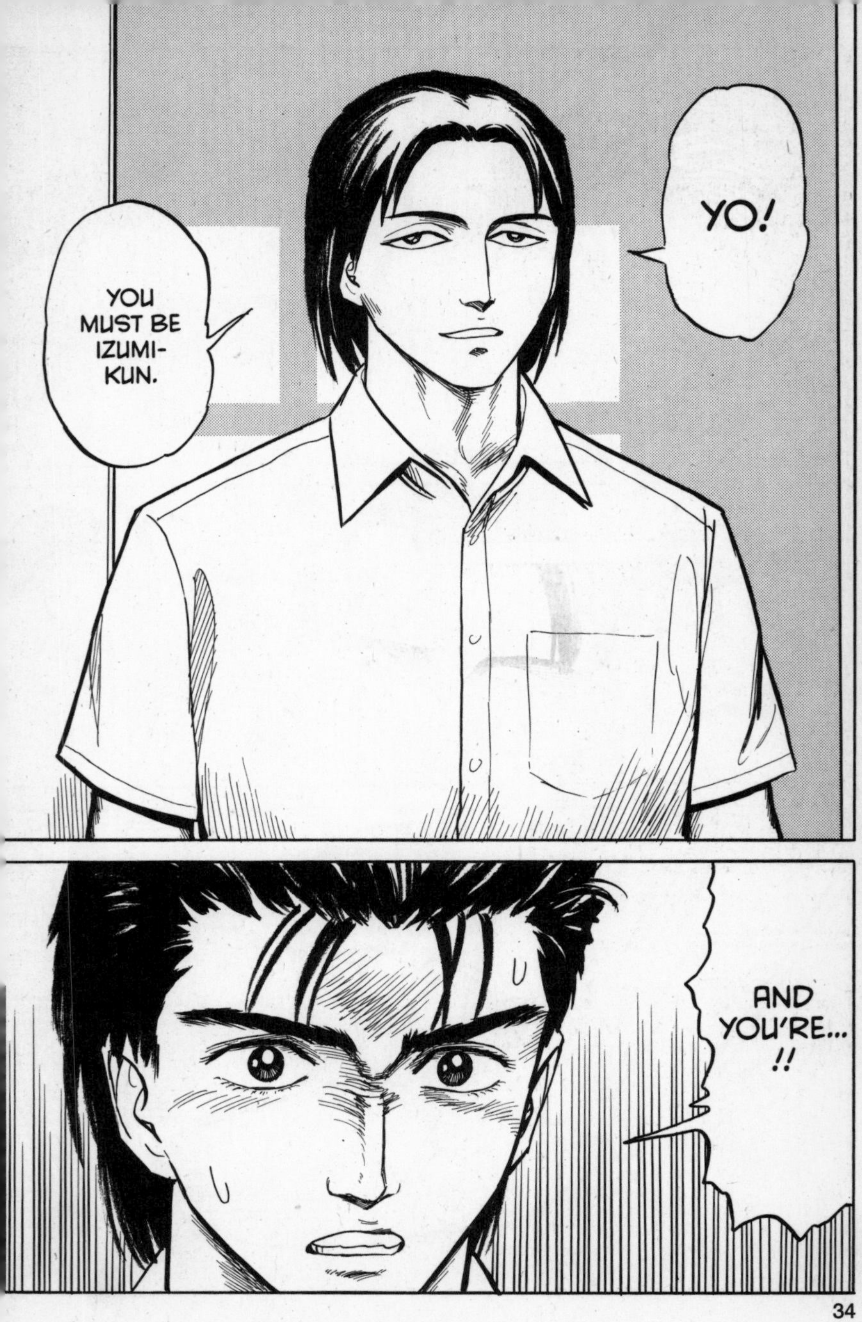
YO!
YOU MUST BE IZUMI-KUN.
AND YOU'RE... !!

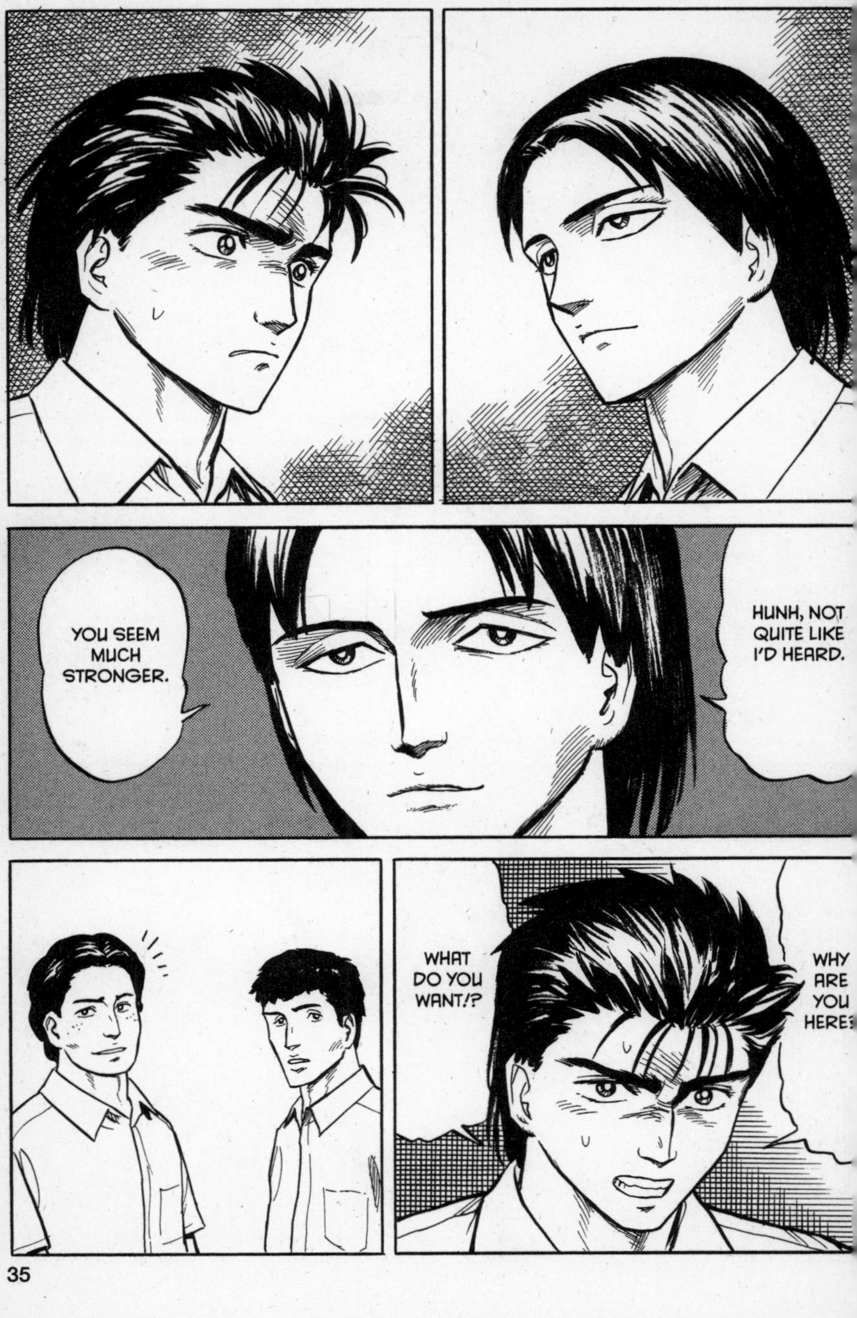
HUNH, NOT QUITE LIKE I'D HEARD.
YOU SEEM MUCH STRONGER.
WHY ARE YOU HERE
WHAT DO YOU WANT!?

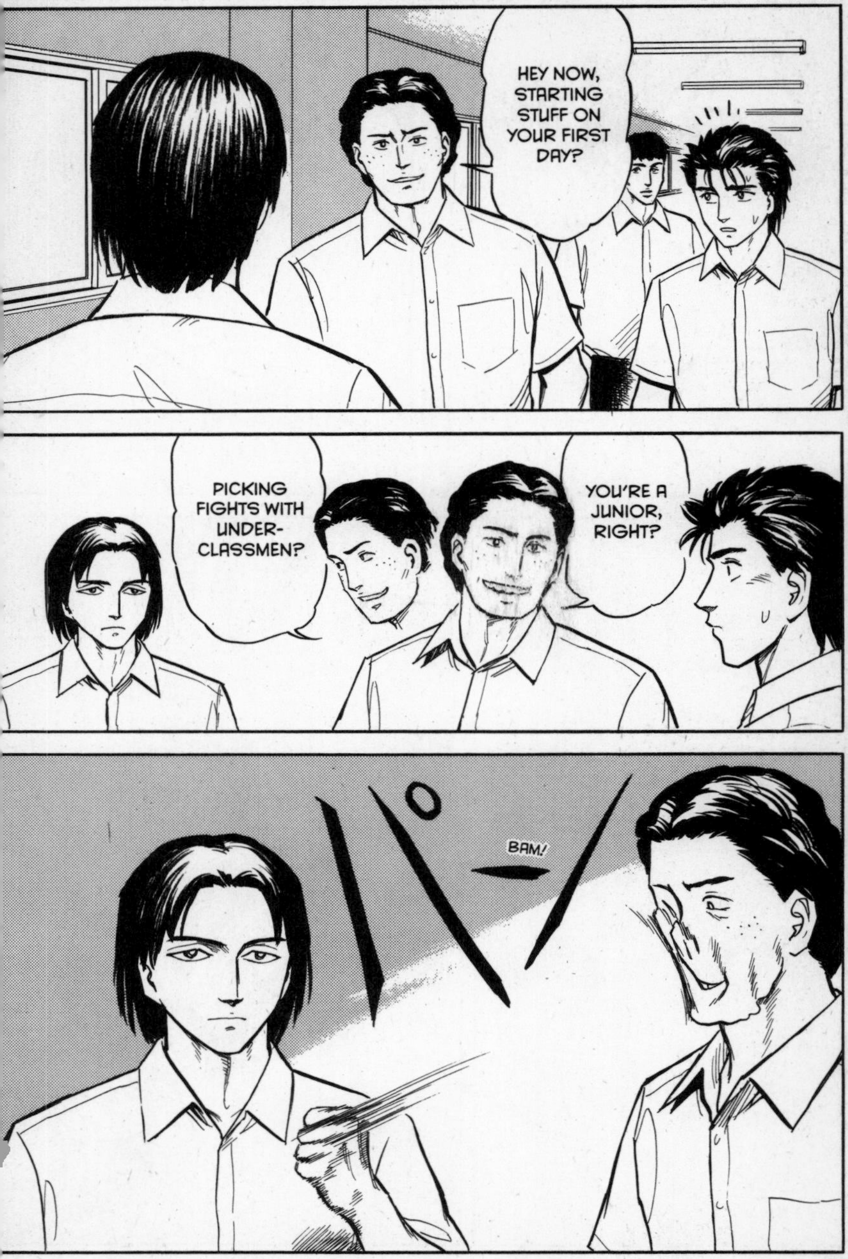
HEY NOW, STARTING STUFF ON YOUR FIRST DAY?
YOU'RE A JUNIOR, RIGHT?
PICKING FIGHTS WITH UNDER-CLASSMEN?
パ
BAM!

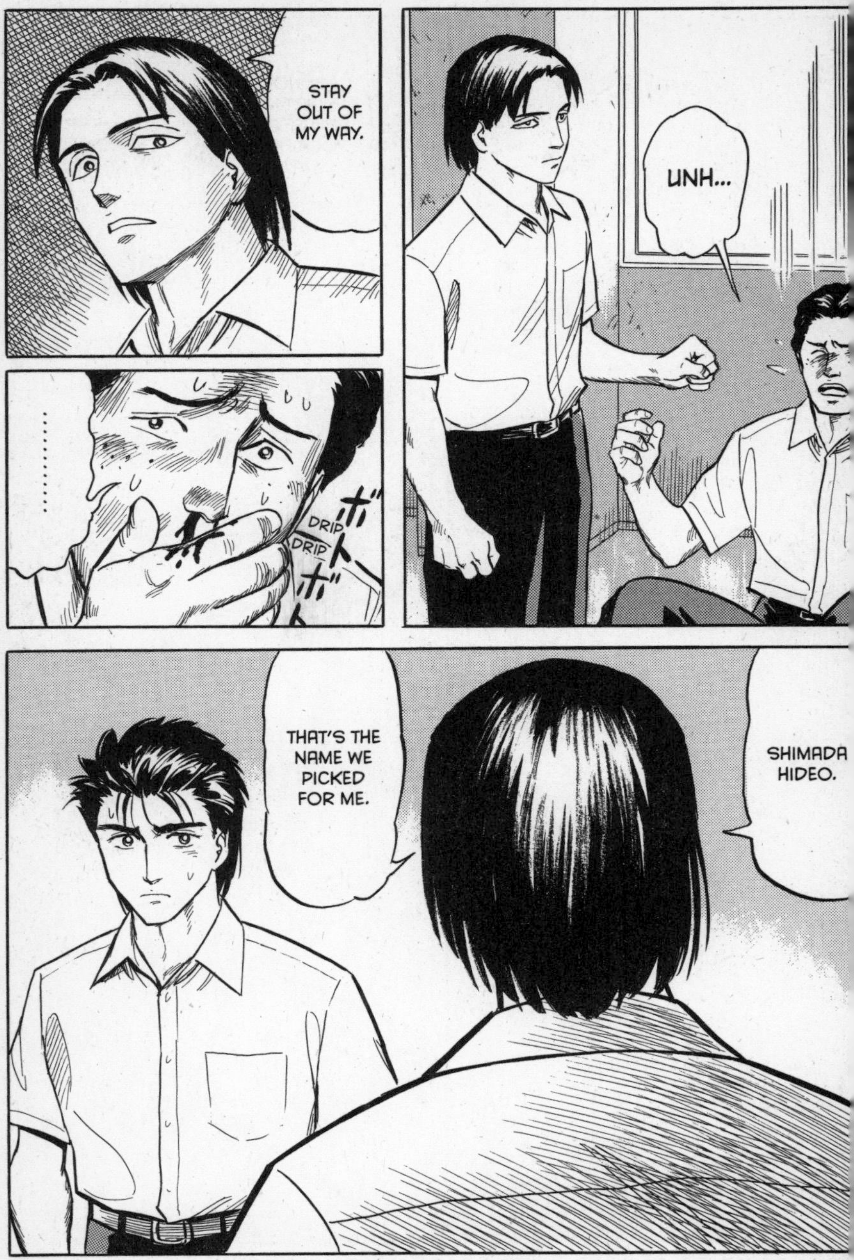
UNH...
STAY OUT OF MY WAY.
......
DRIP
DRIP
SHIMADA HIDEO.
THAT'S THE NAME WE PICKED FOR ME.

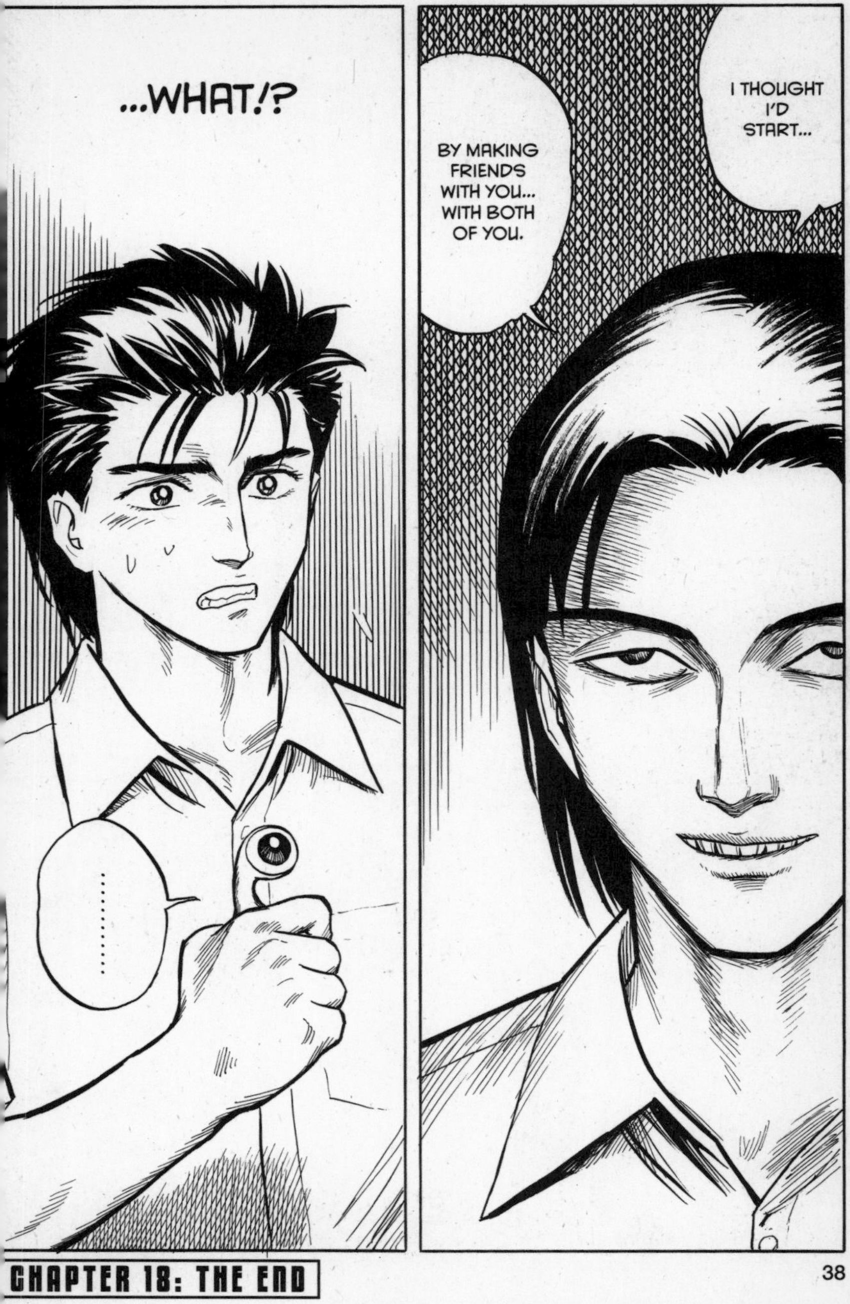
I THOUGHT I'D START...
BY MAKING FRIENDS WITH YOU... WITH BOTH OF YOU.
...WHAT!?
......

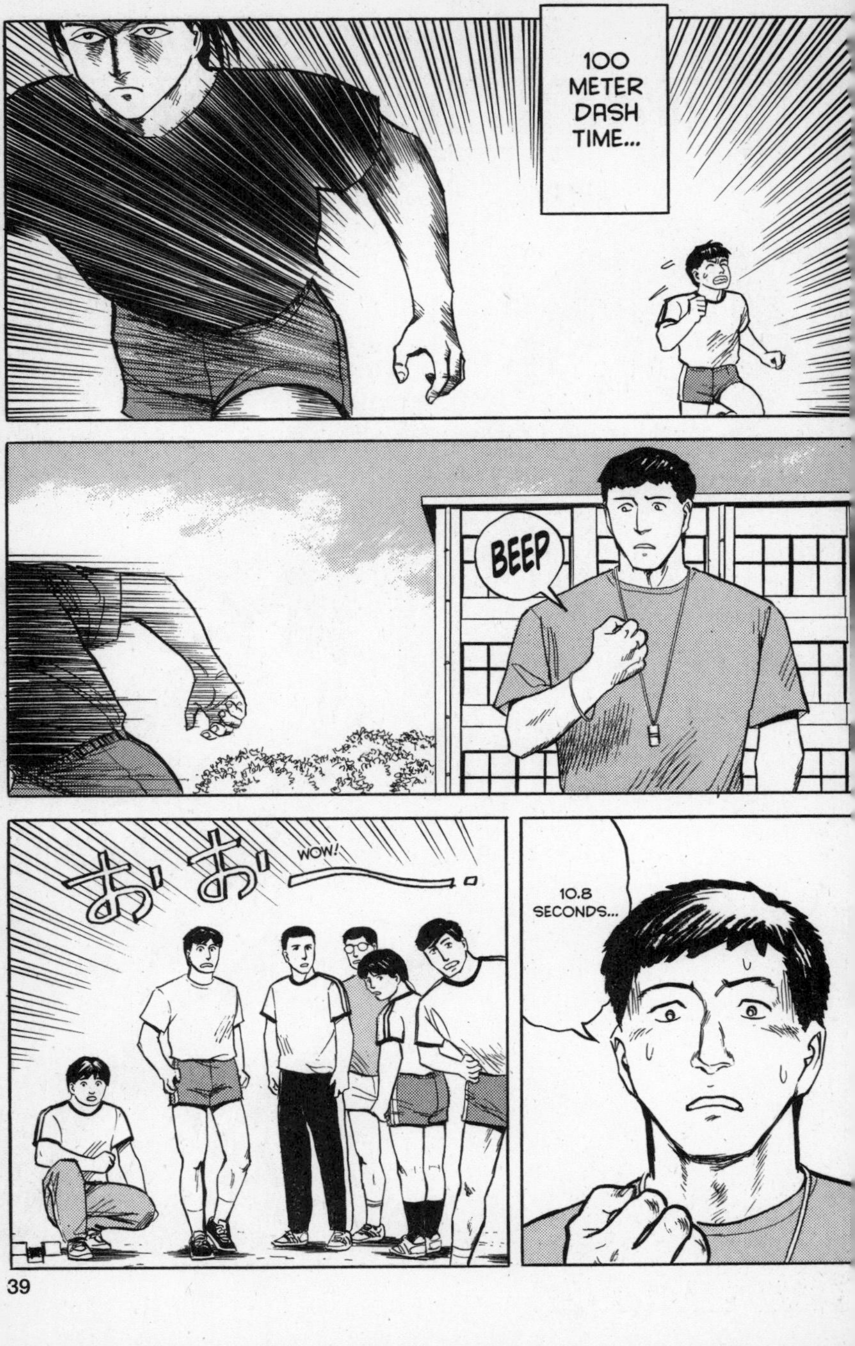
100 METER DASH TIME...
BEEP
10.8 SECONDS...
おおー。
WOW!

CHAPTER 19: SHIMADA HIDEO

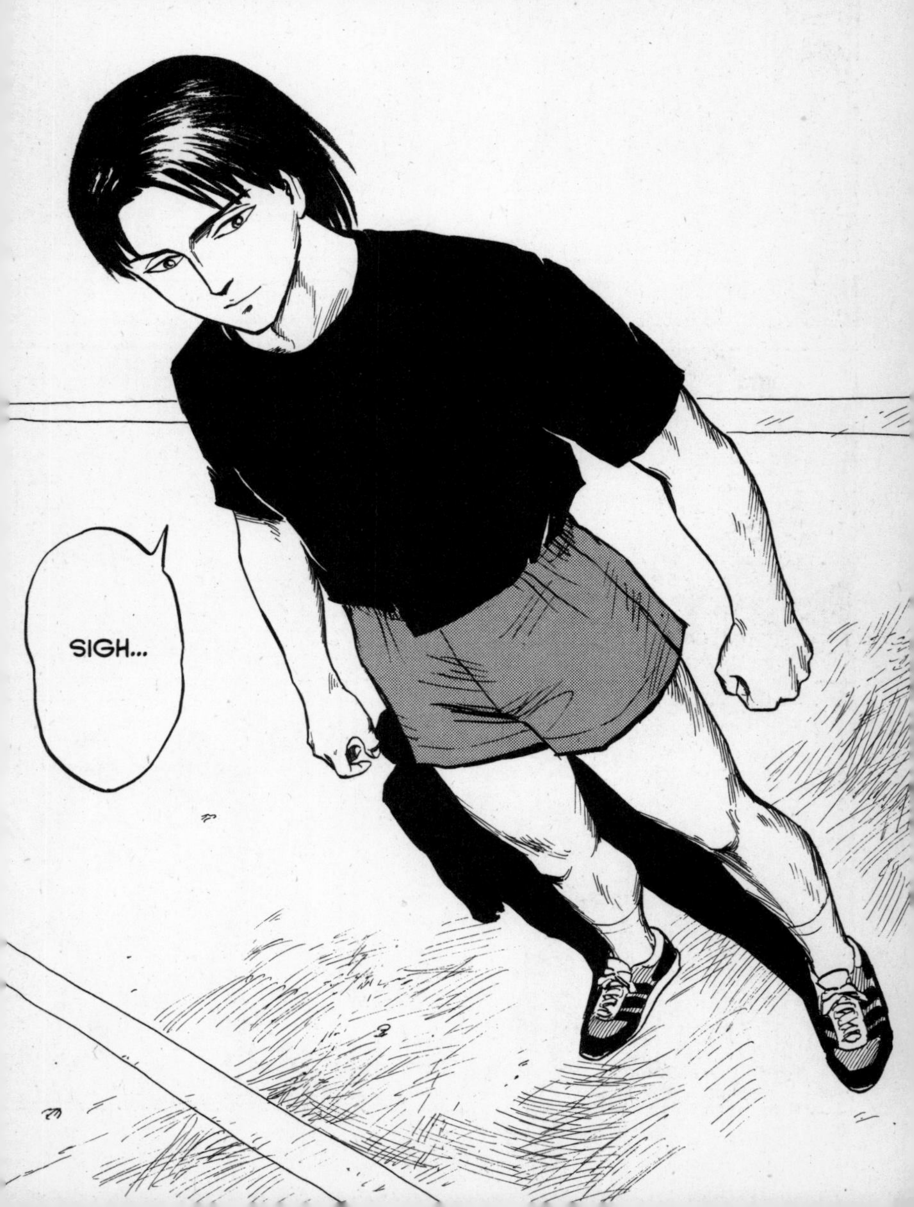
SIGH...

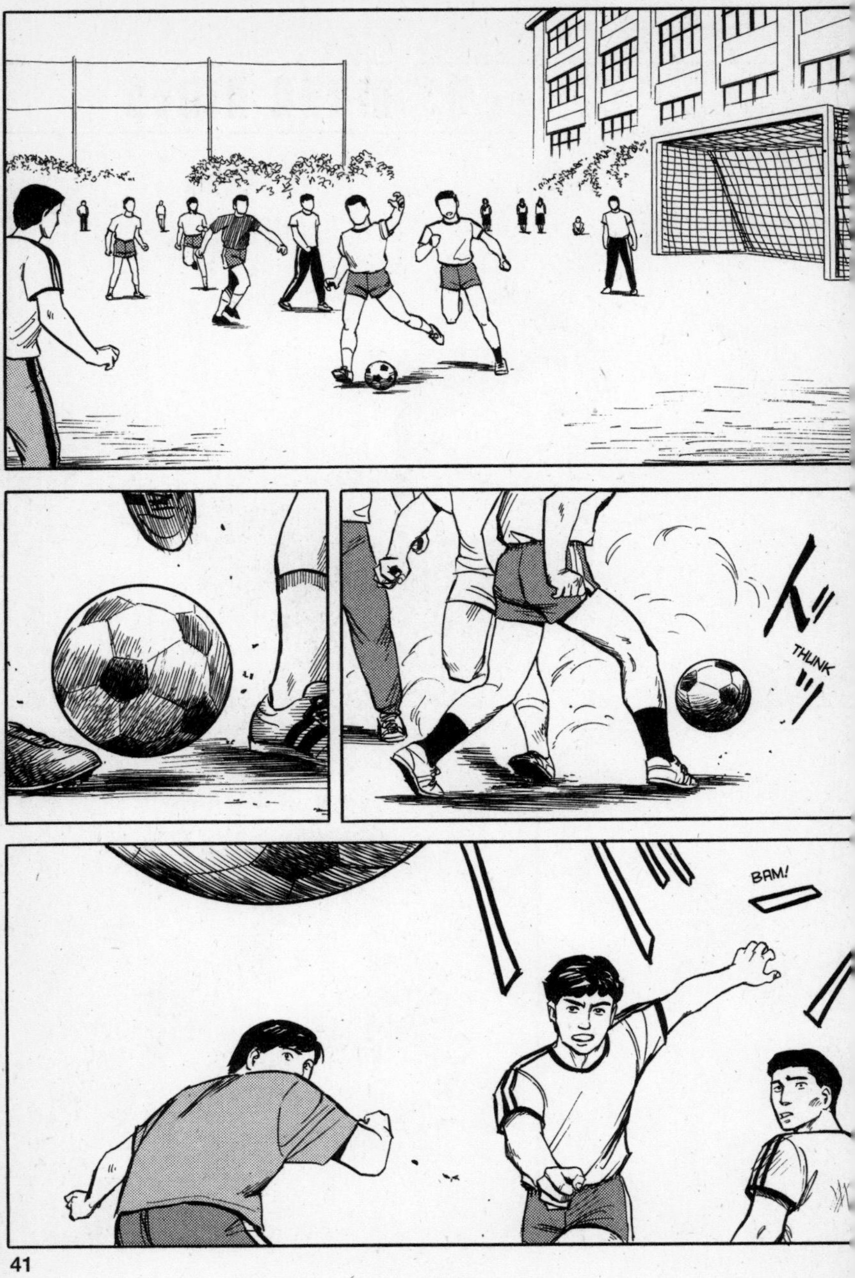
THUNK
BAM!

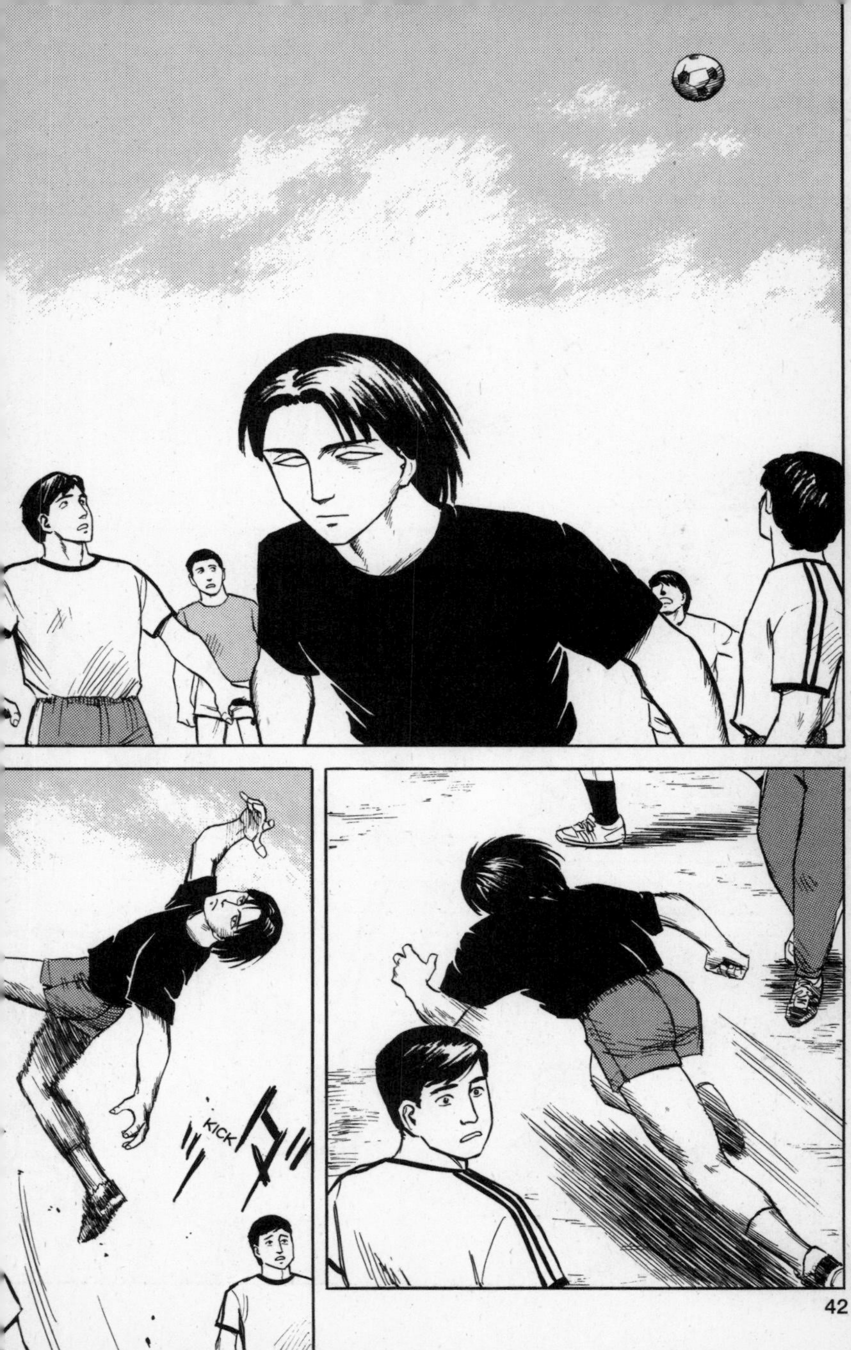
KICK

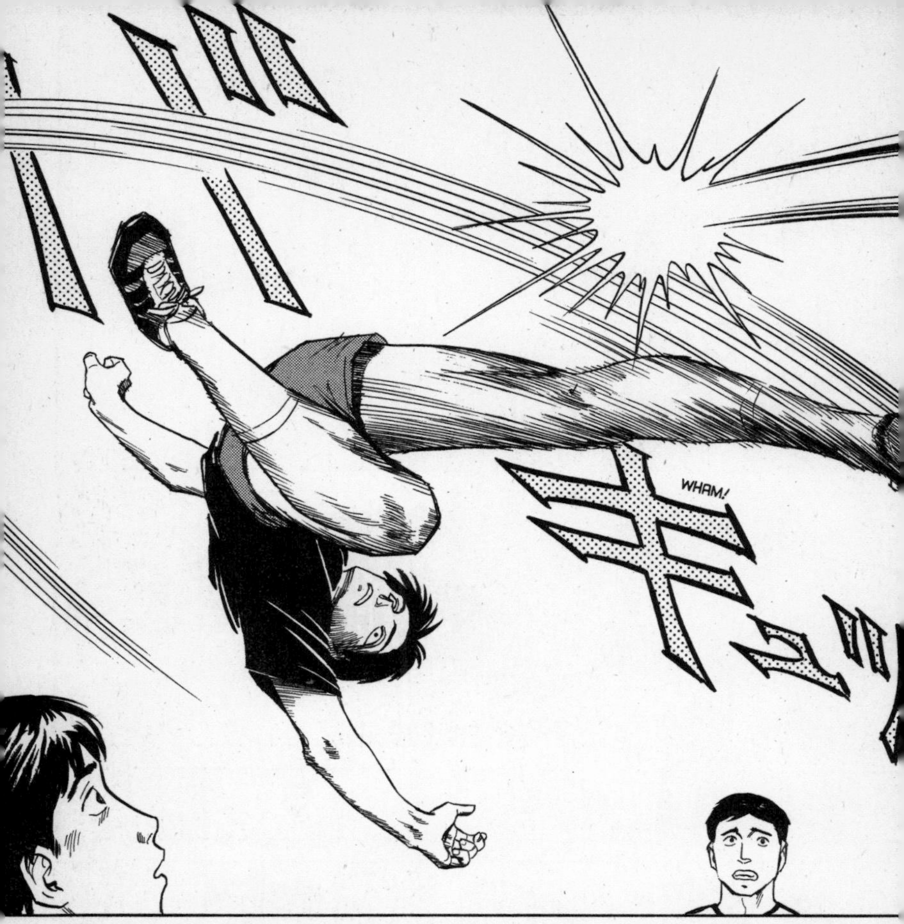
WHAM!

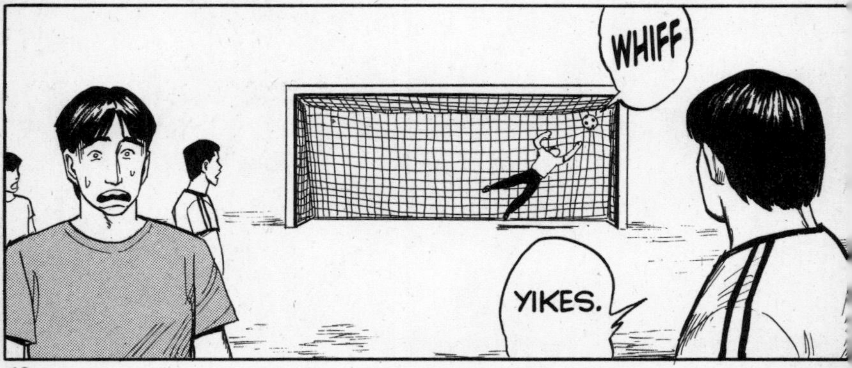
WHIFF
YIKES.

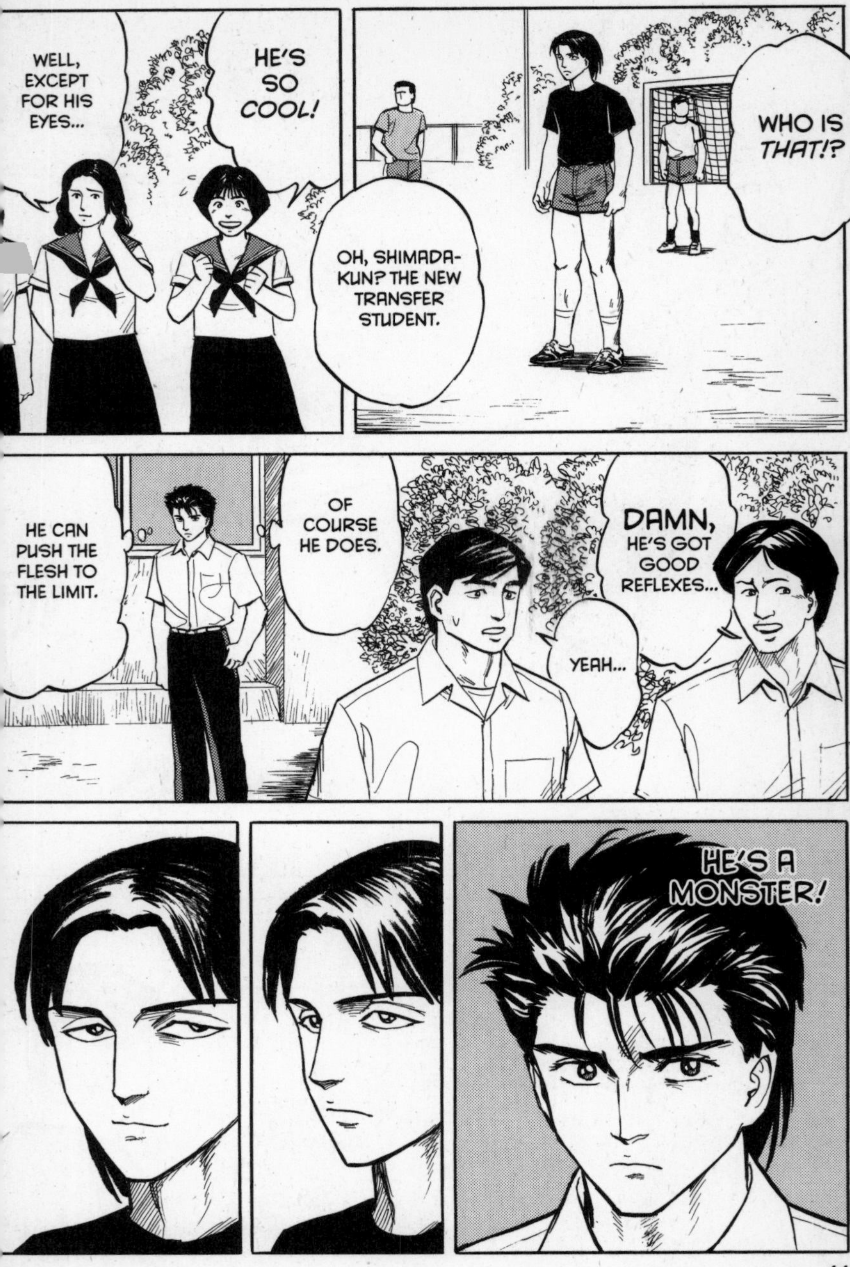
WHO IS THAT!?
OH, SHIMADA-KUN? THE NEW TRANSFER STUDENT.
HE'S SO COOL!
WELL, EXCEPT FOR HIS EYES...
DAMN, HE'S GOT GOOD REFLEXES...
YEAH...
OF COURSE HE DOES.
HE CAN PUSH THE FLESH TO THE LIMIT.
HE'S A MONSTER!

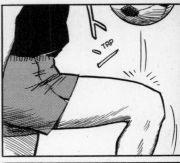

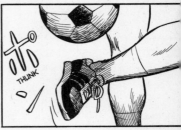

I LIKE SPORTS.

THE MORE YOU MOVE, THE GREATER YOUR CONTROL BECOMES.

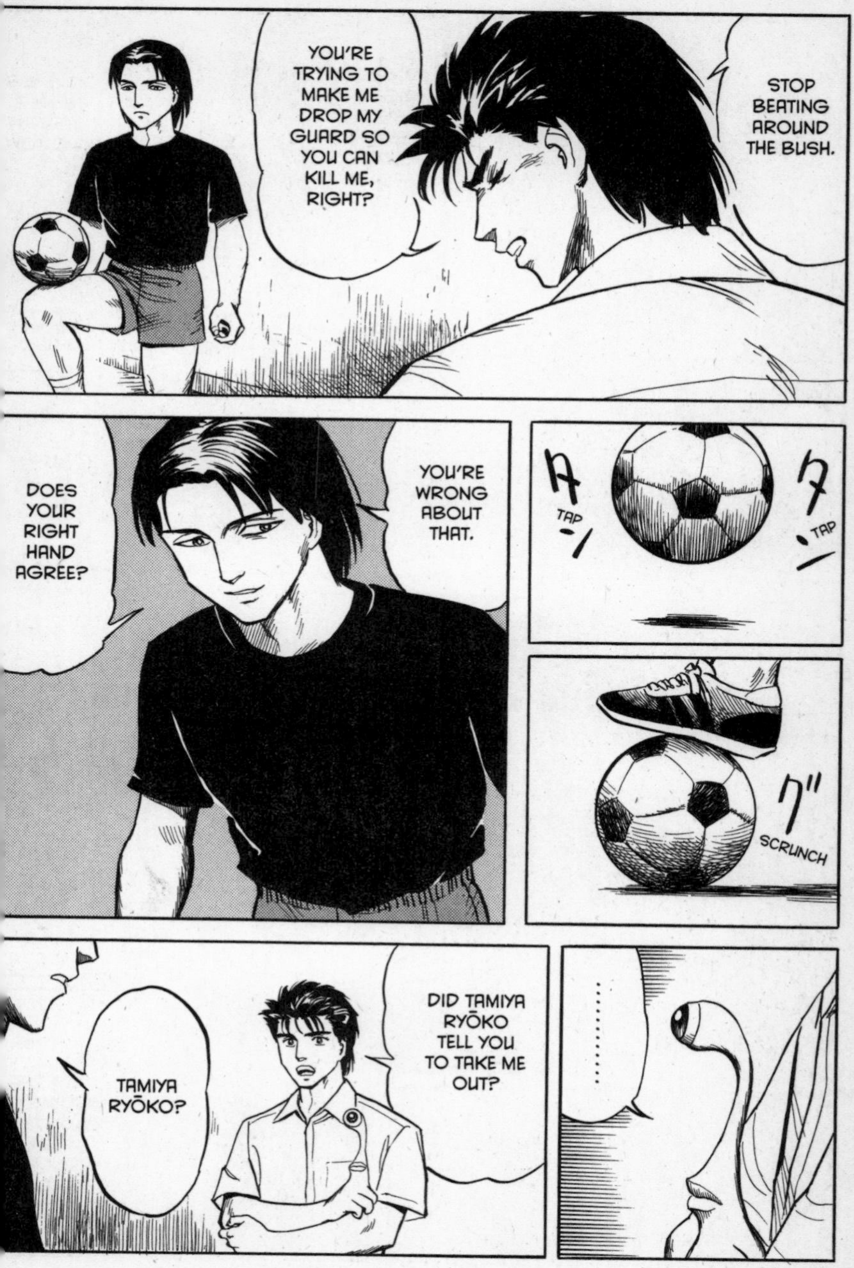
STOP BEATING AROUND THE BUSH.
YOU'RE TRYING TO MAKE ME DROP MY GUARD SO YOU CAN KILL ME, RIGHT?
タ
TAP
タ
TAP
グ
SCRUNCH
YOU'RE WRONG ABOUT THAT.
DOES YOUR RIGHT HAND AGREE?
......
DID TAMIYA RYŌKO TELL YOU TO TAKE ME OUT?
TAMIYA RYŌKO?

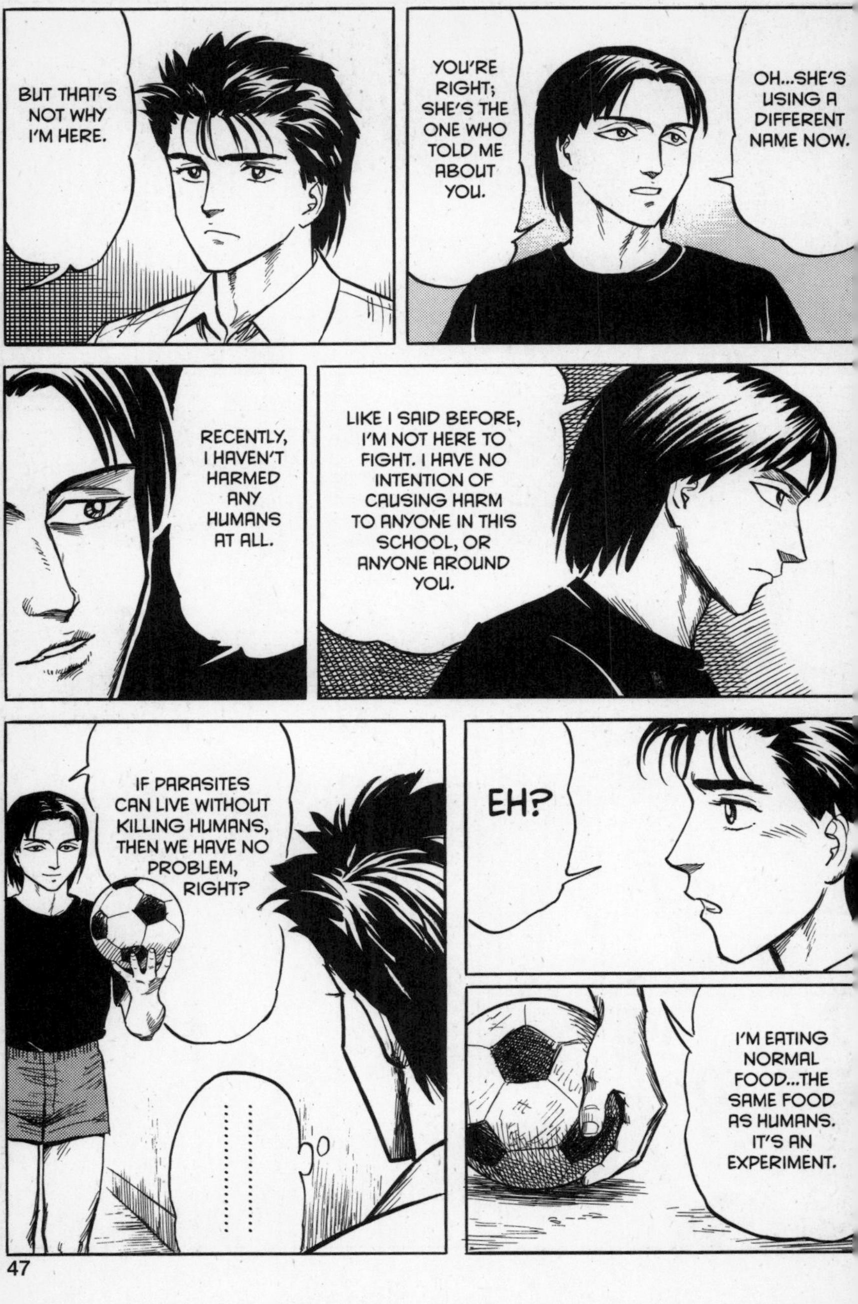
OH...SHE'S USING A DIFFERENT NAME NOW.
YOU'RE RIGHT; SHE'S THE ONE WHO TOLD ME ABOUT YOU.
BUT THAT'S NOT WHY I'M HERE.
LIKE I SAID BEFORE, I'M NOT HERE TO FIGHT. I HAVE NO INTENTION OF CAUSING HARM TO ANYONE IN THIS SCHOOL, OR ANYONE AROUND YOU.
RECENTLY, I HAVEN'T HARMED ANY HUMANS AT ALL.
EH?
I'M EATING NORMAL FOOD...THE SAME FOOD AS HUMANS. IT'S AN EXPERIMENT.
IF PARASITES CAN LIVE WITHOUT KILLING HUMANS, THEN WE HAVE NO PROBLEM, RIGHT?
......

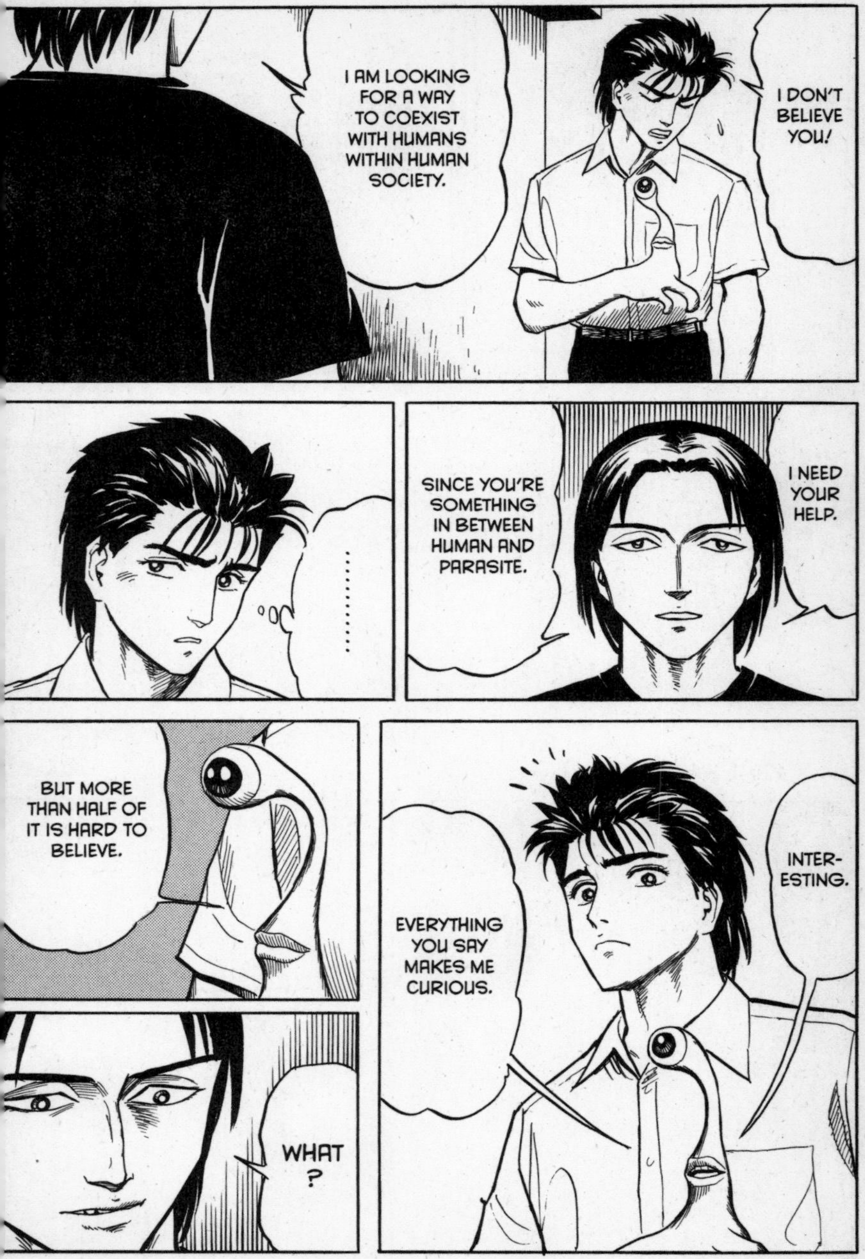
I DON'T BELIEVE YOU!
I AM LOOKING FOR A WAY TO COEXIST WITH HUMANS WITHIN HUMAN SOCIETY.
I NEED YOUR HELP.
SINCE YOU'RE SOMETHING IN BETWEEN HUMAN AND PARASITE.
....
INTER-ESTING.
EVERYTHING YOU SAY MAKES ME CURIOUS.
BUT MORE THAN HALF OF IT IS HARD TO BELIEVE.
WHAT ?

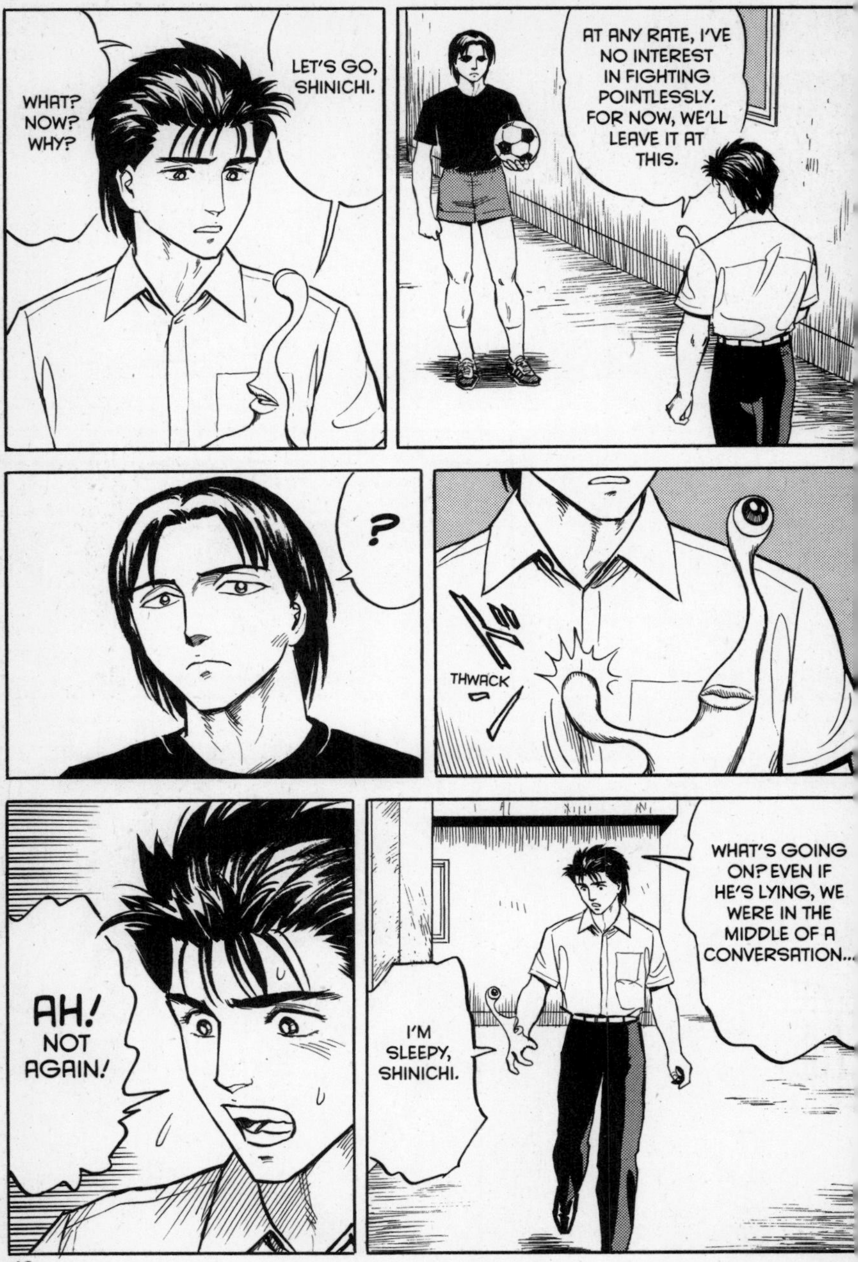

AT ANY RATE, I'VE NO INTEREST IN FIGHTING POINTLESSLY. FOR NOW, WE'LL LEAVE IT AT THIS.
LET'S GO, SHINICHI.
WHAT? NOW? WHY?
THWACK
?
WHAT'S GOING ON? EVEN IF HE'S LYING, WE WERE IN THE MIDDLE OF A CONVERSATION...
I'M SLEEPY, SHINICHI.
AH! NOT AGAIN!

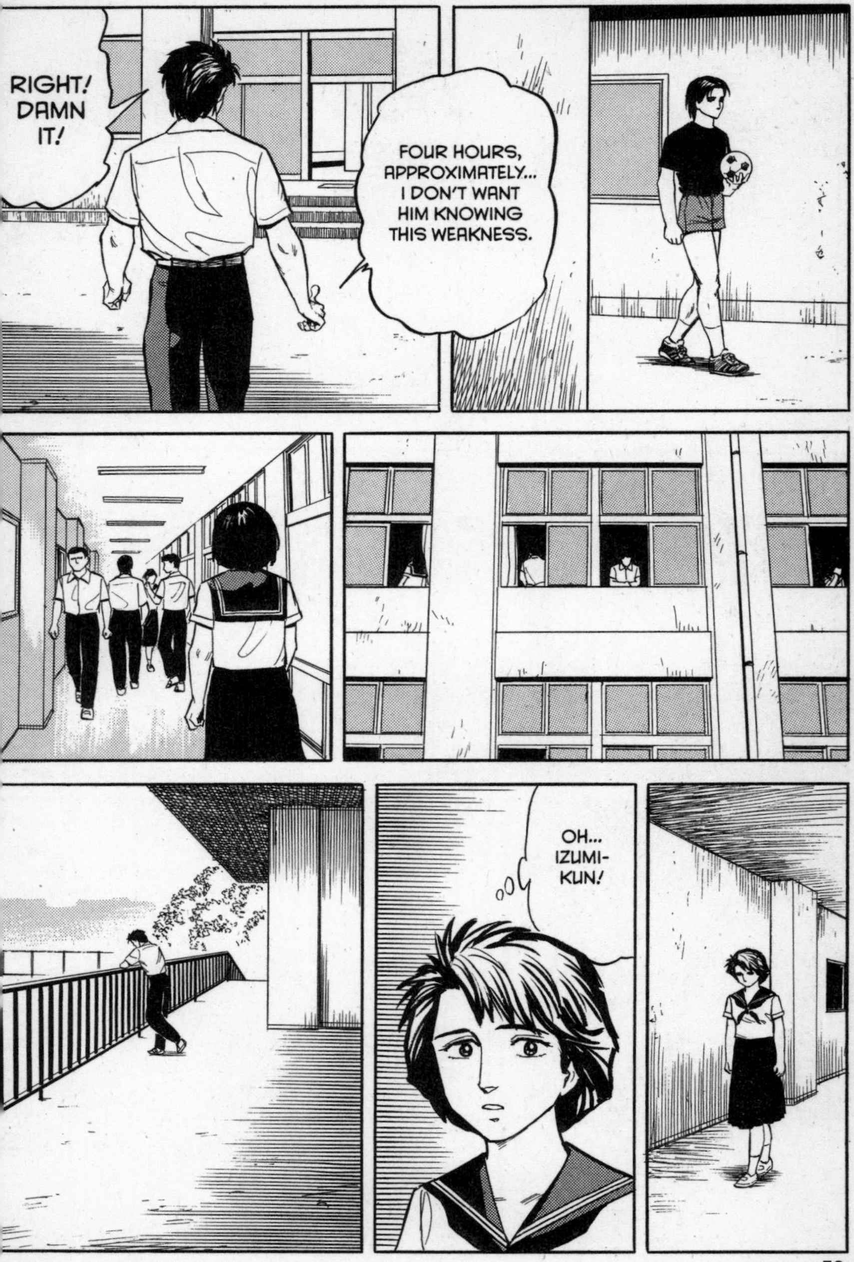
FOUR HOURS, APPROXIMATELY... I DON'T WANT HIM KNOWING THIS WEAKNESS.
RIGHT! DAMN IT!
OH... IZUMI-KUN!

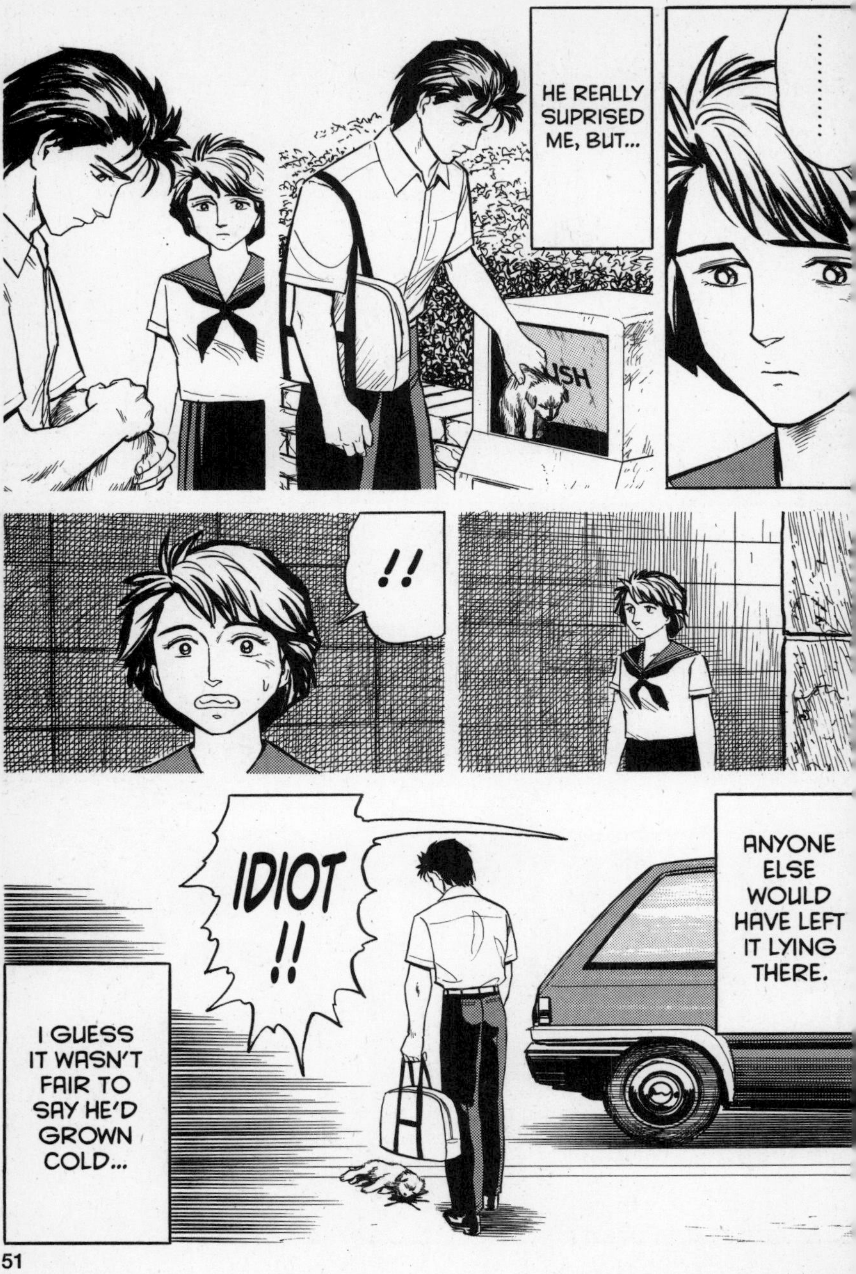
......
HE REALLY SUPRISED ME, BUT...
!!
ANYONE ELSE WOULD HAVE LEFT IT LYING THERE.
IDIOT !!
I GUESS IT WASN'T FAIR TO SAY HE'D GROWN COLD...

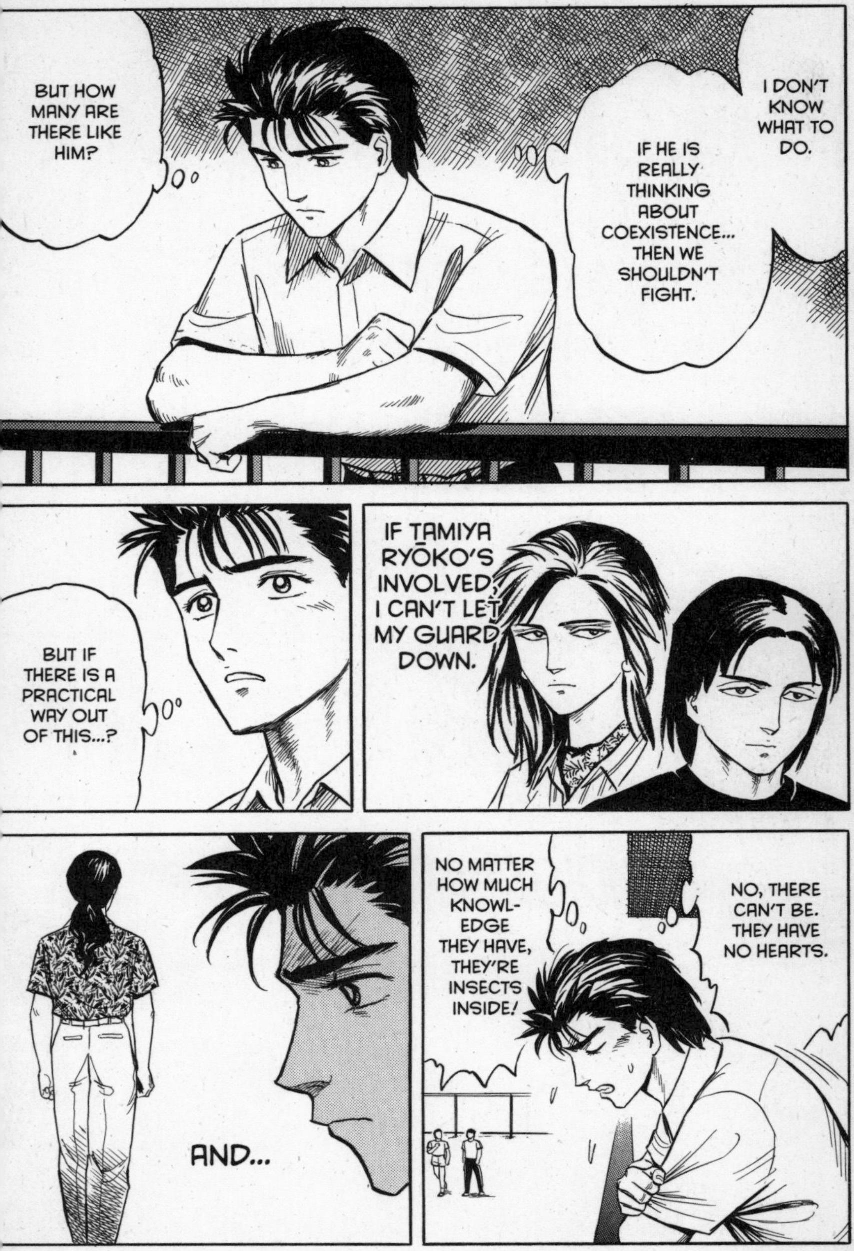
I DON'T KNOW WHAT TO DO.
IF HE IS REALLY THINKING ABOUT COEXISTENCE... THEN WE SHOULDN'T FIGHT.
BUT HOW MANY ARE THERE LIKE HIM?
IF TAMIYA RYŌKO'S INVOLVED, I CAN'T LET MY GUARD DOWN.
BUT IF THERE IS A PRACTICAL WAY OUT OF THIS...?
NO, THERE CAN'T BE. THEY HAVE NO HEARTS.
NO MATTER HOW MUCH KNOWLEDGE THEY HAVE, THEY'RE INSECTS INSIDE!
AND...

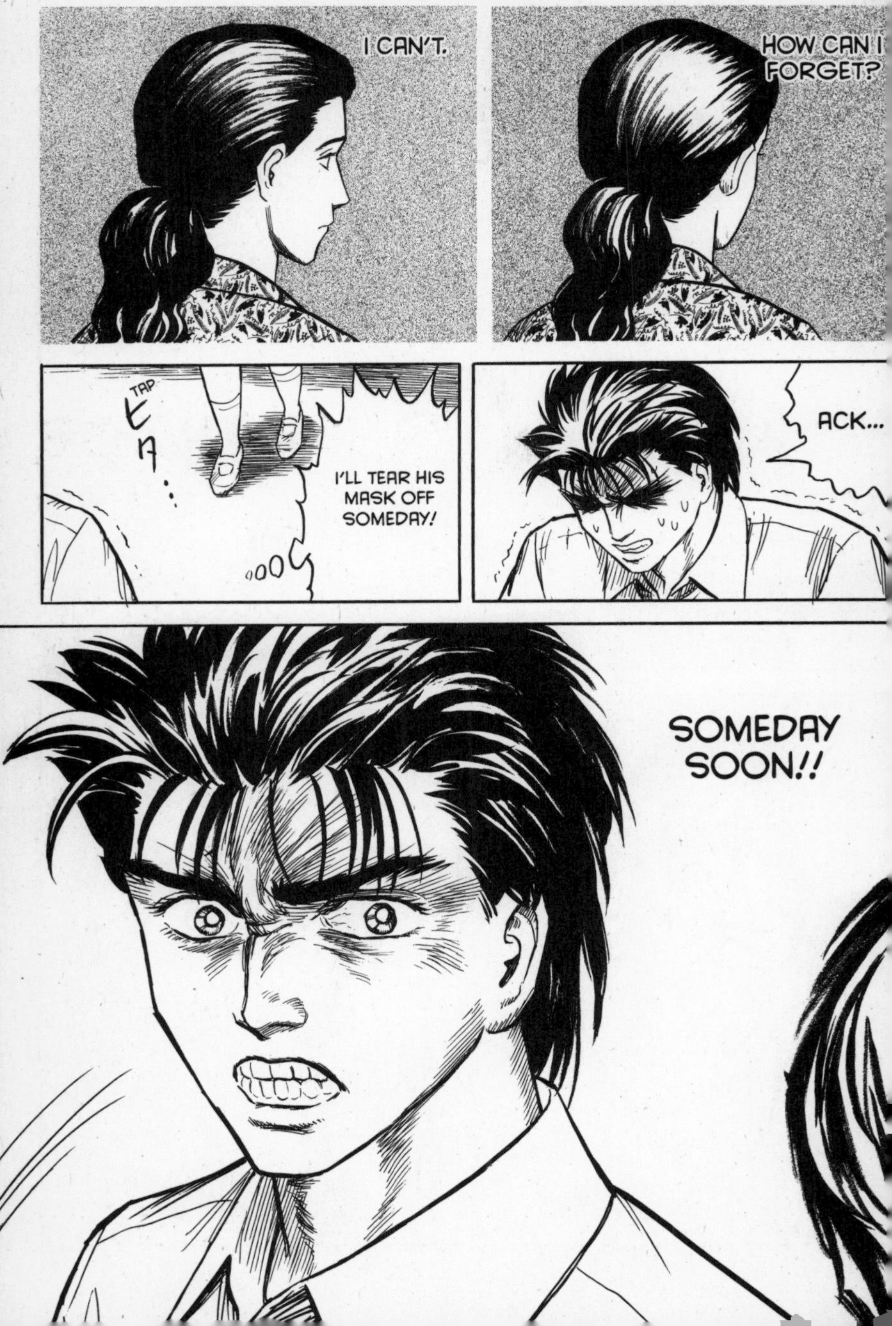
HOW CAN I FORGET?
I CAN'T.
ACK...
TAP
I'LL TEAR HIS MASK OFF SOMEDAY!
SOMEDAY SOON!!

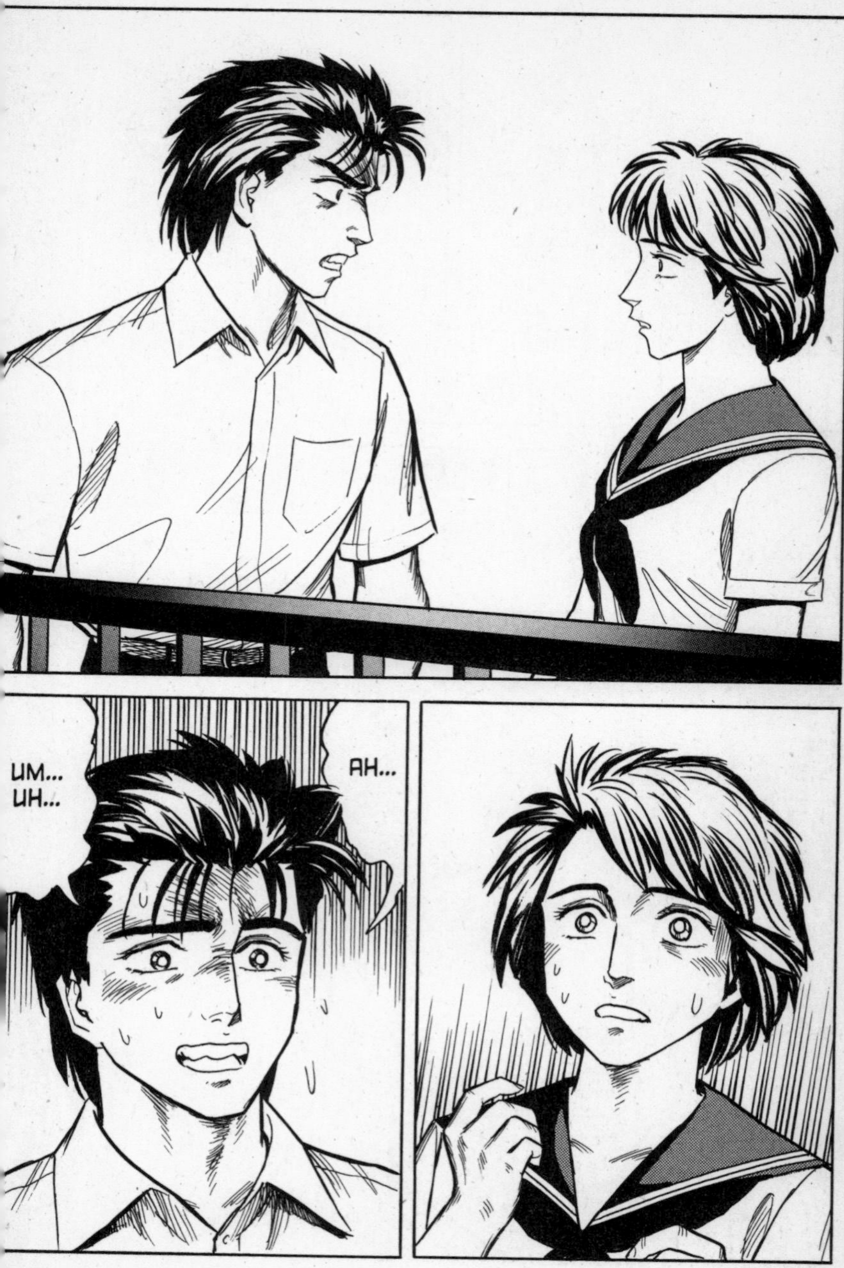
AH...
UM...
UH...

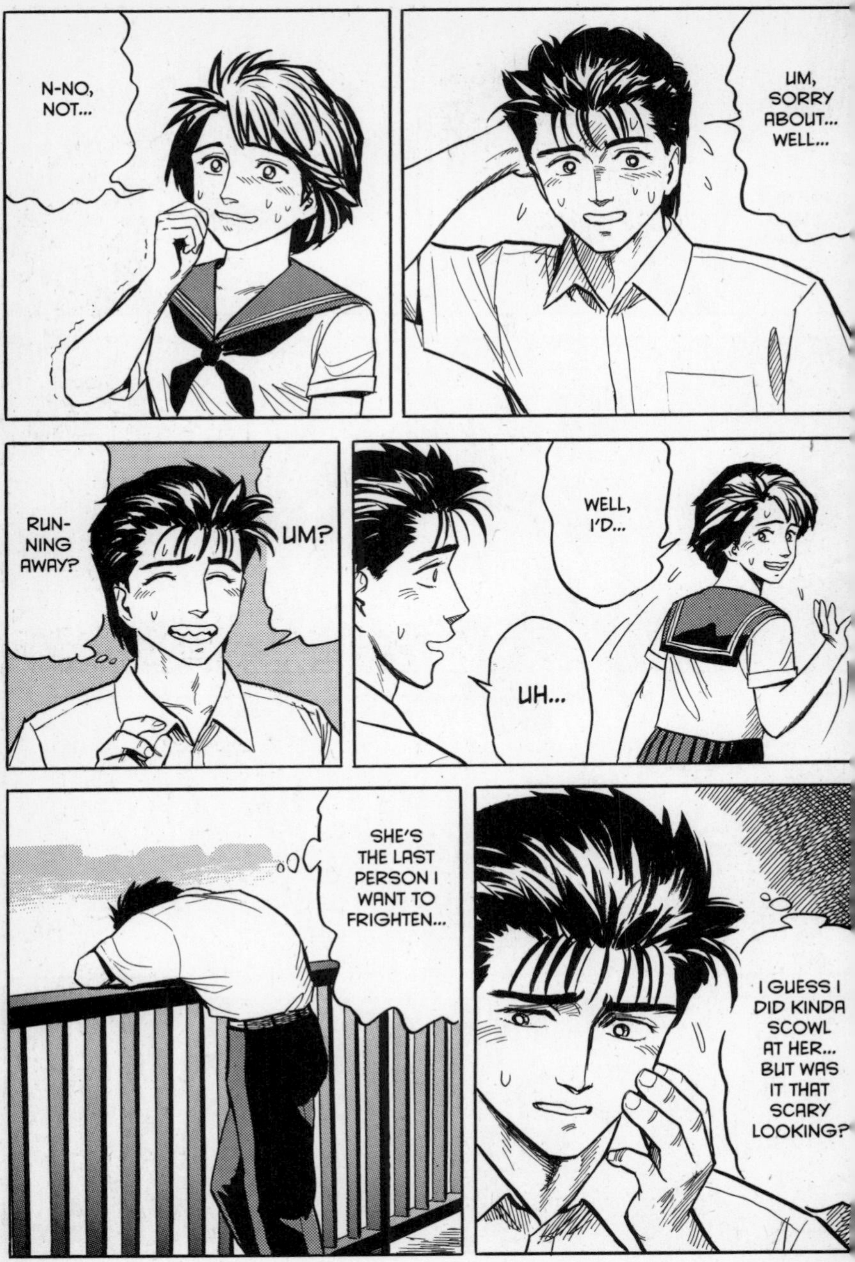
UM, SORRY ABOUT... WELL...
N-NO, NOT...
WELL, I'D...
UH...
UM?
RUN-NING AWAY?
I GUESS I DID KINDA SCOWL AT HER... BUT WAS IT THAT SCARY LOOKING?
SHE'S THE LAST PERSON I WANT TO FRIGHTEN...

HEH HEH... NO, I KNOW...

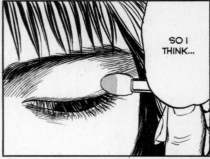

SO I THINK...

I HAVE PSYCHIC POWERS.

TO SENSE THE RED STRING?

THE ABILITY...

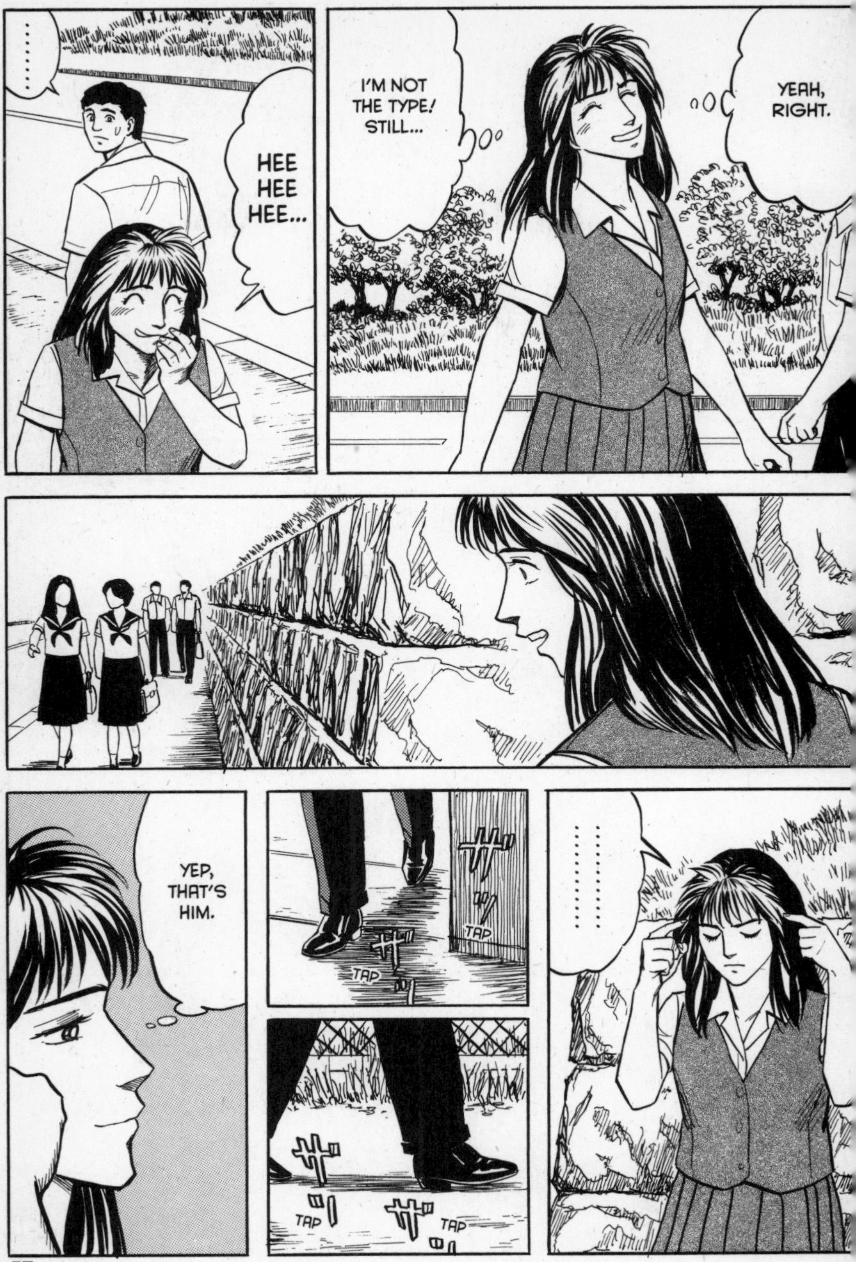

YEAH, RIGHT.
I'M NOT THE TYPE! STILL...
HEE HEE HEE...
......
......
TAP
TAP
TAP
TAP
YEP, THAT'S HIM.

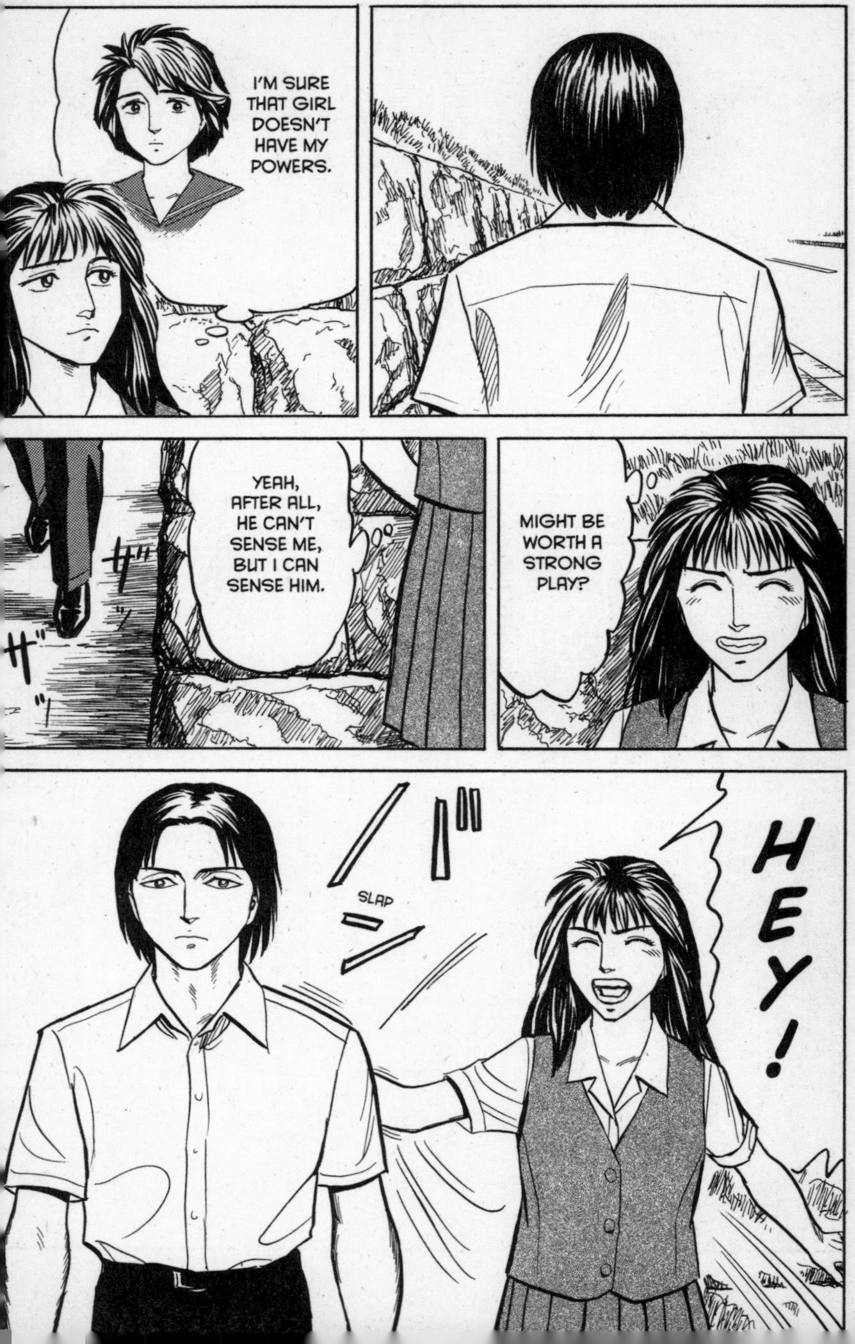
I'M SURE THAT GIRL DOESN'T HAVE MY POWERS.
MIGHT BE WORTH A STRONG PLAY?
YEAH, AFTER ALL, HE CAN'T SENSE ME, BUT I CAN SENSE HIM.
HEY!
SLAP

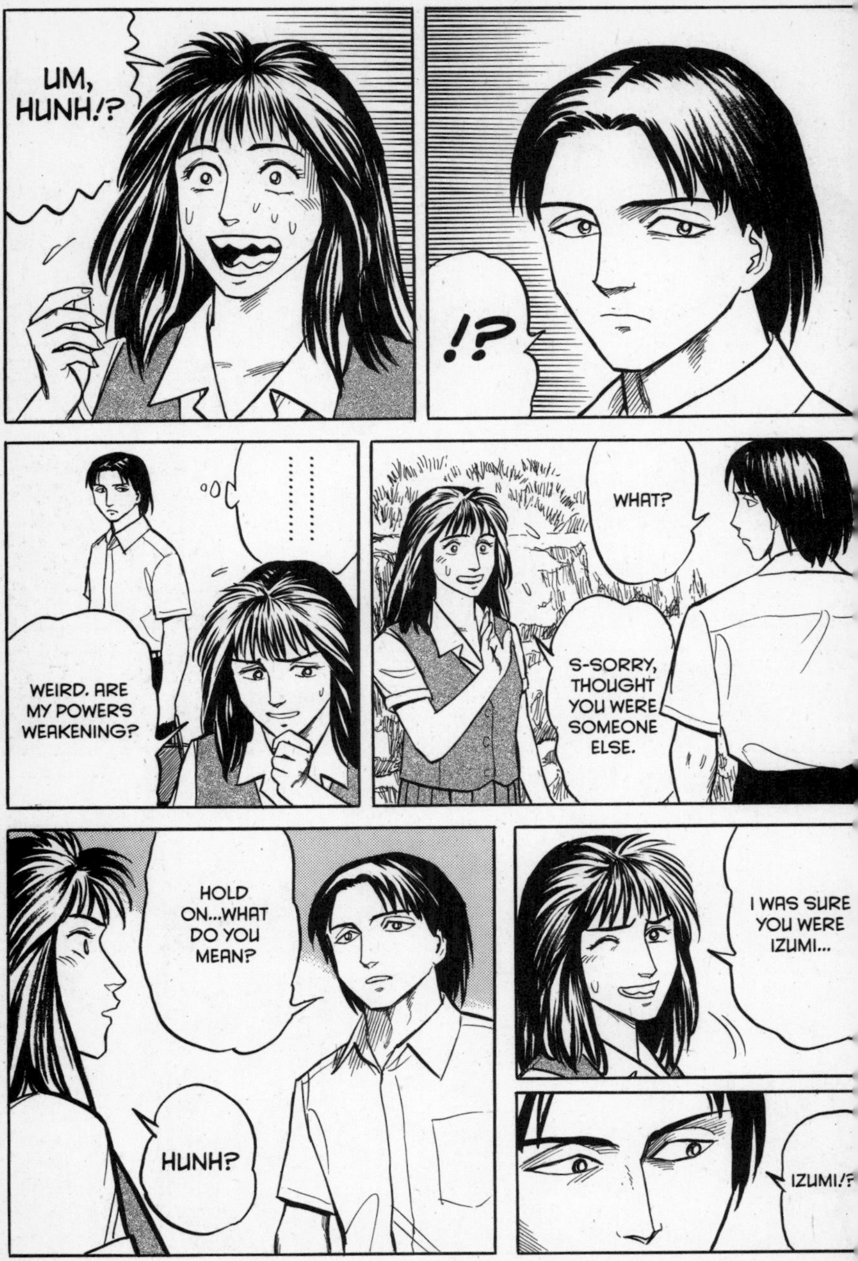
!?
UM, HUNH!?
WHAT?
S-SORRY, THOUGHT YOU WERE SOMEONE ELSE.
......
WEIRD. ARE MY POWERS WEAKENING?
I WAS SURE YOU WERE IZUMI...
IZUMI!?
HOLD ON...WHAT DO YOU MEAN?
HUNH?

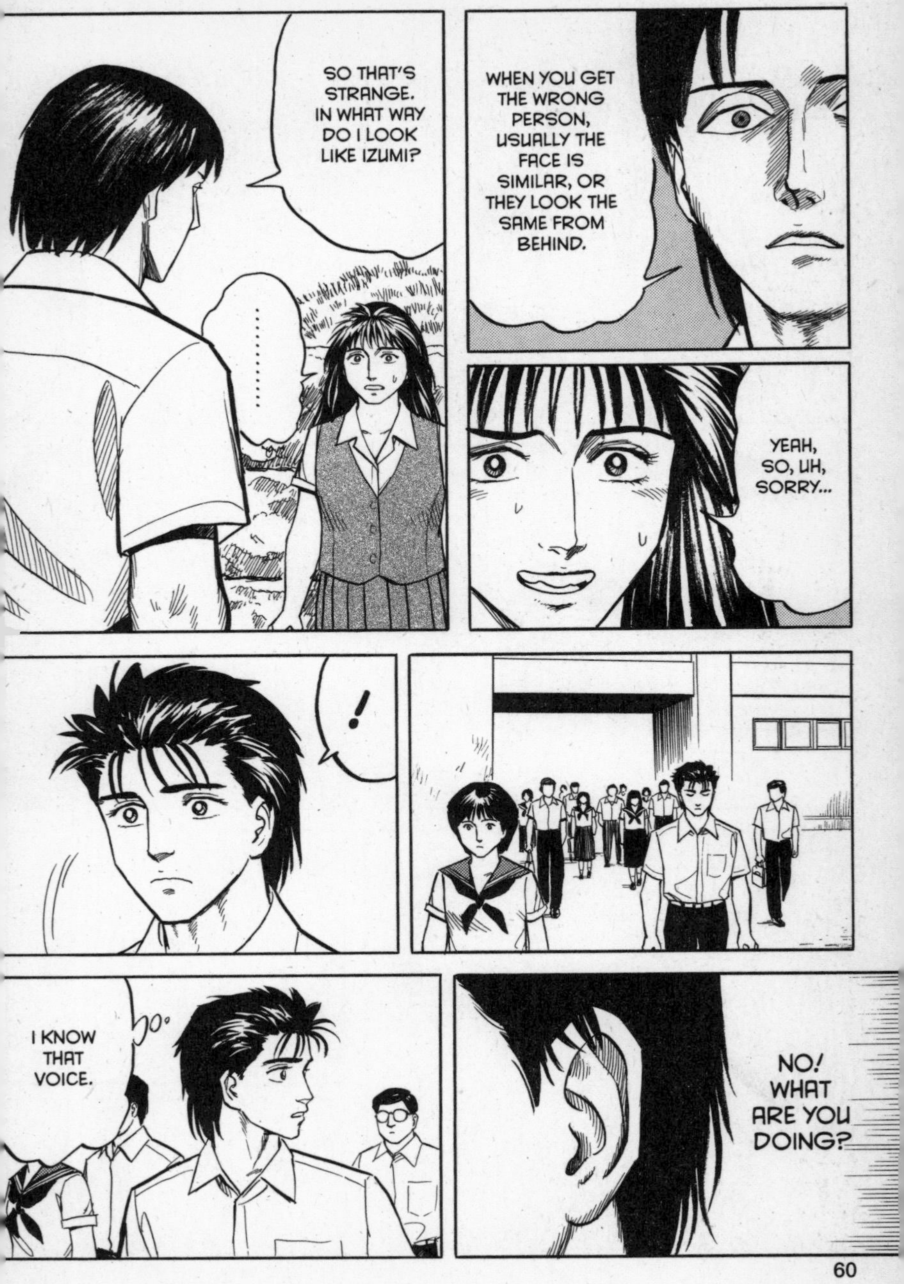
WHEN YOU GET THE WRONG PERSON, USUALLY THE FACE IS SIMILAR, OR THEY LOOK THE SAME FROM BEHIND.
YEAH, SO, UH, SORRY...
SO THAT'S STRANGE. IN WHAT WAY DO I LOOK LIKE IZUMI?
......
!
NO! WHAT ARE YOU DOING?
I KNOW THAT VOICE.

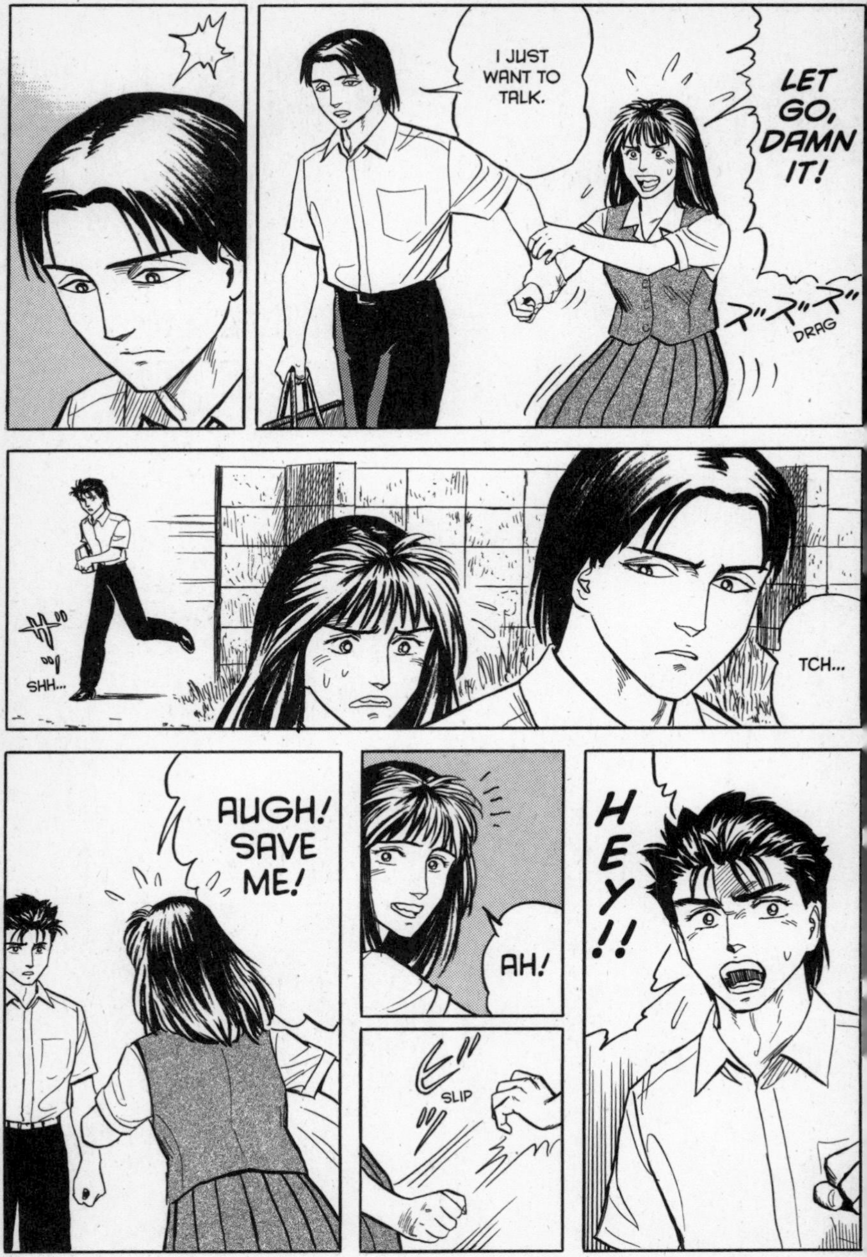
LET GO, DAMN IT!
I JUST WANT TO TALK.
DRAG
TCH...
SHH...
HEY!!
AH!
SLIP
AUGH! SAVE ME!

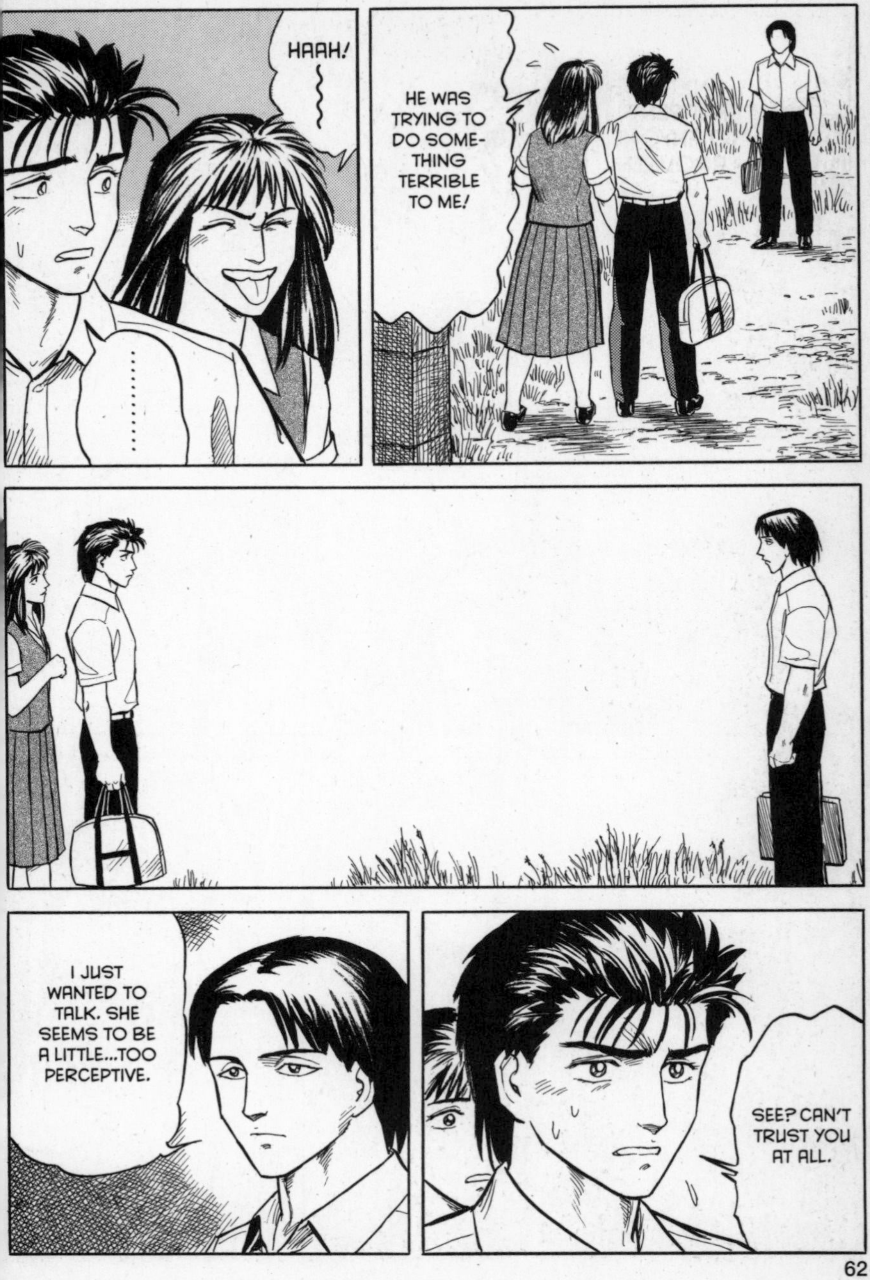
HE WAS TRYING TO DO SOME-THING TERRIBLE TO ME!
HAAH!
......
SEE? CAN'T TRUST YOU AT ALL.
I JUST WANTED TO TALK. SHE SEEMS TO BE A LITTLE...TOO PERCEPTIVE.

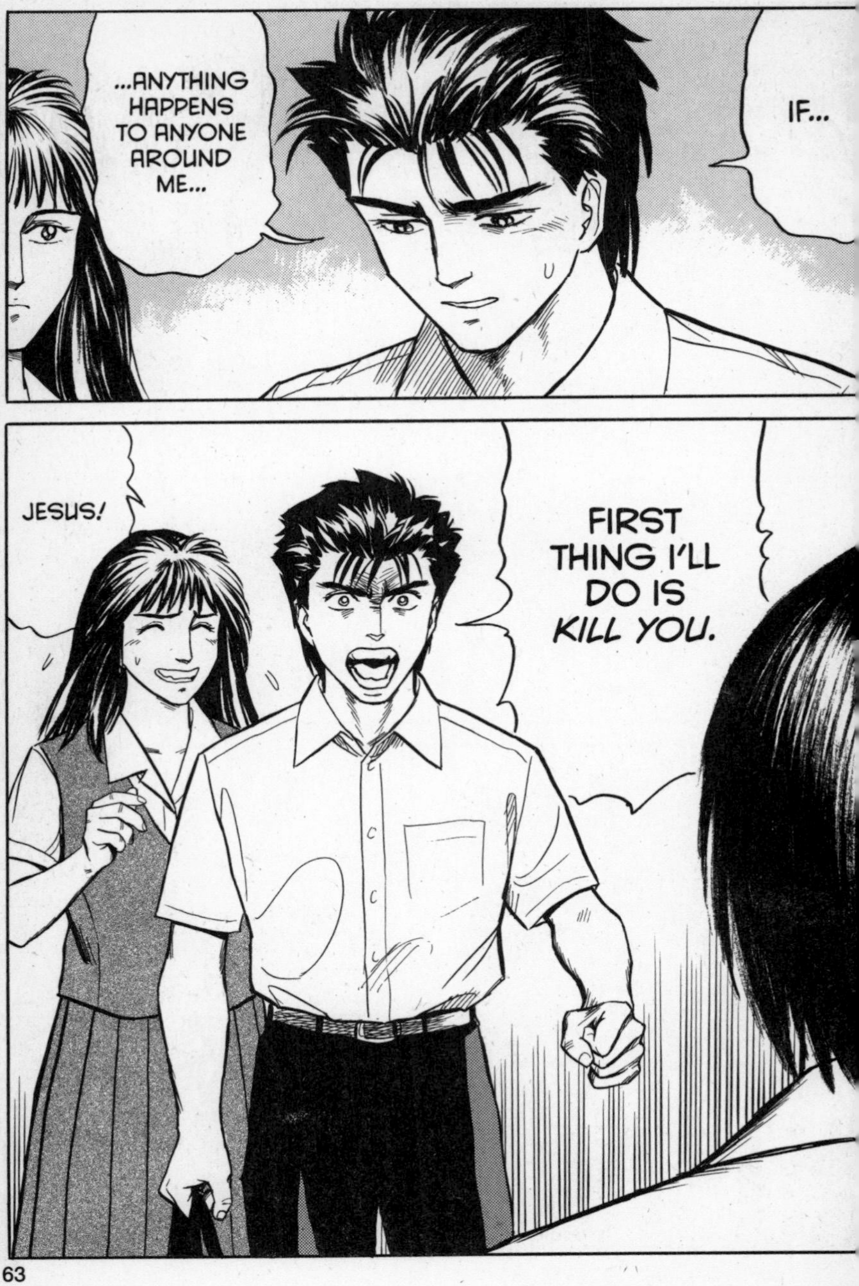
IF...
...ANYTHING HAPPENS TO ANYONE AROUND ME...
FIRST THING I'LL DO IS *KILL YOU.*
JESUS!

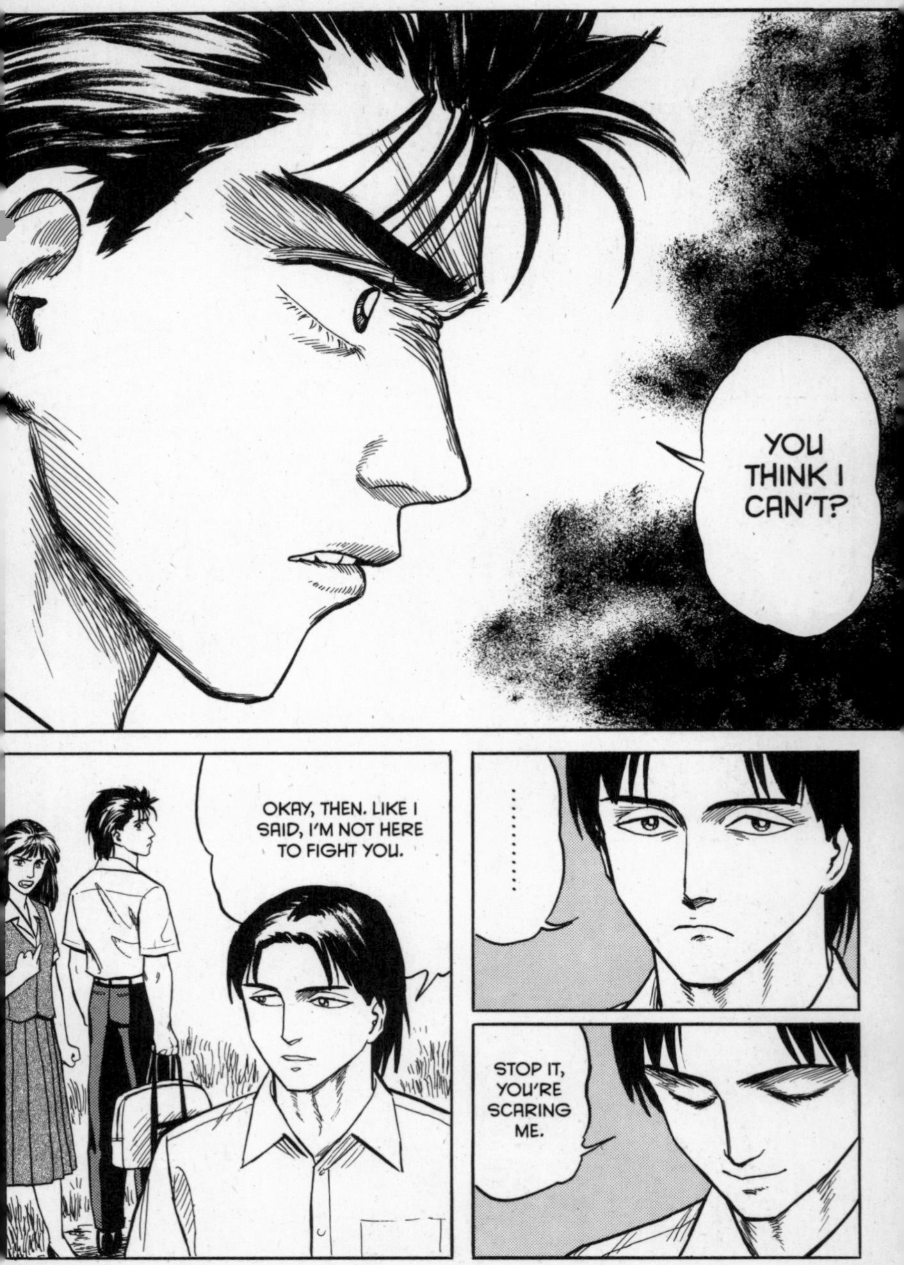
YOU THINK I CAN'T?
......
STOP IT, YOU'RE SCARING ME.
OKAY, THEN. LIKE I SAID, I'M NOT HERE TO FIGHT YOU.

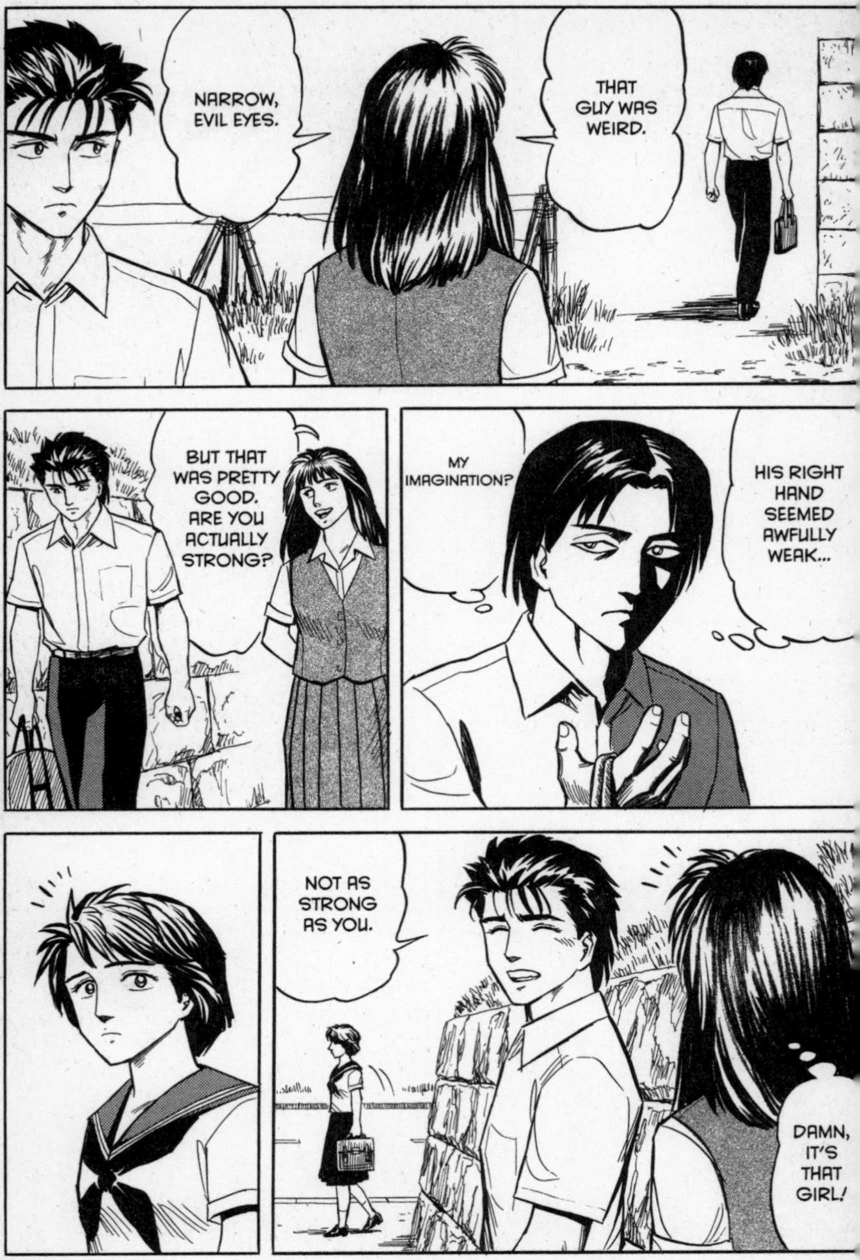
THAT GUY WAS WEIRD.
NARROW, EVIL EYES.
HIS RIGHT HAND SEEMED AWFULLY WEAK...
MY IMAGINATION?
BUT THAT WAS PRETTY GOOD. ARE YOU ACTUALLY STRONG?
NOT AS STRONG AS YOU.
DAMN, IT'S THAT GIRL!

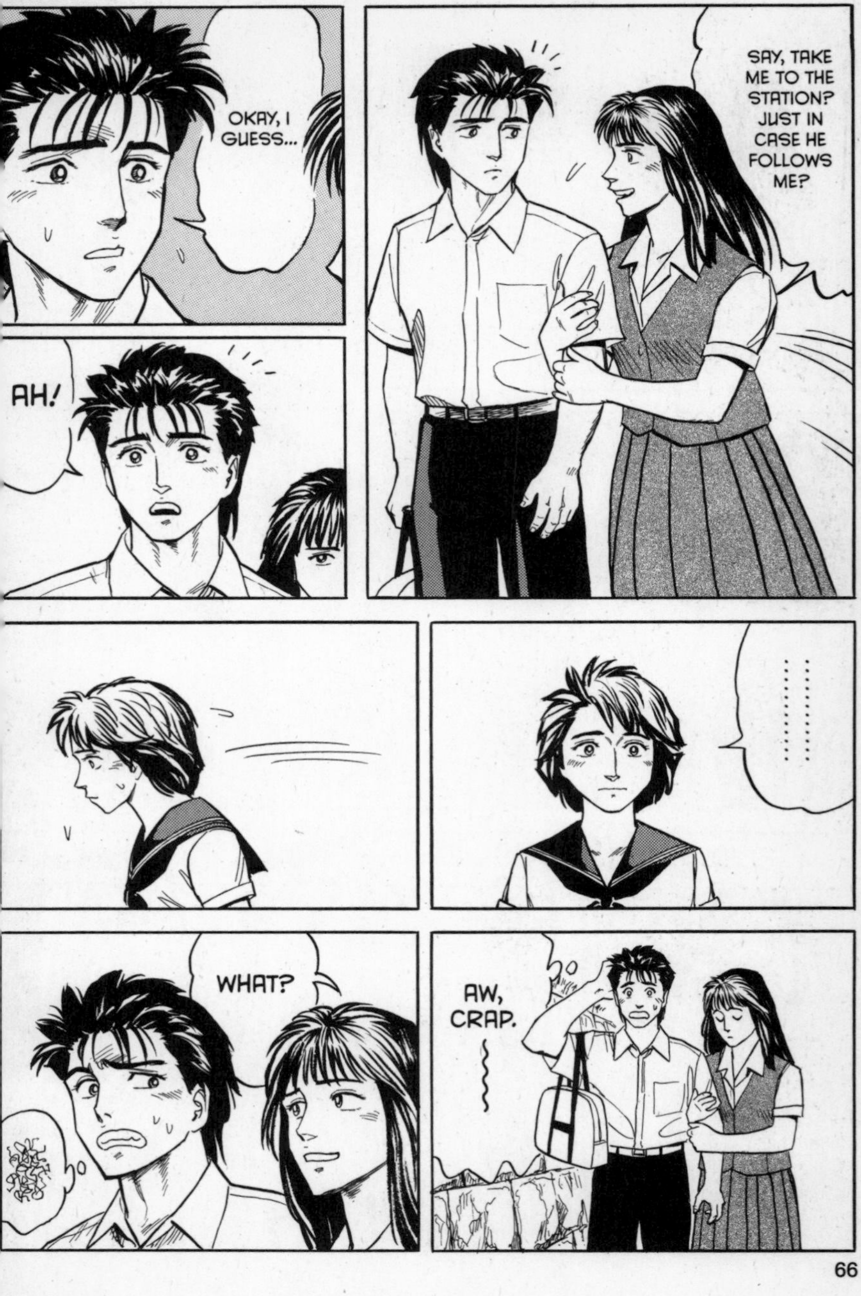
SAY, TAKE ME TO THE STATION? JUST IN CASE HE FOLLOWS ME?
OKAY, I GUESS...
AH!
......
AW, CRAP.
WHAT?

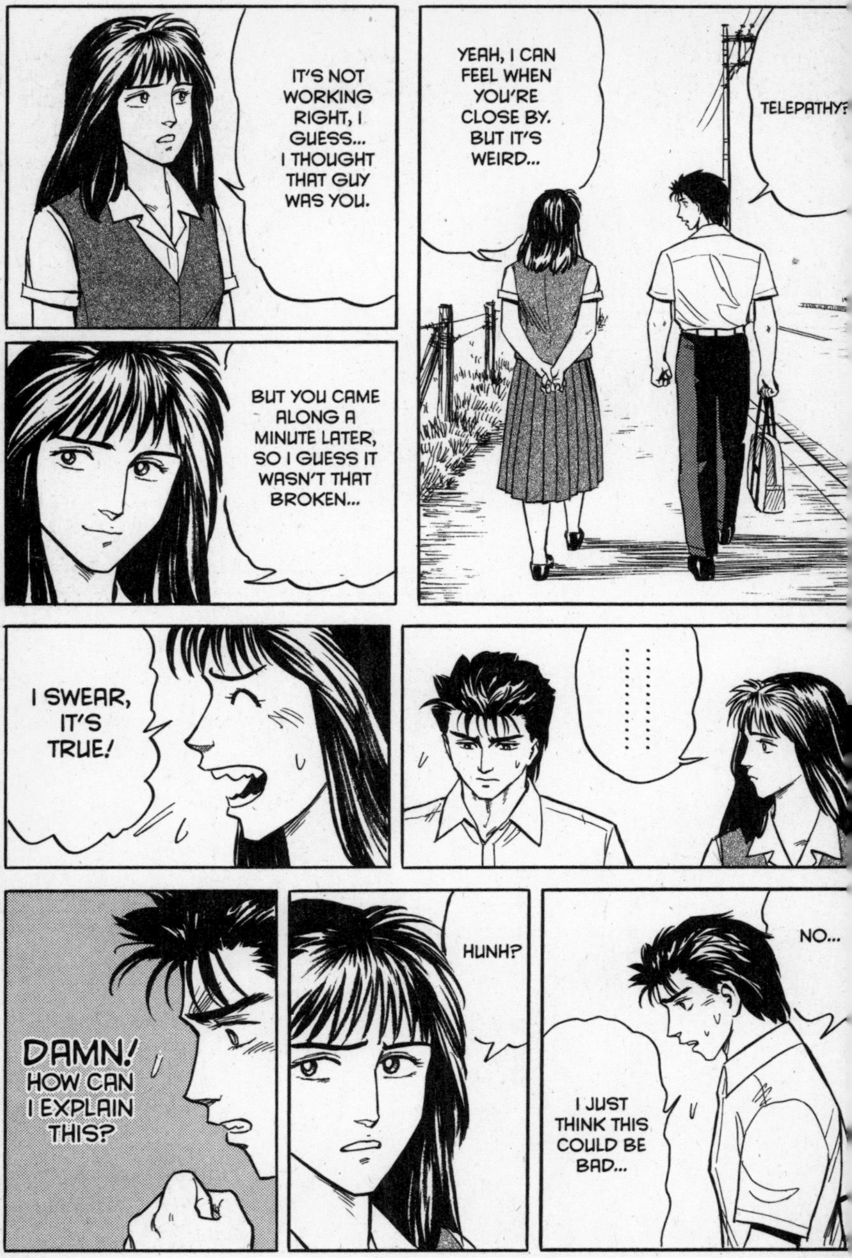
TELEPATHY?
YEAH, I CAN FEEL WHEN YOU'RE CLOSE BY. BUT IT'S WEIRD...
IT'S NOT WORKING RIGHT, I GUESS... I THOUGHT THAT GUY WAS YOU.
BUT YOU CAME ALONG A MINUTE LATER, SO I GUESS IT WASN'T THAT BROKEN...
......
I SWEAR, IT'S TRUE!
NO...
I JUST THINK THIS COULD BE BAD...
HUNH?
DAMN! HOW CAN I EXPLAIN THIS?

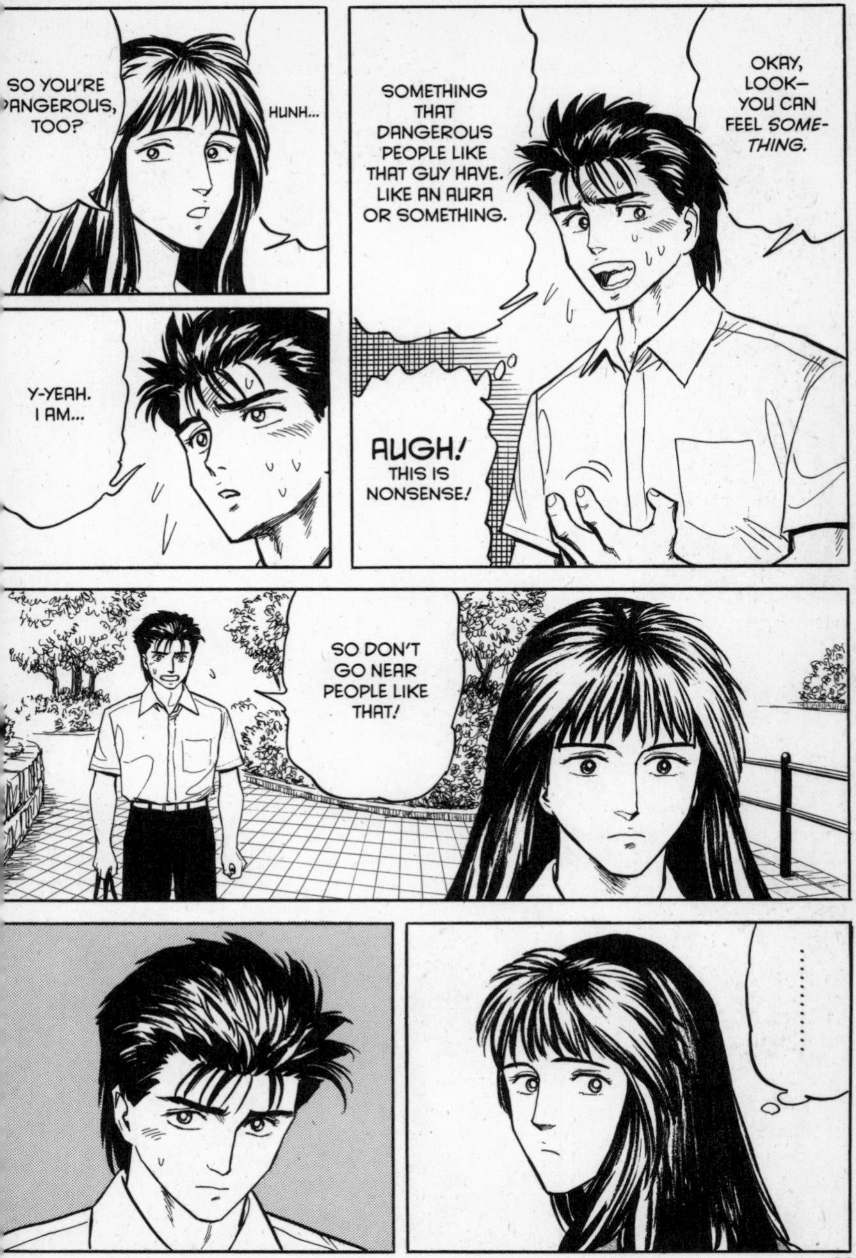

OKAY, LOOK— YOU CAN FEEL *SOMETHING.*
SOMETHING THAT DANGEROUS PEOPLE LIKE THAT GUY HAVE. LIKE AN AURA OR SOMETHING.
AUGH! THIS IS NONSENSE!
HUNH...
SO YOU'RE DANGEROUS, TOO?
Y-YEAH. I AM...
SO DON'T GO NEAR PEOPLE LIKE THAT!
......

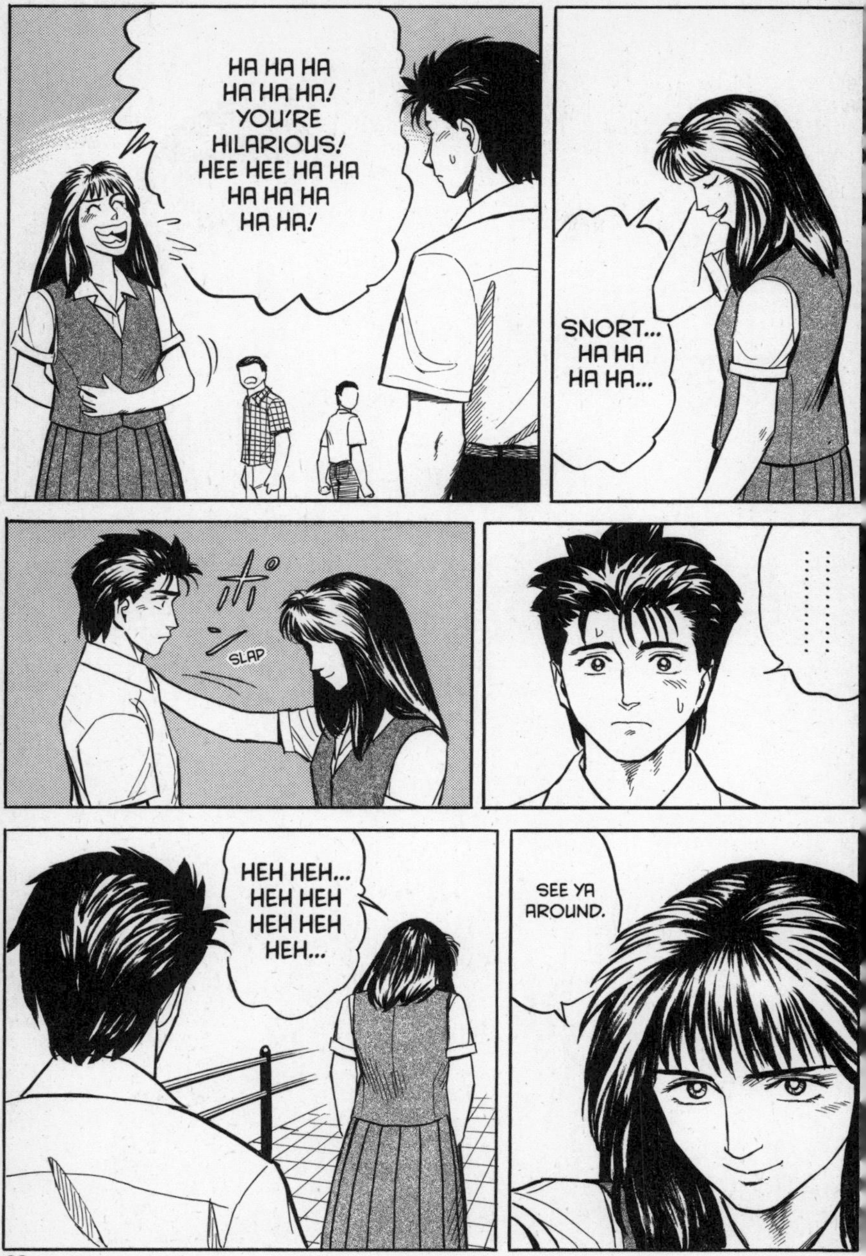
SNORT... HA HA HA HA...
HA HA HA HA HA HA! YOU'RE HILARIOUS! HEE HEE HA HA HA HA HA HA HA!
......
SLAP
SEE YA AROUND.
HEH HEH... HEH HEH HEH HEH HEH...

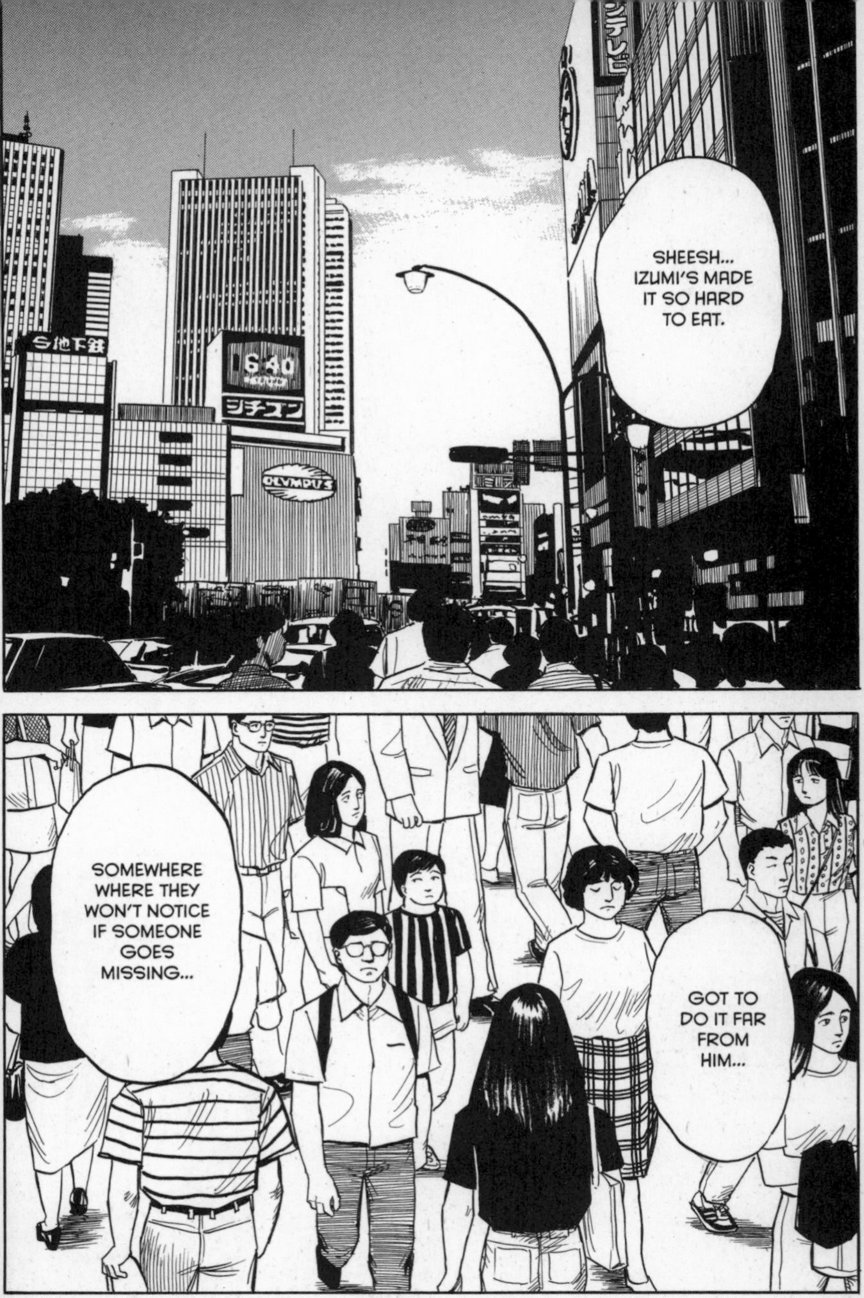
SHEESH... IZUMI'S MADE IT SO HARD TO EAT.
GOT TO DO IT FAR FROM HIM...
SOMEWHERE WHERE THEY WON'T NOTICE IF SOMEONE GOES MISSING...

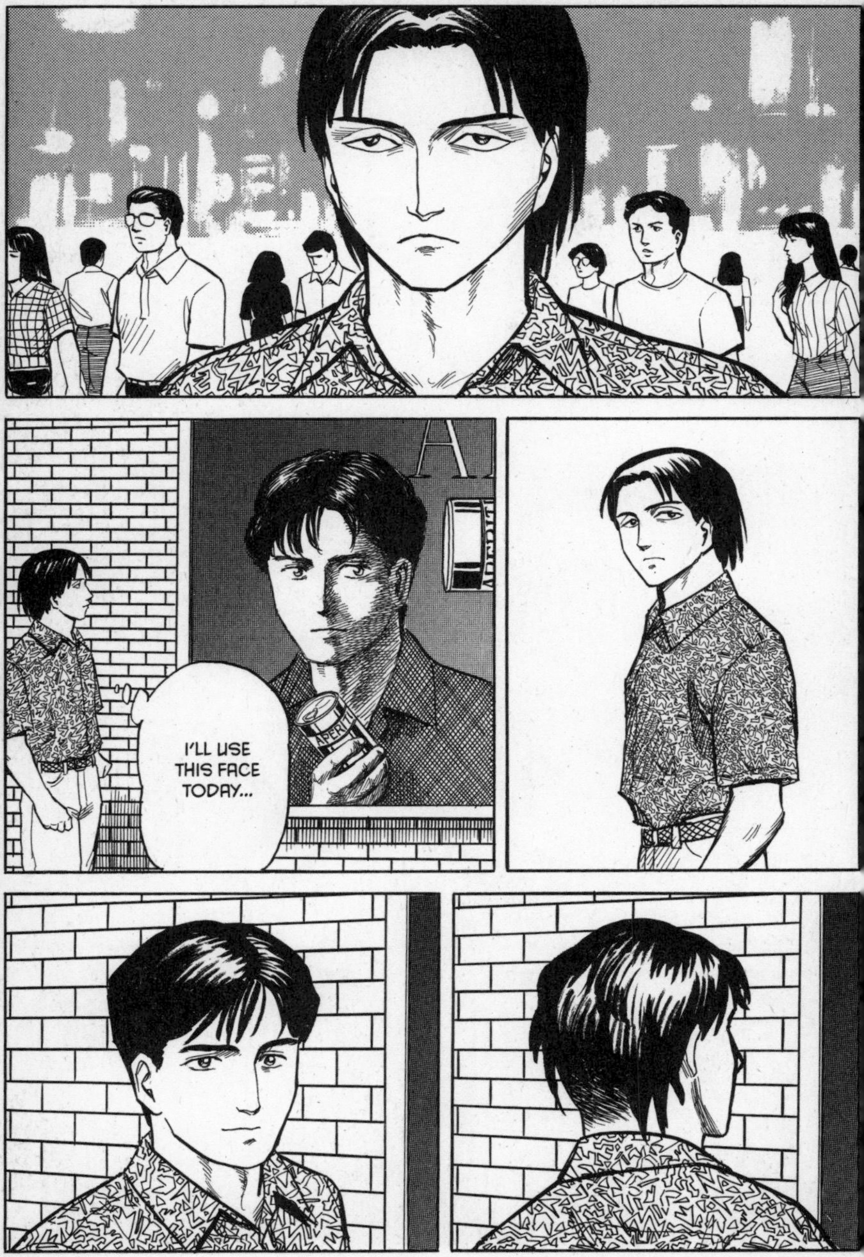
I'LL USE
THIS FACE
TODAY...

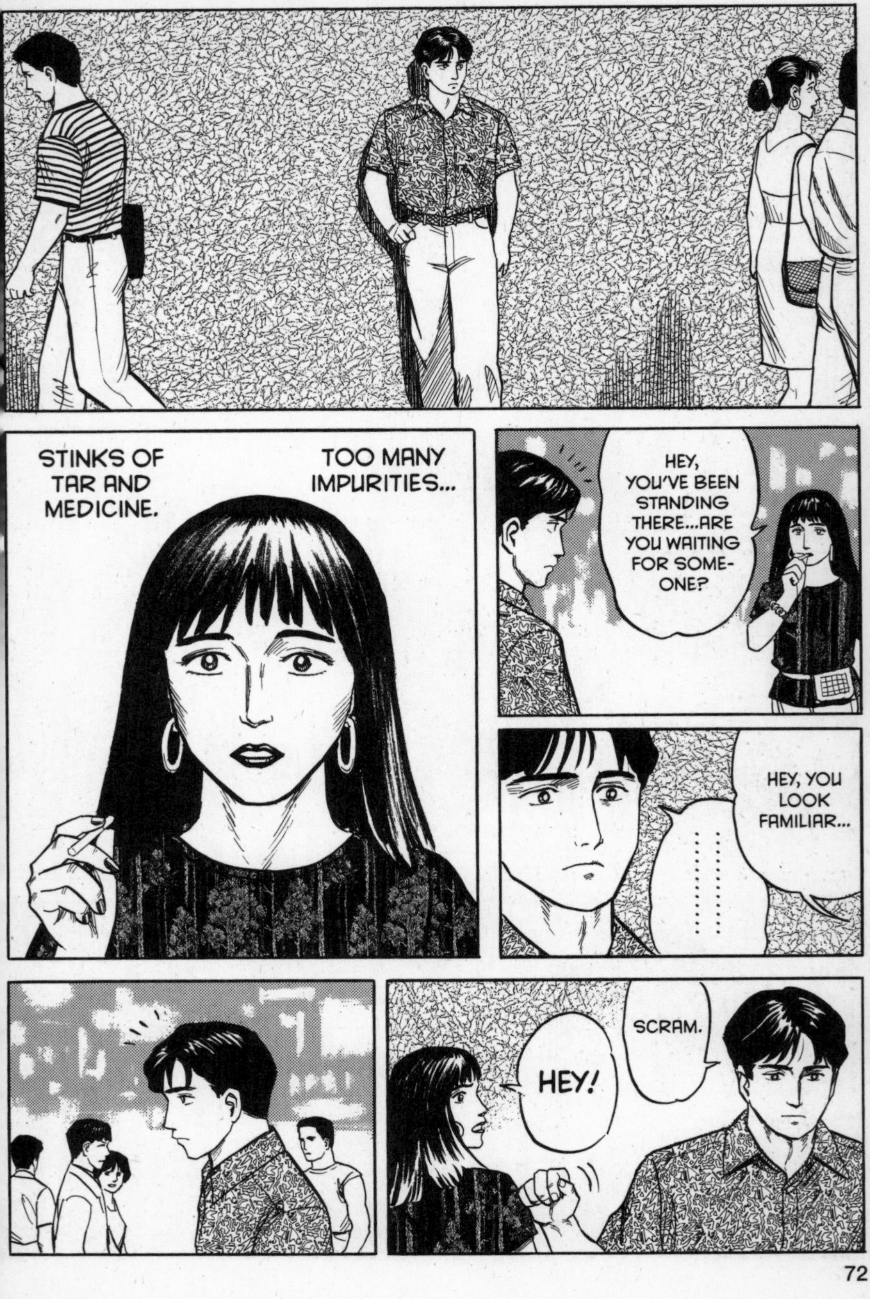
HEY, YOU'VE BEEN STANDING THERE...ARE YOU WAITING FOR SOME-ONE?
HEY, YOU LOOK FAMILIAR...
......
TOO MANY IMPURITIES...
STINKS OF TAR AND MEDICINE.
SCRAM.
HEY!

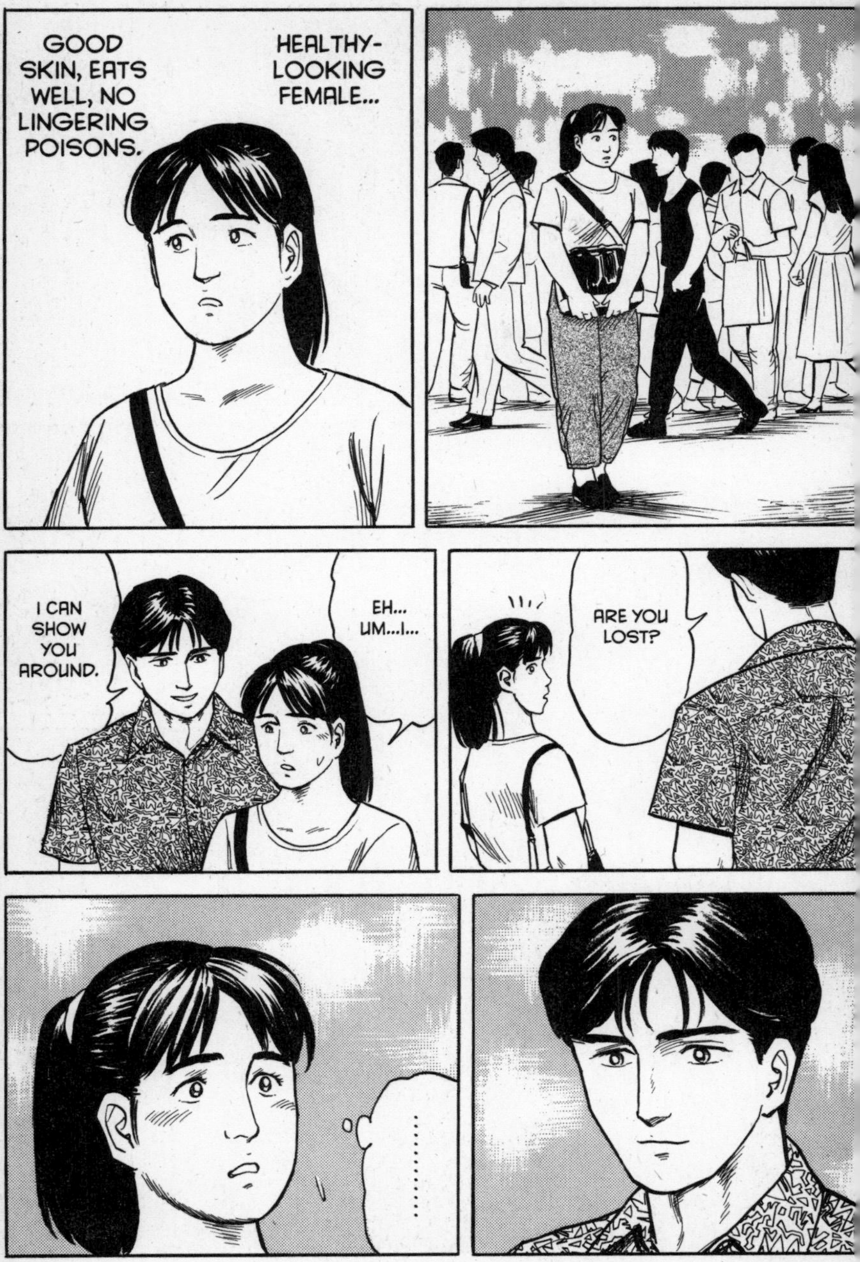
HEALTHY-LOOKING FEMALE...
GOOD SKIN, EATS WELL, NO LINGERING POISONS.
ARE YOU LOST?
EH... UM...I...
I CAN SHOW YOU AROUND.
....

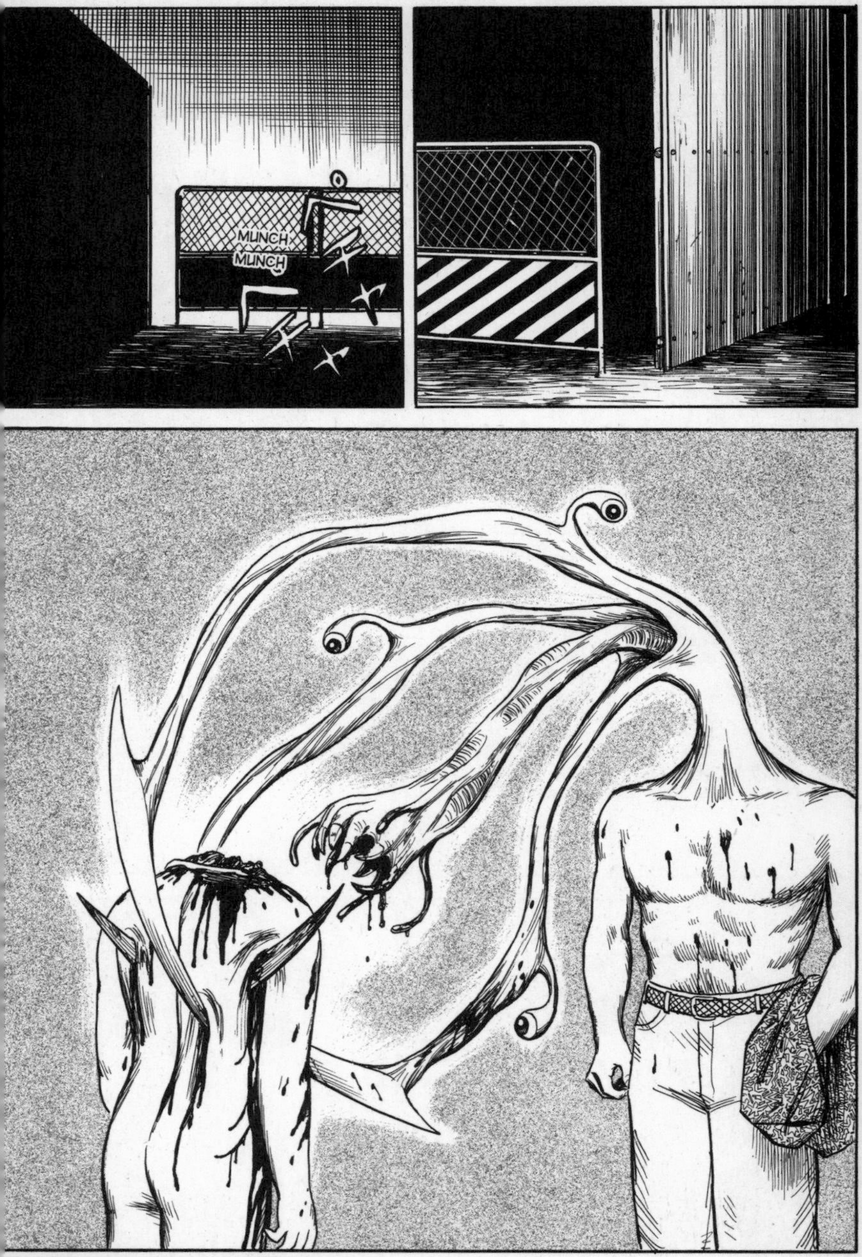
MUNCH
MUNCH

CHAPTER 19: THE END

CHAPTER 20: SIGNS

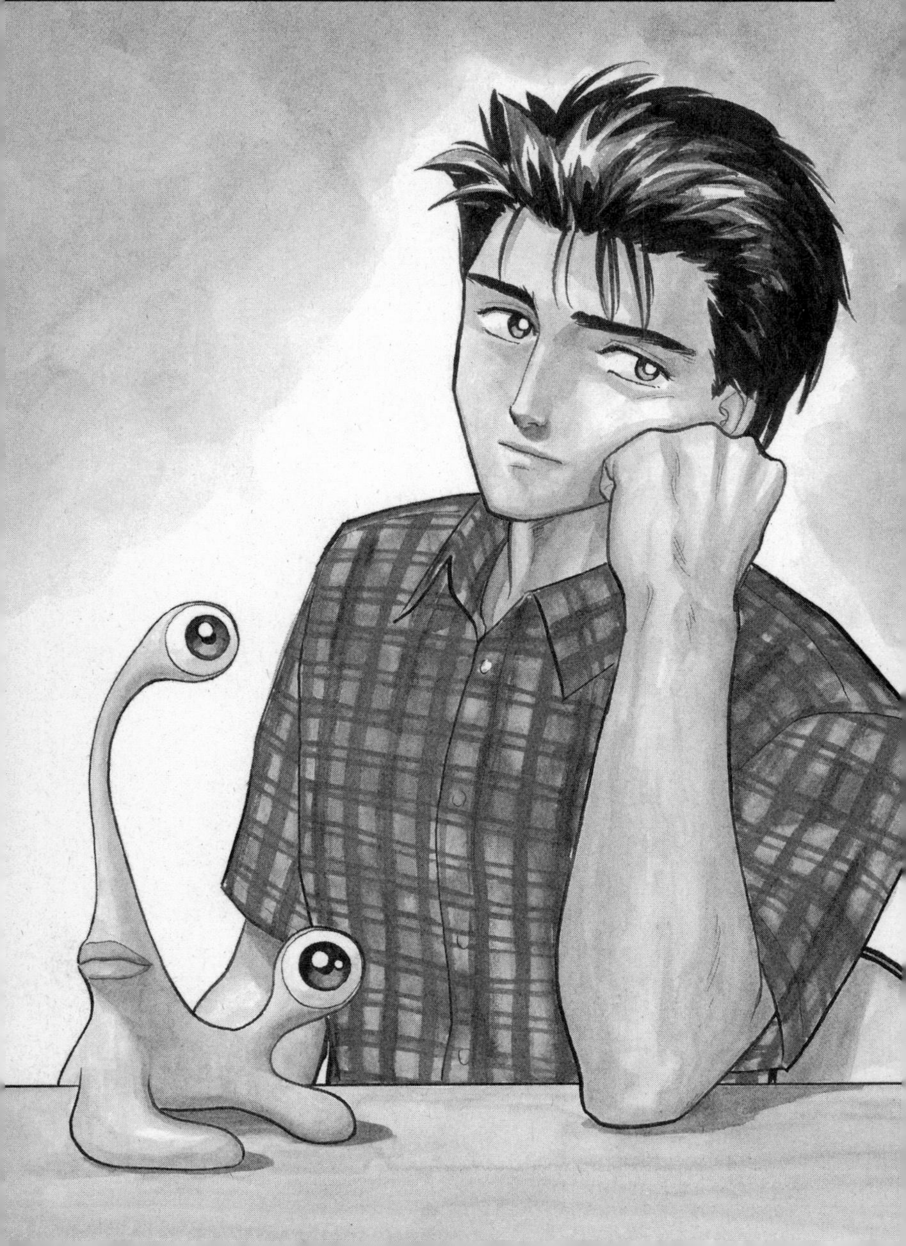

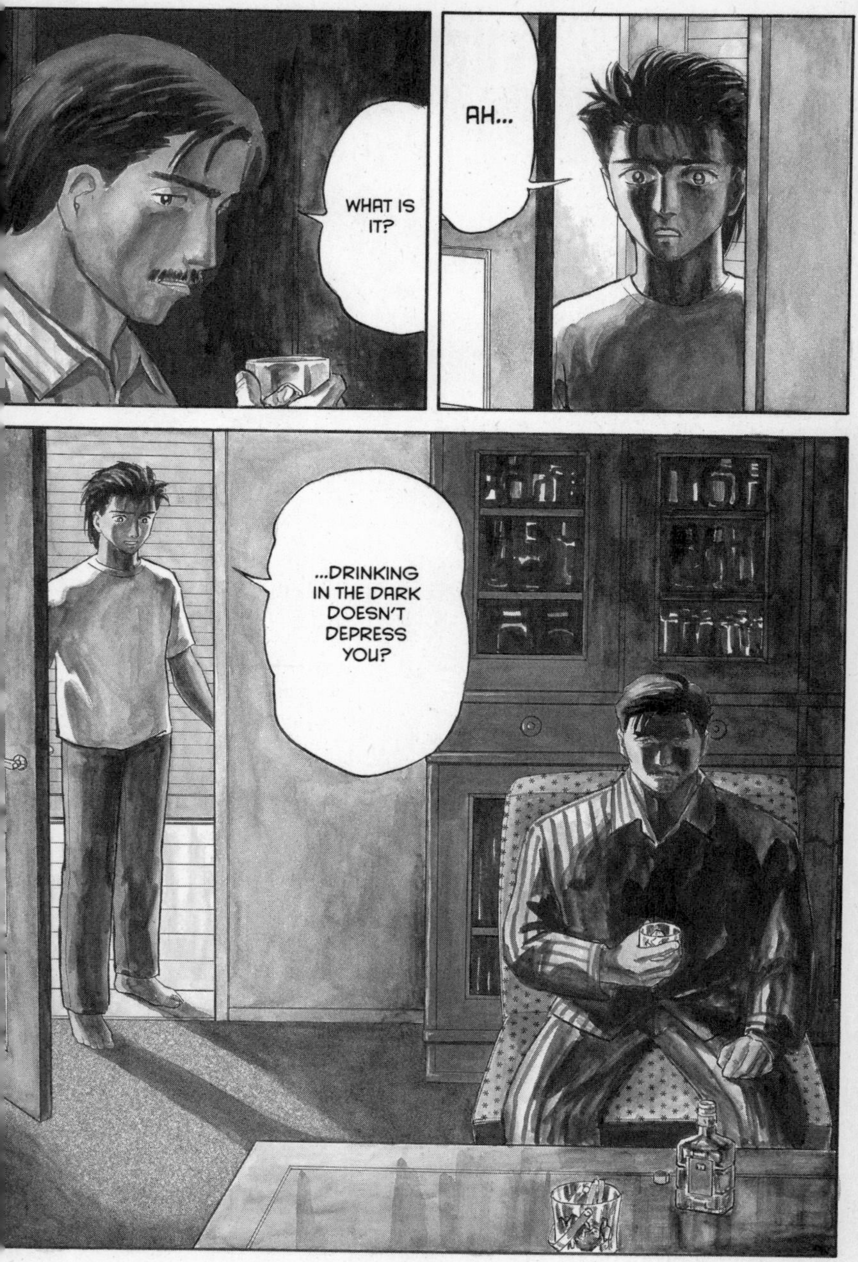
AH...
WHAT IS IT?
...DRINKING IN THE DARK DOESN'T DEPRESS YOU?

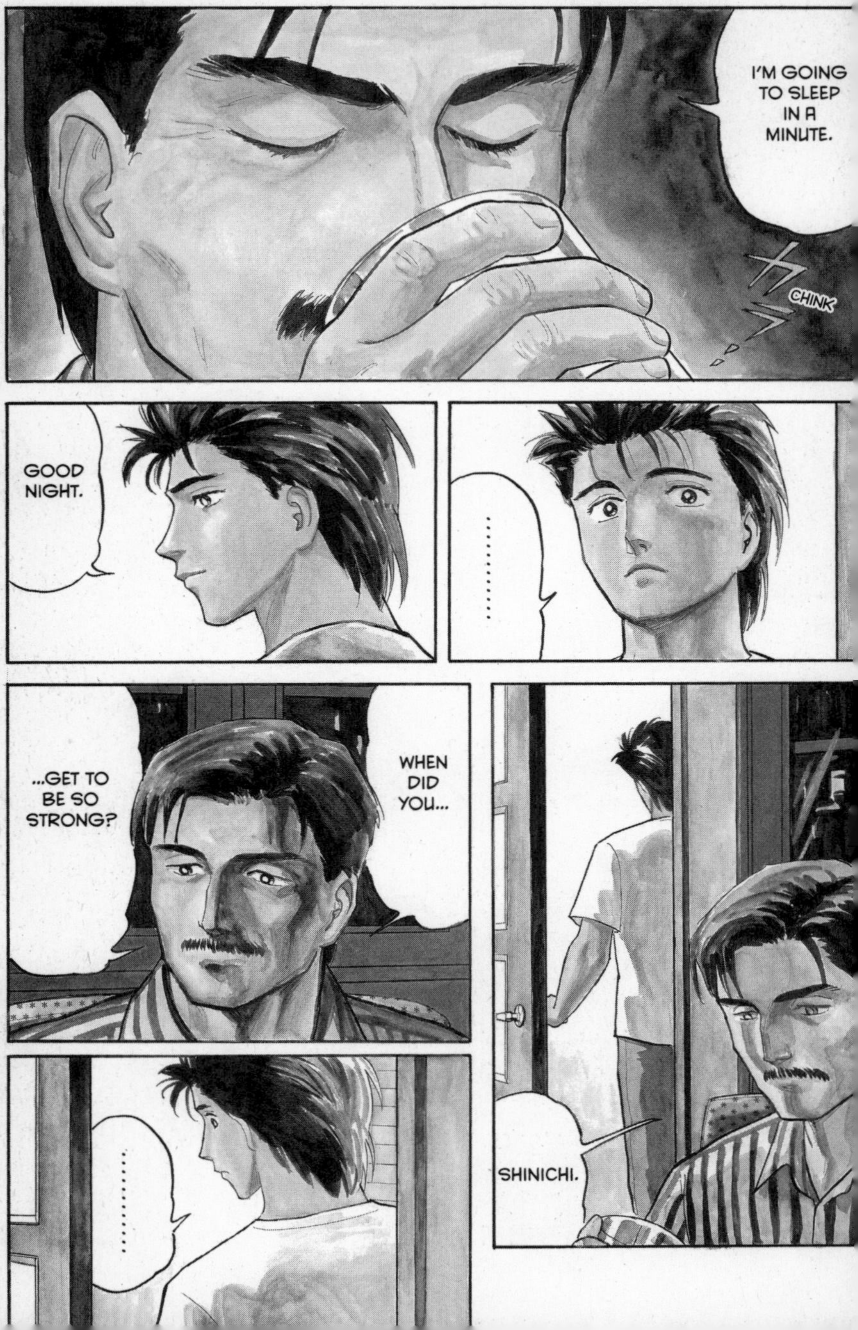
I'M GOING TO SLEEP IN A MINUTE.
CHINK
......
GOOD NIGHT.
SHINICHI.
WHEN DID YOU...
...GET TO BE SO STRONG?
......

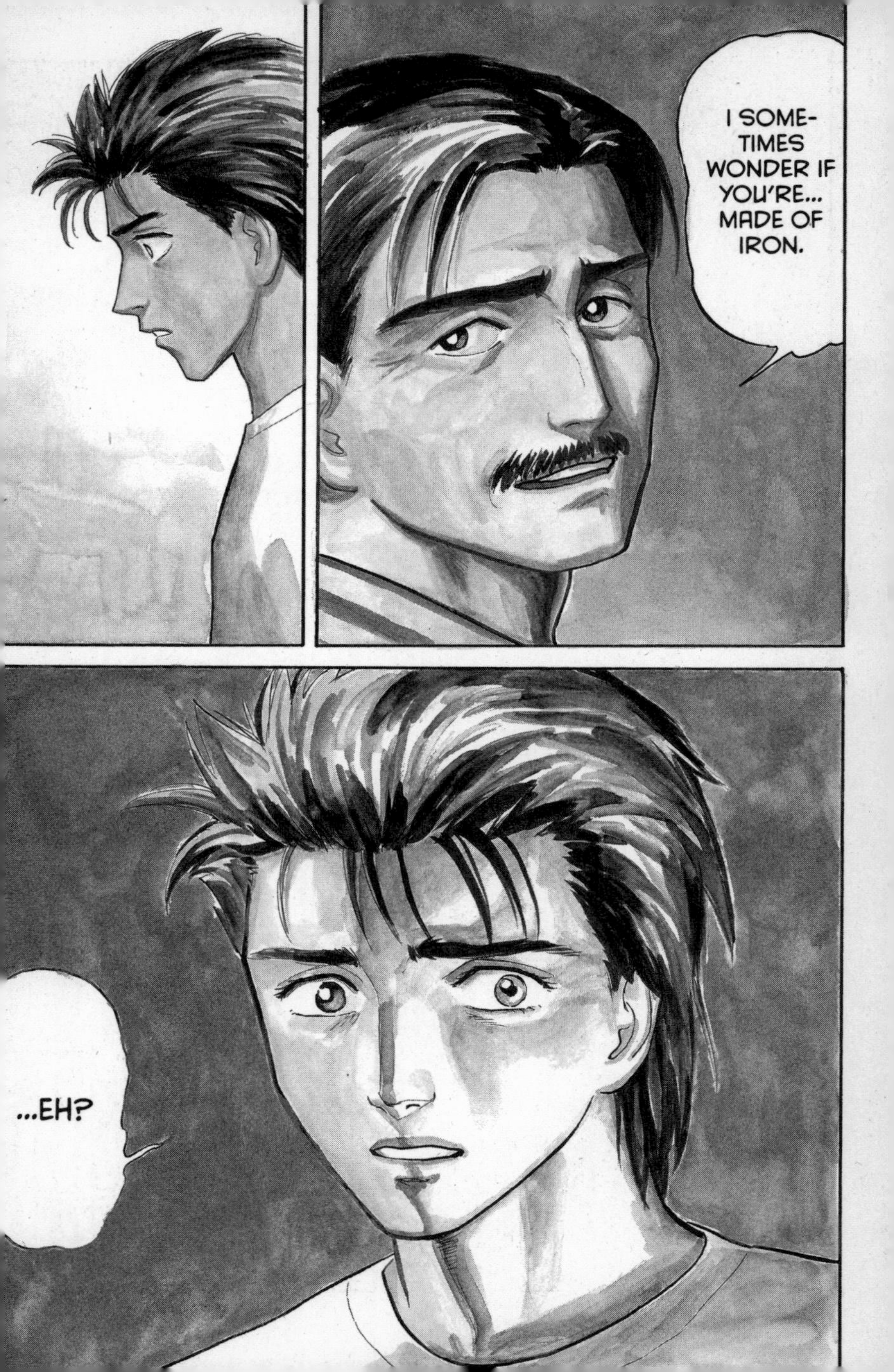
I SOME-TIMES WONDER IF YOU'RE... MADE OF IRON.
...EH?

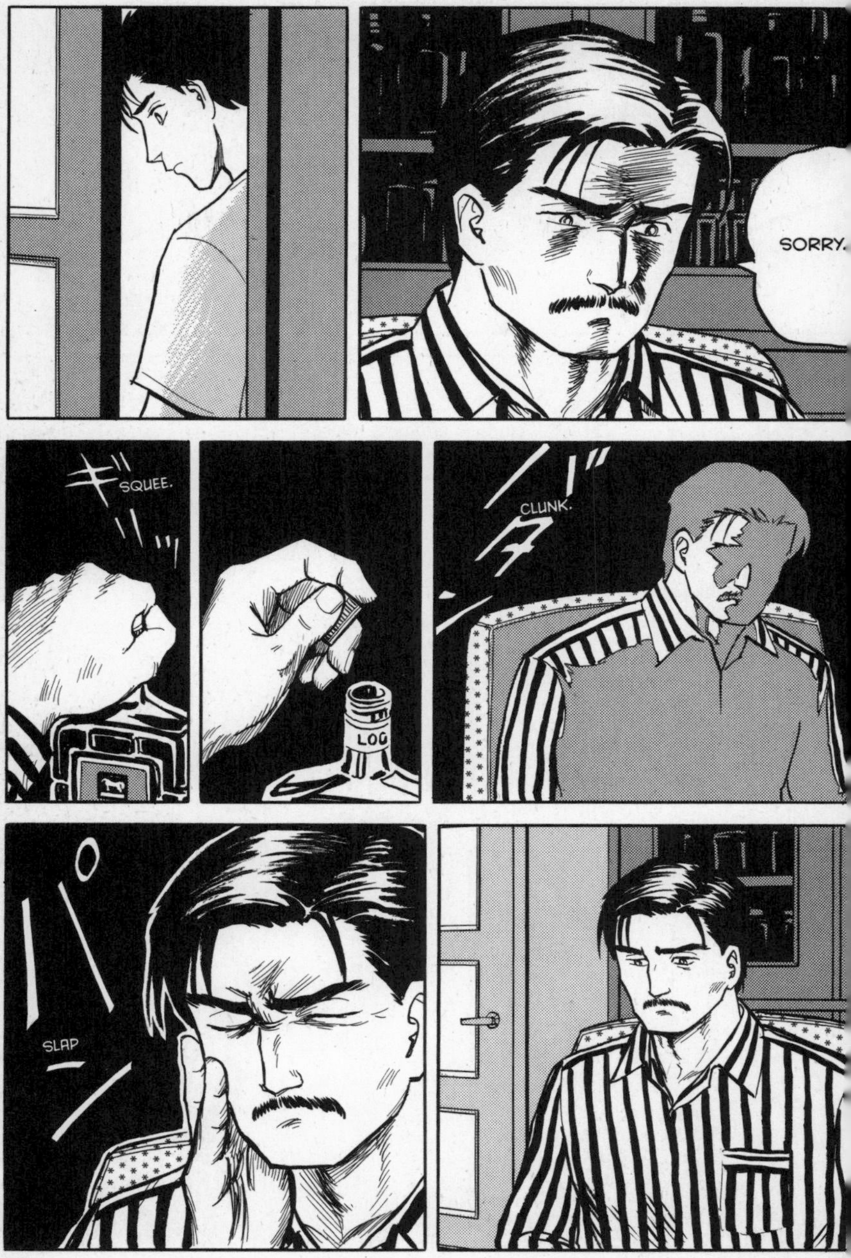
SORRY.
CLUNK.
LOG
SQUEE.
SLAP

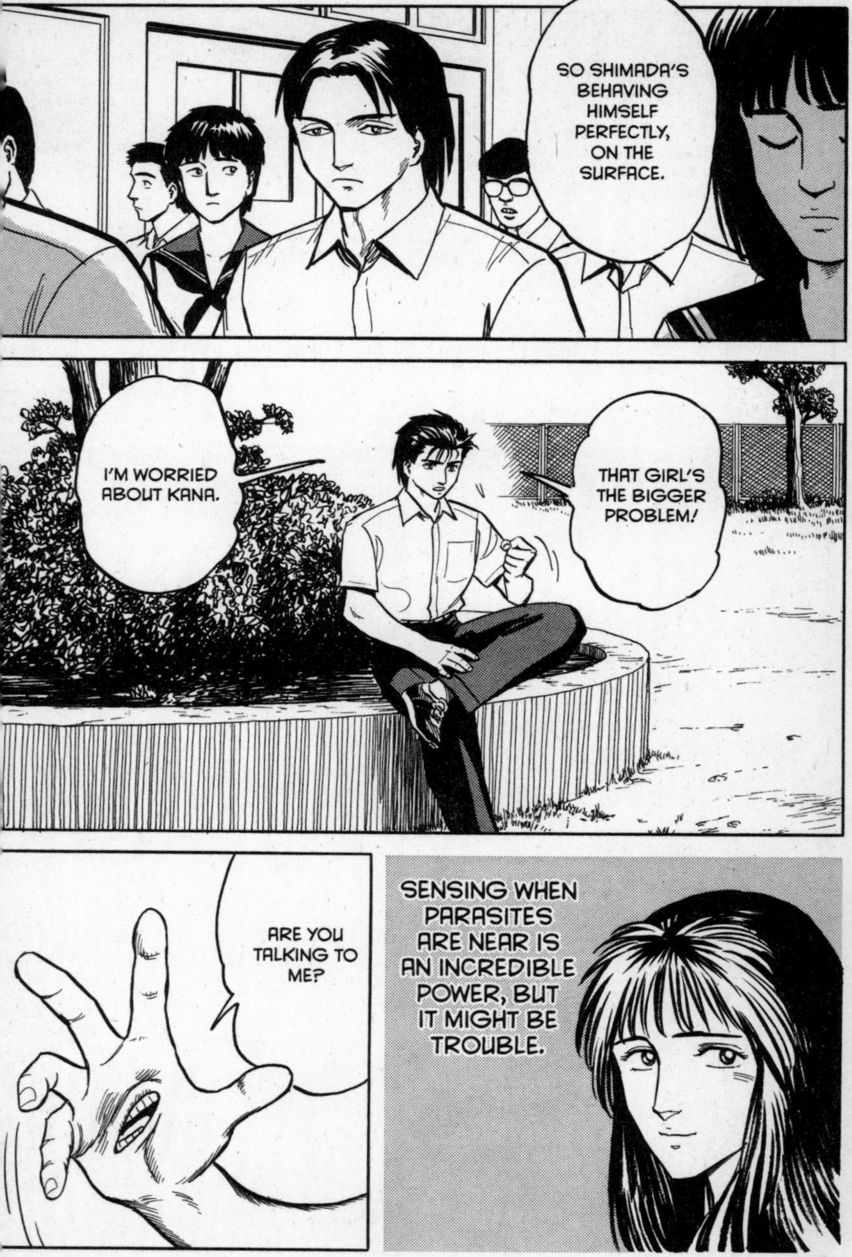
SO SHIMADA'S BEHAVING HIMSELF PERFECTLY, ON THE SURFACE.
THAT GIRL'S THE BIGGER PROBLEM!
I'M WORRIED ABOUT KANA.
SENSING WHEN PARASITES ARE NEAR IS AN INCREDIBLE POWER, BUT IT MIGHT BE TROUBLE.
ARE YOU TALKING TO ME?

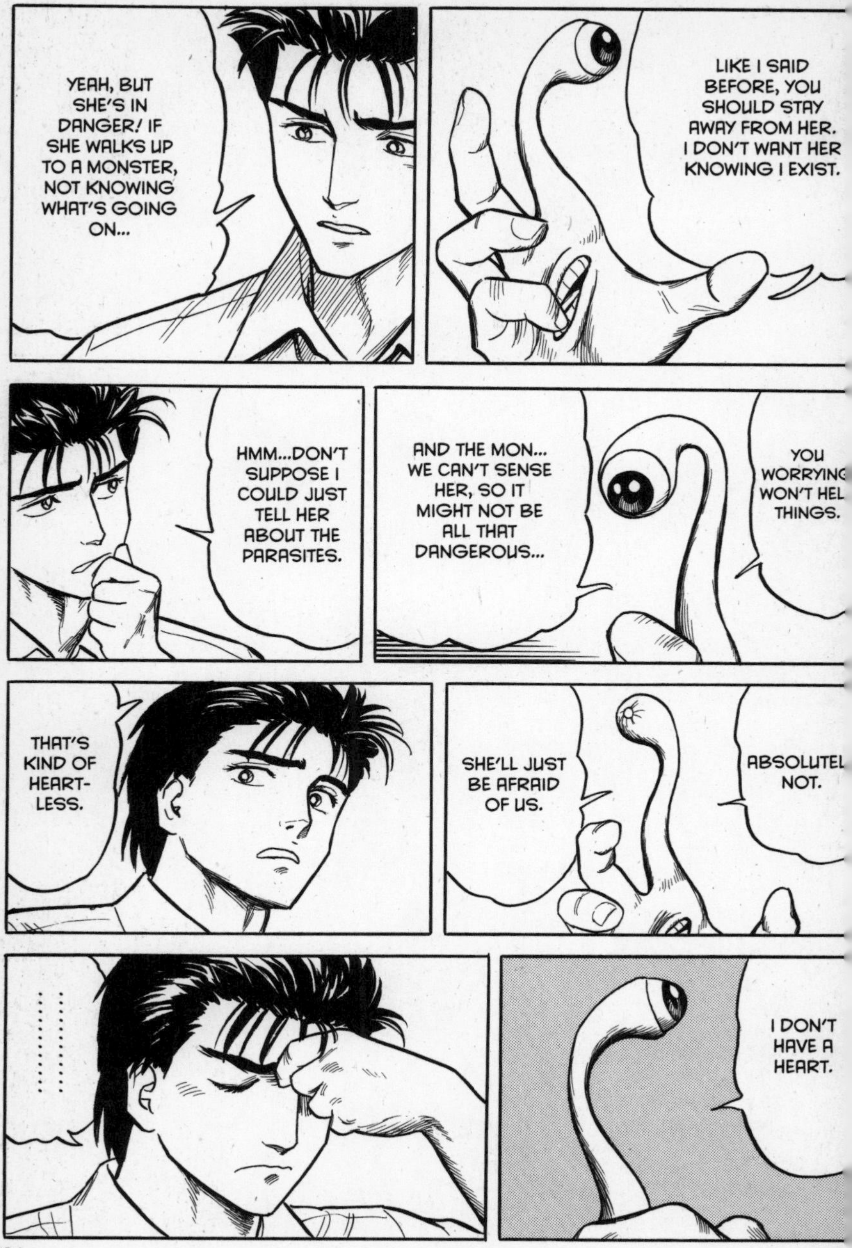
LIKE I SAID BEFORE, YOU SHOULD STAY AWAY FROM HER. I DON'T WANT HER KNOWING I EXIST.
YEAH, BUT SHE'S IN DANGER! IF SHE WALKS UP TO A MONSTER, NOT KNOWING WHAT'S GOING ON...
YOU WORRYING WON'T HEL THINGS.
AND THE MON... WE CAN'T SENSE HER, SO IT MIGHT NOT BE ALL THAT DANGEROUS...
HMM...DON'T SUPPOSE I COULD JUST TELL HER ABOUT THE PARASITES.
ABSOLUTEL NOT.
SHE'LL JUST BE AFRAID OF US.
THAT'S KIND OF HEART-LESS.
I DON'T HAVE A HEART.
......

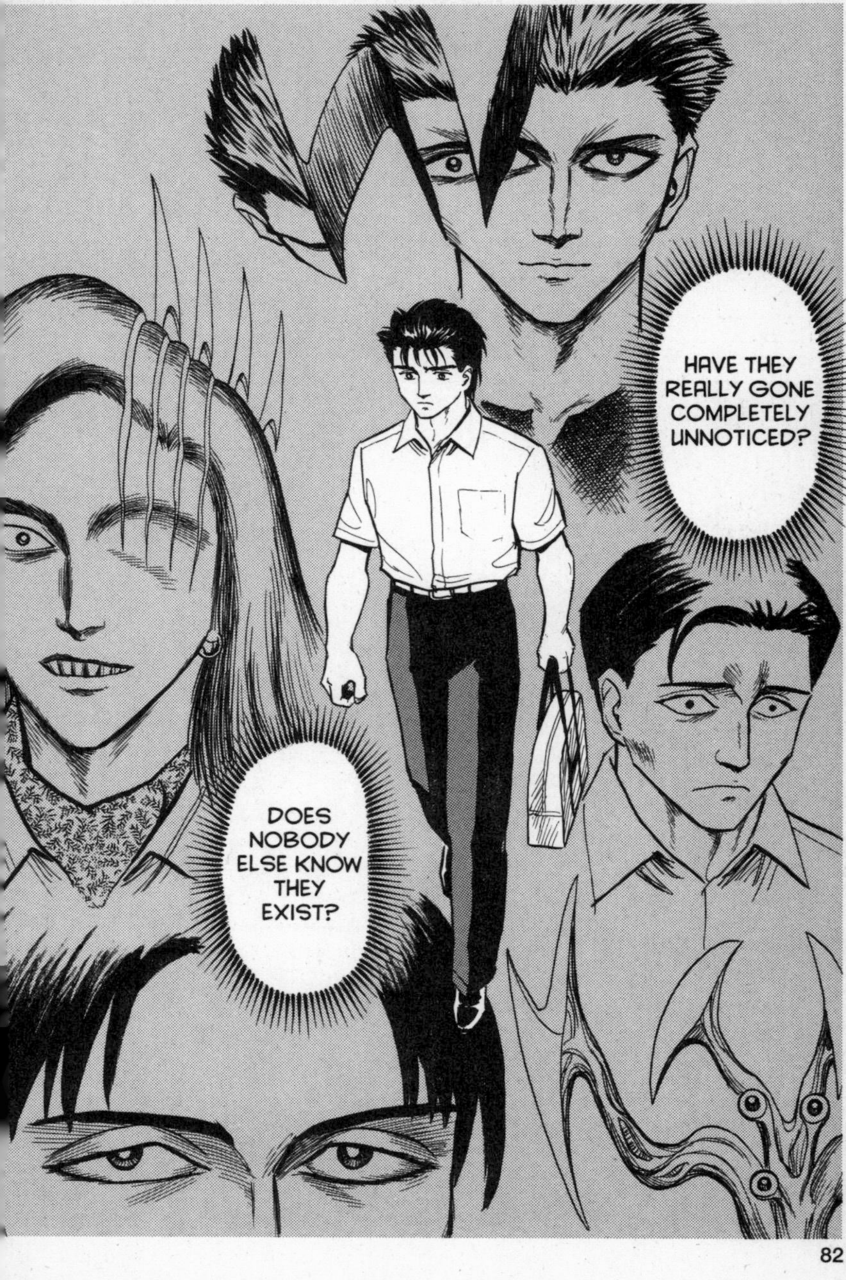
HAVE THEY REALLY GONE COMPLETELY UNNOTICED?
DOES NOBODY ELSE KNOW THEY EXIST?

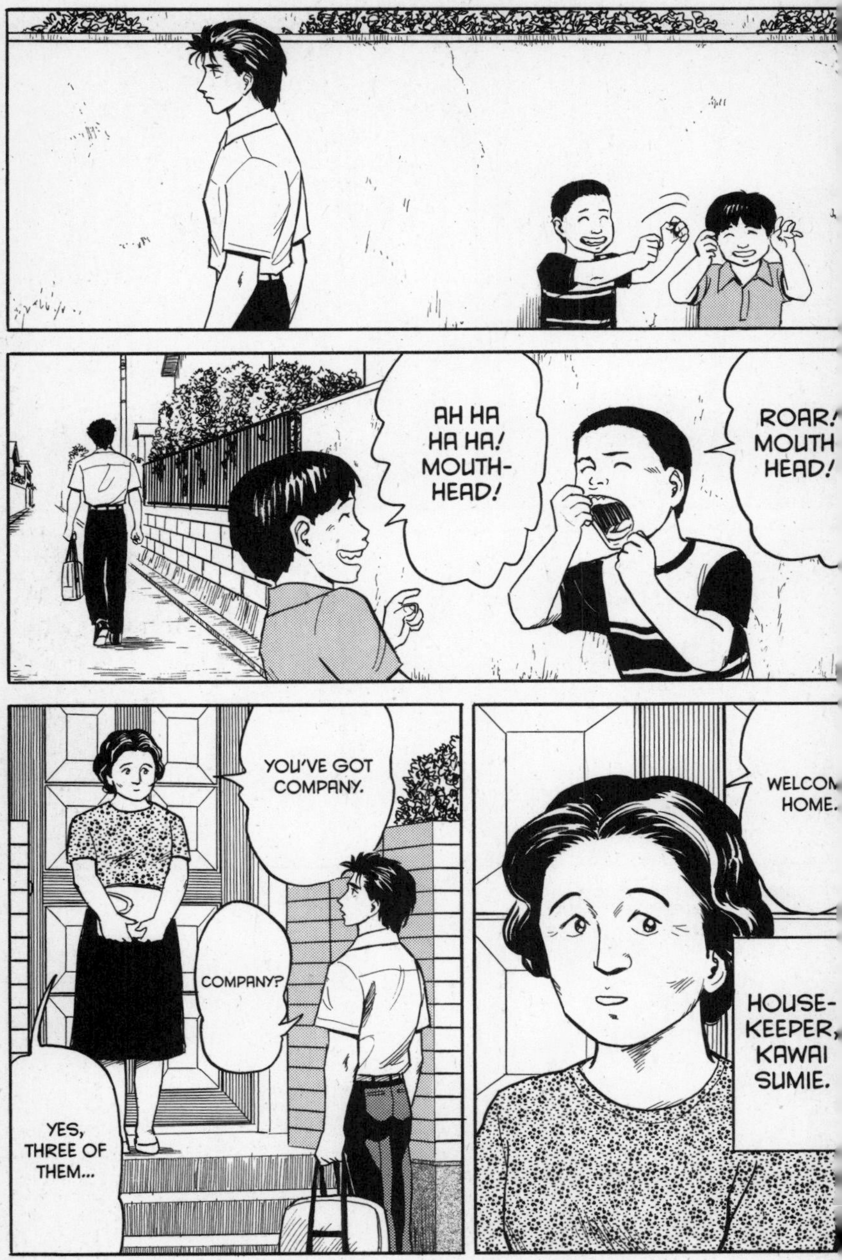
ROAR! MOUTH HEAD!
AH HA HA HA! MOUTH-HEAD!
WELCOM HOME.
HOUSE-KEEPER, KAWAI SUMIE.
YOU'VE GOT COMPANY.
COMPANY?
YES, THREE OF THEM...

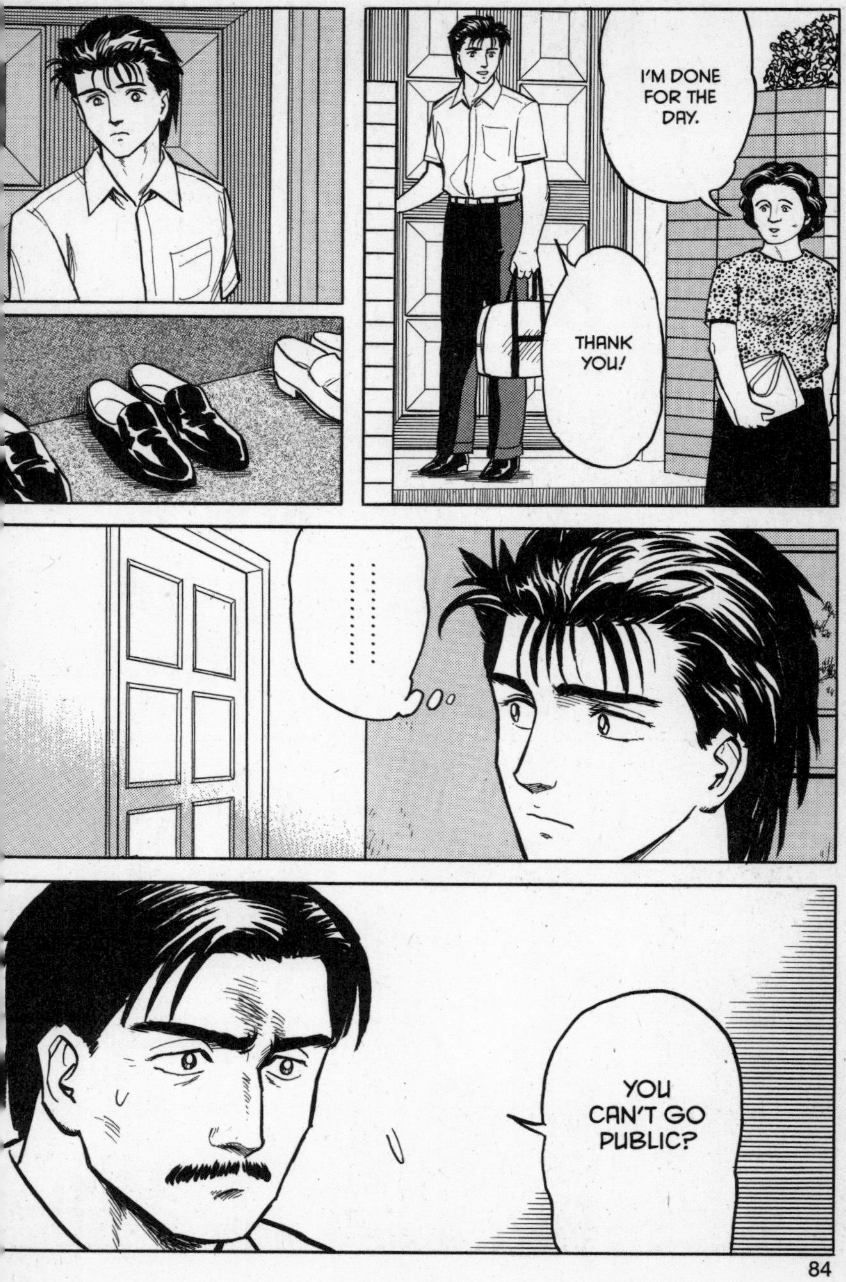
I'M DONE FOR THE DAY.
THANK YOU!
……
YOU CAN'T GO PUBLIC?

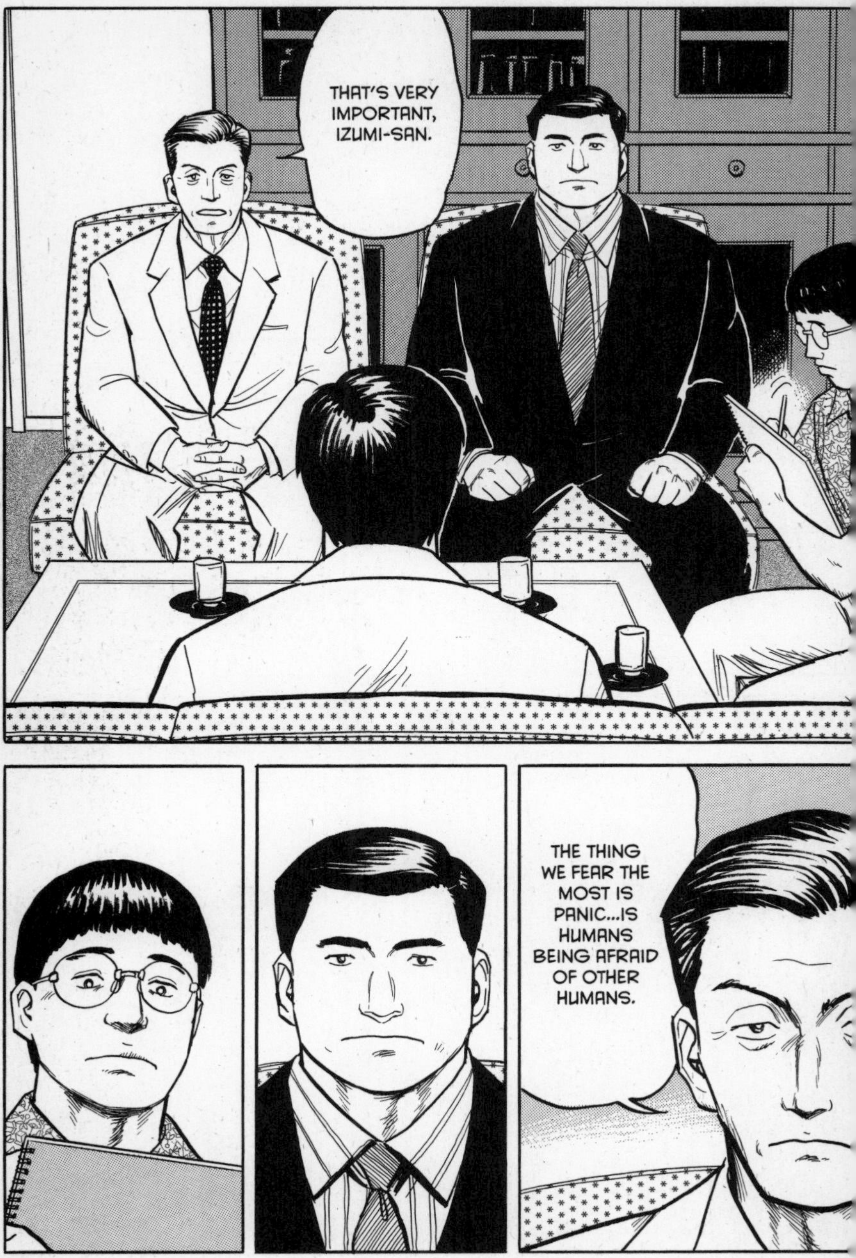
THAT'S VERY IMPORTANT, IZUMI-SAN.
THE THING WE FEAR THE MOST IS PANIC...IS HUMANS BEING AFRAID OF OTHER HUMANS.

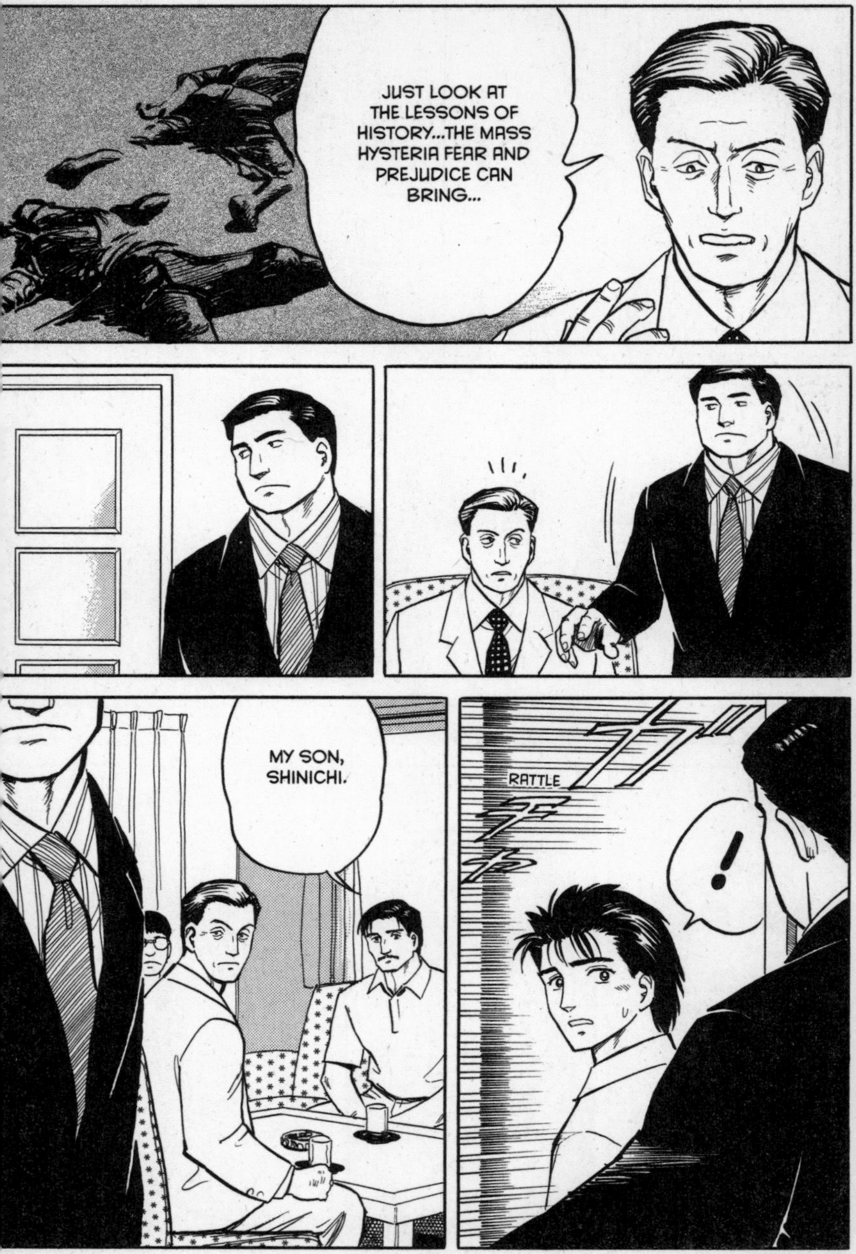
JUST LOOK AT THE LESSONS OF HISTORY...THE MASS HYSTERIA FEAR AND PREJUDICE CAN BRING...
RATTLE
!
MY SON, SHINICHI.

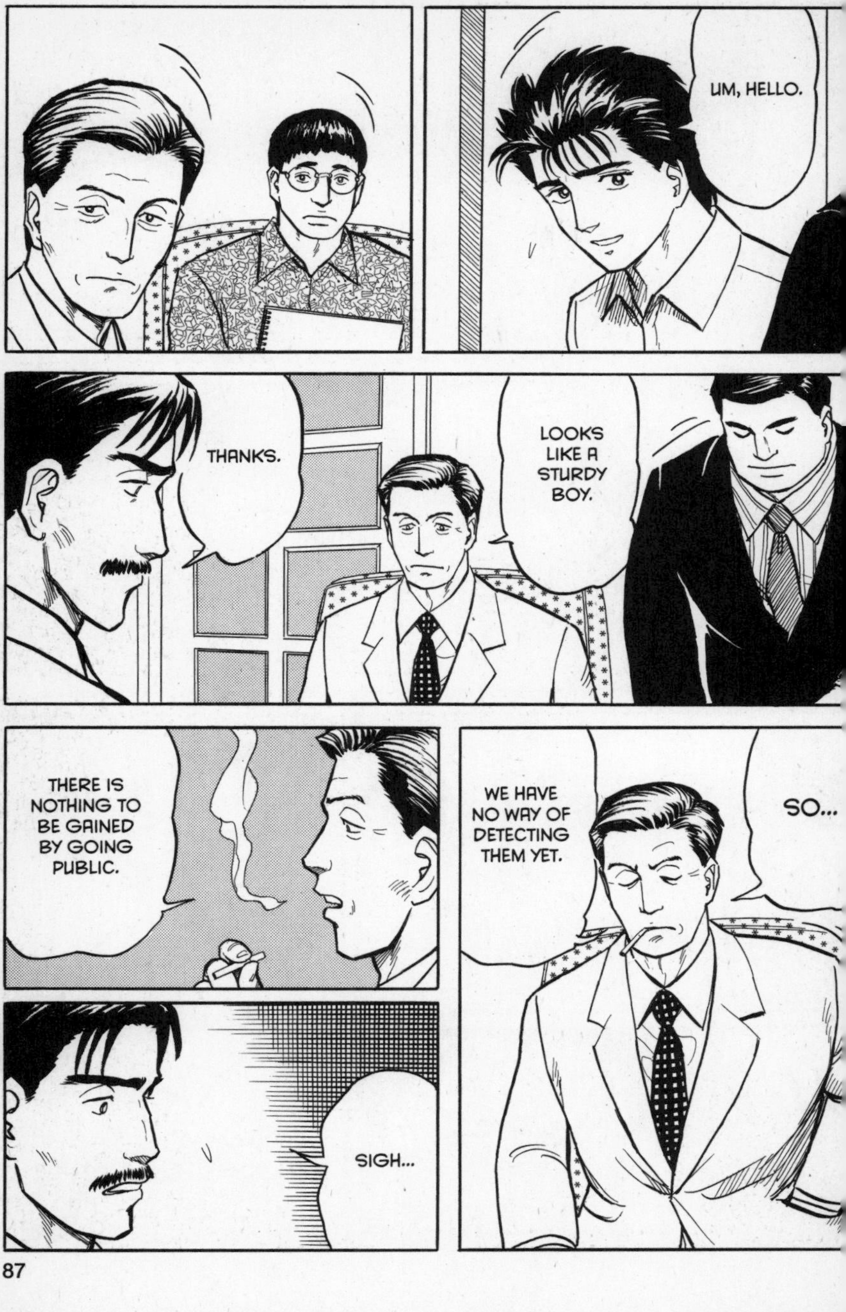
UM, HELLO.
LOOKS LIKE A STURDY BOY.
THANKS.
SO...
WE HAVE NO WAY OF DETECTING THEM YET.
THERE IS NOTHING TO BE GAINED BY GOING PUBLIC.
SIGH...

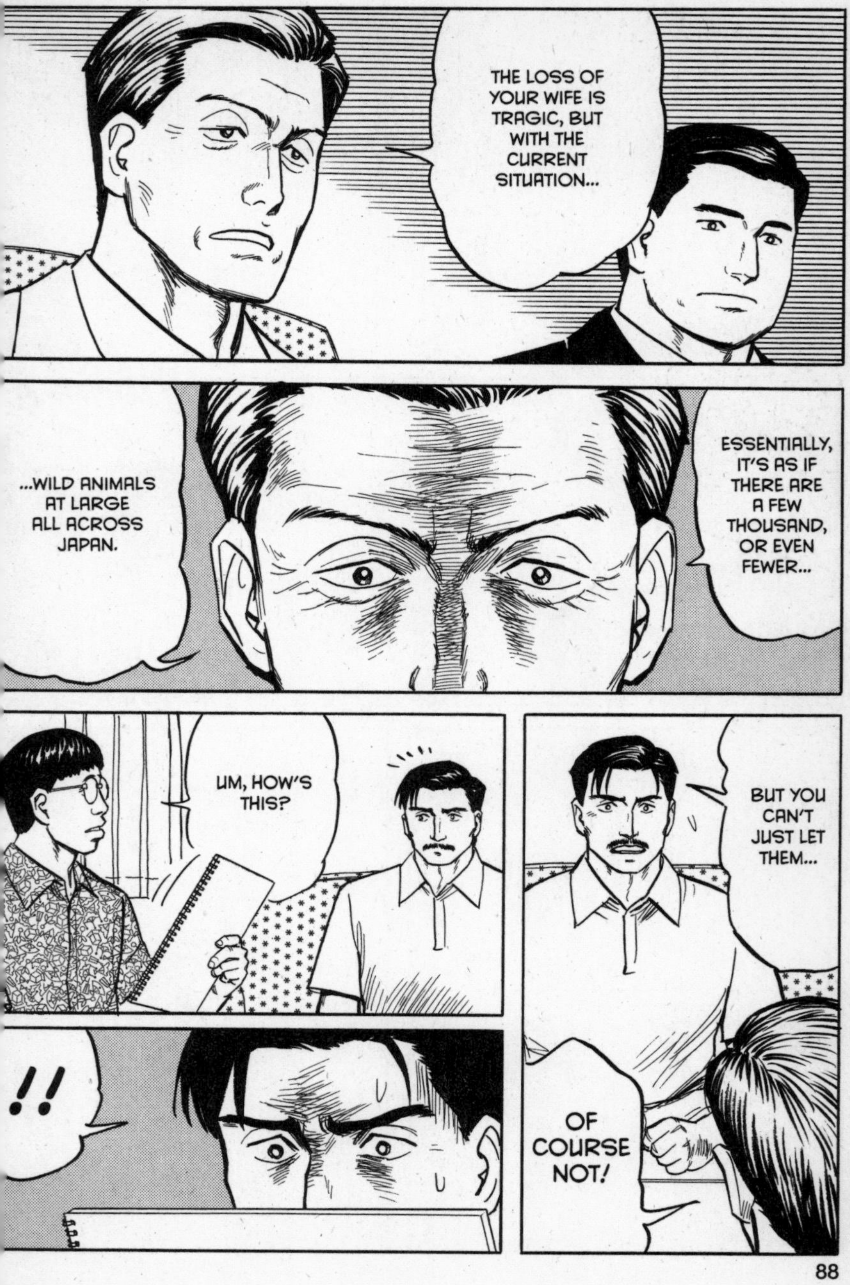
THE LOSS OF YOUR WIFE IS TRAGIC, BUT WITH THE CURRENT SITUATION...
ESSENTIALLY, IT'S AS IF THERE ARE A FEW THOUSAND, OR EVEN FEWER...
...WILD ANIMALS AT LARGE ALL ACROSS JAPAN.
BUT YOU CAN'T JUST LET THEM...
OF COURSE NOT!
UM, HOW'S THIS?
!!

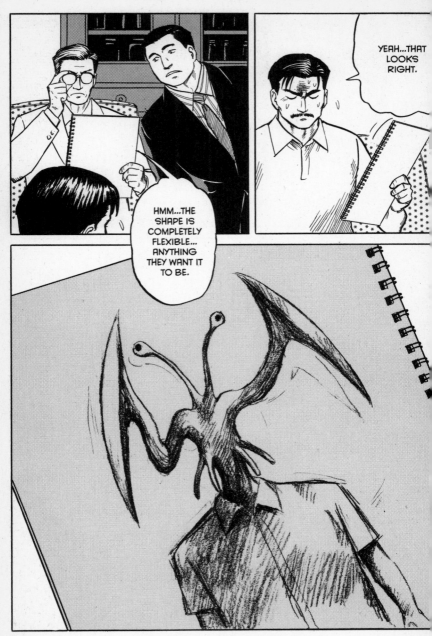

YEAH...THAT LOOKS RIGHT.

HMM...THE SHAPE IS COMPLETELY FLEXIBLE... ANYTHING THEY WANT IT TO BE.

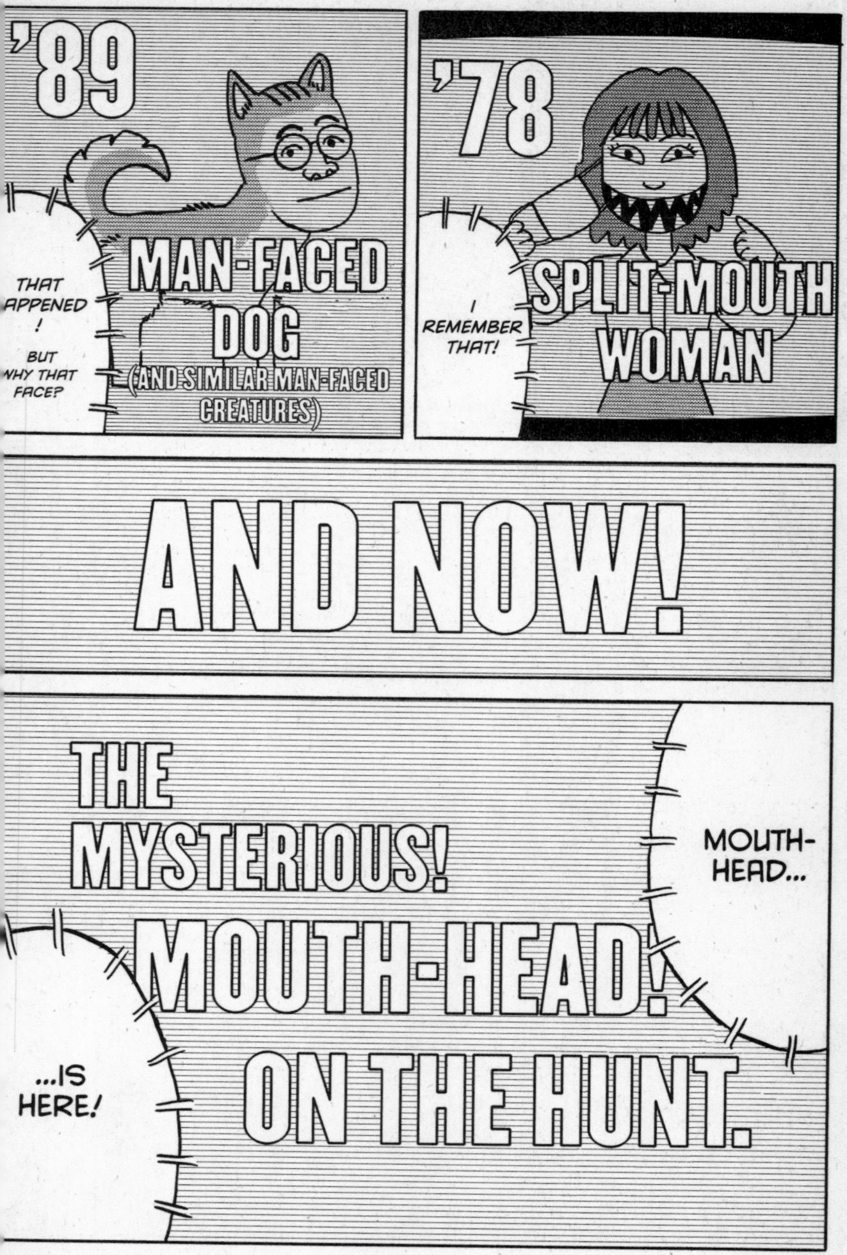
'78
SPLIT-MOUTH WOMAN
I REMEMBER THAT!
'89
MAN-FACED DOG
(AND SIMILAR MAN-FACED CREATURES)
THAT APPENED!
BUT WHY THAT FACE?
AND NOW!
MOUTH-HEAD...
THE MYSTERIOUS!
MOUTH-HEAD!
ON THE HUNT.
...IS HERE!

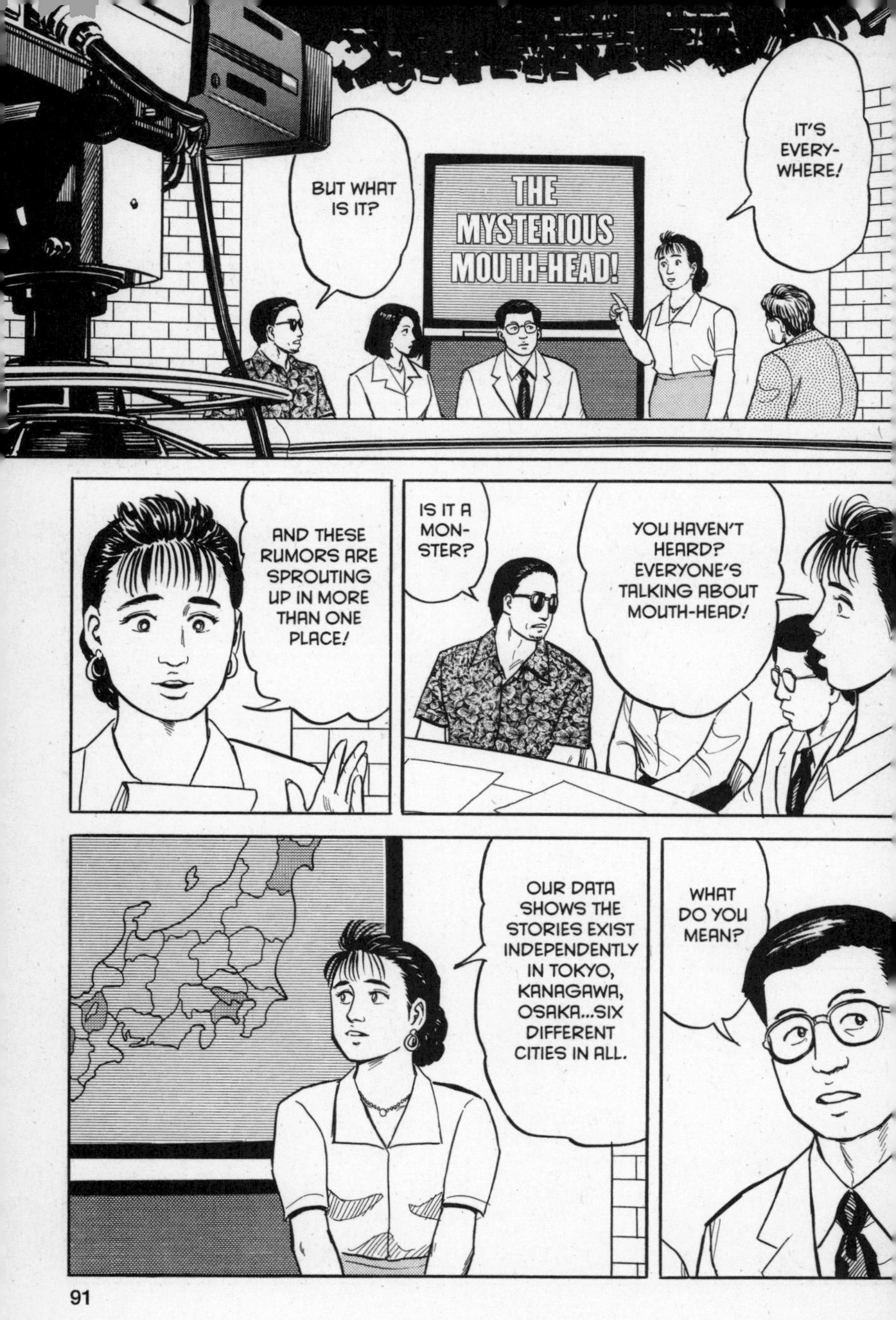
IT'S EVERY-WHERE!
THE MYSTERIOUS MOUTH-HEAD!
BUT WHAT IS IT?
YOU HAVEN'T HEARD? EVERYONE'S TALKING ABOUT MOUTH-HEAD!
IS IT A MON-STER?
AND THESE RUMORS ARE SPROUTING UP IN MORE THAN ONE PLACE!
WHAT DO YOU MEAN?
OUR DATA SHOWS THE STORIES EXIST INDEPENDENTLY IN TOKYO, KANAGAWA, OSAKA...SIX DIFFERENT CITIES IN ALL.

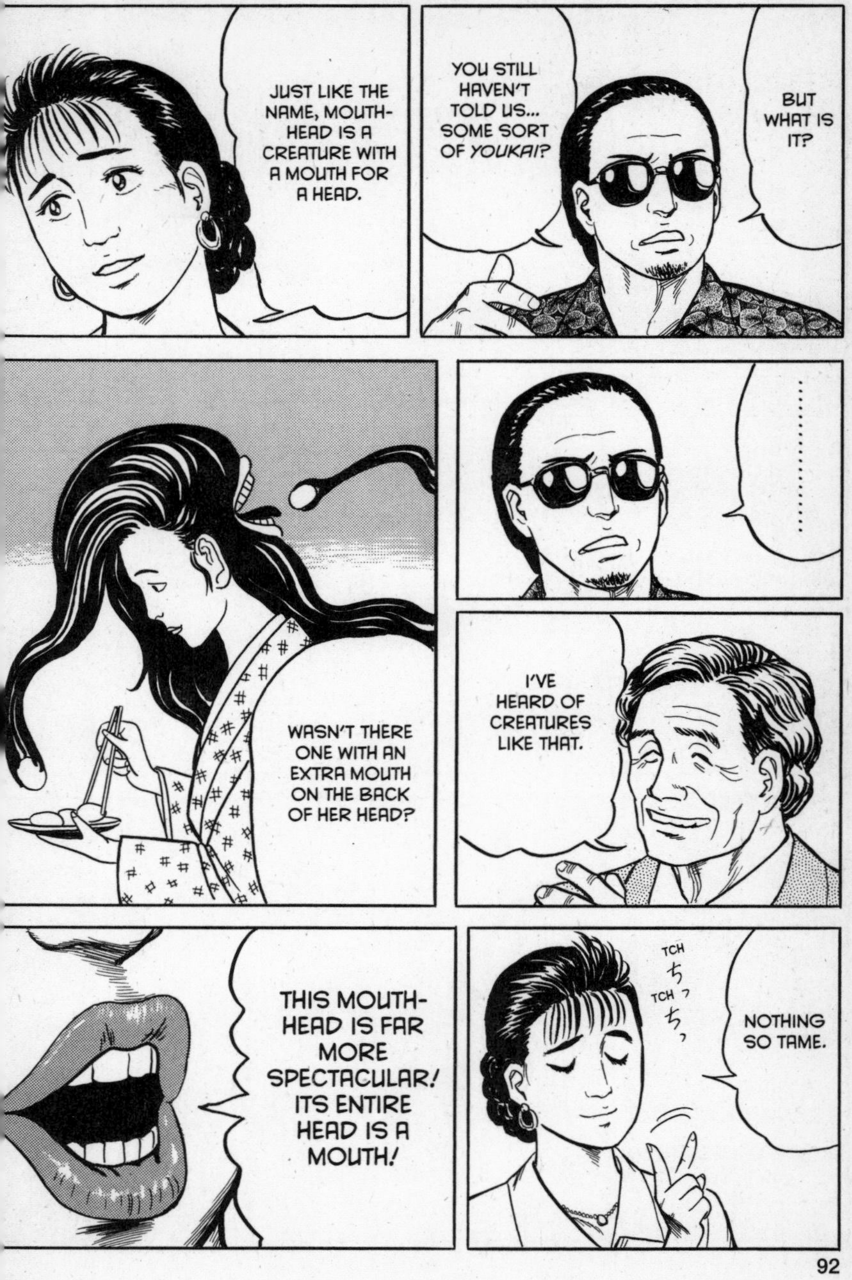
BUT WHAT IS IT?
YOU STILL HAVEN'T TOLD US... SOME SORT OF *YOUKAI*?
JUST LIKE THE NAME, MOUTH-HEAD IS A CREATURE WITH A MOUTH FOR A HEAD.
......
I'VE HEARD OF CREATURES LIKE THAT.
WASN'T THERE ONE WITH AN EXTRA MOUTH ON THE BACK OF HER HEAD?
NOTHING SO TAME.
TCH ちっ TCH ちっ
THIS MOUTH-HEAD IS FAR MORE SPECTACULAR! ITS ENTIRE HEAD IS A MOUTH!

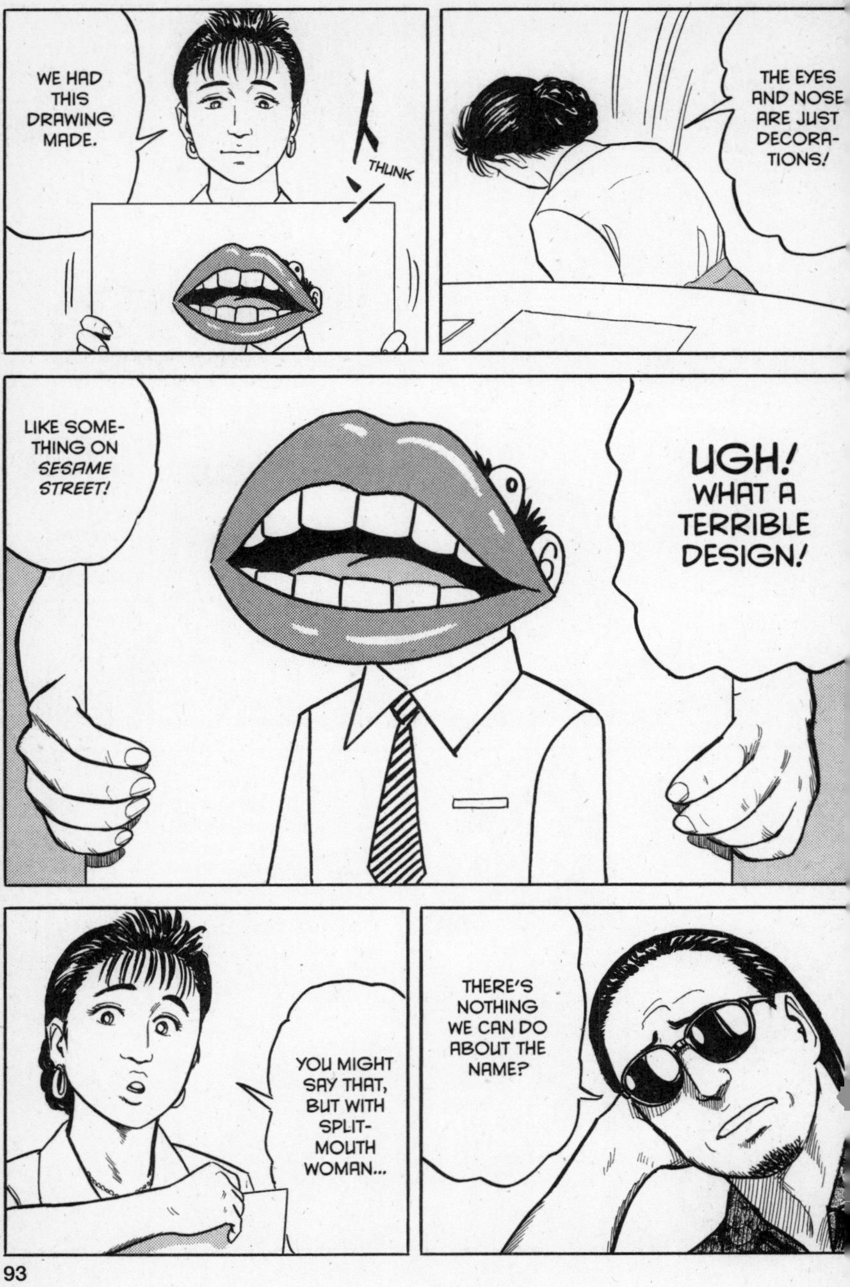
THE EYES AND NOSE ARE JUST DECORATIONS!
WE HAD THIS DRAWING MADE.
THUNK
UGH! WHAT A TERRIBLE DESIGN!
LIKE SOMETHING ON *SESAME STREET*!
THERE'S NOTHING WE CAN DO ABOUT THE NAME?
YOU MIGHT SAY THAT, BUT WITH SPLIT-MOUTH WOMAN...

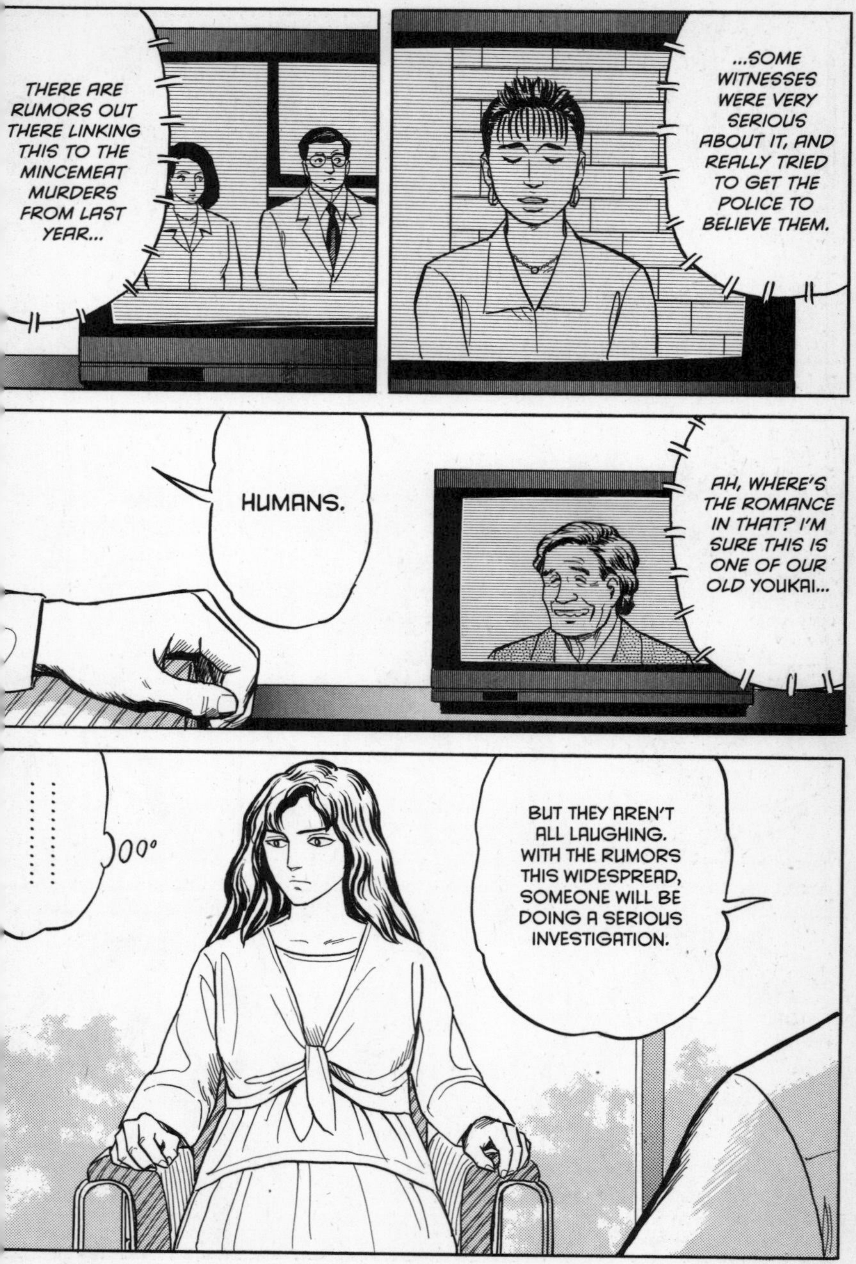
...SOME WITNESSES WERE VERY SERIOUS ABOUT IT, AND REALLY TRIED TO GET THE POLICE TO BELIEVE THEM.
THERE ARE RUMORS OUT THERE LINKING THIS TO THE MINCEMEAT MURDERS FROM LAST YEAR...
AH, WHERE'S THE ROMANCE IN THAT? I'M SURE THIS IS ONE OF OUR OLD YOUKAI...
HUMANS.
BUT THEY AREN'T ALL LAUGHING. WITH THE RUMORS THIS WIDESPREAD, SOMEONE WILL BE DOING A SERIOUS INVESTIGATION.

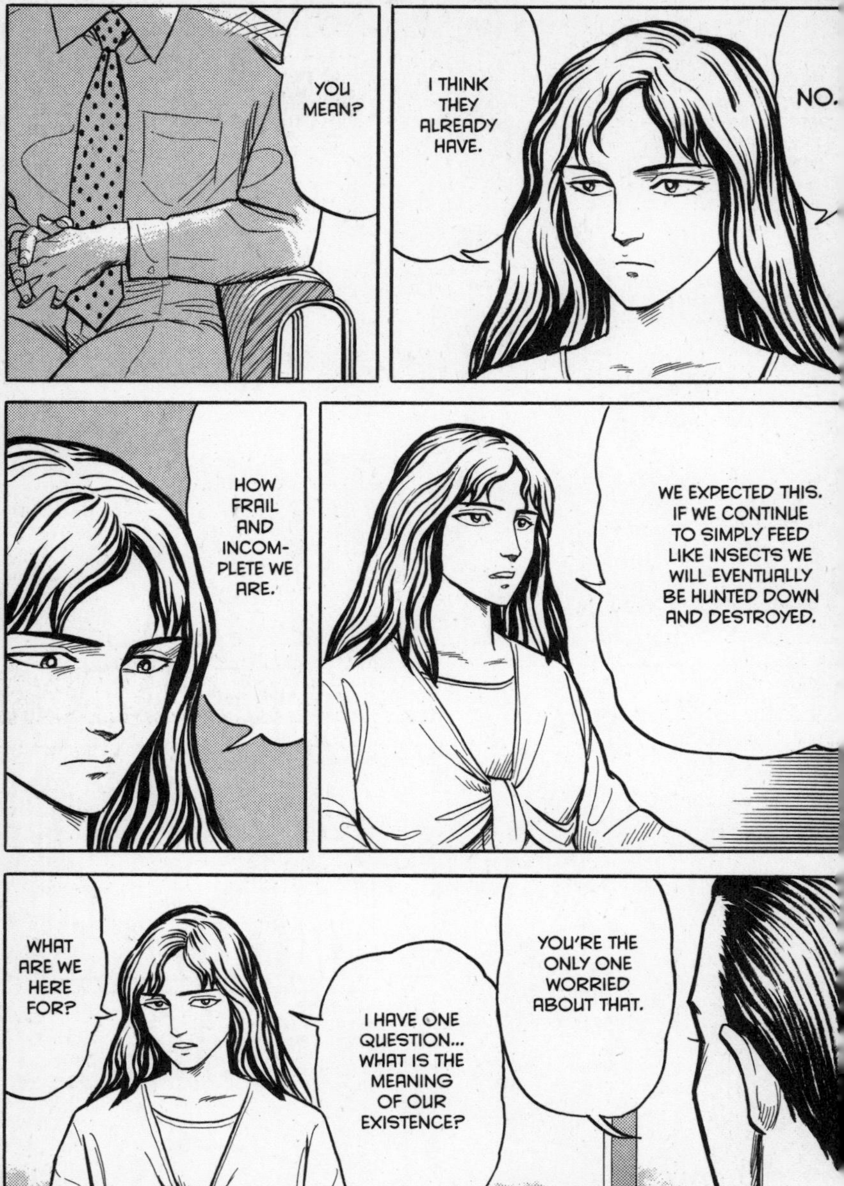
NO.
I THINK THEY ALREADY HAVE.
YOU MEAN?
WE EXPECTED THIS. IF WE CONTINUE TO SIMPLY FEED LIKE INSECTS WE WILL EVENTUALLY BE HUNTED DOWN AND DESTROYED.
HOW FRAIL AND INCOMPLETE WE ARE.
YOU'RE THE ONLY ONE WORRIED ABOUT THAT.
I HAVE ONE QUESTION... WHAT IS THE MEANING OF OUR EXISTENCE?
WHAT ARE WE HERE FOR?

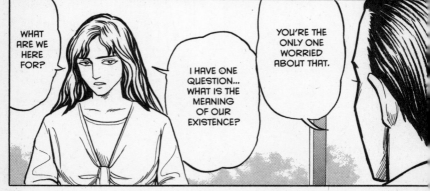

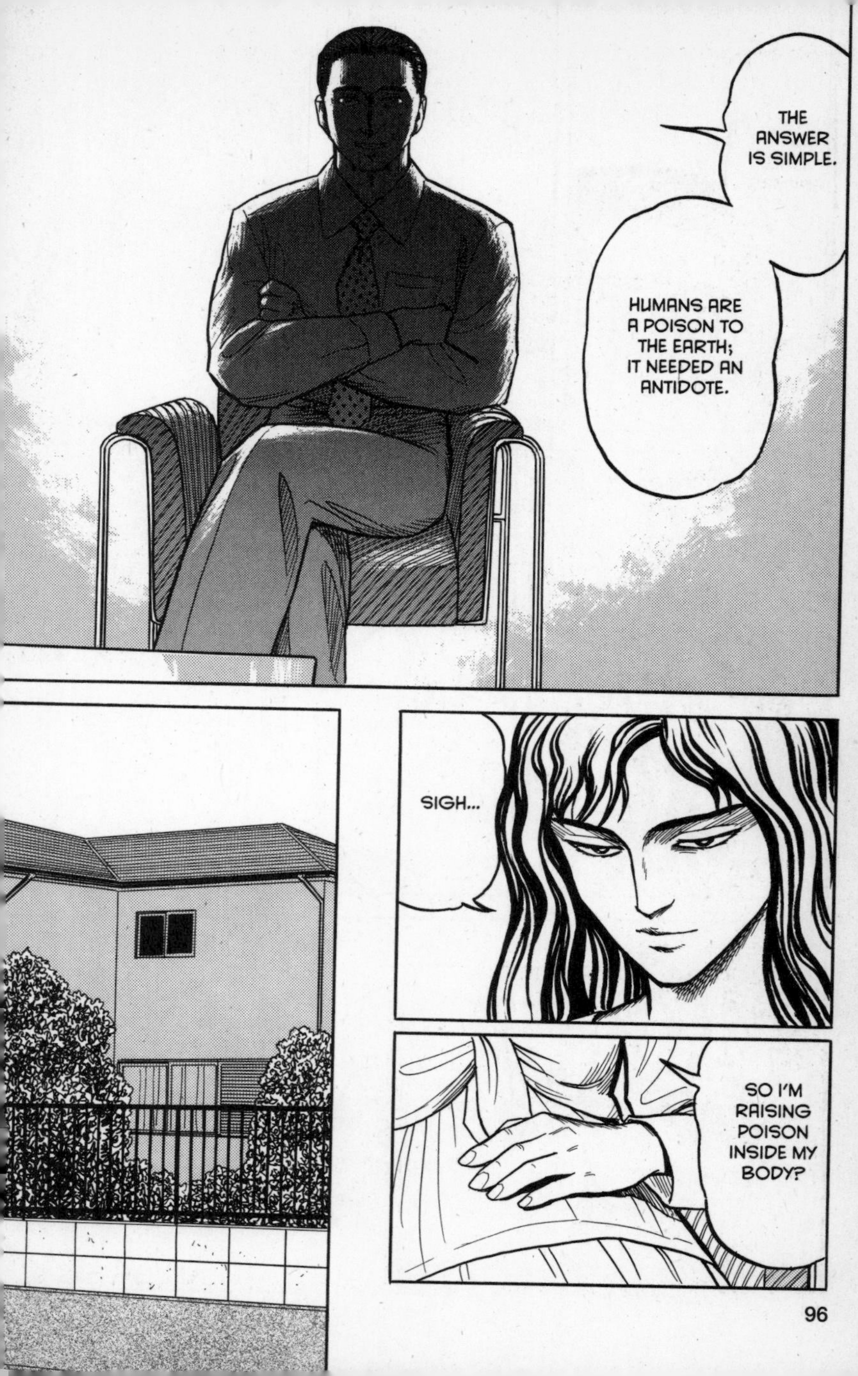
THE ANSWER IS SIMPLE.
HUMANS ARE A POISON TO THE EARTH; IT NEEDED AN ANTIDOTE.
SIGH...
SO I'M RAISING POISON INSIDE MY BODY?

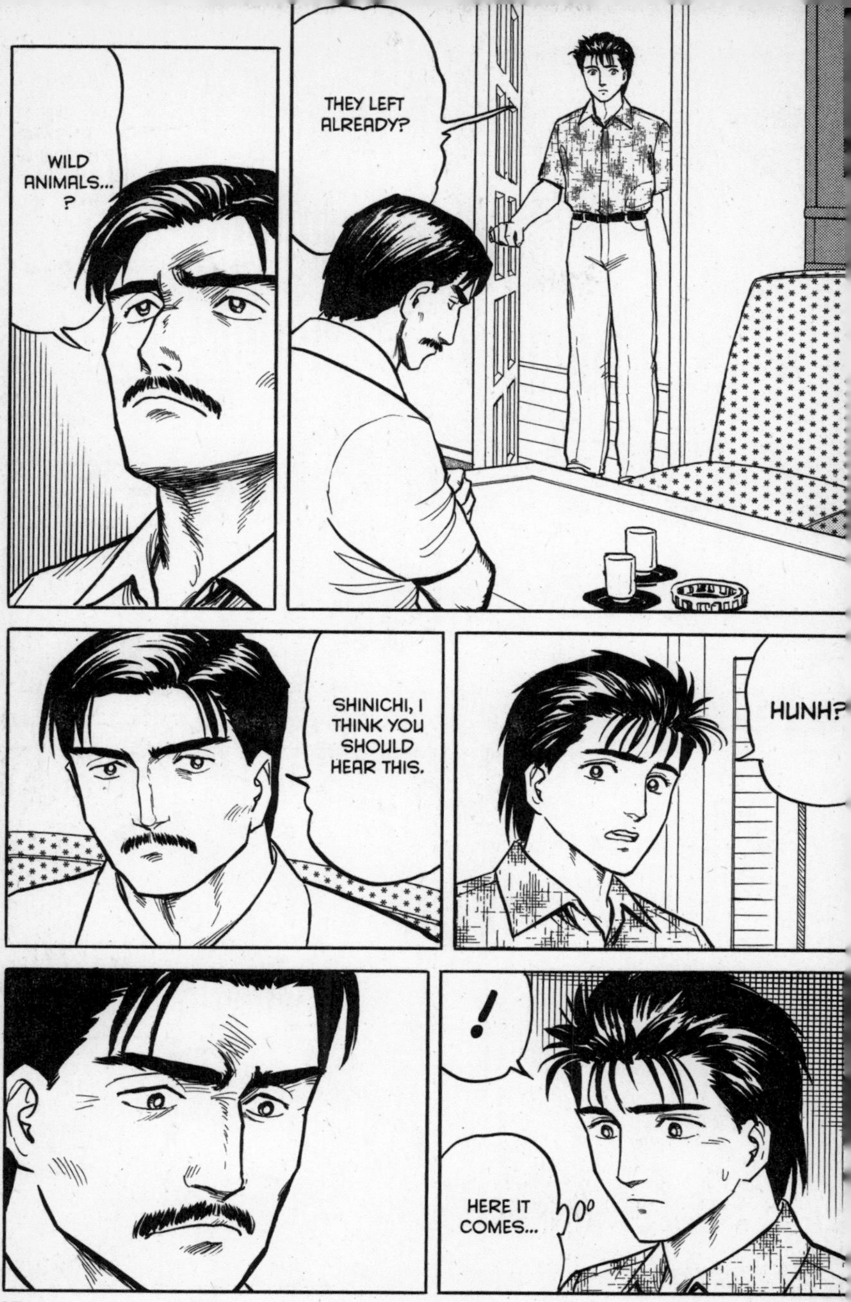
THEY LEFT ALREADY?
WILD ANIMALS... ?
HUNH?
SHINICHI, I THINK YOU SHOULD HEAR THIS.
!
HERE IT COMES...

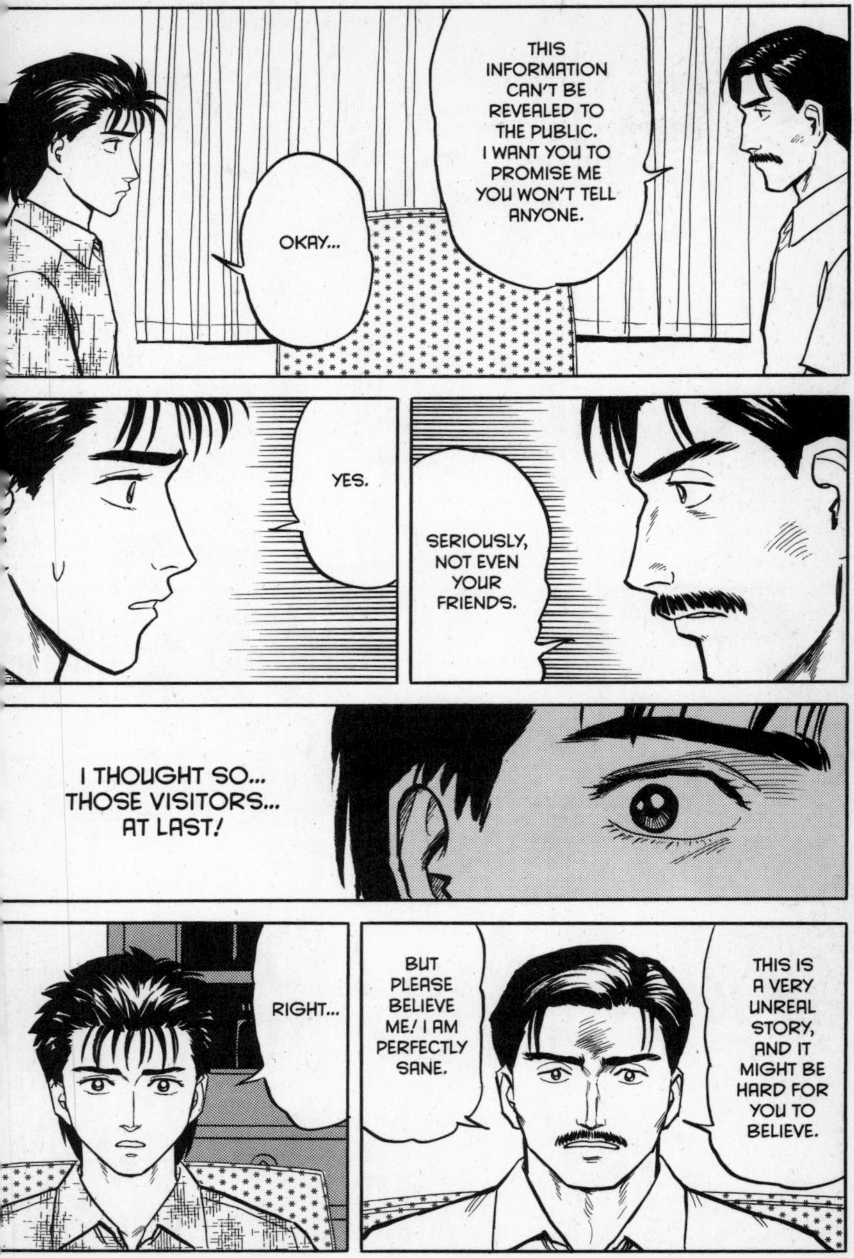
THIS INFORMATION CAN'T BE REVEALED TO THE PUBLIC. I WANT YOU TO PROMISE ME YOU WON'T TELL ANYONE.
OKAY...
SERIOUSLY, NOT EVEN YOUR FRIENDS.
YES.
I THOUGHT SO... THOSE VISITORS... AT LAST!
THIS IS A VERY UNREAL STORY, AND IT MIGHT BE HARD FOR YOU TO BELIEVE.
BUT PLEASE BELIEVE ME! I AM PERFECTLY SANE.
RIGHT...

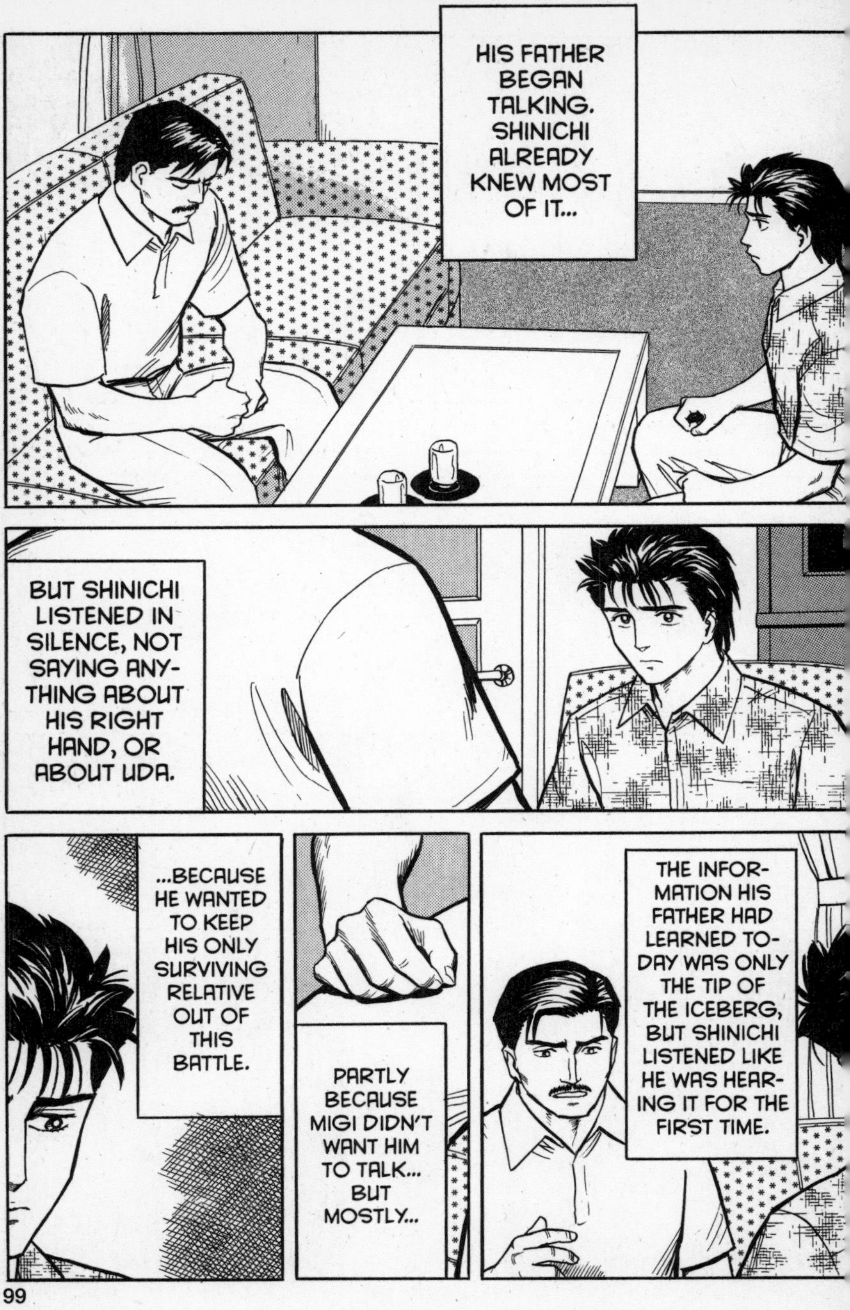
HIS FATHER BEGAN TALKING. SHINICHI ALREADY KNEW MOST OF IT...
BUT SHINICHI LISTENED IN SILENCE, NOT SAYING ANY-THING ABOUT HIS RIGHT HAND, OR ABOUT UDA.
THE INFOR-MATION HIS FATHER HAD LEARNED TO-DAY WAS ONLY THE TIP OF THE ICEBERG, BUT SHINICHI LISTENED LIKE HE WAS HEAR-ING IT FOR THE FIRST TIME.
PARTLY BECAUSE MIGI DIDN'T WANT HIM TO TALK... BUT MOSTLY...
...BECAUSE HE WANTED TO KEEP HIS ONLY SURVIVING RELATIVE OUT OF THIS BATTLE.

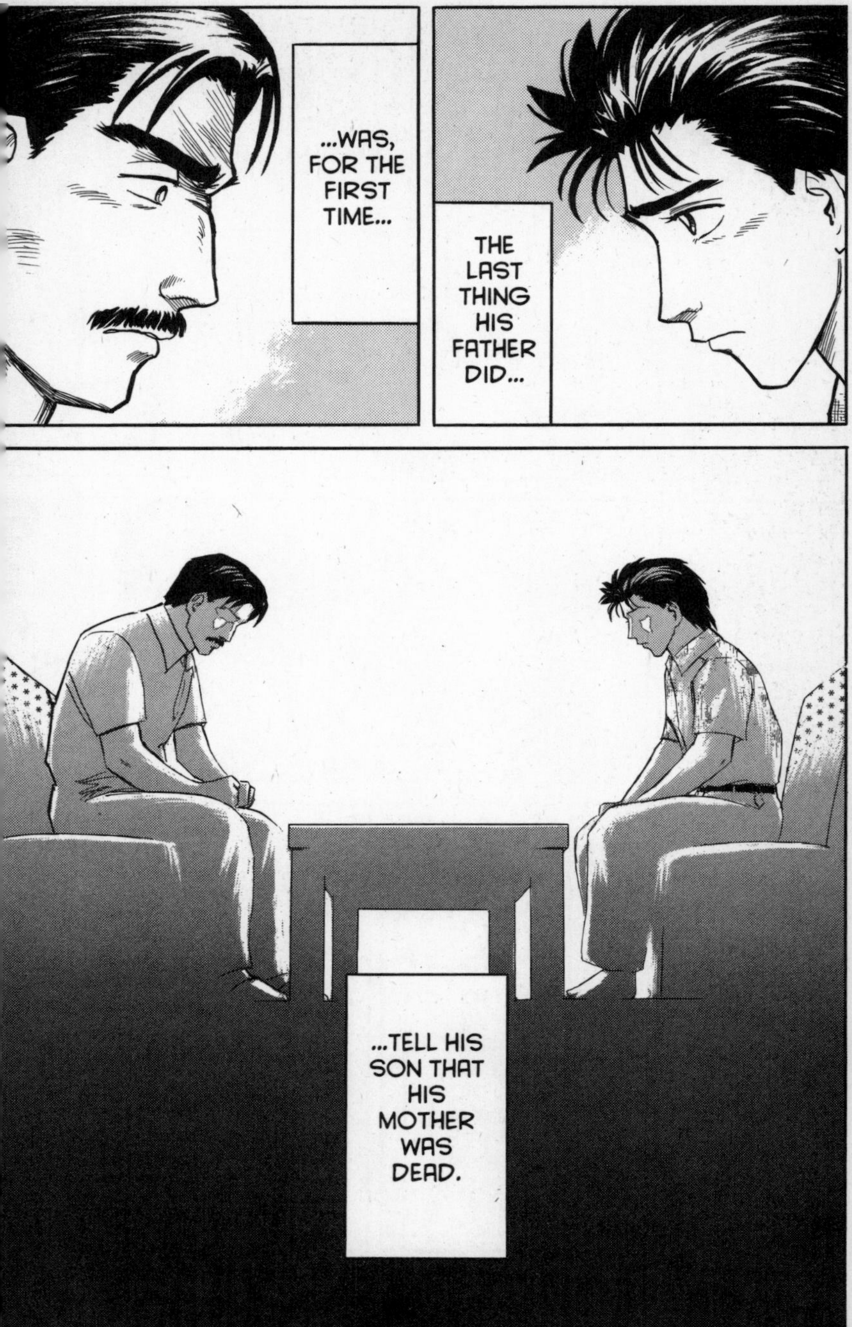
THE LAST THING HIS FATHER DID...
...WAS, FOR THE FIRST TIME...
...TELL HIS SON THAT HIS MOTHER WAS DEAD.

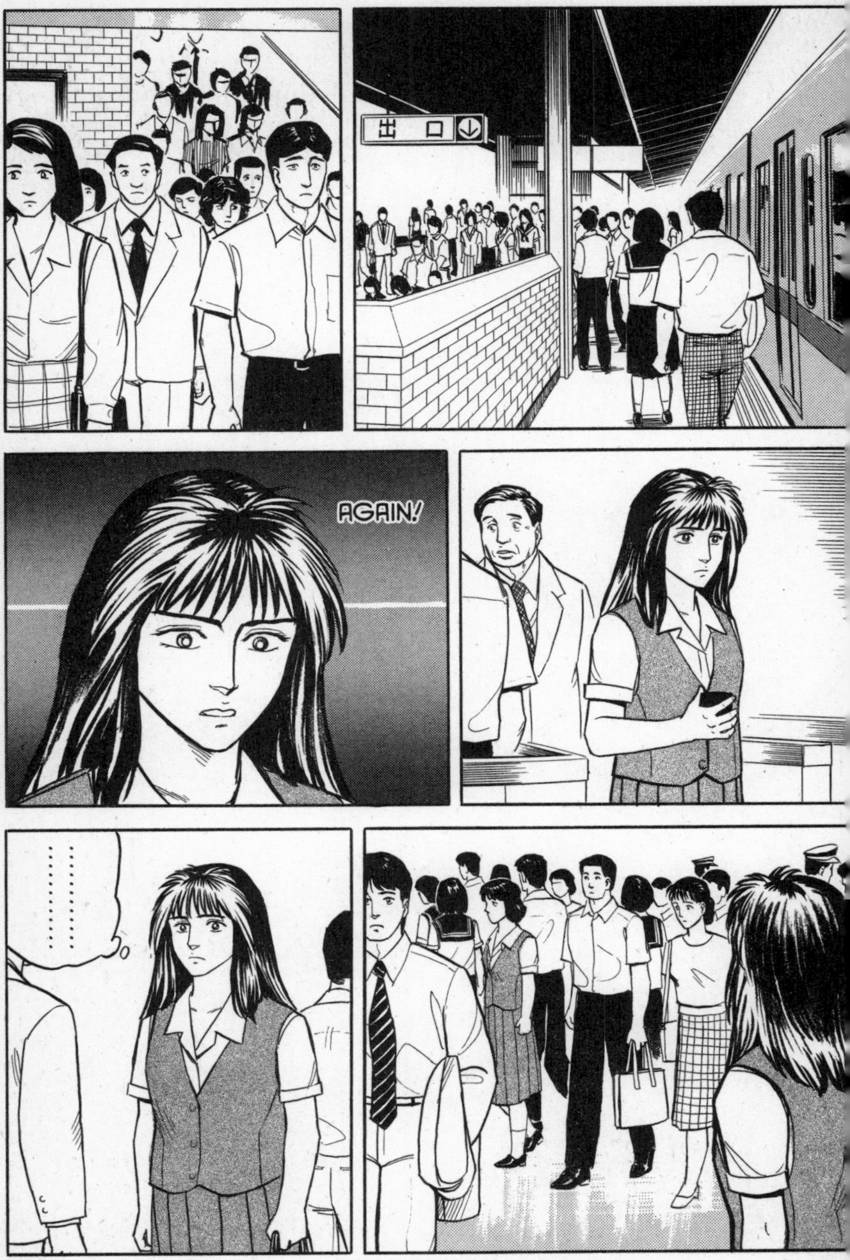
出口
AGAIN!
......

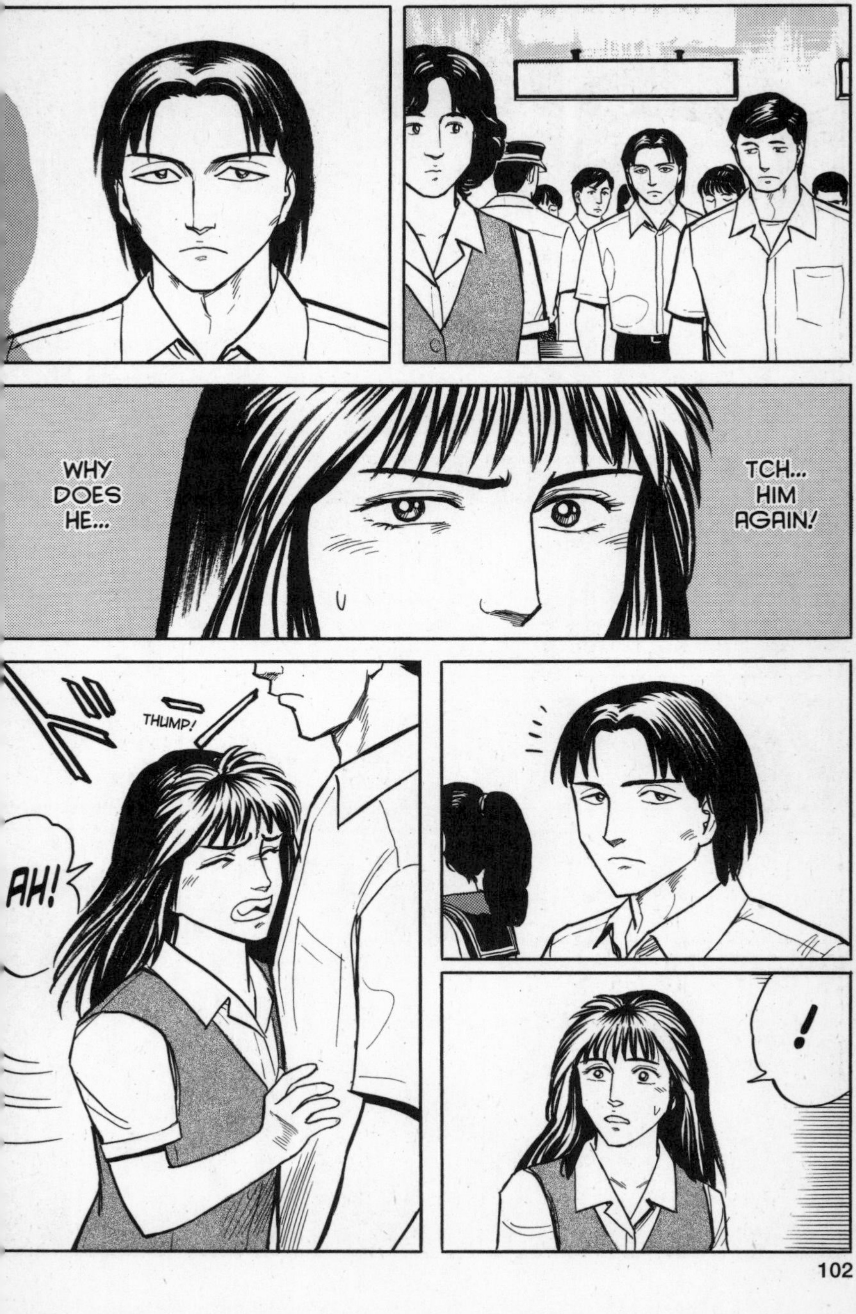
TCH... HIM AGAIN!
WHY DOES HE...
!
THUMP!
AH!

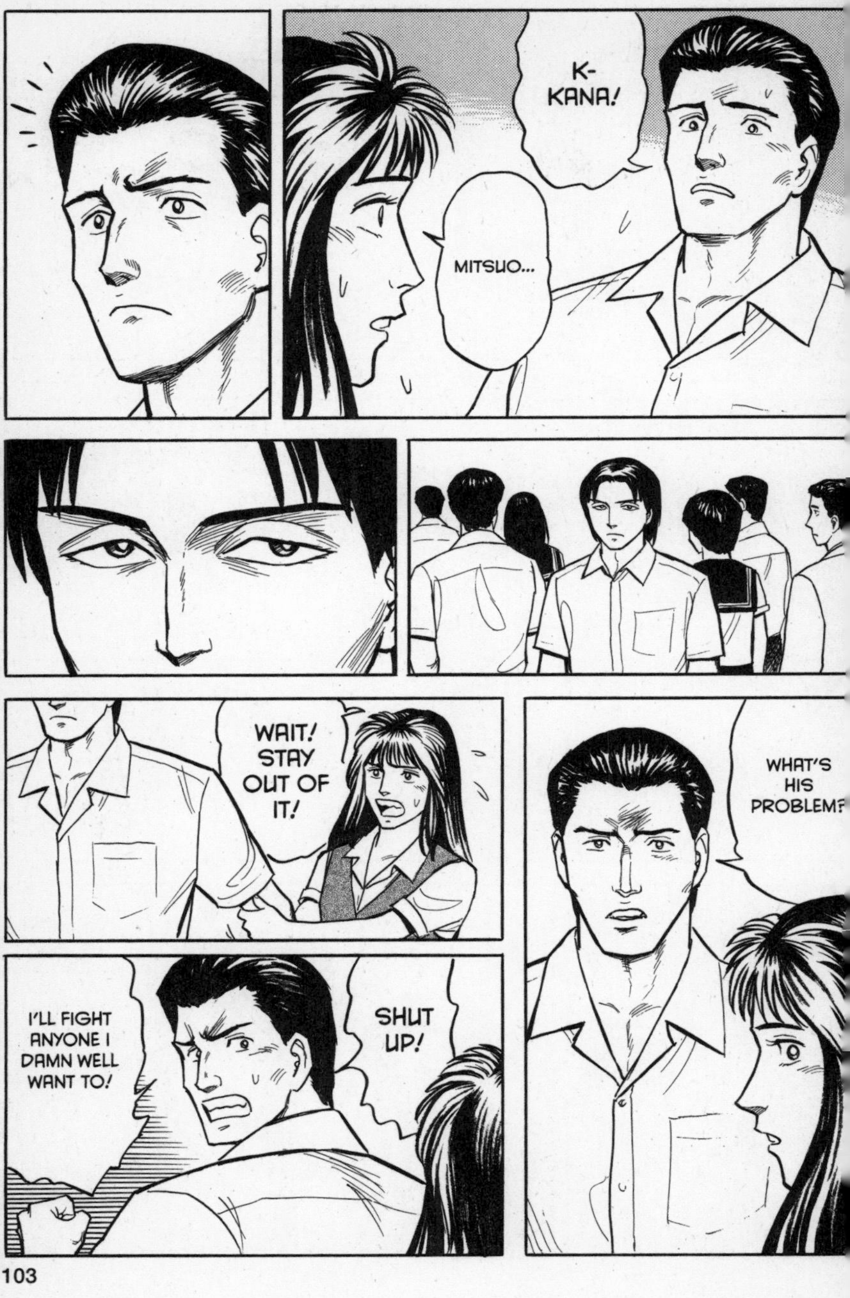

K-KANA!
MITSUO...
WHAT'S HIS PROBLEM?
WAIT! STAY OUT OF IT!
SHUT UP!
I'LL FIGHT ANYONE I DAMN WELL WANT TO!

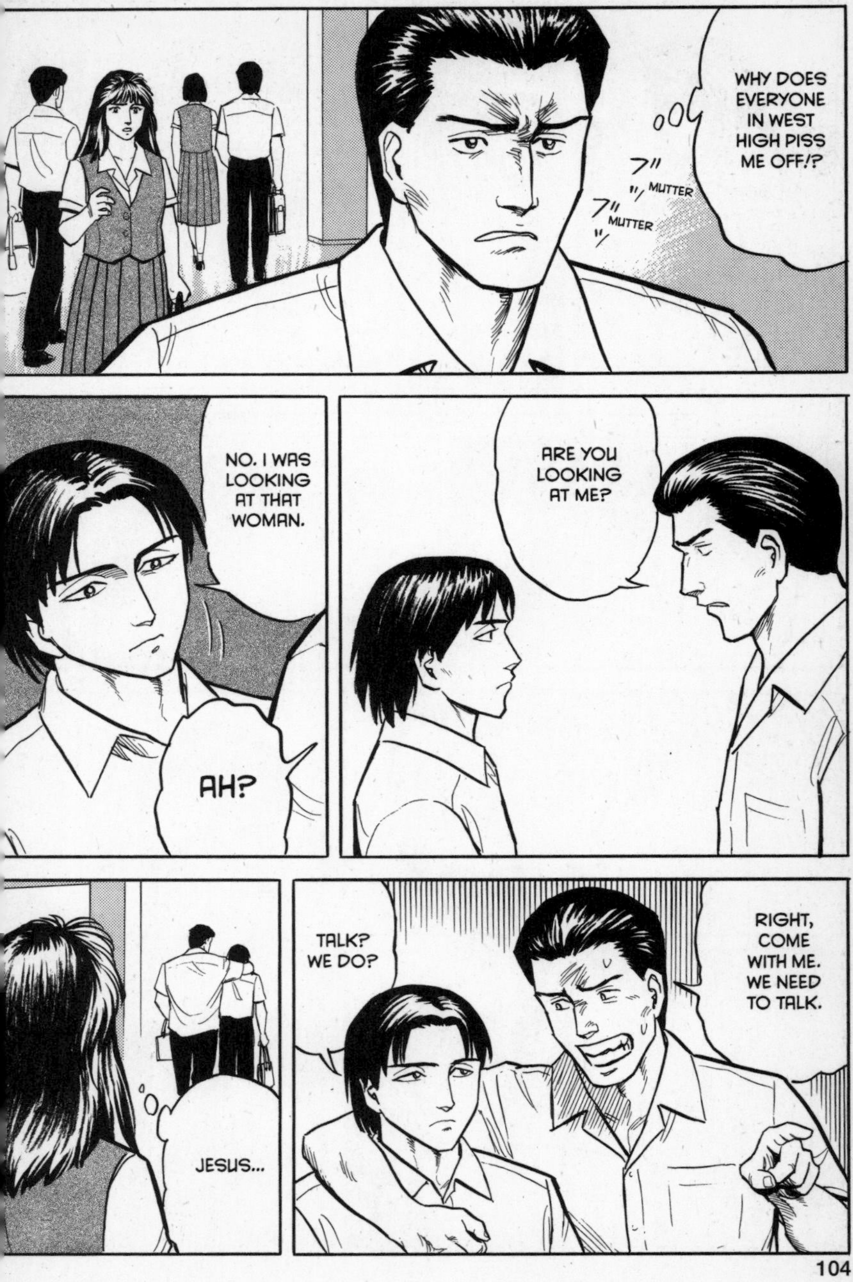
WHY DOES EVERYONE IN WEST HIGH PISS ME OFF!?
MUTTER
MUTTER
ARE YOU LOOKING AT ME?
NO. I WAS LOOKING AT THAT WOMAN.
AH?
RIGHT, COME WITH ME. WE NEED TO TALK.
TALK? WE DO?
JESUS...

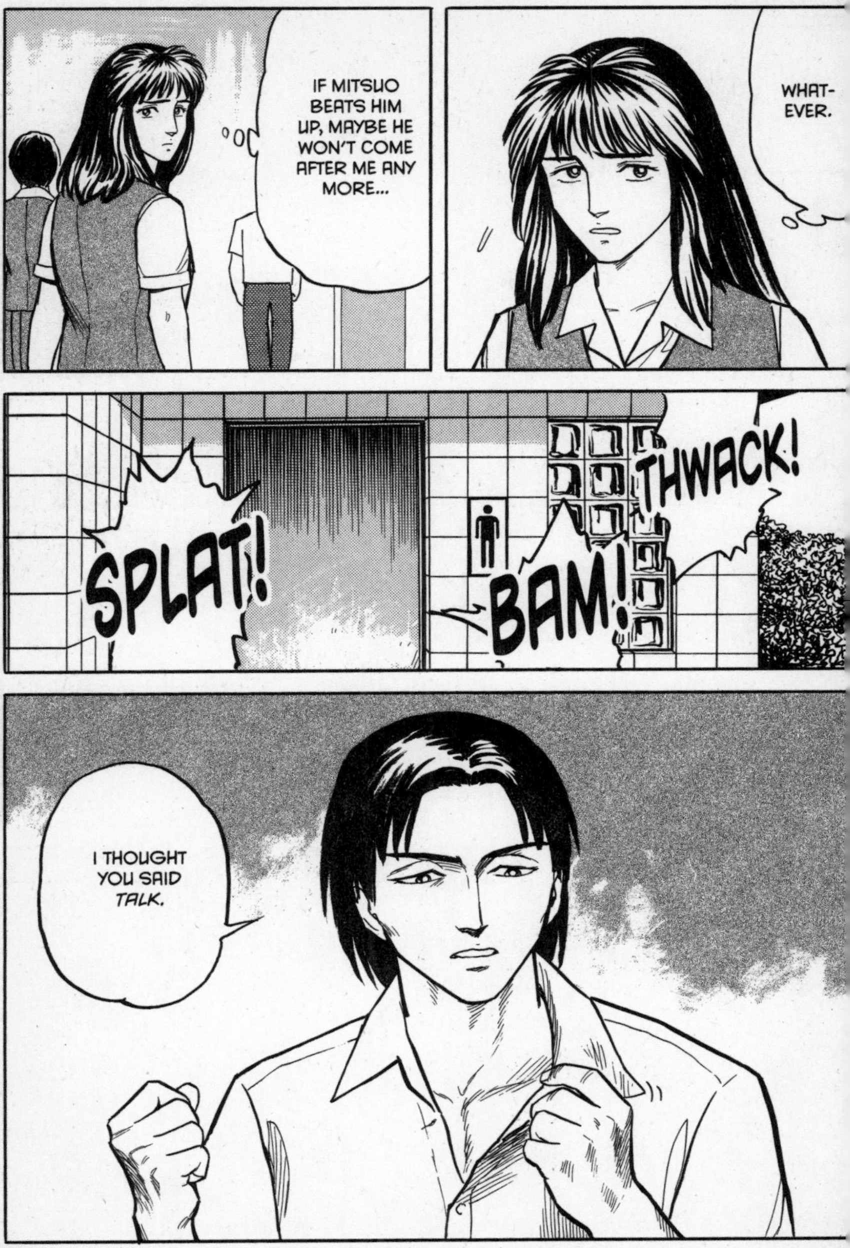
WHAT-EVER.
IF MITSUO BEATS HIM UP, MAYBE HE WON'T COME AFTER ME ANY MORE...
THWACK!
BAM!
SPLAT!
I THOUGHT YOU SAID *TALK*.

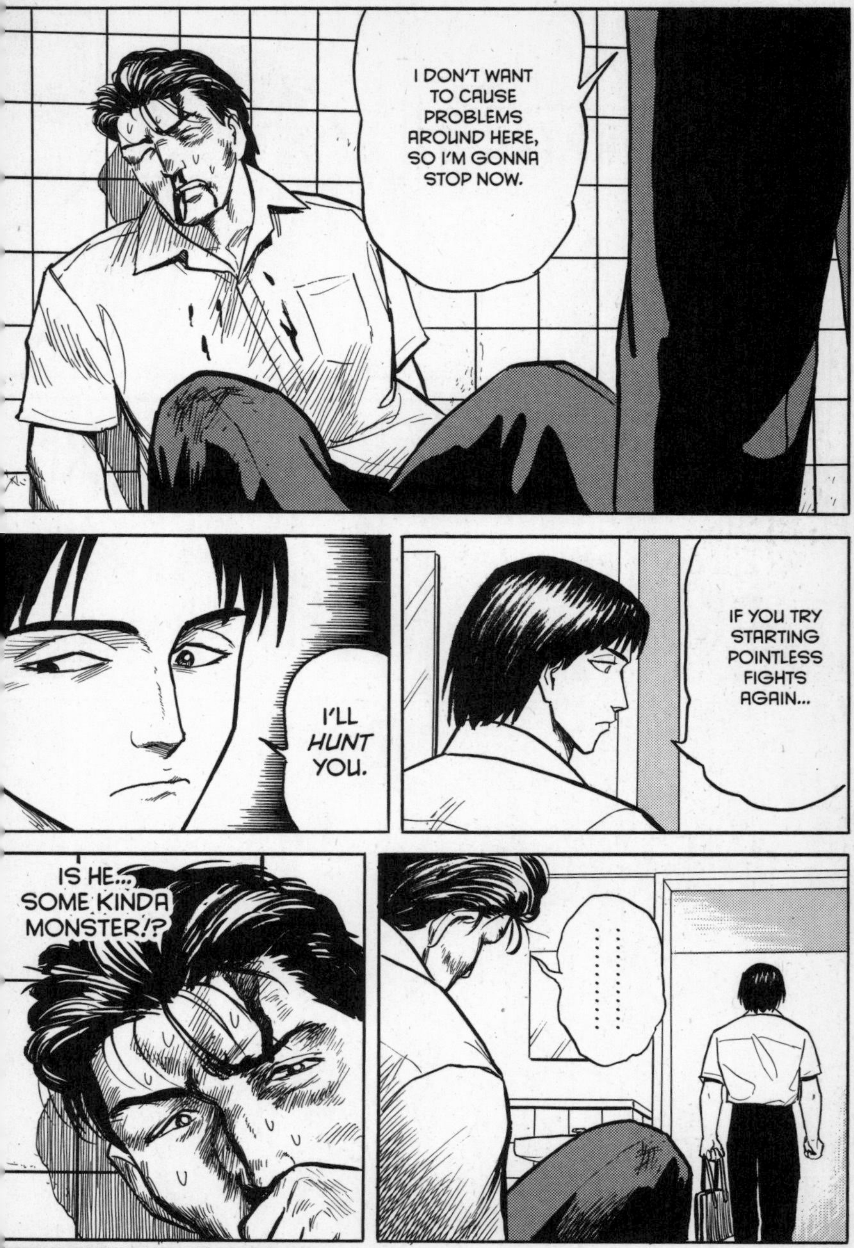
I DON'T WANT TO CAUSE PROBLEMS AROUND HERE, SO I'M GONNA STOP NOW.
IF YOU TRY STARTING POINTLESS FIGHTS AGAIN...
I'LL *HUNT* YOU.
......
IS HE... SOME KINDA MONSTER!?

CHAPTER 21: OBSERVATION

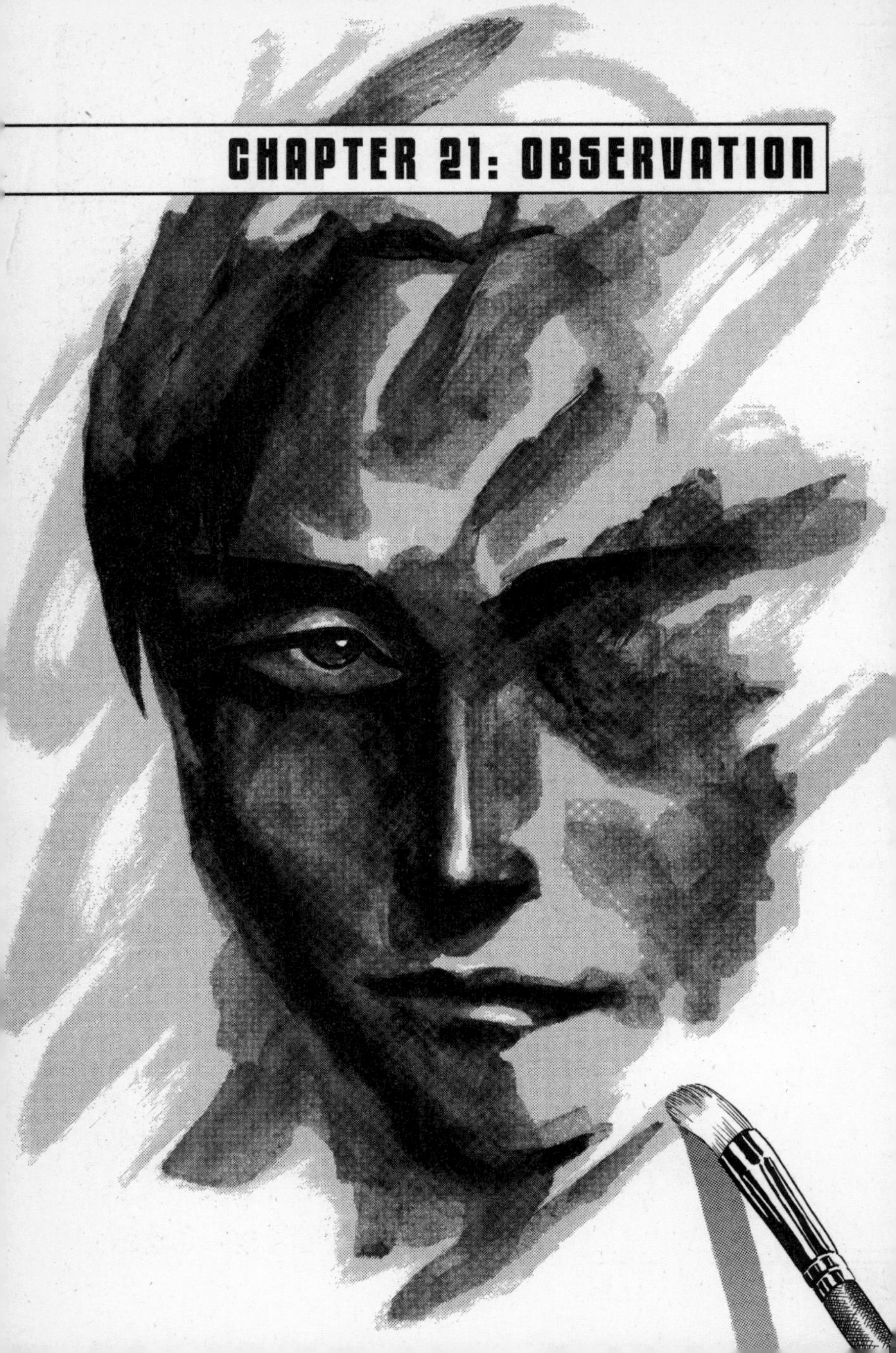

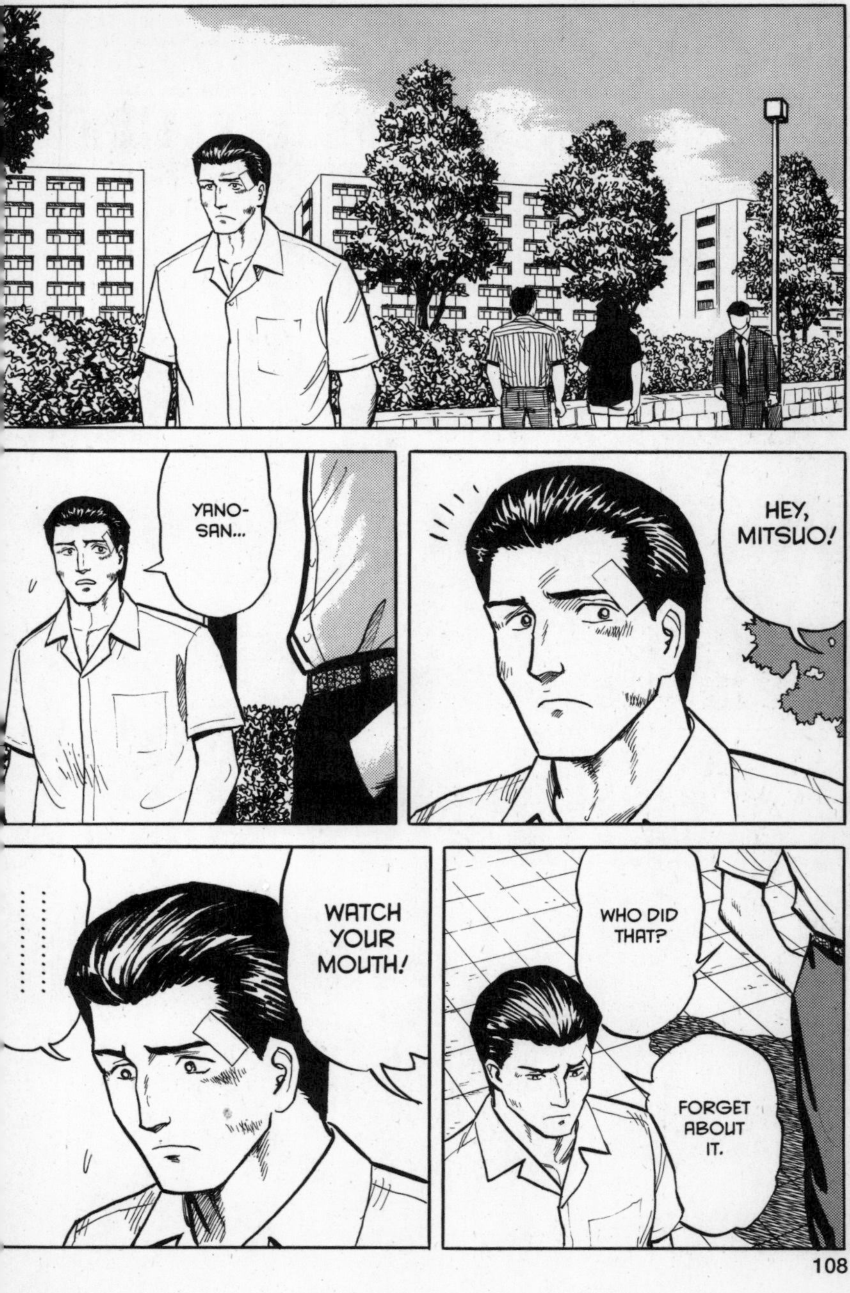
HEY, MITSUO!
YANO-SAN...
WHO DID THAT?
FORGET ABOUT IT.
WATCH YOUR MOUTH!
......

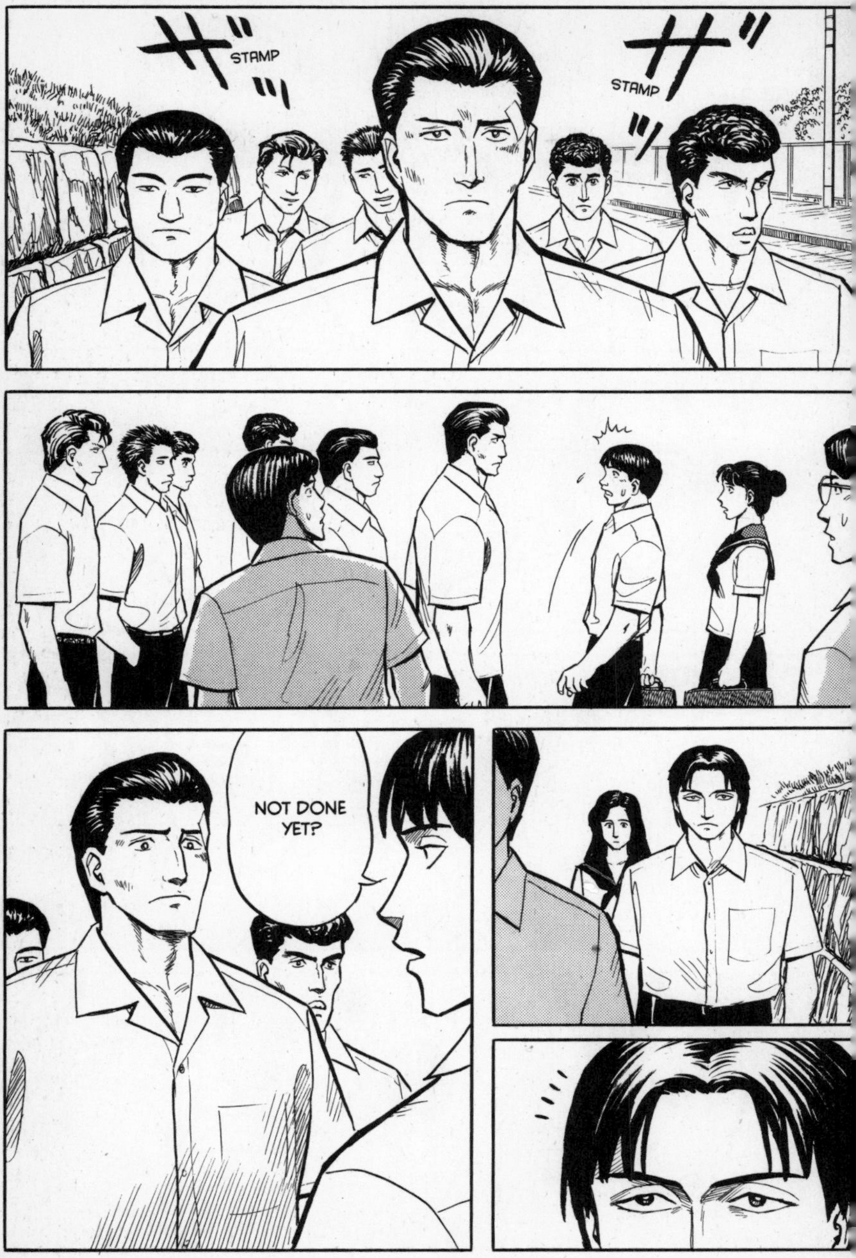
ザッ
STAMP
ザッ
STAMP
NOT DONE YET?

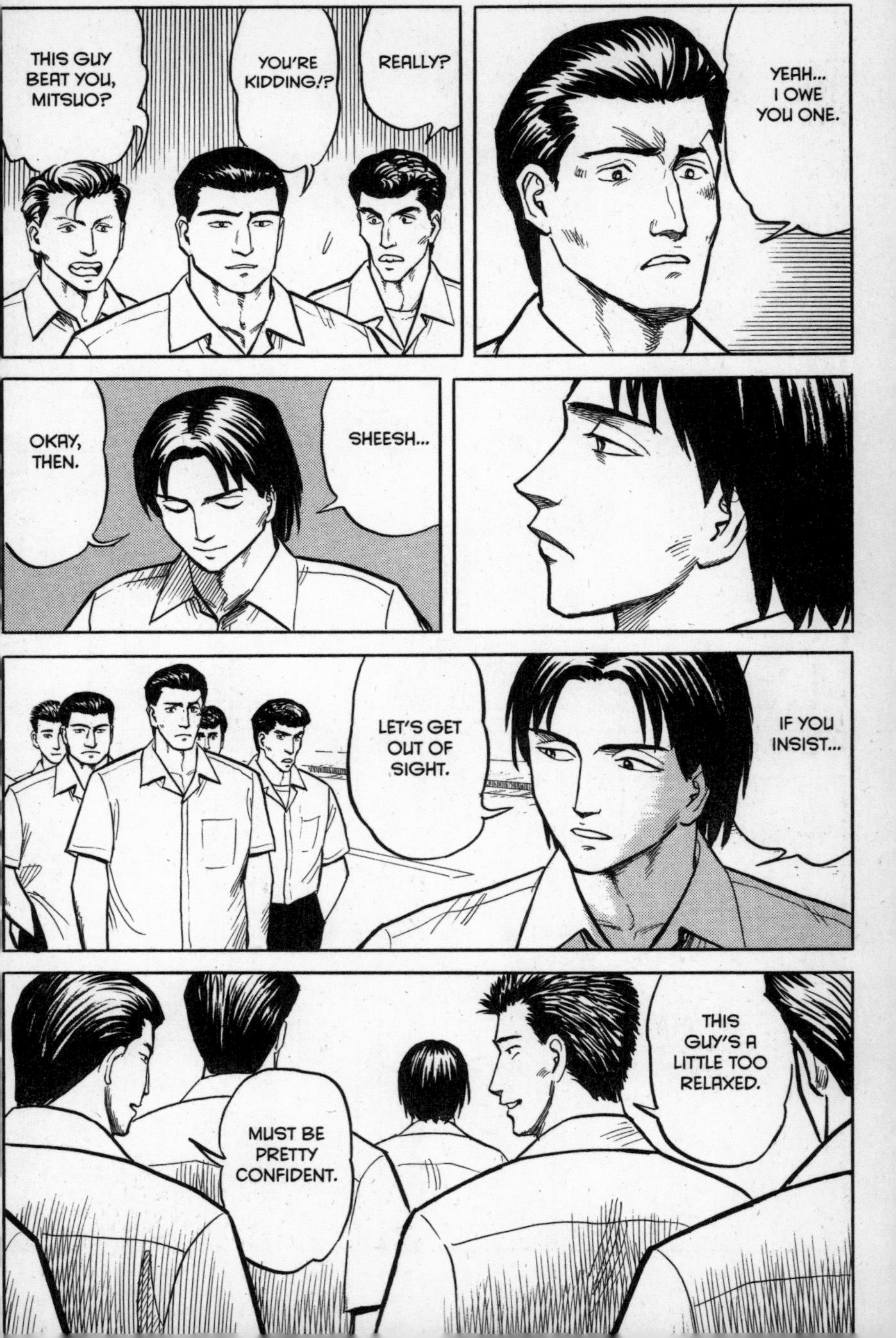
YEAH... I OWE YOU ONE.
REALLY?
YOU'RE KIDDING!?
THIS GUY BEAT YOU, MITSUO?
SHEESH...
OKAY, THEN.
IF YOU INSIST...
LET'S GET OUT OF SIGHT.
THIS GUY'S A LITTLE TOO RELAXED.
MUST BE PRETTY CONFIDENT.

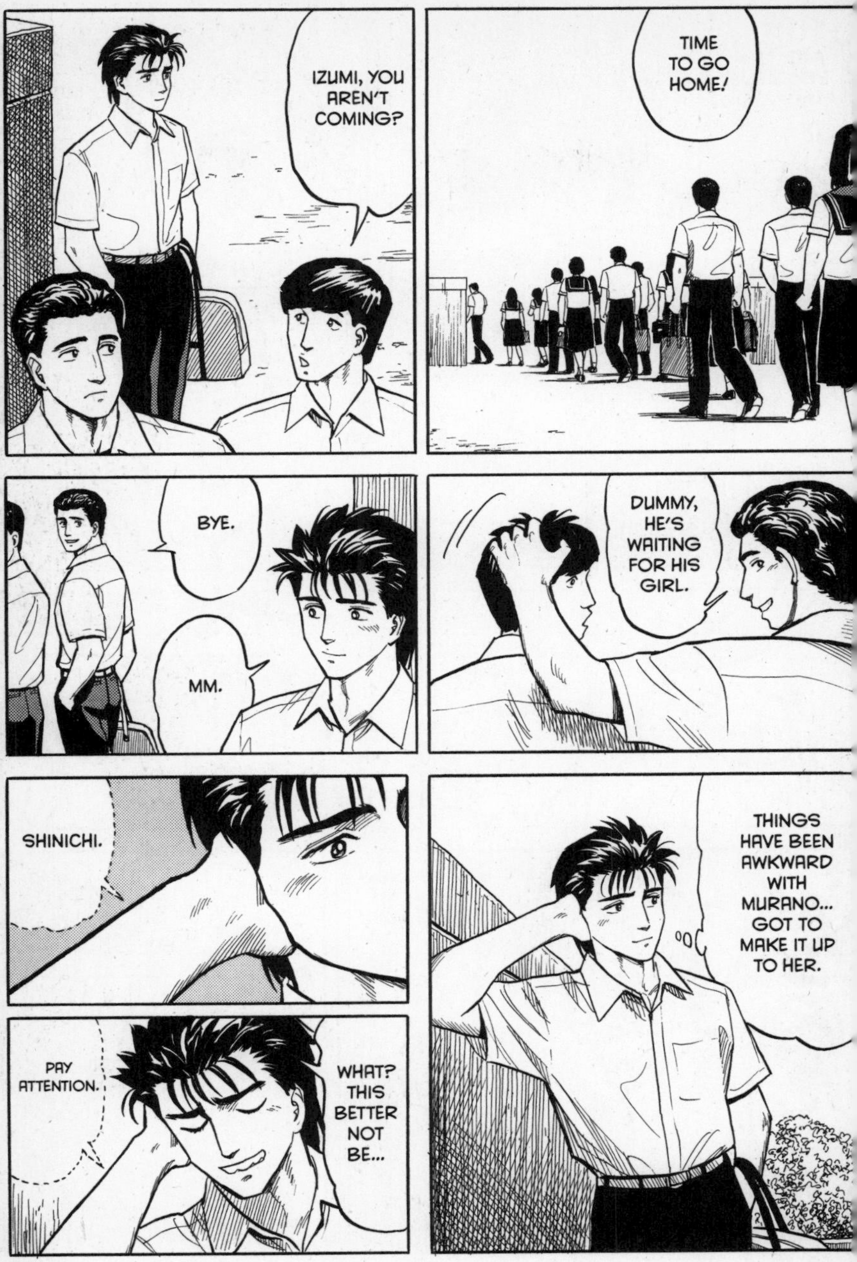
TIME TO GO HOME!
IZUMI, YOU AREN'T COMING?
DUMMY, HE'S WAITING FOR HIS GIRL.
BYE.
MM.
THINGS HAVE BEEN AWKWARD WITH MURANO... GOT TO MAKE IT UP TO HER.
SHINICHI.
WHAT? THIS BETTER NOT BE...
PAY ATTENTION.

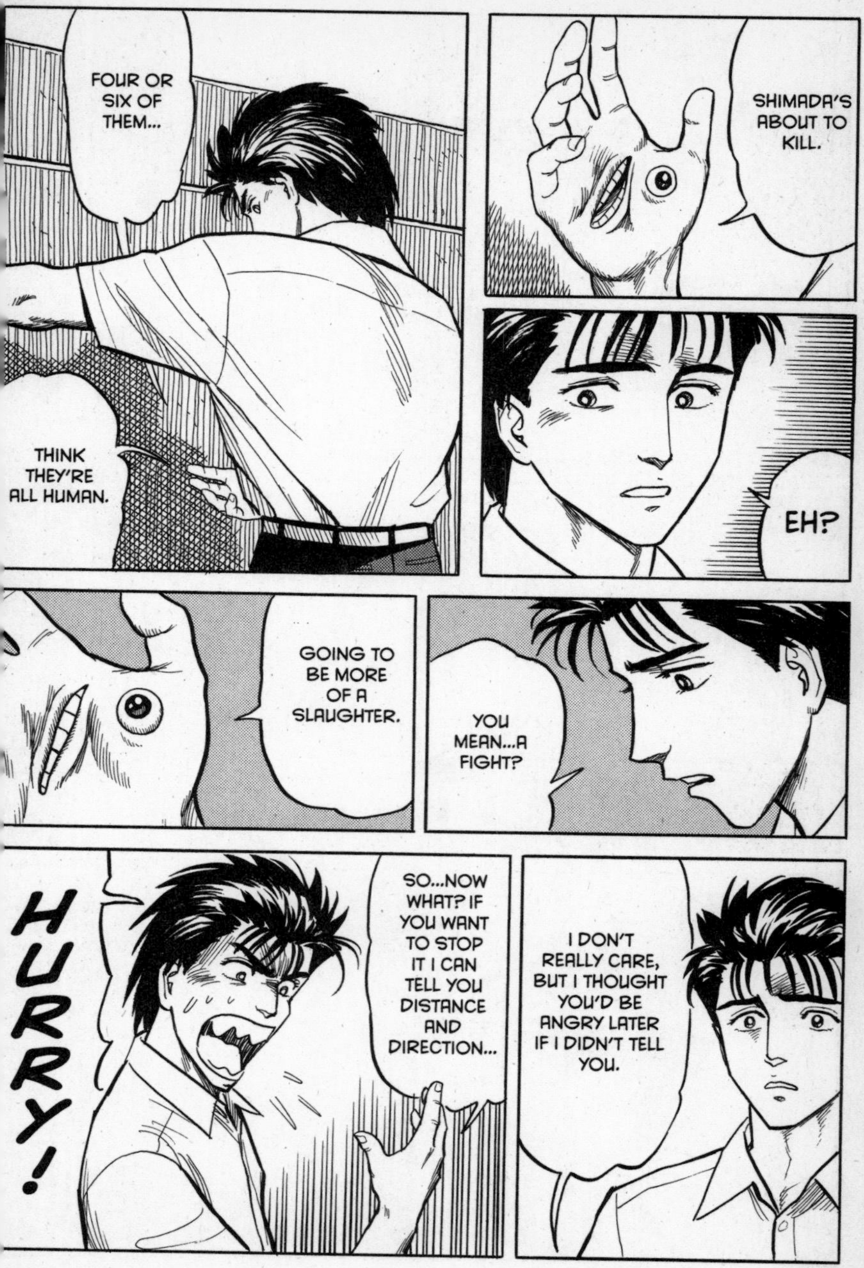
SHIMADA'S ABOUT TO KILL.
EH?
FOUR OR SIX OF THEM...
THINK THEY'RE ALL HUMAN.
YOU MEAN...A FIGHT?
GOING TO BE MORE OF A SLAUGHTER.
I DON'T REALLY CARE, BUT I THOUGHT YOU'D BE ANGRY LATER IF I DIDN'T TELL YOU.
SO...NOW WHAT? IF YOU WANT TO STOP IT I CAN TELL YOU DISTANCE AND DIRECTION...
HURRY!

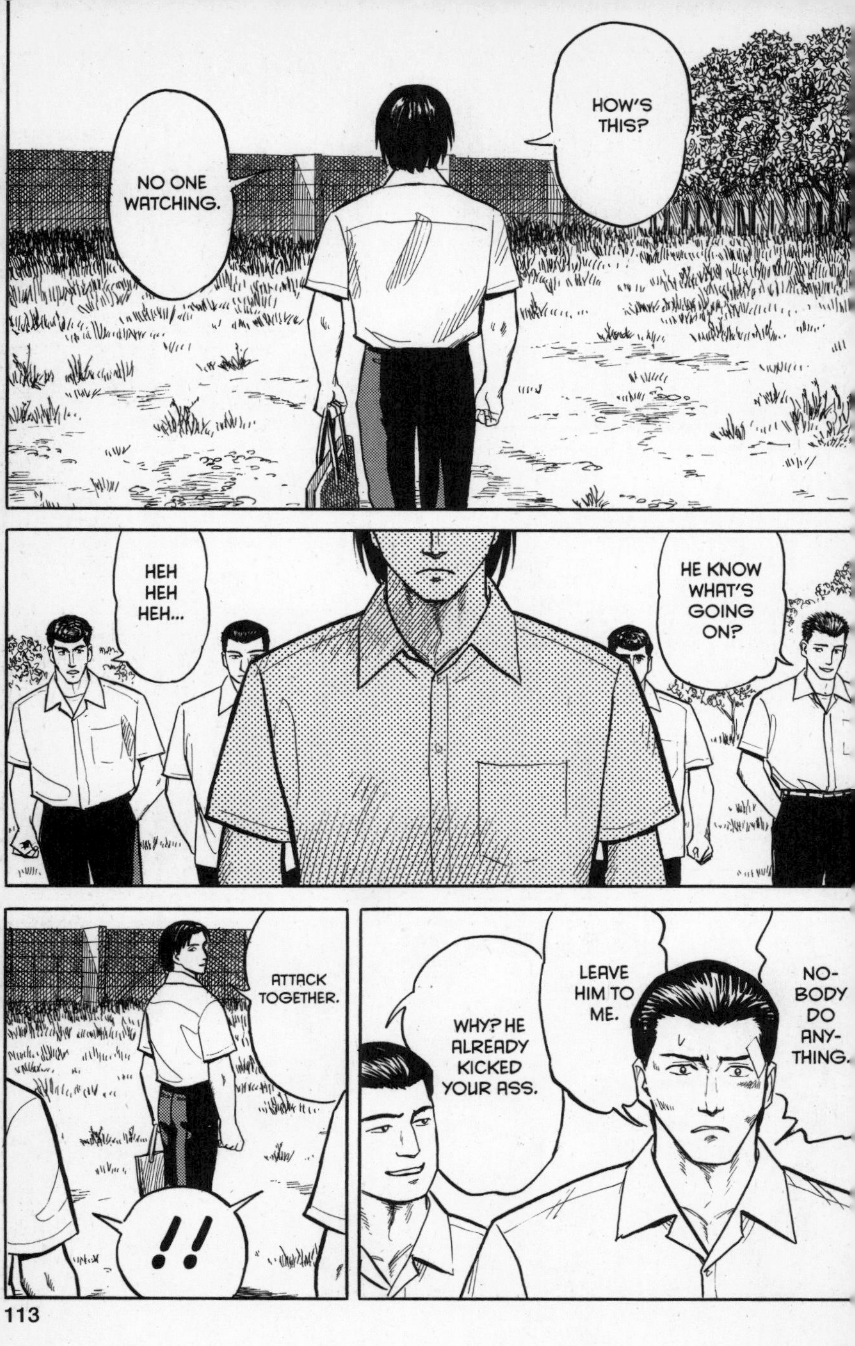
HOW'S THIS?
NO ONE WATCHING.
HE KNOW WHAT'S GOING ON?
HEH HEH HEH...
NO-BODY DO ANY-THING.
LEAVE HIM TO ME.
WHY? HE ALREADY KICKED YOUR ASS.
ATTACK TOGETHER.
!!

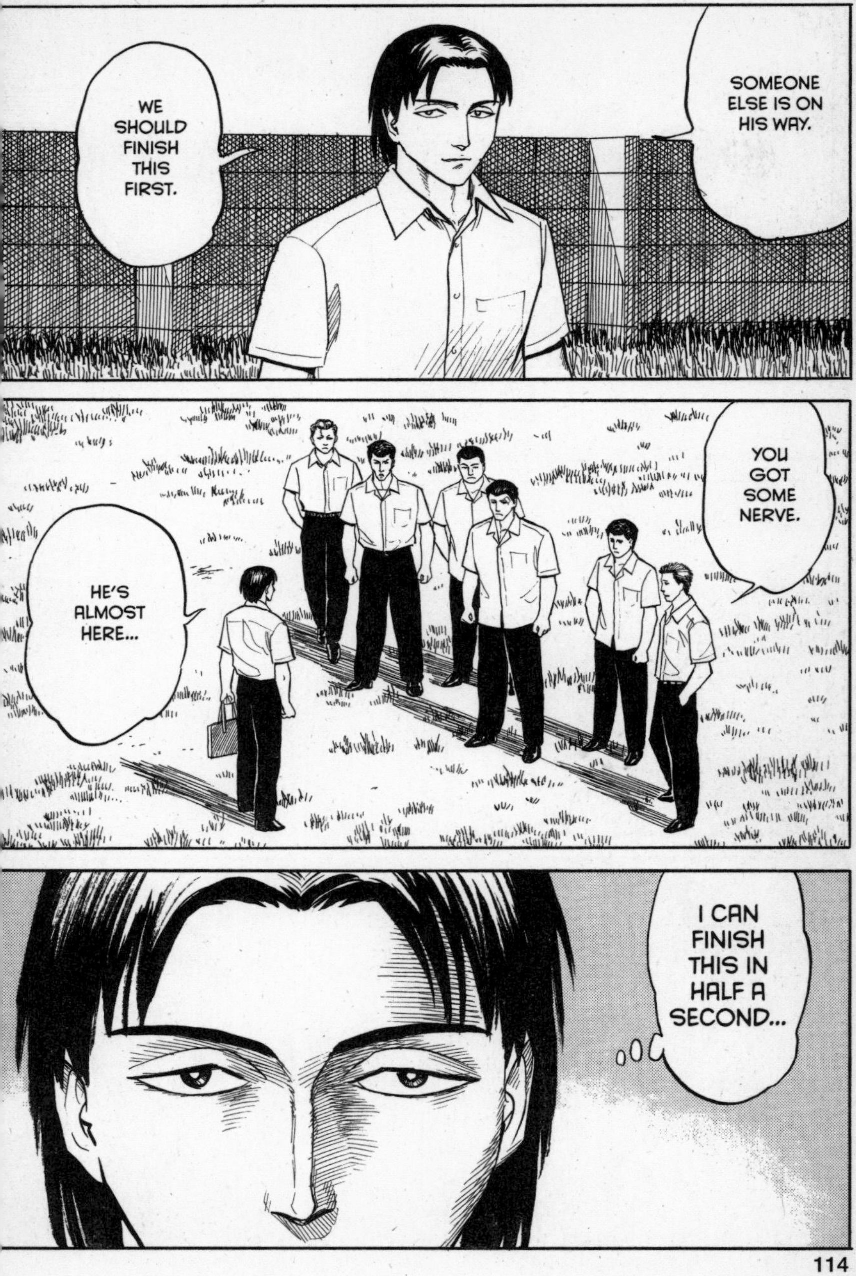
SOMEONE ELSE IS ON HIS WAY.
WE SHOULD FINISH THIS FIRST.
YOU GOT SOME NERVE.
HE'S ALMOST HERE...
I CAN FINISH THIS IN HALF A SECOND...

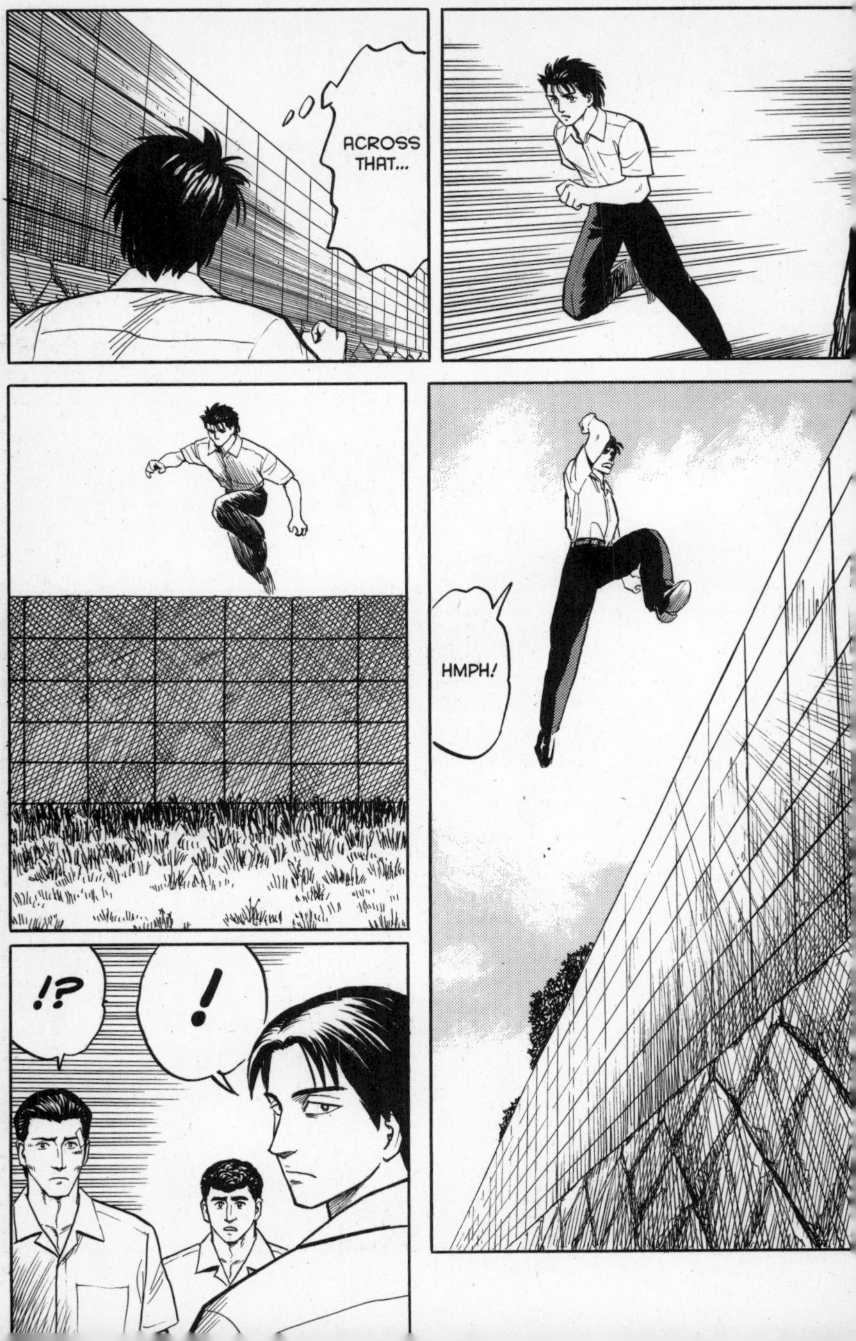
ACROSS THAT...
HMPH!
!
!?

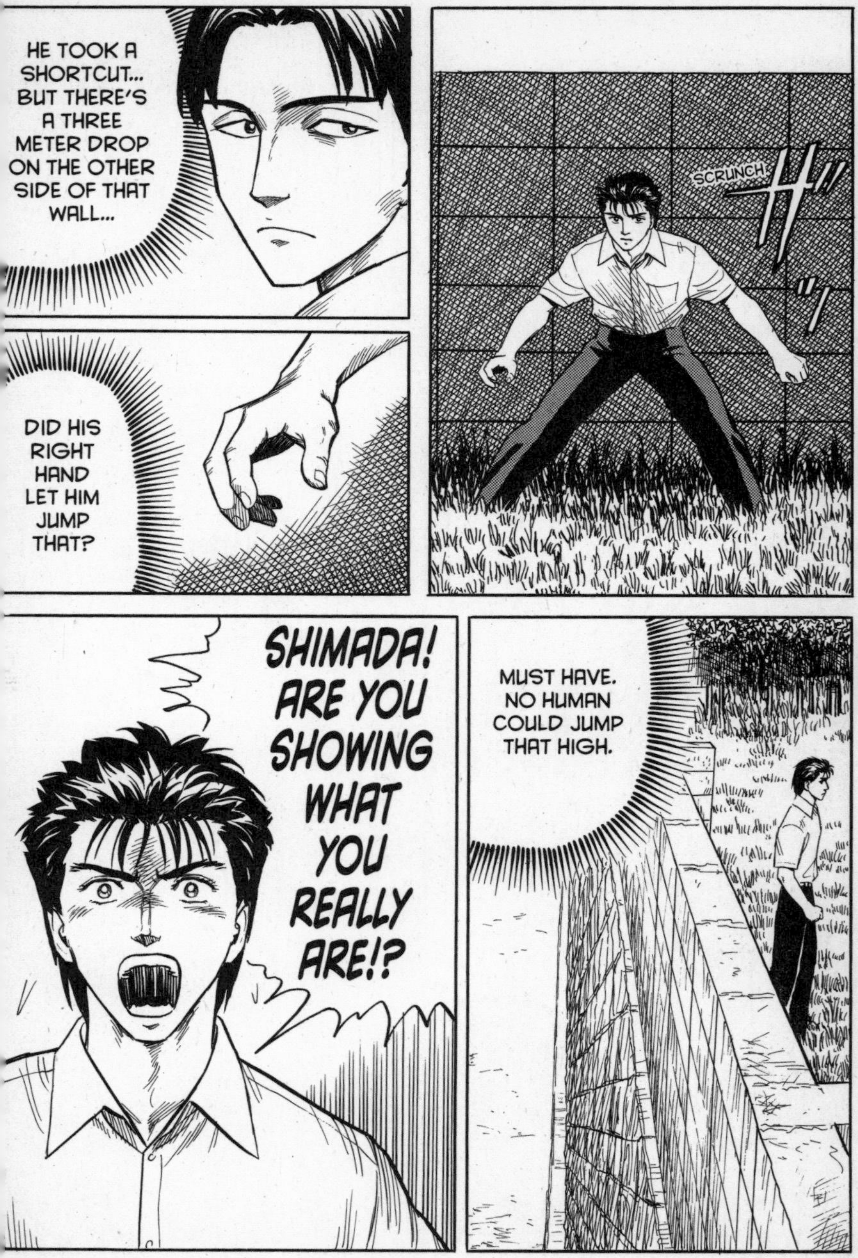
SCRUNCH
HE TOOK A SHORTCUT... BUT THERE'S A THREE METER DROP ON THE OTHER SIDE OF THAT WALL...
DID HIS RIGHT HAND LET HIM JUMP THAT?
MUST HAVE. NO HUMAN COULD JUMP THAT HIGH.
SHIMADA! ARE YOU SHOWING WHAT YOU REALLY ARE!?

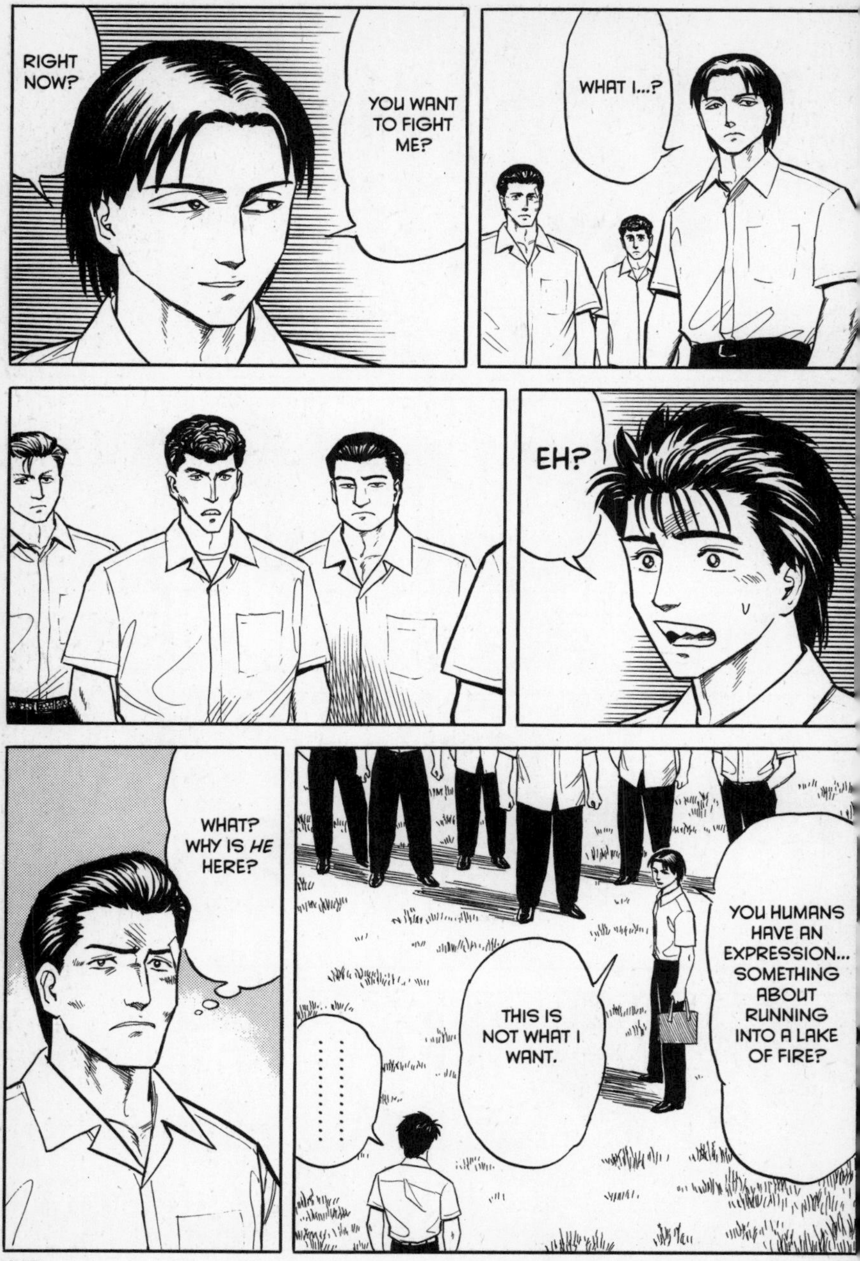
WHAT I...?
YOU WANT TO FIGHT ME?
RIGHT NOW?
EH?
YOU HUMANS HAVE AN EXPRESSION... SOMETHING ABOUT RUNNING INTO A LAKE OF FIRE?
THIS IS NOT WHAT I WANT.
......
WHAT? WHY IS *HE* HERE?

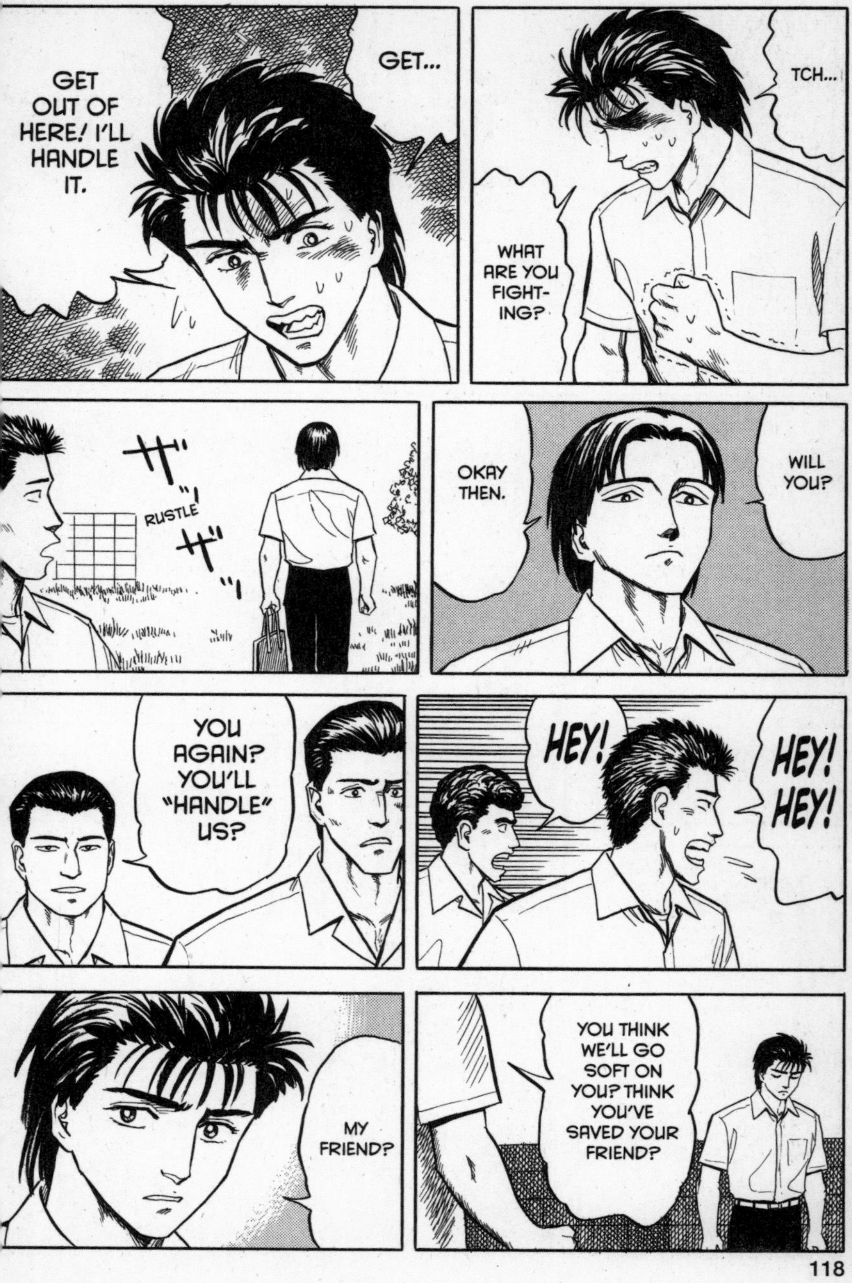
TCH...
WHAT ARE YOU FIGHT-ING?
GET...
GET OUT OF HERE! I'LL HANDLE IT.
WILL YOU?
OKAY THEN.
ザ
RUSTLE
ザ
HEY! HEY!
HEY!
YOU AGAIN? YOU'LL "HANDLE" US?
YOU THINK WE'LL GO SOFT ON YOU? THINK YOU'VE SAVED YOUR FRIEND?
MY FRIEND?

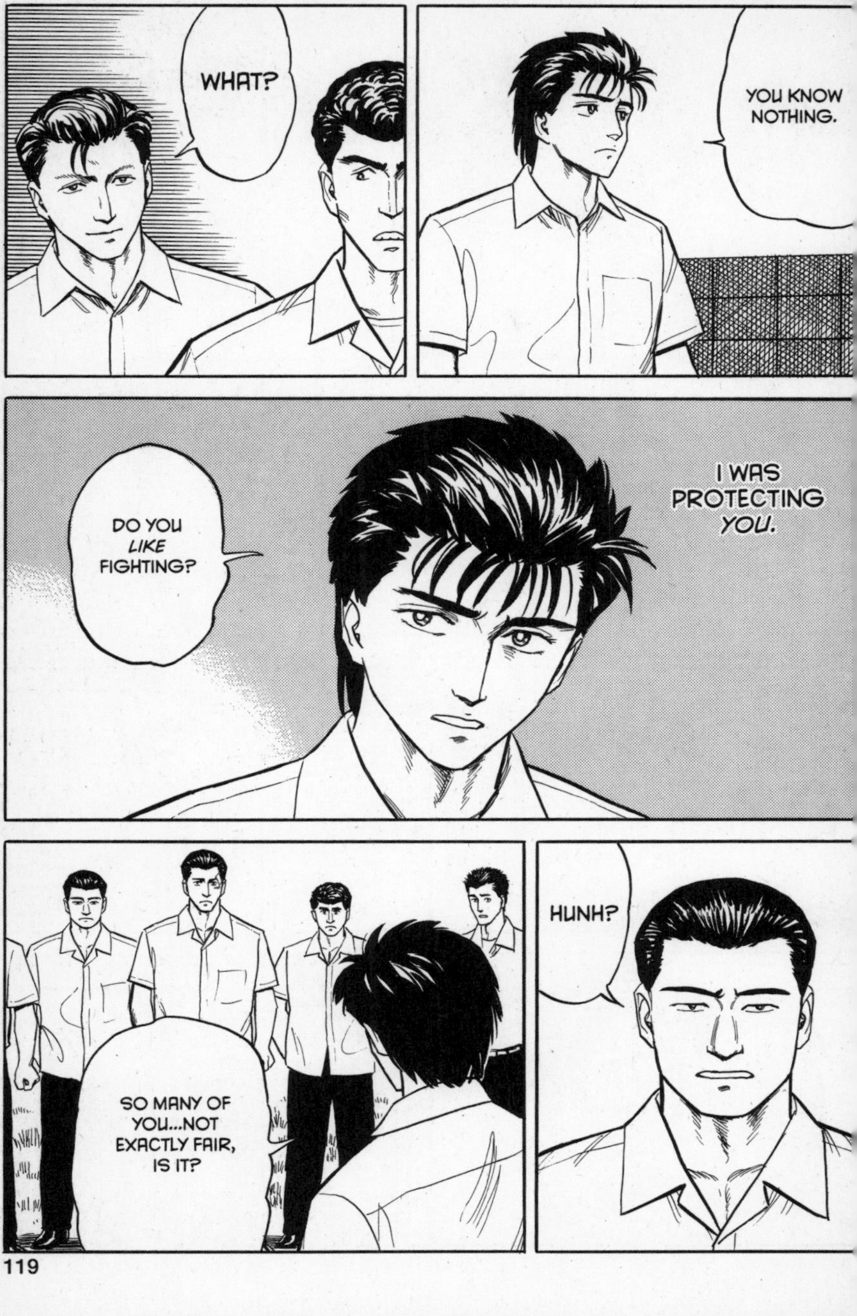
YOU KNOW NOTHING.
WHAT?
I WAS PROTECTING *YOU.*
DO YOU *LIKE* FIGHTING?
HUNH?
SO MANY OF YOU...NOT EXACTLY FAIR, IS IT?

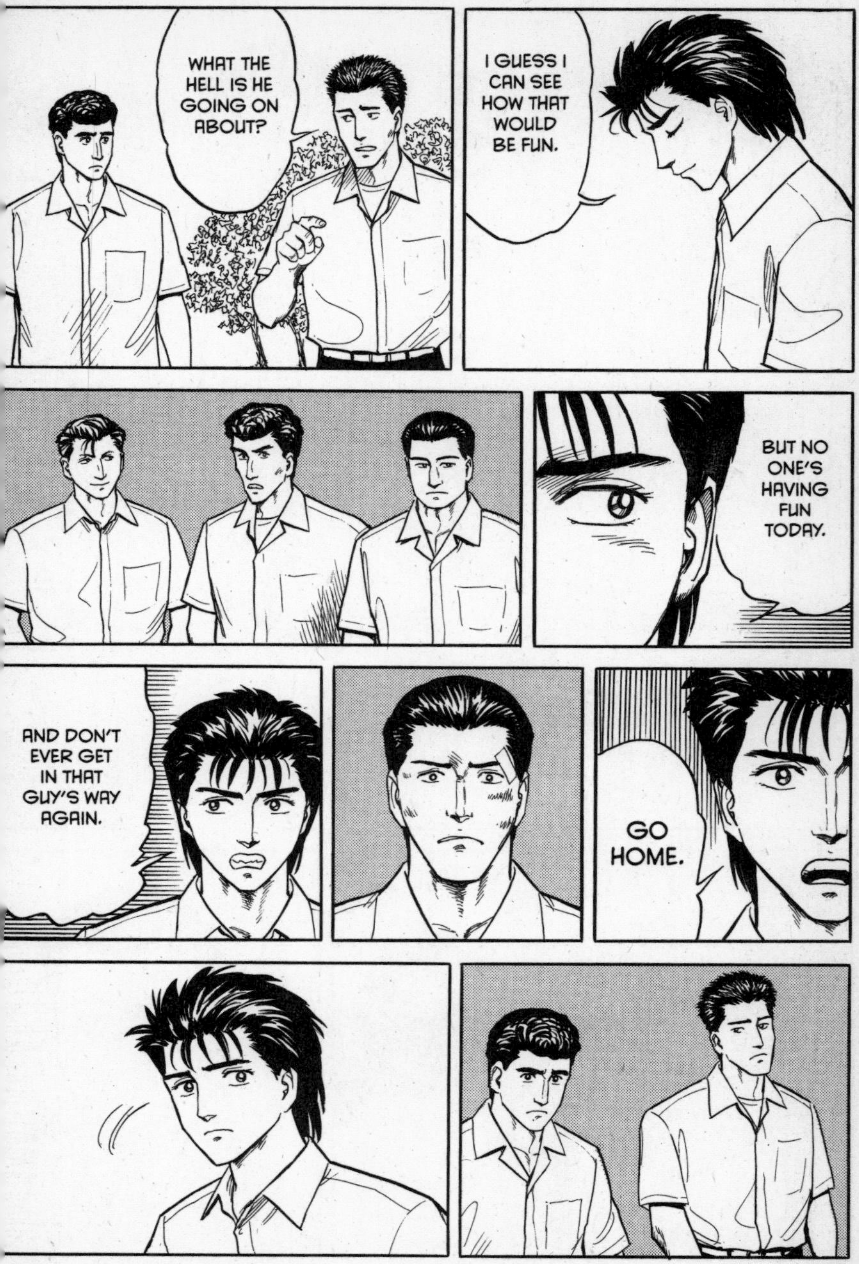
I GUESS I CAN SEE HOW THAT WOULD BE FUN.
WHAT THE HELL IS HE GOING ON ABOUT?
BUT NO ONE'S HAVING FUN TODAY.
GO HOME.
AND DON'T EVER GET IN THAT GUY'S WAY AGAIN.

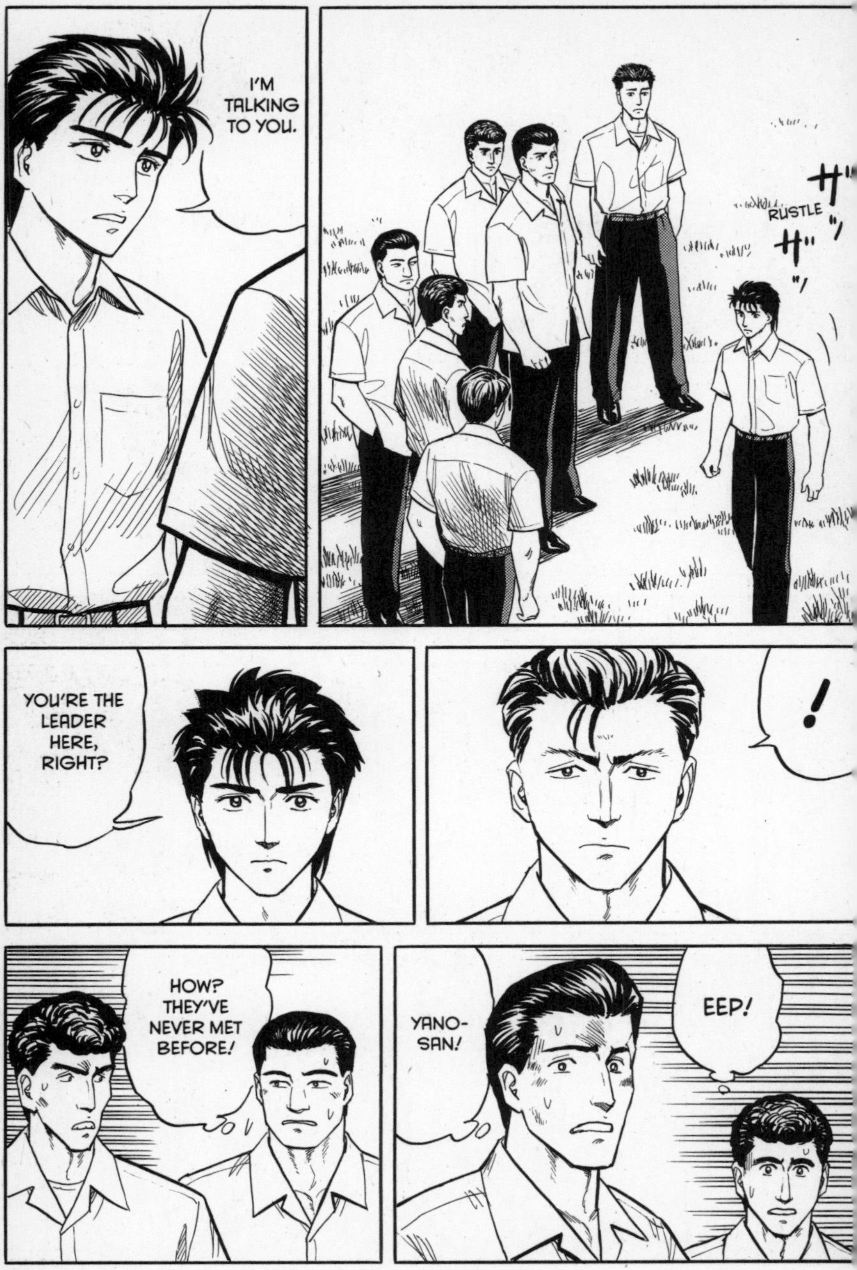
ザッ
ザッ
RUSTLE
I'M TALKING TO YOU.
!
YOU'RE THE LEADER HERE, RIGHT?
EEP!
YANO-SAN!
HOW? THEY'VE NEVER MET BEFORE!

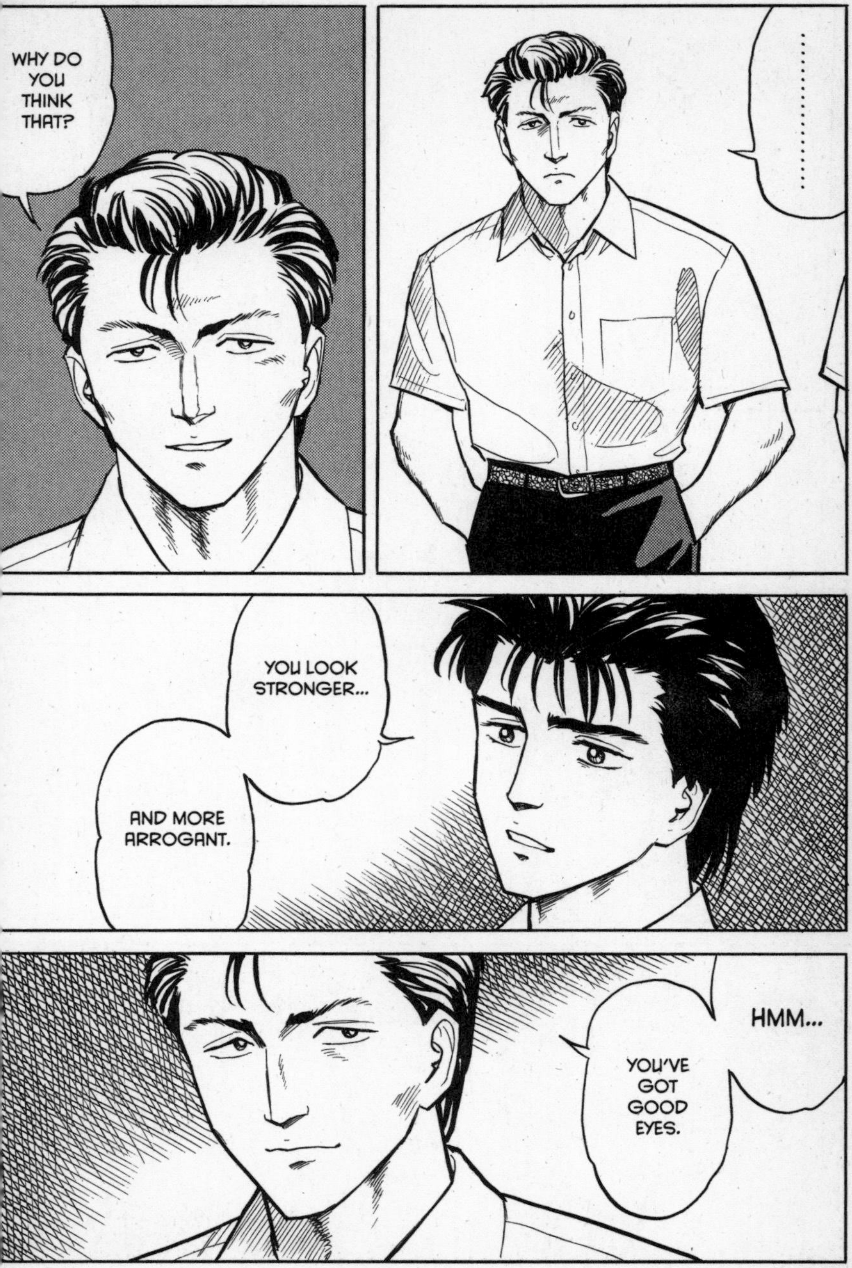
......
WHY DO YOU THINK THAT?
YOU LOOK STRONGER...
AND MORE ARROGANT.
HMM...
YOU'VE GOT GOOD EYES.

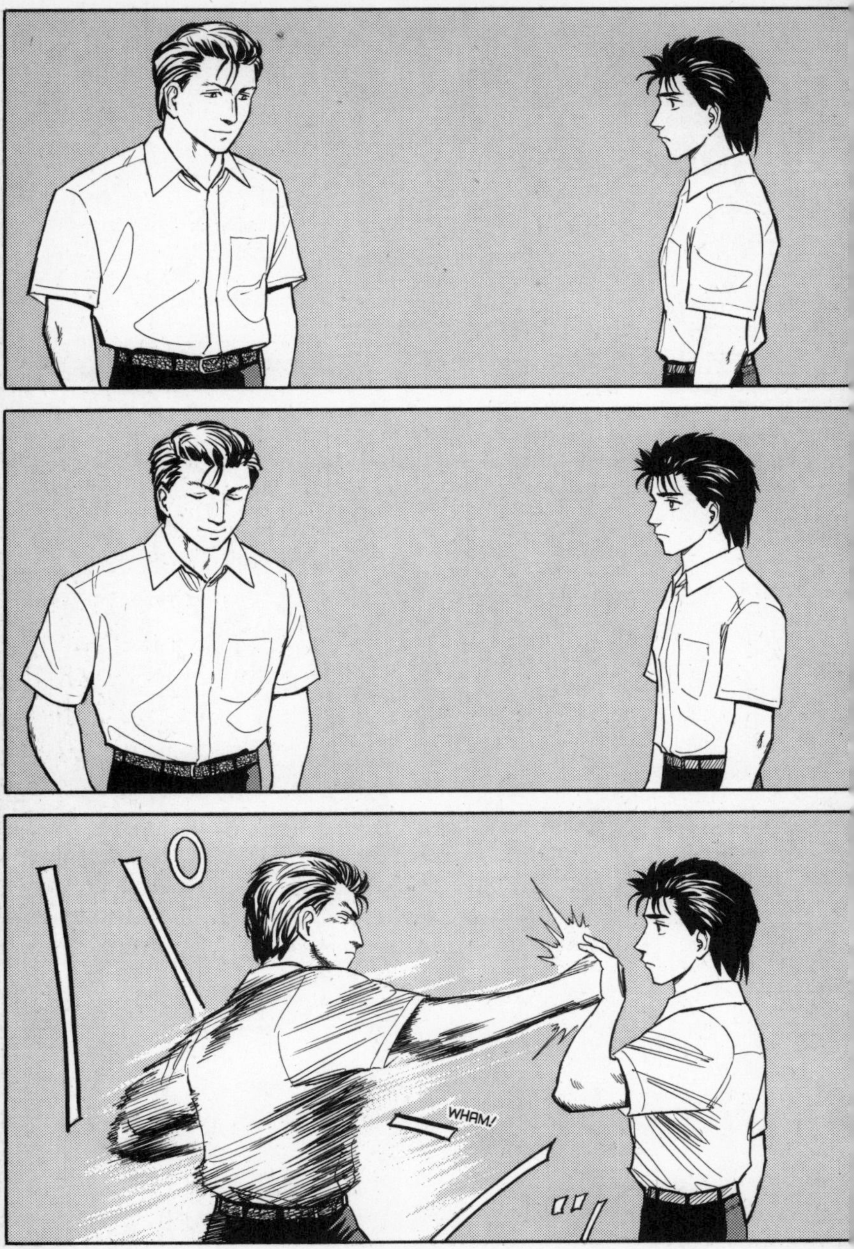
WHAM!

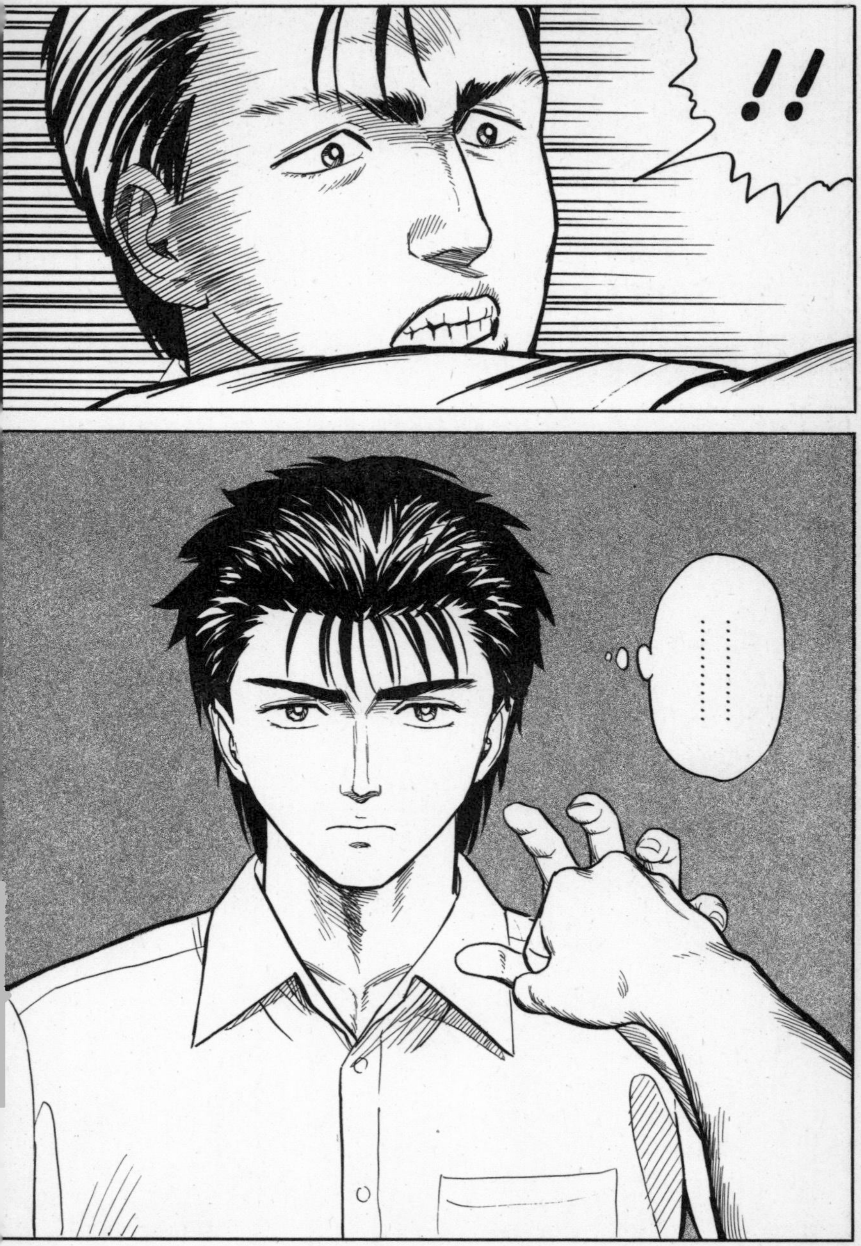
!!
……

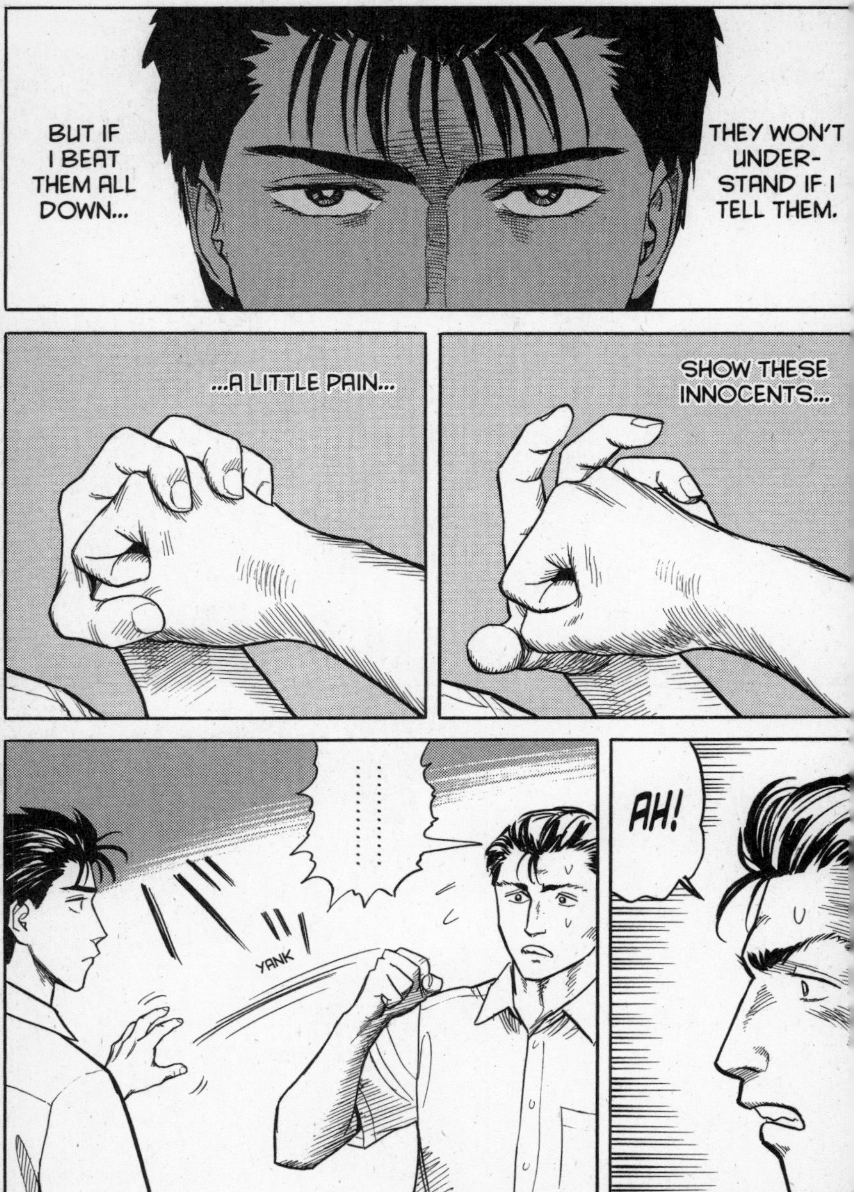
THEY WON'T UNDER-STAND IF I TELL THEM.
BUT IF I BEAT THEM ALL DOWN...
SHOW THESE INNOCENTS...
...A LITTLE PAIN...
AH!
......
YANK

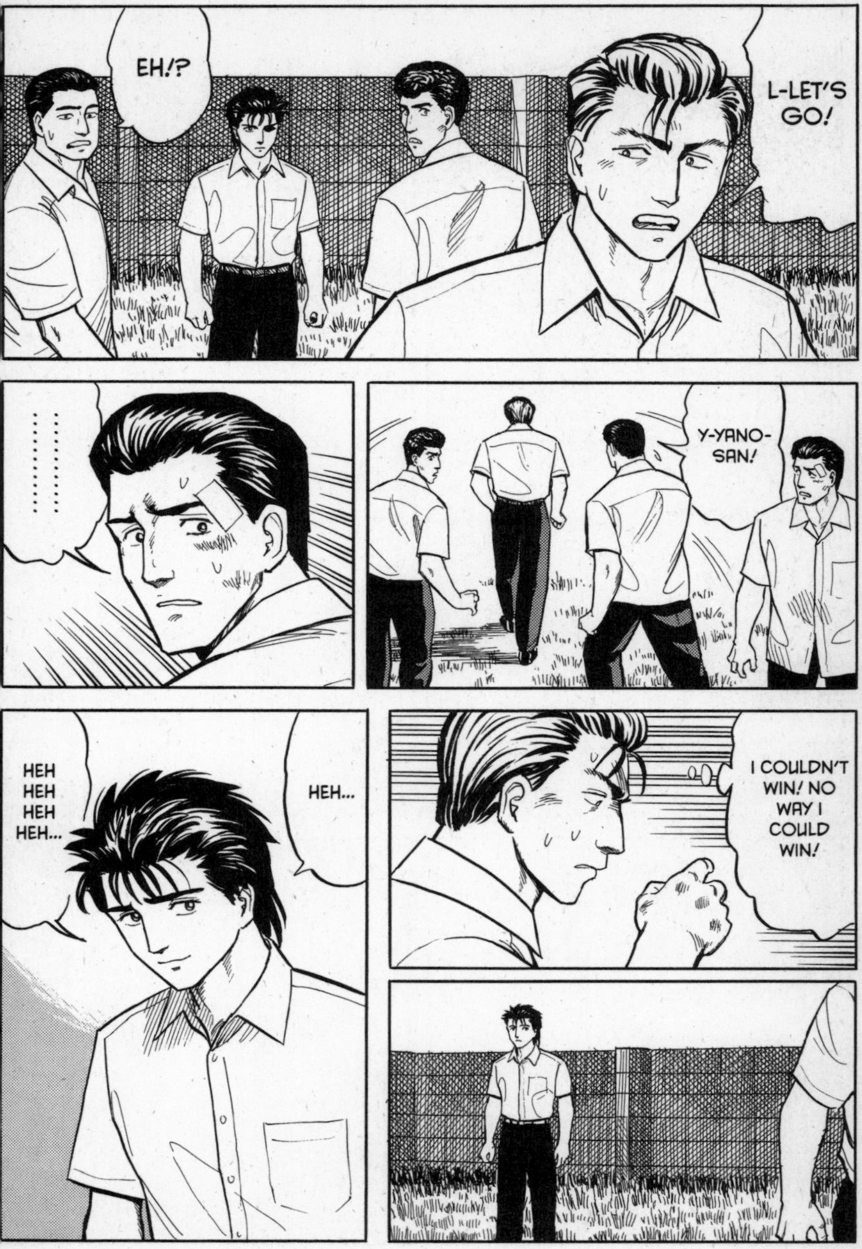
L-LET'S GO!
EH!?
Y-YANO-SAN!
......
I COULDN'T WIN! NO WAY I COULD WIN!
HEH...
HEH HEH HEH HEH...

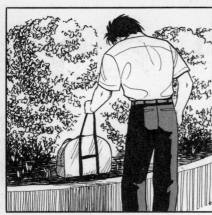

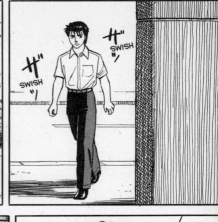

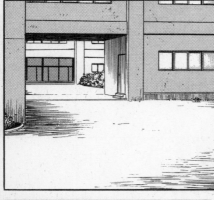

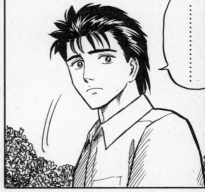

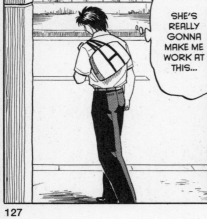

SWISH
SWISH
......
SO MUCH FOR WAITING...
SHE'S REALLY GONNA MAKE ME WORK AT THIS...

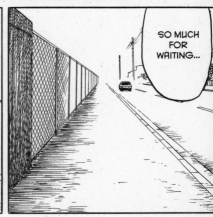

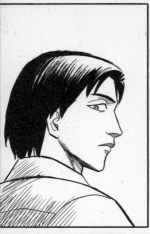

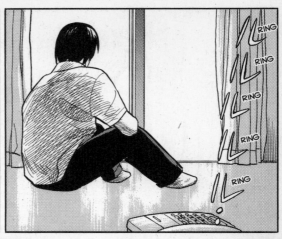

RING
RING
RING
RING
RING
HOW ARE THINGS?
NOT A PROBLEM.
BUT IT'S HARD TO EAT.
YES... BUT KEEP THINGS QUIET.

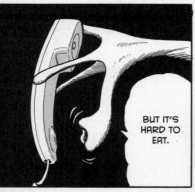

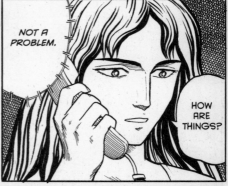

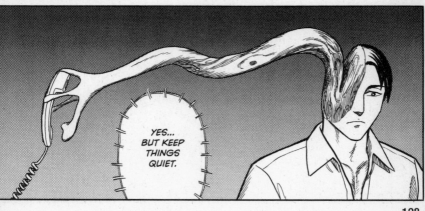

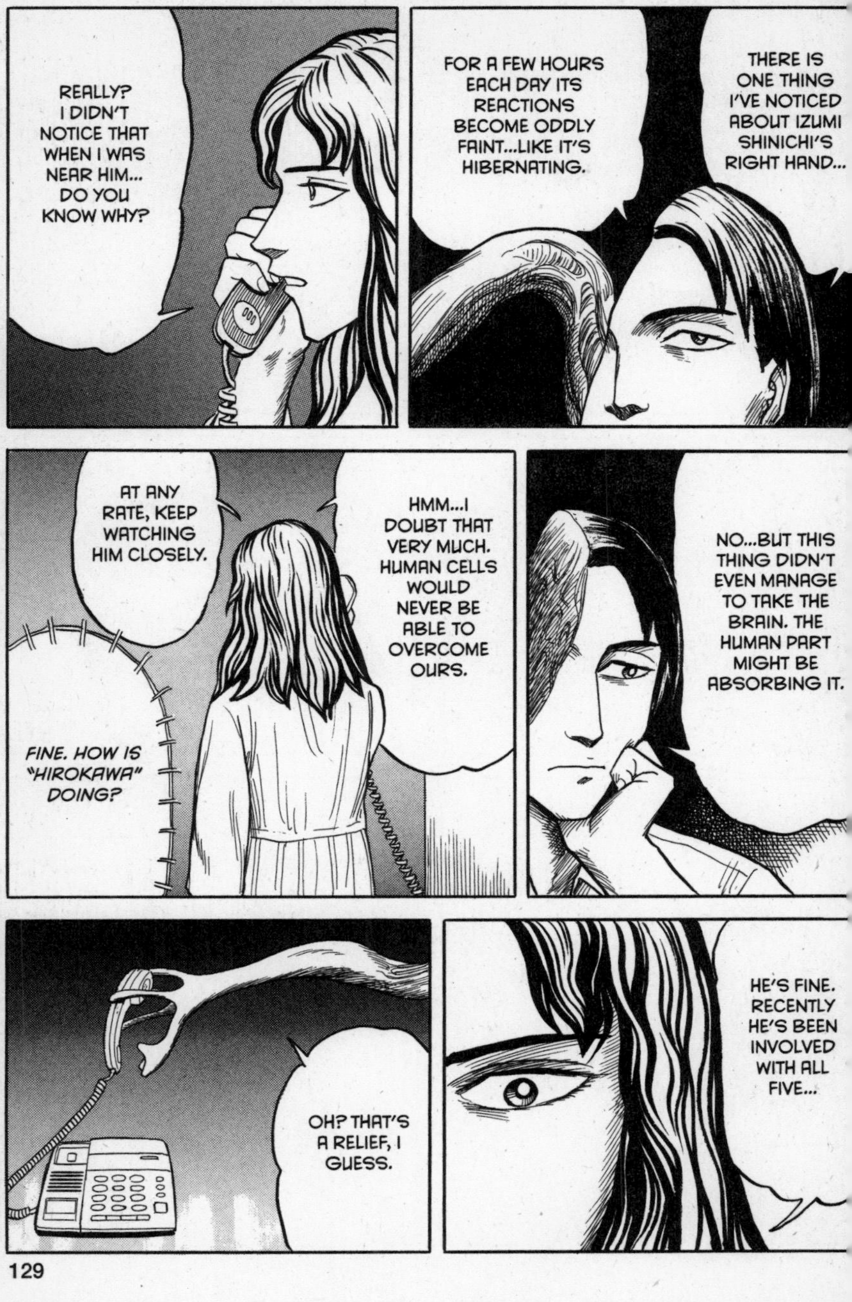
THERE IS ONE THING I'VE NOTICED ABOUT IZUMI SHINICHI'S RIGHT HAND...
FOR A FEW HOURS EACH DAY ITS REACTIONS BECOME ODDLY FAINT...LIKE IT'S HIBERNATING.
REALLY? I DIDN'T NOTICE THAT WHEN I WAS NEAR HIM... DO YOU KNOW WHY?
NO...BUT THIS THING DIDN'T EVEN MANAGE TO TAKE THE BRAIN. THE HUMAN PART MIGHT BE ABSORBING IT.
HMM...I DOUBT THAT VERY MUCH. HUMAN CELLS WOULD NEVER BE ABLE TO OVERCOME OURS.
AT ANY RATE, KEEP WATCHING HIM CLOSELY.
FINE. HOW IS "HIROKAWA" DOING?
HE'S FINE. RECENTLY HE'S BEEN INVOLVED WITH ALL FIVE...
OH? THAT'S A RELIEF, I GUESS.

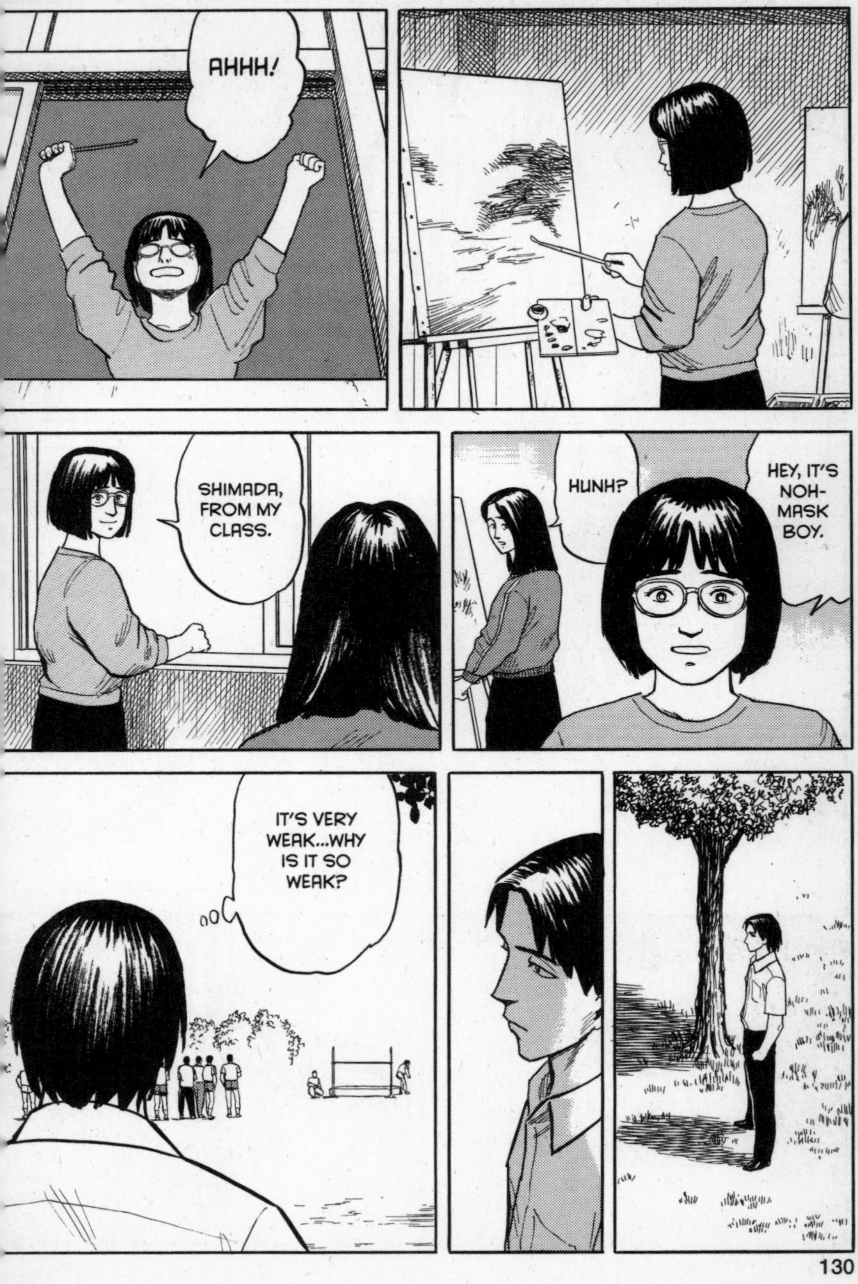
AHHH!
HEY, IT'S NOH-MASK BOY.
HUNH?
SHIMADA, FROM MY CLASS.
IT'S VERY WEAK...WHY IS IT SO WEAK?

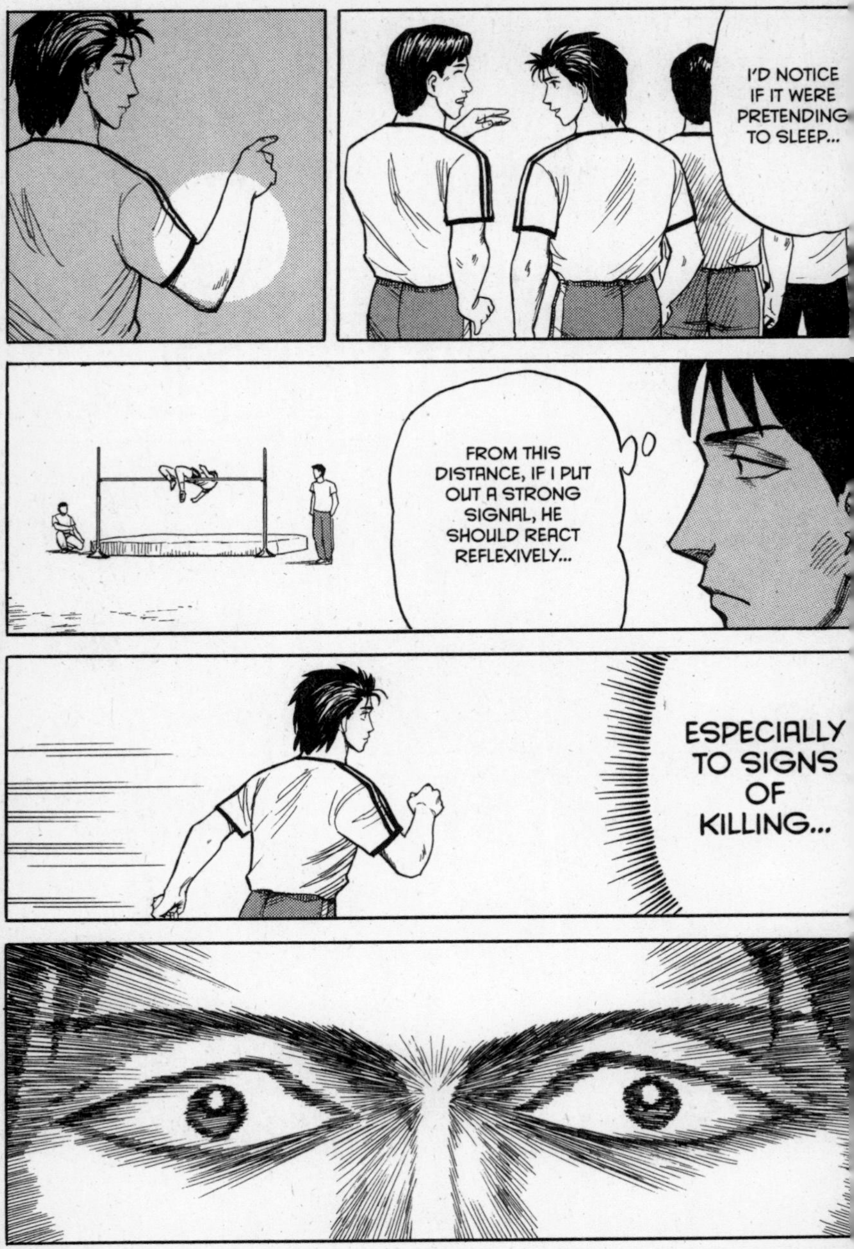
I'D NOTICE IF IT WERE PRETENDING TO SLEEP...
FROM THIS DISTANCE, IF I PUT OUT A STRONG SIGNAL, HE SHOULD REACT REFLEXIVELY...
ESPECIALLY TO SIGNS OF KILLING...

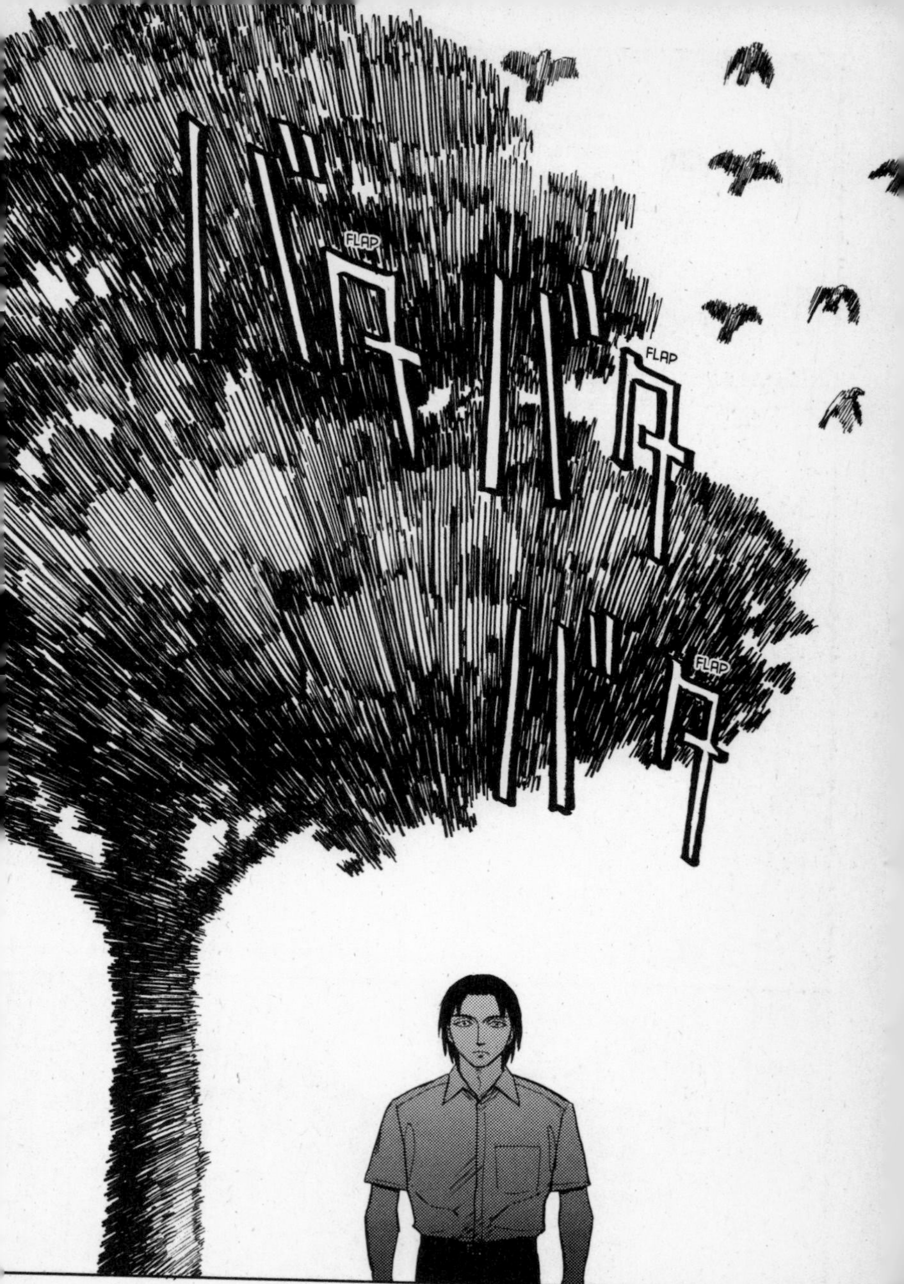
バサ
FLAP
バサ
FLAP
バサ
FLAP

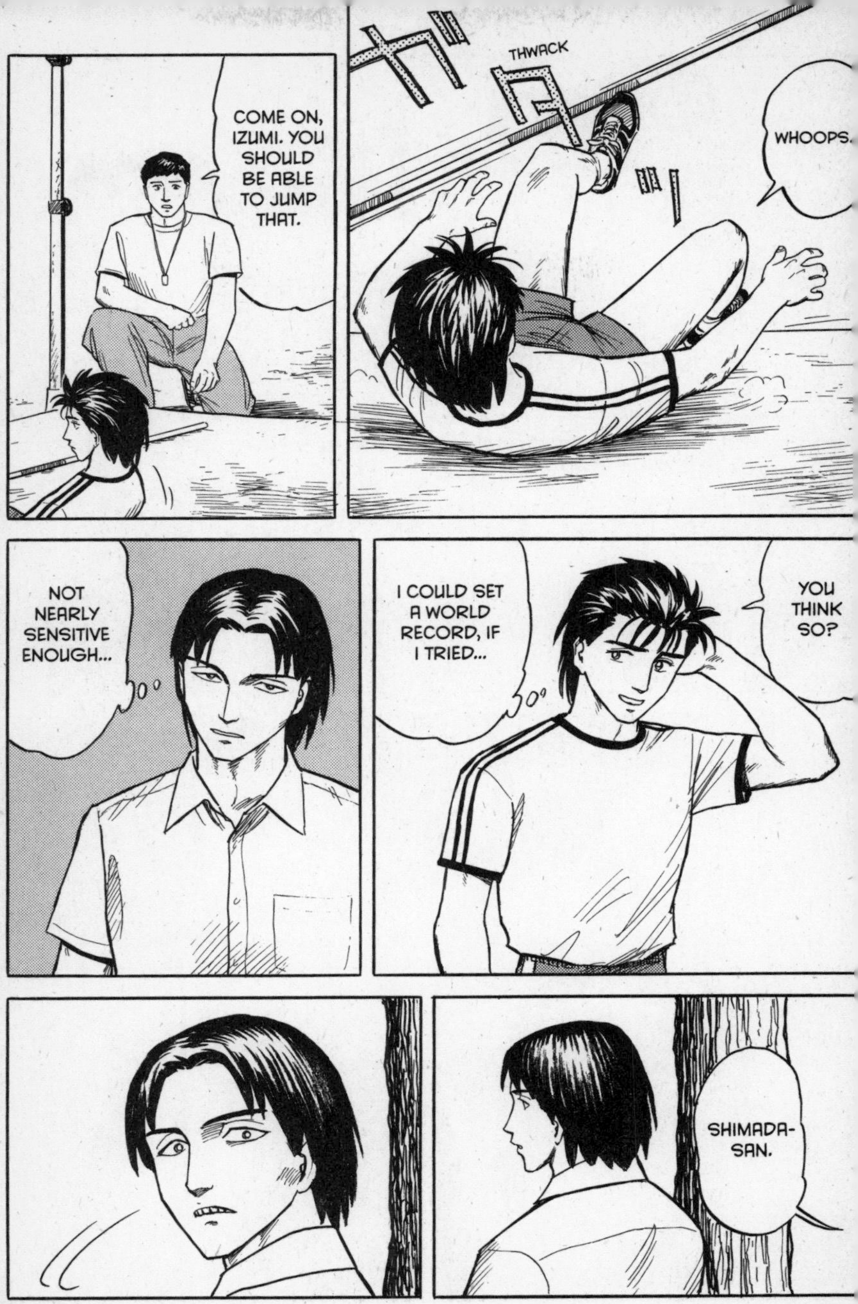
THWACK
WHOOPS.
COME ON, IZUMI. YOU SHOULD BE ABLE TO JUMP THAT.
YOU THINK SO?
I COULD SET A WORLD RECORD, IF I TRIED...
NOT NEARLY SENSITIVE ENOUGH...
SHIMADA-SAN.

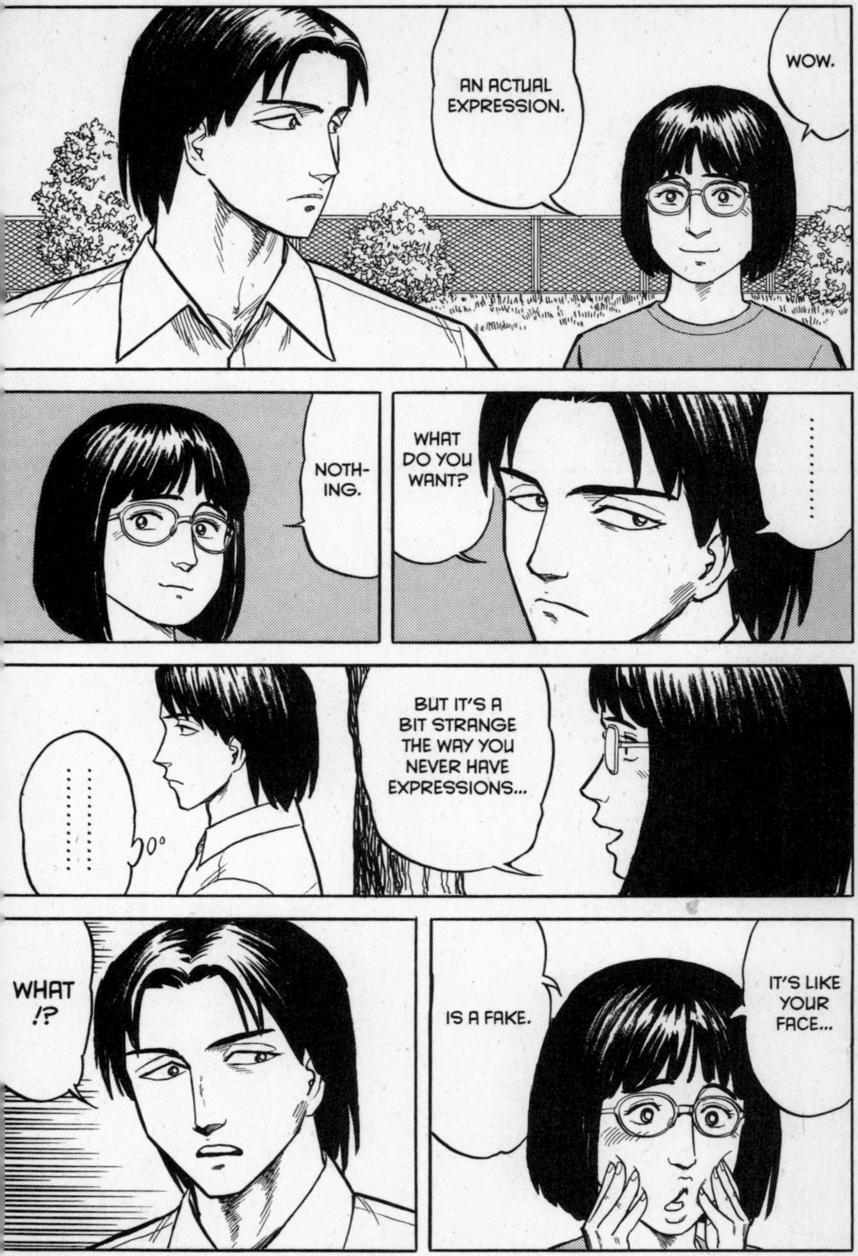
WOW.
AN ACTUAL EXPRESSION.
......
WHAT DO YOU WANT?
NOTH-ING.
BUT IT'S A BIT STRANGE THE WAY YOU NEVER HAVE EXPRESSIONS...
......
IT'S LIKE YOUR FACE...
IS A FAKE.
WHAT !?

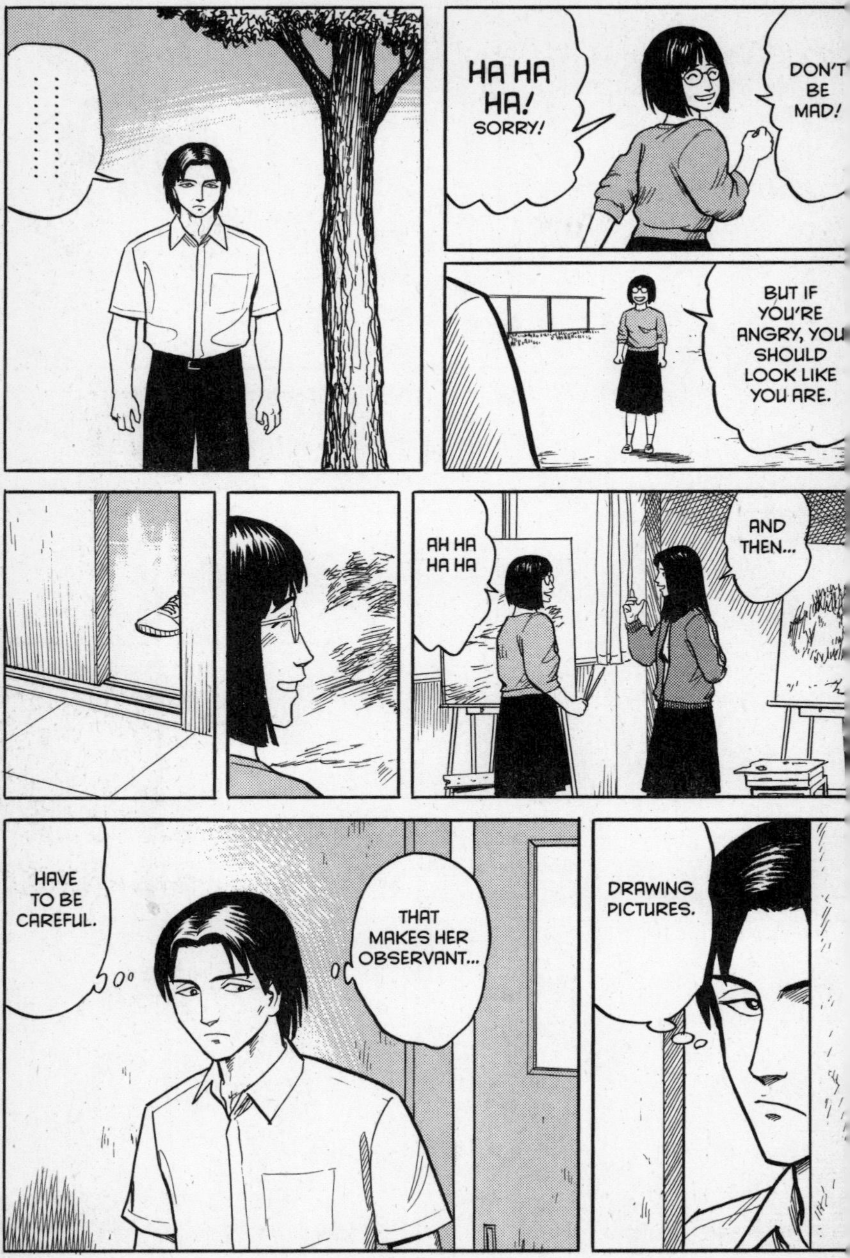
DON'T BE MAD!
HA HA HA! SORRY!
BUT IF YOU'RE ANGRY, YOU SHOULD LOOK LIKE YOU ARE.
......
AND THEN...
AH HA HA HA
DRAWING PICTURES.
THAT MAKES HER OBSERVANT...
HAVE TO BE CAREFUL.

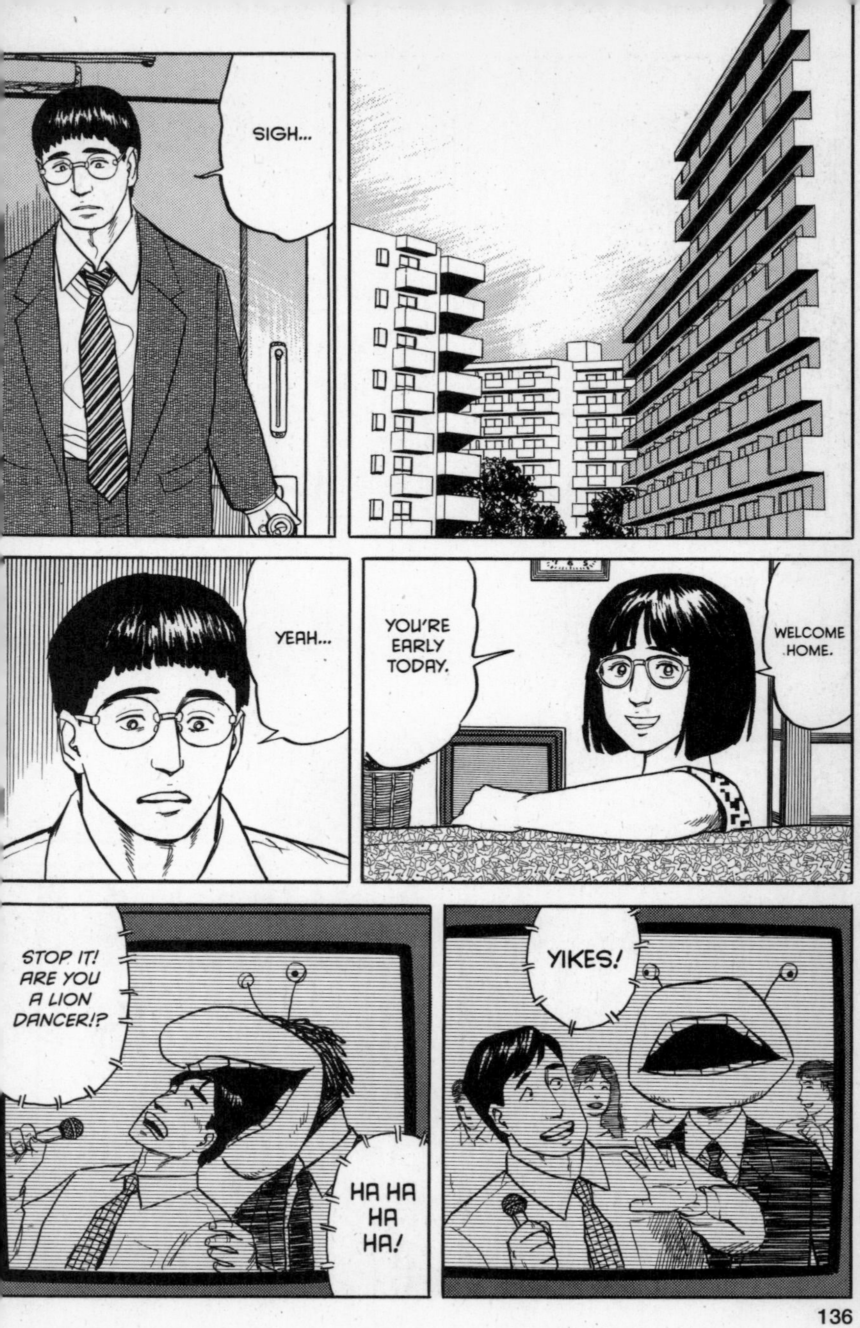
SIGH...
WELCOME HOME.
YOU'RE EARLY TODAY.
YEAH...
YIKES!
STOP IT! ARE YOU A LION DANCER!?
HA HA HA HA!

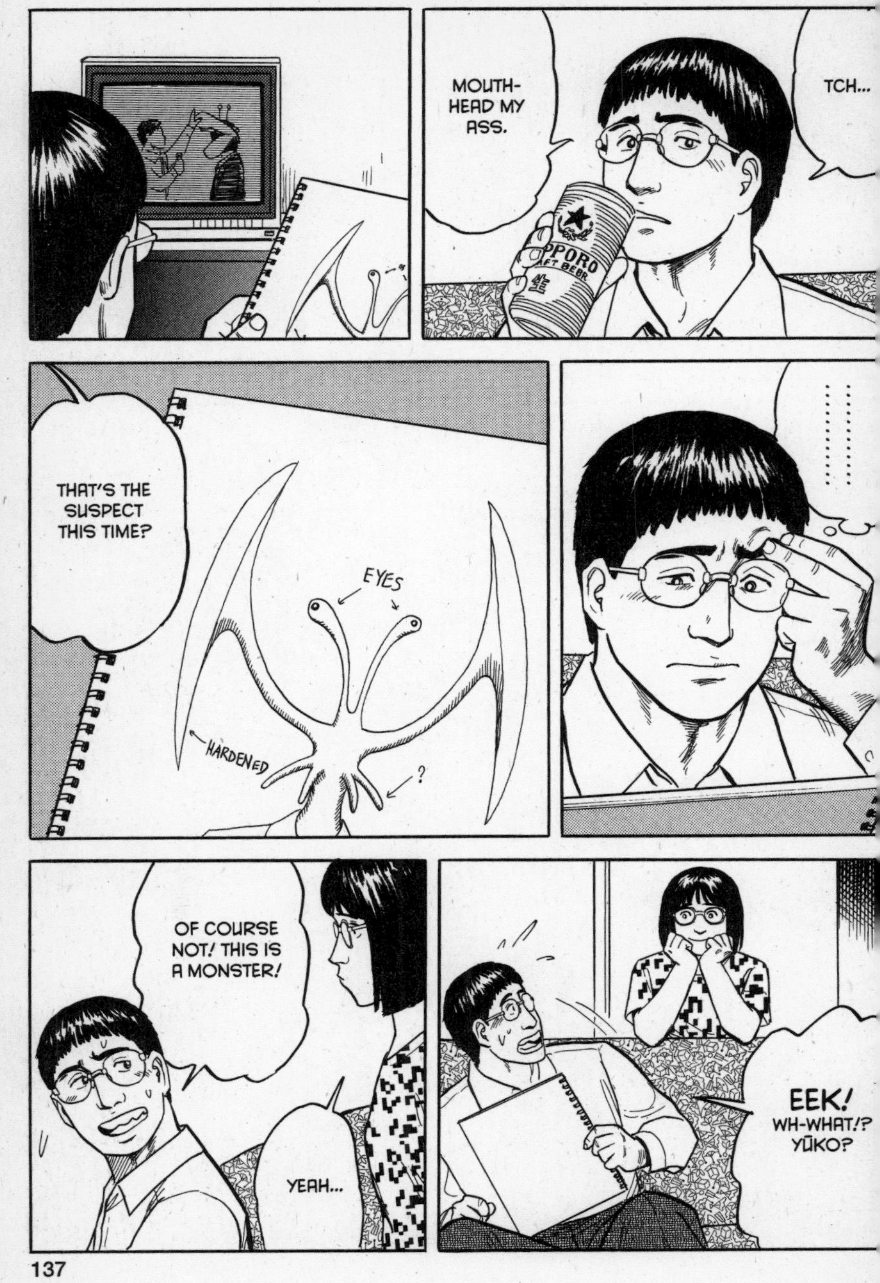
TCH...
MOUTH-HEAD MY ASS.
......
THAT'S THE SUSPECT THIS TIME?
EYES
HARDENED
?
EEK! WH-WHAT!? YŪKO?
OF COURSE NOT! THIS IS A MONSTER!
YEAH...

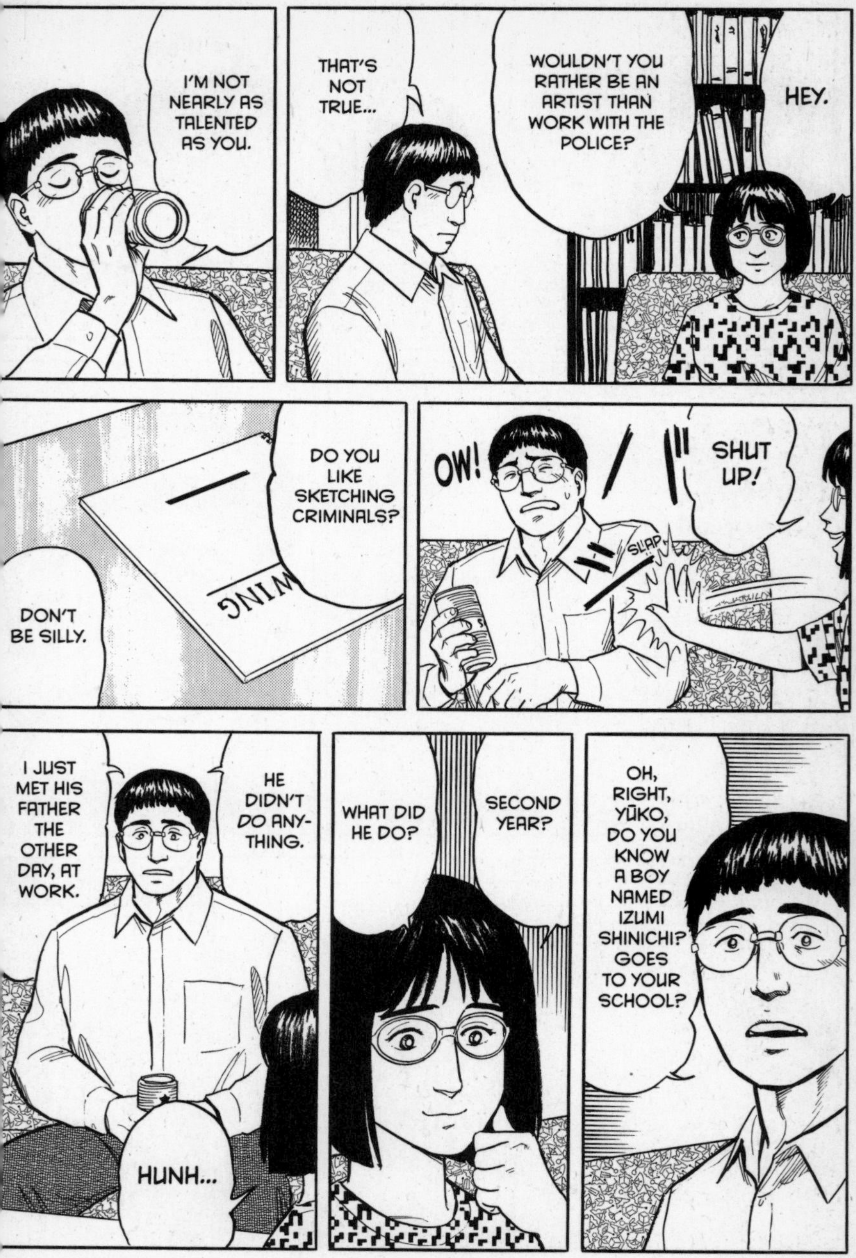
HEY.
WOULDN'T YOU RATHER BE AN ARTIST THAN WORK WITH THE POLICE?
THAT'S NOT TRUE...
I'M NOT NEARLY AS TALENTED AS YOU.
SHUT UP!
OW!
SLAP
DO YOU LIKE SKETCHING CRIMINALS?
DON'T BE SILLY.
OH, RIGHT, YŪKO, DO YOU KNOW A BOY NAMED IZUMI SHINICHI? GOES TO YOUR SCHOOL?
SECOND YEAR?
WHAT DID HE DO?
HE DIDN'T *DO* ANYTHING.
I JUST MET HIS FATHER THE OTHER DAY, AT WORK.
HUNH...

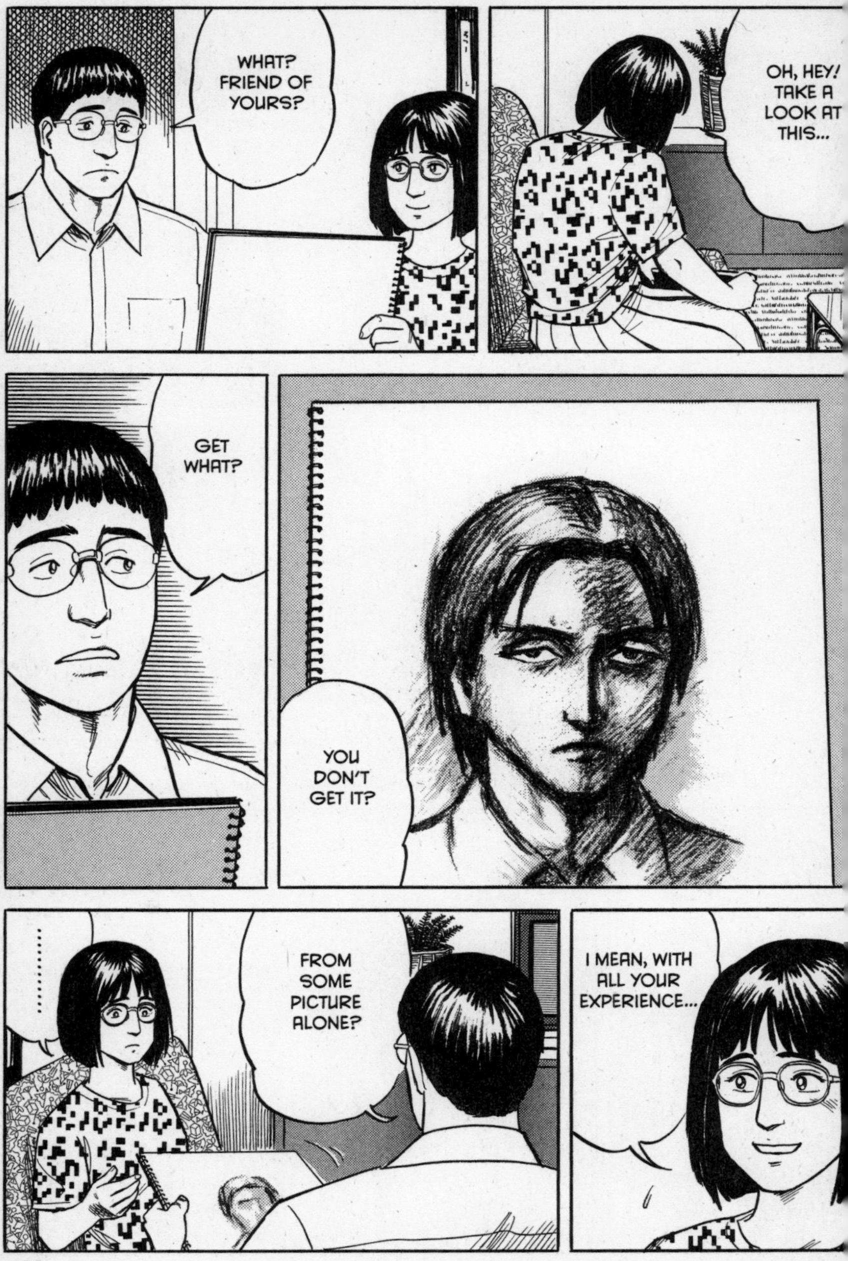
OH, HEY! TAKE A LOOK AT THIS...
WHAT? FRIEND OF YOURS?
YOU DON'T GET IT?
GET WHAT?
I MEAN, WITH ALL YOUR EXPERIENCE...
FROM SOME PICTURE ALONE?
....

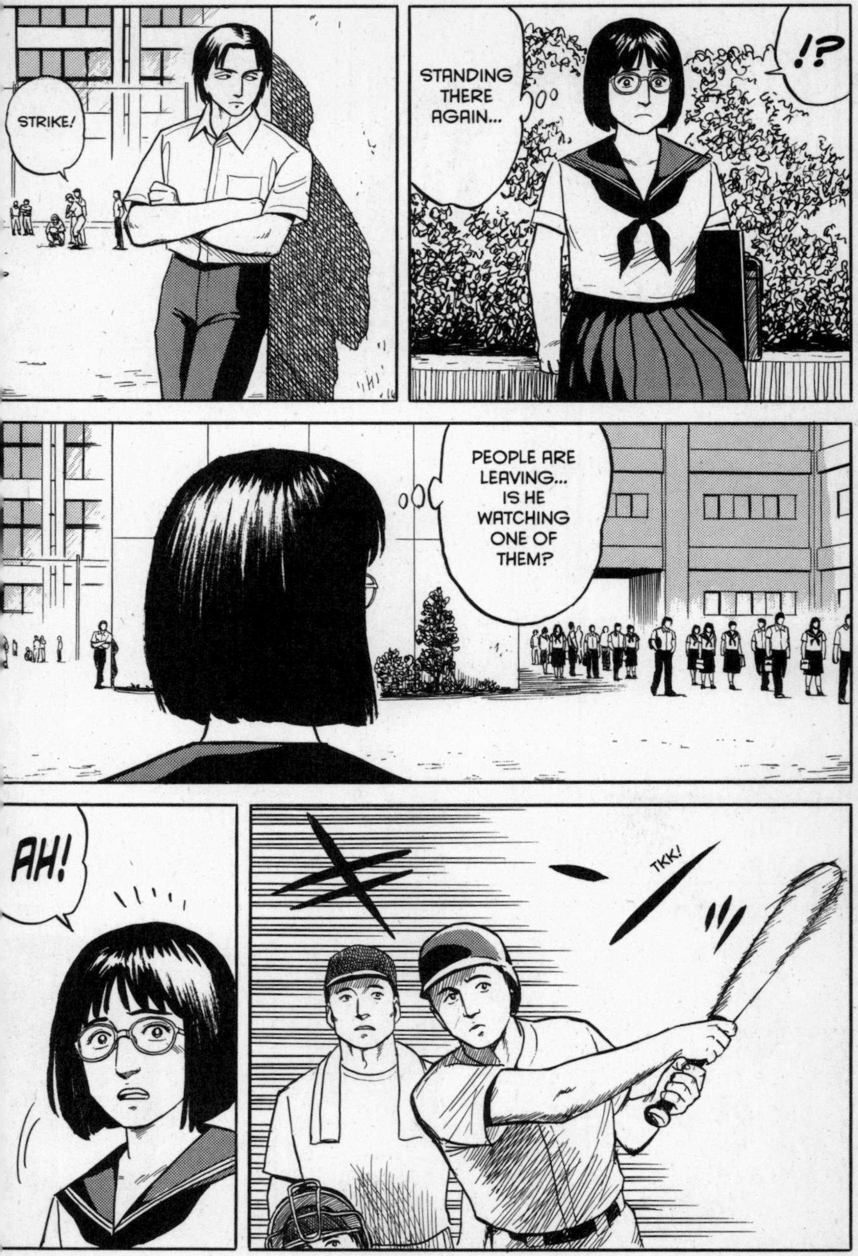
!?
STANDING THERE AGAIN...
STRIKE!
PEOPLE ARE LEAVING... IS HE WATCHING ONE OF THEM?
TKK!
AH!

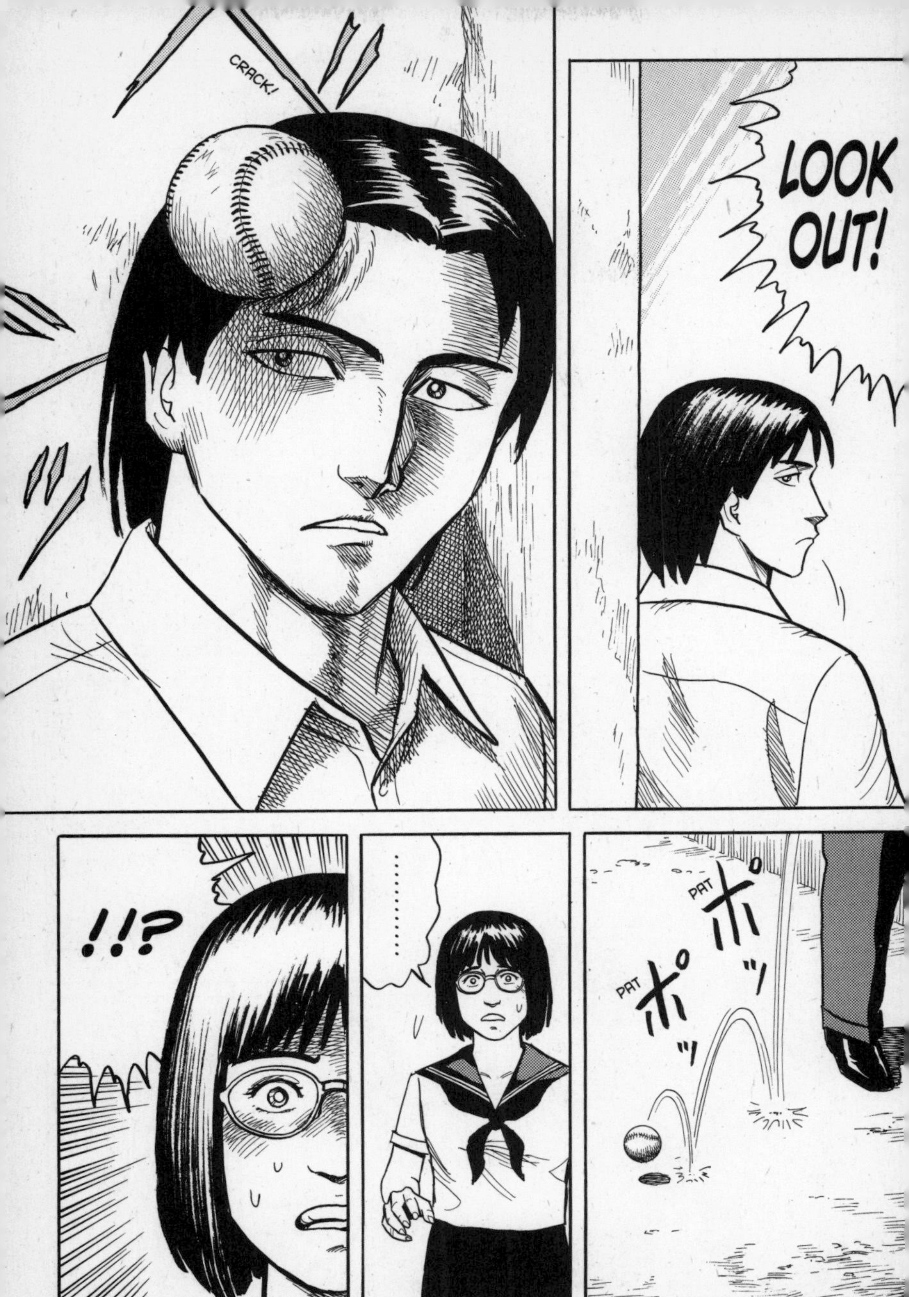
LOOK OUT!
CRACK!
PAT
ポッ
PAT
ポッ
......
!!?

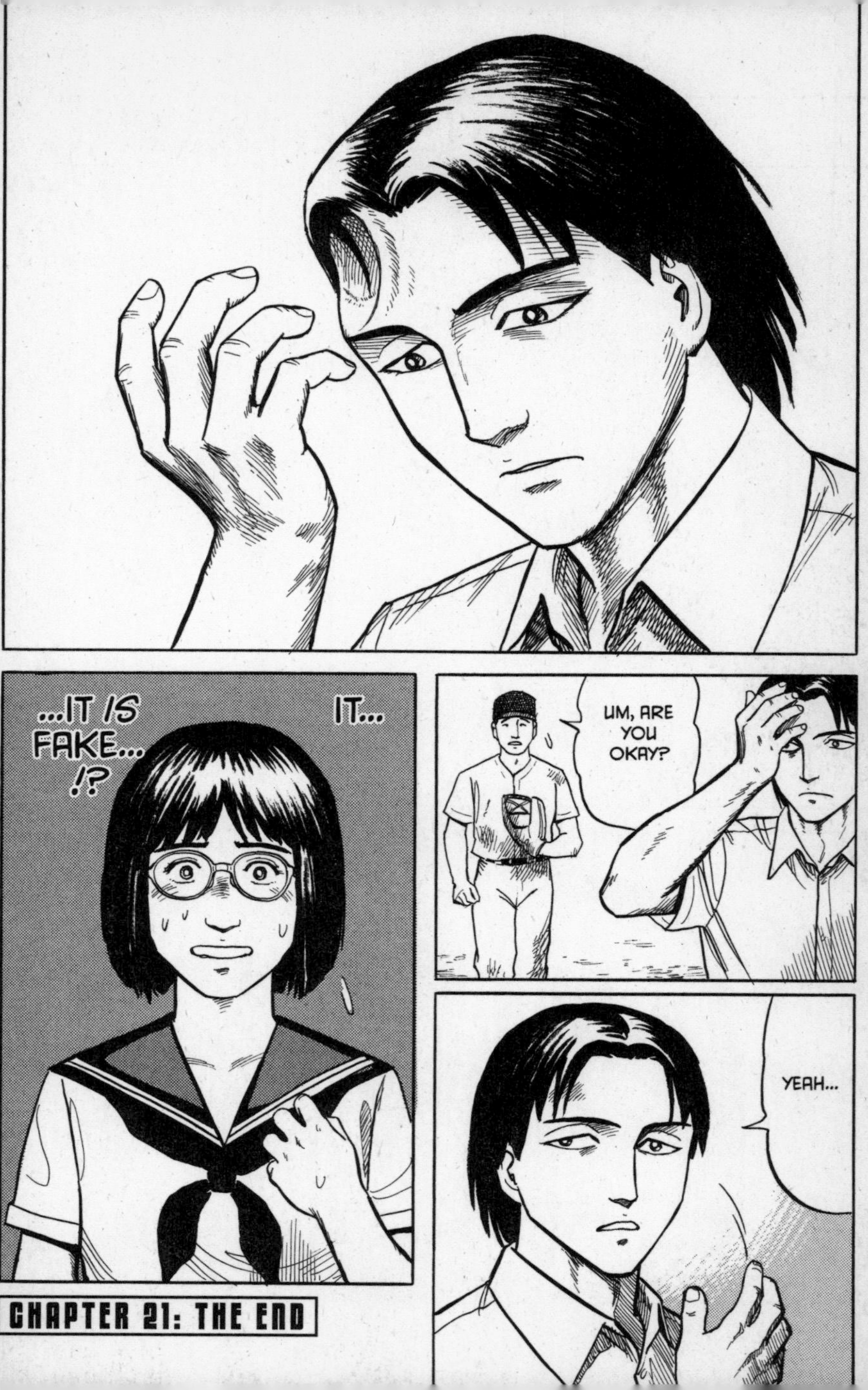
UM, ARE YOU OKAY?
YEAH...
IT...
...IT IS FAKE...!?

CHAPTER 21: THE END

CHAPTER 22: FISSURE

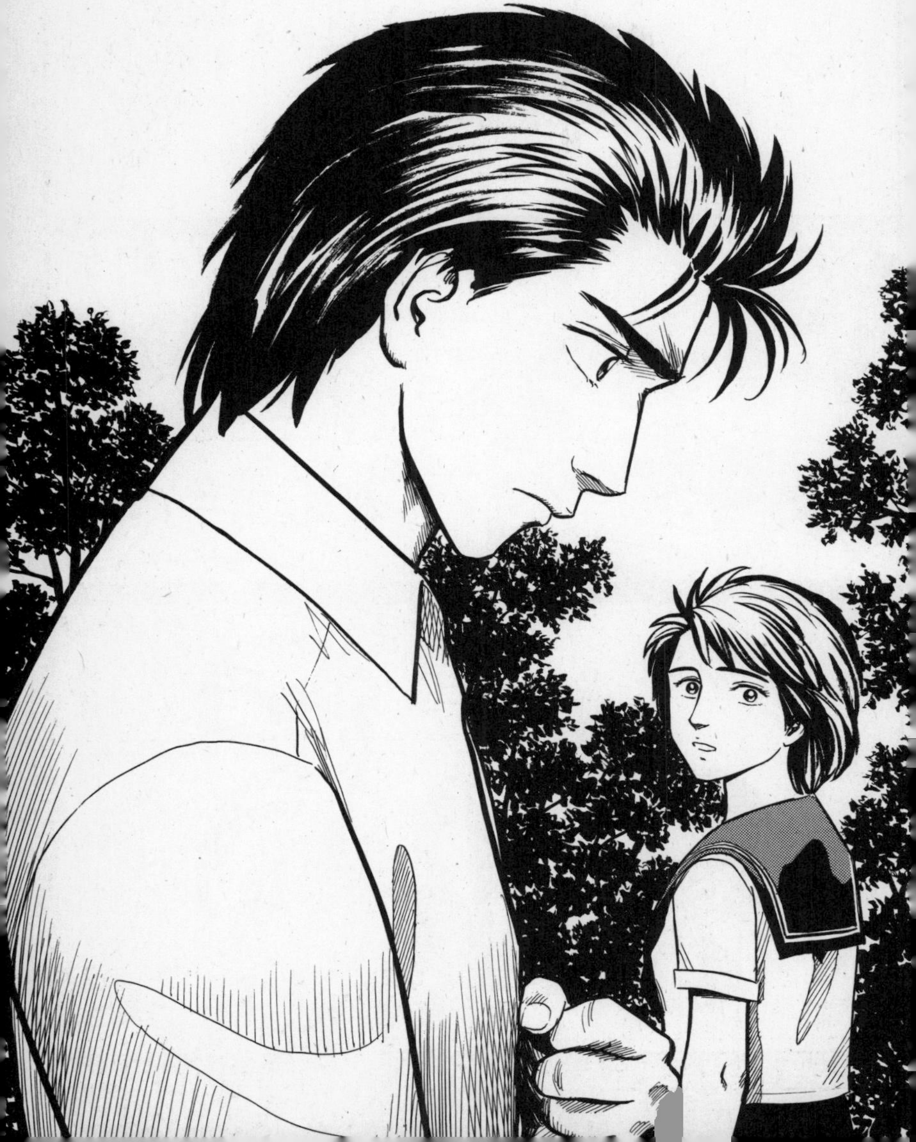

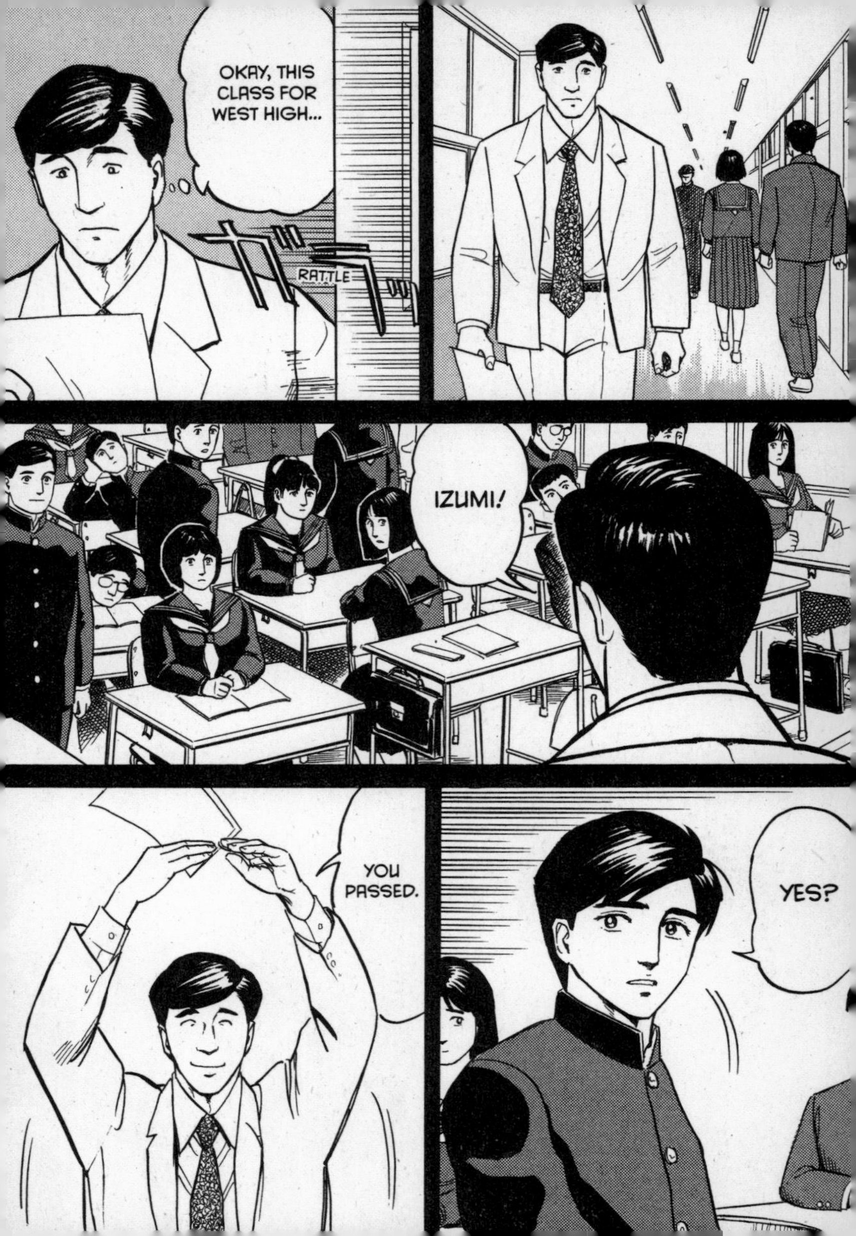
OKAY, THIS CLASS FOR WEST HIGH...
RATTLE
IZUMI!
YES?
YOU PASSED.

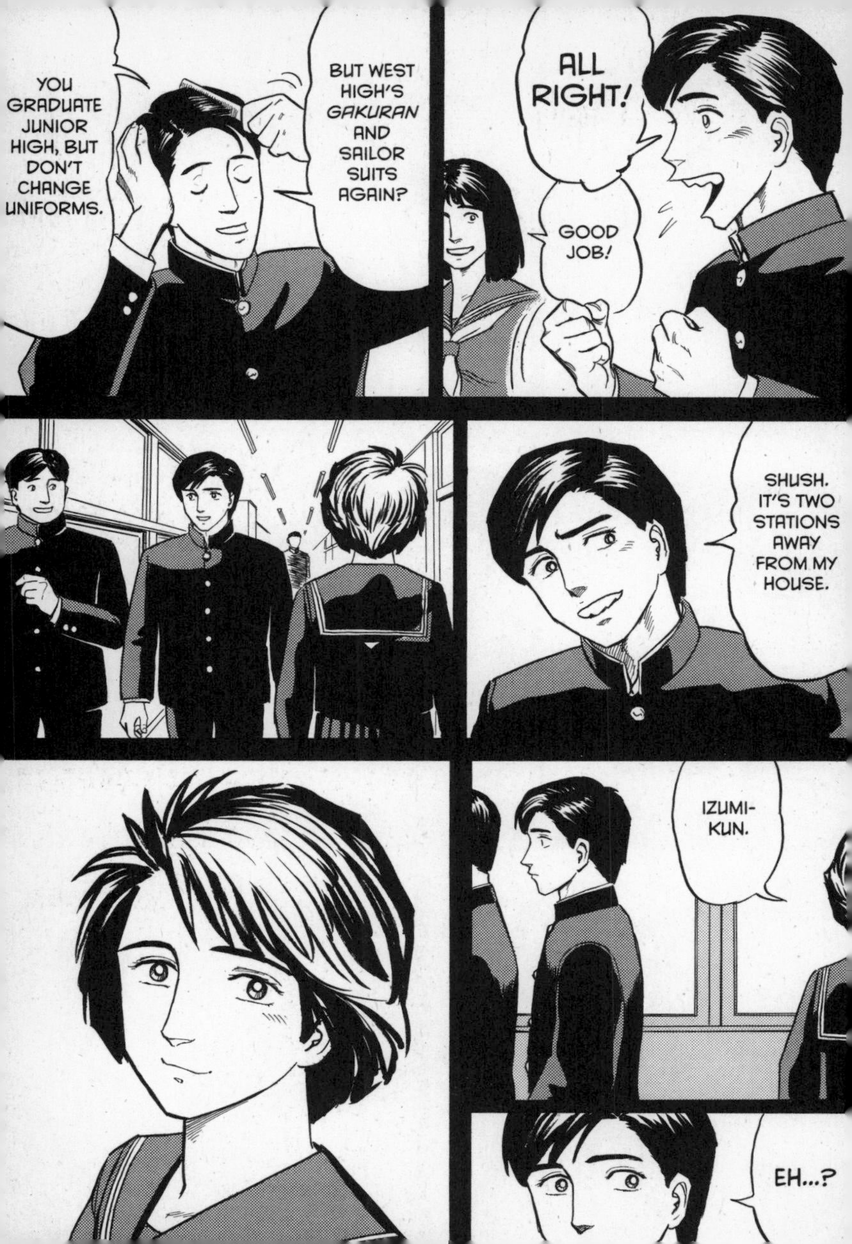
ALL RIGHT!
GOOD JOB!
BUT WEST HIGH'S *GAKURAN* AND SAILOR SUITS AGAIN?
YOU GRADUATE JUNIOR HIGH, BUT DON'T CHANGE UNIFORMS.
SHUSH. IT'S TWO STATIONS AWAY FROM MY HOUSE.
IZUMI-KUN.
EH...?

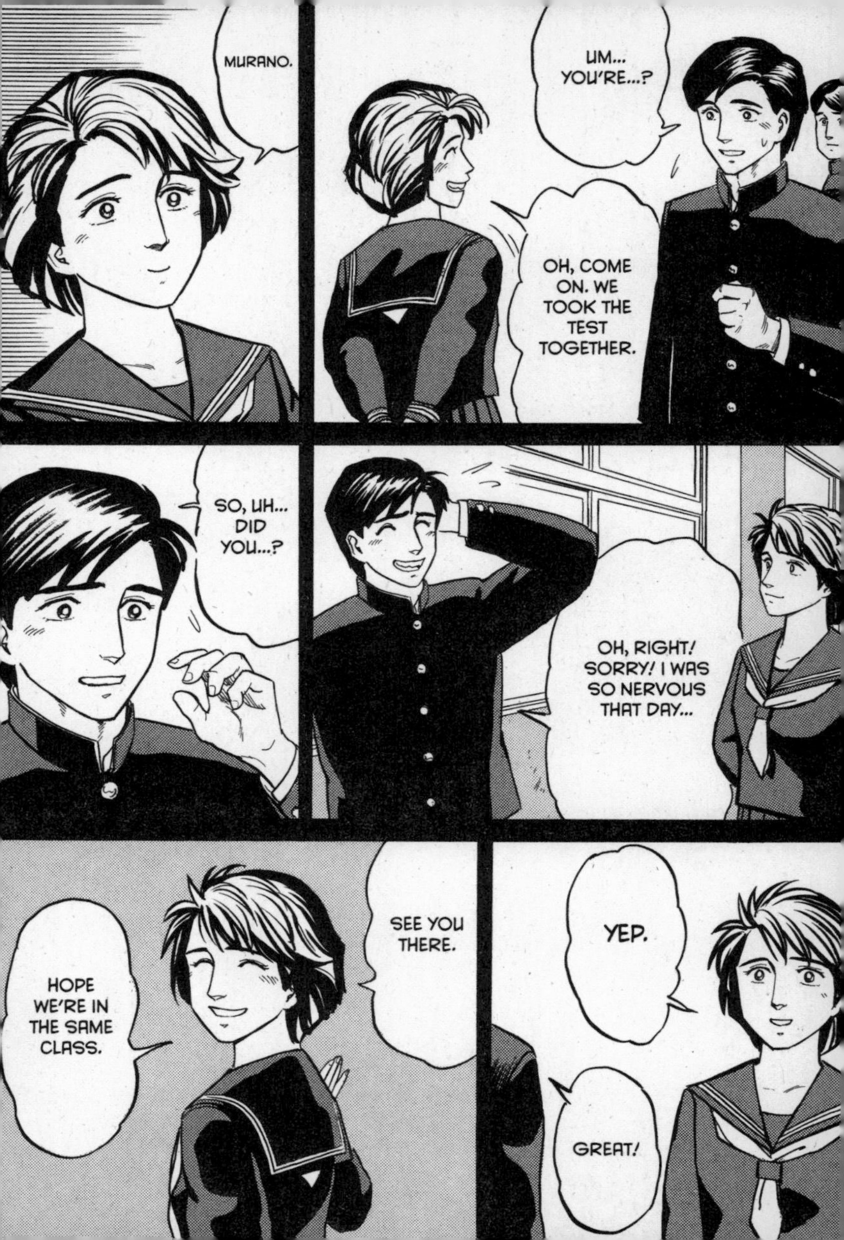
UM... YOU'RE...?
OH, COME ON. WE TOOK THE TEST TOGETHER.
MURANO.
OH, RIGHT! SORRY! I WAS SO NERVOUS THAT DAY...
SO, UH... DID YOU...?
YEP.
GREAT!
SEE YOU THERE.
HOPE WE'RE IN THE SAME CLASS.

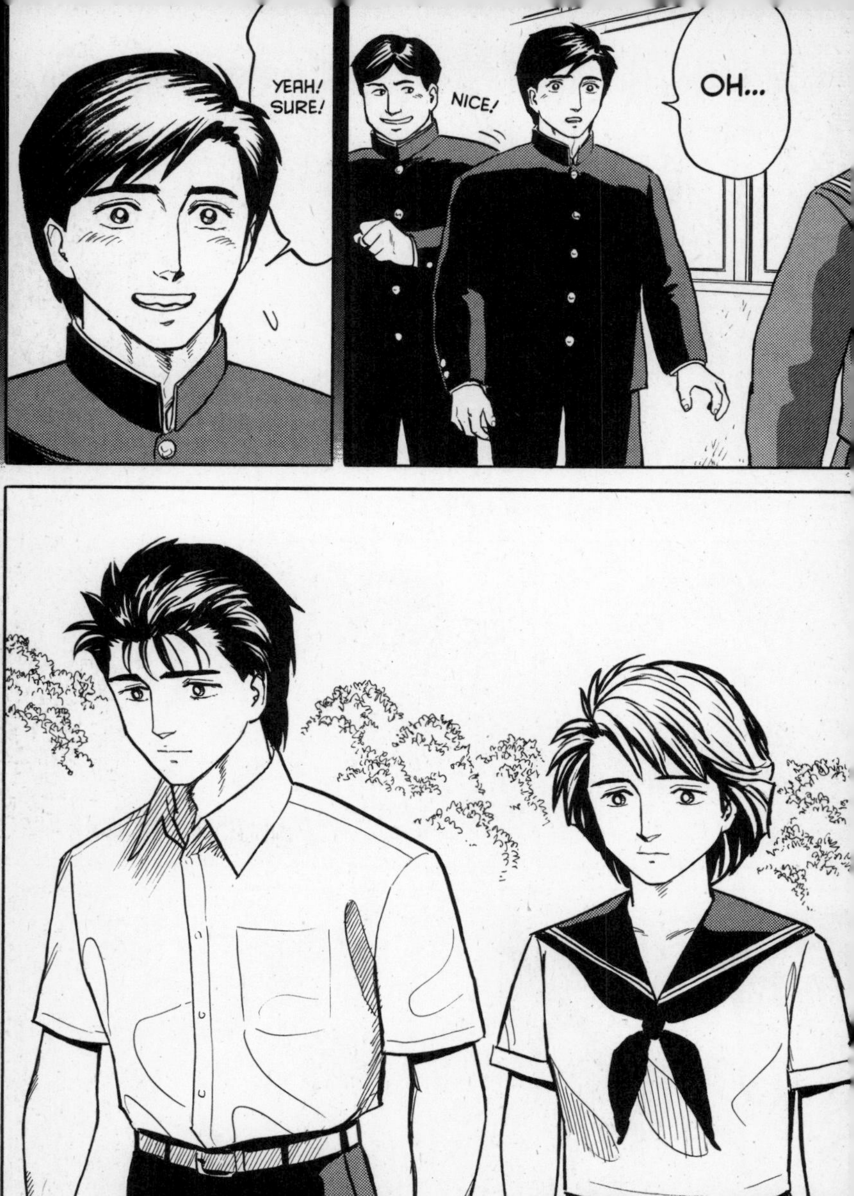
OH...
NICE!
YEAH! SURE!

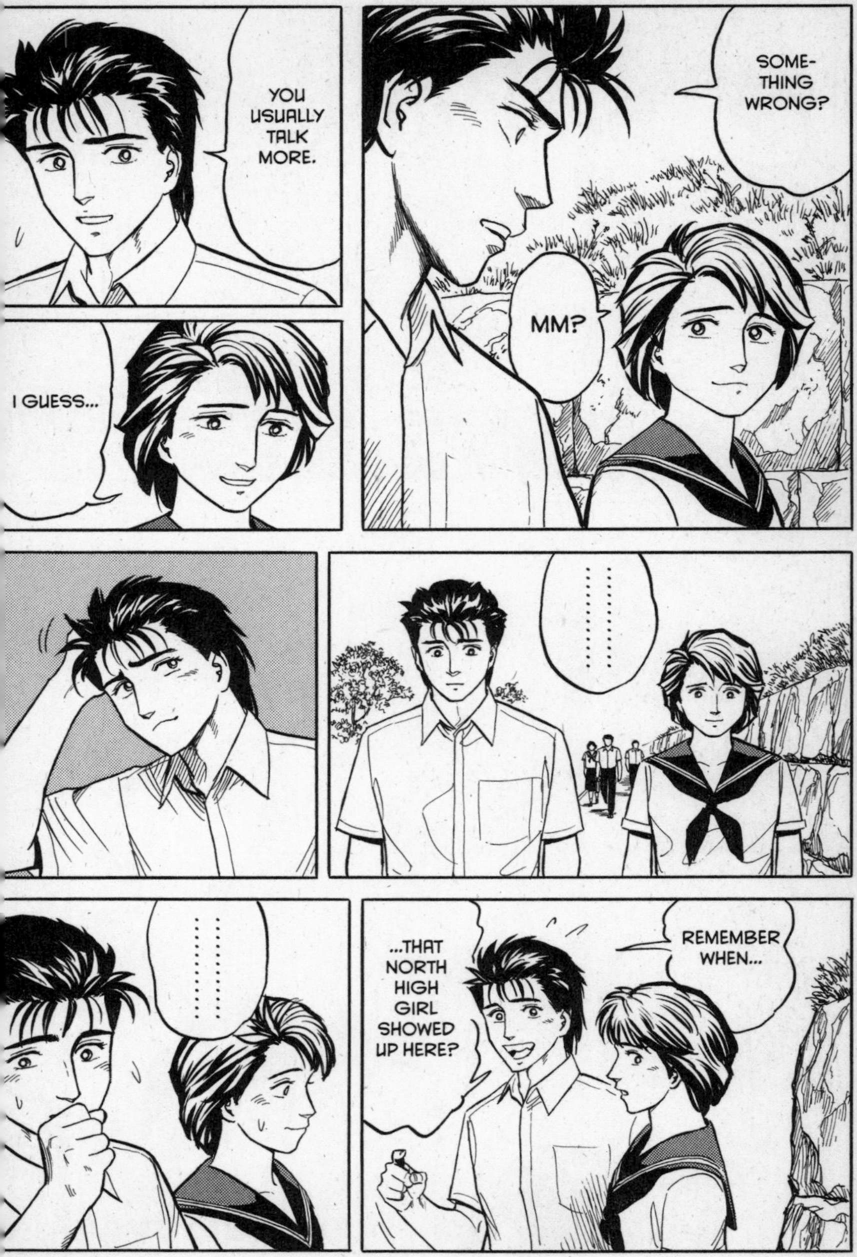
SOME-THING WRONG?
MM?
YOU USUALLY TALK MORE.
I GUESS...
......
REMEMBER WHEN...
...THAT NORTH HIGH GIRL SHOWED UP HERE?
......

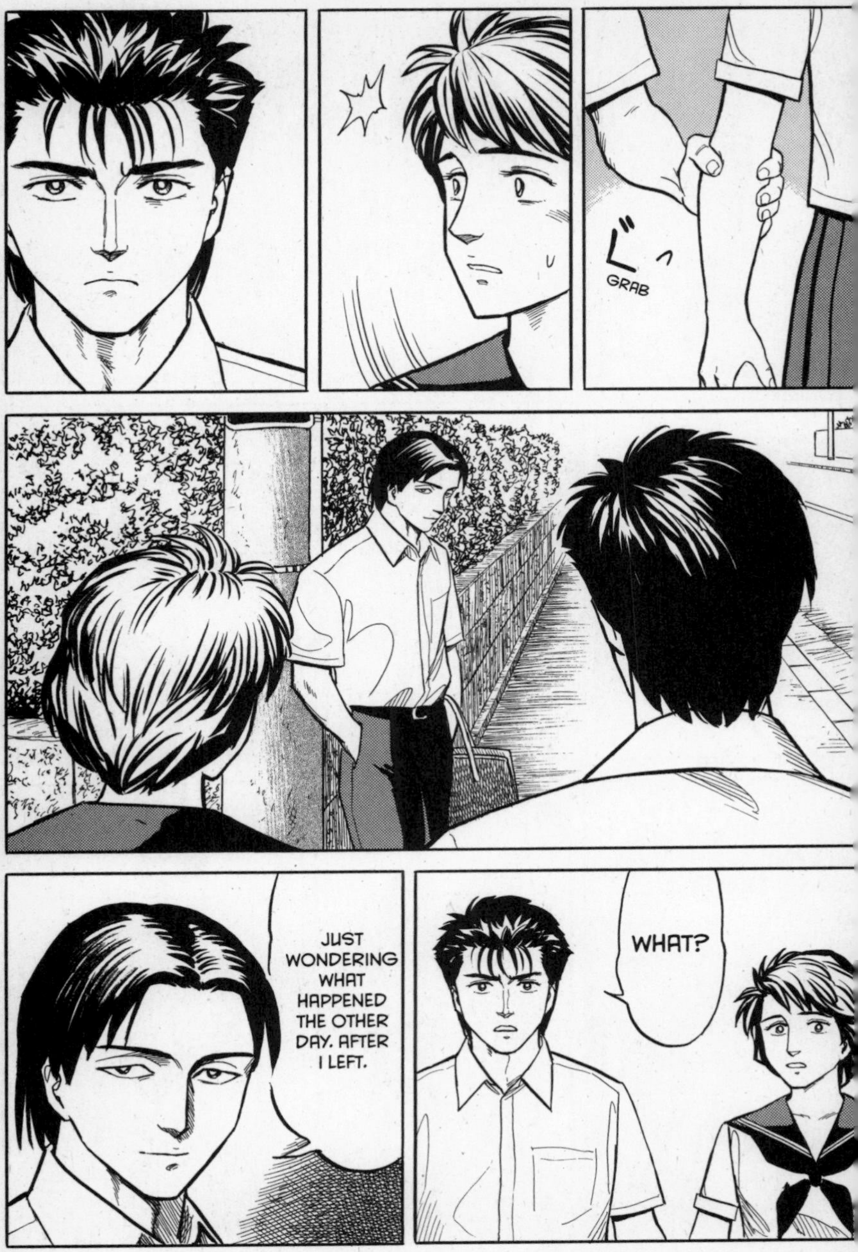
GRAB
WHAT?
JUST WONDERING WHAT HAPPENED THE OTHER DAY. AFTER I LEFT.

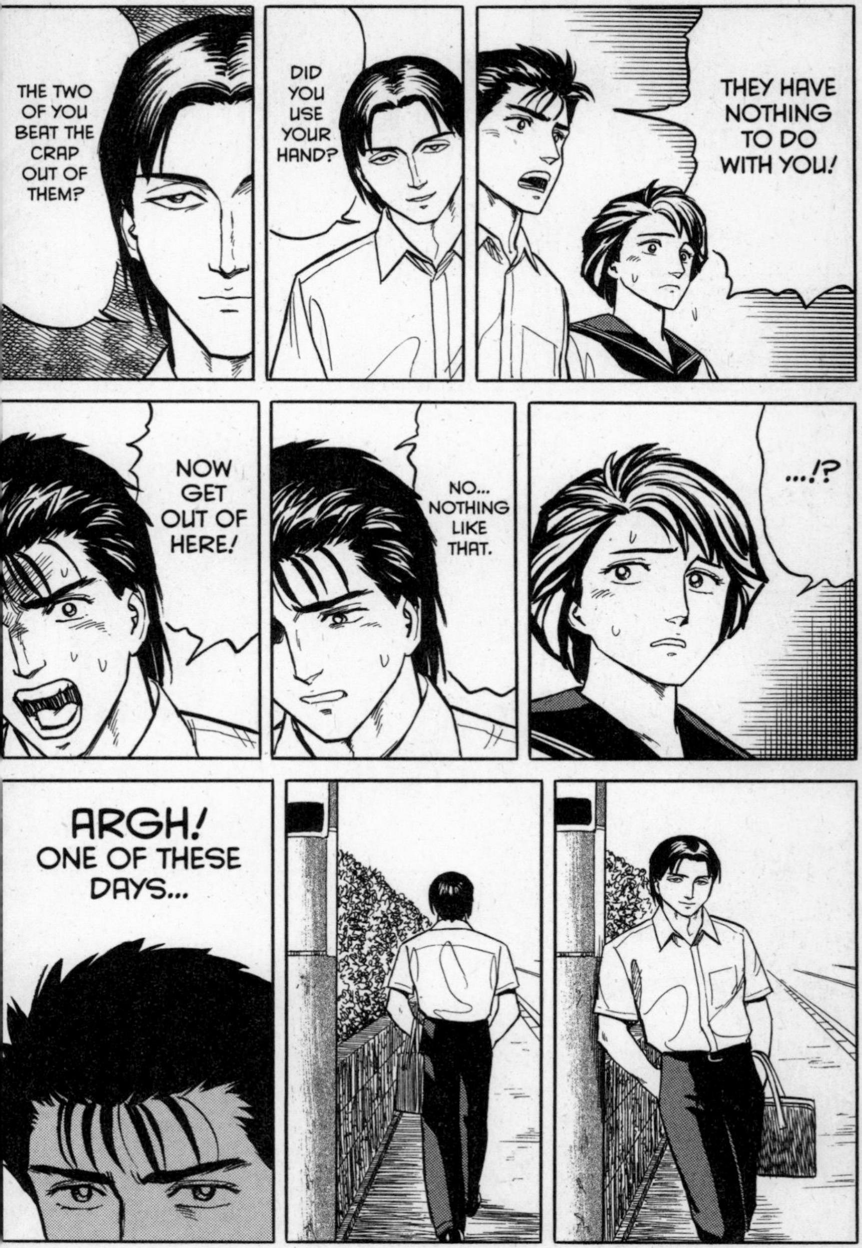
THEY HAVE NOTHING TO DO WITH YOU!
DID YOU USE YOUR HAND?
THE TWO OF YOU BEAT THE CRAP OUT OF THEM?
...!?
NO... NOTHING LIKE THAT.
NOW GET OUT OF HERE!
ARGH! ONE OF THESE DAYS...

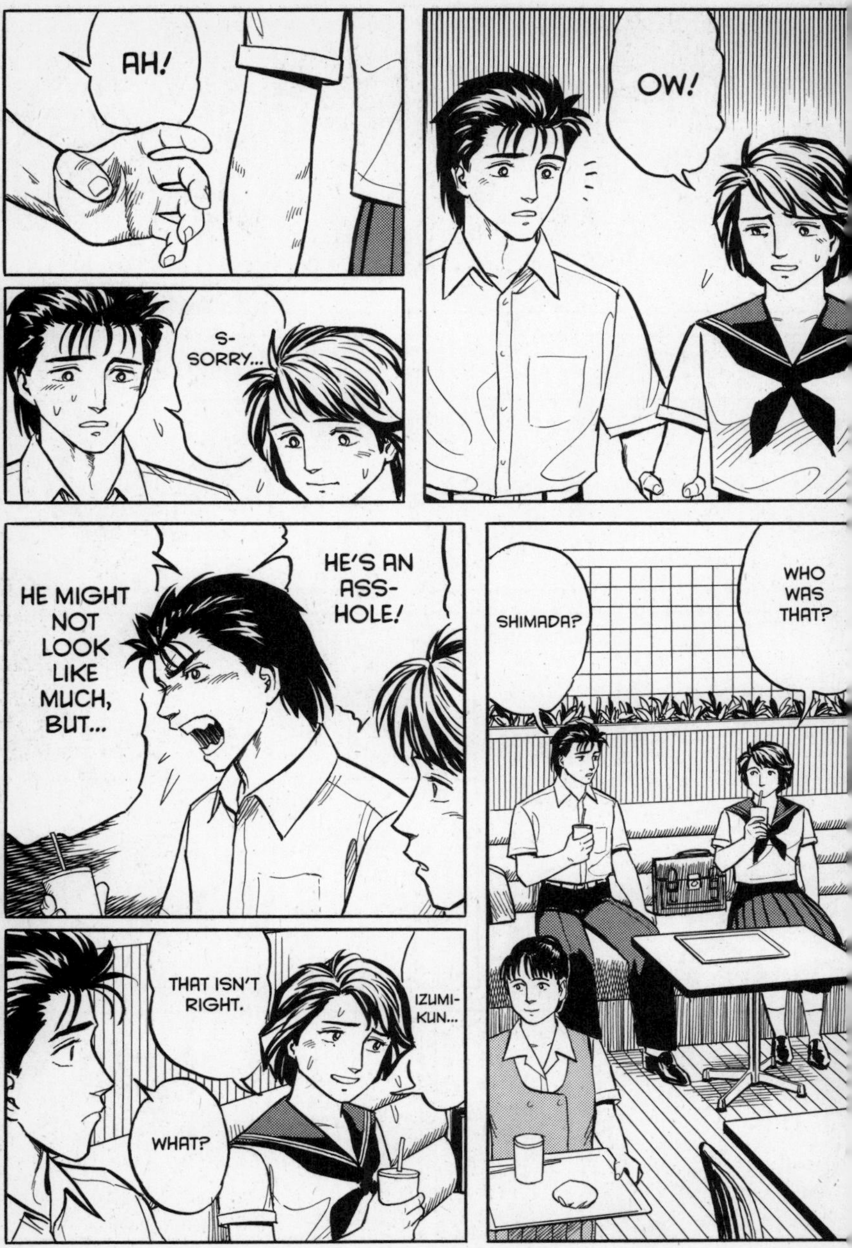
OW!
AH!
S-SORRY...
WHO WAS THAT?
SHIMADA?
HE'S AN ASS-HOLE!
HE MIGHT NOT LOOK LIKE MUCH, BUT...
IZUMI-KUN...
THAT ISN'T RIGHT.
WHAT?

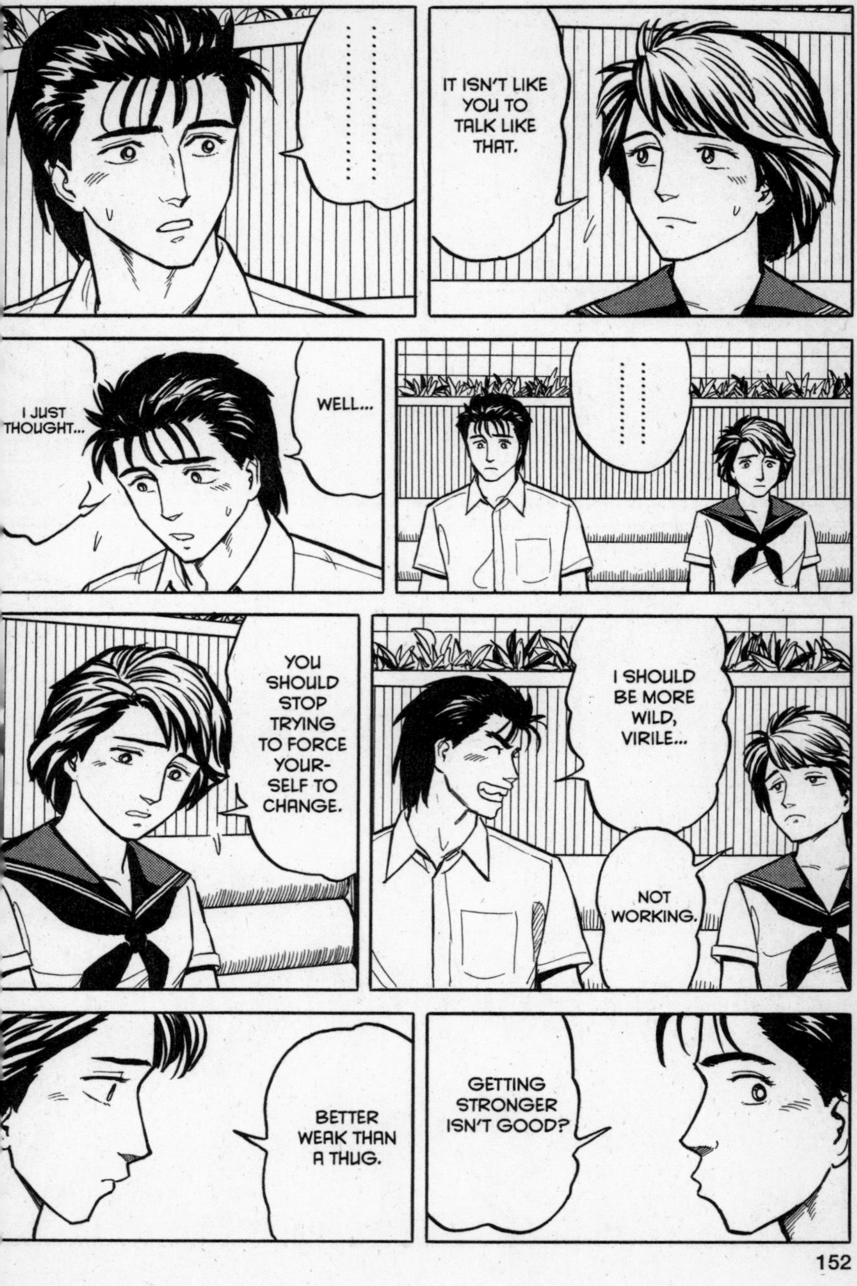
IT ISN'T LIKE YOU TO TALK LIKE THAT.
......
......
WELL...
I JUST THOUGHT...
I SHOULD BE MORE WILD, VIRILE...
NOT WORKING.
YOU SHOULD STOP TRYING TO FORCE YOUR-SELF TO CHANGE.
GETTING STRONGER ISN'T GOOD?
BETTER WEAK THAN A THUG.

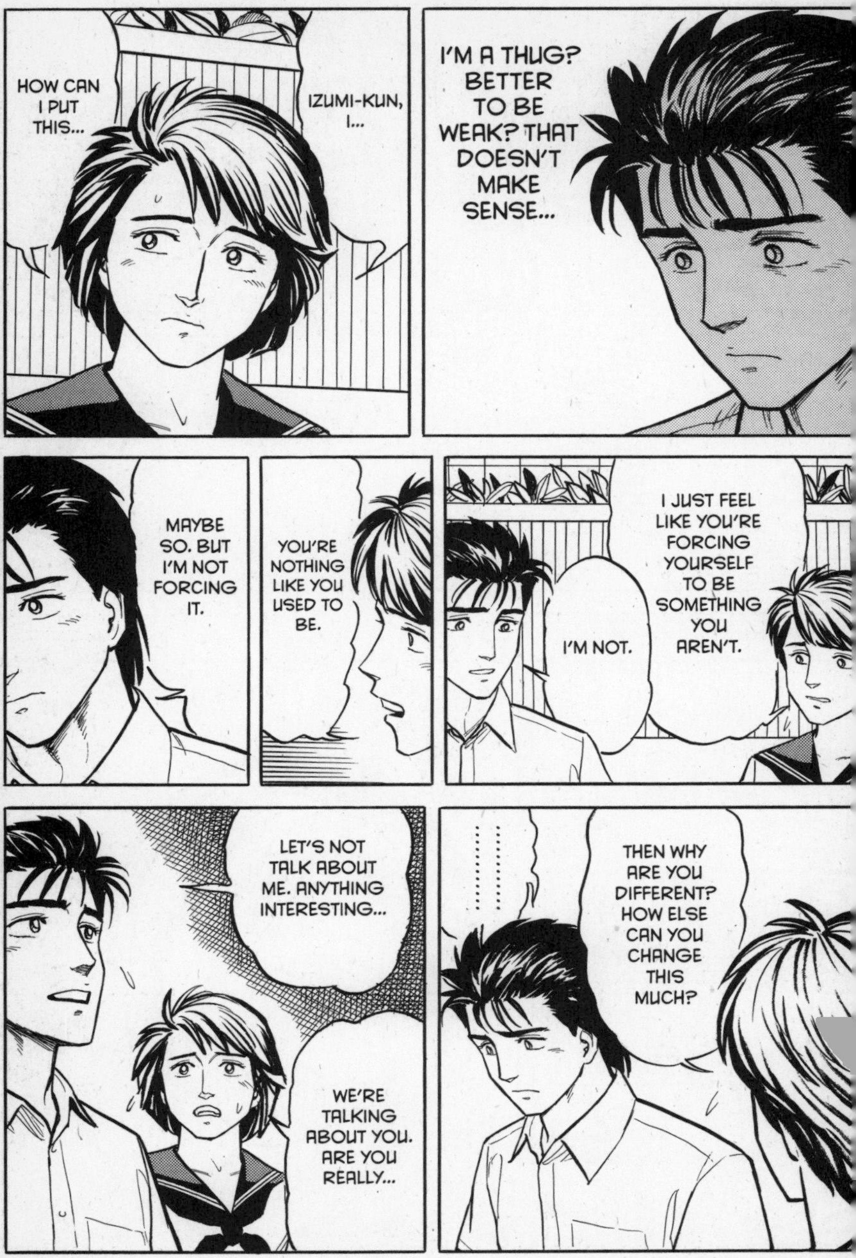
I'M A THUG? BETTER TO BE WEAK? THAT DOESN'T MAKE SENSE...
IZUMI-KUN, I...
HOW CAN I PUT THIS...
I JUST FEEL LIKE YOU'RE FORCING YOURSELF TO BE SOMETHING YOU AREN'T.
I'M NOT.
YOU'RE NOTHING LIKE YOU USED TO BE.
MAYBE SO. BUT I'M NOT FORCING IT.
THEN WHY ARE YOU DIFFERENT? HOW ELSE CAN YOU CHANGE THIS MUCH?
......
LET'S NOT TALK ABOUT ME. ANYTHING INTERESTING...
WE'RE TALKING ABOUT YOU. ARE YOU REALLY...

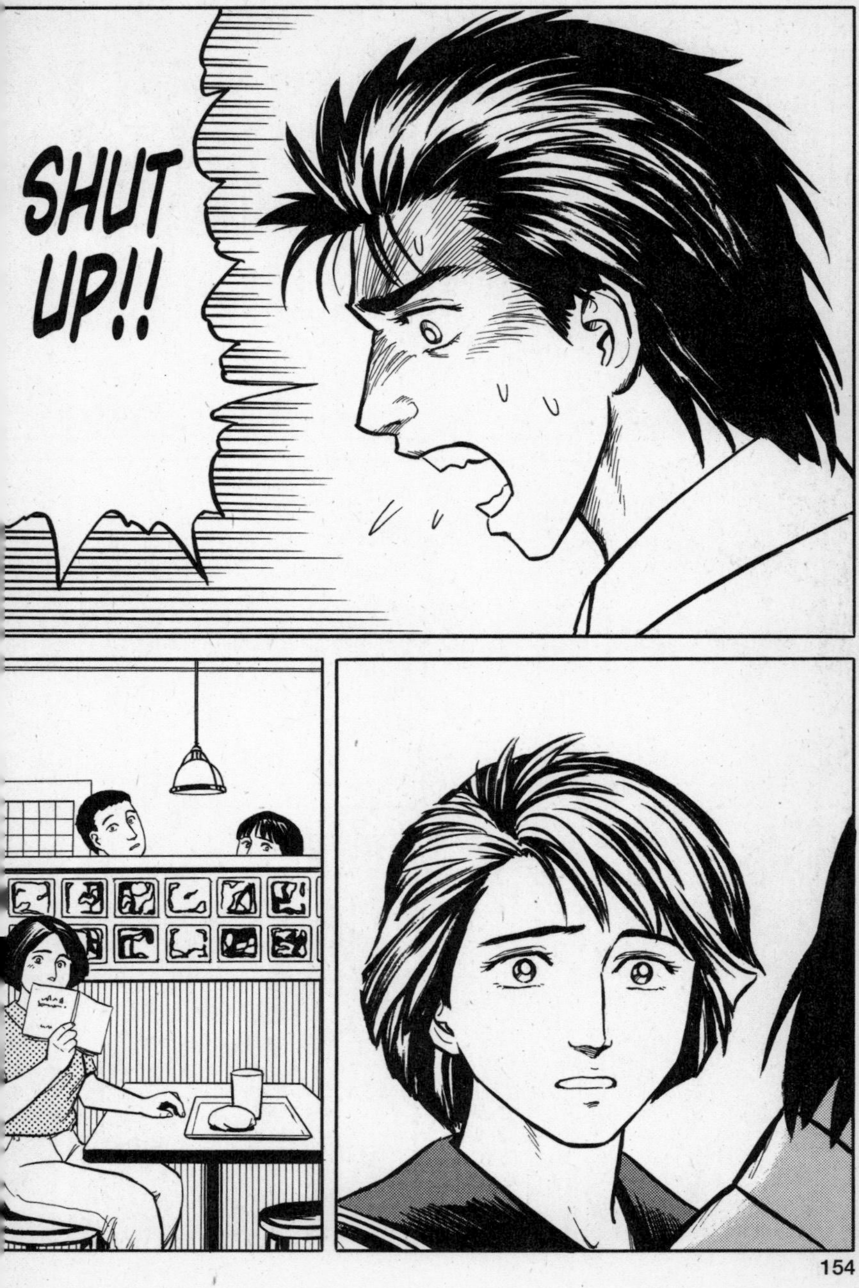
SHUT UP!!

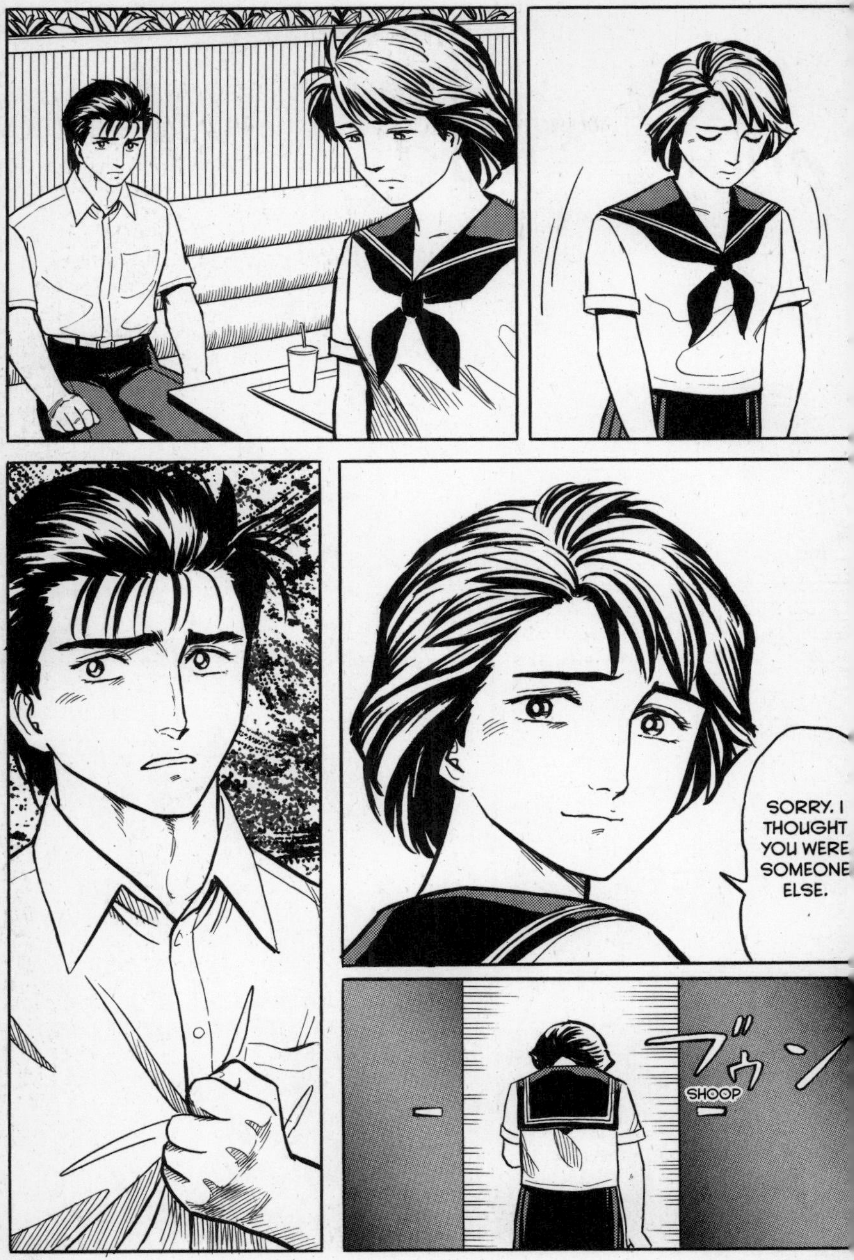
SORRY. I THOUGHT YOU WERE SOMEONE ELSE.
ヴゥン
SHOOP

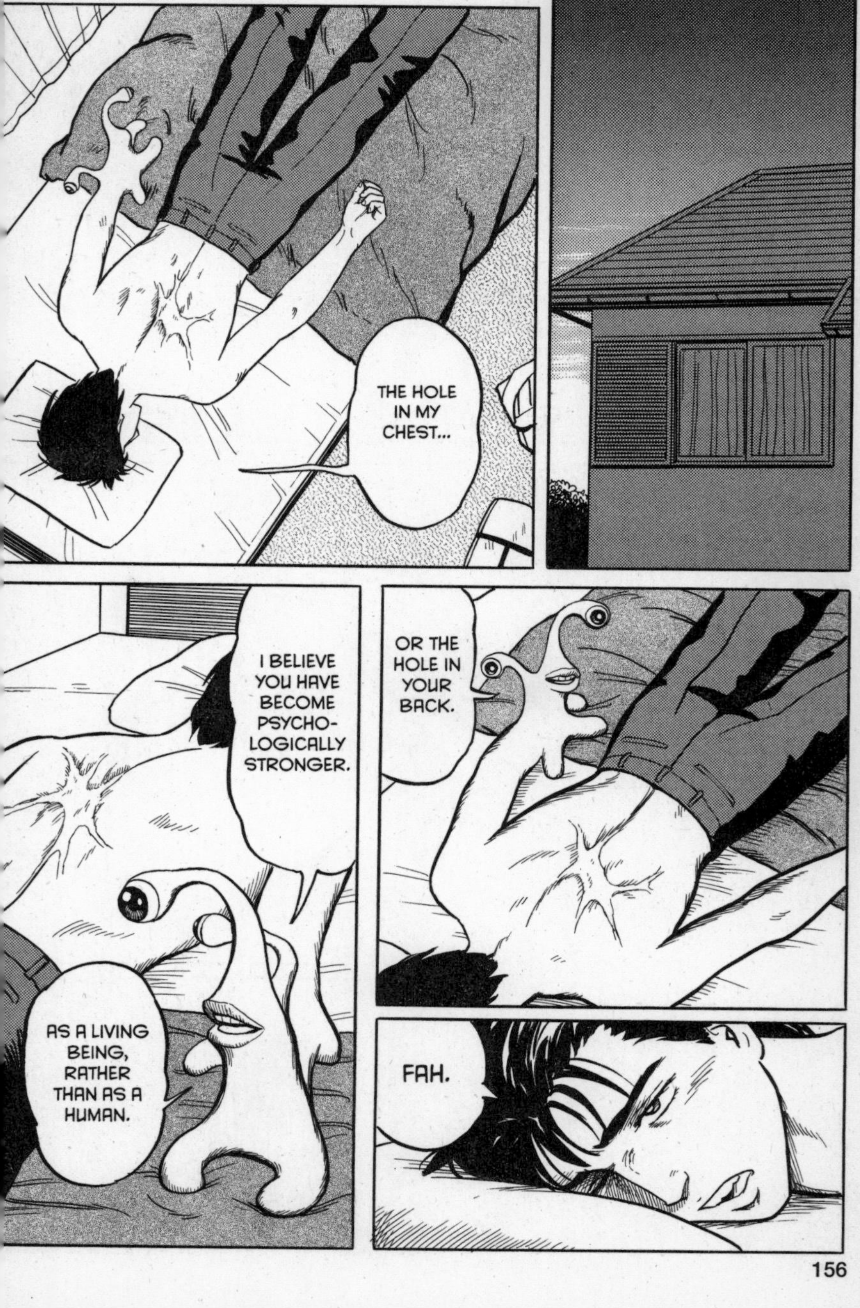

THE HOLE IN MY CHEST...
OR THE HOLE IN YOUR BACK.
FAH.
I BELIEVE YOU HAVE BECOME PSYCHO-LOGICALLY STRONGER.
AS A LIVING BEING, RATHER THAN AS A HUMAN.

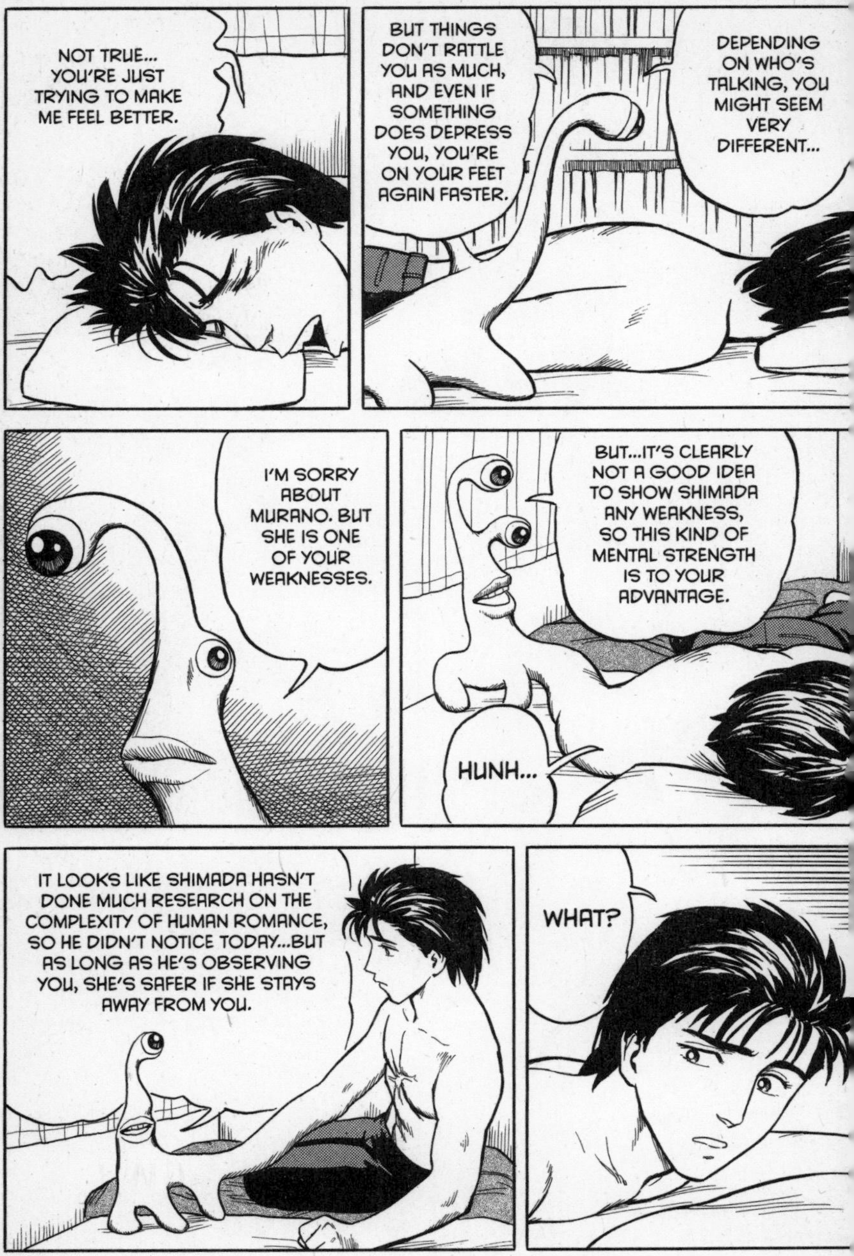
DEPENDING ON WHO'S TALKING, YOU MIGHT SEEM VERY DIFFERENT...
BUT THINGS DON'T RATTLE YOU AS MUCH, AND EVEN IF SOMETHING DOES DEPRESS YOU, YOU'RE ON YOUR FEET AGAIN FASTER.
NOT TRUE... YOU'RE JUST TRYING TO MAKE ME FEEL BETTER.
BUT...IT'S CLEARLY NOT A GOOD IDEA TO SHOW SHIMADA ANY WEAKNESS, SO THIS KIND OF MENTAL STRENGTH IS TO YOUR ADVANTAGE.
HUNH...
I'M SORRY ABOUT MURANO. BUT SHE IS ONE OF YOUR WEAKNESSES.
WHAT?
IT LOOKS LIKE SHIMADA HASN'T DONE MUCH RESEARCH ON THE COMPLEXITY OF HUMAN ROMANCE, SO HE DIDN'T NOTICE TODAY...BUT AS LONG AS HE'S OBSERVING YOU, SHE'S SAFER IF SHE STAYS AWAY FROM YOU.

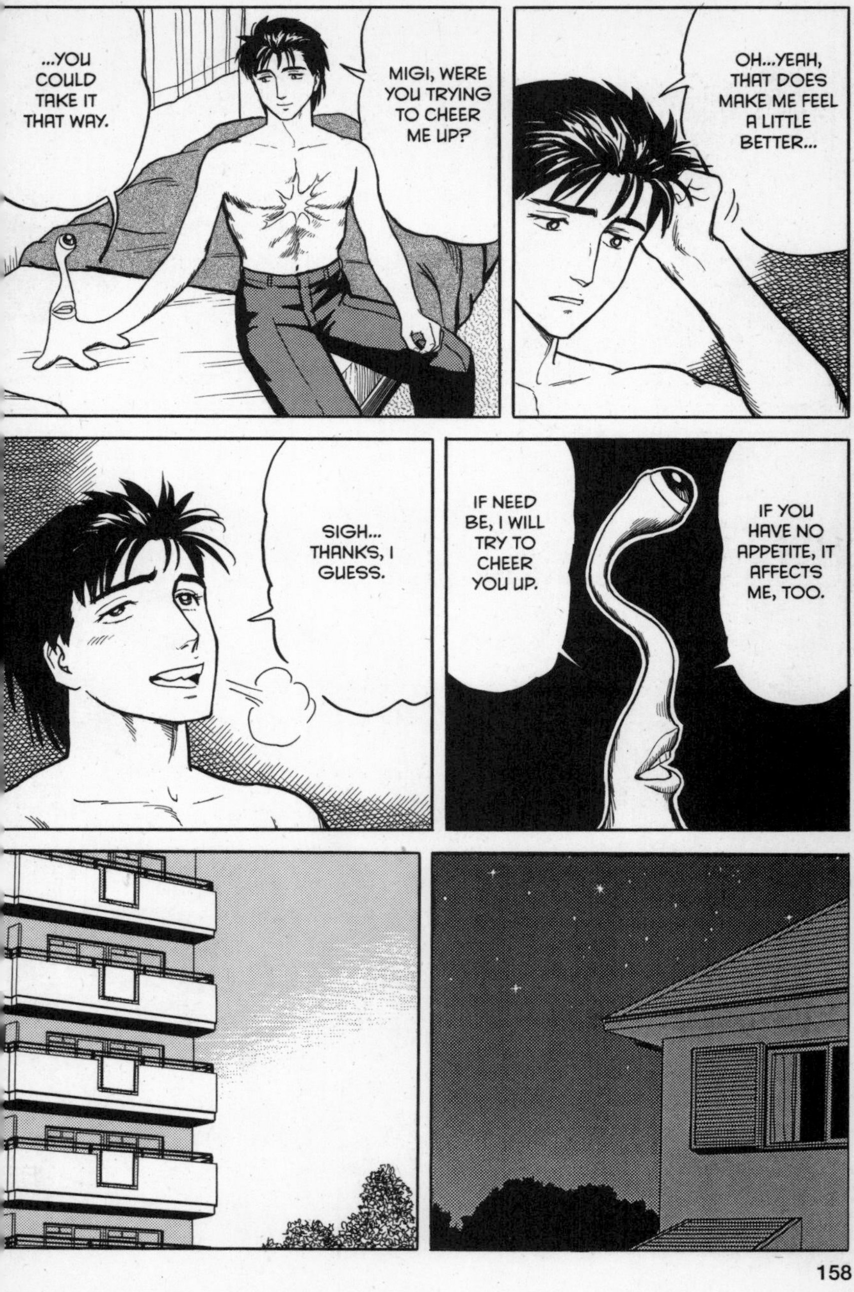
OH...YEAH, THAT DOES MAKE ME FEEL A LITTLE BETTER...
MIGI, WERE YOU TRYING TO CHEER ME UP?
...YOU COULD TAKE IT THAT WAY.
IF YOU HAVE NO APPETITE, IT AFFECTS ME, TOO.
IF NEED BE, I WILL TRY TO CHEER YOU UP.
SIGH... THANKS, I GUESS.

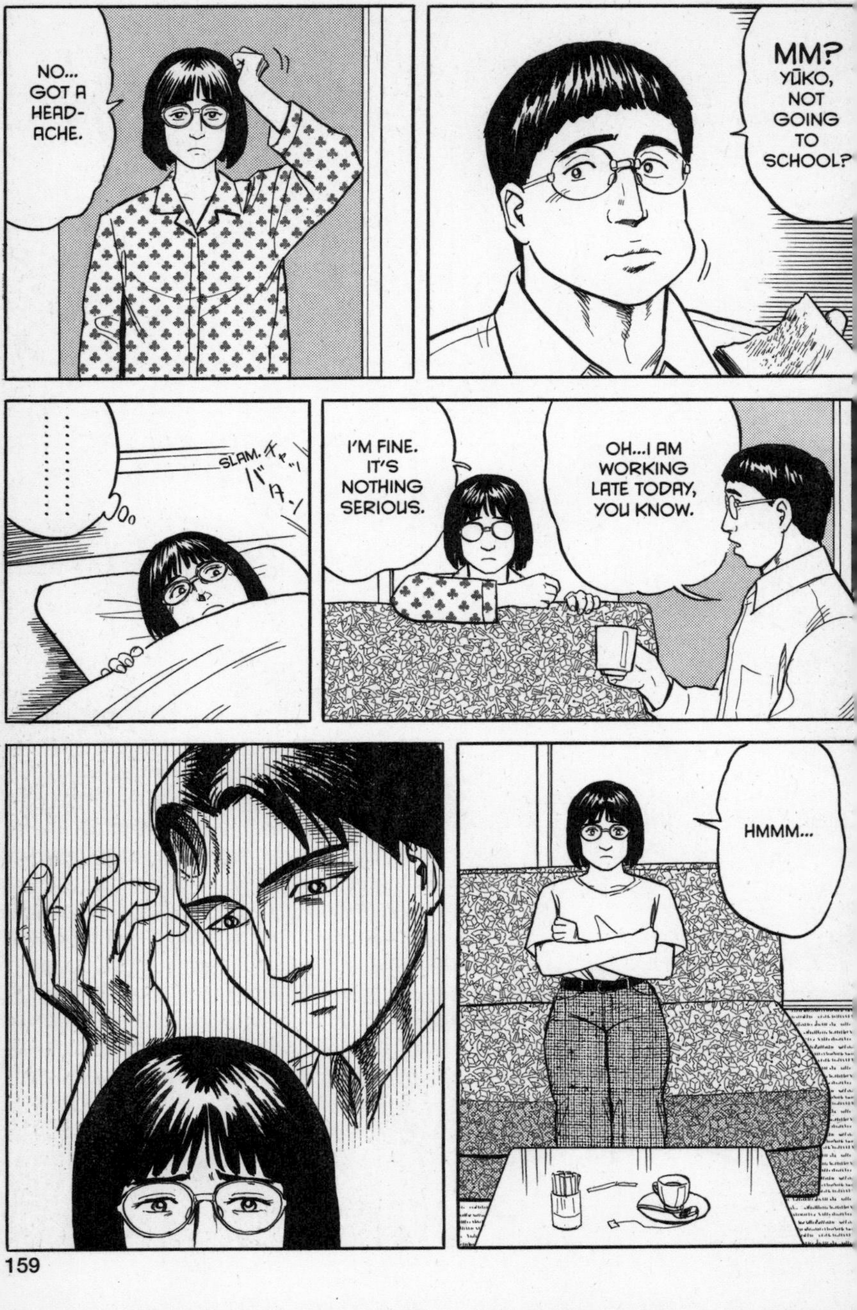

MM? YŪKO, NOT GOING TO SCHOOL?
NO... GOT A HEAD-ACHE.
OH...I AM WORKING LATE TODAY, YOU KNOW.
I'M FINE. IT'S NOTHING SERIOUS.
......
SLAM.
HMMM...

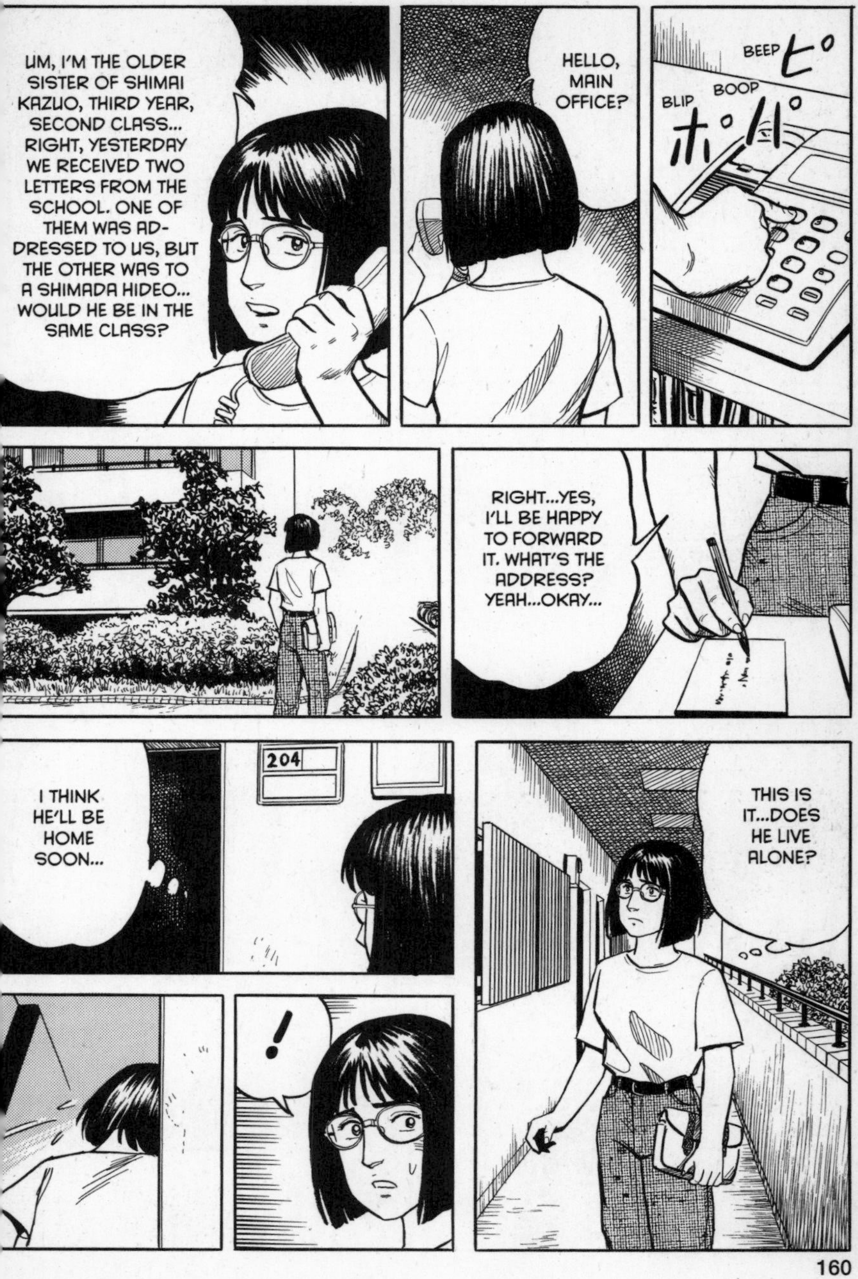
BEEP
ピ
BOOP
BLIP
ポパ
HELLO, MAIN OFFICE?
UM, I'M THE OLDER SISTER OF SHIMAI KAZUO, THIRD YEAR, SECOND CLASS... RIGHT, YESTERDAY WE RECEIVED TWO LETTERS FROM THE SCHOOL. ONE OF THEM WAS AD-DRESSED TO US, BUT THE OTHER WAS TO A SHIMADA HIDEO... WOULD HE BE IN THE SAME CLASS?
RIGHT...YES, I'LL BE HAPPY TO FORWARD IT. WHAT'S THE ADDRESS? YEAH...OKAY...
THIS IS IT...DOES HE LIVE ALONE?
204
I THINK HE'LL BE HOME SOON...
!

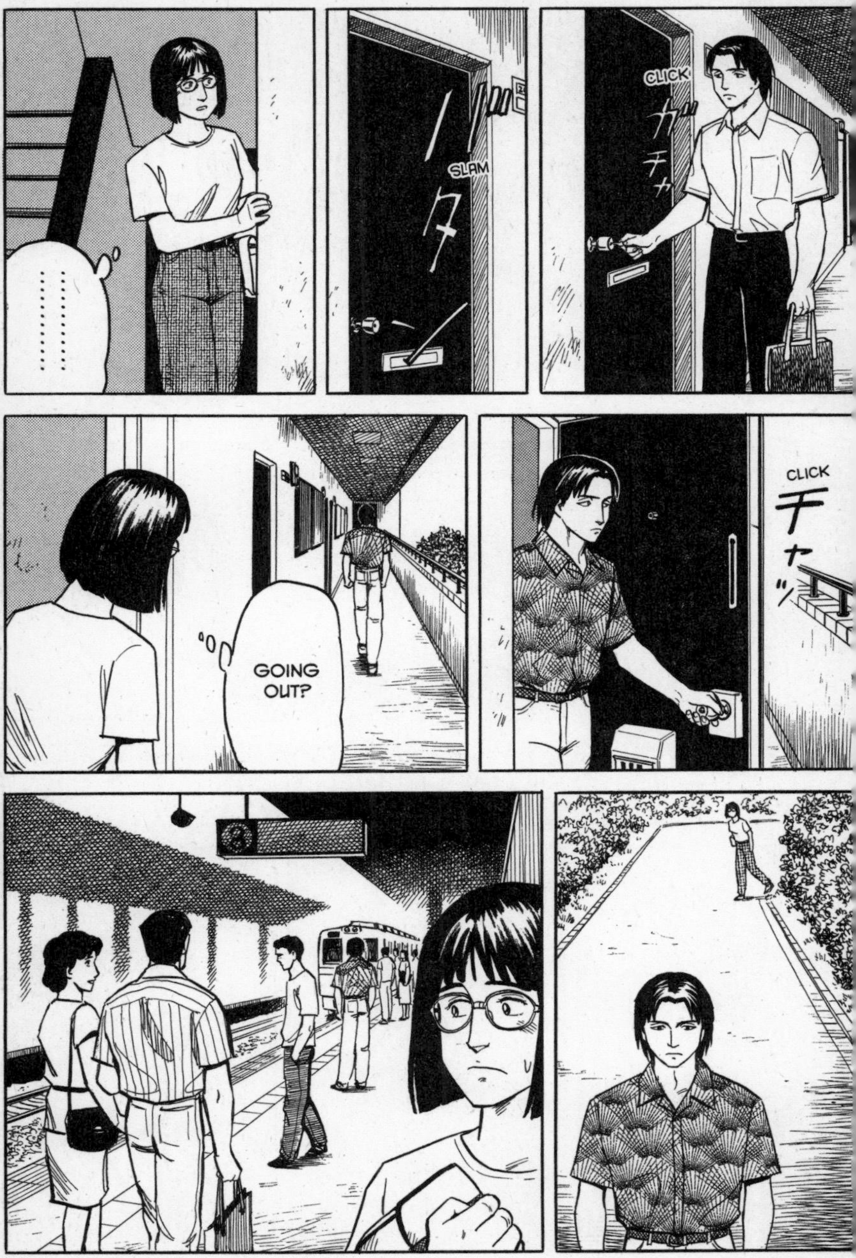
CLICK
ガチャ
SLAM
バタン
CLICK
チャッ
GOING OUT?

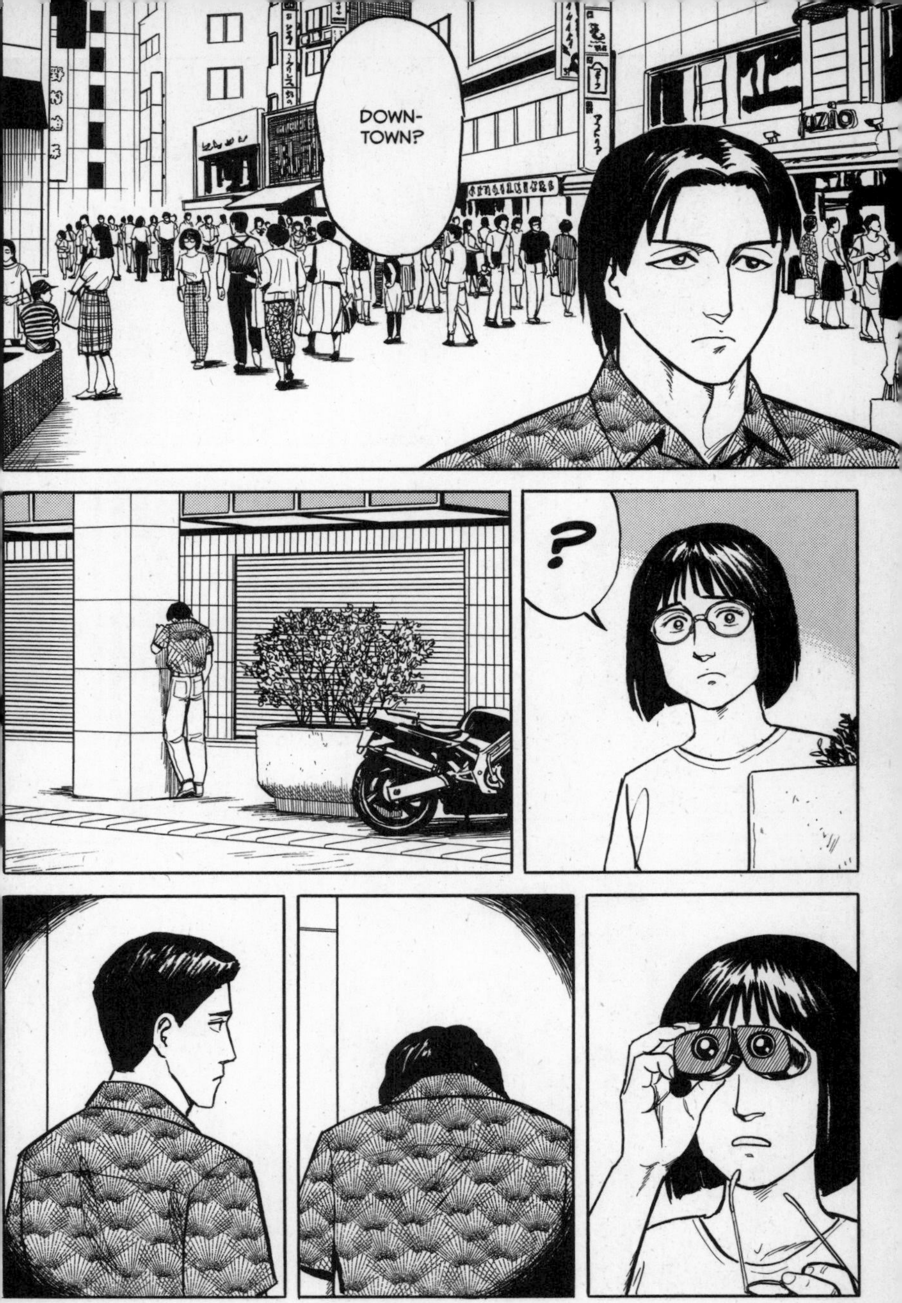
DOWN-
TOWN?
?

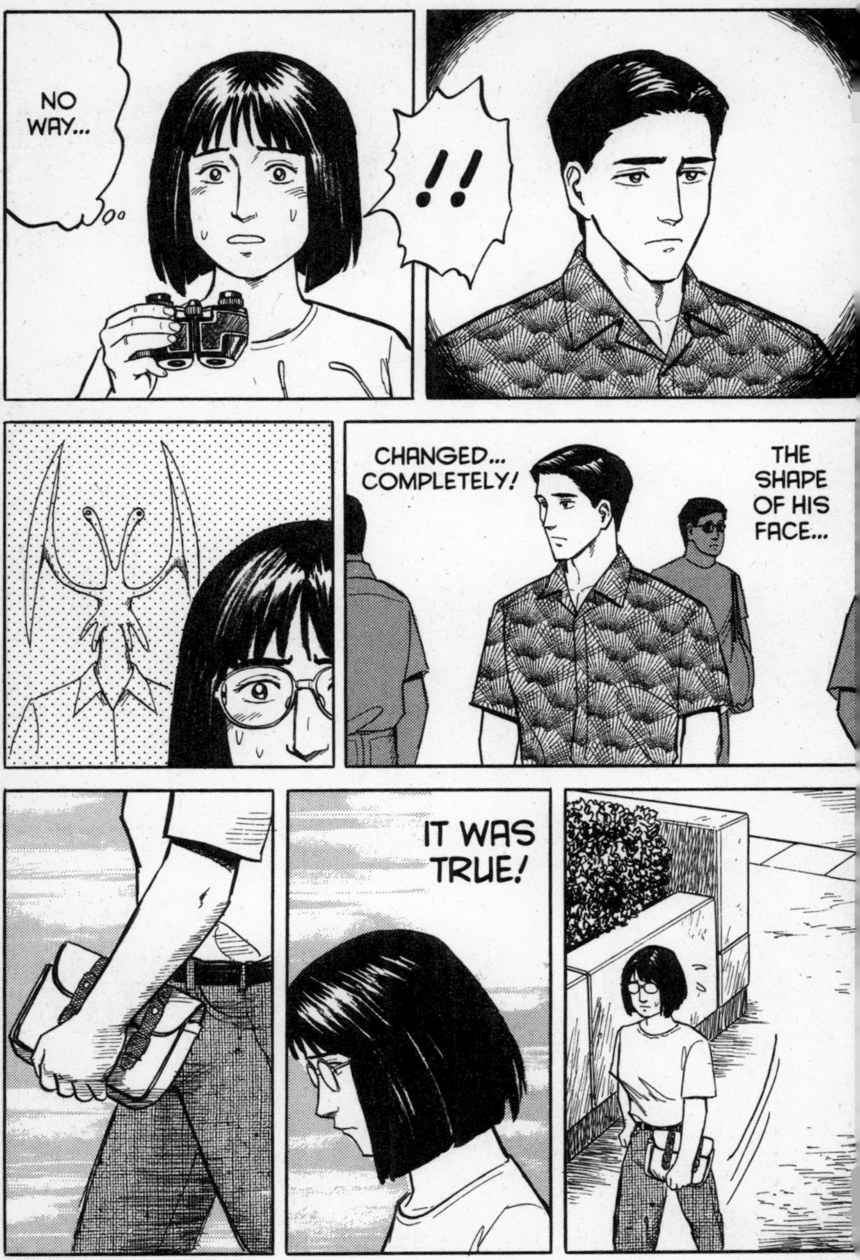
!!
NO WAY...
THE SHAPE OF HIS FACE...
CHANGED... COMPLETELY!
IT WAS TRUE!

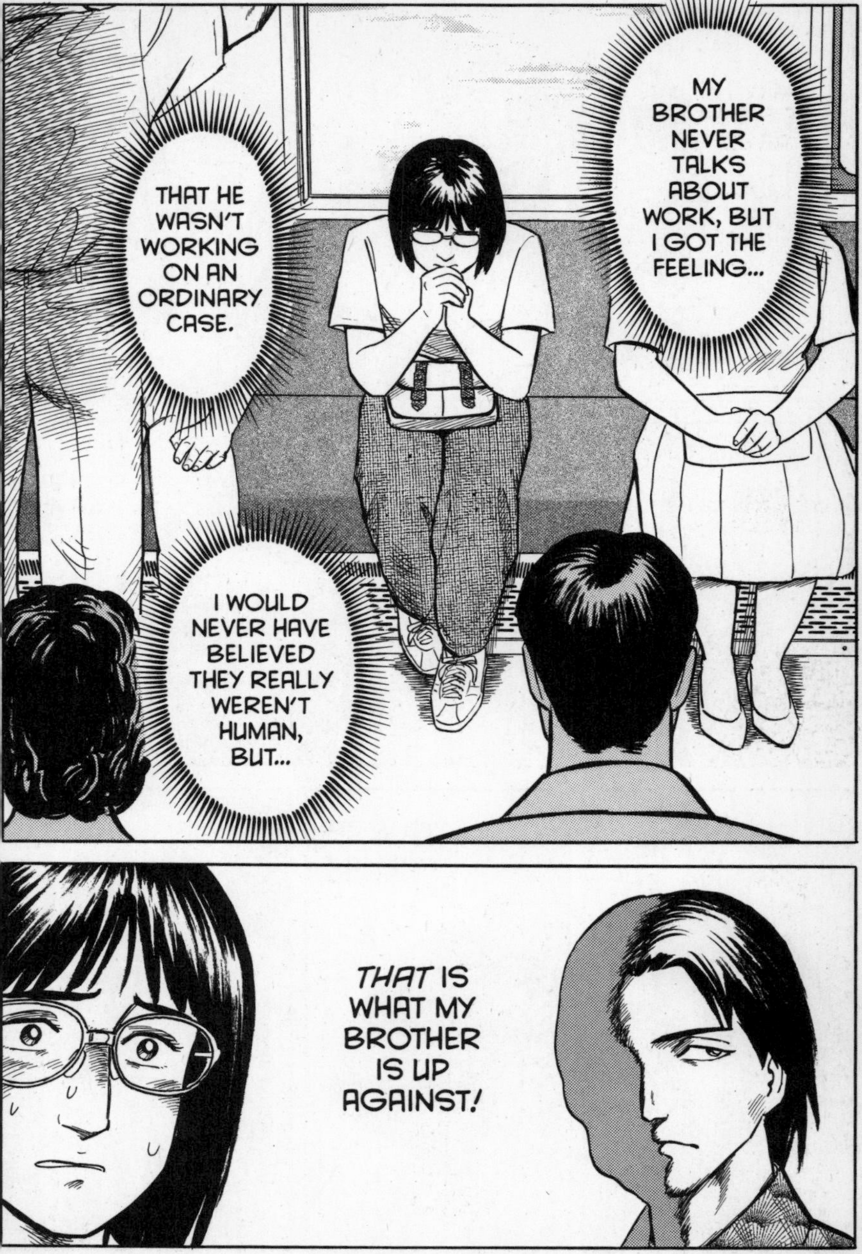
MY BROTHER NEVER TALKS ABOUT WORK, BUT I GOT THE FEELING...
THAT HE WASN'T WORKING ON AN ORDINARY CASE.
I WOULD NEVER HAVE BELIEVED THEY REALLY WEREN'T HUMAN, BUT...
THAT IS WHAT MY BROTHER IS UP AGAINST!

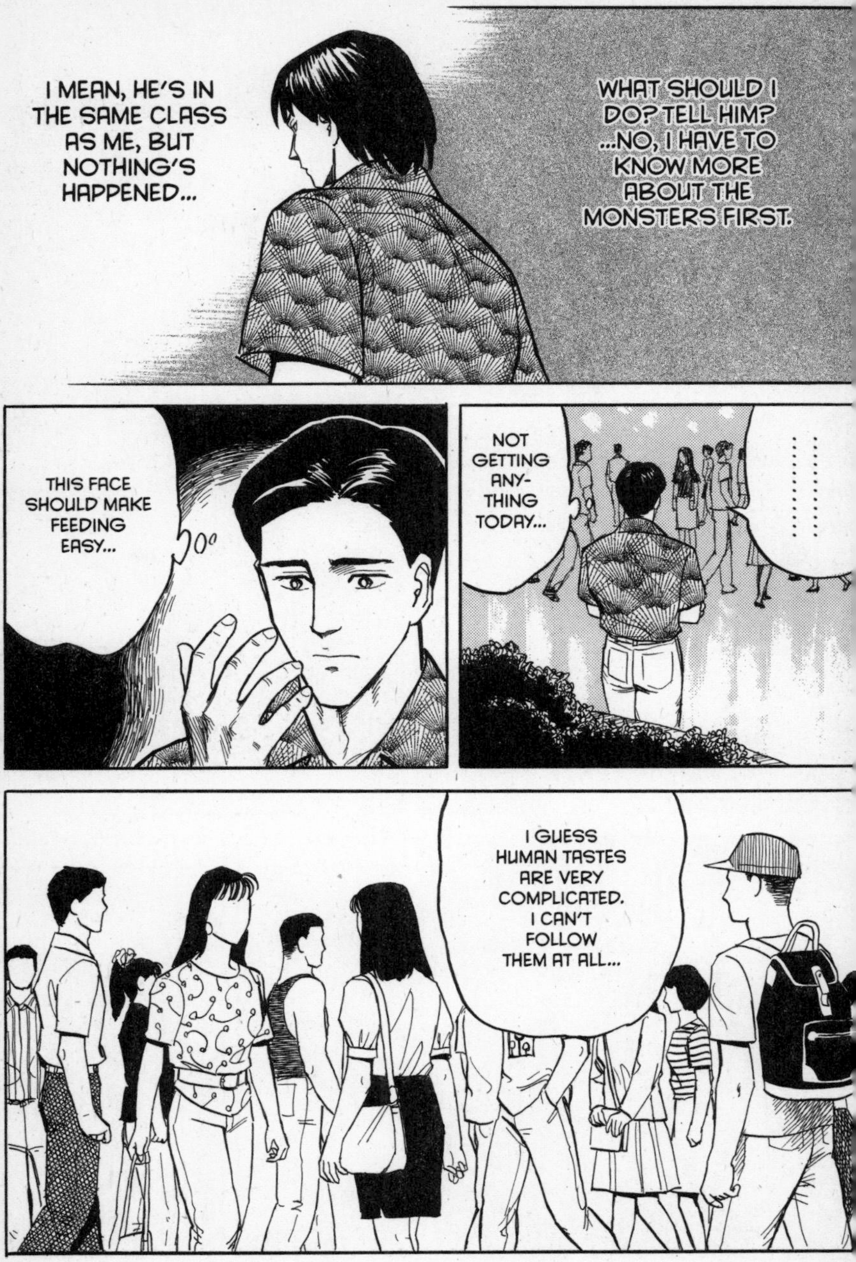

WHAT SHOULD I DO? TELL HIM? ...NO, I HAVE TO KNOW MORE ABOUT THE MONSTERS FIRST.
I MEAN, HE'S IN THE SAME CLASS AS ME, BUT NOTHING'S HAPPENED...
......
NOT GETTING ANY-THING TODAY...
THIS FACE SHOULD MAKE FEEDING EASY...
I GUESS HUMAN TASTES ARE VERY COMPLICATED. I CAN'T FOLLOW THEM AT ALL...

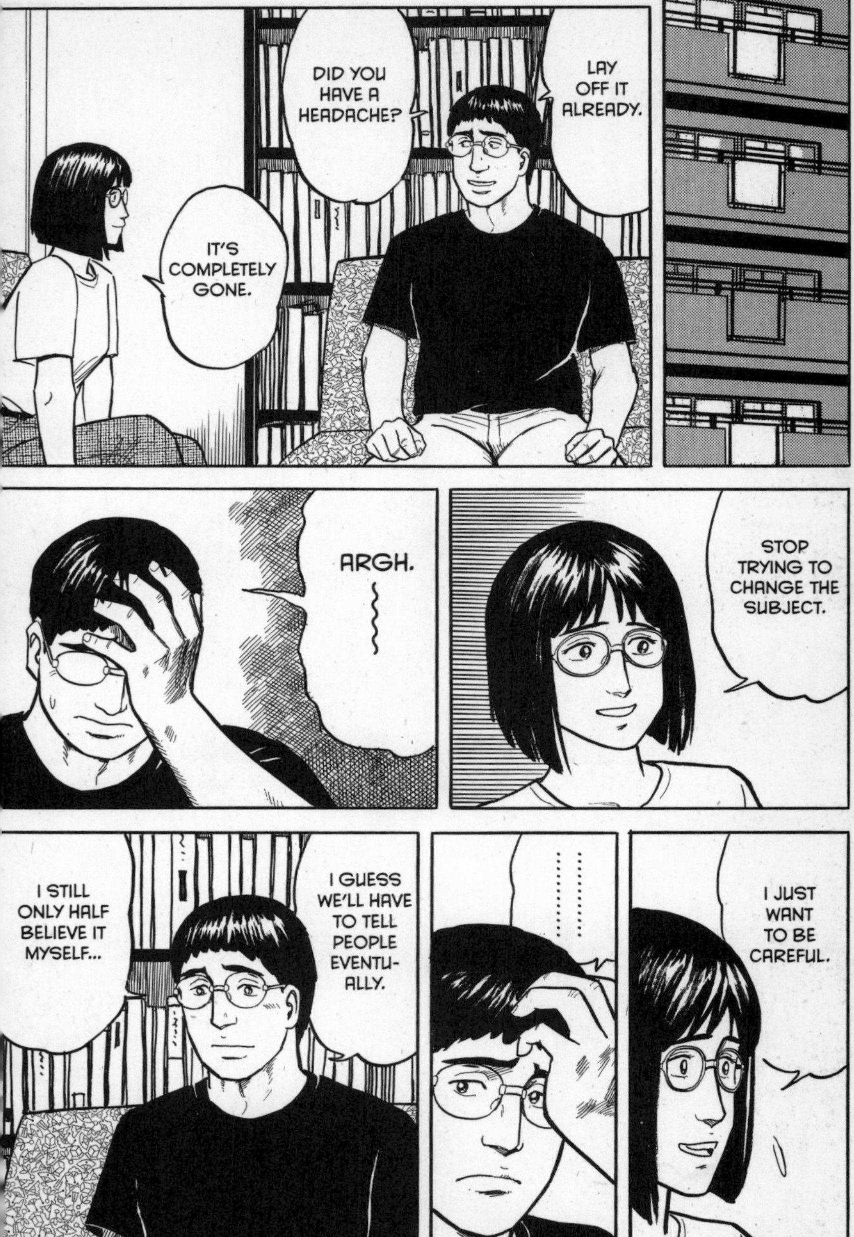
LAY OFF IT ALREADY.
DID YOU HAVE A HEADACHE?
IT'S COMPLETELY GONE.
STOP TRYING TO CHANGE THE SUBJECT.
ARGH.
I JUST WANT TO BE CAREFUL.
......
I GUESS WE'LL HAVE TO TELL PEOPLE EVENTU-ALLY.
I STILL ONLY HALF BELIEVE IT MYSELF...

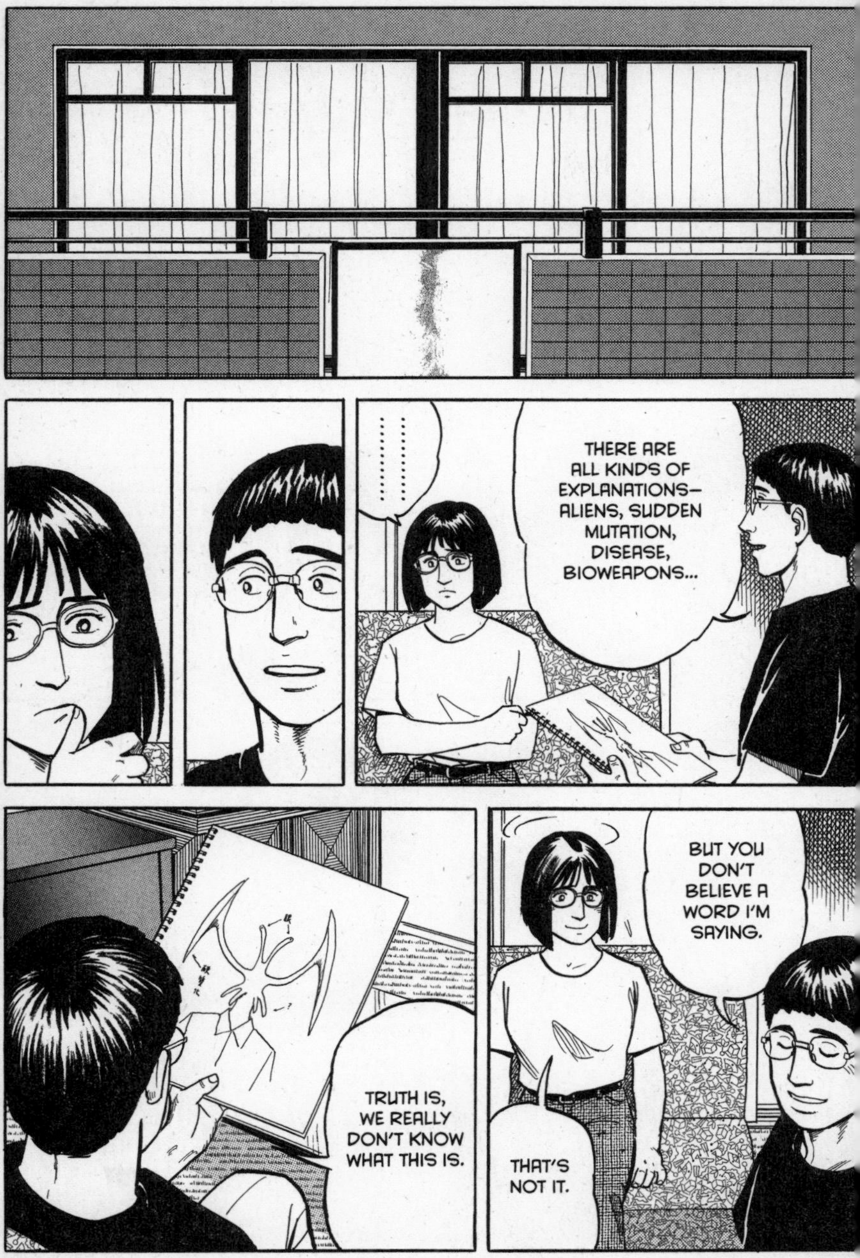

THERE ARE ALL KINDS OF EXPLANATIONS— ALIENS, SUDDEN MUTATION, DISEASE, BIOWEAPONS...
......
BUT YOU DON'T BELIEVE A WORD I'M SAYING.
THAT'S NOT IT.
TRUTH IS, WE REALLY DON'T KNOW WHAT THIS IS.

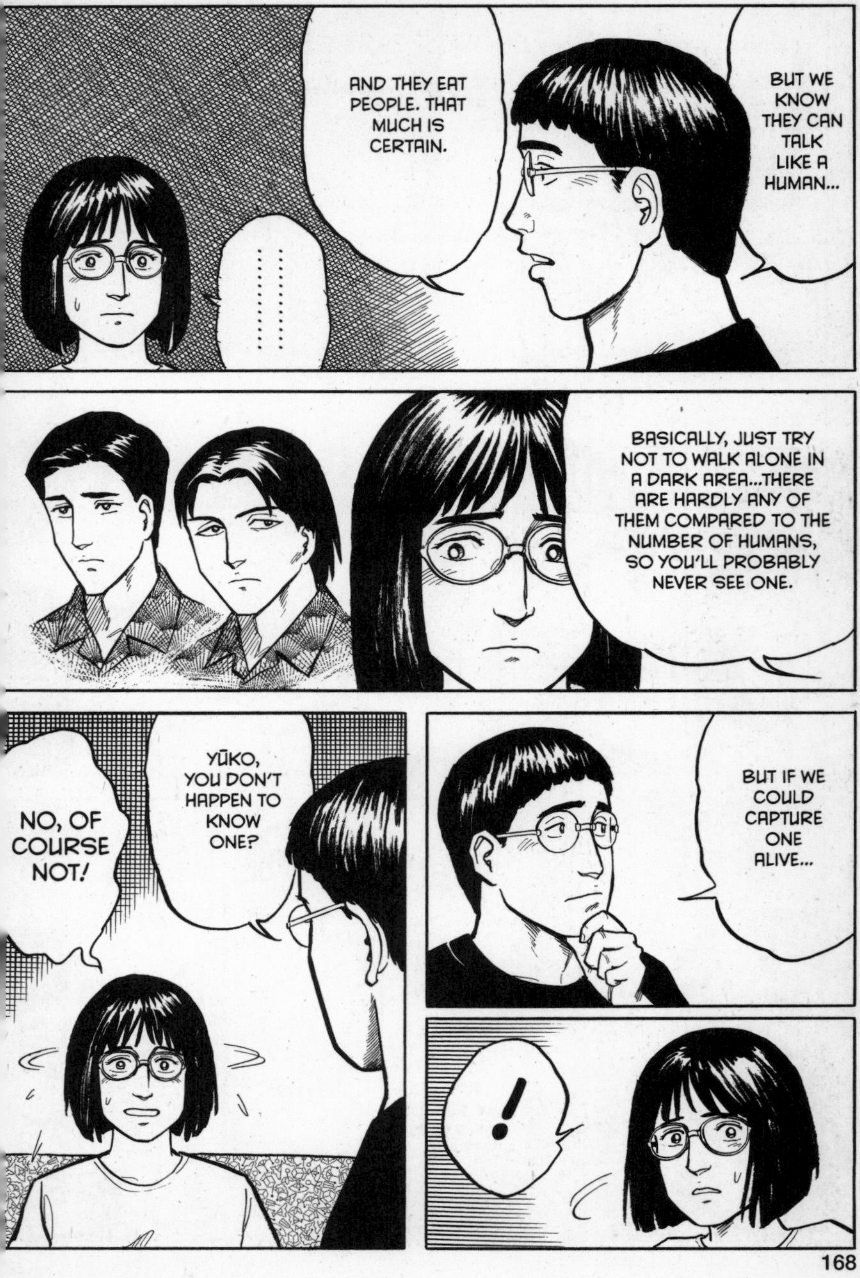
BUT WE KNOW THEY CAN TALK LIKE A HUMAN...
AND THEY EAT PEOPLE. THAT MUCH IS CERTAIN.
......
BASICALLY, JUST TRY NOT TO WALK ALONE IN A DARK AREA...THERE ARE HARDLY ANY OF THEM COMPARED TO THE NUMBER OF HUMANS, SO YOU'LL PROBABLY NEVER SEE ONE.
BUT IF WE COULD CAPTURE ONE ALIVE...
!
YŪKO, YOU DON'T HAPPEN TO KNOW ONE?
NO, OF COURSE NOT!

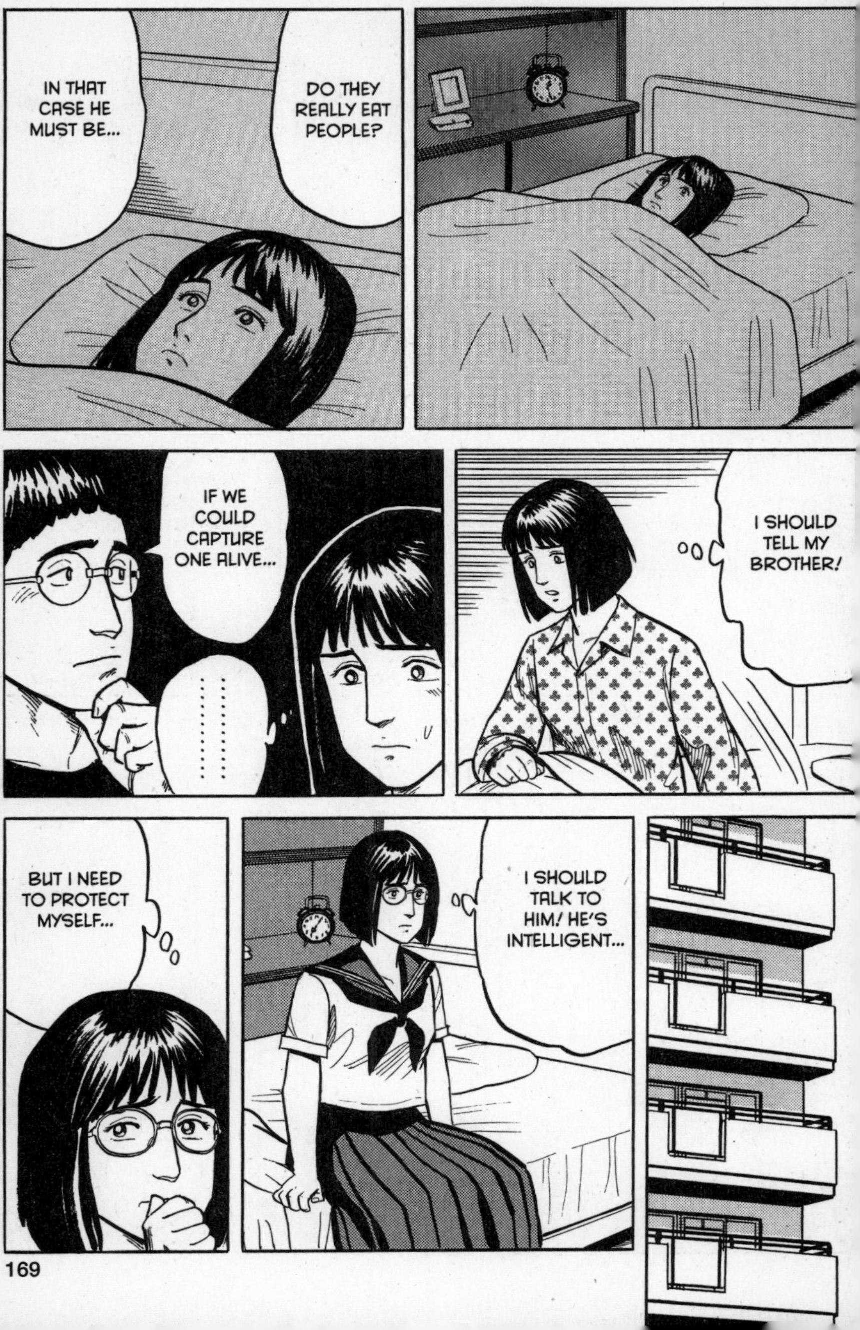
DO THEY REALLY EAT PEOPLE?
IN THAT CASE HE MUST BE...
I SHOULD TELL MY BROTHER!
IF WE COULD CAPTURE ONE ALIVE...
......
I SHOULD TALK TO HIM! HE'S INTELLIGENT...
BUT I NEED TO PROTECT MYSELF...

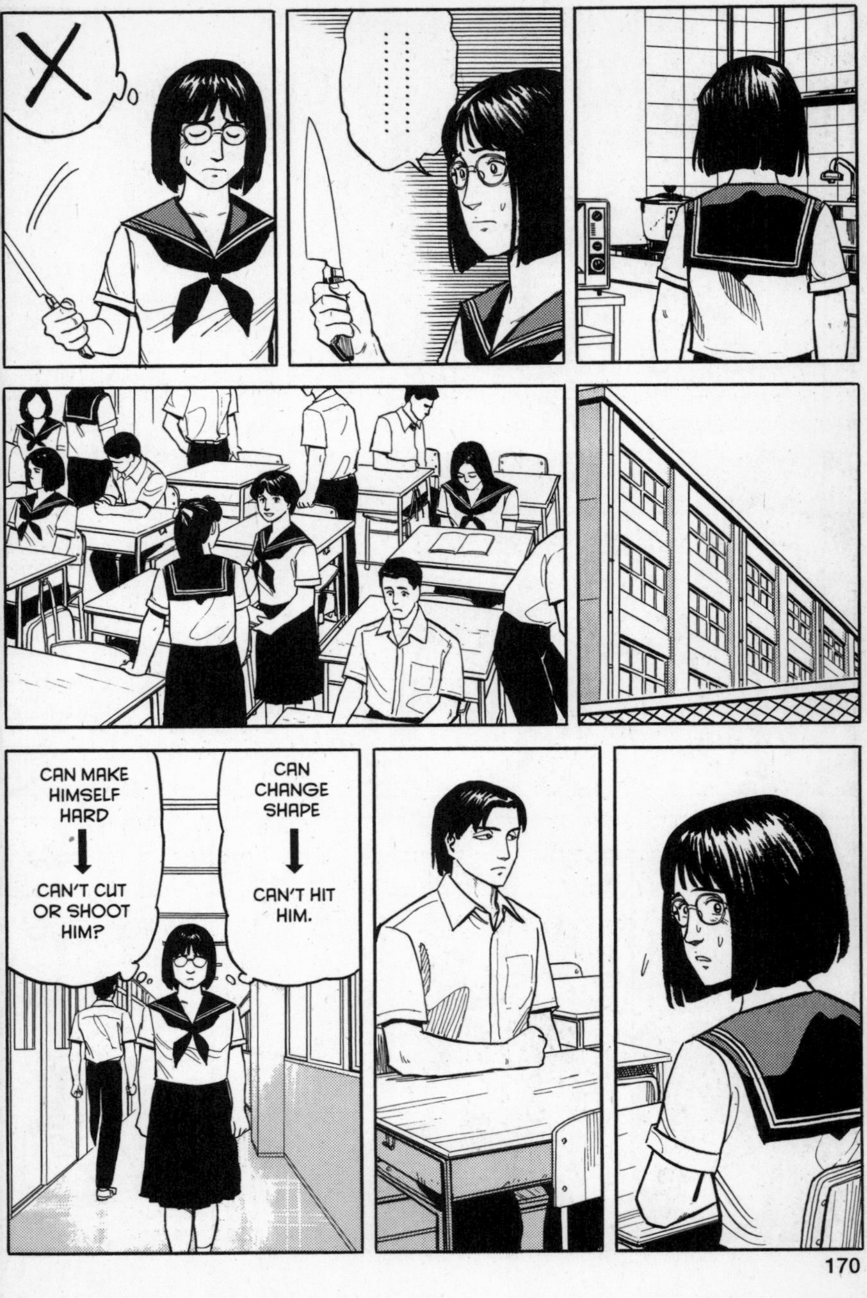
......
CAN CHANGE SHAPE
CAN'T HIT HIM.
CAN MAKE HIMSELF HARD
CAN'T CUT OR SHOOT HIM?

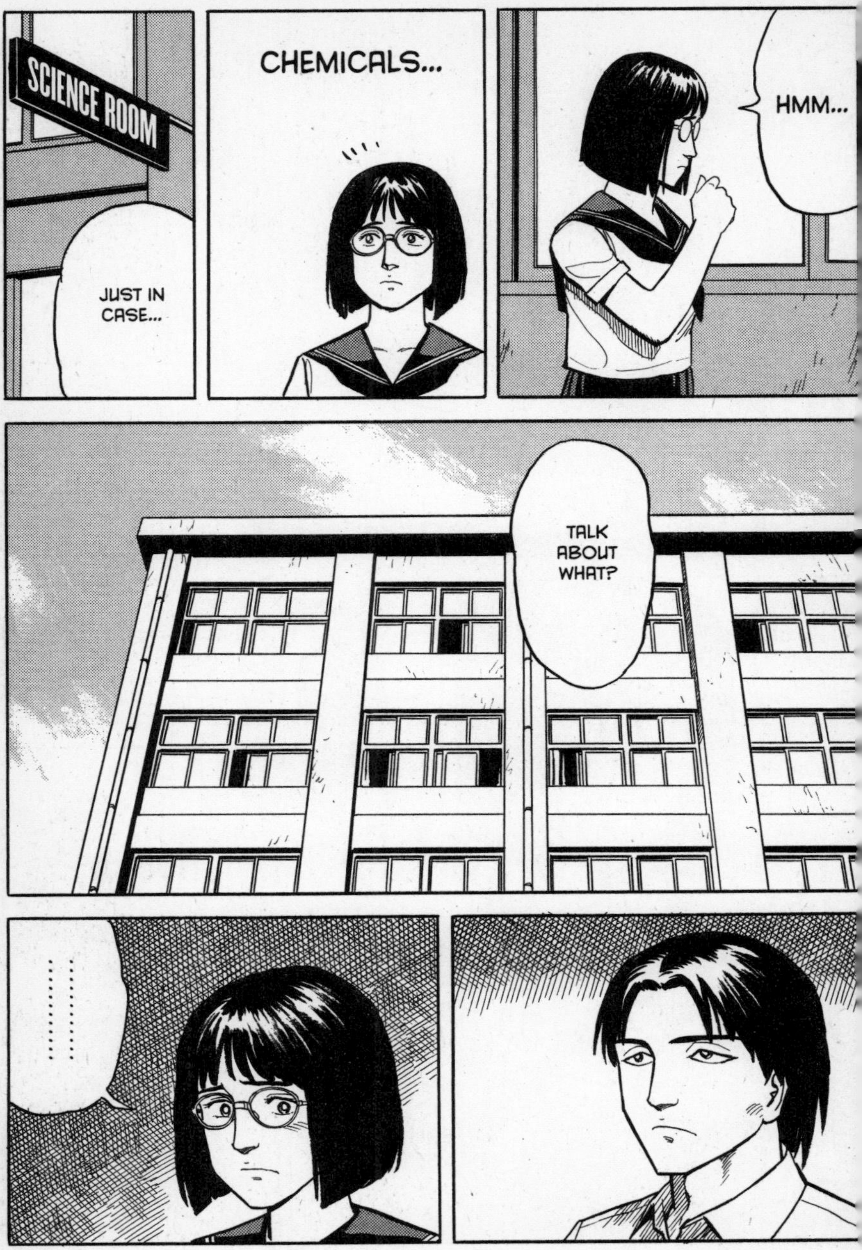
HMM...
CHEMICALS...
SCIENCE ROOM
JUST IN CASE...
TALK ABOUT WHAT?
......

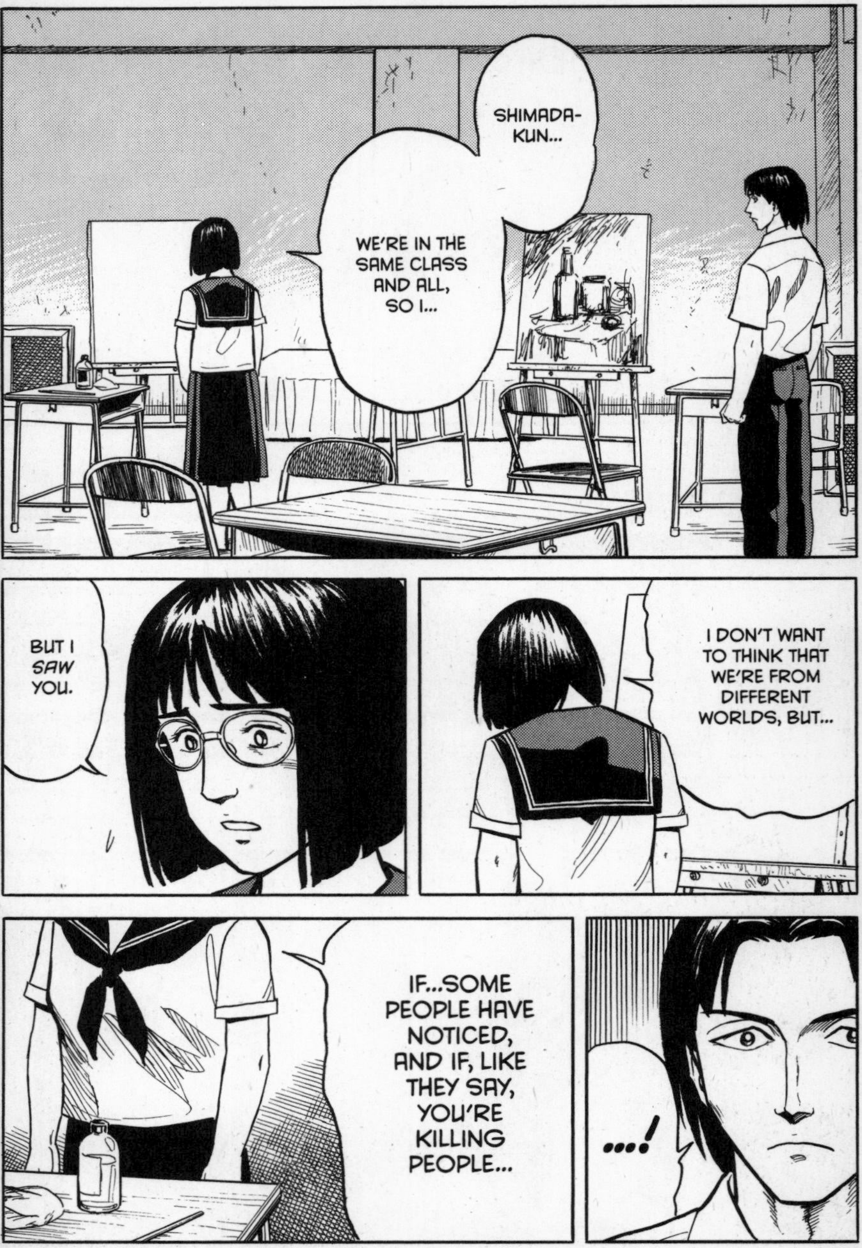
SHIMADA-KUN...
WE'RE IN THE SAME CLASS AND ALL, SO I...
I DON'T WANT TO THINK THAT WE'RE FROM DIFFERENT WORLDS, BUT...
BUT I *SAW* YOU.
...!
IF...SOME PEOPLE HAVE NOTICED, AND IF, LIKE THEY SAY, YOU'RE KILLING PEOPLE...

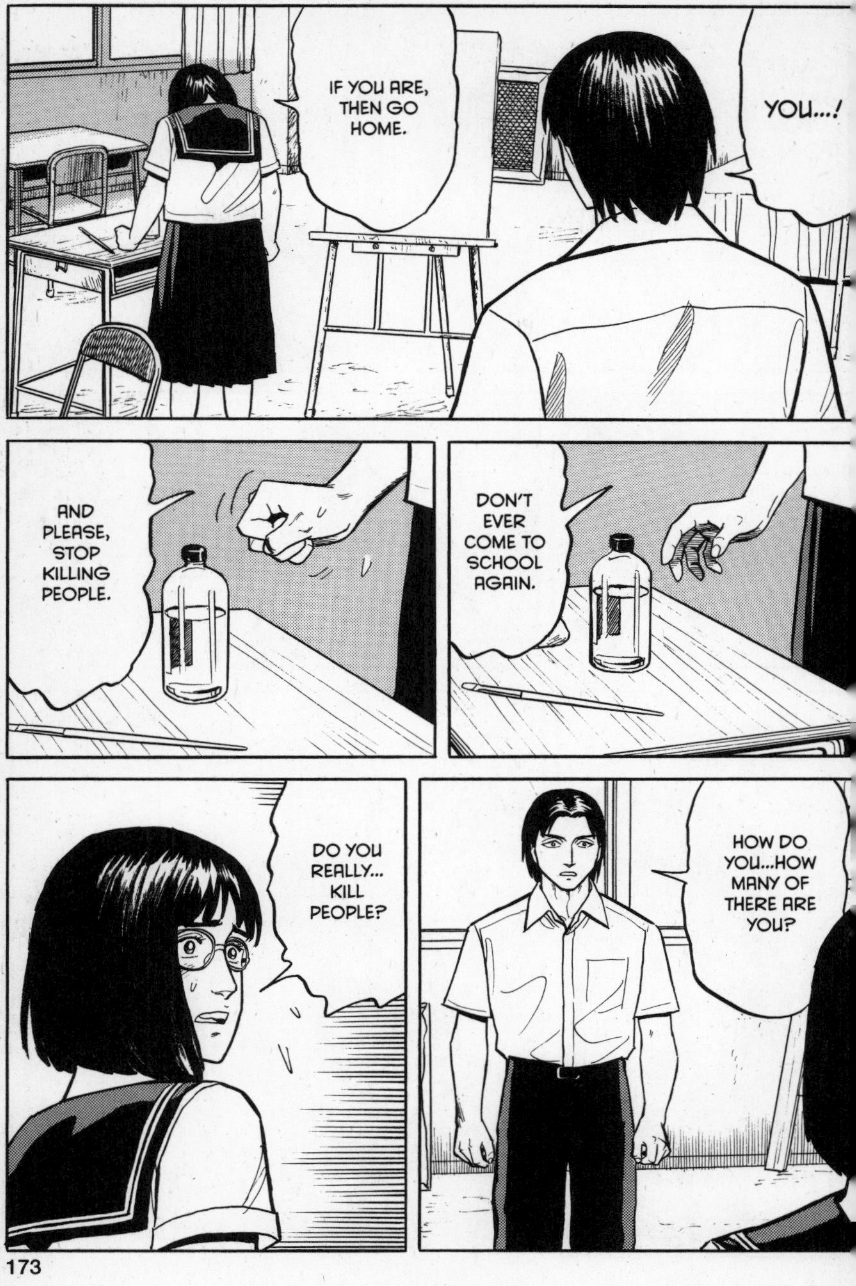
YOU...!
IF YOU ARE, THEN GO HOME.
DON'T EVER COME TO SCHOOL AGAIN.
AND PLEASE, STOP KILLING PEOPLE.
HOW DO YOU...HOW MANY OF THERE ARE YOU?
DO YOU REALLY... KILL PEOPLE?

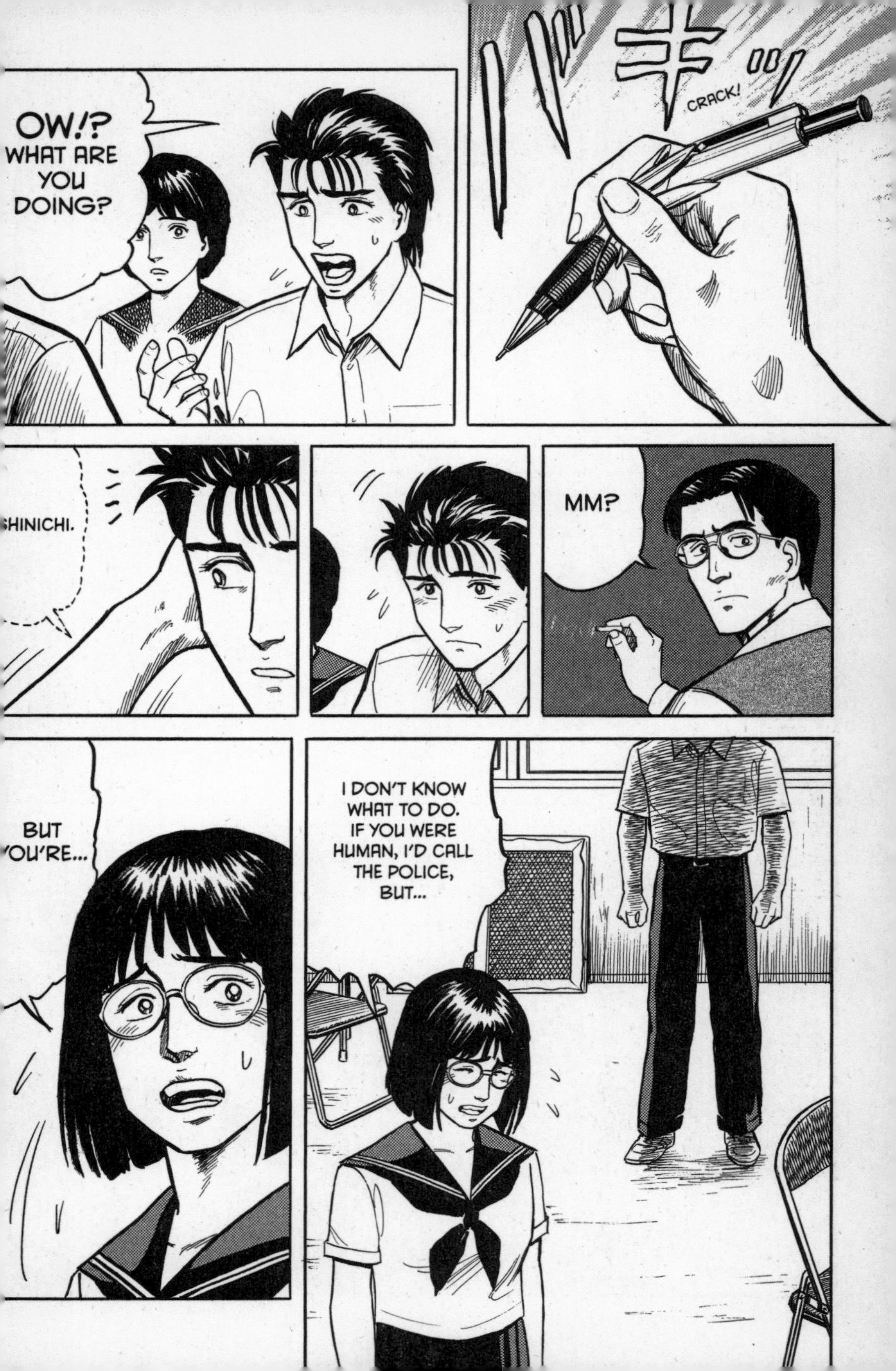

バキッ
CRACK!
OW!? WHAT ARE YOU DOING?
MM?
SHINICHI.
I DON'T KNOW WHAT TO DO. IF YOU WERE HUMAN, I'D CALL THE POLICE, BUT...
BUT YOU'RE...

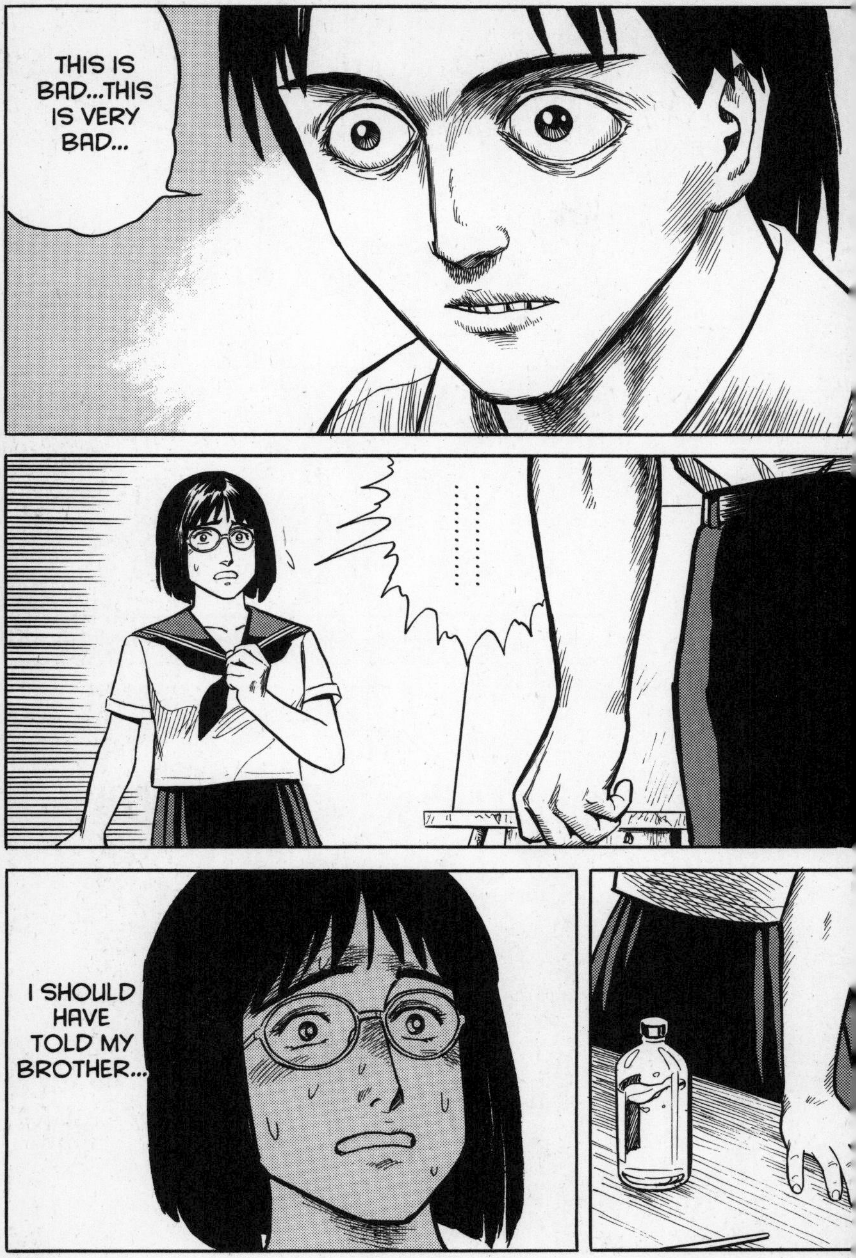
THIS IS BAD...THIS IS VERY BAD...
I SHOULD HAVE TOLD MY BROTHER...

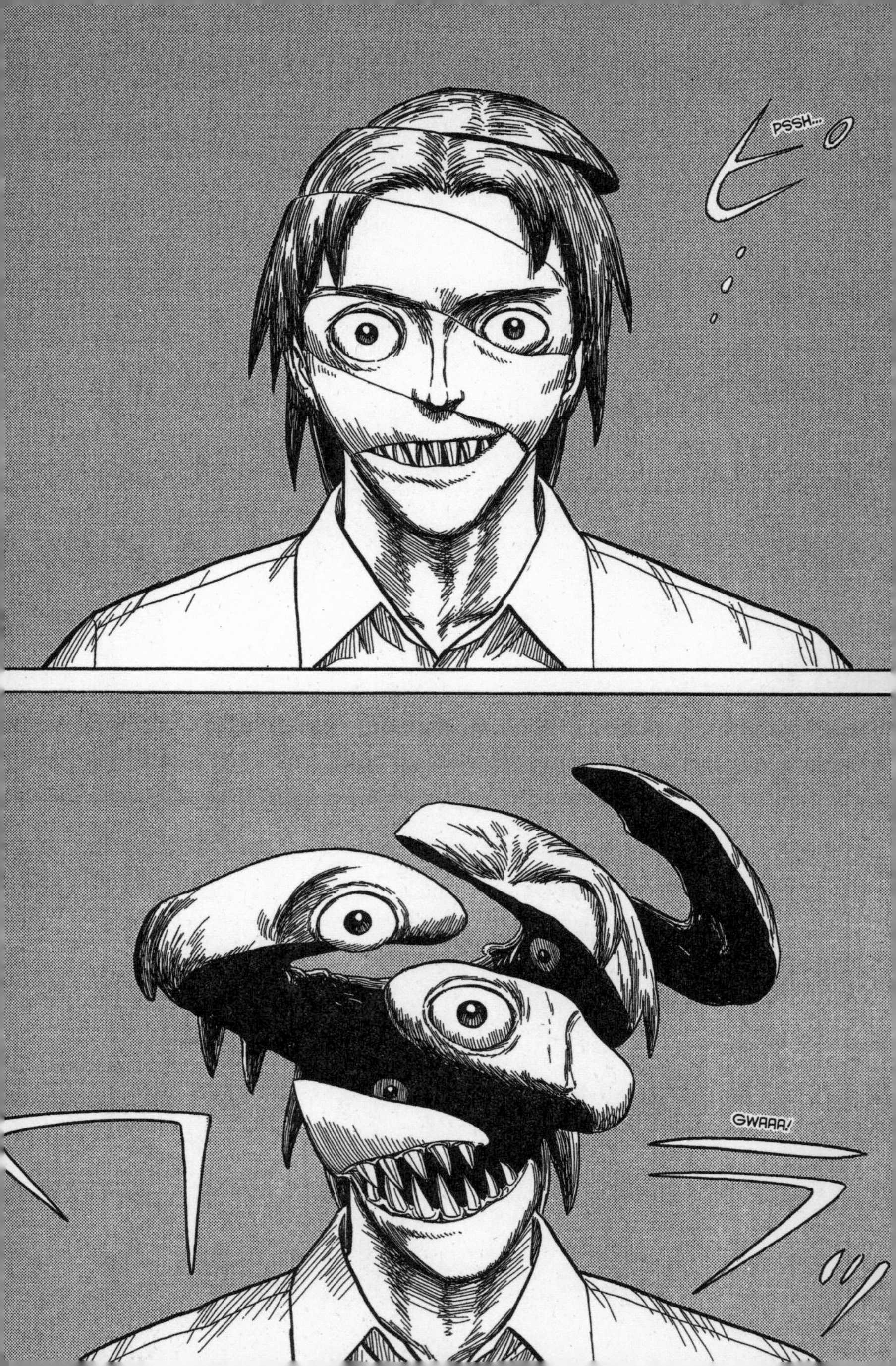
PSSH...
GWAAA!

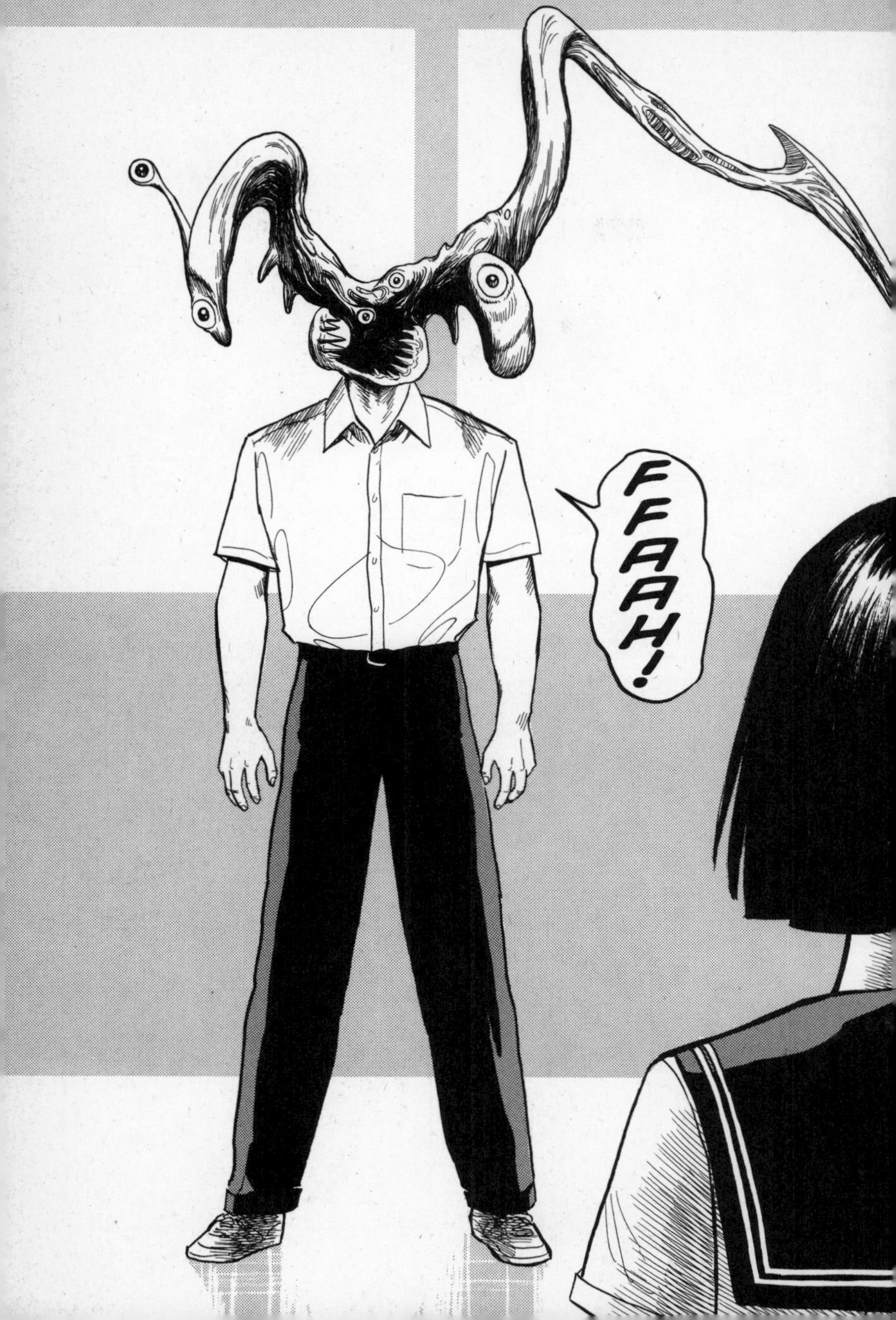
FFAAH!

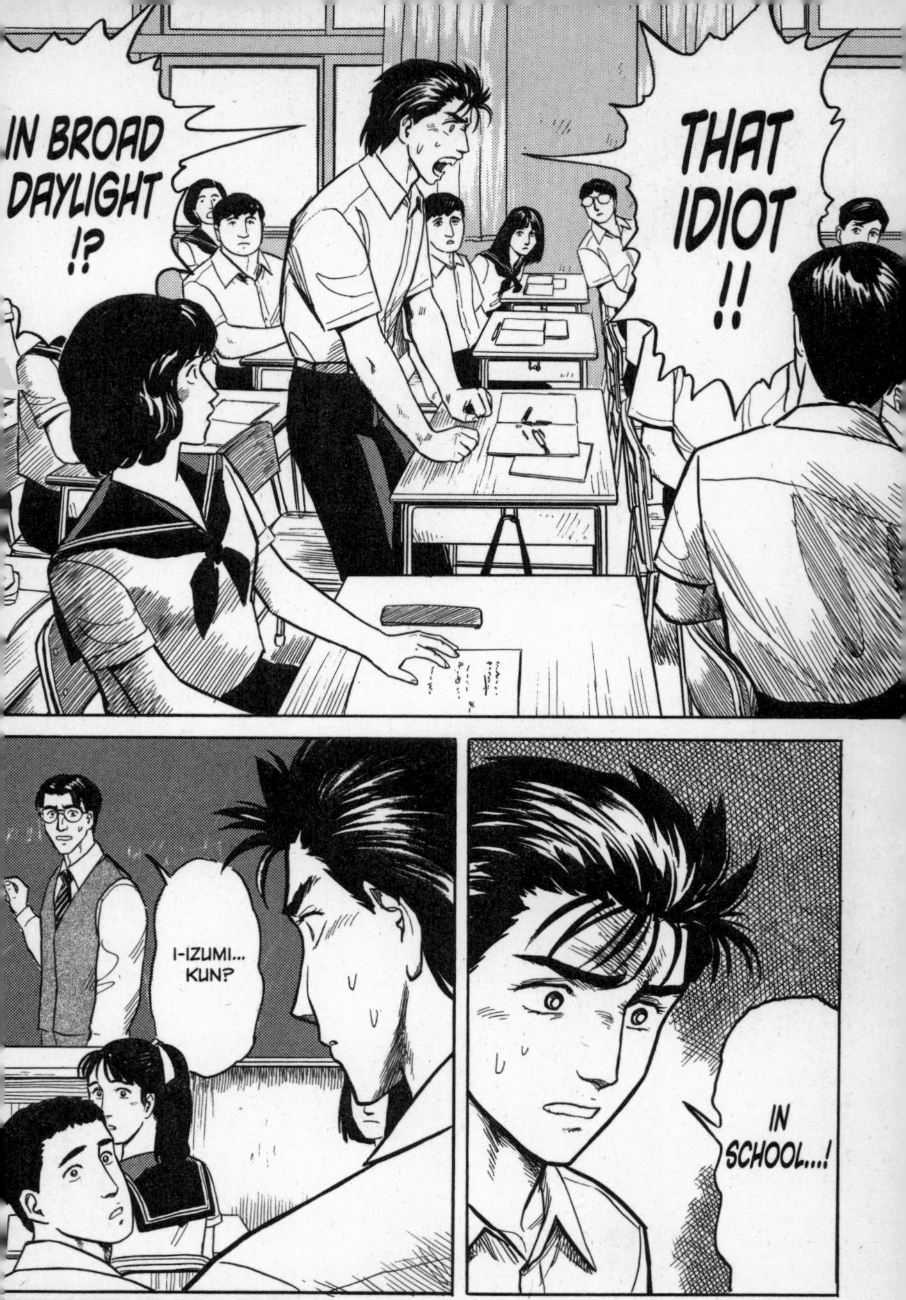
THAT IDIOT !!
IN BROAD DAYLIGHT !?
IN SCHOOL...!
I-IZUMI... KUN?

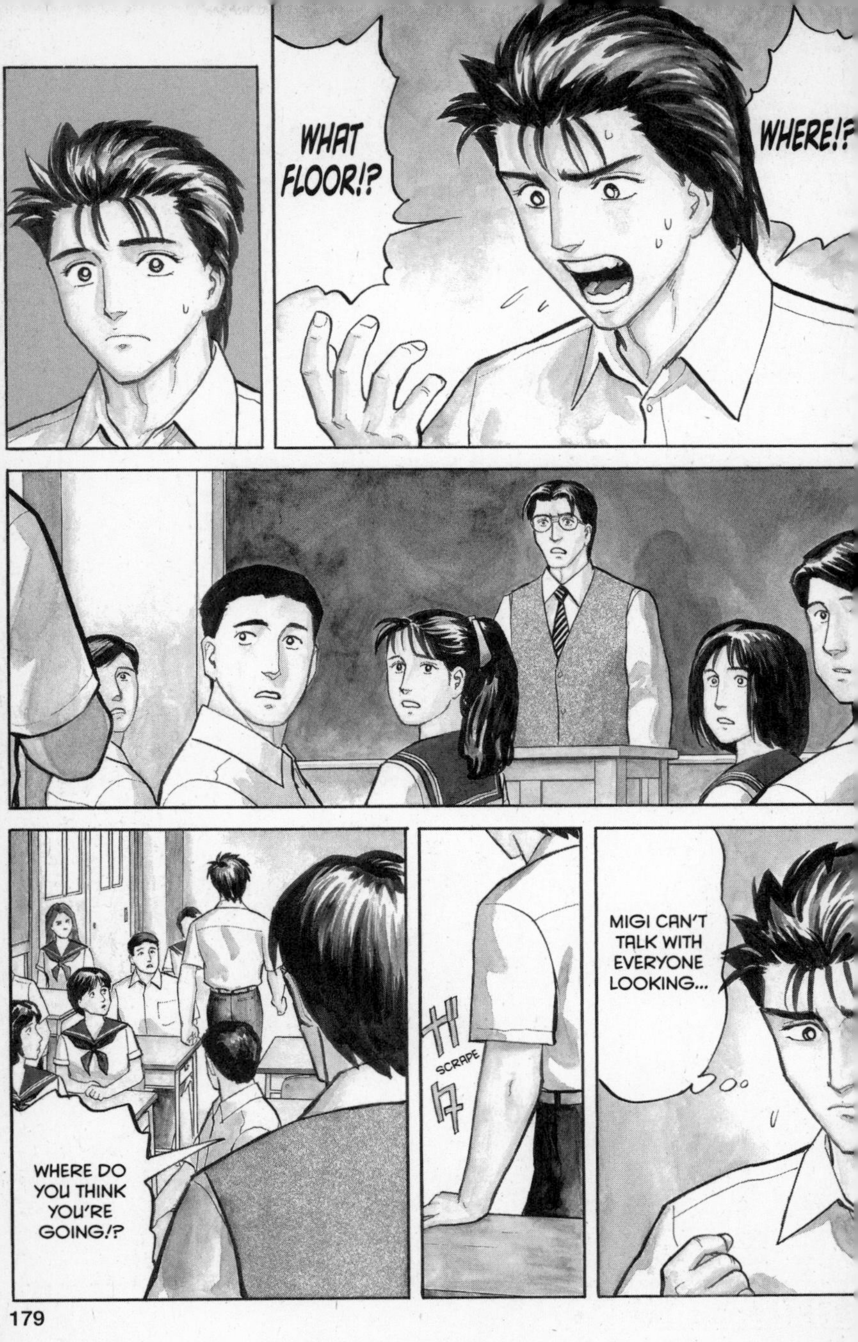
WHERE!?
WHAT FLOOR!?
MIGI CAN'T TALK WITH EVERYONE LOOKING...
SCRAPE
WHERE DO YOU THINK YOU'RE GOING!?

CHAPTER 23: CONFUSION AND SLAUGHTER

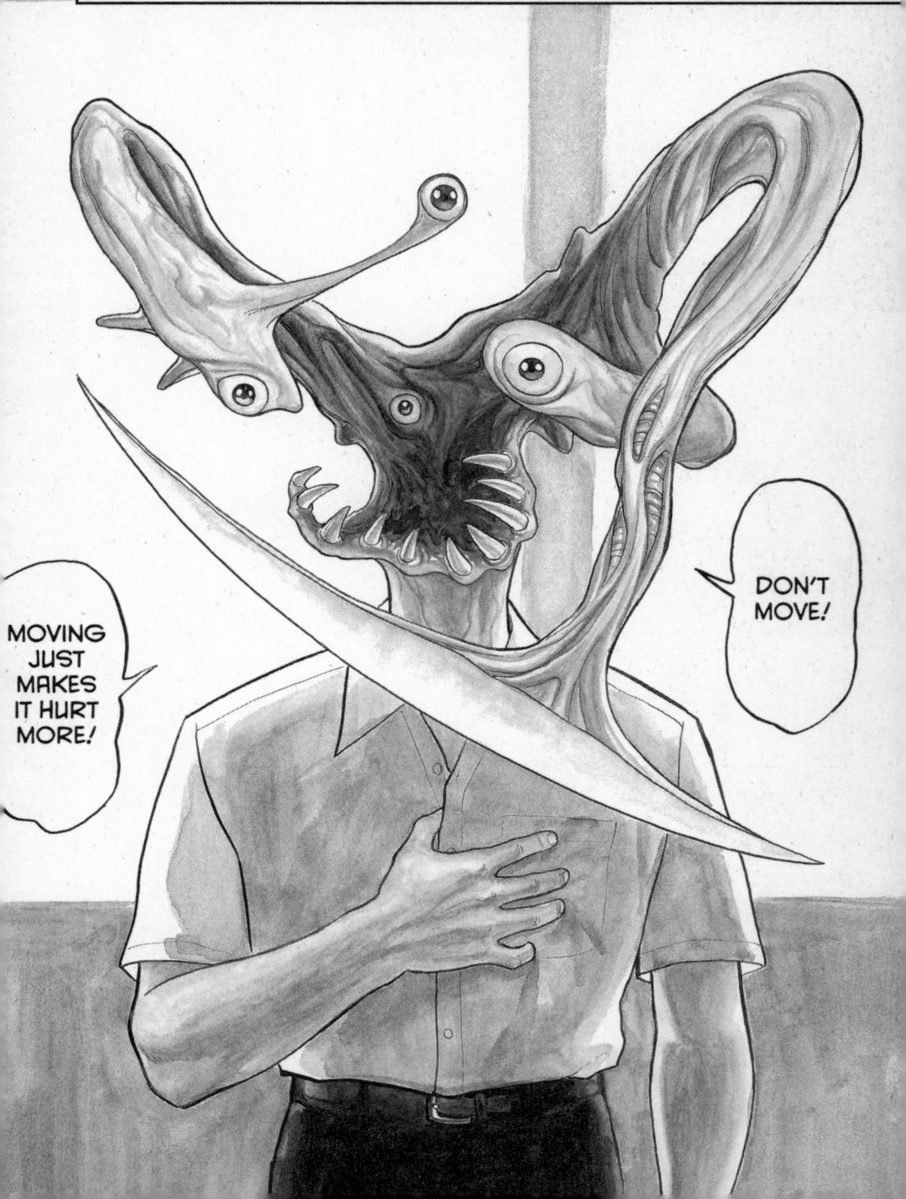
DON'T MOVE!
MOVING JUST MAKES IT HURT MORE!

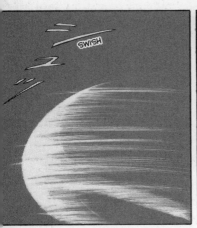

SWISH

EEK...
AHH...

CLANG

GLUG

!

ROLL

181

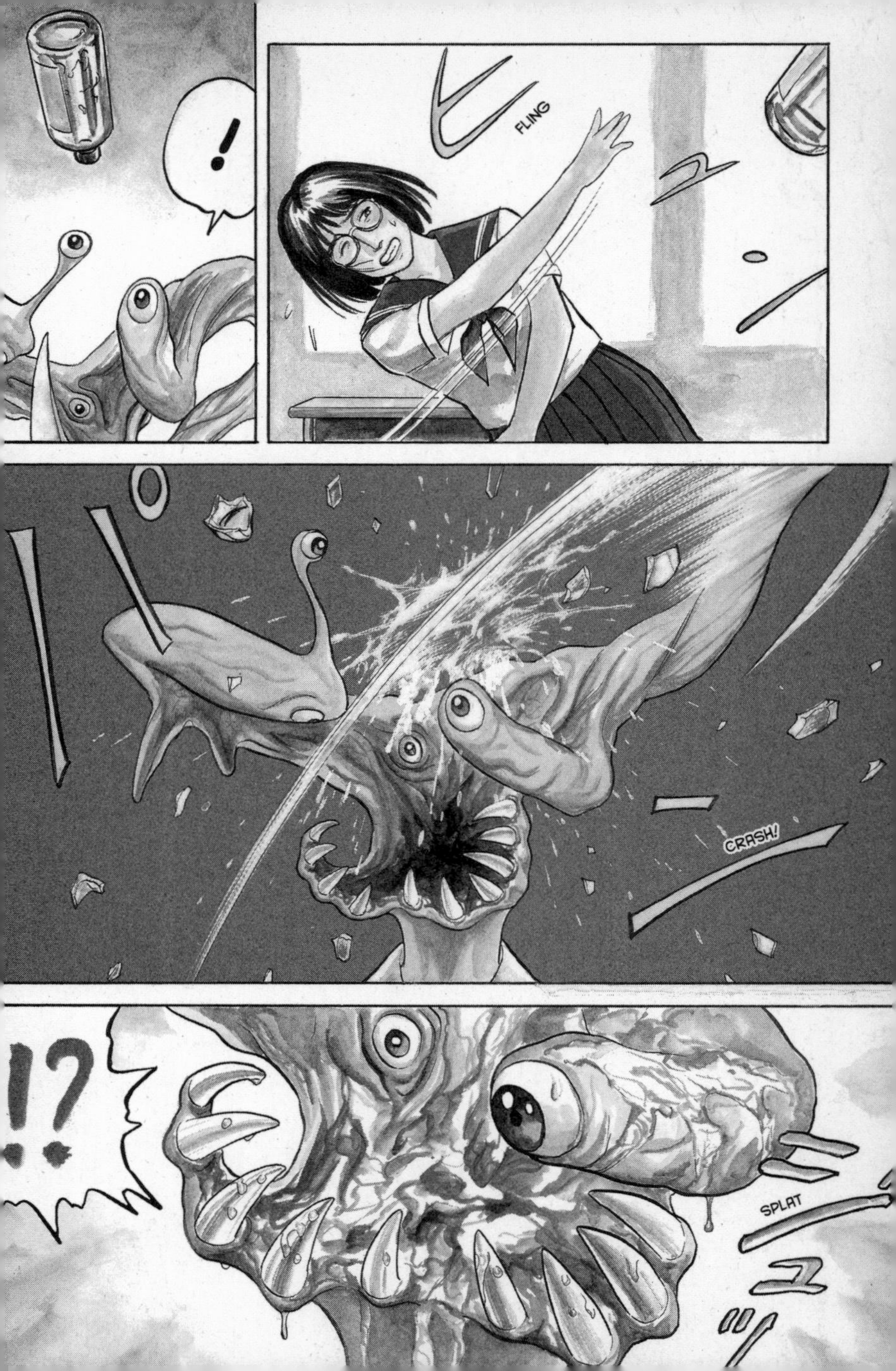
FLING
!
CRASH!
!?
SPLAT

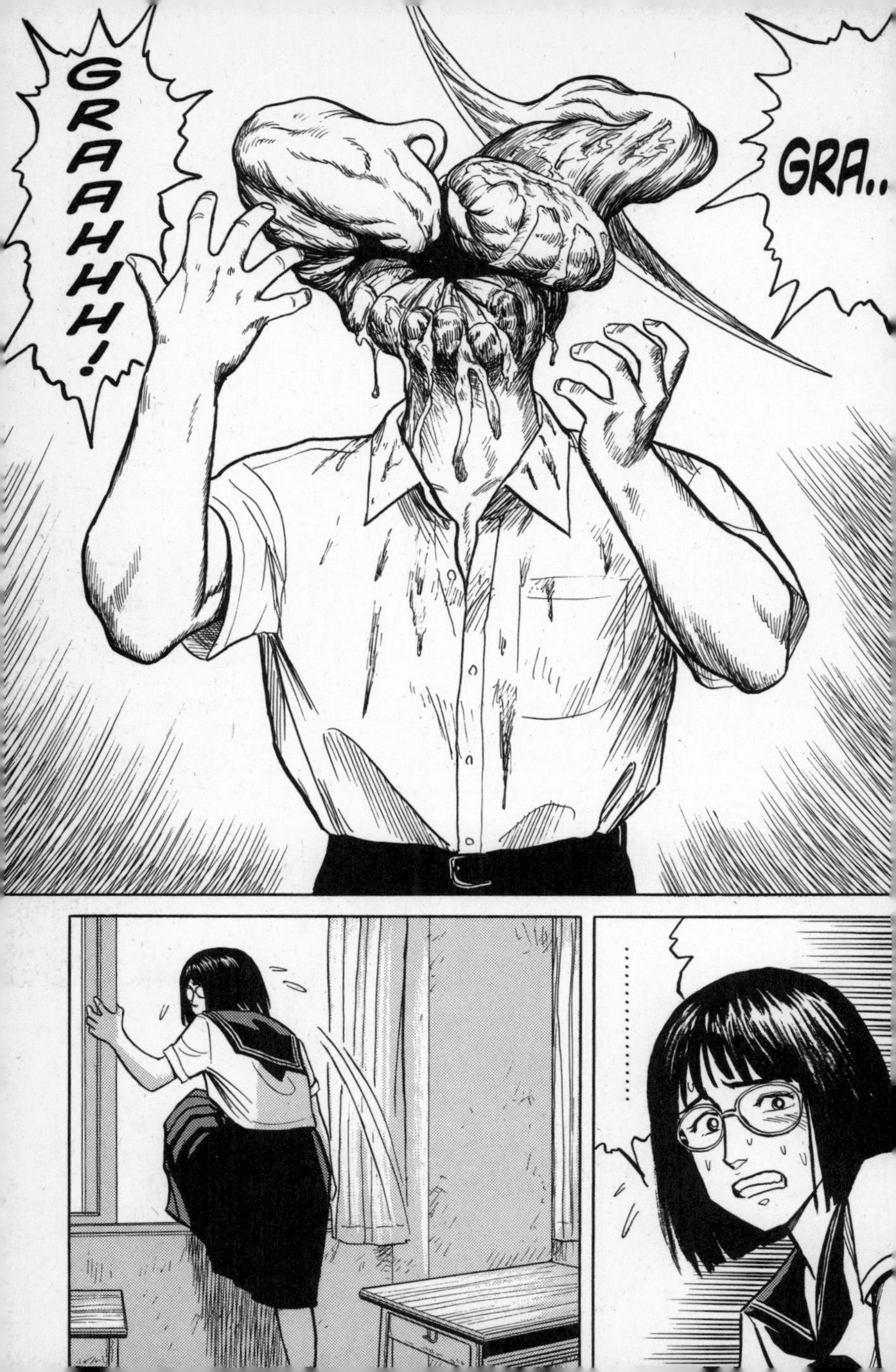
GRA..
GRAAHHH!
......

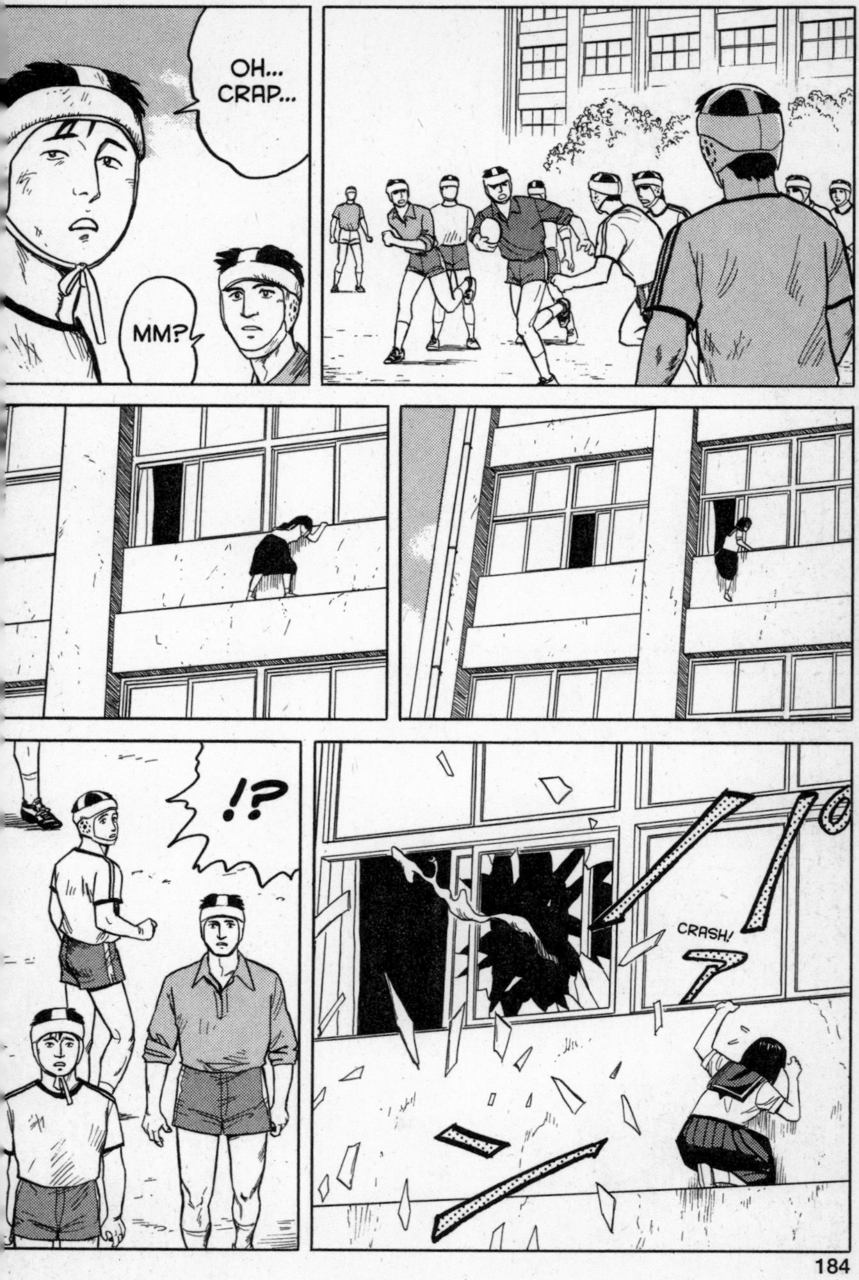
OH... CRAP...
MM?
CRASH!
!?

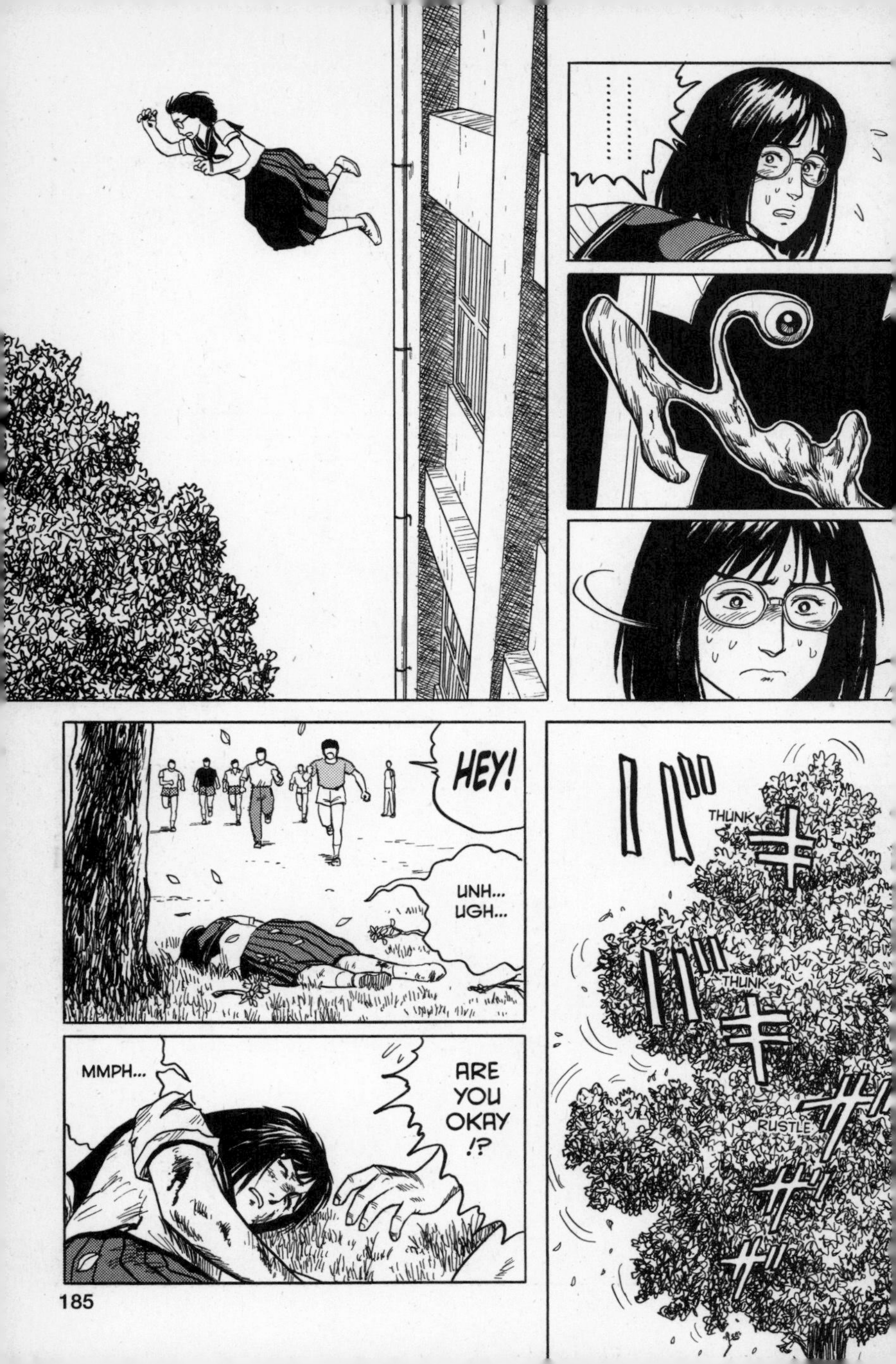

......
THUNK
THUNK
RUSTLE
HEY!
UNH... UGH...
ARE YOU OKAY!?
MMPH...

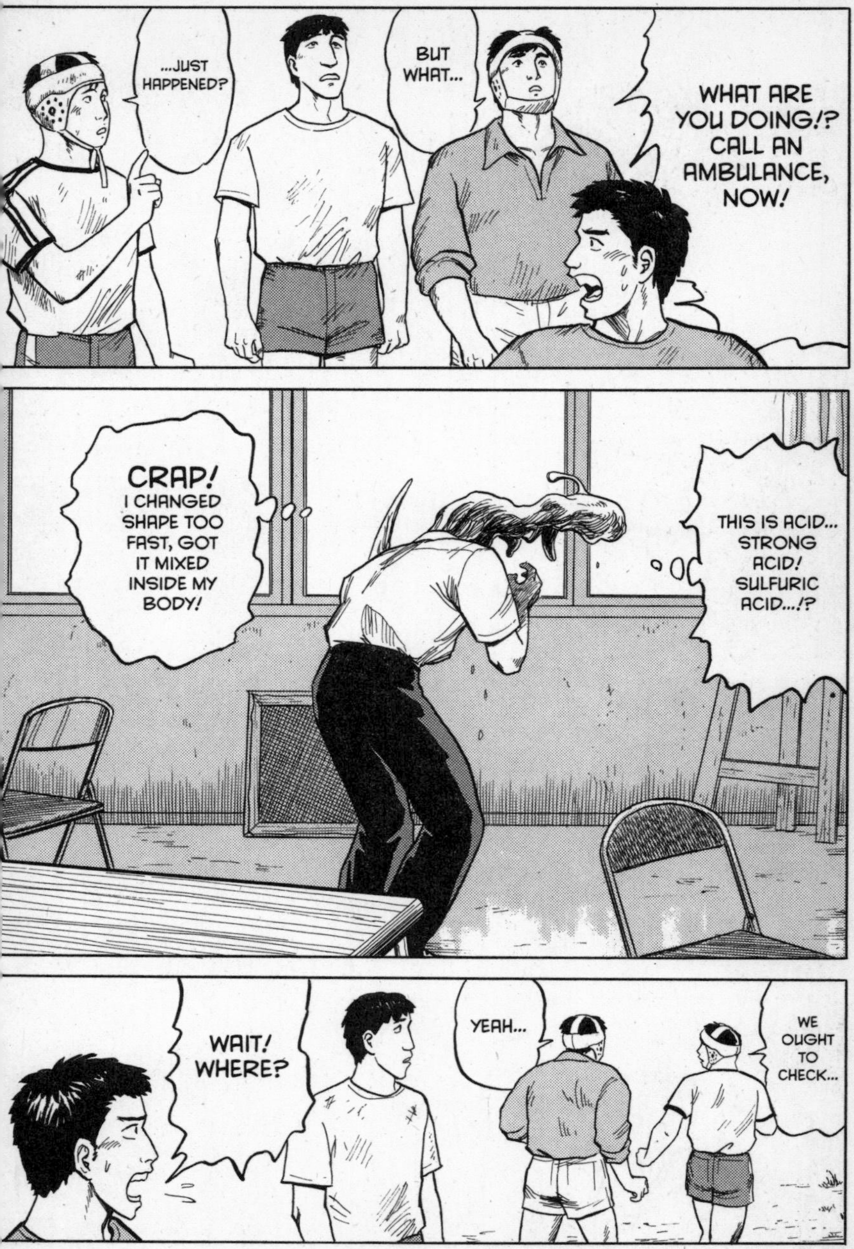
WHAT ARE YOU DOING!? CALL AN AMBULANCE, NOW!
BUT WHAT...
...JUST HAPPENED?
THIS IS ACID... STRONG ACID! SULFURIC ACID...!?
CRAP! I CHANGED SHAPE TOO FAST, GOT IT MIXED INSIDE MY BODY!
WE OUGHT TO CHECK...
YEAH...
WAIT! WHERE?

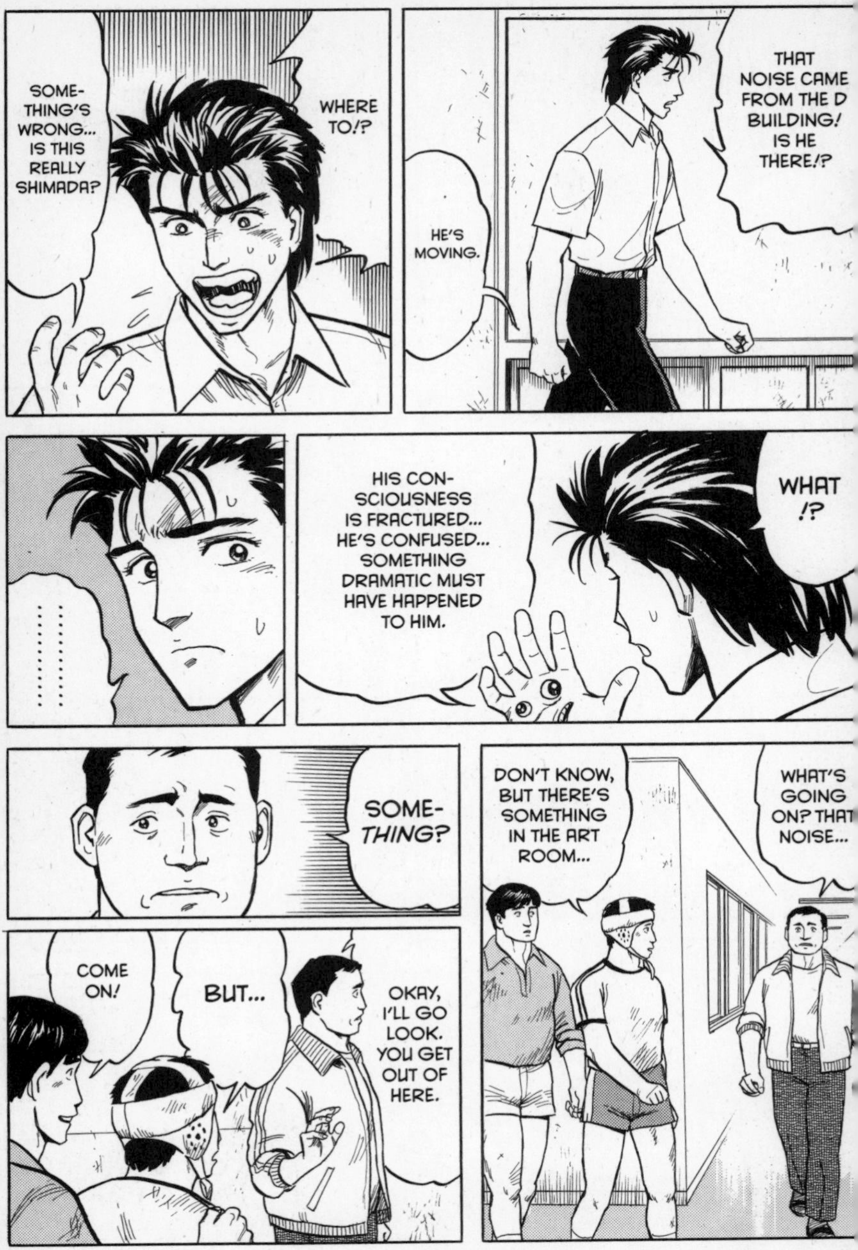
THAT NOISE CAME FROM THE D BUILDING! IS HE THERE!?
HE'S MOVING.
WHERE TO!?
SOME-THING'S WRONG... IS THIS REALLY SHIMADA?
WHAT !?
HIS CON-SCIOUSNESS IS FRACTURED... HE'S CONFUSED... SOMETHING DRAMATIC MUST HAVE HAPPENED TO HIM.
......
WHAT'S GOING ON? THAT NOISE...
DON'T KNOW, BUT THERE'S SOMETHING IN THE ART ROOM...
SOME-*THING*?
OKAY, I'LL GO LOOK. YOU GET OUT OF HERE.
BUT...
COME ON!

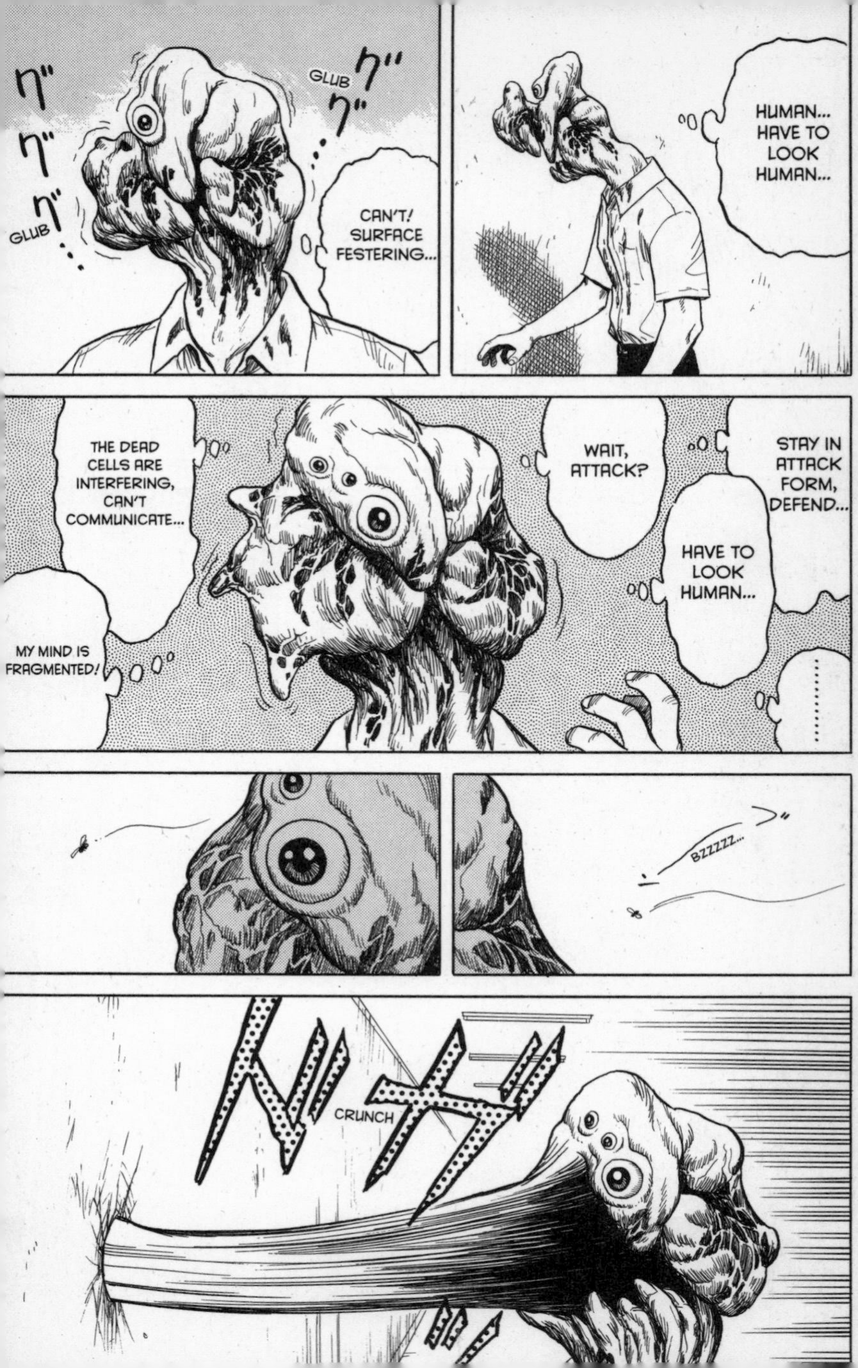
HUMAN... HAVE TO LOOK HUMAN...
GLUB
GLUB
CAN'T! SURFACE FESTERING...
STAY IN ATTACK FORM, DEFEND...
WAIT, ATTACK?
HAVE TO LOOK HUMAN...
......
THE DEAD CELLS ARE INTERFERING, CAN'T COMMUNICATE...
MY MIND IS FRAGMENTED!
BZZZZZ...
CRUNCH

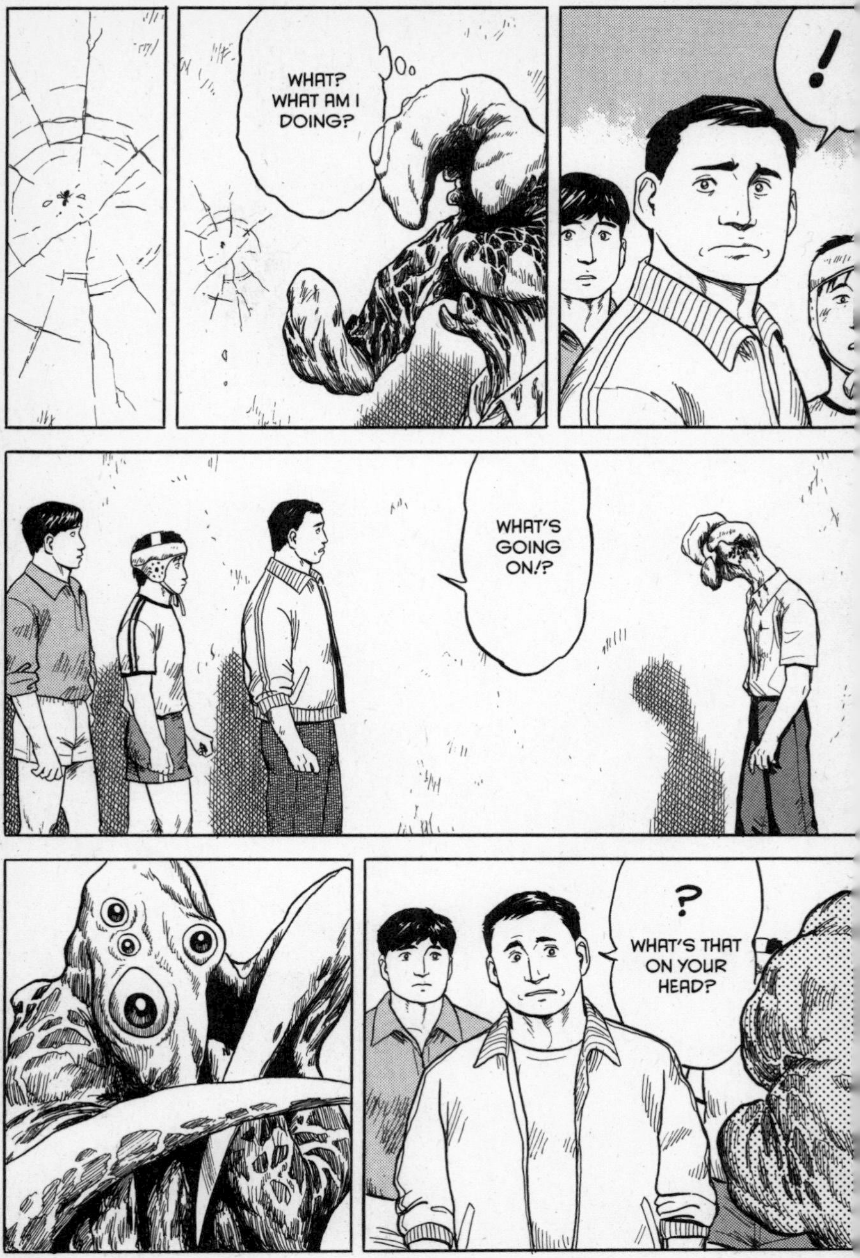
!
WHAT? WHAT AM I DOING?
WHAT'S GOING ON!?
?
WHAT'S THAT ON YOUR HEAD?

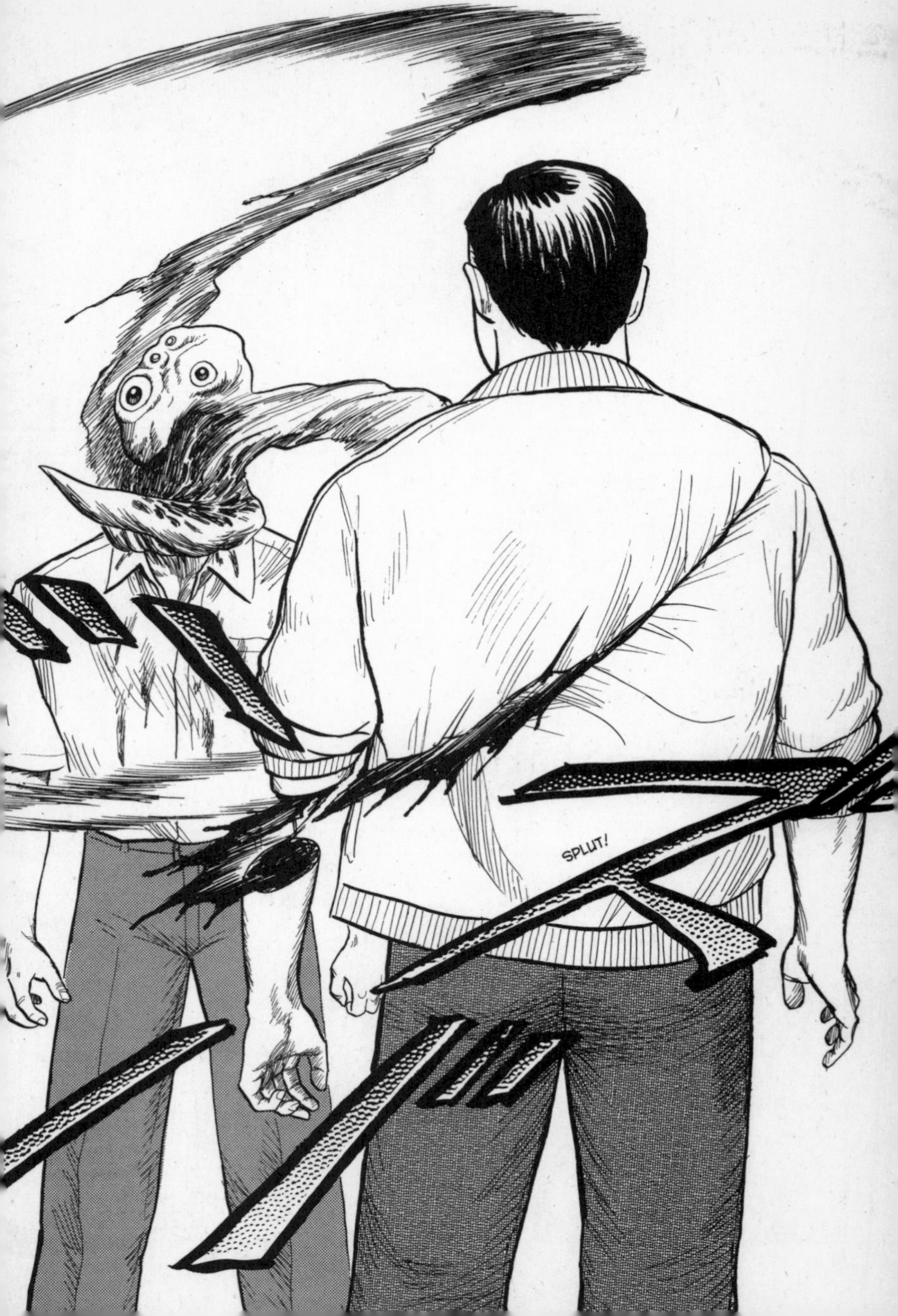
SPLUT!

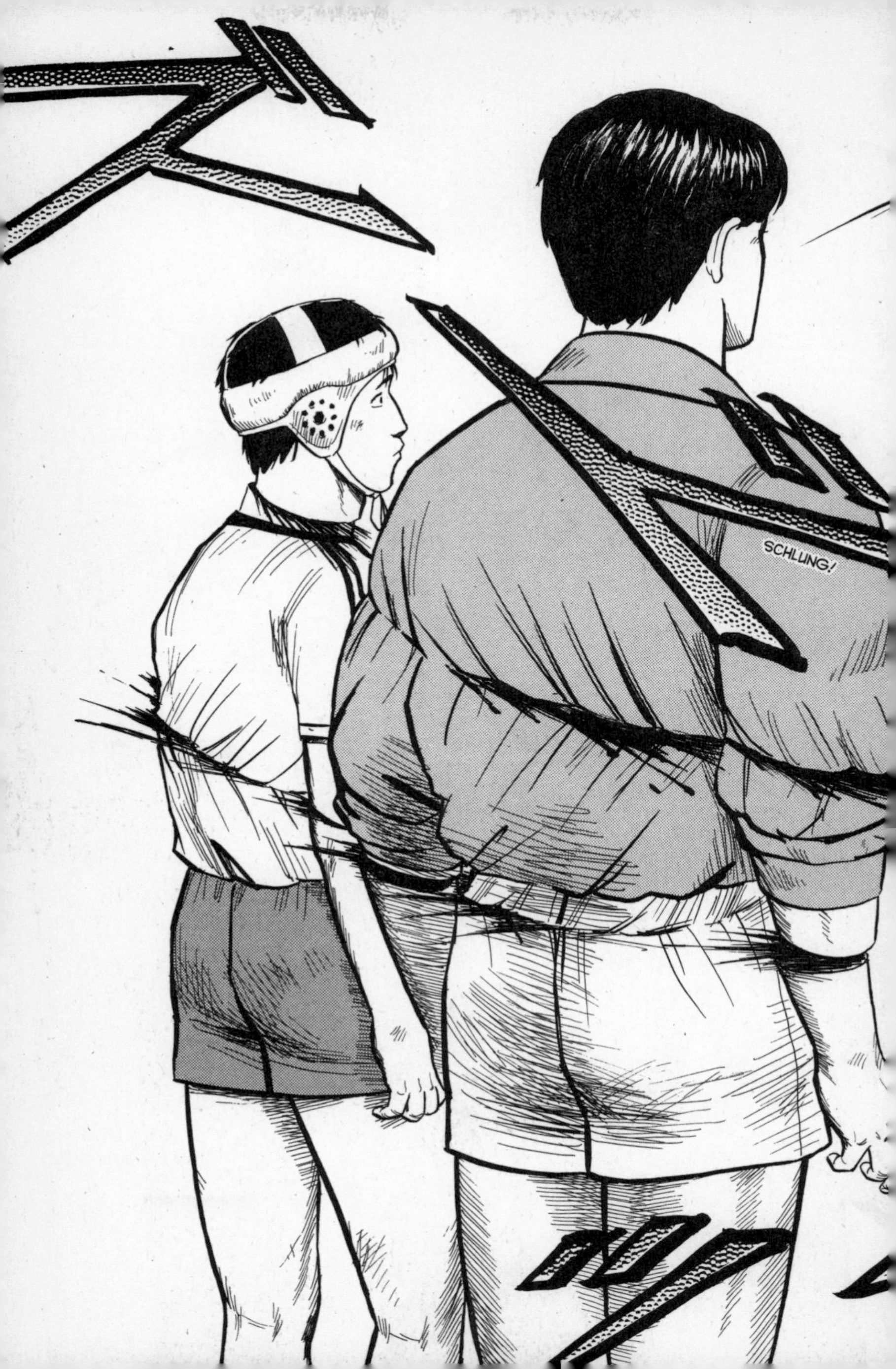
SCHLUNG!

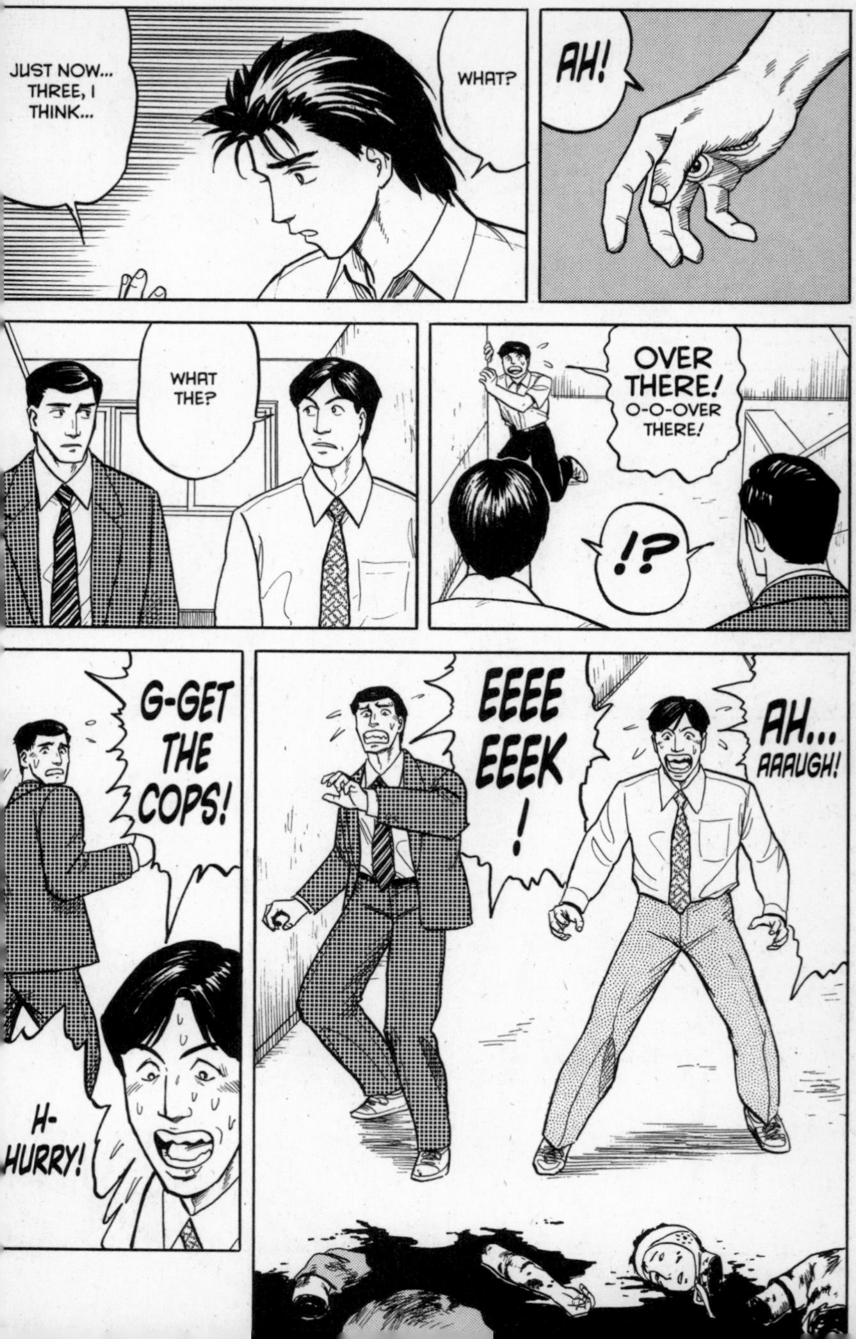
AH!
WHAT?
JUST NOW... THREE, I THINK...
OVER THERE! O-O-OVER THERE!
!?
WHAT THE?
AH... AAAUGH!
EEEE EEEK!
G-GET THE COPS!
H-HURRY!

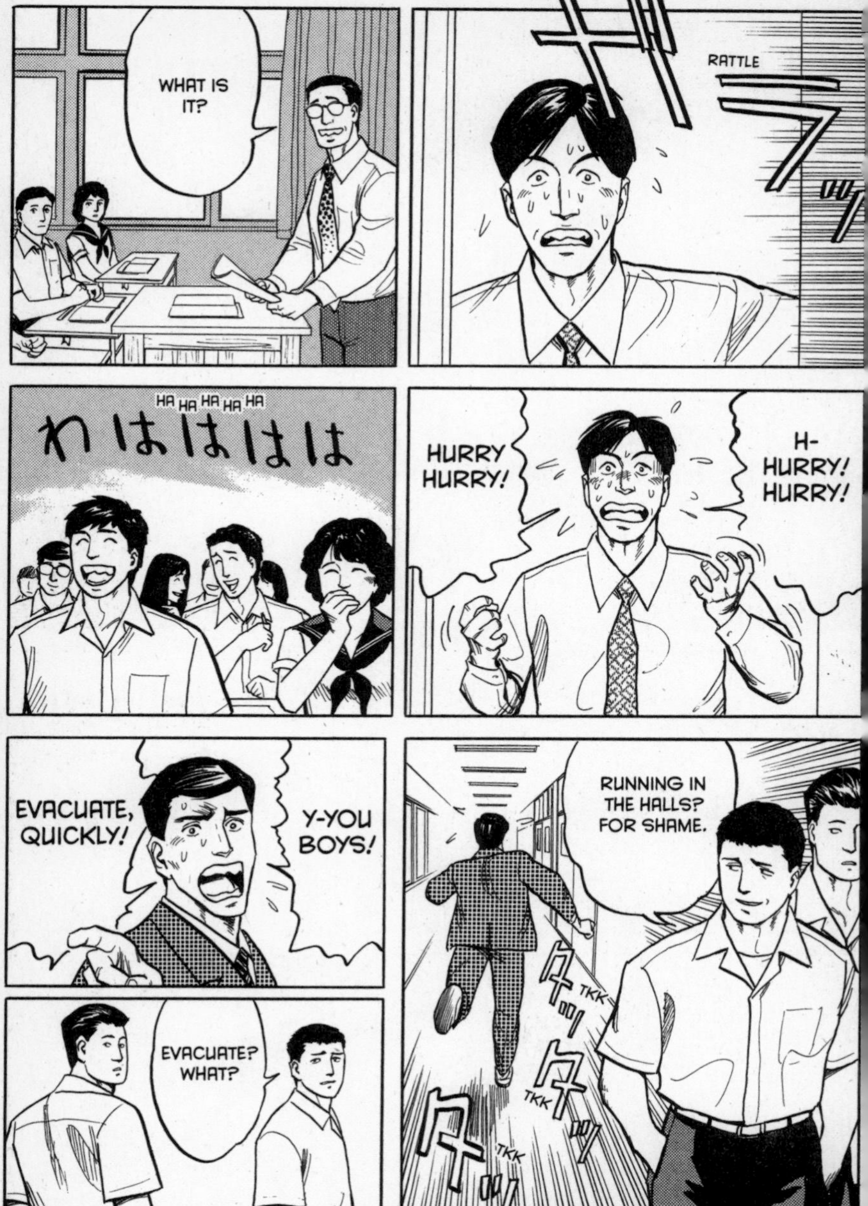

ガラッ
RATTLE
WHAT IS IT?
H-HURRY! HURRY!
HURRY HURRY!
わはははは
HA HA HA HA HA
RUNNING IN THE HALLS? FOR SHAME.
タッ
TKK
タッ
TKK
タッ
TKK
Y-YOU BOYS!
EVACUATE, QUICKLY!
EVACUATE? WHAT?

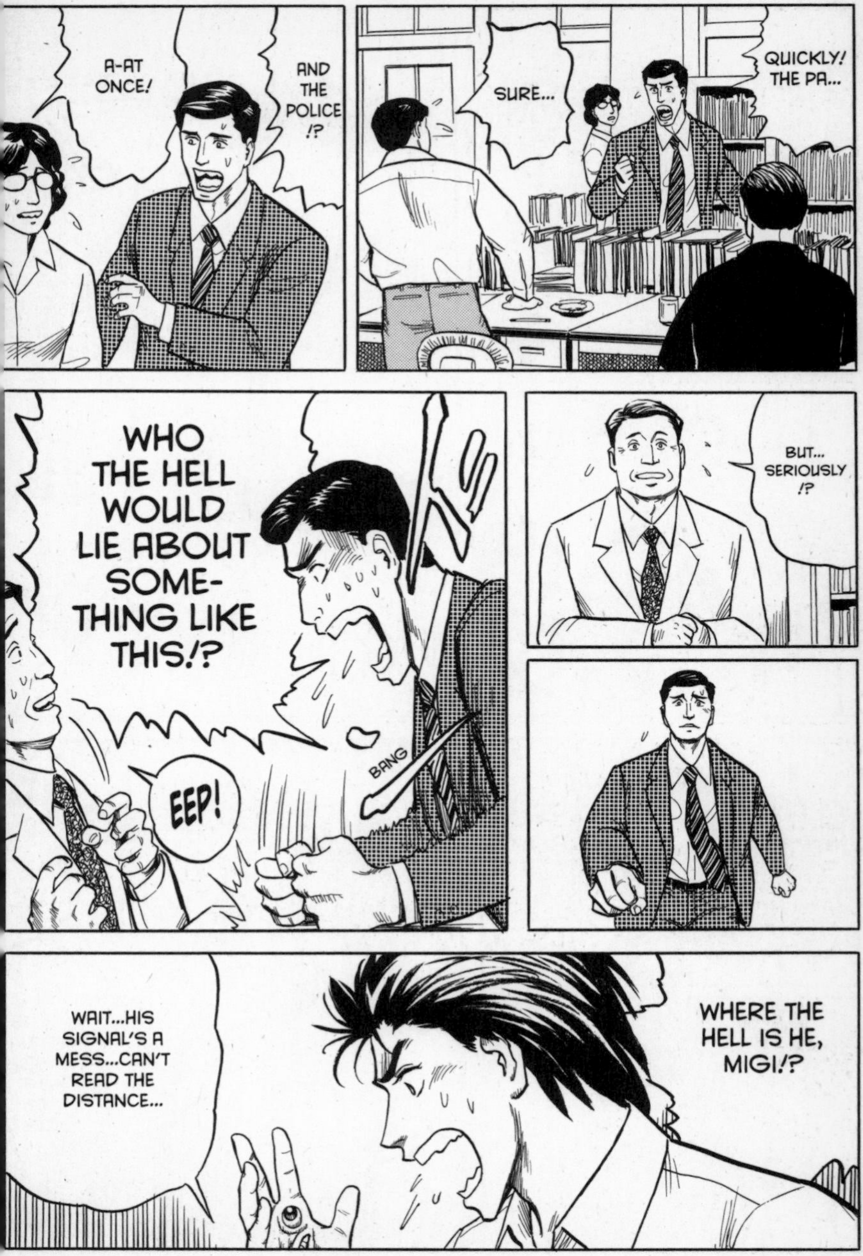
QUICKLY! THE PA...
SURE...
AND THE POLICE !?
A-AT ONCE!
BUT... SERIOUSLY !?
WHO THE HELL WOULD LIE ABOUT SOME-THING LIKE THIS!?
BANG
EEP!
WHERE THE HELL IS HE, MIGI!?
WAIT...HIS SIGNAL'S A MESS...CAN'T READ THE DISTANCE...

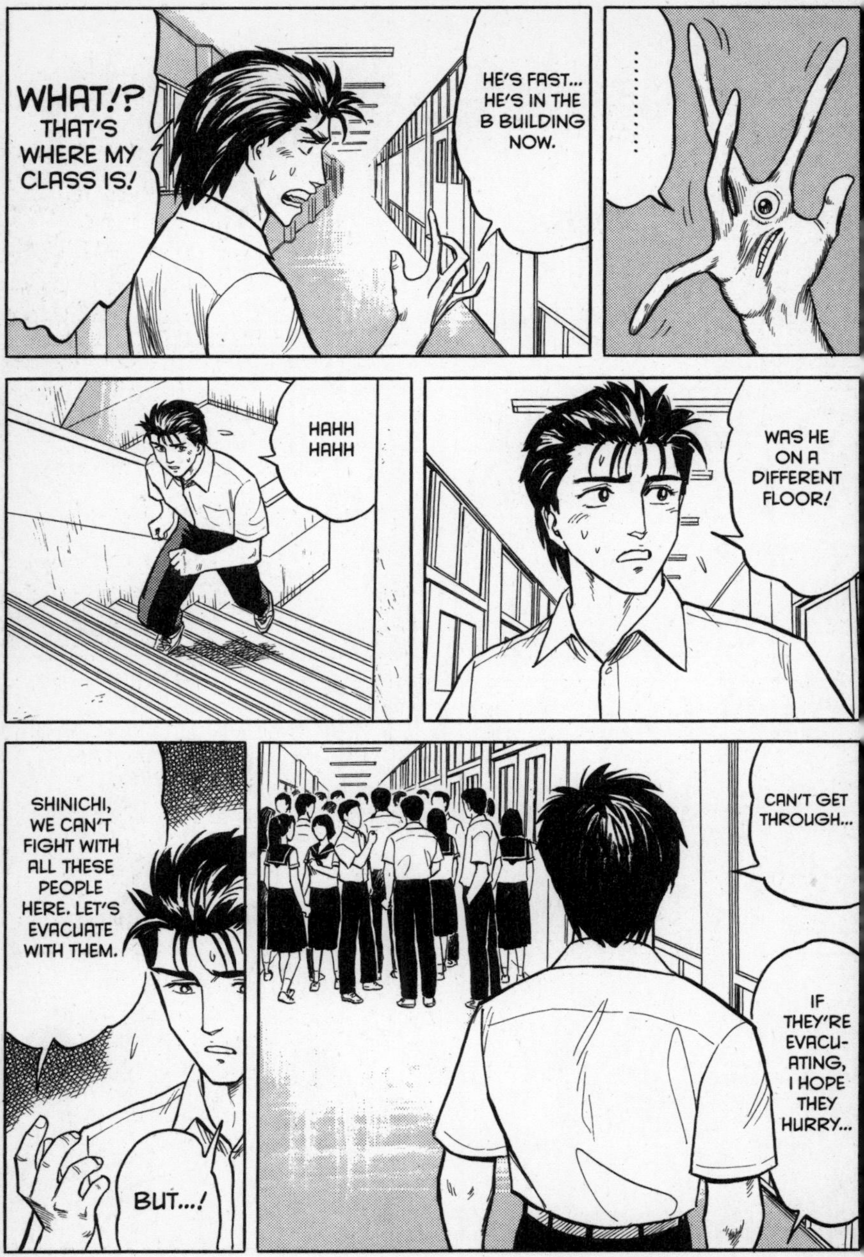
......
HE'S FAST... HE'S IN THE B BUILDING NOW.
WHAT!? THAT'S WHERE MY CLASS IS!
WAS HE ON A DIFFERENT FLOOR!
HAHH HAHH
CAN'T GET THROUGH...
IF THEY'RE EVACU-ATING, I HOPE THEY HURRY...
SHINICHI, WE CAN'T FIGHT WITH ALL THESE PEOPLE HERE. LET'S EVACUATE WITH THEM.
BUT...!

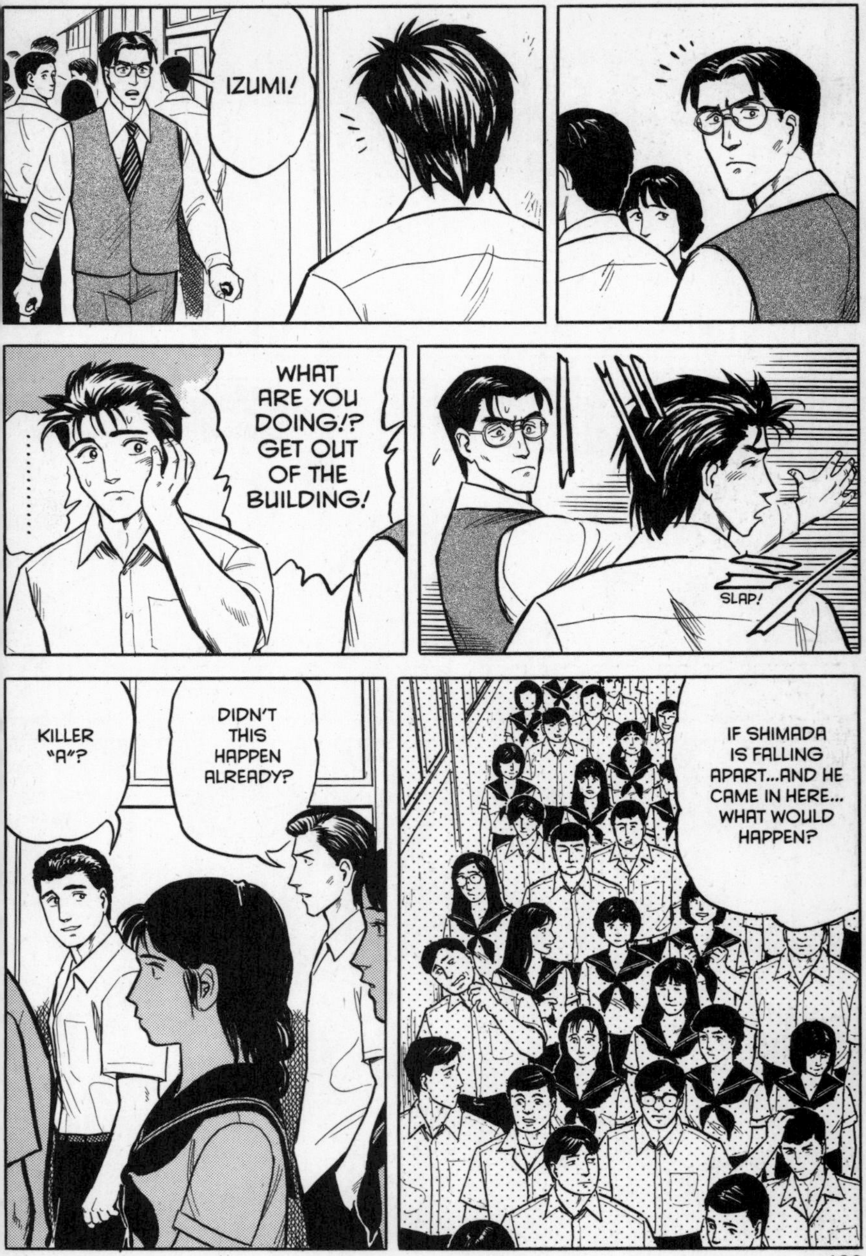
IZUMI!
SLAP!
WHAT ARE YOU DOING!? GET OUT OF THE BUILDING!
......
IF SHIMADA IS FALLING APART...AND HE CAME IN HERE... WHAT WOULD HAPPEN?
DIDN'T THIS HAPPEN ALREADY?
KILLER "A"?

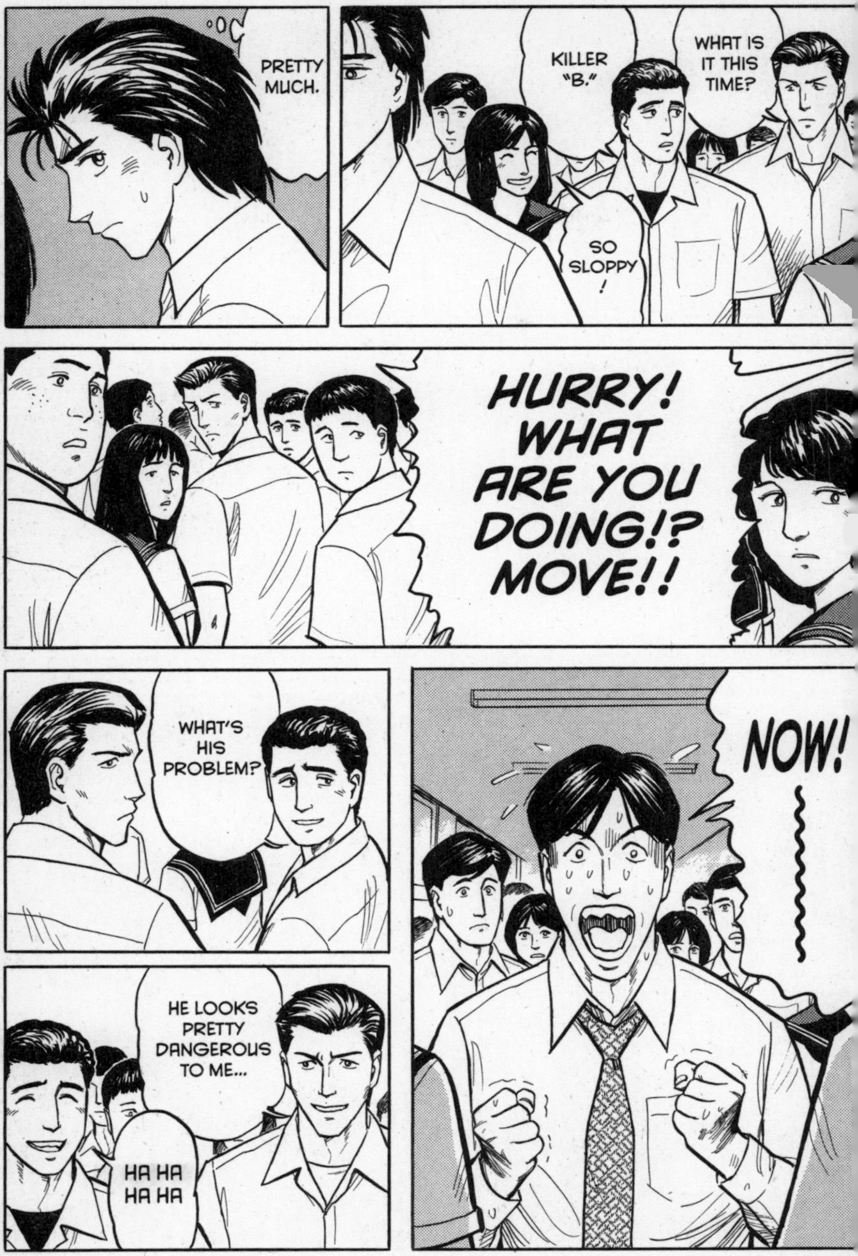
WHAT IS IT THIS TIME?
KILLER "B."
SO SLOPPY!
PRETTY MUCH.
HURRY! WHAT ARE YOU DOING!? MOVE!!
NOW!
WHAT'S HIS PROBLEM?
HE LOOKS PRETTY DANGEROUS TO ME...
HA HA HA HA

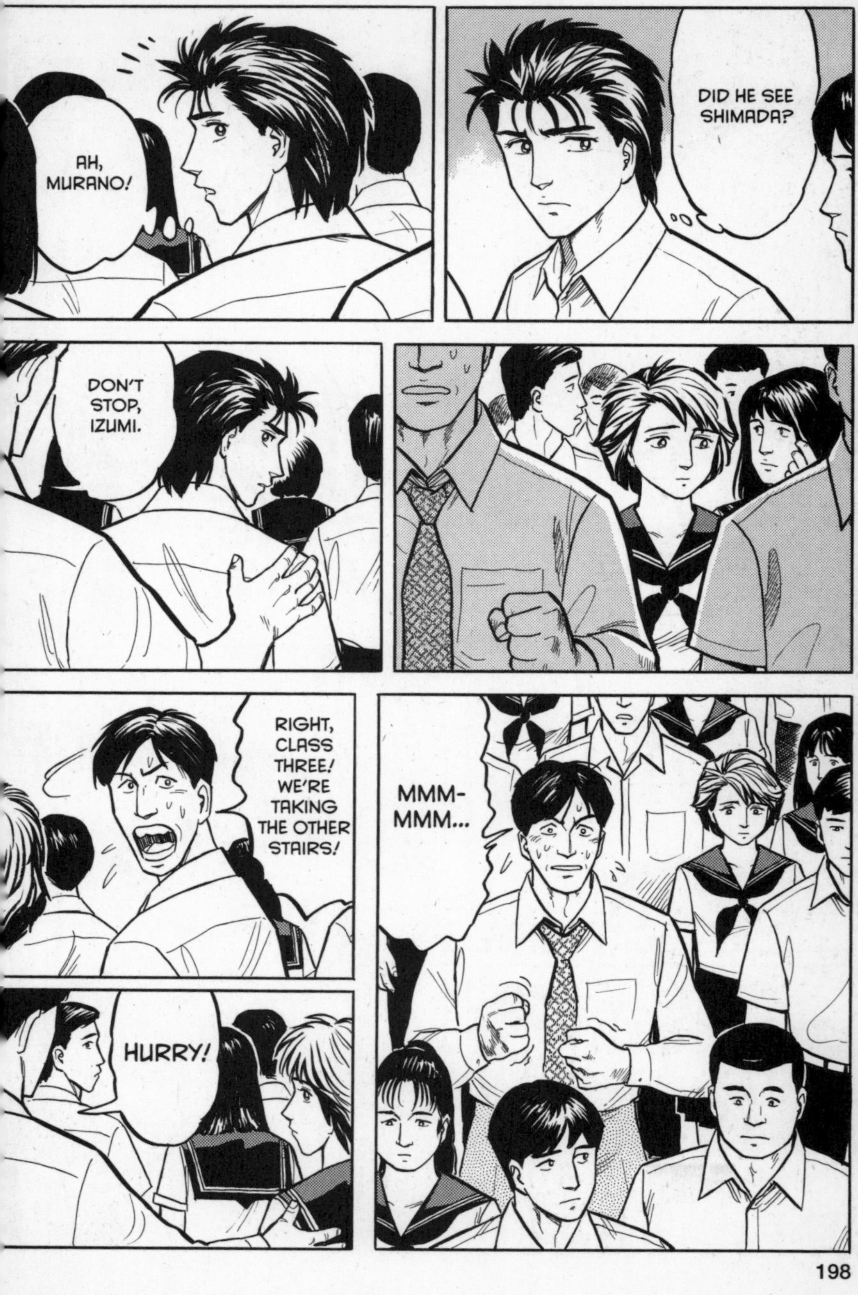
DID HE SEE SHIMADA?
AH, MURANO!
DON'T STOP, IZUMI.
MMM-MMM...
RIGHT, CLASS THREE! WE'RE TAKING THE OTHER STAIRS!
HURRY!

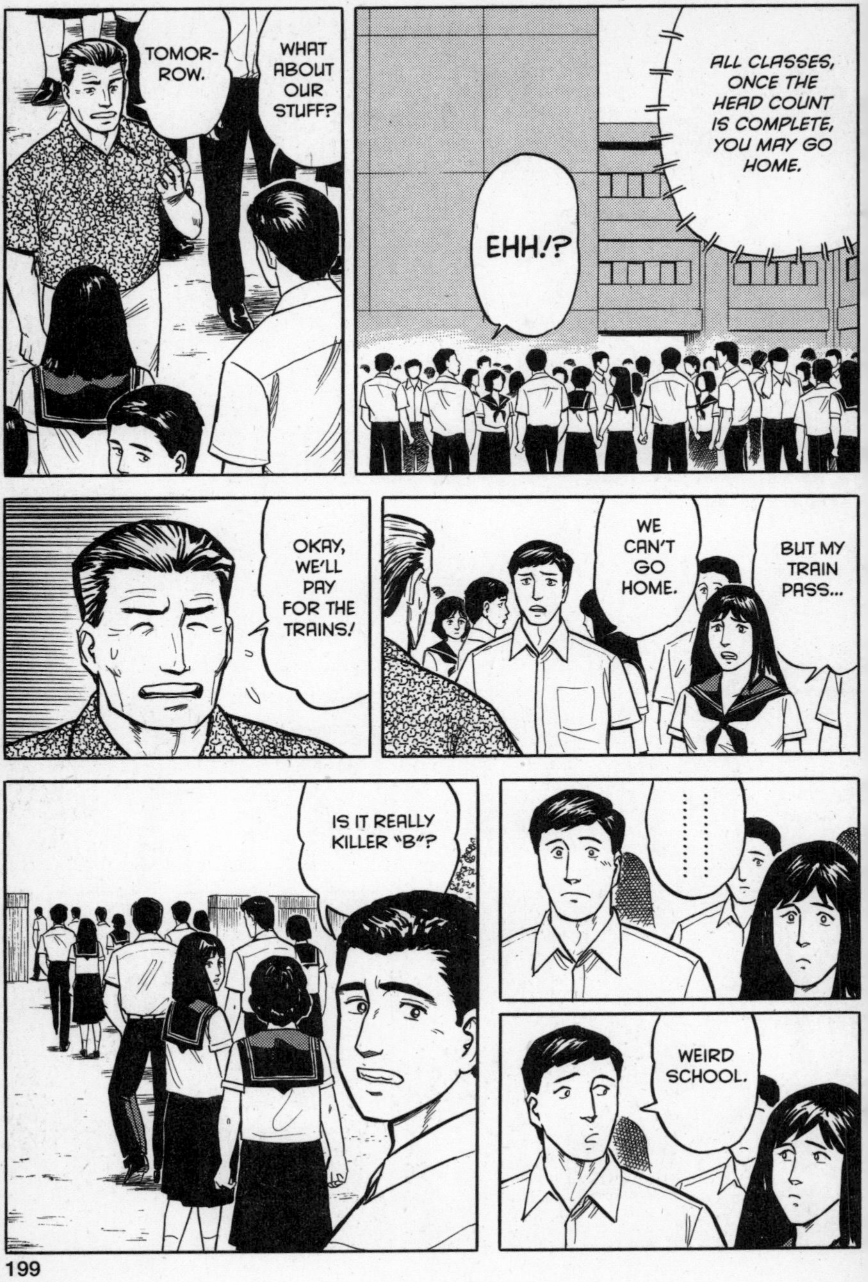
ALL CLASSES, ONCE THE HEAD COUNT IS COMPLETE, YOU MAY GO HOME.
EHH!?
WHAT ABOUT OUR STUFF?
TOMOR-ROW.
BUT MY TRAIN PASS...
WE CAN'T GO HOME.
OKAY, WE'LL PAY FOR THE TRAINS!
......
WEIRD SCHOOL.
IS IT REALLY KILLER "B"?

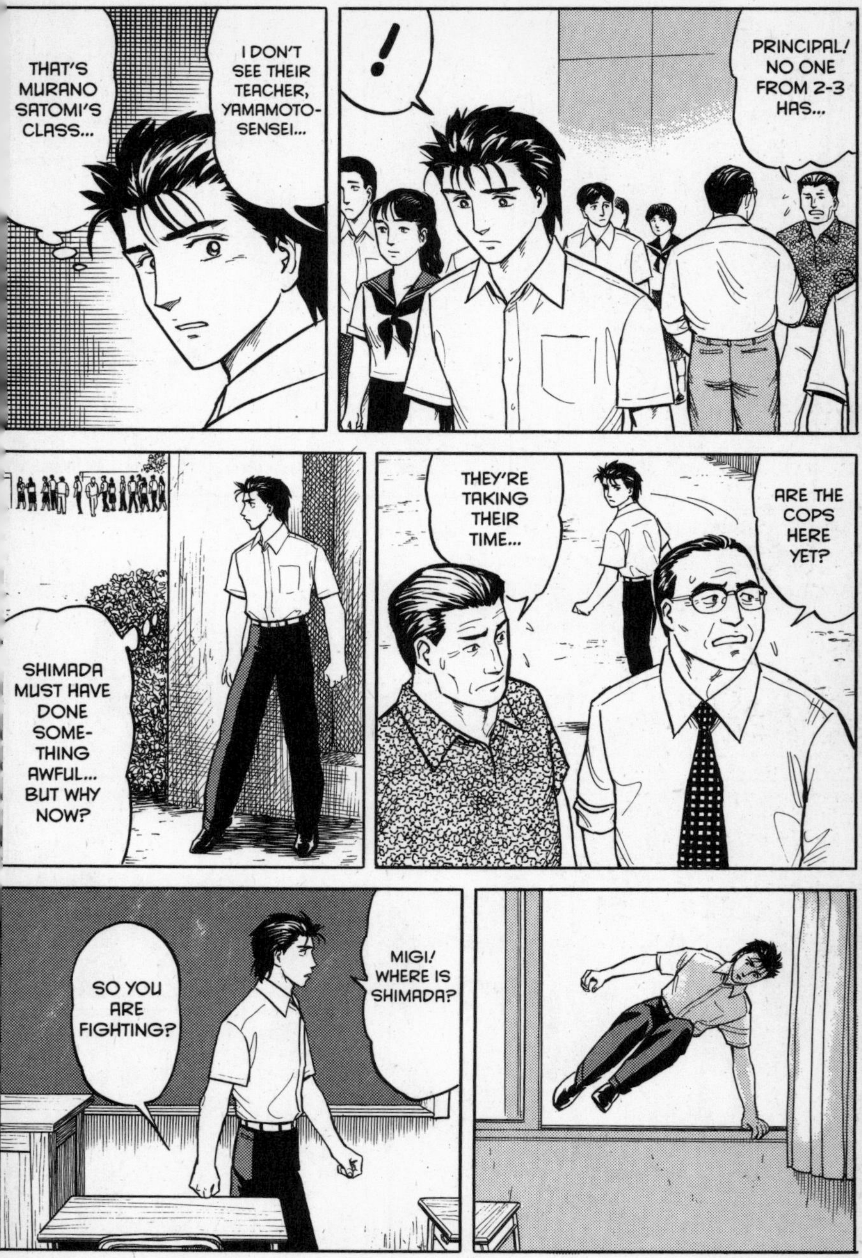
PRINCIPAL! NO ONE FROM 2-3 HAS...
!
I DON'T SEE THEIR TEACHER, YAMAMOTO-SENSEI...
THAT'S MURANO SATOMI'S CLASS...
ARE THE COPS HERE YET?
THEY'RE TAKING THEIR TIME...
SHIMADA MUST HAVE DONE SOME-THING AWFUL... BUT WHY NOW?
MIGI! WHERE IS SHIMADA?
SO YOU ARE FIGHTING?

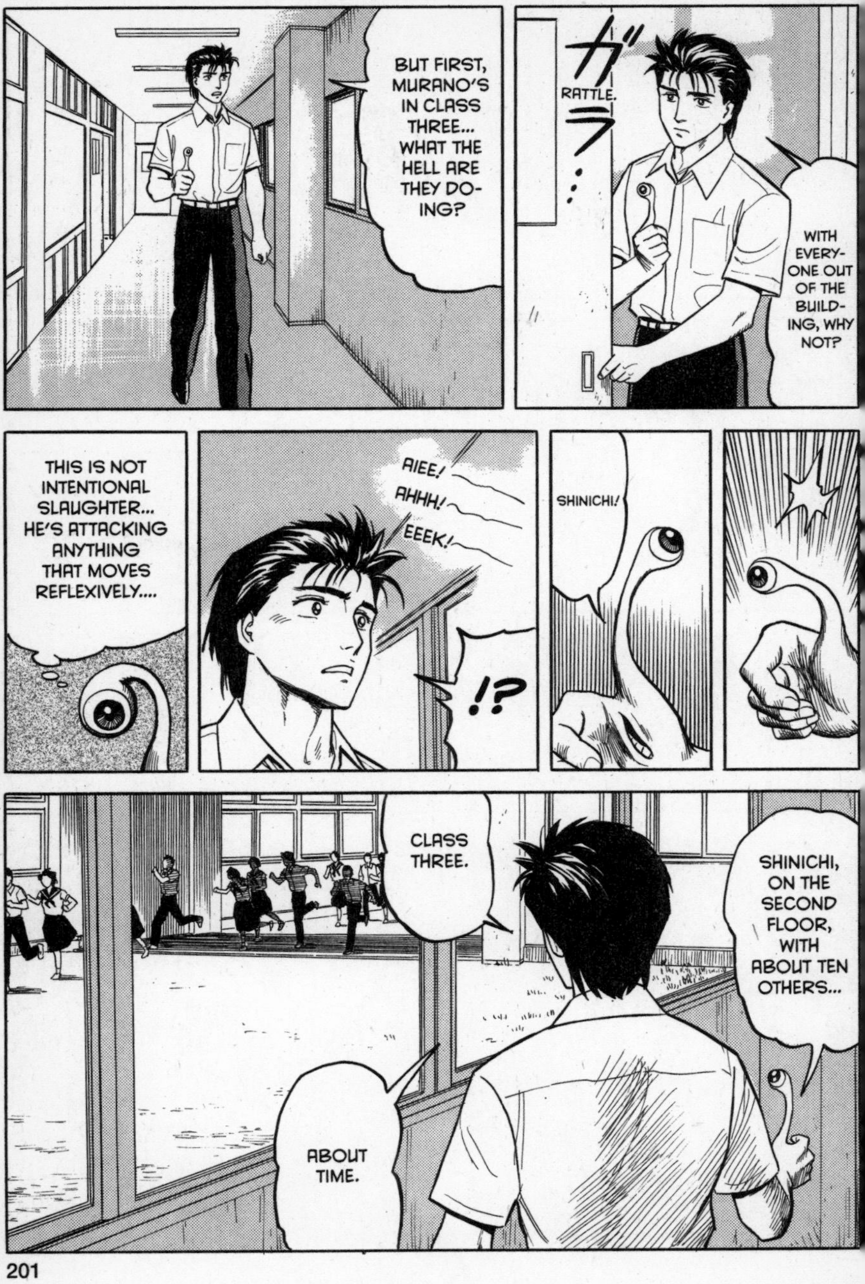

ガラ...
RATTLE.
WITH EVERYONE OUT OF THE BUILDING, WHY NOT?
BUT FIRST, MURANO'S IN CLASS THREE... WHAT THE HELL ARE THEY DOING?
SHINICHI!
AIEE!
AHHH!
EEEK!
!?
THIS IS NOT INTENTIONAL SLAUGHTER... HE'S ATTACKING ANYTHING THAT MOVES REFLEXIVELY....
SHINICHI, ON THE SECOND FLOOR, WITH ABOUT TEN OTHERS...
CLASS THREE.
ABOUT TIME.

UH-
OH.

BUT
NOT
HERE.

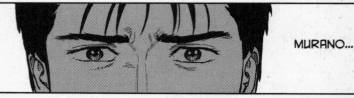

MURANO...

SORRY...I
THOUGHT
YOU WERE
SOMEONE
ELSE.

SHUT
UP!!

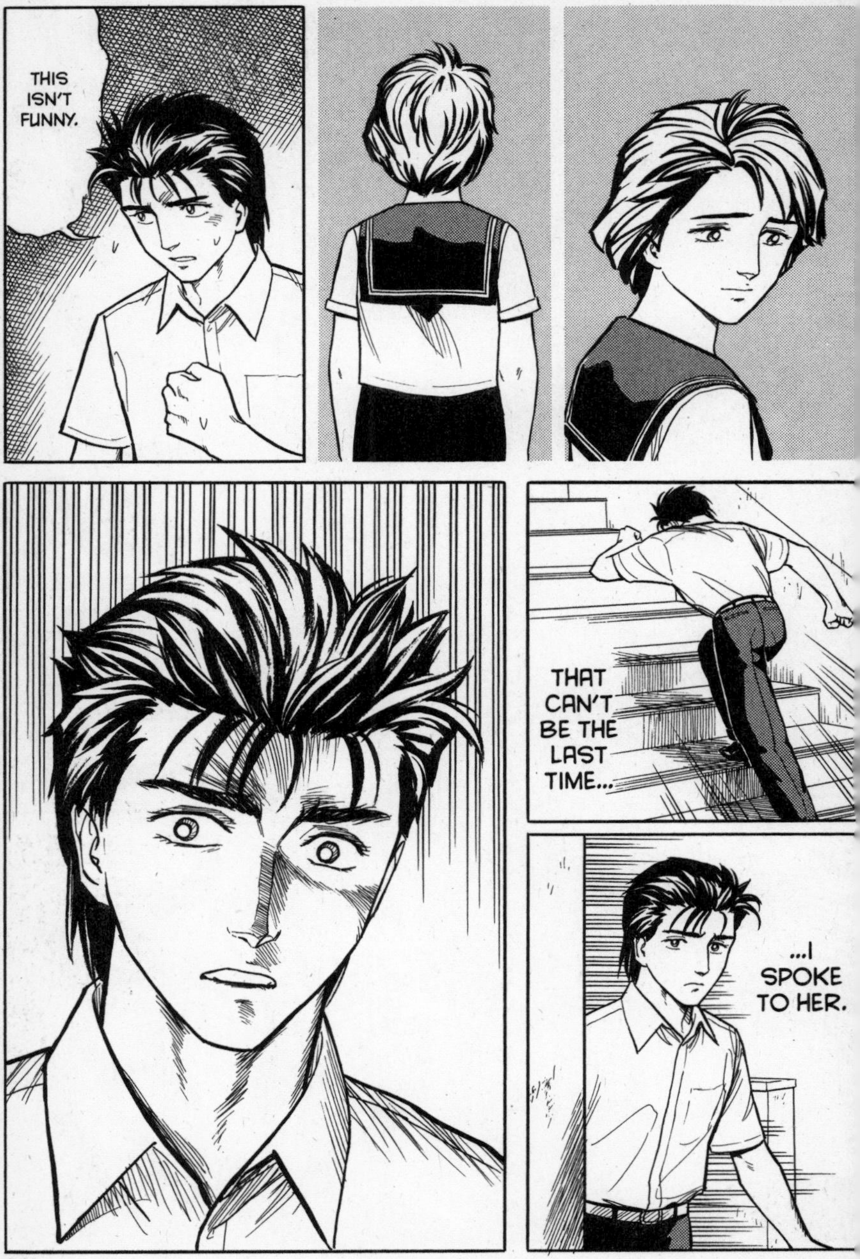
THIS ISN'T FUNNY.
THAT CAN'T BE THE LAST TIME...
...I SPOKE TO HER.

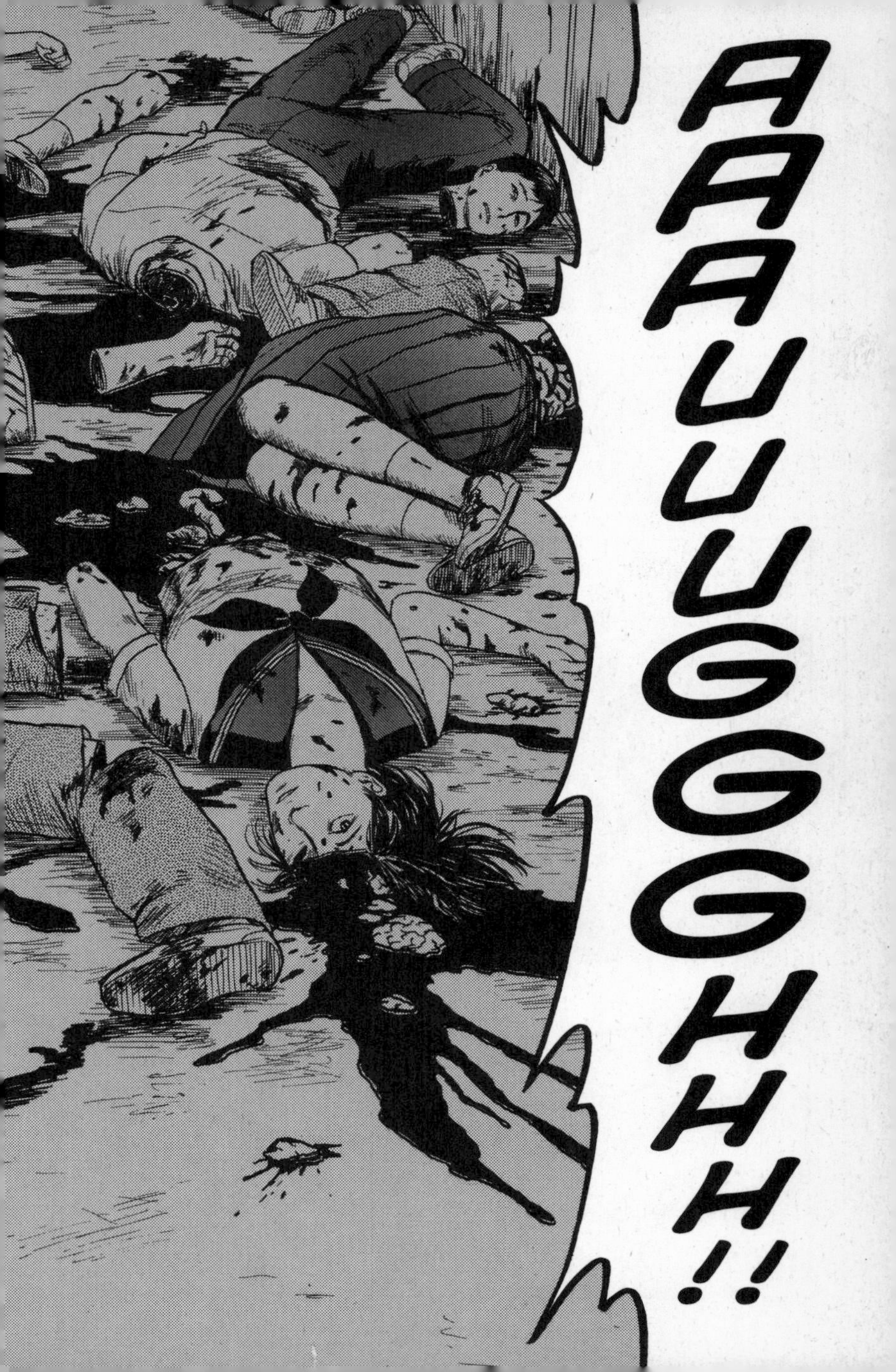
AAAUUUGGGHHH!!

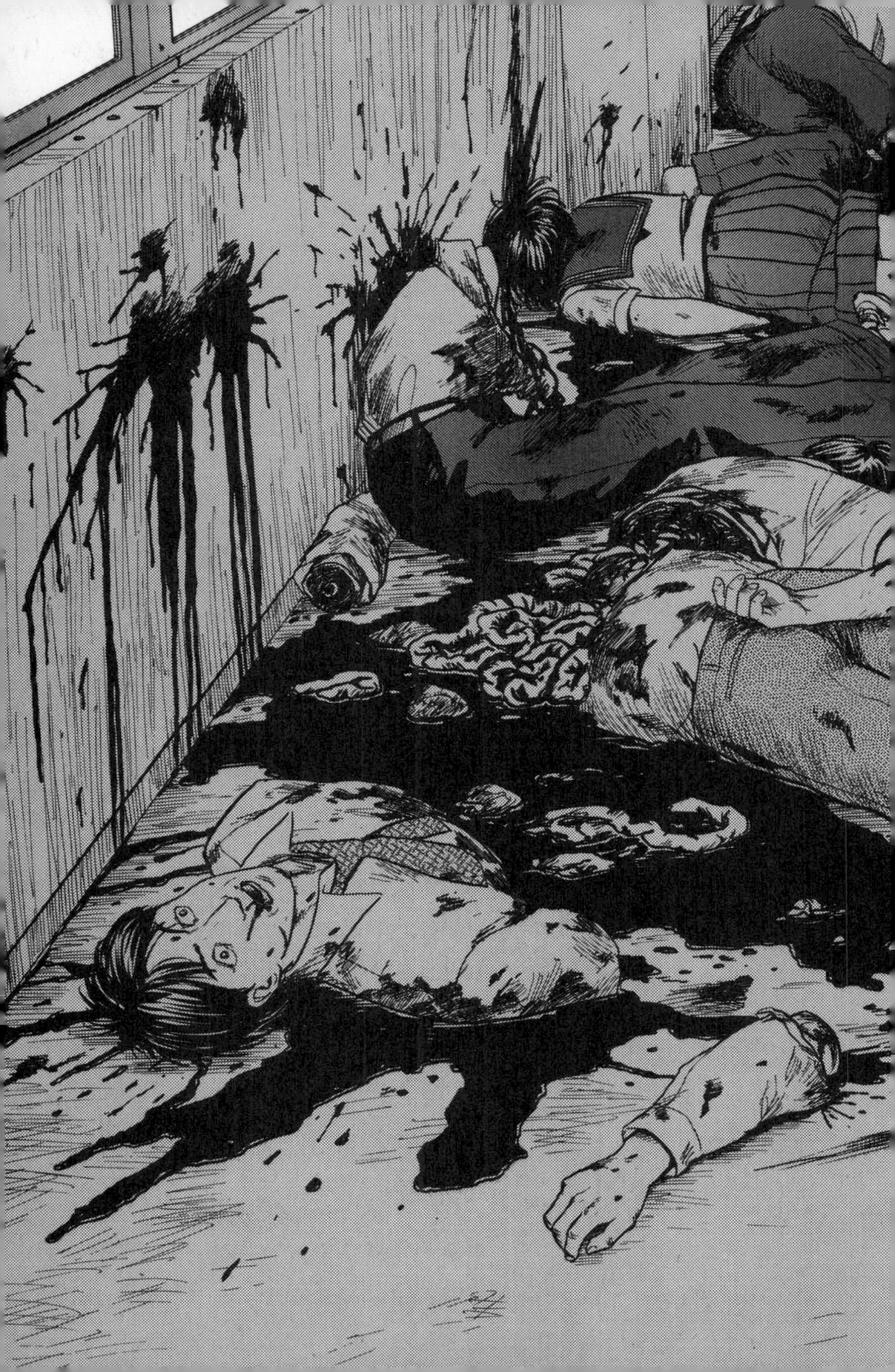

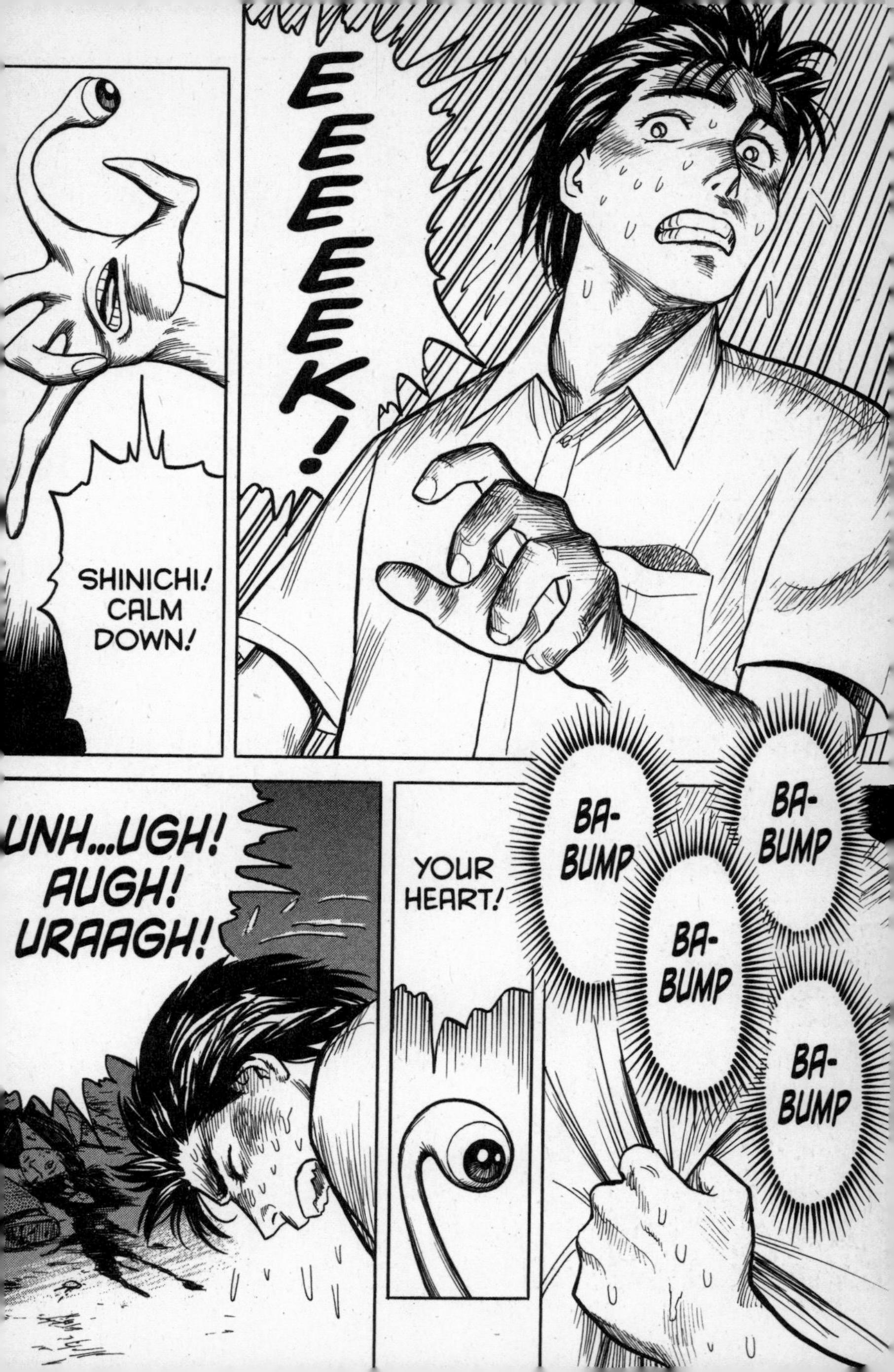
EEEEEK!
SHINICHI! CALM DOWN!
BA-BUMP
BA-BUMP
BA-BUMP
BA-BUMP
YOUR HEART!
UNH...UGH! AUGH! URAAGH!

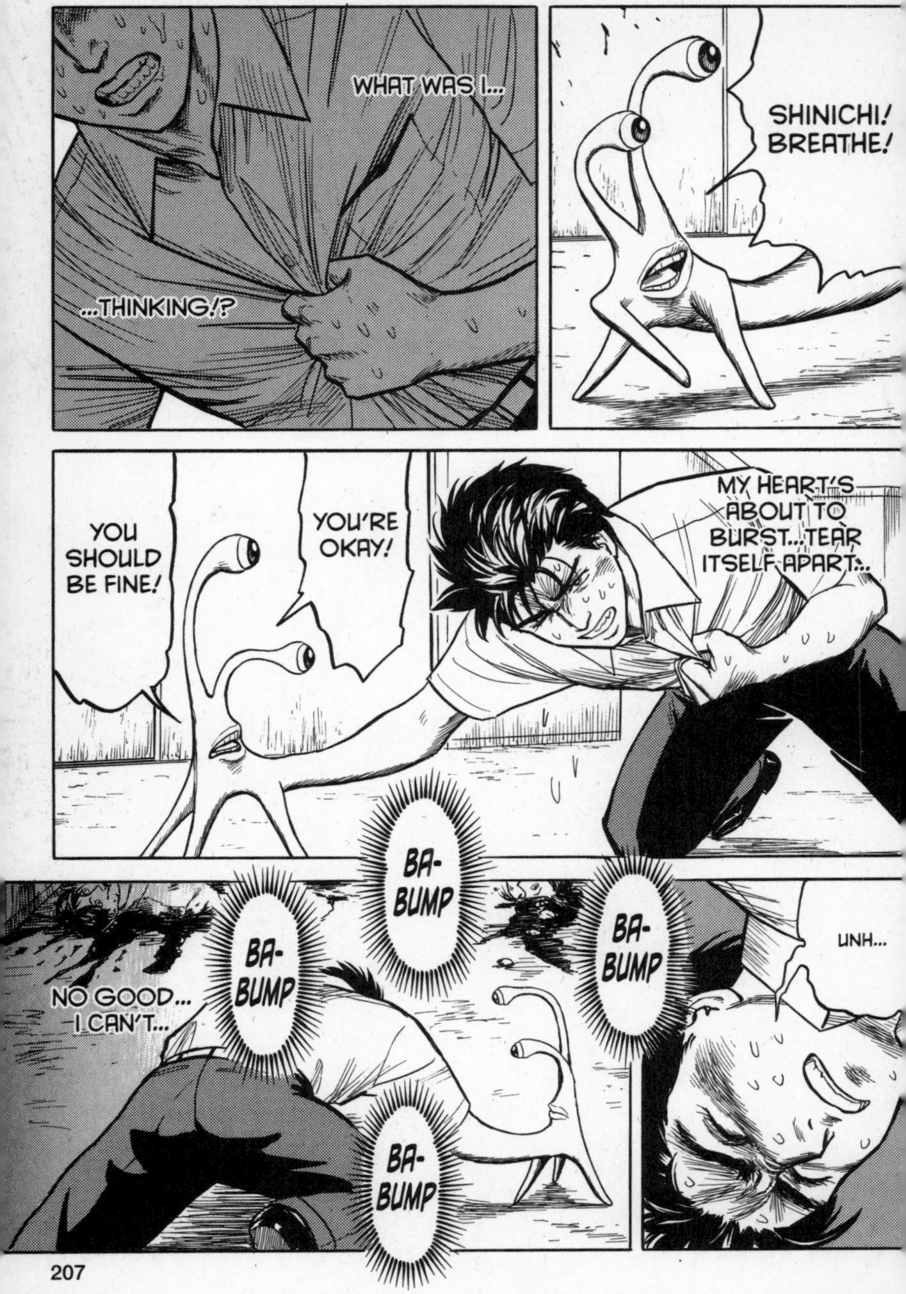
SHINICHI! BREATHE!
WHAT WAS I...
...THINKING!?
MY HEART'S ABOUT TO BURST... TEAR ITSELF APART...
YOU'RE OKAY!
YOU SHOULD BE FINE!
UNH...
BA-BUMP
BA-BUMP
BA-BUMP
BA-BUMP
NO GOOD... I CAN'T...

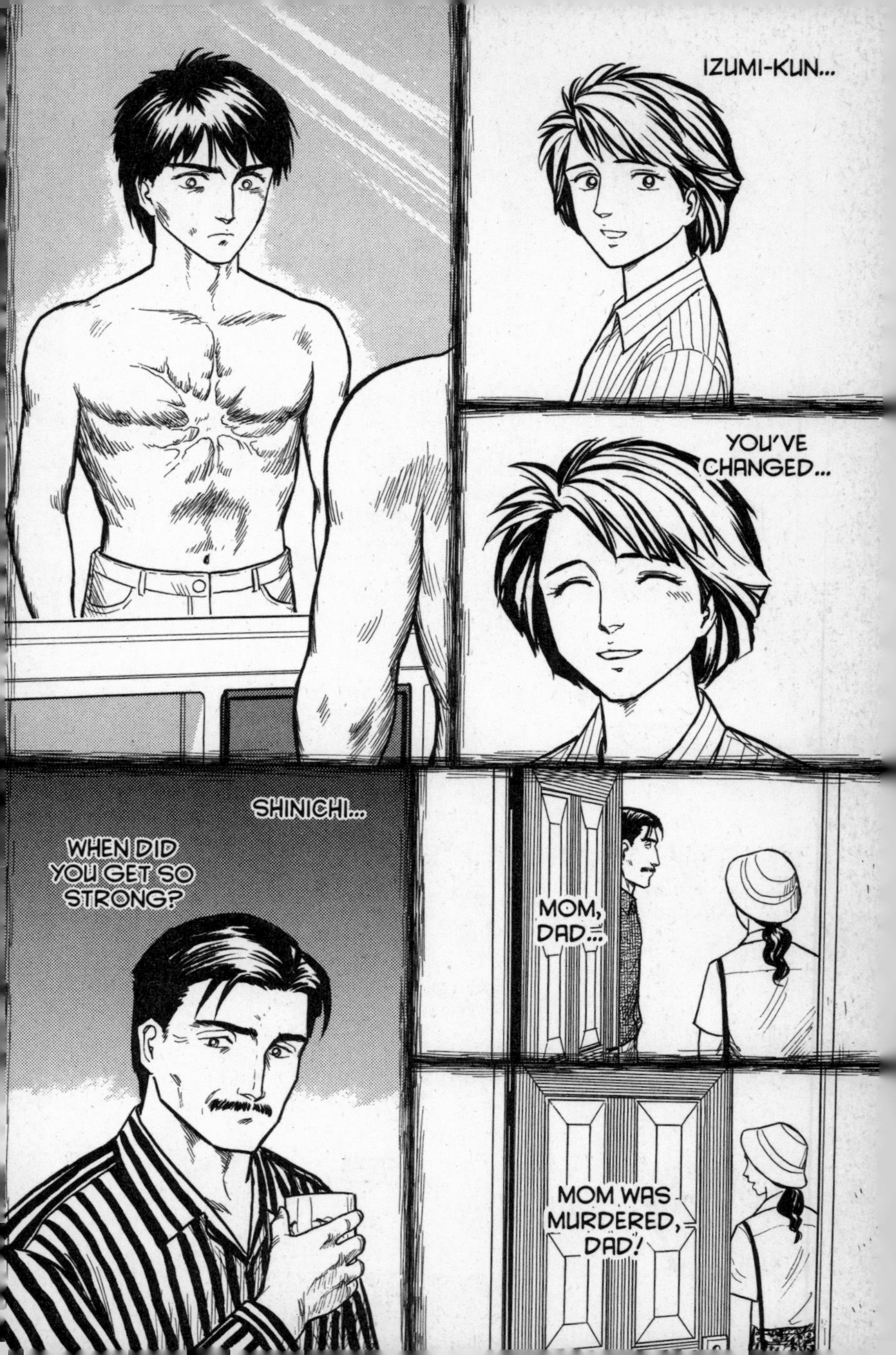
IZUMI-KUN...
YOU'VE CHANGED...
MOM, DAD...
MOM WAS MURDERED, DAD!
SHINICHI...
WHEN DID YOU GET SO STRONG?

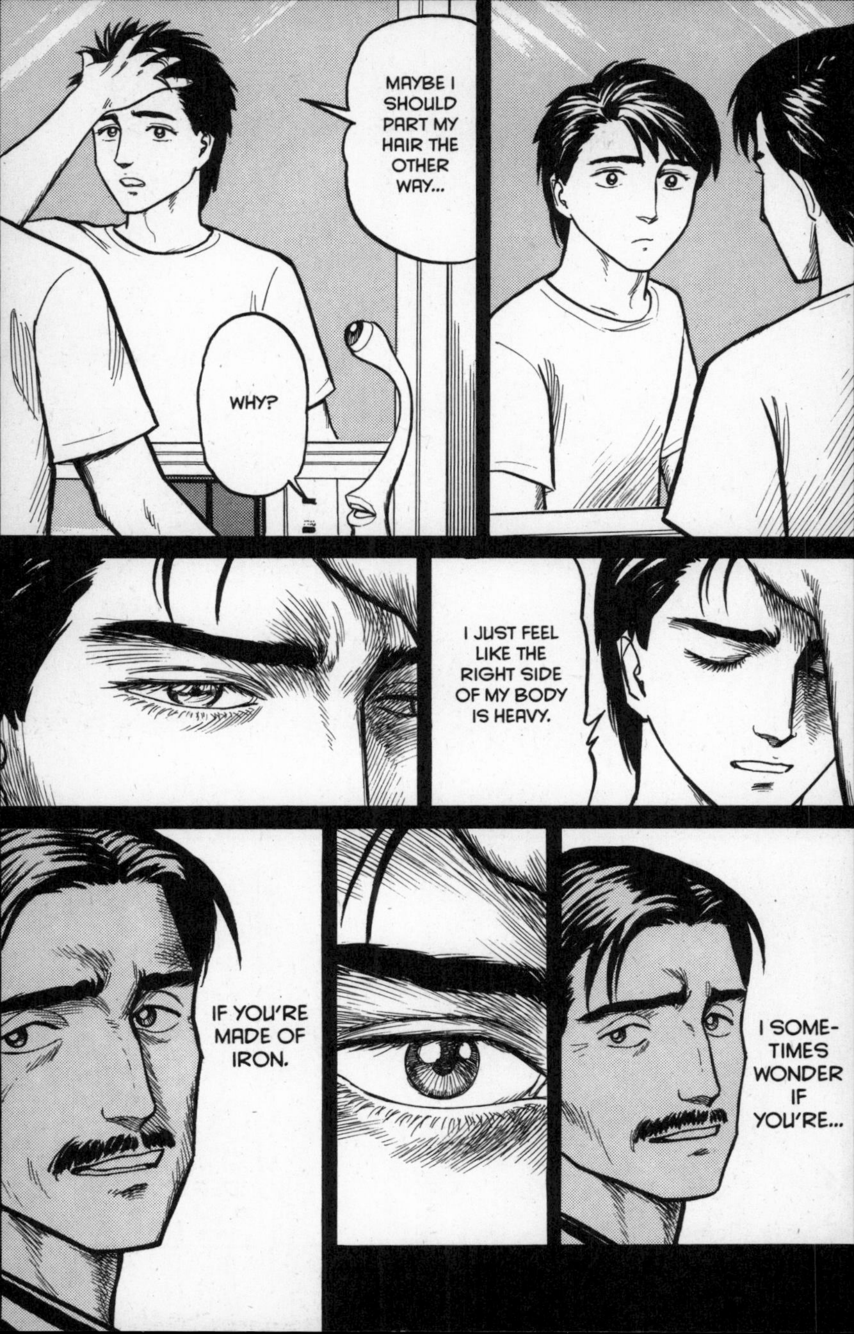
MAYBE I SHOULD PART MY HAIR THE OTHER WAY...
WHY?
I JUST FEEL LIKE THE RIGHT SIDE OF MY BODY IS HEAVY.
I SOME-TIMES WONDER IF YOU'RE...
IF YOU'RE MADE OF IRON.

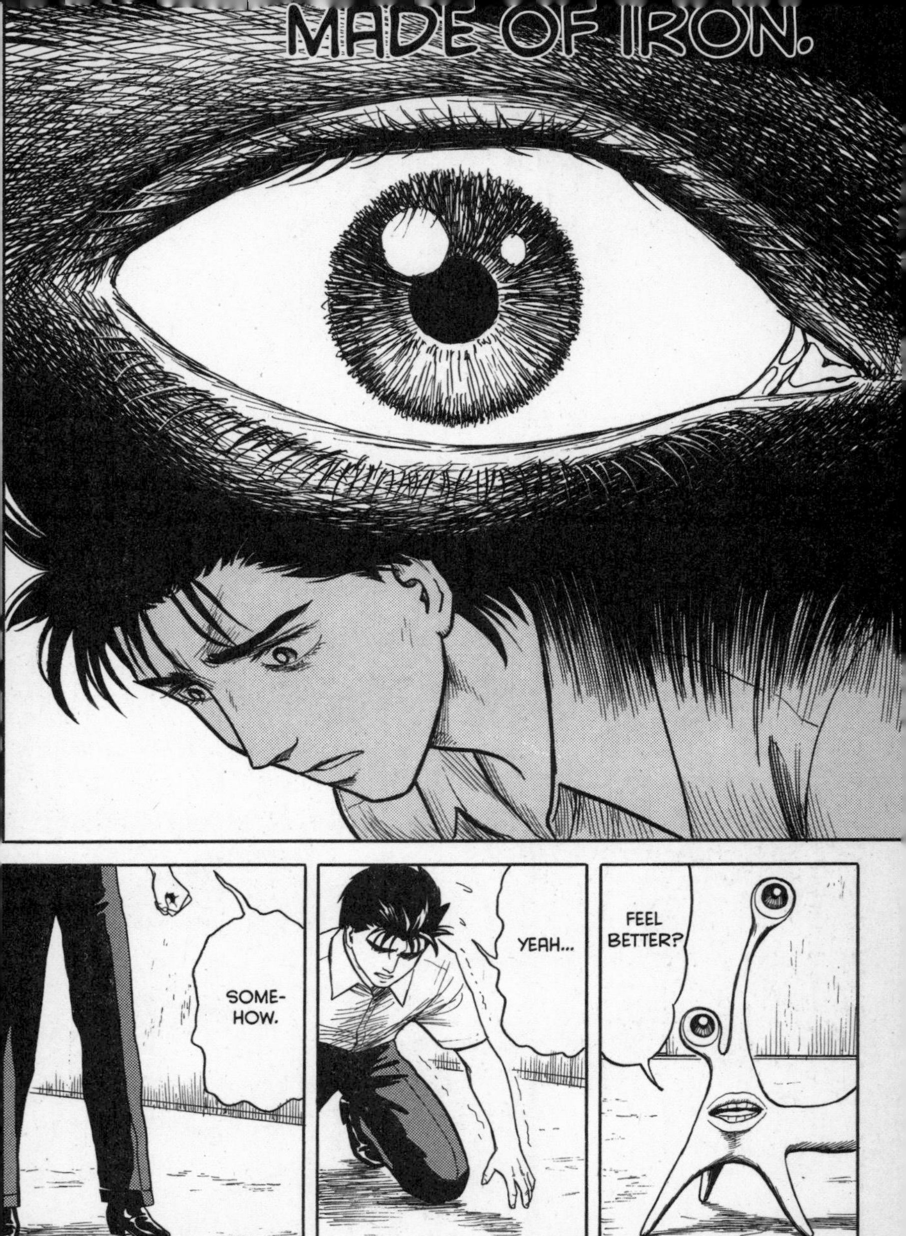

MADE OF IRON.

SOME-
HOW.

YEAH...

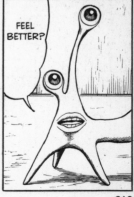

FEEL
BETTER?

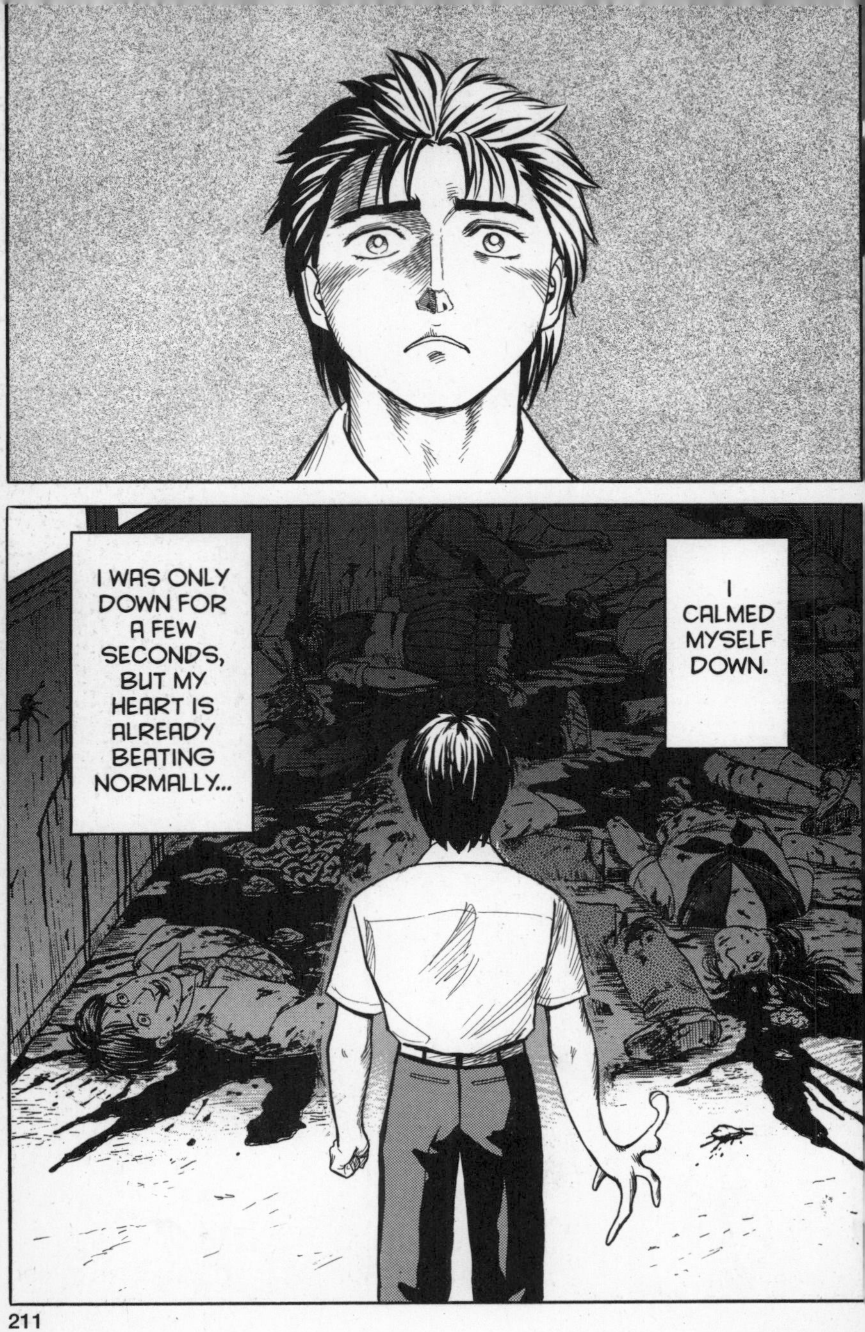
I CALMED MYSELF DOWN.
I WAS ONLY DOWN FOR A FEW SECONDS, BUT MY HEART IS ALREADY BEATING NORMALLY...

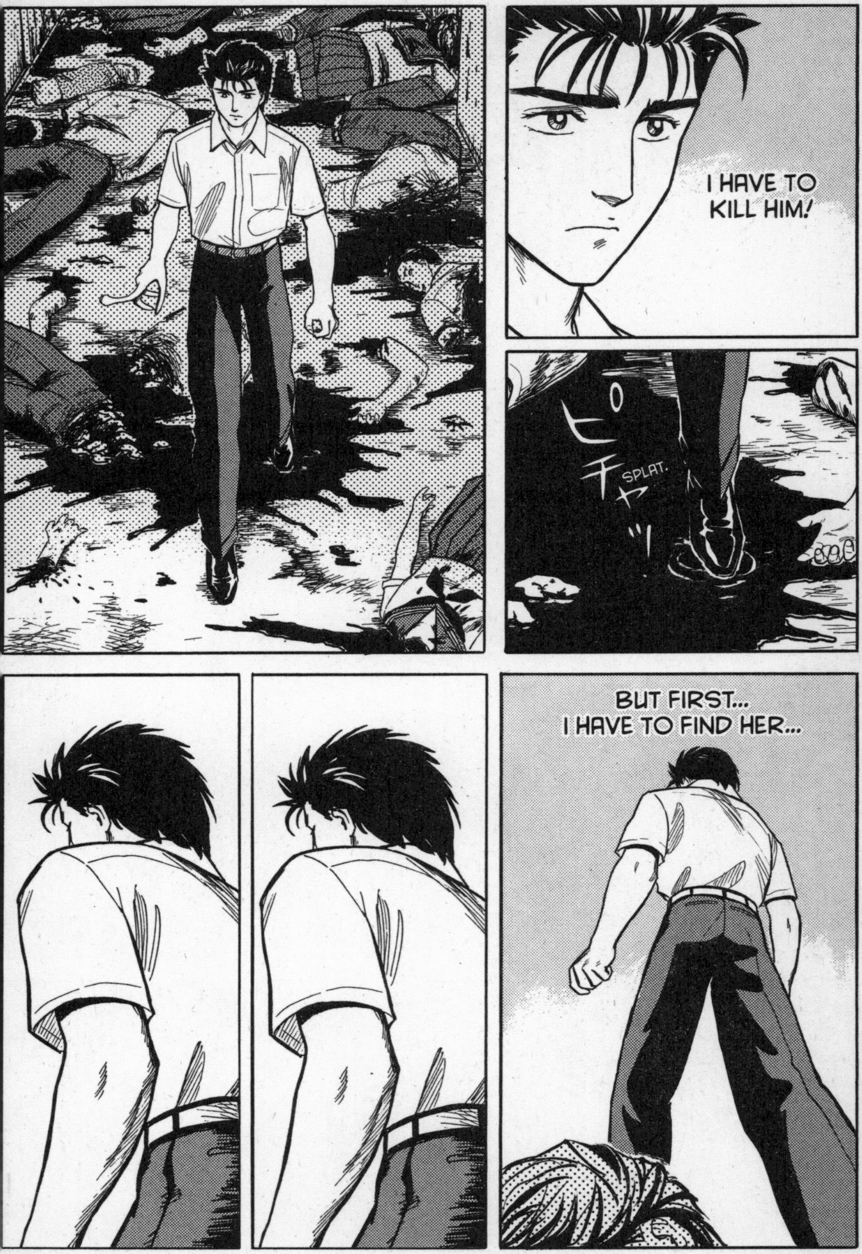
I HAVE TO
KILL HIM!
ピチャッ
SPLAT.
BUT FIRST...
I HAVE TO FIND HER...

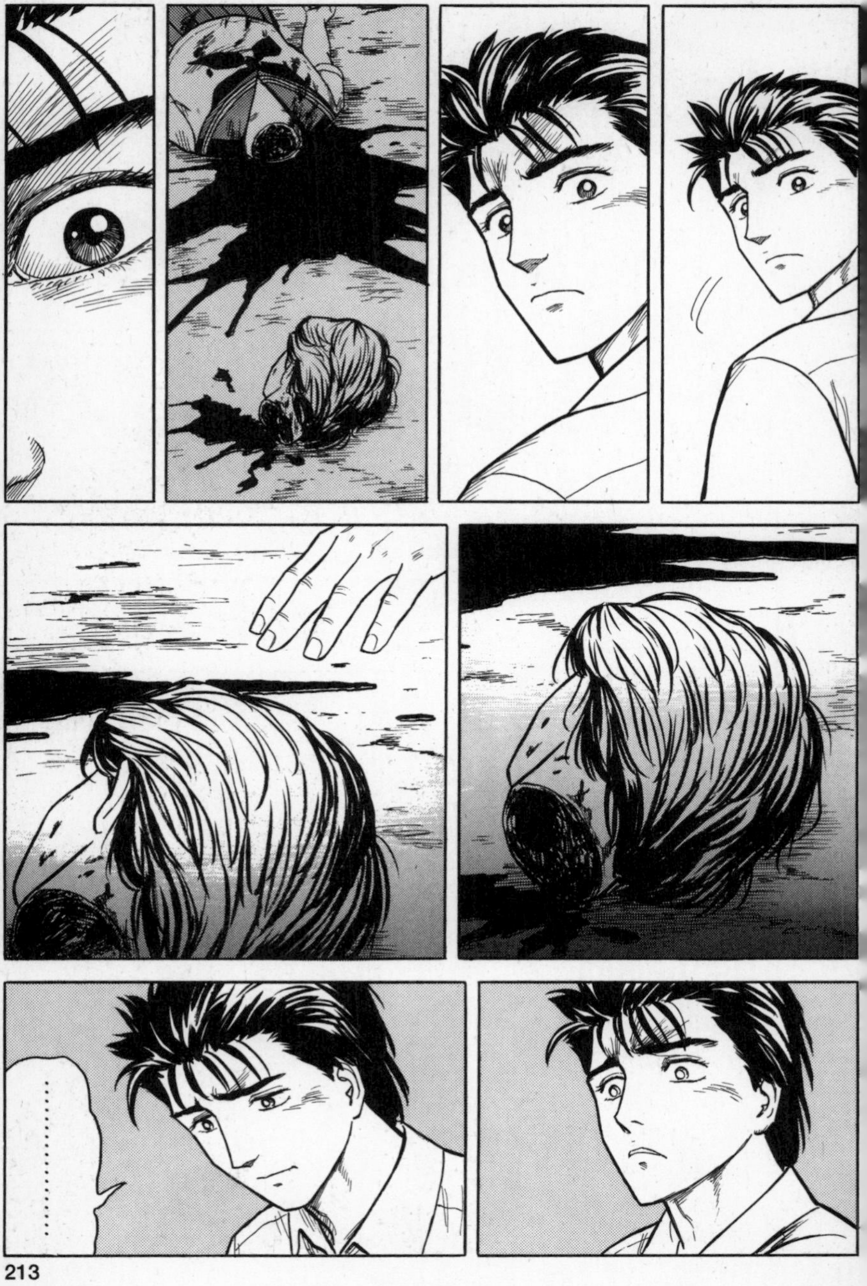
……

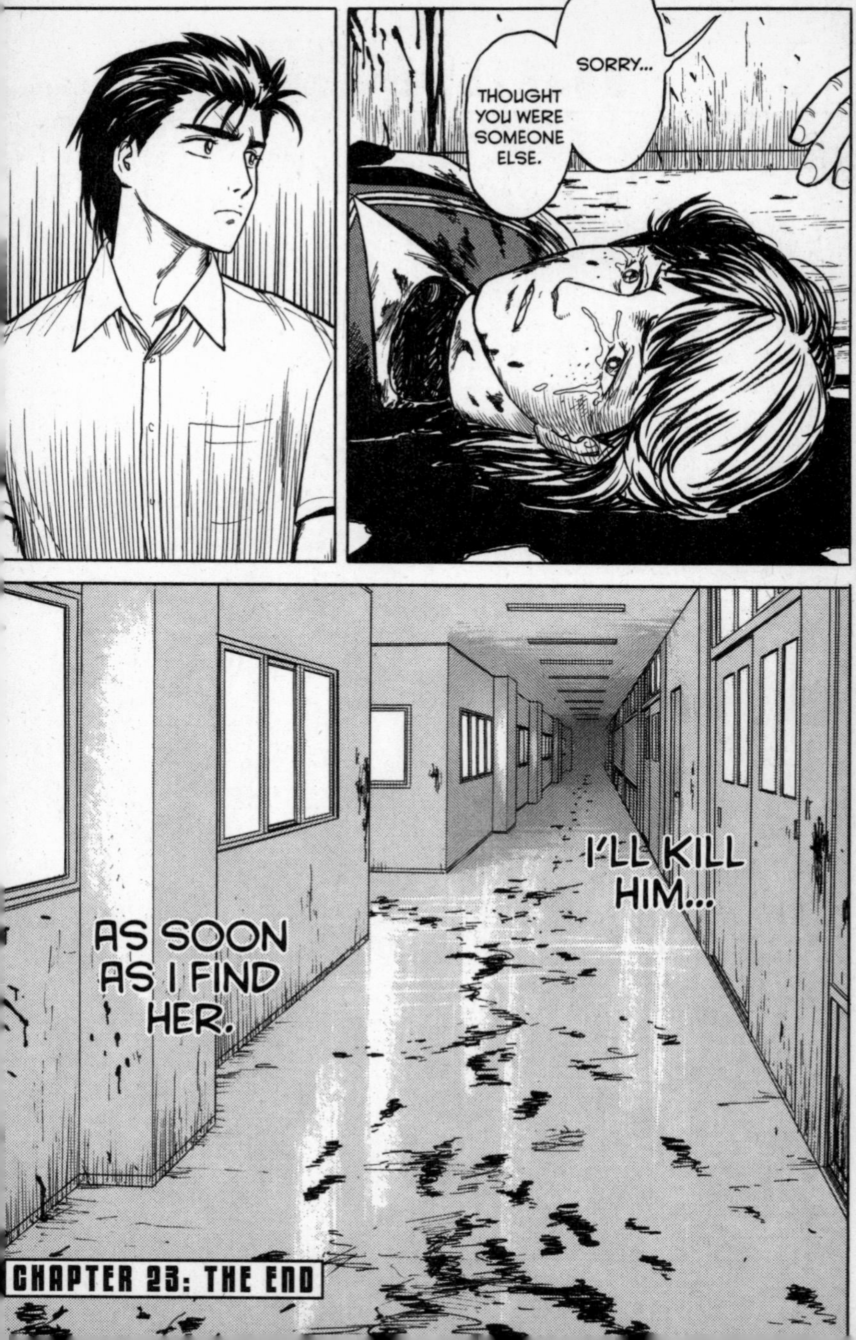
SORRY... THOUGHT YOU WERE SOMEONE ELSE.
I'LL KILL HIM...
AS SOON AS I FIND HER.
CHAPTER 23: THE END

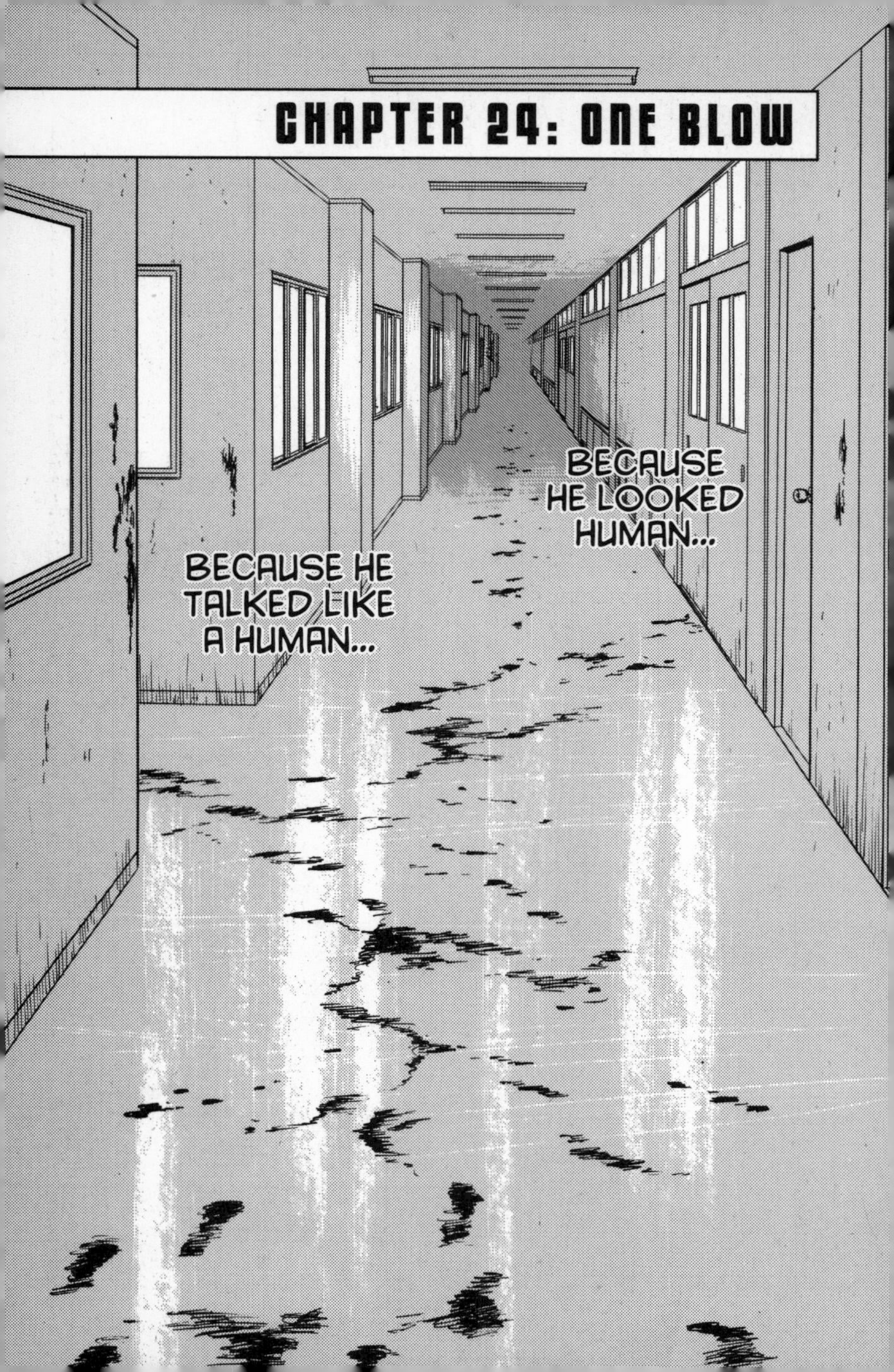
CHAPTER 24: ONE BLOW
BECAUSE HE LOOKED HUMAN...
BECAUSE HE TALKED LIKE A HUMAN...

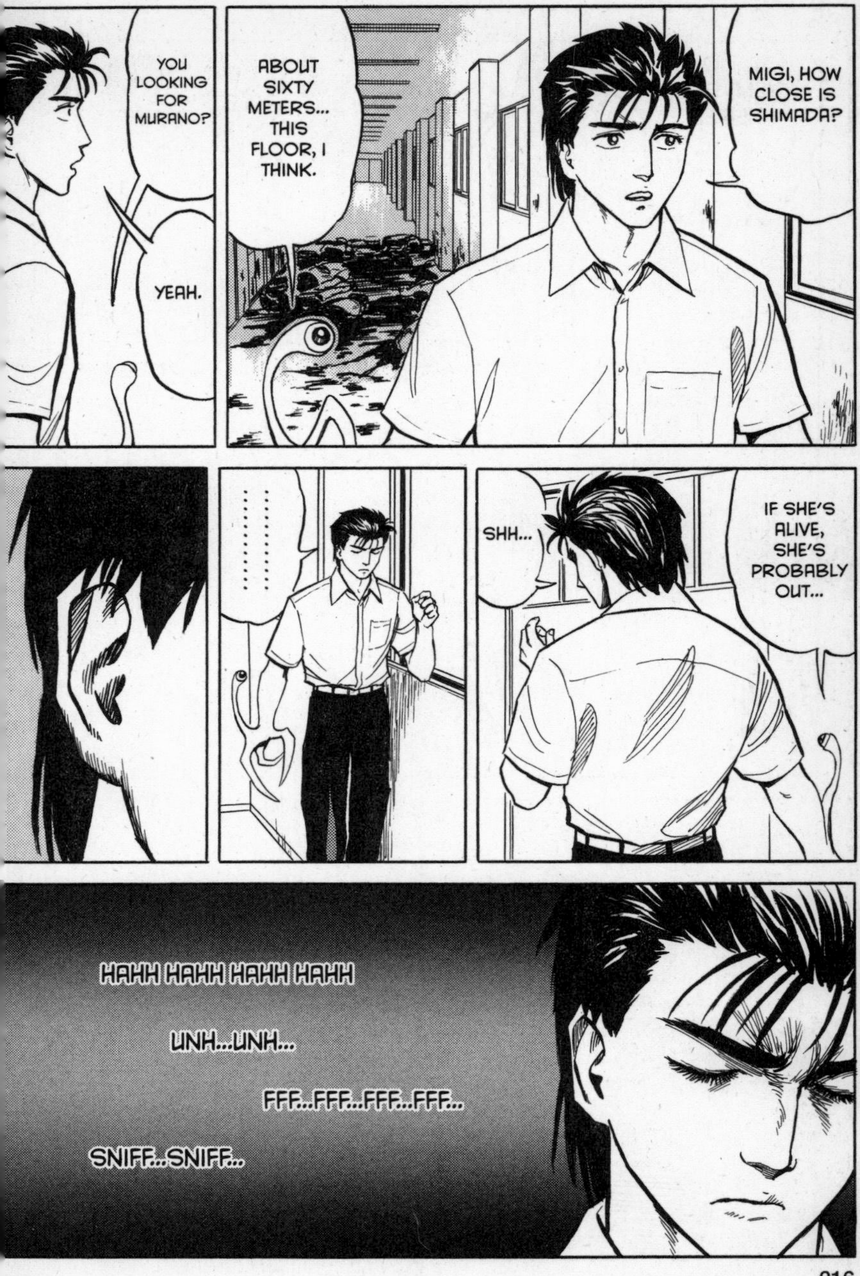
MIGI, HOW CLOSE IS SHIMADA?
ABOUT SIXTY METERS... THIS FLOOR, I THINK.
YOU LOOKING FOR MURANO?
YEAH.
IF SHE'S ALIVE, SHE'S PROBABLY OUT...
SHH...
......
HAHH HAHH HAHH HAHH
UNH...UNH...
FFF...FFF...FFF...FFF...
SNIFF...SNIFF...

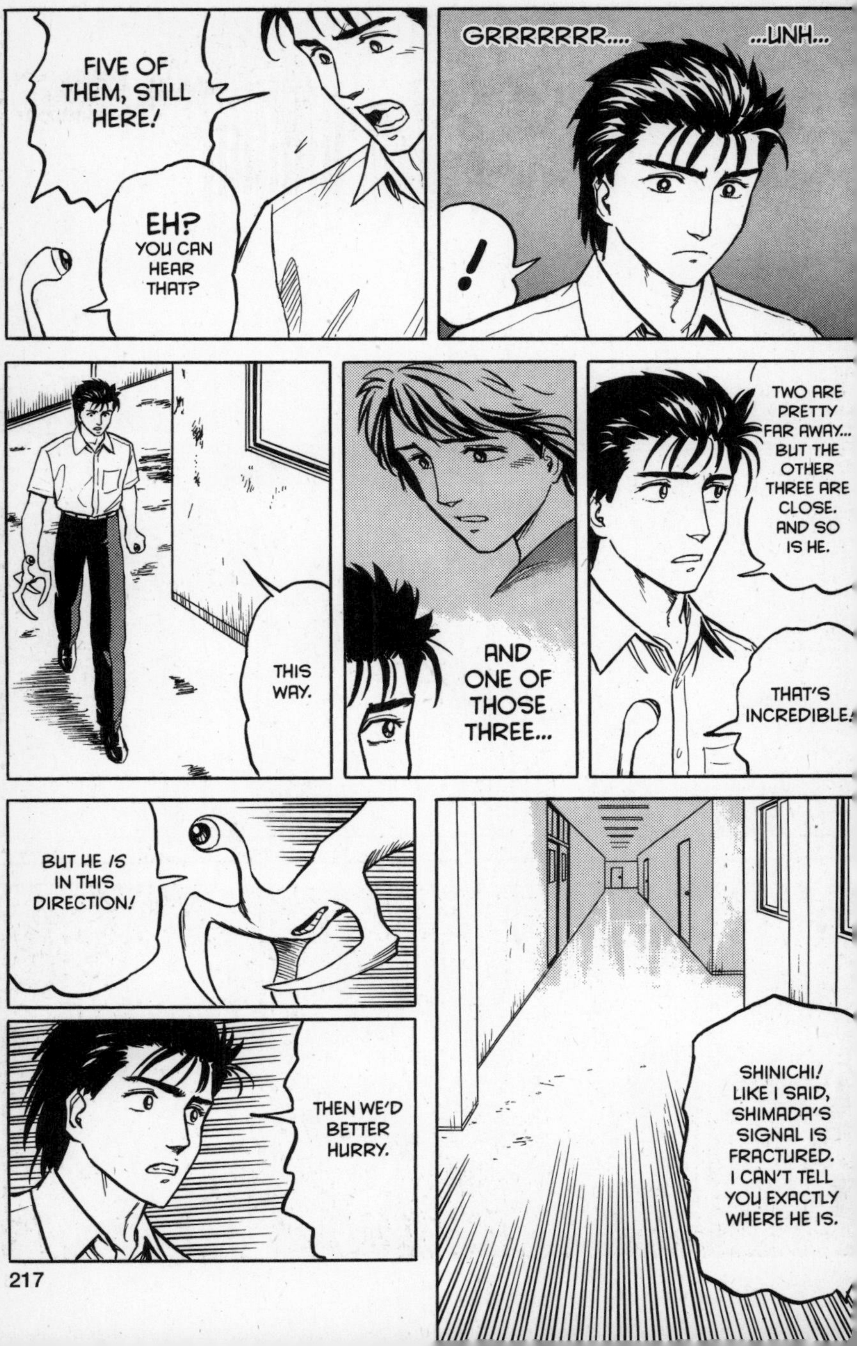
...UNH...
GRRRRRRR....
!
FIVE OF THEM, STILL HERE!
EH? YOU CAN HEAR THAT?
TWO ARE PRETTY FAR AWAY... BUT THE OTHER THREE ARE CLOSE. AND SO IS HE.
THAT'S INCREDIBLE!
AND ONE OF THOSE THREE...
THIS WAY.
SHINICHI! LIKE I SAID, SHIMADA'S SIGNAL IS FRACTURED. I CAN'T TELL YOU EXACTLY WHERE HE IS.
BUT HE *IS* IN THIS DIRECTION!
THEN WE'D BETTER HURRY.

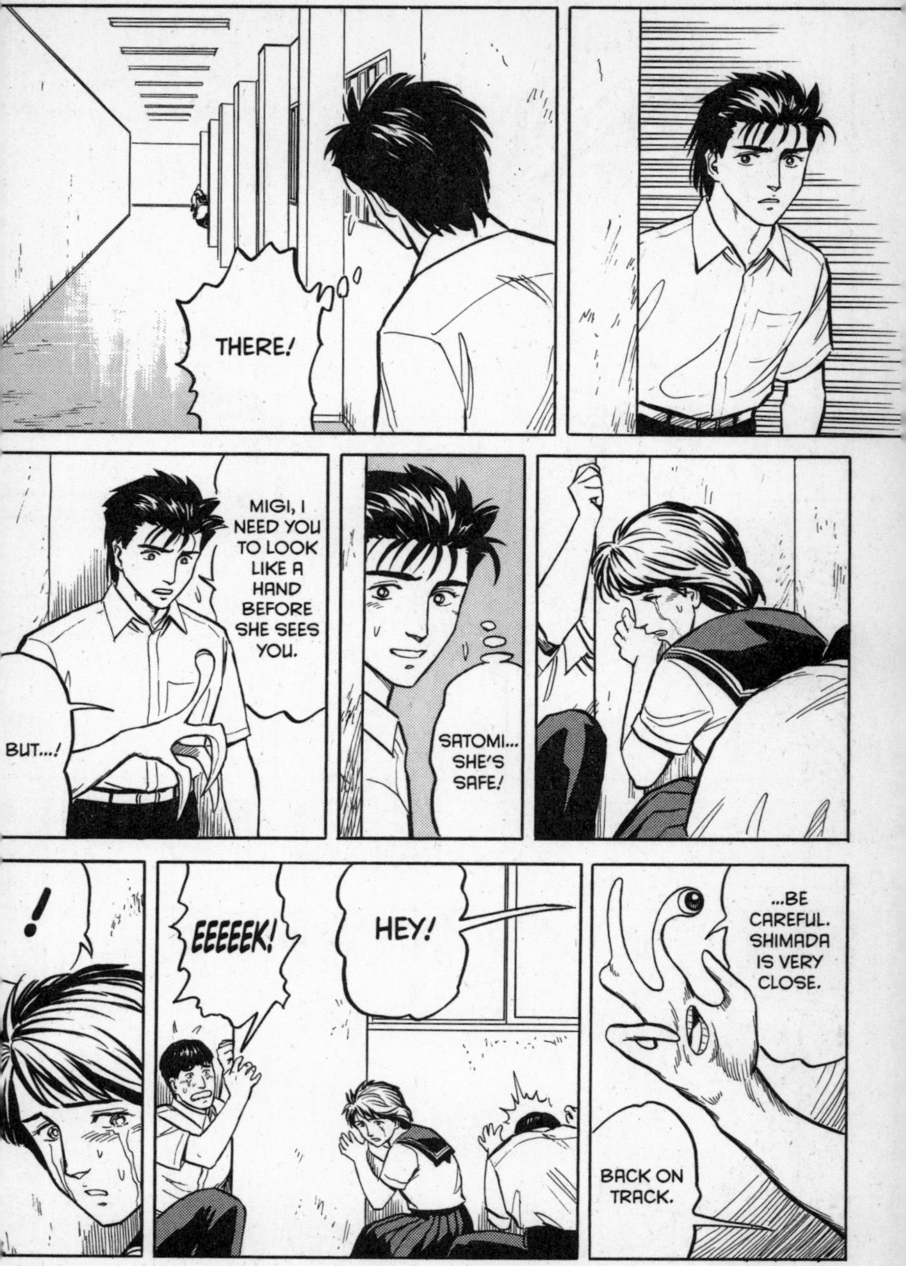
THERE!
SATOMI... SHE'S SAFE!
MIGI, I NEED YOU TO LOOK LIKE A HAND BEFORE SHE SEES YOU.
BUT...!
...BE CAREFUL. SHIMADA IS VERY CLOSE.
BACK ON TRACK.
HEY!
EEEEEK!
!

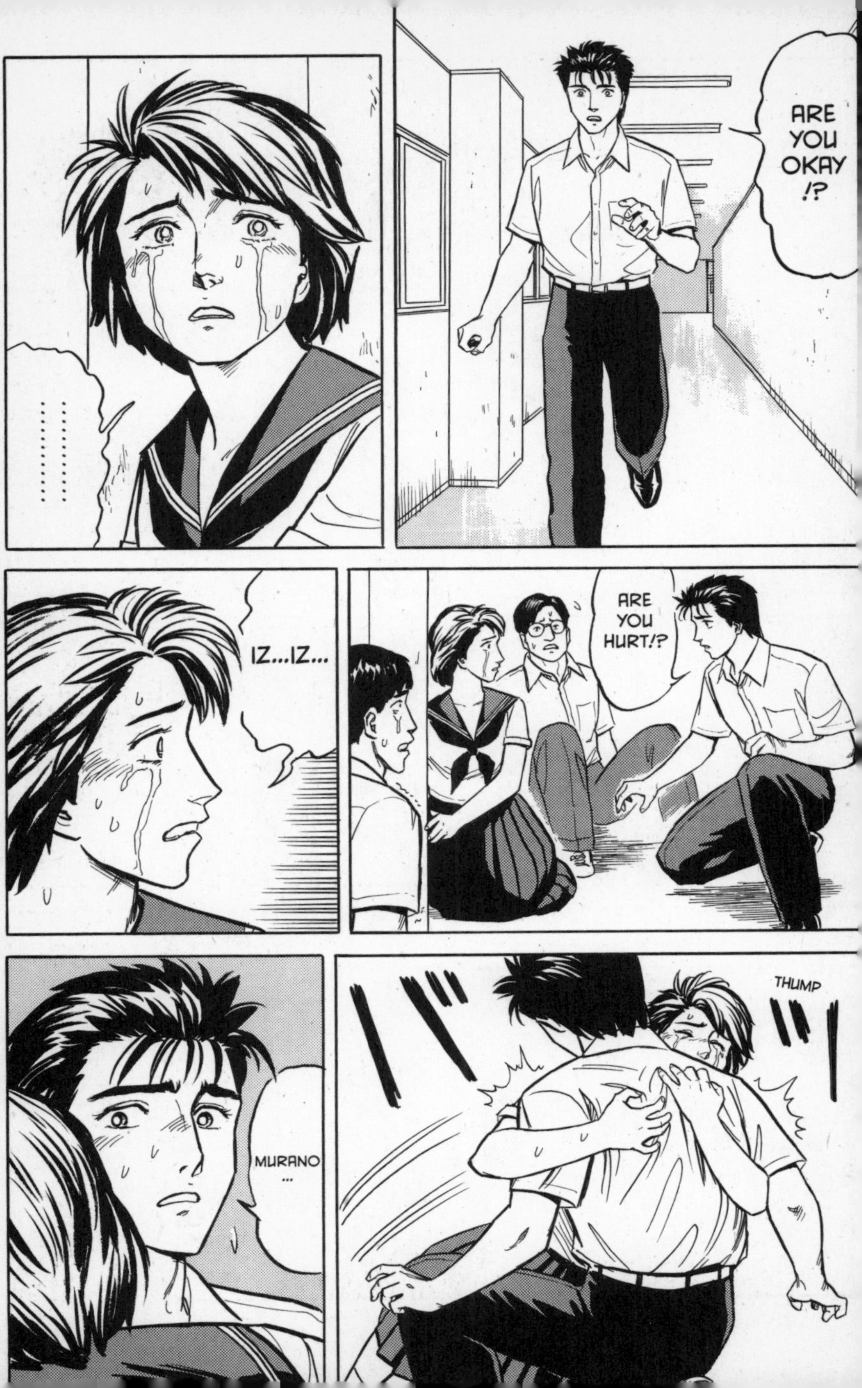
ARE YOU OKAY !?
......
ARE YOU HURT!?
IZ...IZ...
THUMP
MURANO ...

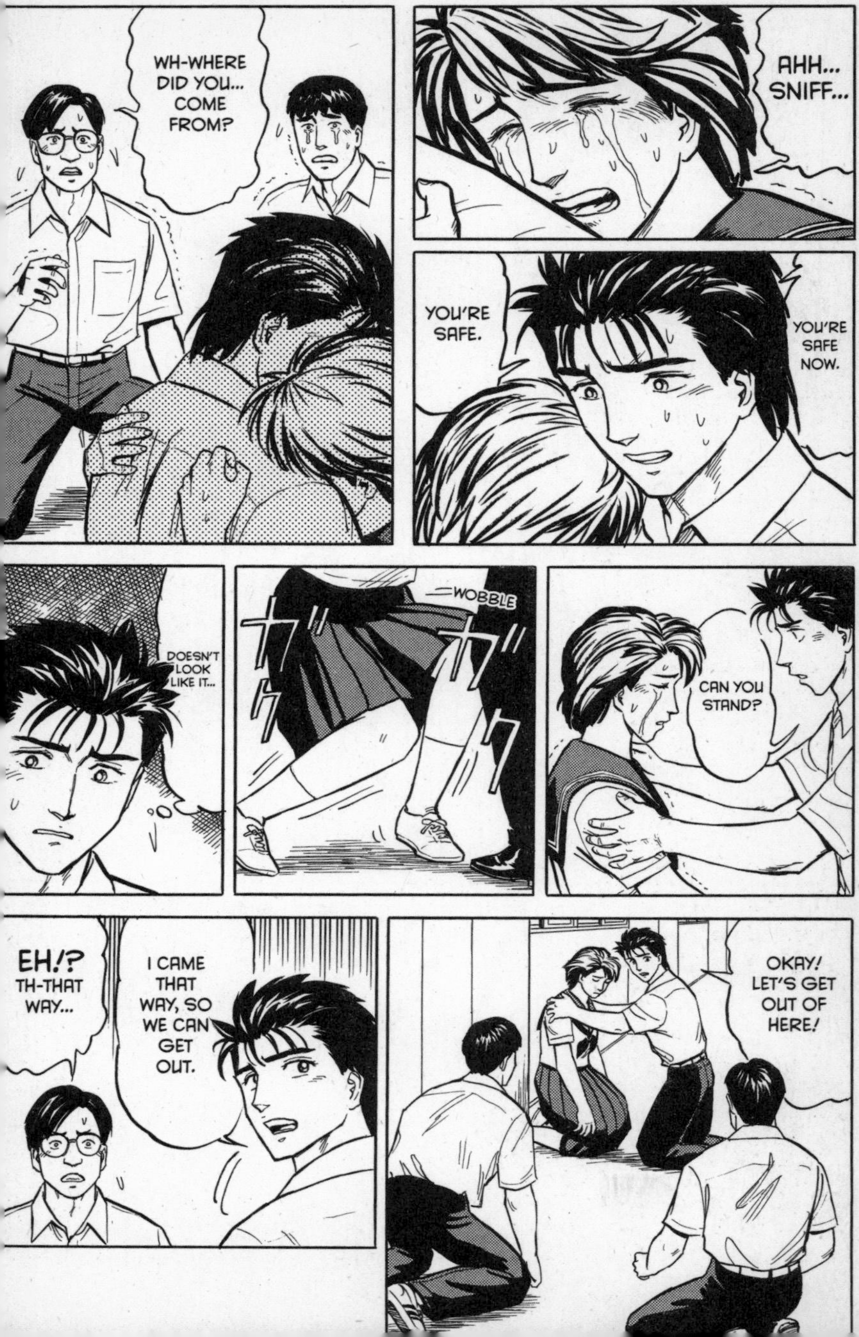
AHH... SNIFF...
YOU'RE SAFE.
YOU'RE SAFE NOW.
WH-WHERE DID YOU... COME FROM?
CAN YOU STAND?
WOBBLE
ガクガク
DOESN'T LOOK LIKE IT...
OKAY! LET'S GET OUT OF HERE!
I CAME THAT WAY, SO WE CAN GET OUT.
EH!? TH-THAT WAY...

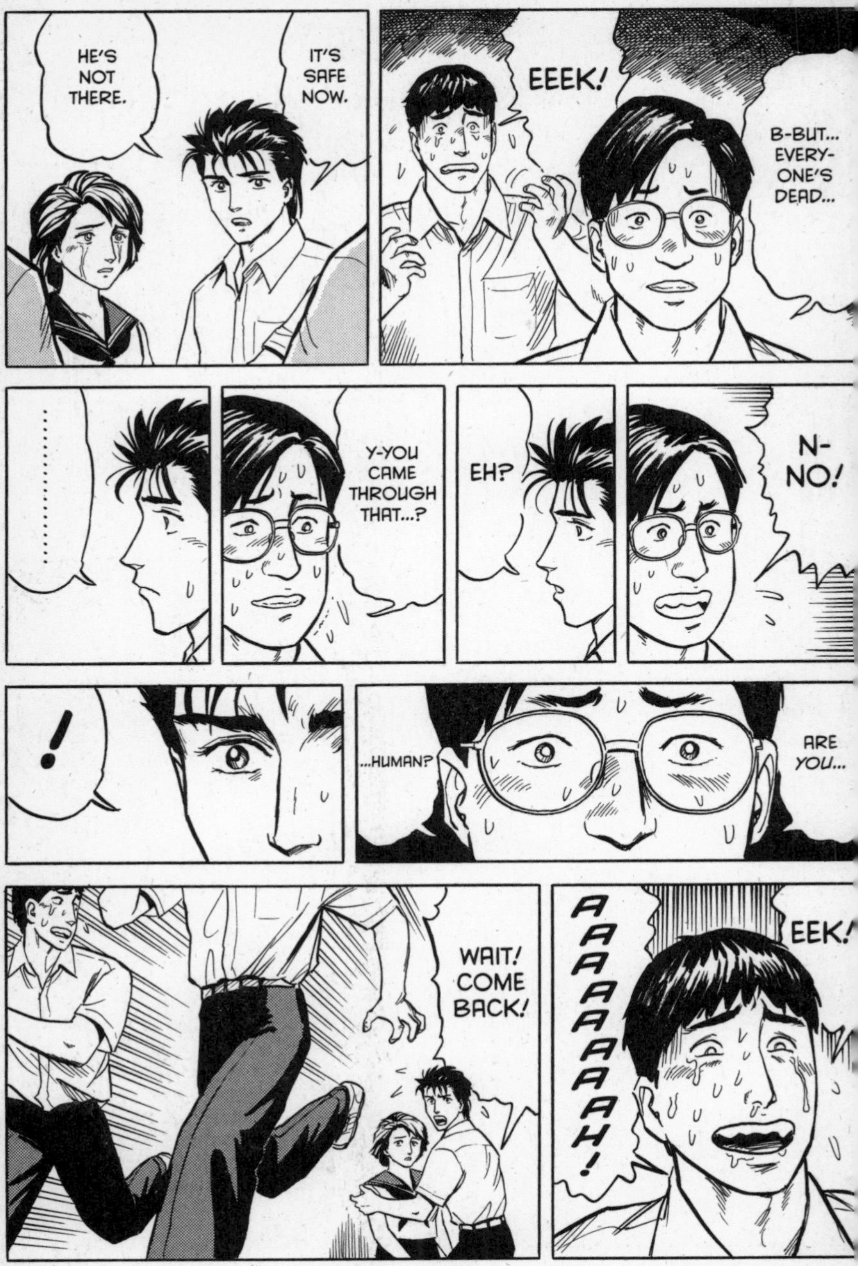
EEEK!
B-BUT... EVERYONE'S DEAD...
IT'S SAFE NOW.
HE'S NOT THERE.
N-NO!
EH?
Y-YOU CAME THROUGH THAT...?
......
ARE YOU...
...HUMAN?
!
EEK!
AAAAAAAAH!
WAIT! COME BACK!

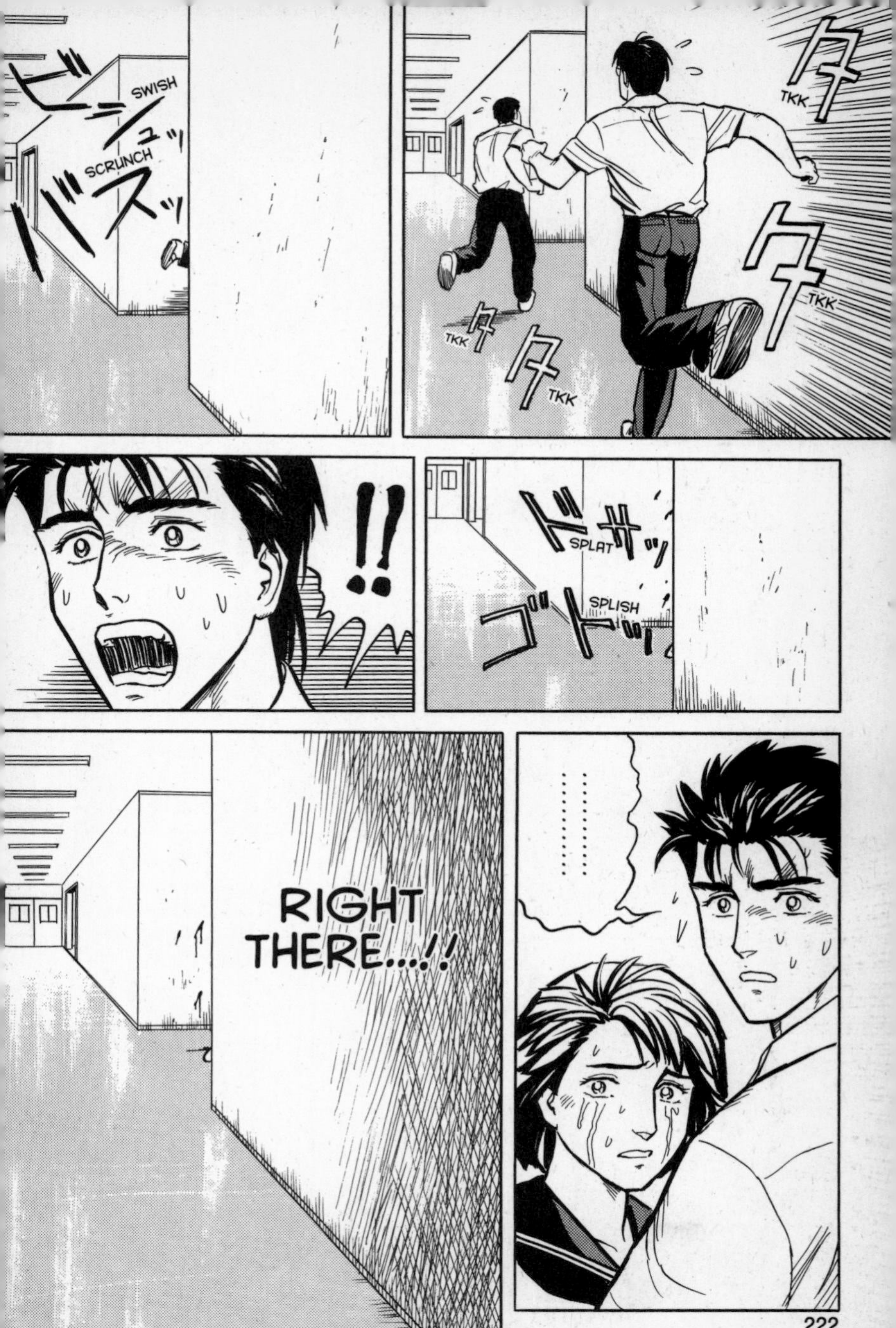
TKK
TKK
TKK
TKK
SWISH
SCRUNCH
SPLAT
SPLISH
!!
......
RIGHT THERE...!!

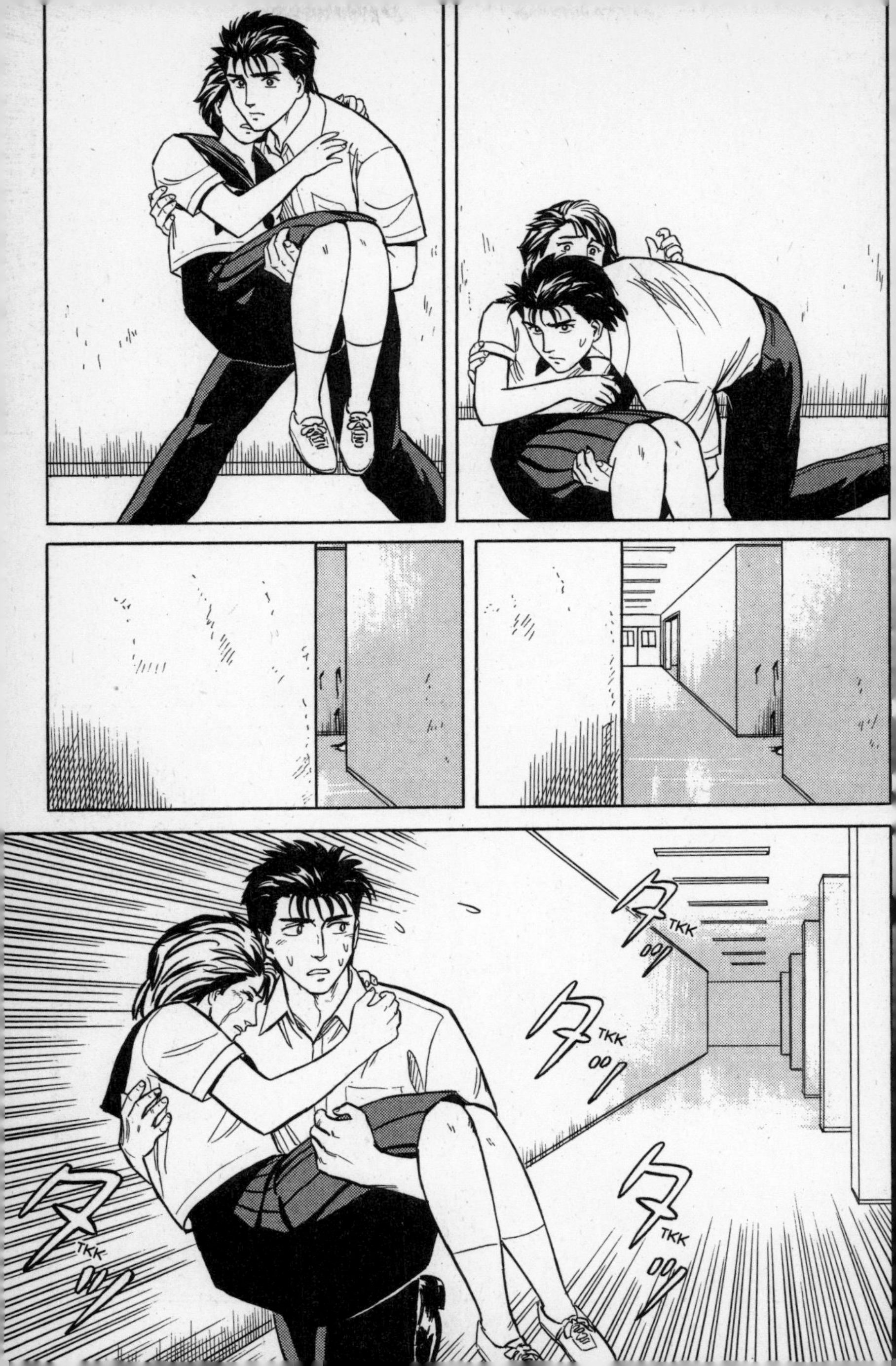
タッ
TKK
タッ
TKK
タッ
TKK
タッ
TKK

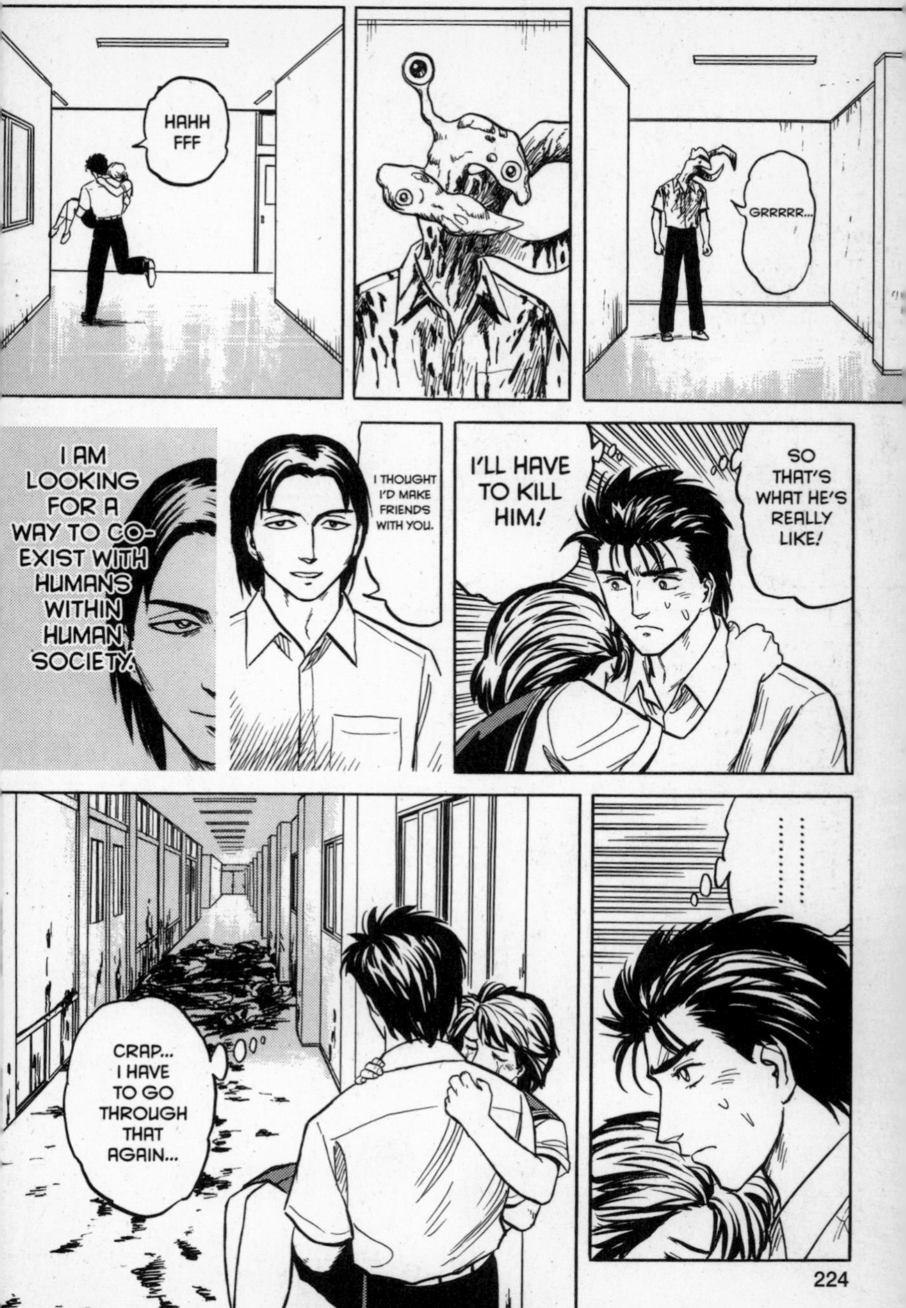
GRRRRR...
HAHH FFF
SO THAT'S WHAT HE'S REALLY LIKE!
I'LL HAVE TO KILL HIM!
I THOUGHT I'D MAKE FRIENDS WITH YOU.
I AM LOOKING FOR A WAY TO CO-EXIST WITH HUMANS WITHIN HUMAN SOCIETY.
......
CRAP... I HAVE TO GO THROUGH THAT AGAIN...

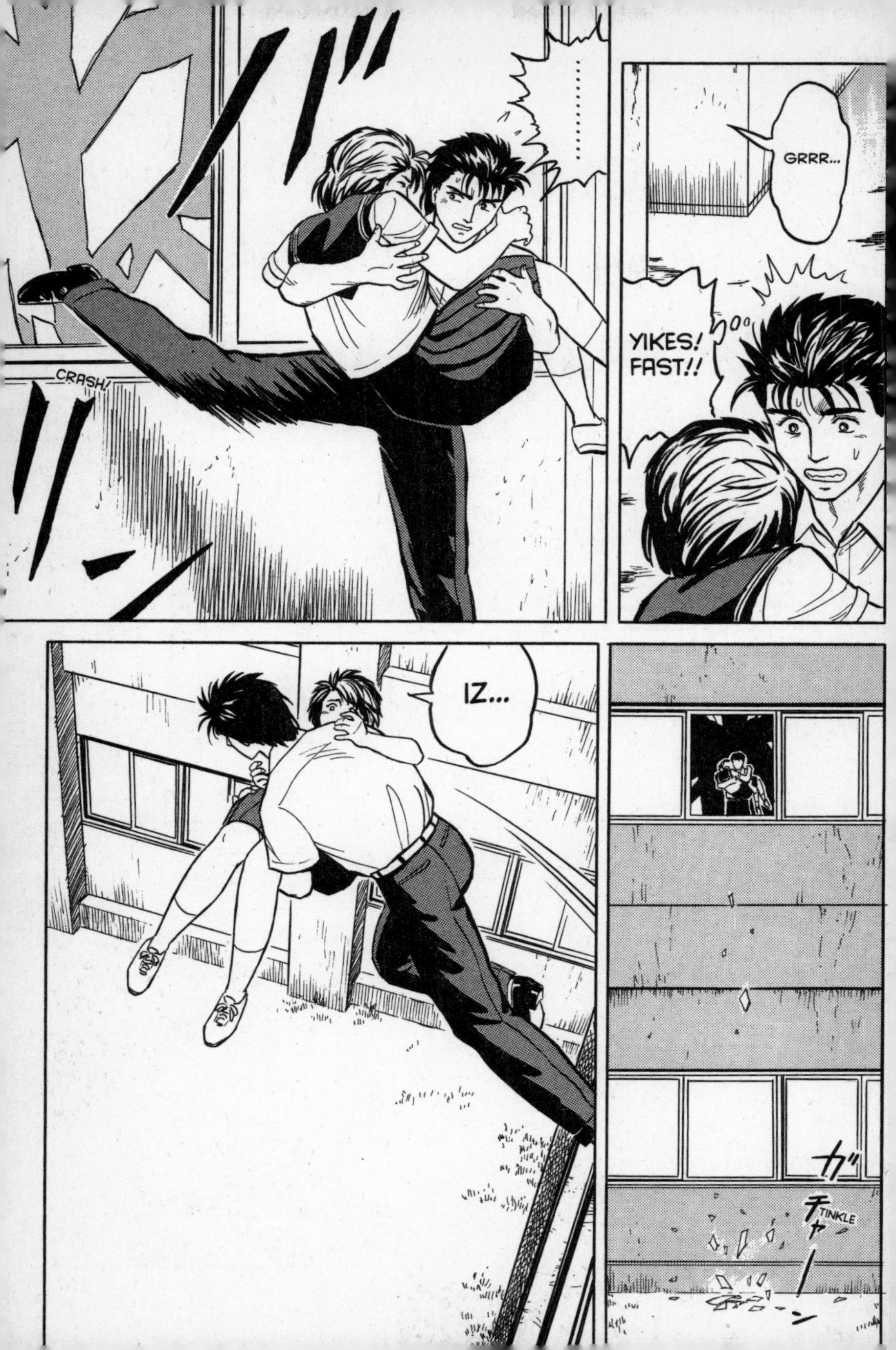
GRRR...
YIKES! FAST!!
CRASH!
TINKLE
IZ...

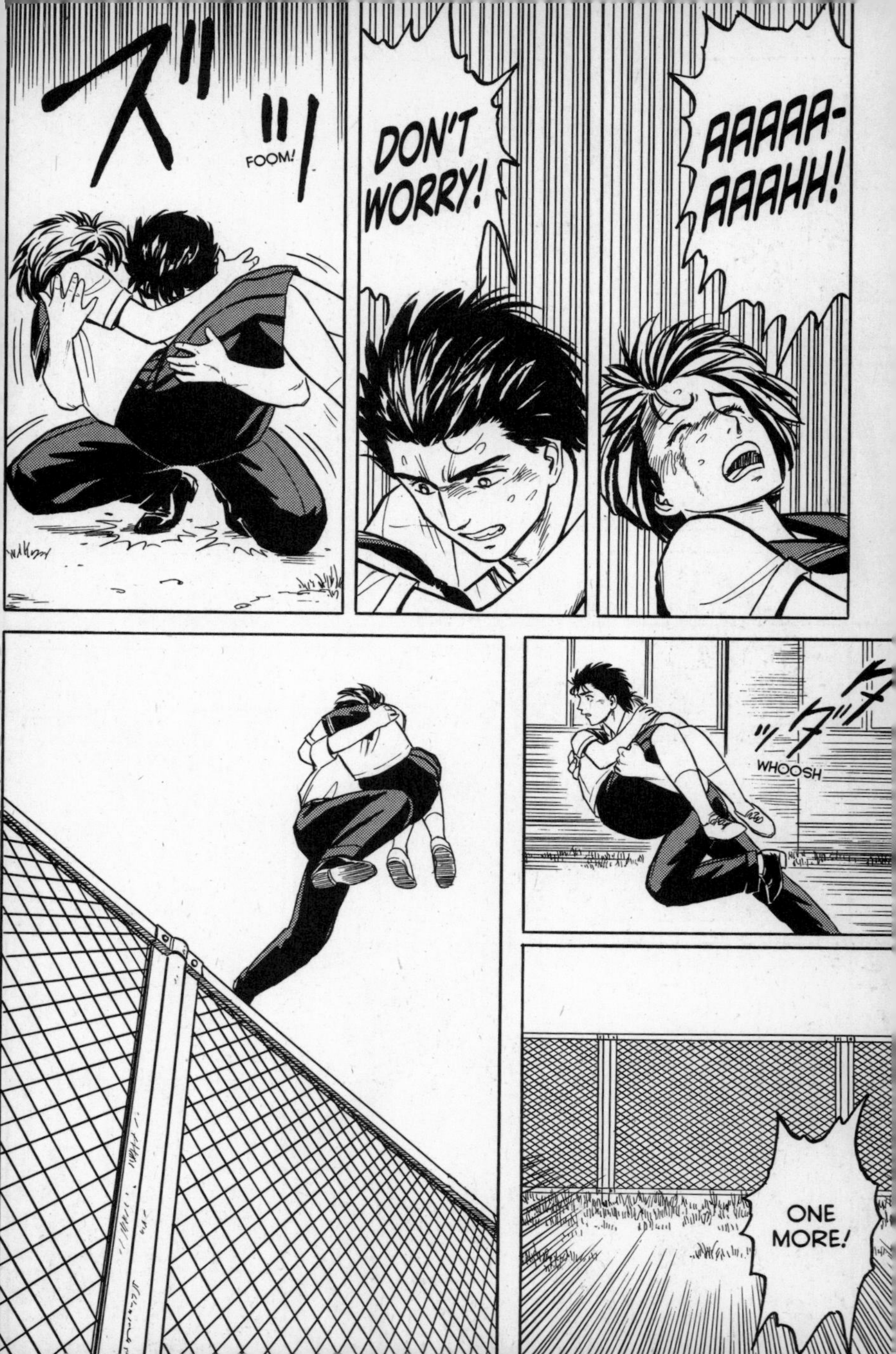
AAAAA-AAAAHH!
DON'T WORRY!
ズ!!
FOOM!
ドダッ
WHOOSH
ONE MORE!

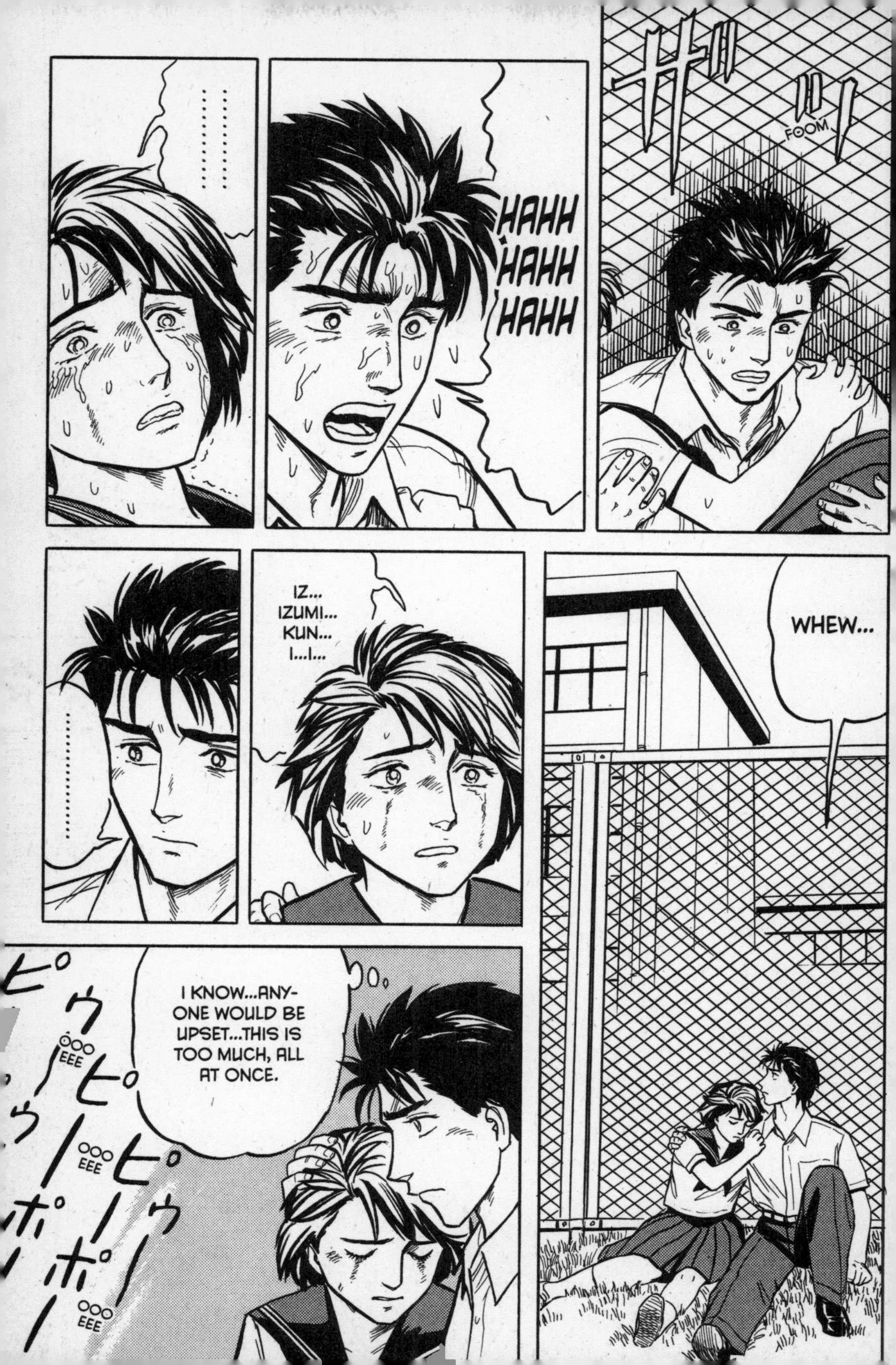
FOOM
HAHH HAHH HAHH
......
WHEW...
IZ... IZUMI... KUN... I...I...
......
I KNOW...ANY-ONE WOULD BE UPSET...THIS IS TOO MUCH, ALL AT ONCE.
OOO EEE
OOO EEE
OOO EEE

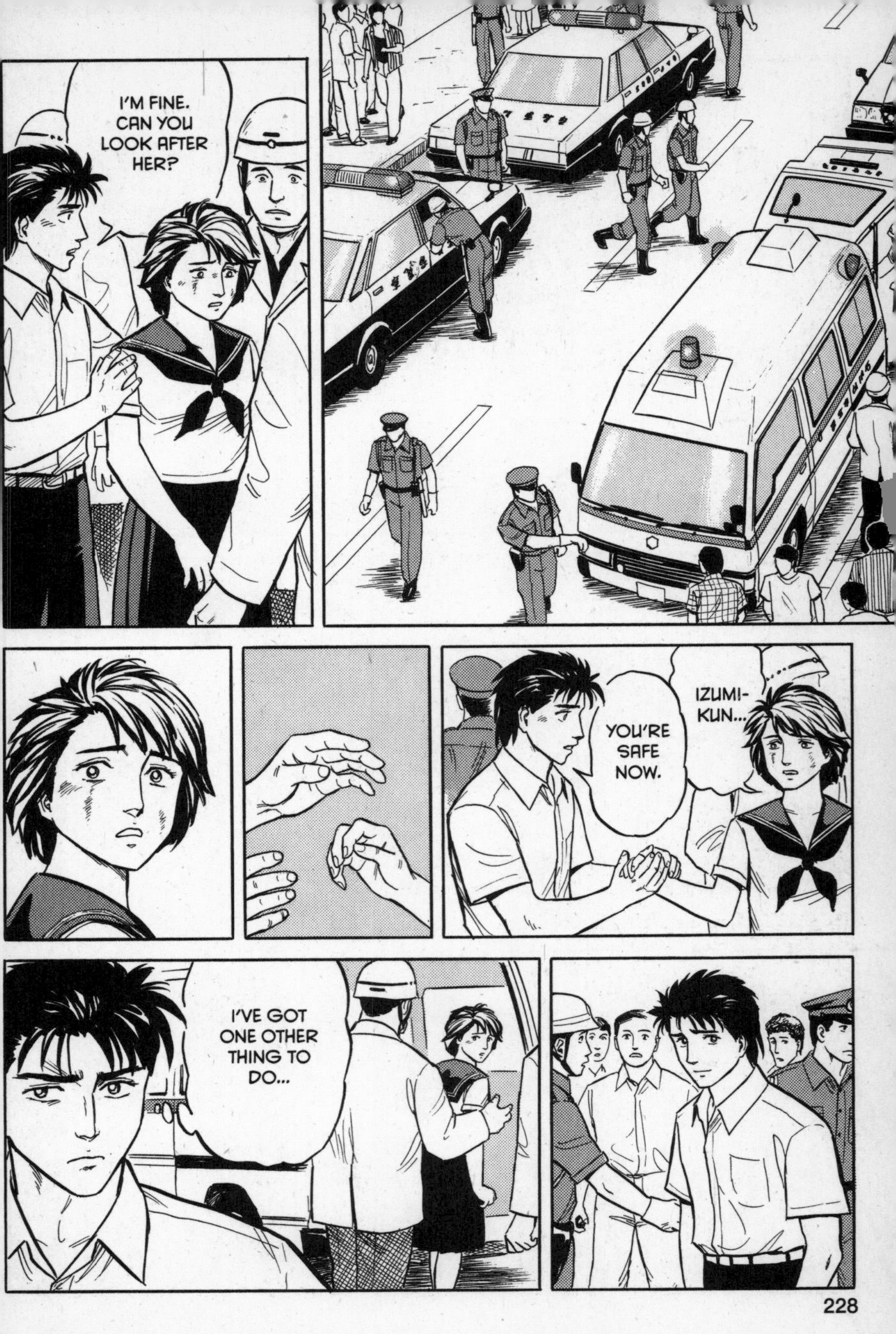
I'M FINE. CAN YOU LOOK AFTER HER?
IZUMI-KUN...
YOU'RE SAFE NOW.
I'VE GOT ONE OTHER THING TO DO...

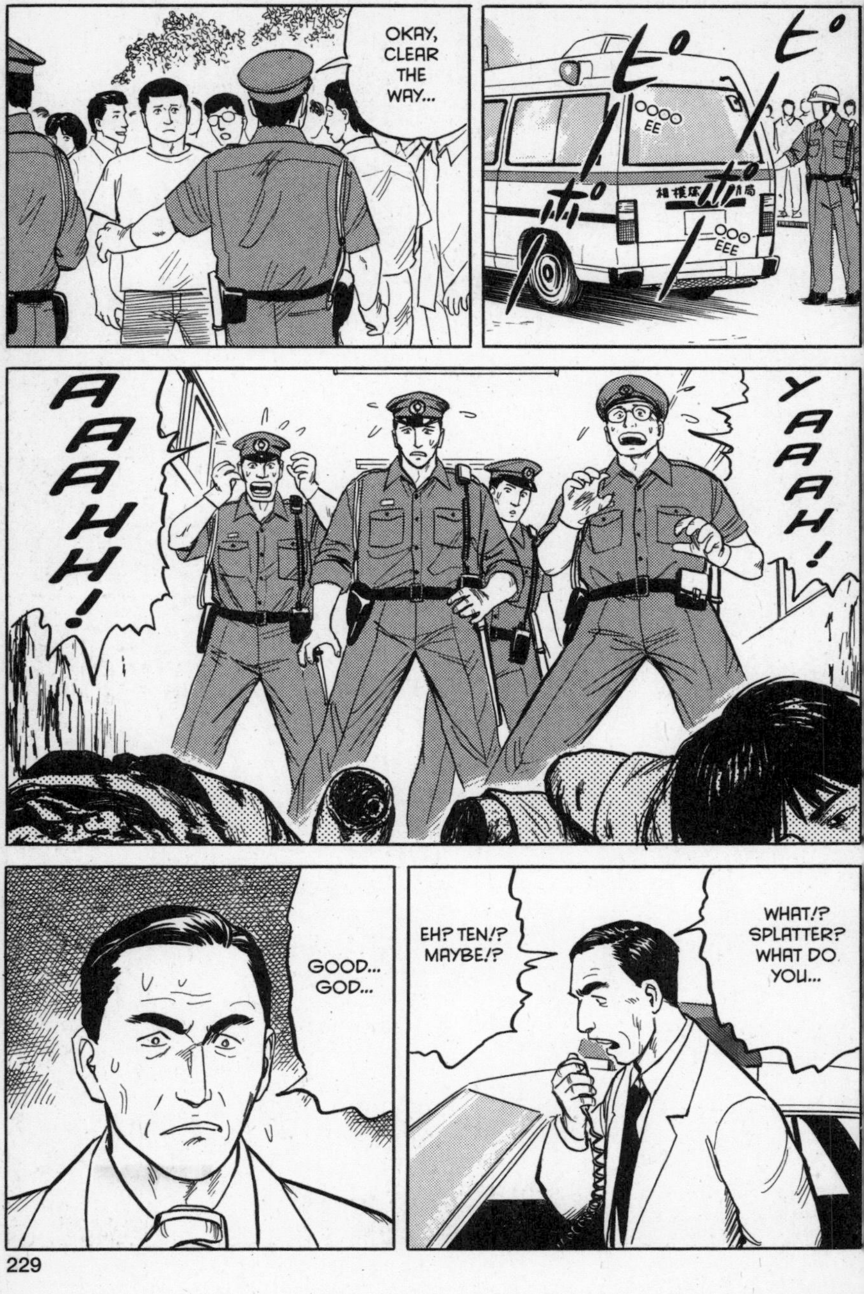
OKAY, CLEAR THE WAY...
YAAAAH!
AAAAHH!
WHAT!? SPLATTER? WHAT DO YOU...
EH? TEN!? MAYBE!?
GOOD... GOD...

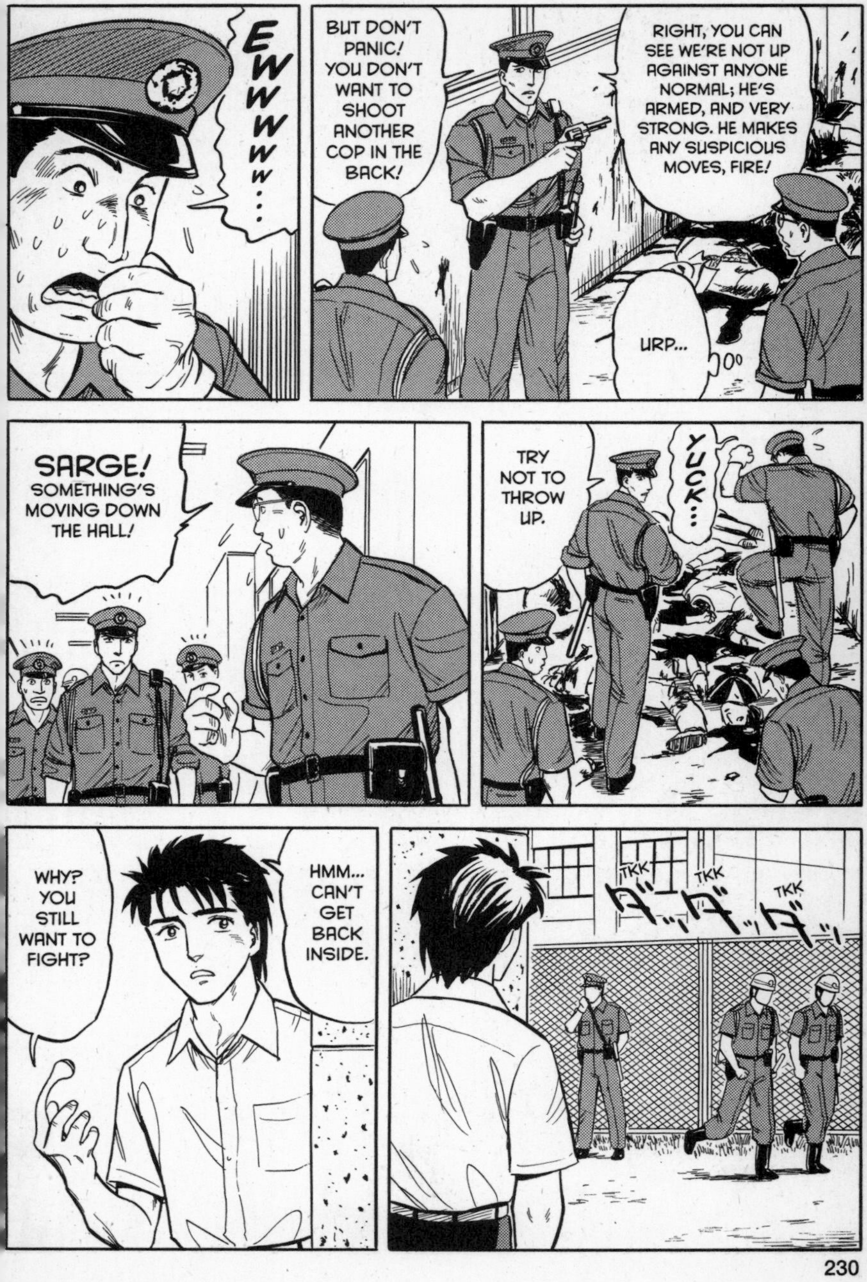
RIGHT, YOU CAN SEE WE'RE NOT UP AGAINST ANYONE NORMAL; HE'S ARMED, AND VERY STRONG. HE MAKES ANY SUSPICIOUS MOVES, FIRE!
BUT DON'T PANIC! YOU DON'T WANT TO SHOOT ANOTHER COP IN THE BACK!
URP...
EWWWWWW...
YUCK...
TRY NOT TO THROW UP.
SARGE! SOMETHING'S MOVING DOWN THE HALL!
TKK
TKK
TKK
HMM... CAN'T GET BACK INSIDE.
WHY? YOU STILL WANT TO FIGHT?

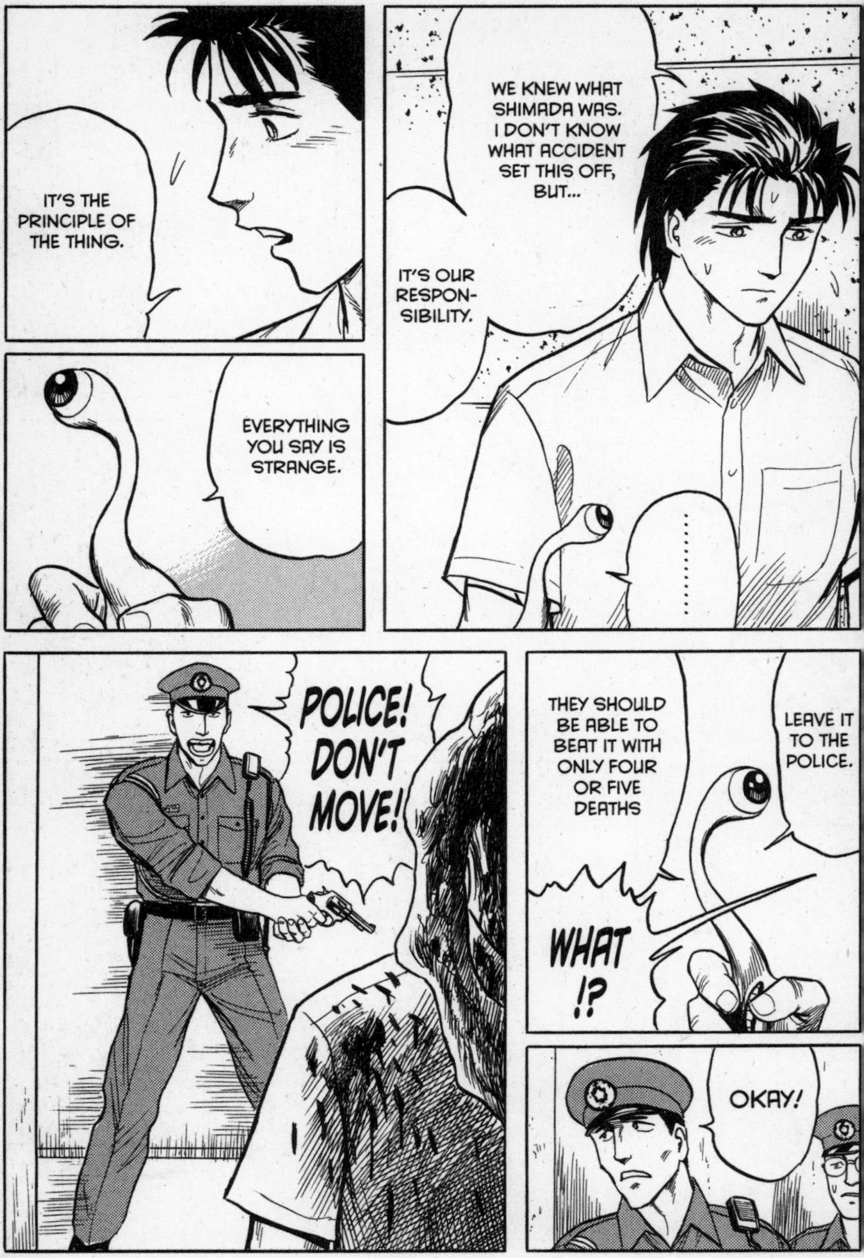
WE KNEW WHAT SHIMADA WAS. I DON'T KNOW WHAT ACCIDENT SET THIS OFF, BUT...
IT'S OUR RESPONSIBILITY.
IT'S THE PRINCIPLE OF THE THING.
EVERYTHING YOU SAY IS STRANGE.
LEAVE IT TO THE POLICE.
THEY SHOULD BE ABLE TO BEAT IT WITH ONLY FOUR OR FIVE DEATHS
WHAT !?
OKAY!
POLICE! DON'T MOVE!

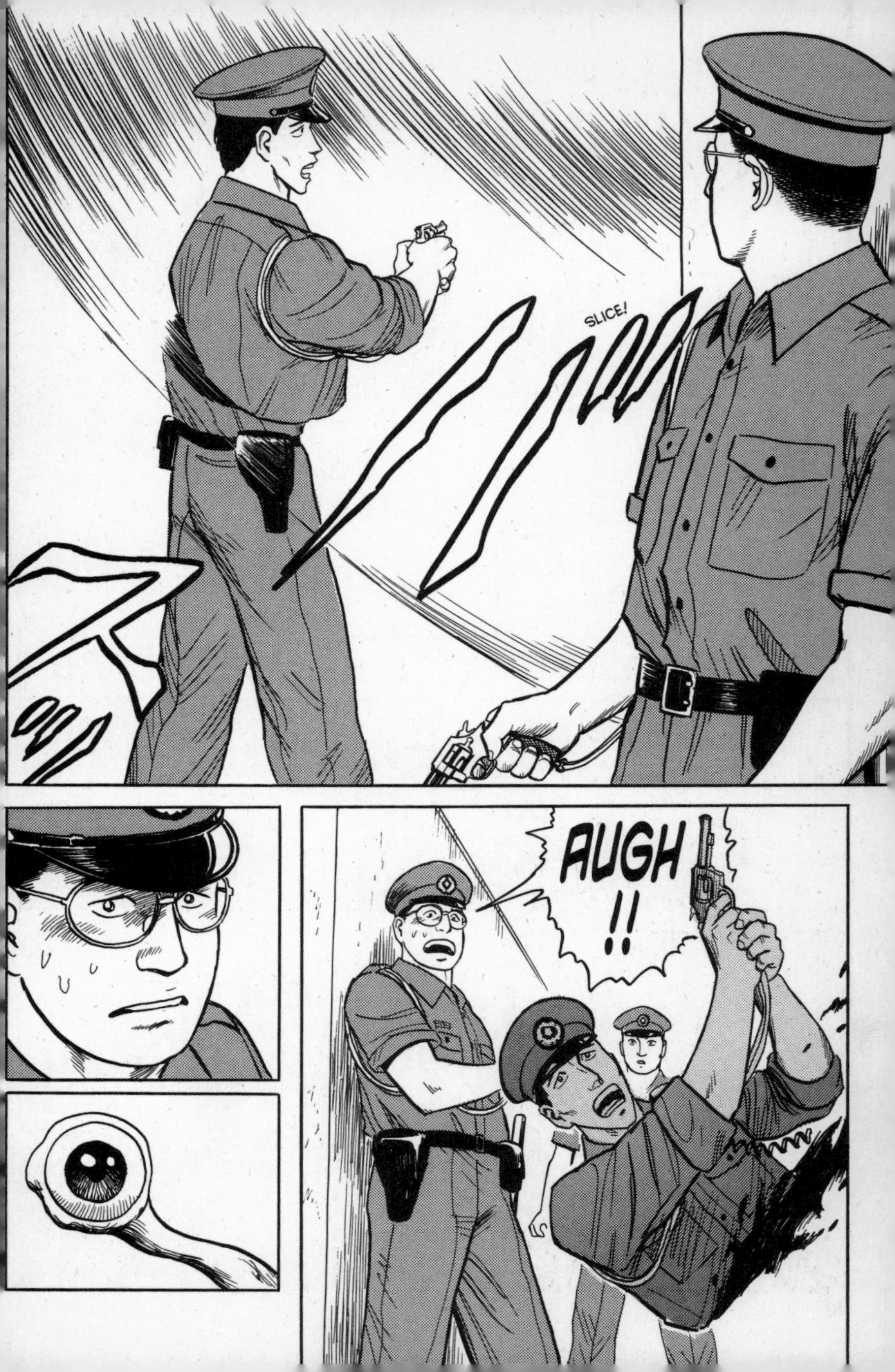
SLICE!
AUGH !!

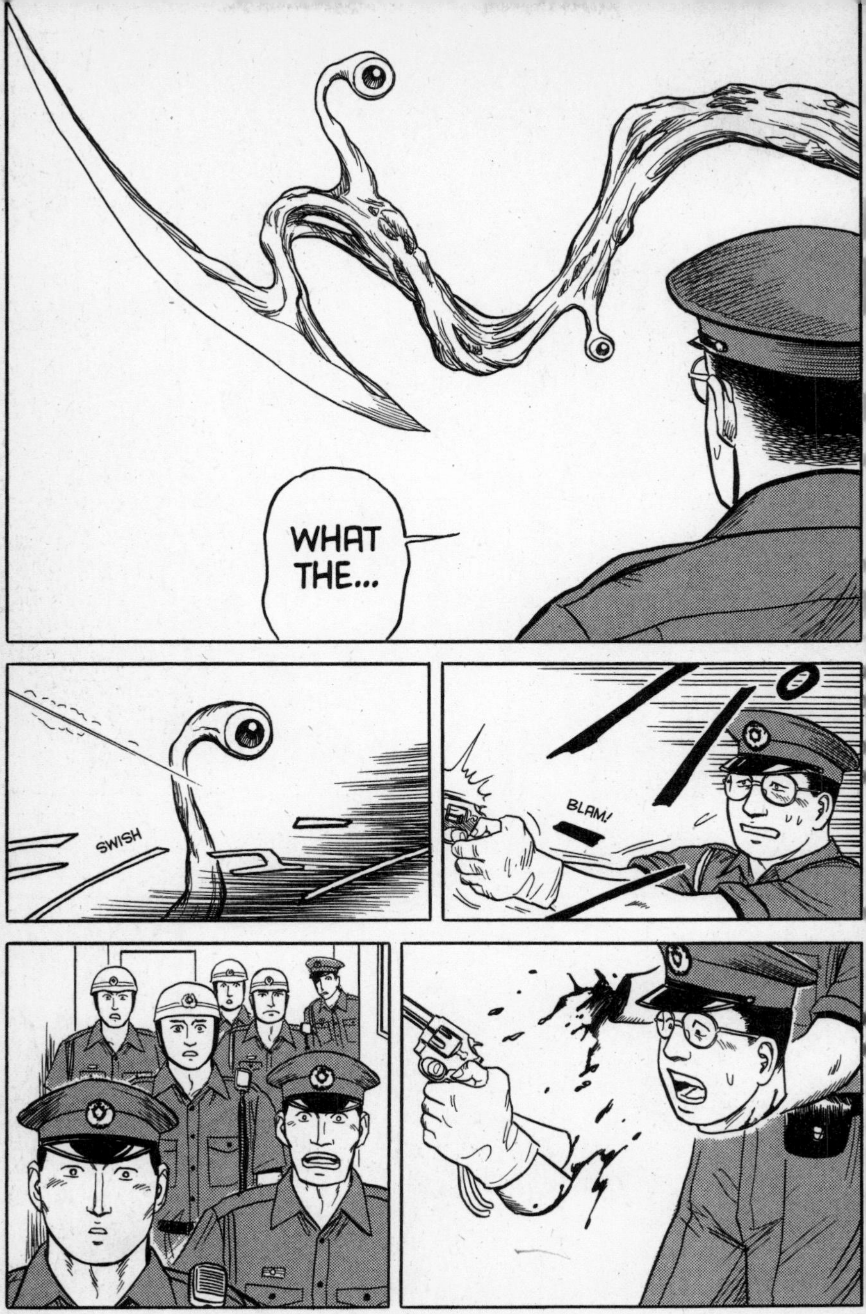
WHAT THE...
BLAM!
SWISH

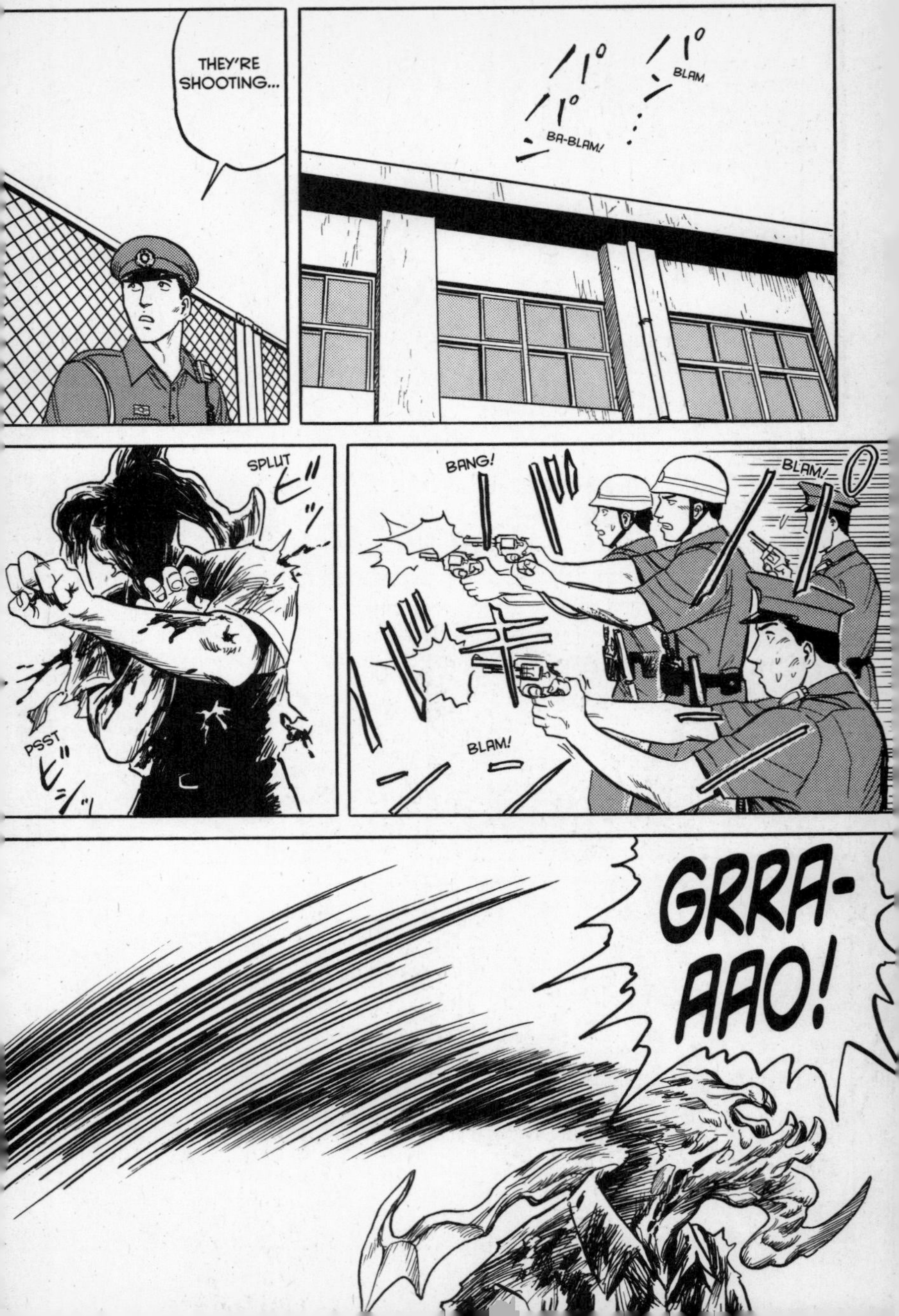
BLAM
BA-BLAM!
THEY'RE SHOOTING...
BLAM!
BANG!
BLAM!
SPLUT
PSST
GRRA-AAO!

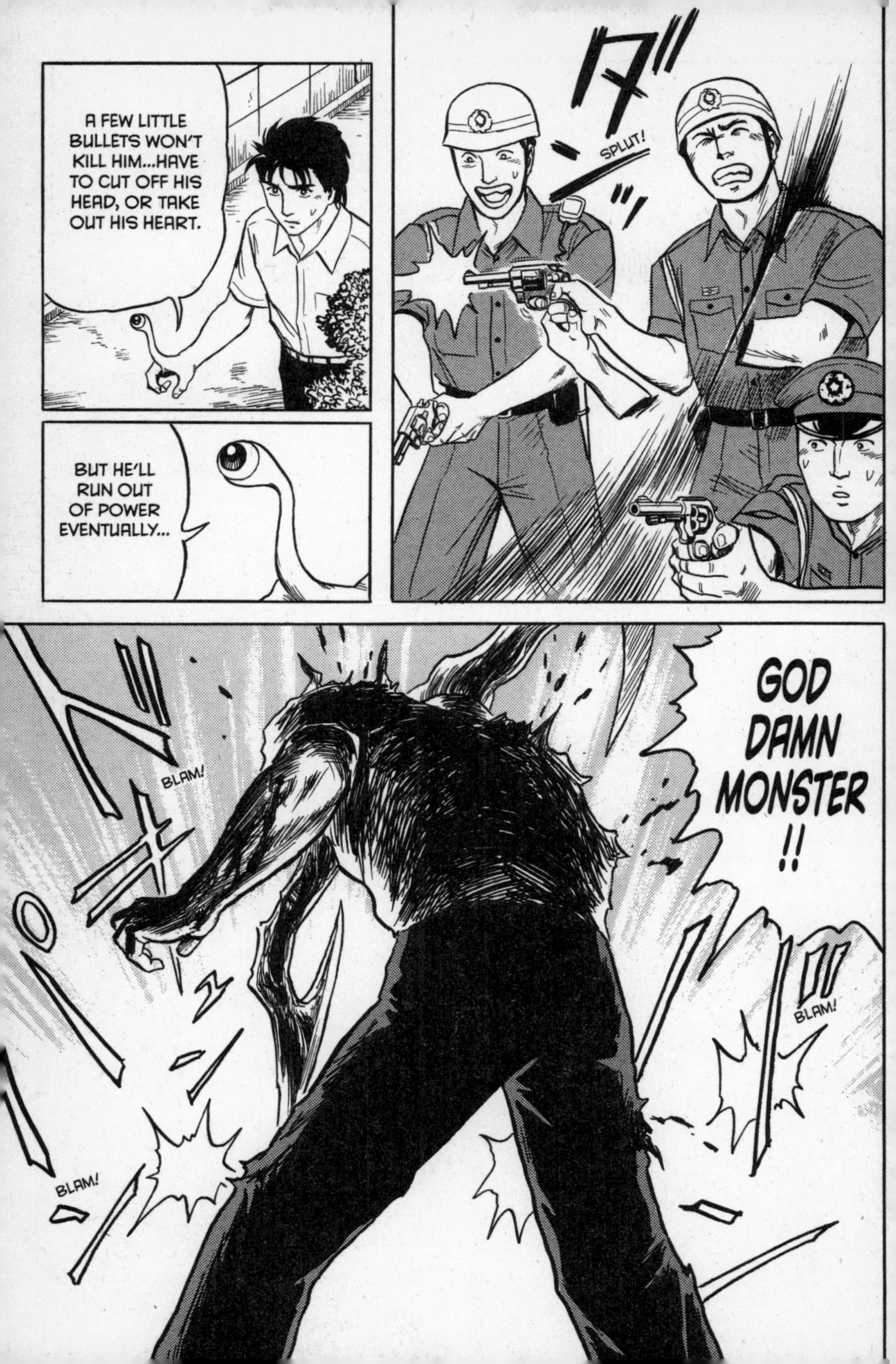
SPLUT!
A FEW LITTLE BULLETS WON'T KILL HIM...HAVE TO CUT OFF HIS HEAD, OR TAKE OUT HIS HEART.
BUT HE'LL RUN OUT OF POWER EVENTUALLY...
GOD DAMN MONSTER !!
BLAM!
BLAM!
BLAM!

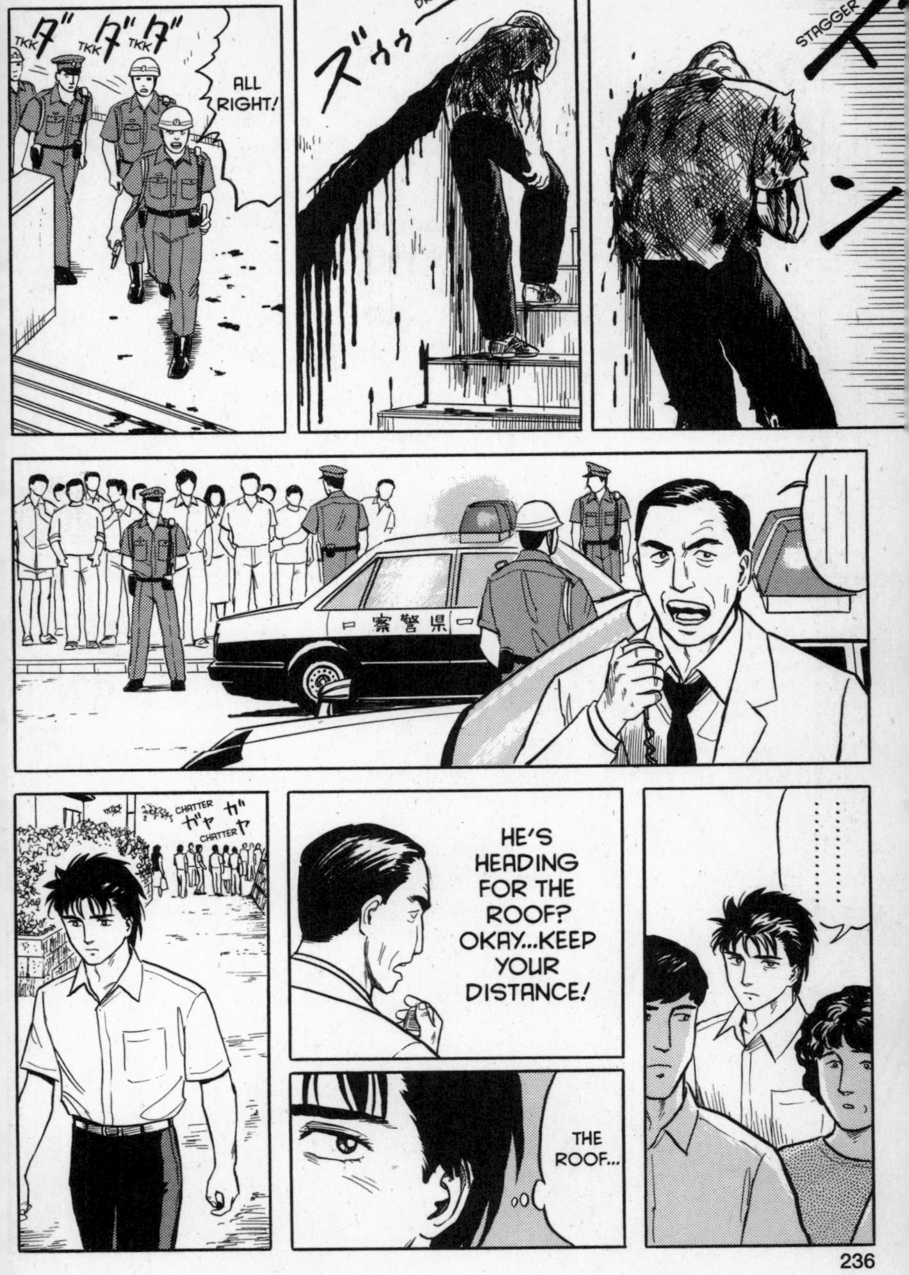

STAGGER
DRAG
ズウゥ
TKK TKK TKK
ダダダ
ALL RIGHT!
県警察
......
HE'S HEADING FOR THE ROOF? OKAY...KEEP YOUR DISTANCE!
THE ROOF...
CHATTER CHATTER
ガヤガヤ

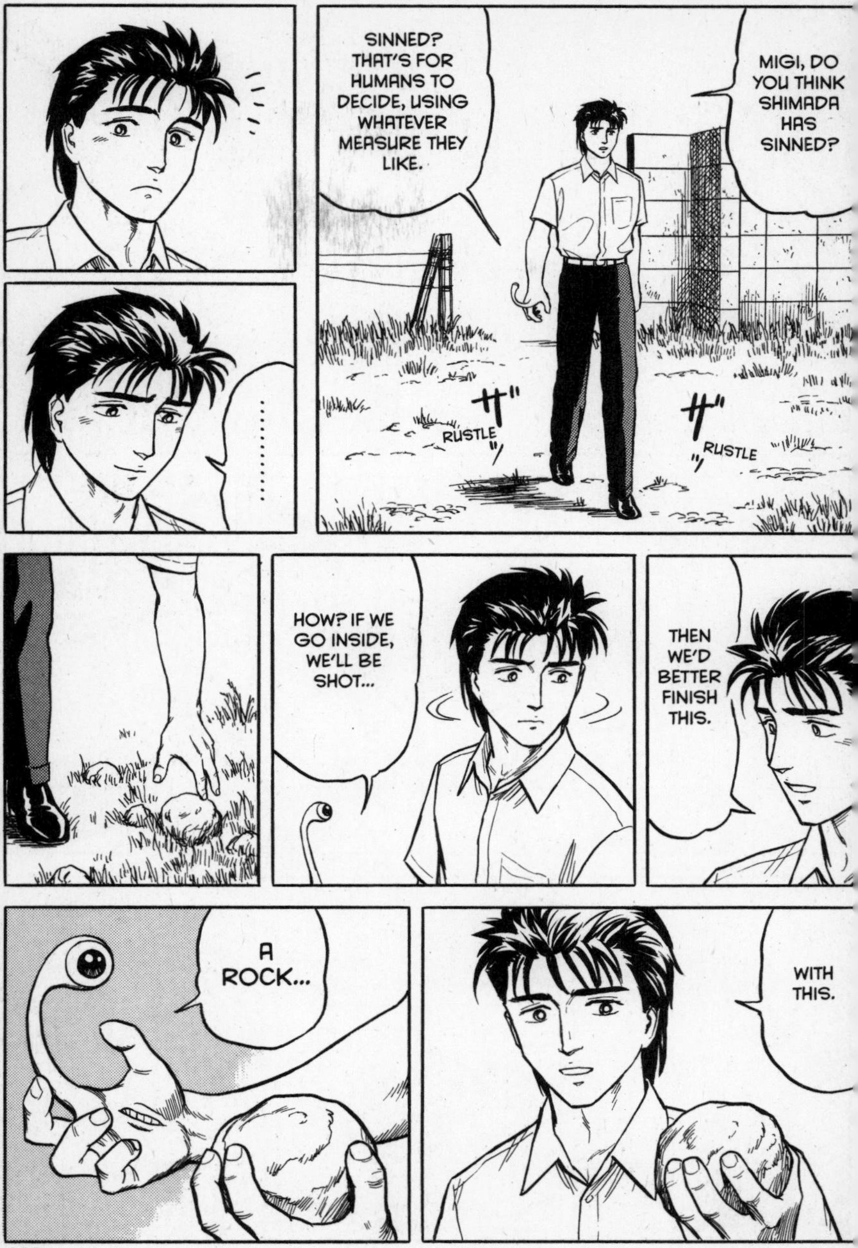
MIGI, DO YOU THINK SHIMADA HAS SINNED?
SINNED? THAT'S FOR HUMANS TO DECIDE, USING WHATEVER MEASURE THEY LIKE.
ザ" RUSTLE
ザ" RUSTLE
....
THEN WE'D BETTER FINISH THIS.
HOW? IF WE GO INSIDE, WE'LL BE SHOT...
WITH THIS.
A ROCK...

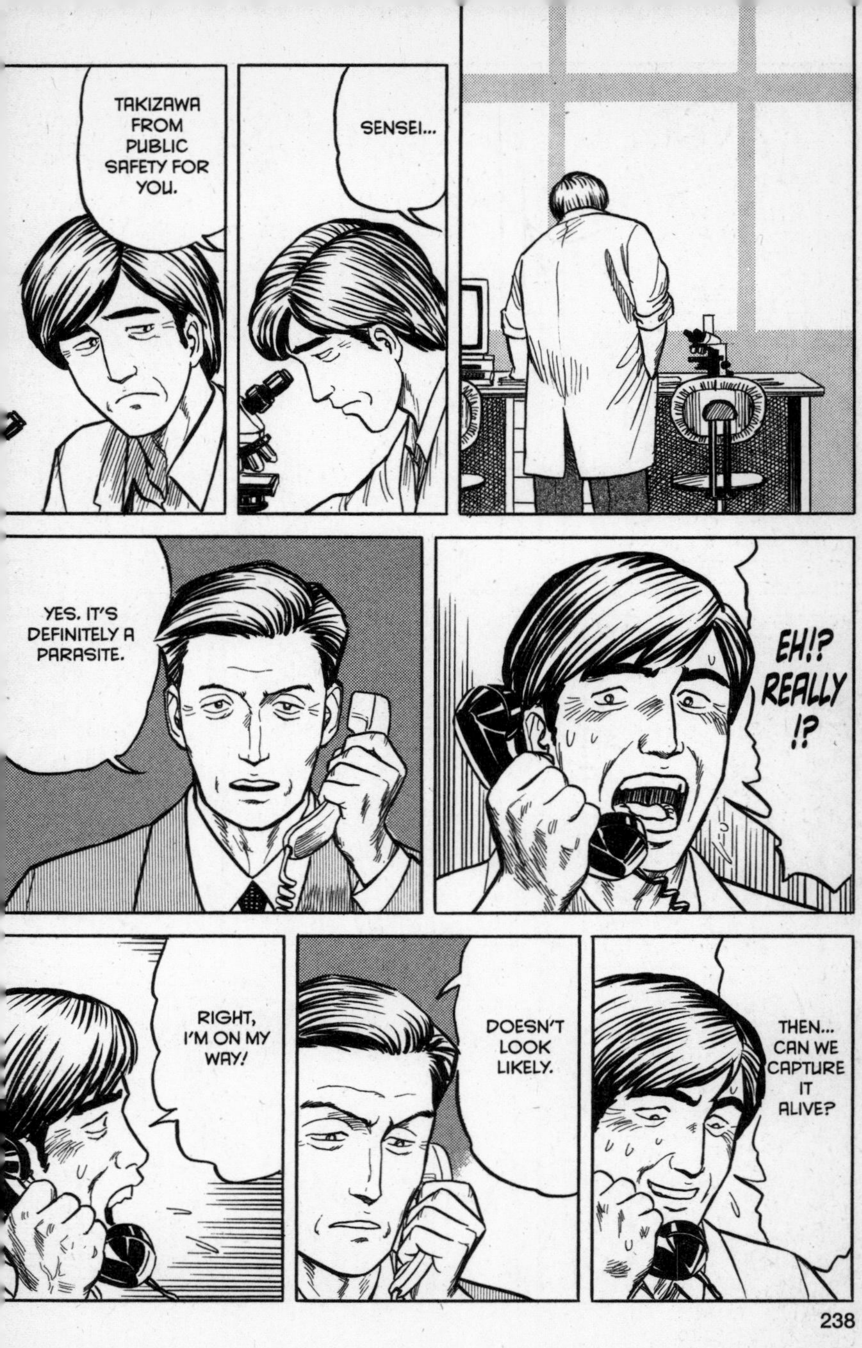
SENSEI...
TAKIZAWA FROM PUBLIC SAFETY FOR YOU.
EH!? REALLY!?
YES. IT'S DEFINITELY A PARASITE.
THEN... CAN WE CAPTURE IT ALIVE?
DOESN'T LOOK LIKELY.
RIGHT, I'M ON MY WAY!

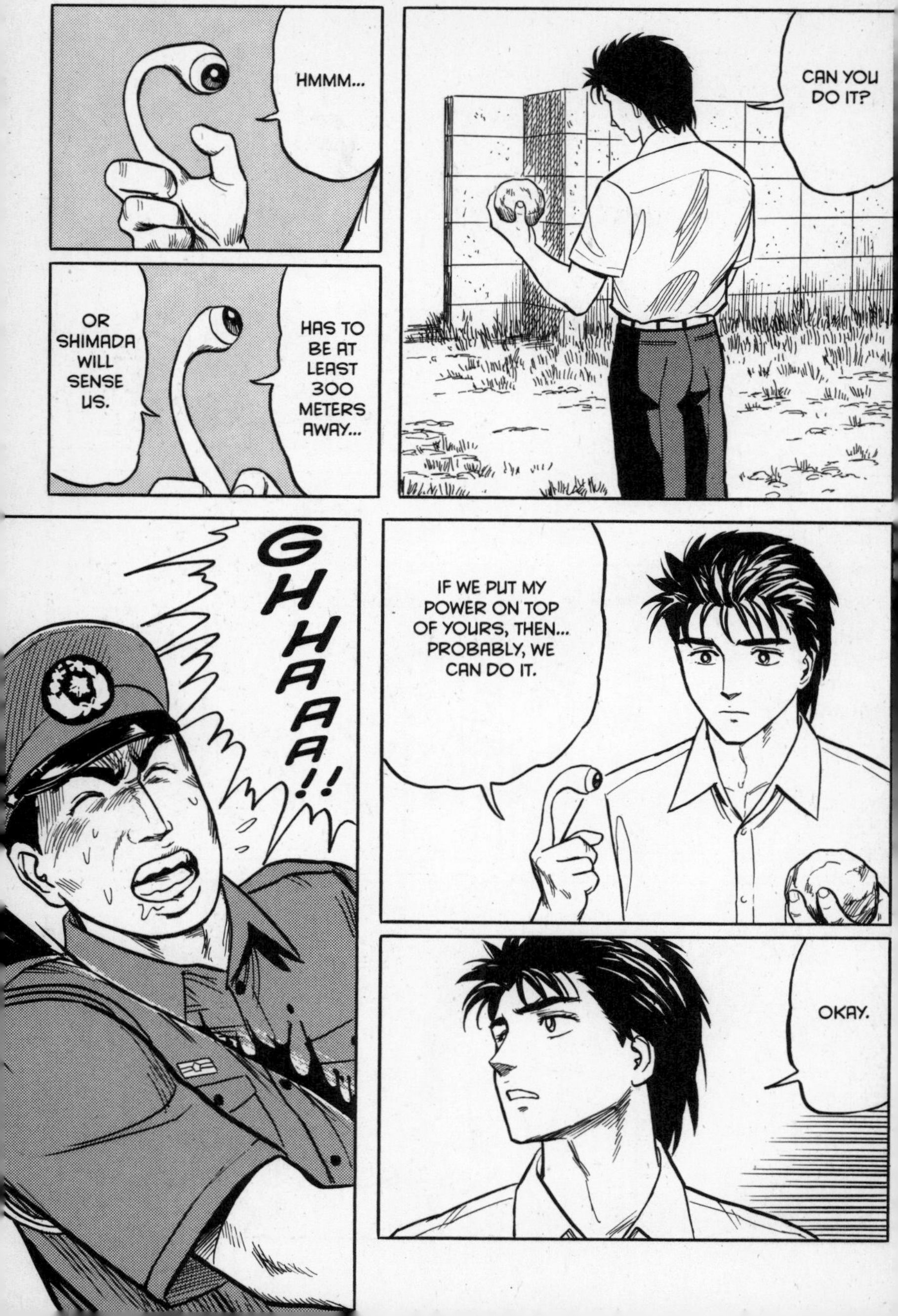
CAN YOU DO IT?
HMMM...
HAS TO BE AT LEAST 300 METERS AWAY...
OR SHIMADA WILL SENSE US.
IF WE PUT MY POWER ON TOP OF YOURS, THEN... PROBABLY, WE CAN DO IT.
OKAY.
GHHAAAA!!

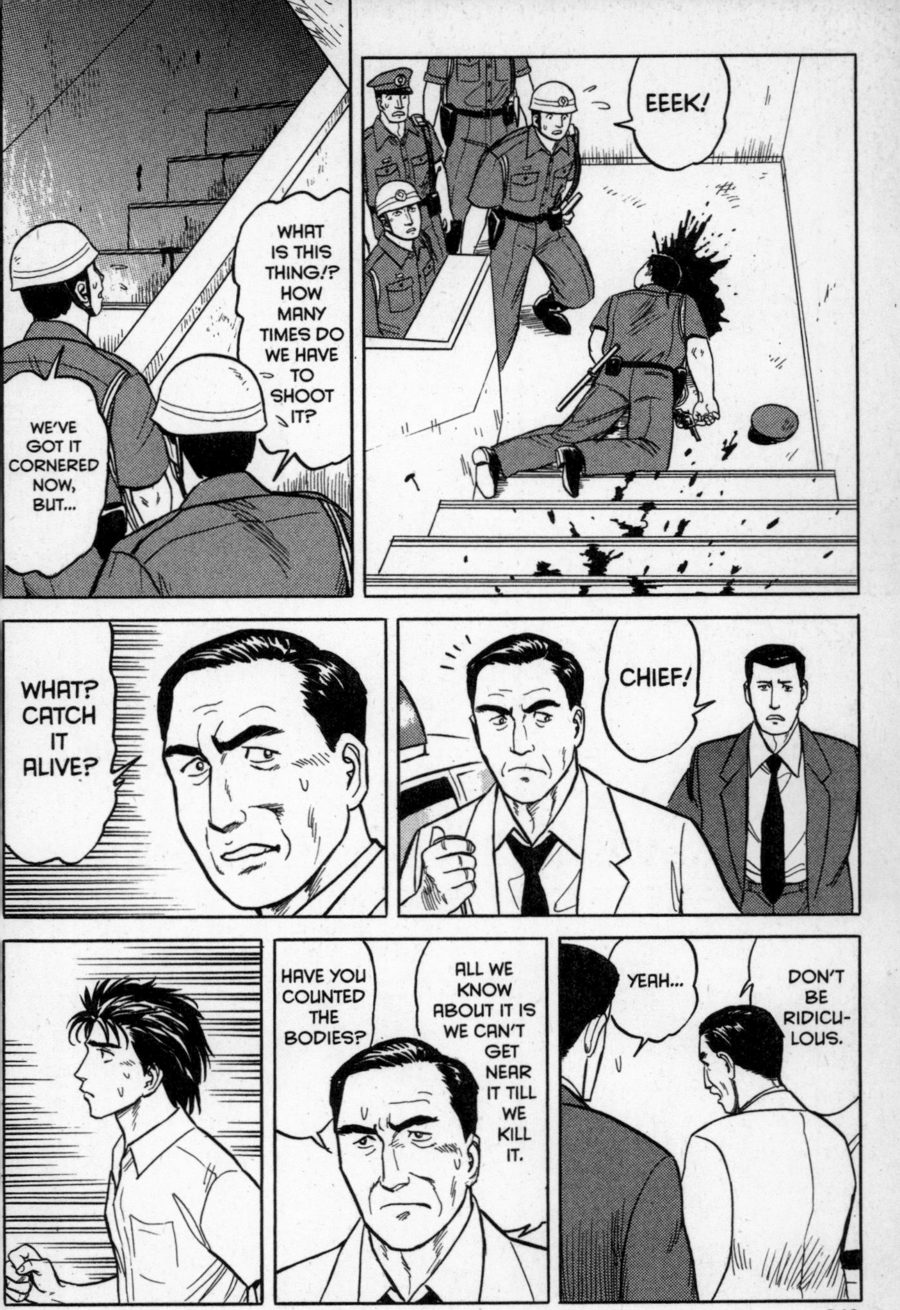
EEEK!
WHAT IS THIS THING!? HOW MANY TIMES DO WE HAVE TO SHOOT IT?
WE'VE GOT IT CORNERED NOW, BUT...
CHIEF!
WHAT? CATCH IT ALIVE?
DON'T BE RIDICU-LOUS.
YEAH...
ALL WE KNOW ABOUT IT IS WE CAN'T GET NEAR IT TILL WE KILL IT.
HAVE YOU COUNTED THE BODIES?

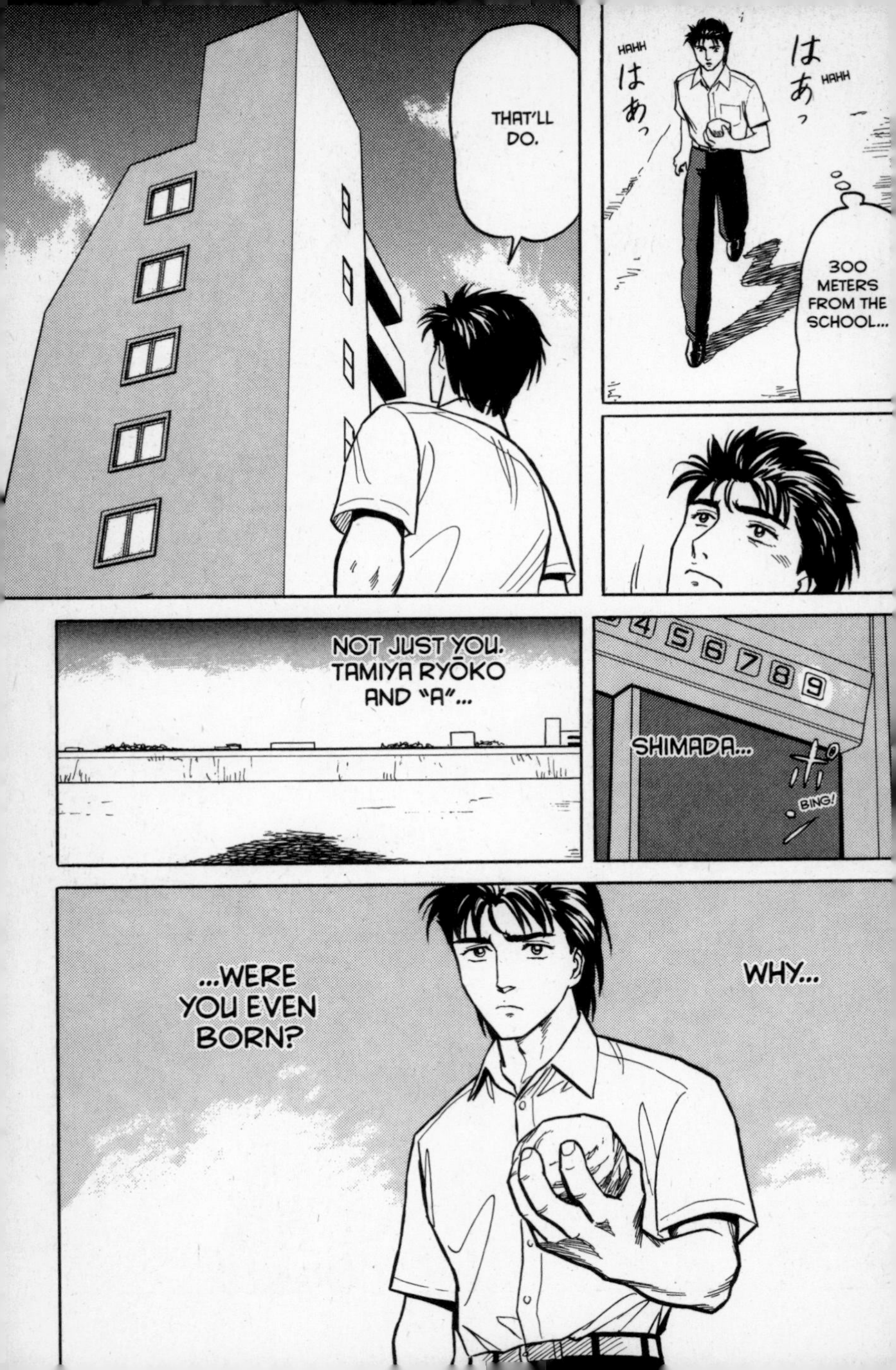
はあっ
HAHH
はあっ
HAHH
300 METERS FROM THE SCHOOL...
THAT'LL DO.
SHIMADA...
ポ
BING!
NOT JUST YOU. TAMIYA RYŌKO AND "A"...
WHY...
...WERE YOU EVEN BORN?

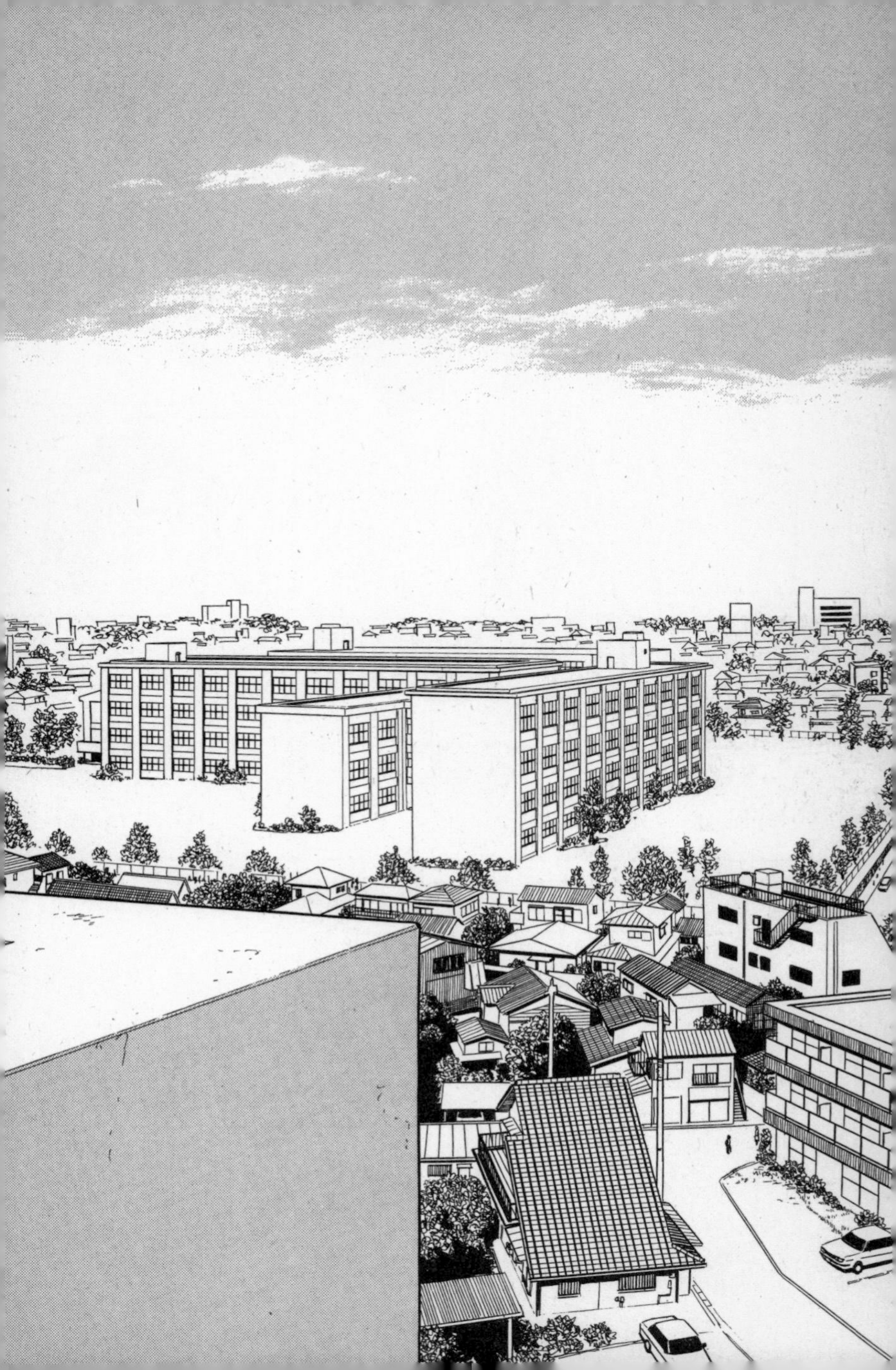

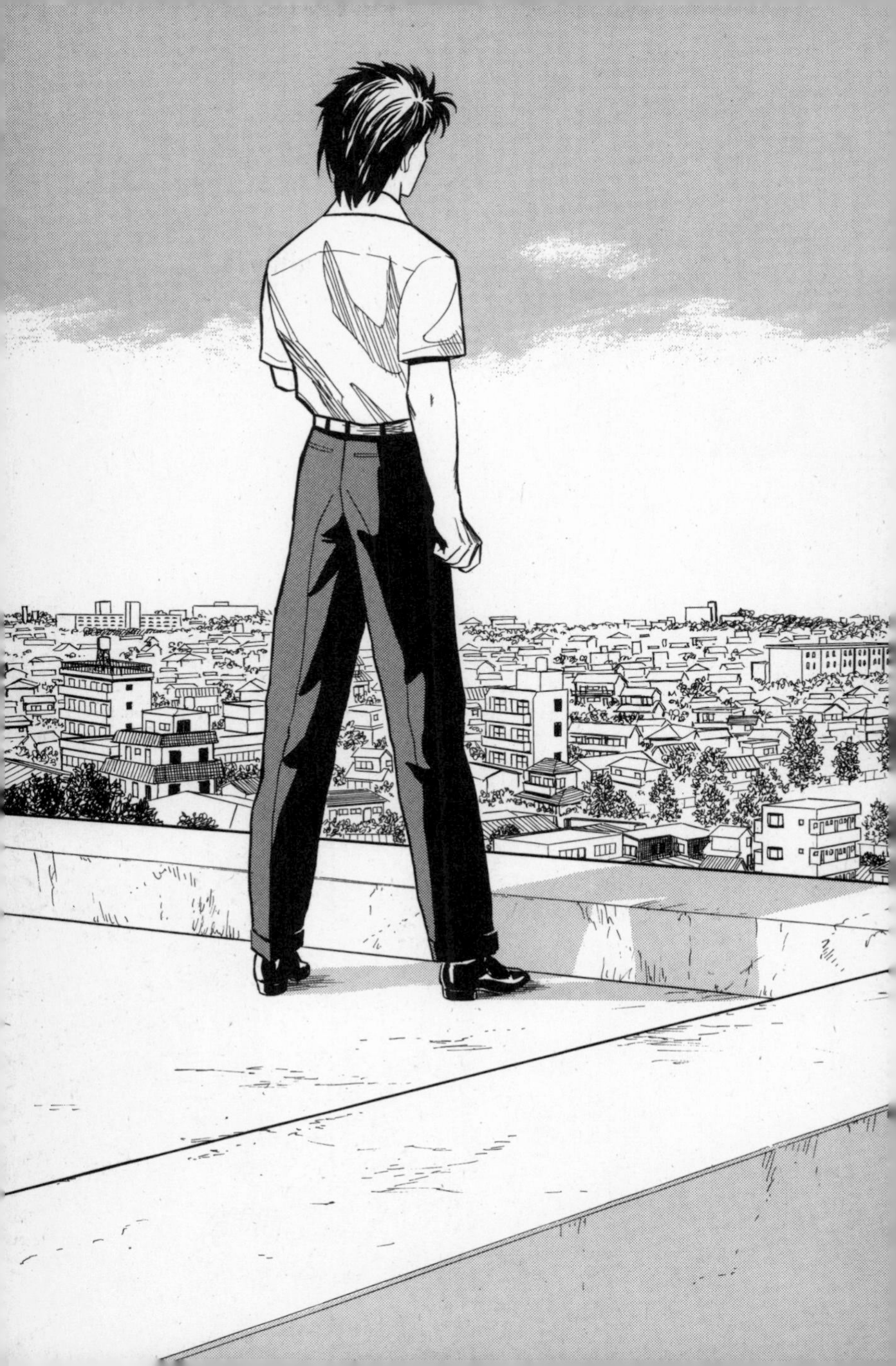

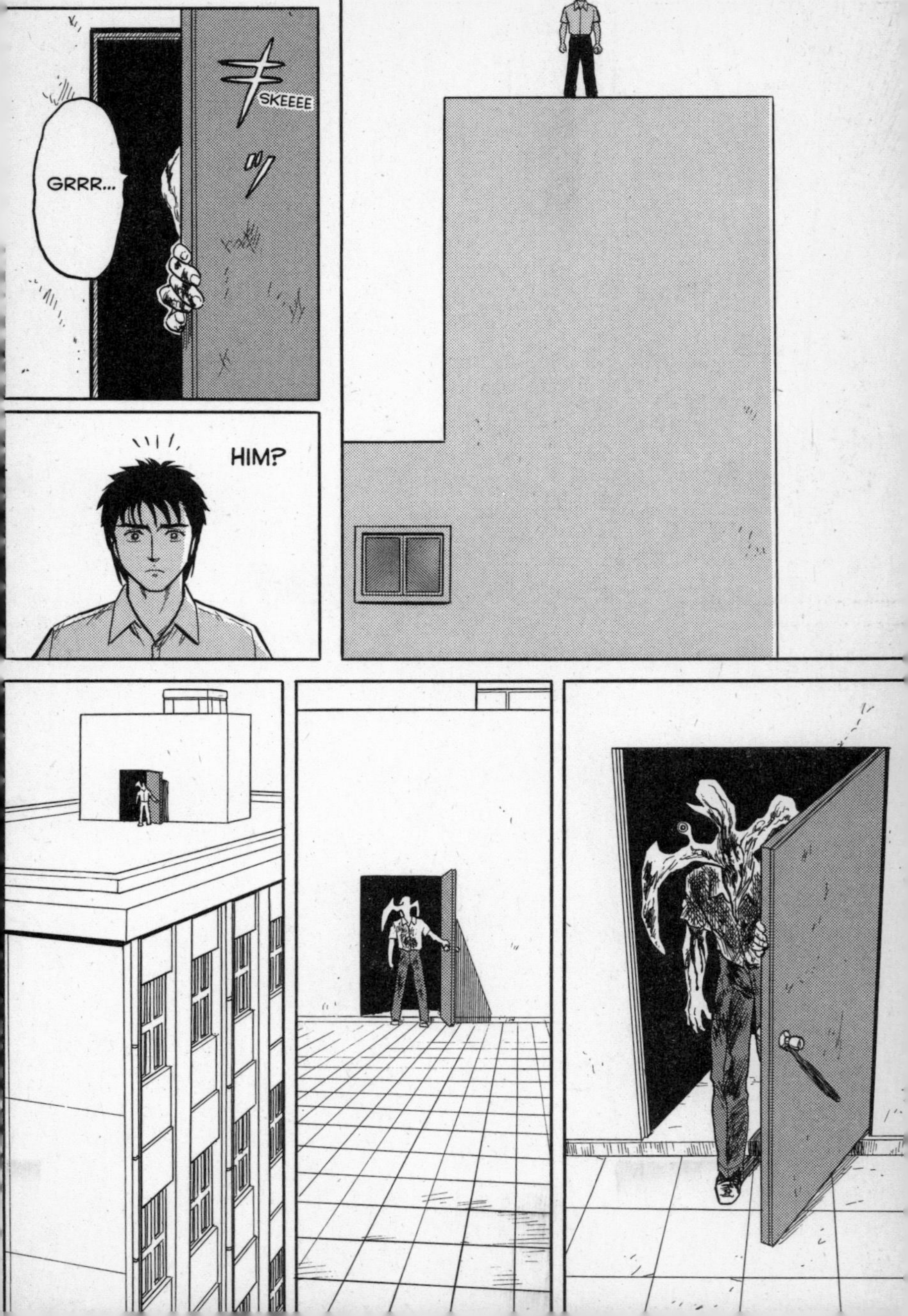
SKEEEE
GRRR...
HIM?

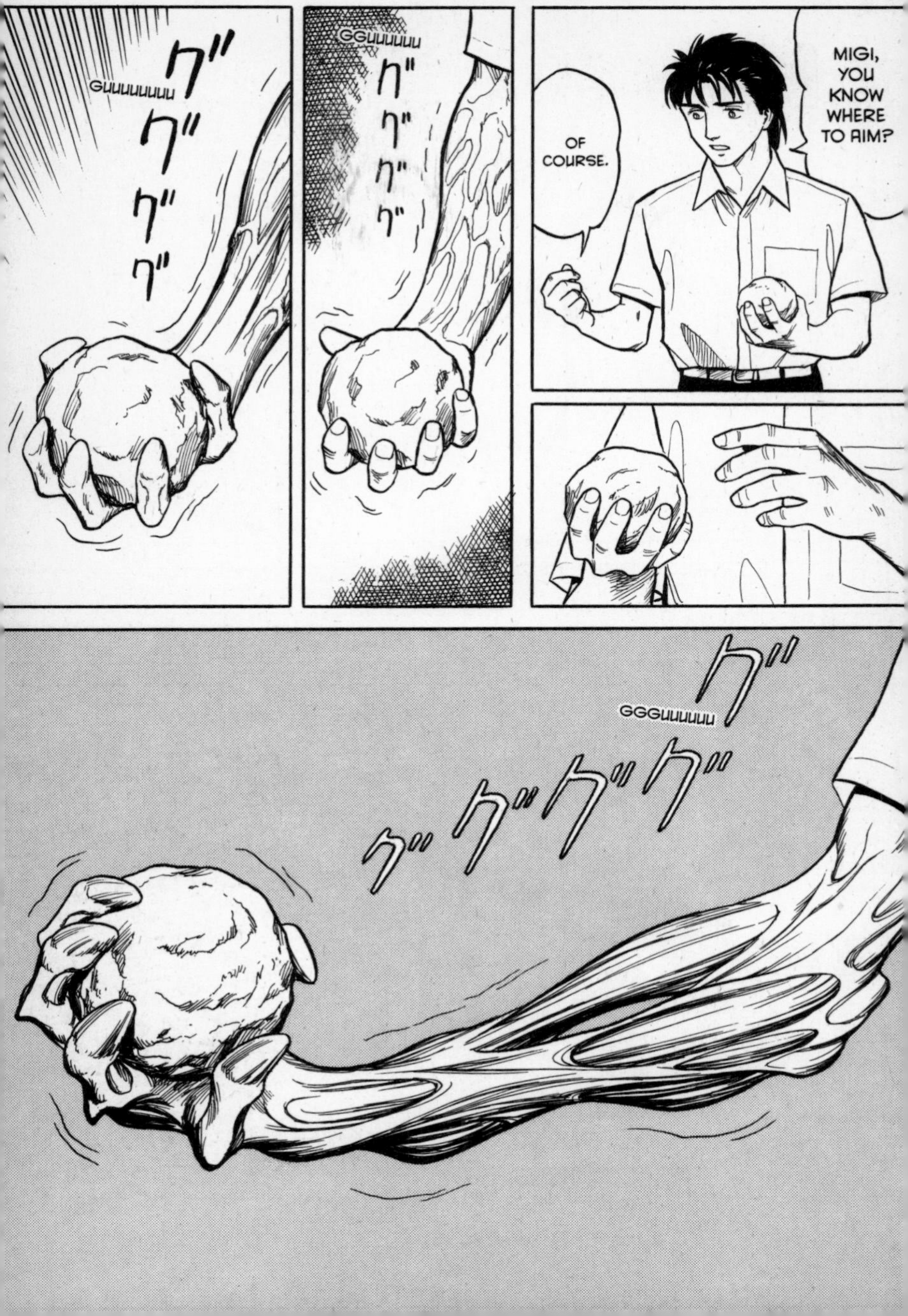
MIGI, YOU KNOW WHERE TO AIM?
OF COURSE.
GGuuuuuu
グ グ グ グ
Guuuuuuuu
グ グ グ グ
GGGuuuuuu
グ グ グ グ グ

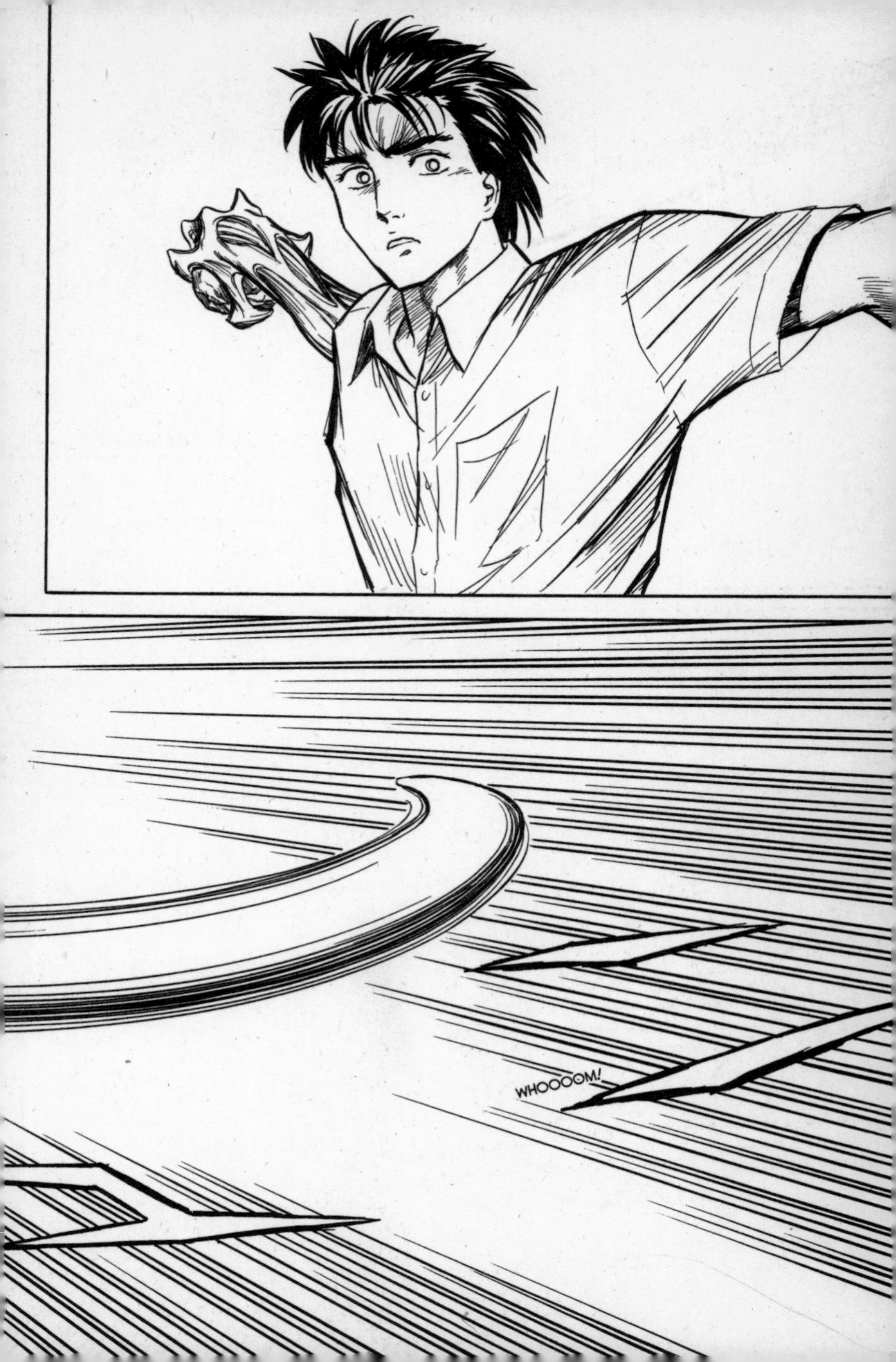
WHOOOOM!

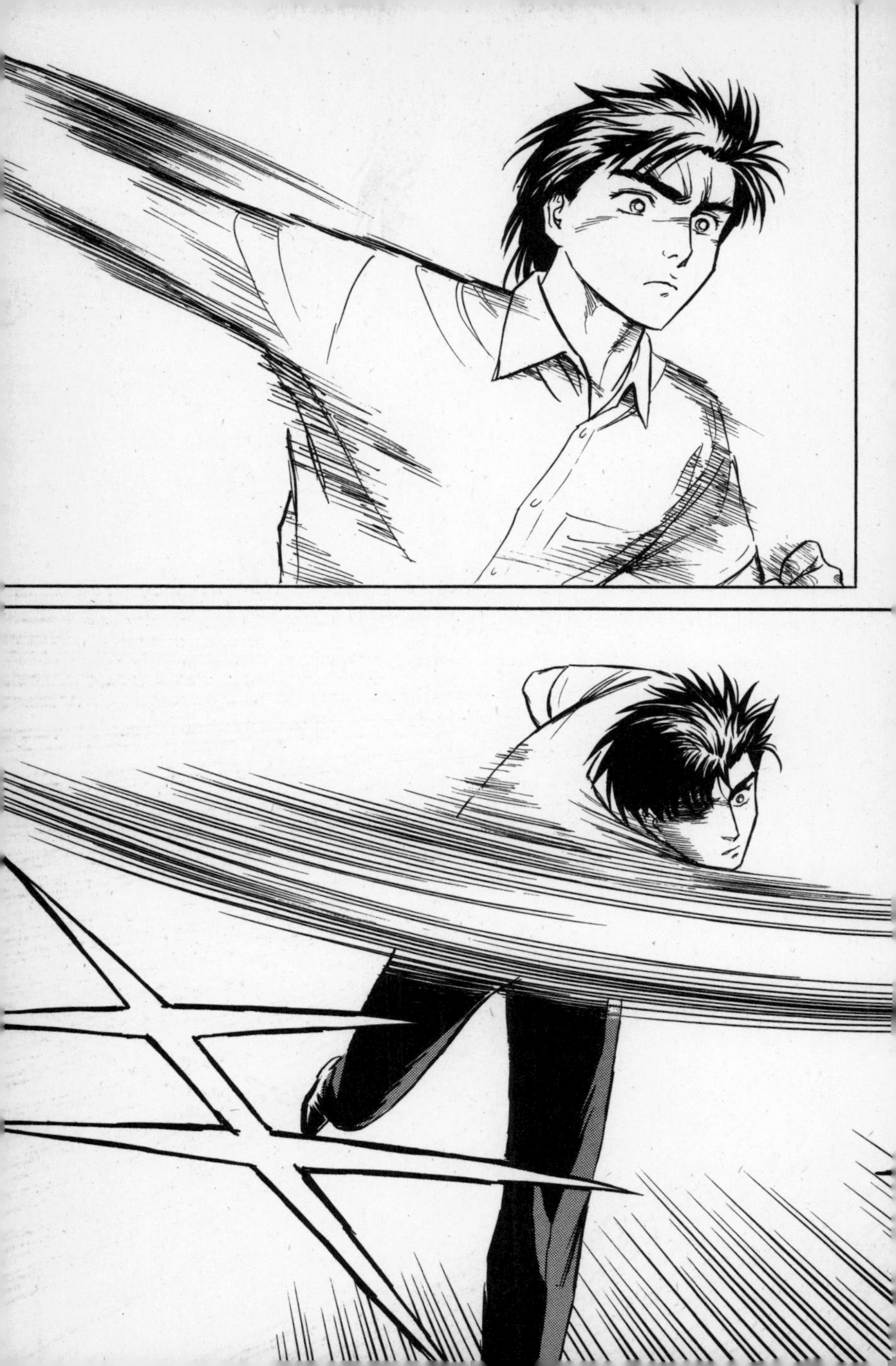

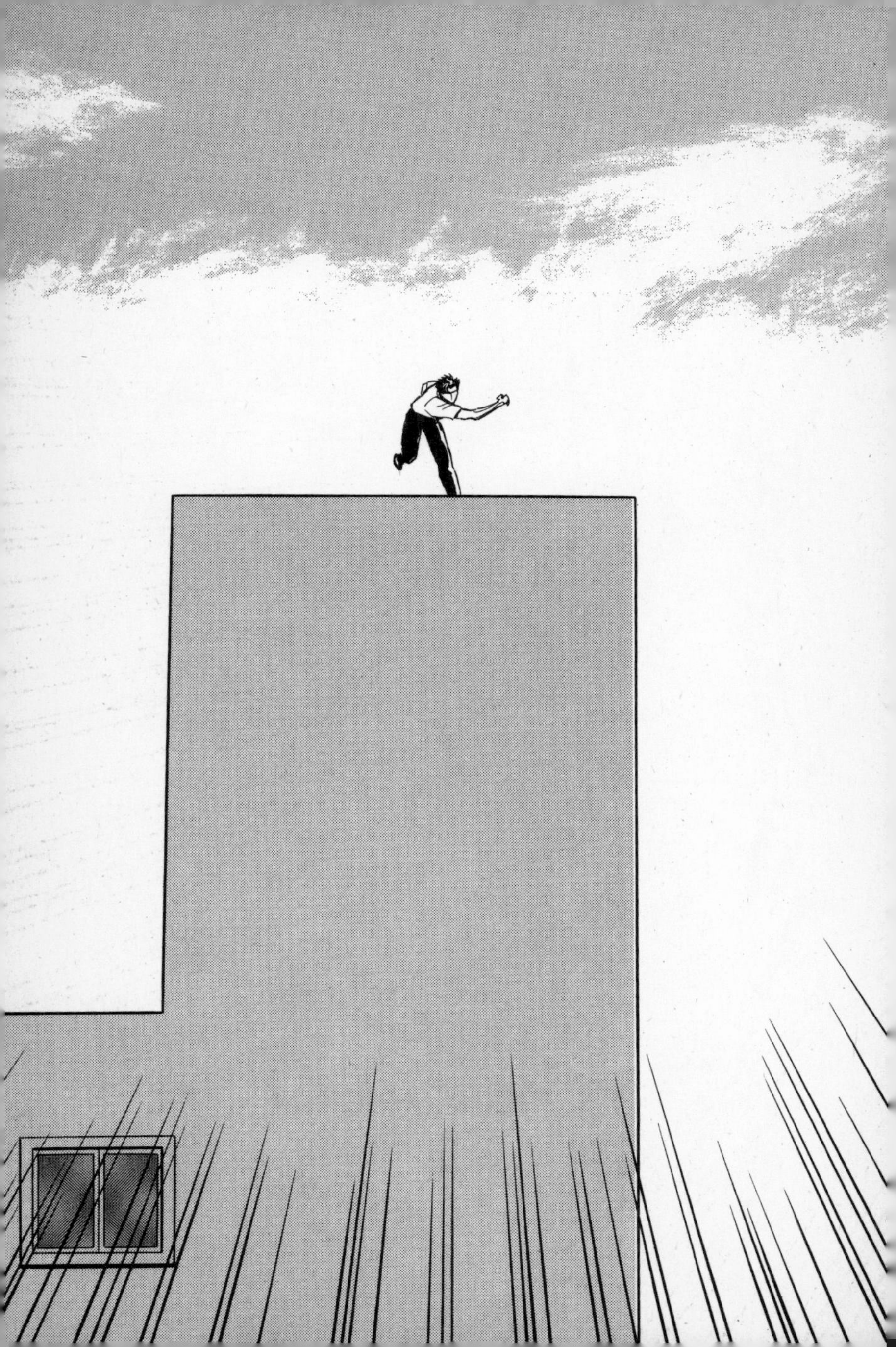

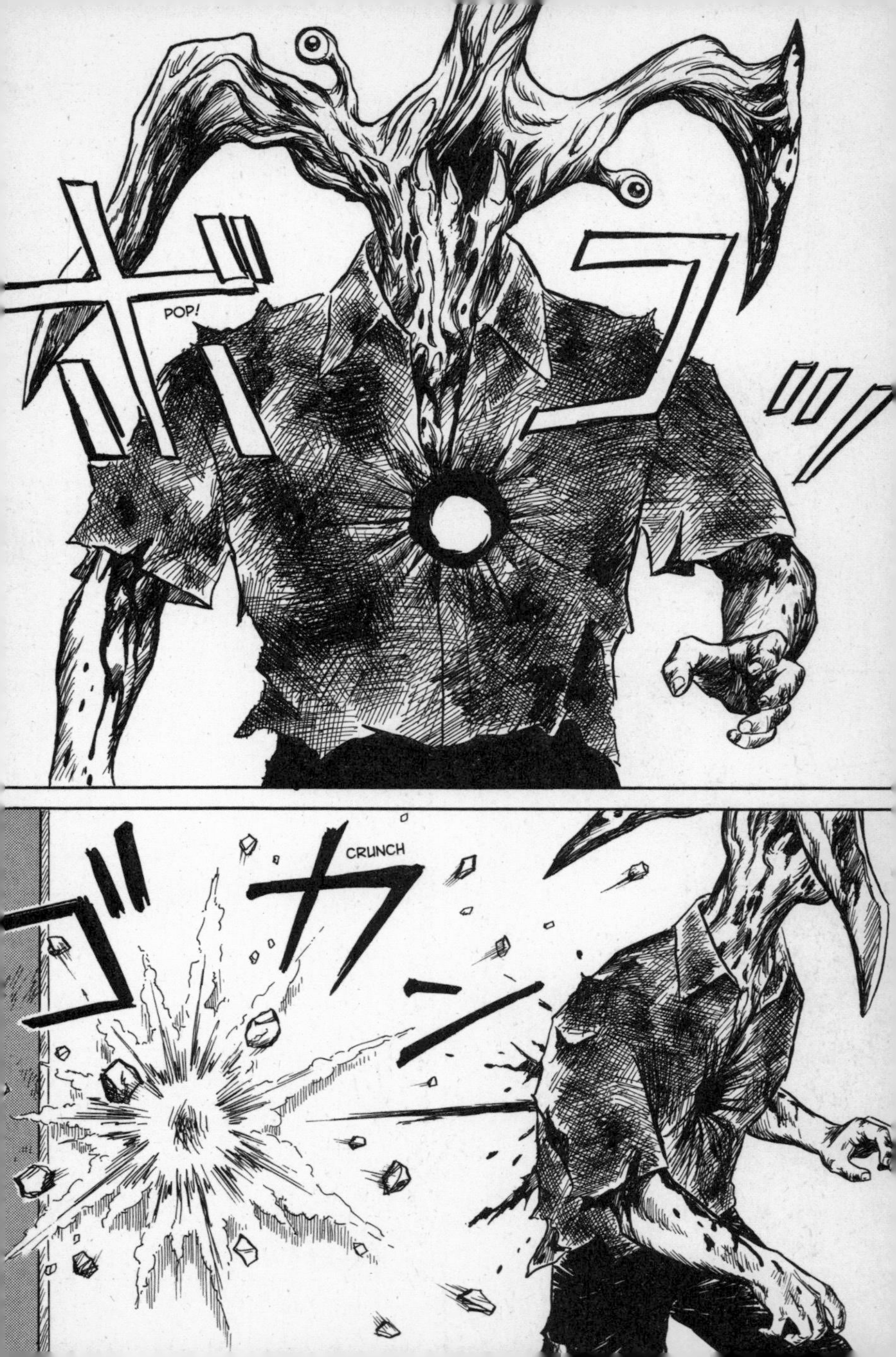
POP!
CRUNCH

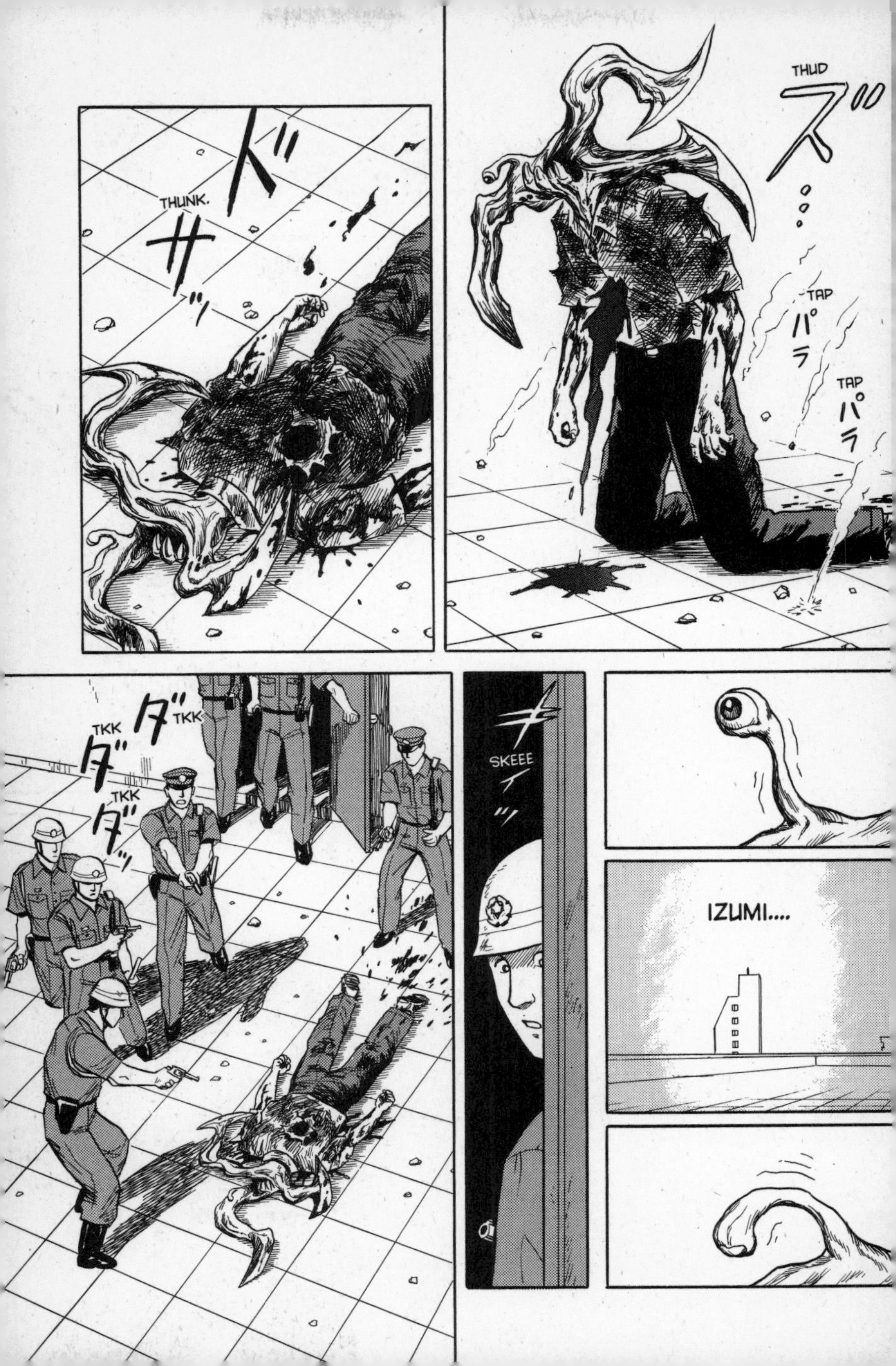
THUD
TAP
TAP
THUNK.
IZUMI....
SKEEE
TKK
TKK
TKK

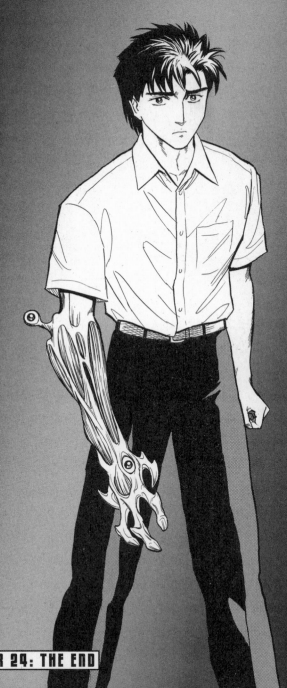

CHAPTER 24: THE END

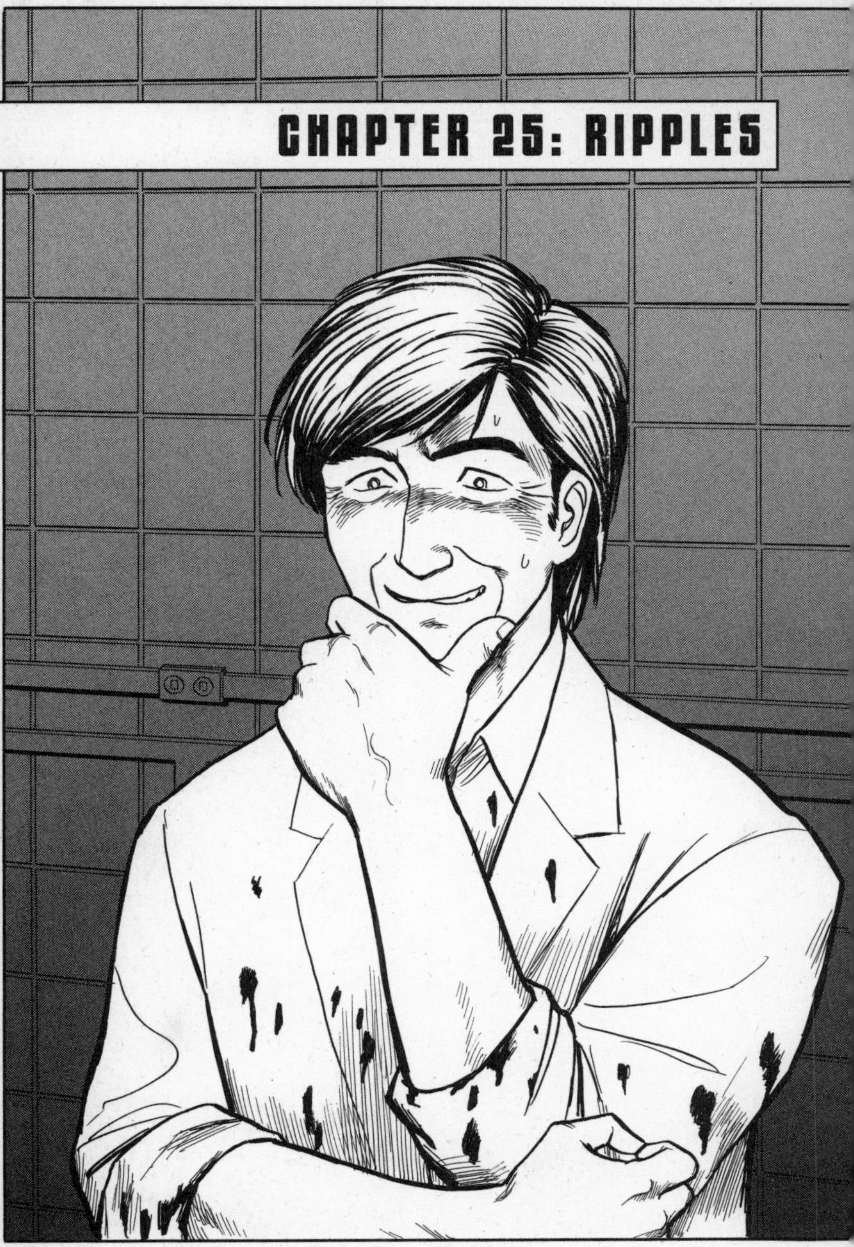
CHAPTER 25: RIPPLES

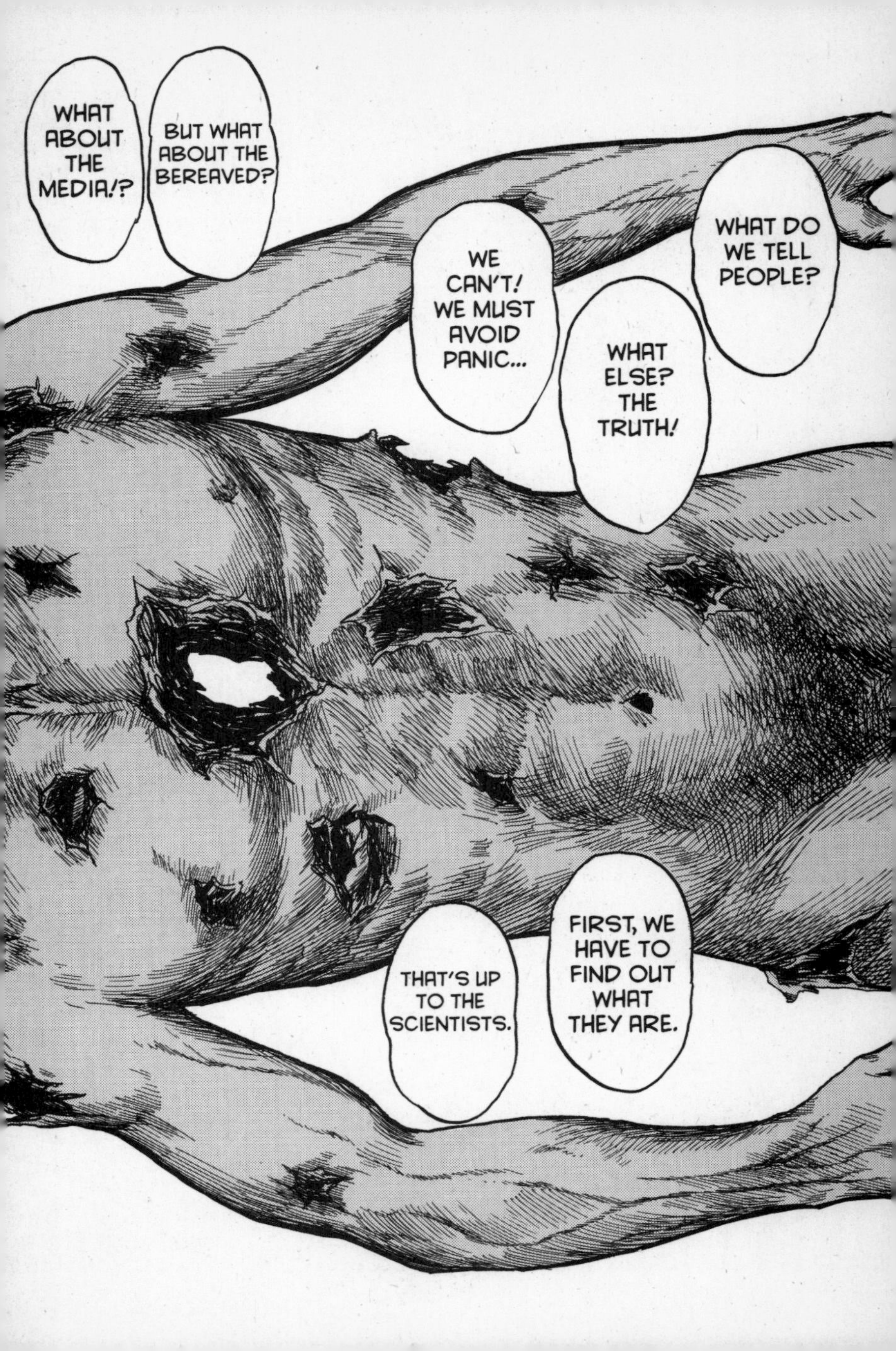

WHAT DO WE TELL PEOPLE?
WHAT ELSE? THE TRUTH!
WE CAN'T! WE MUST AVOID PANIC...
BUT WHAT ABOUT THE BEREAVED?
WHAT ABOUT THE MEDIA!?
FIRST, WE HAVE TO FIND OUT WHAT THEY ARE.
THAT'S UP TO THE SCIENTISTS.

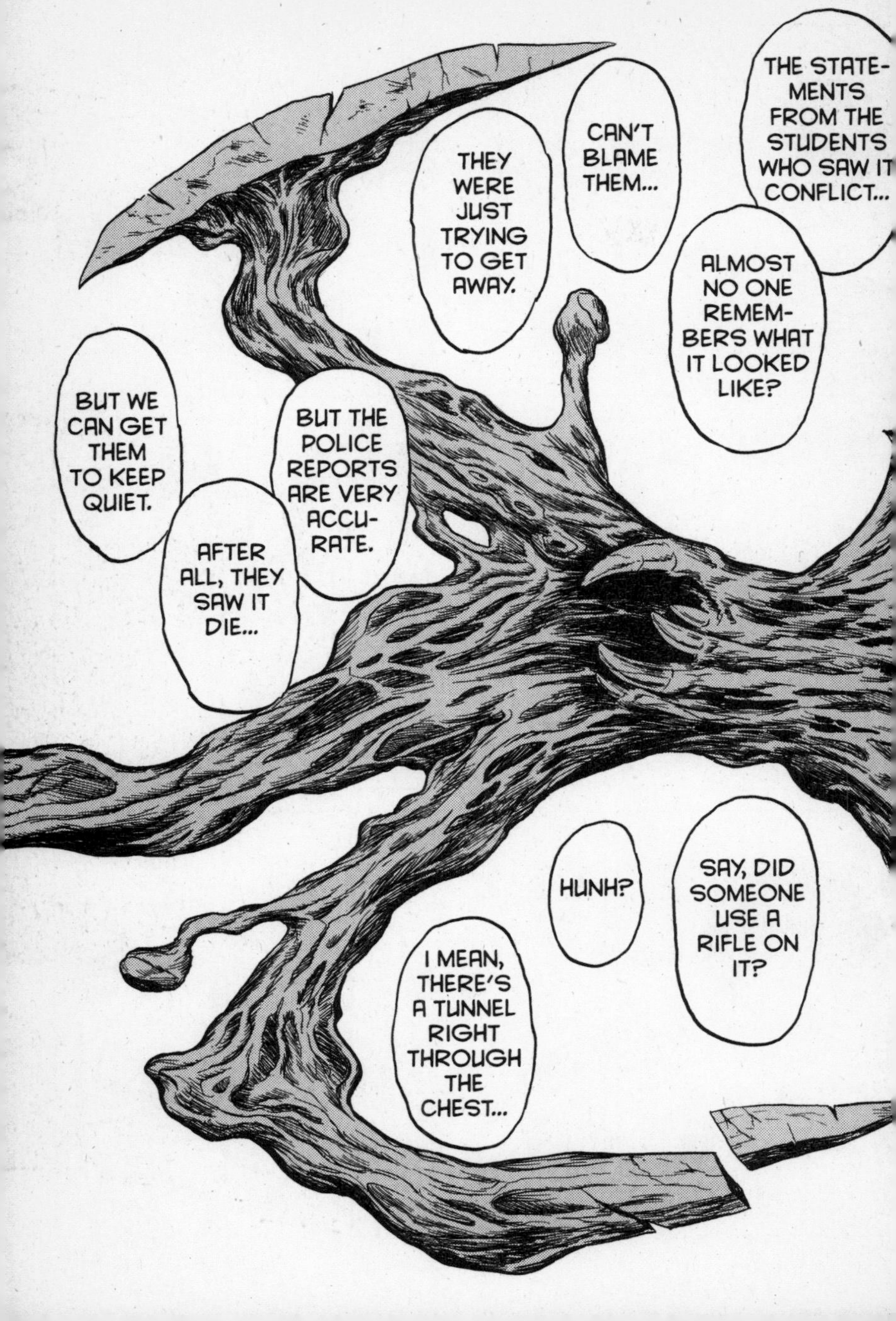
THE STATEMENTS FROM THE STUDENTS WHO SAW IT CONFLICT...
ALMOST NO ONE REMEMBERS WHAT IT LOOKED LIKE?
CAN'T BLAME THEM...
THEY WERE JUST TRYING TO GET AWAY.
BUT THE POLICE REPORTS ARE VERY ACCURATE.
AFTER ALL, THEY SAW IT DIE...
BUT WE CAN GET THEM TO KEEP QUIET.
SAY, DID SOMEONE USE A RIFLE ON IT?
HUNH?
I MEAN, THERE'S A TUNNEL RIGHT THROUGH THE CHEST...

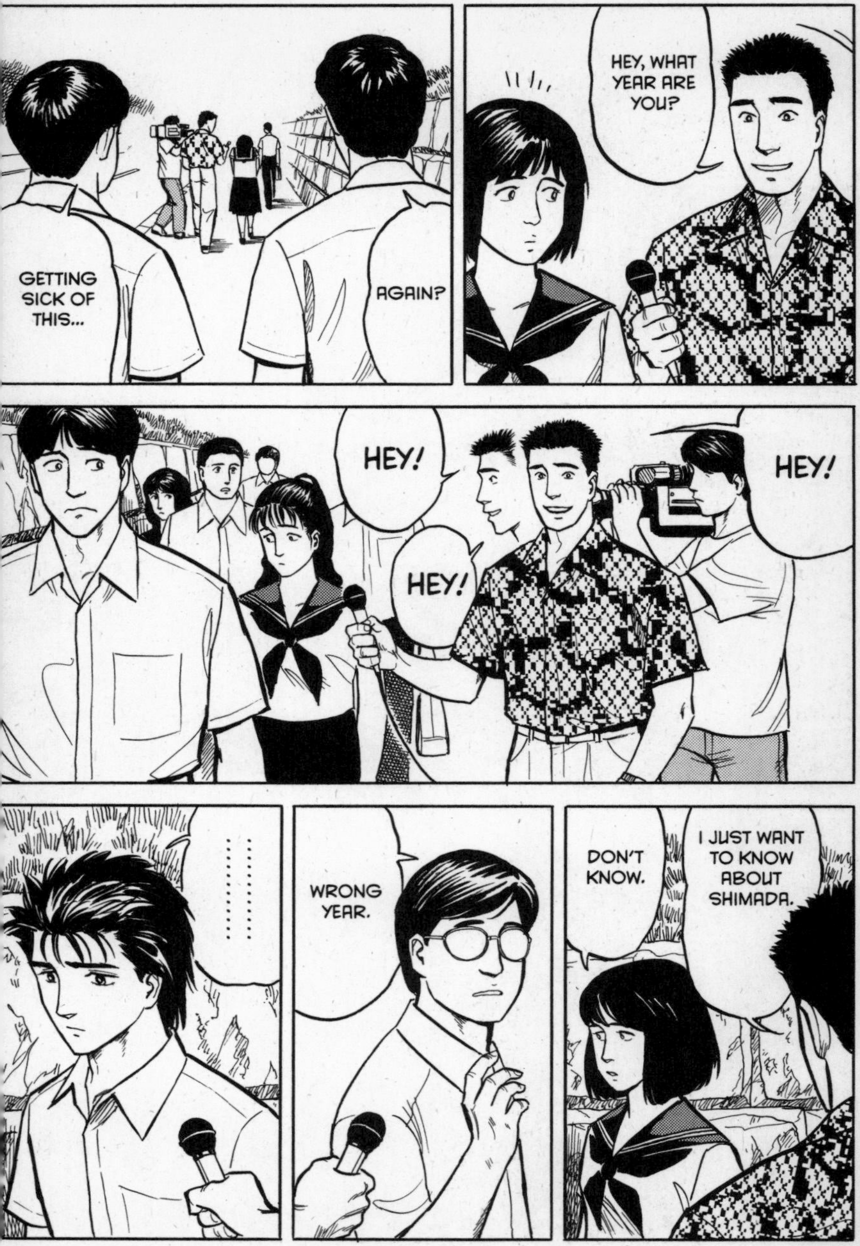
HEY, WHAT YEAR ARE YOU?
AGAIN?
GETTING SICK OF THIS...
HEY!
HEY!
HEY!
I JUST WANT TO KNOW ABOUT SHIMADA.
DON'T KNOW.
WRONG YEAR.
......

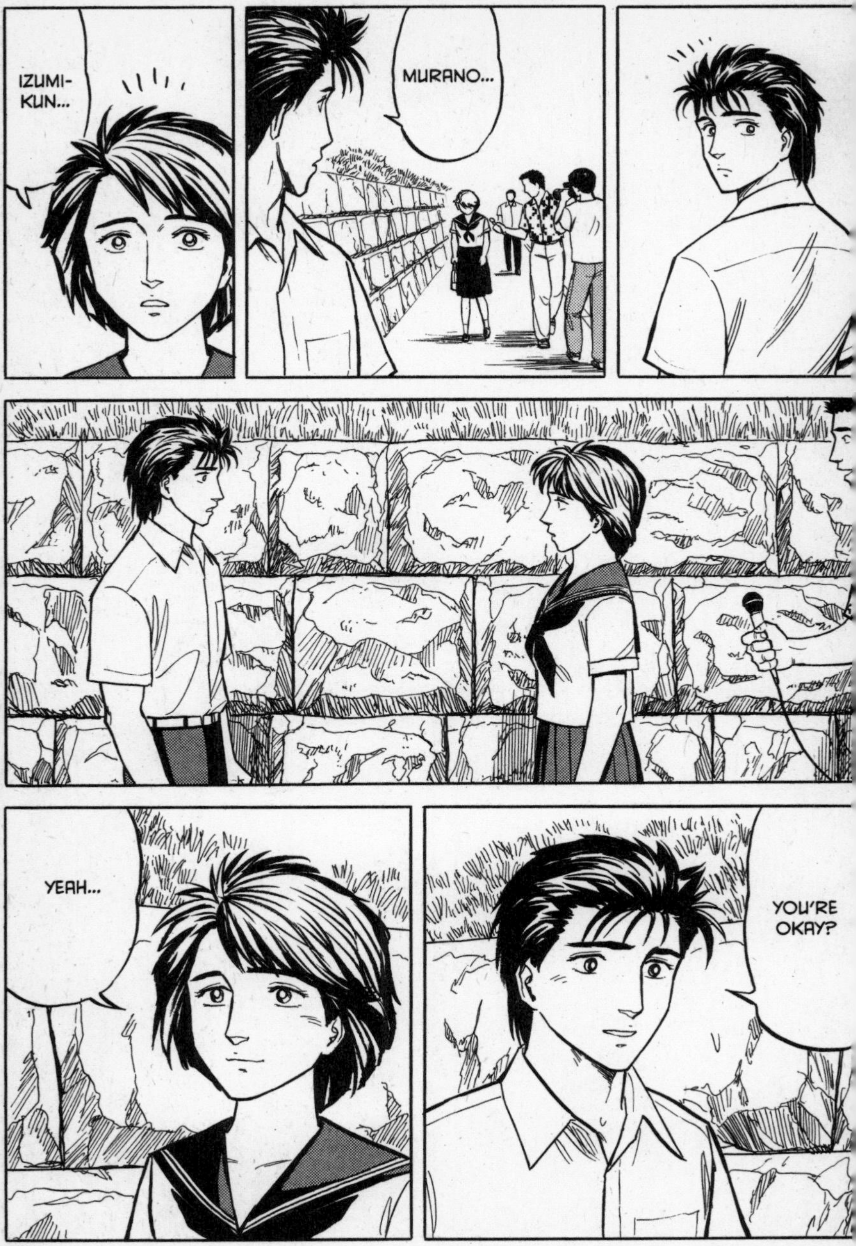
MURANO...
IZUMI-KUN...
YOU'RE OKAY?
YEAH...

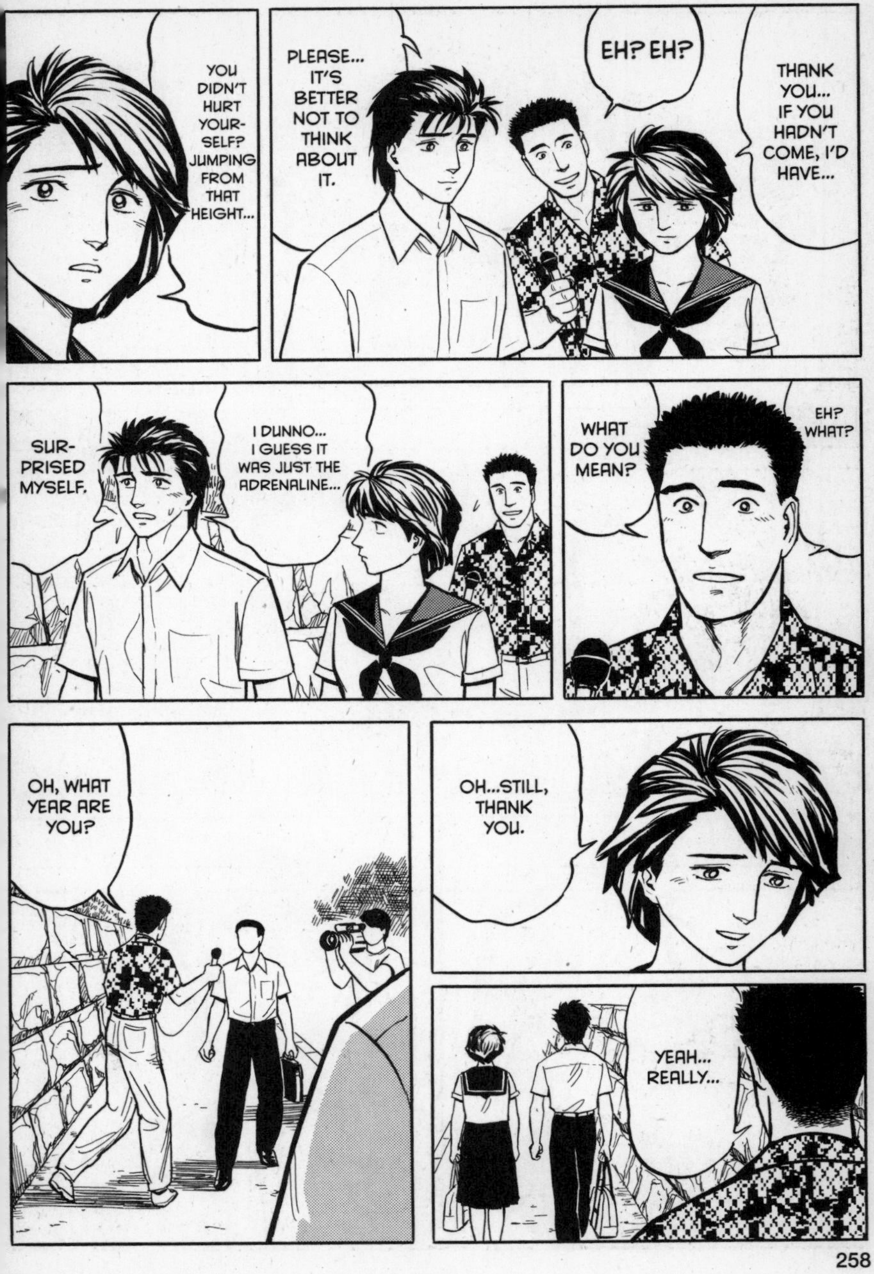
THANK YOU... IF YOU HADN'T COME, I'D HAVE...
EH? EH?
PLEASE... IT'S BETTER NOT TO THINK ABOUT IT.
YOU DIDN'T HURT YOURSELF? JUMPING FROM THAT HEIGHT...
EH? WHAT?
WHAT DO YOU MEAN?
I DUNNO... I GUESS IT WAS JUST THE ADRENALINE...
SURPRISED MYSELF.
OH...STILL, THANK YOU.
YEAH... REALLY...
OH, WHAT YEAR ARE YOU?

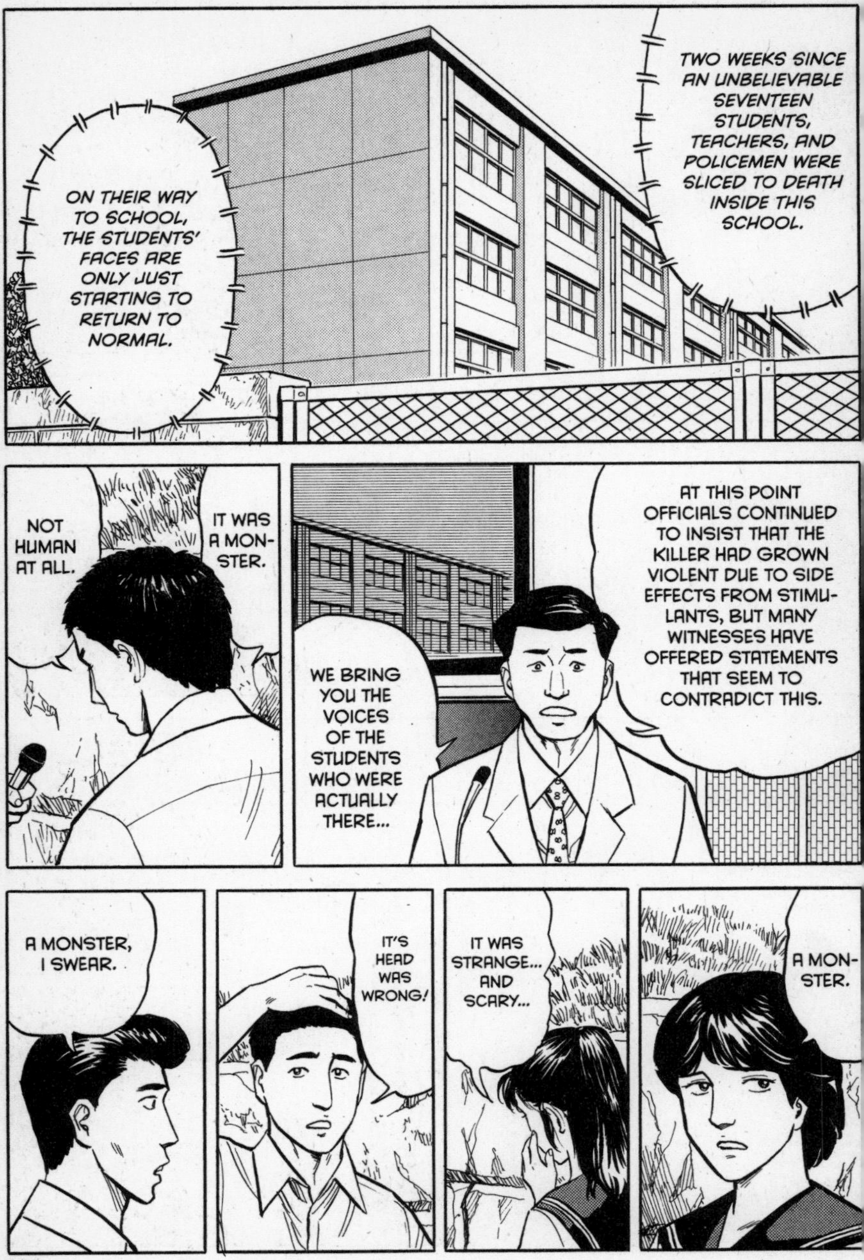
TWO WEEKS SINCE AN UNBELIEVABLE SEVENTEEN STUDENTS, TEACHERS, AND POLICEMEN WERE SLICED TO DEATH INSIDE THIS SCHOOL.
ON THEIR WAY TO SCHOOL, THE STUDENTS' FACES ARE ONLY JUST STARTING TO RETURN TO NORMAL.
AT THIS POINT OFFICIALS CONTINUED TO INSIST THAT THE KILLER HAD GROWN VIOLENT DUE TO SIDE EFFECTS FROM STIMULANTS, BUT MANY WITNESSES HAVE OFFERED STATEMENTS THAT SEEM TO CONTRADICT THIS.
WE BRING YOU THE VOICES OF THE STUDENTS WHO WERE ACTUALLY THERE...
IT WAS A MONSTER.
NOT HUMAN AT ALL.
A MONSTER.
IT WAS STRANGE... AND SCARY...
IT'S HEAD WAS WRONG!
A MONSTER, I SWEAR.

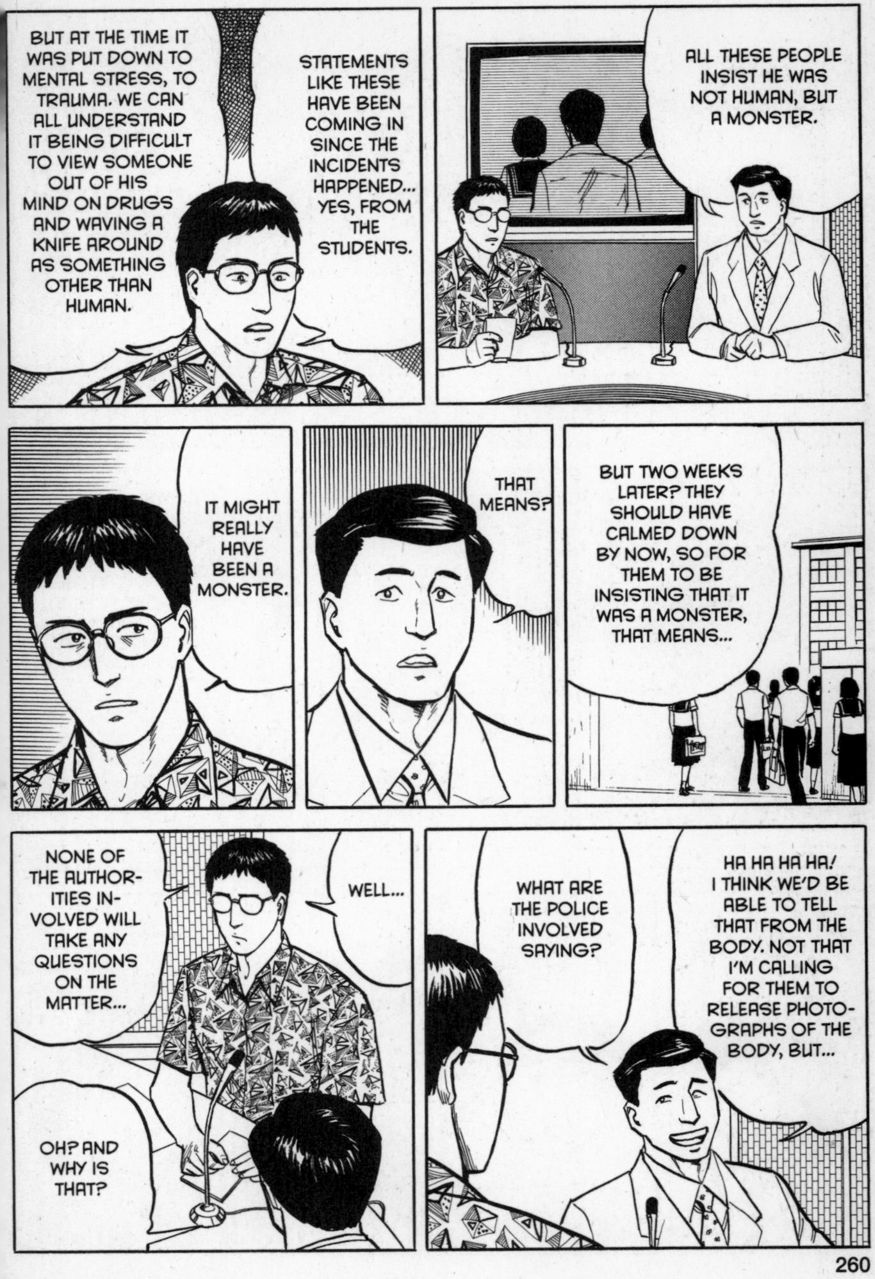
ALL THESE PEOPLE INSIST HE WAS NOT HUMAN, BUT A MONSTER.
STATEMENTS LIKE THESE HAVE BEEN COMING IN SINCE THE INCIDENTS HAPPENED... YES, FROM THE STUDENTS.
BUT AT THE TIME IT WAS PUT DOWN TO MENTAL STRESS, TO TRAUMA. WE CAN ALL UNDERSTAND IT BEING DIFFICULT TO VIEW SOMEONE OUT OF HIS MIND ON DRUGS AND WAVING A KNIFE AROUND AS SOMETHING OTHER THAN HUMAN.
BUT TWO WEEKS LATER? THEY SHOULD HAVE CALMED DOWN BY NOW, SO FOR THEM TO BE INSISTING THAT IT WAS A MONSTER, THAT MEANS...
THAT MEANS?
IT MIGHT REALLY HAVE BEEN A MONSTER.
HA HA HA HA! I THINK WE'D BE ABLE TO TELL THAT FROM THE BODY. NOT THAT I'M CALLING FOR THEM TO RELEASE PHOTO-GRAPHS OF THE BODY, BUT...
WHAT ARE THE POLICE INVOLVED SAYING?
WELL...
NONE OF THE AUTHOR-ITIES IN-VOLVED WILL TAKE ANY QUESTIONS ON THE MATTER...
OH? AND WHY IS THAT?

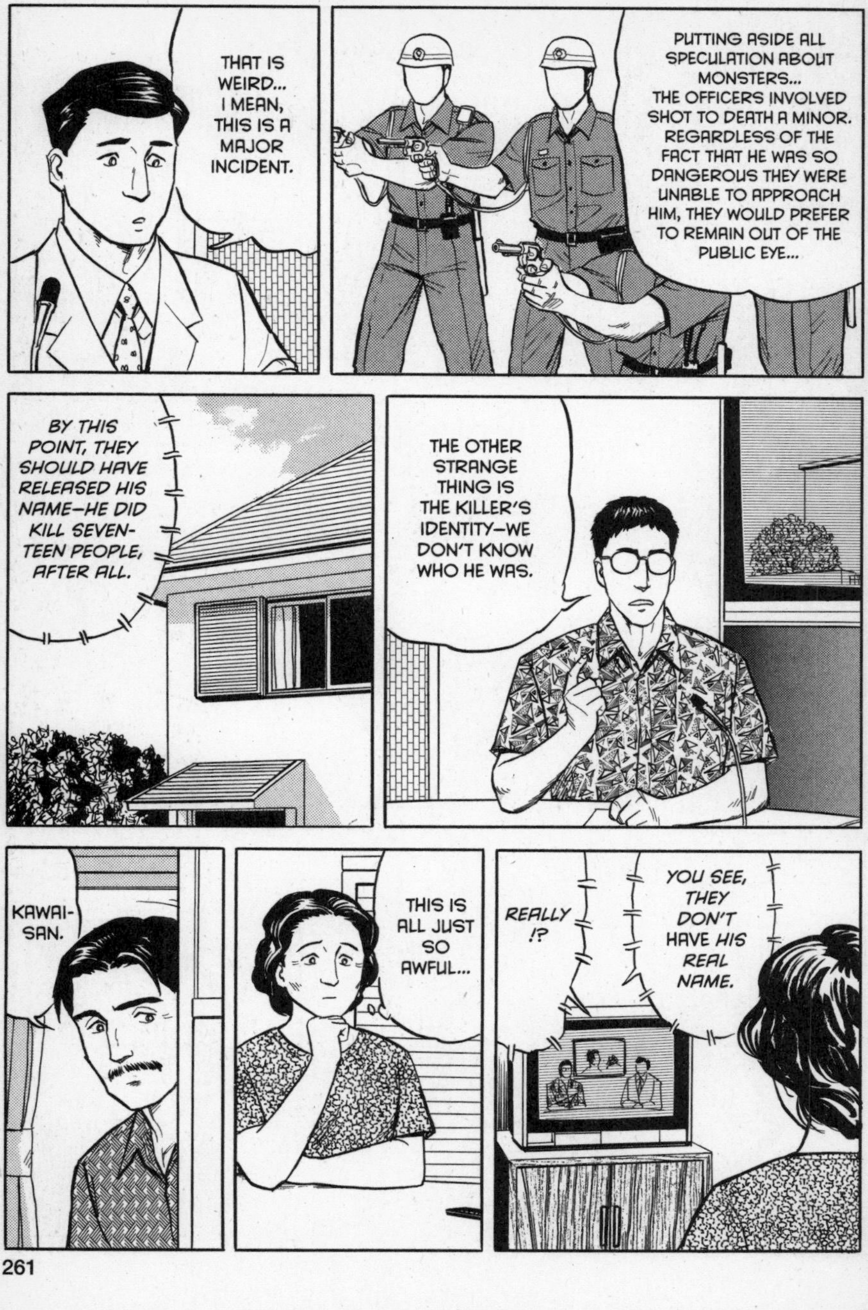
PUTTING ASIDE ALL SPECULATION ABOUT MONSTERS... THE OFFICERS INVOLVED SHOT TO DEATH A MINOR. REGARDLESS OF THE FACT THAT HE WAS SO DANGEROUS THEY WERE UNABLE TO APPROACH HIM, THEY WOULD PREFER TO REMAIN OUT OF THE PUBLIC EYE...
THAT IS WEIRD... I MEAN, THIS IS A MAJOR INCIDENT.
THE OTHER STRANGE THING IS THE KILLER'S IDENTITY—WE DON'T KNOW WHO HE WAS.
BY THIS POINT, THEY SHOULD HAVE RELEASED HIS NAME—HE DID KILL SEVENTEEN PEOPLE, AFTER ALL.
YOU SEE, THEY DON'T HAVE HIS REAL NAME.
REALLY!?
THIS IS ALL JUST SO AWFUL...
KAWAI-SAN.

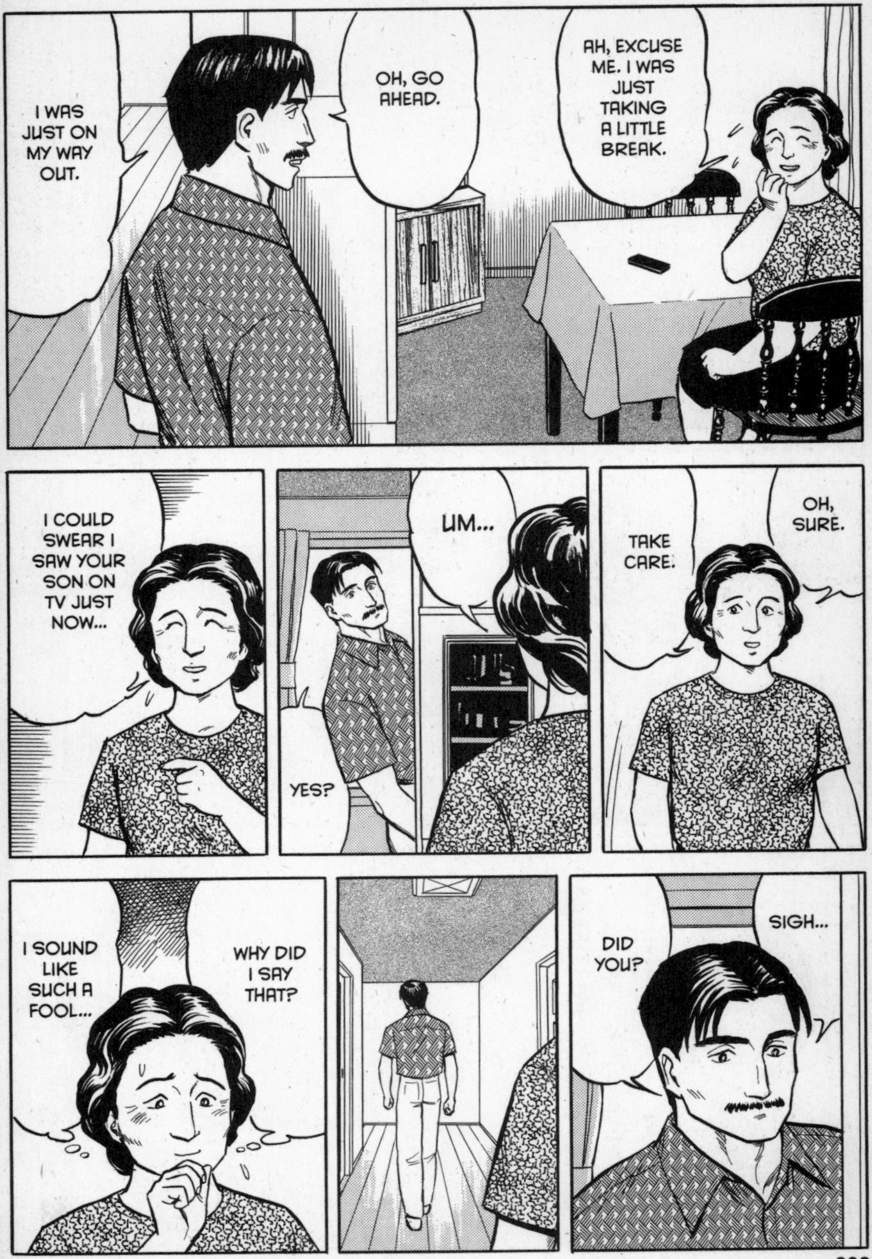
AH, EXCUSE ME. I WAS JUST TAKING A LITTLE BREAK.
OH, GO AHEAD.
I WAS JUST ON MY WAY OUT.
OH, SURE.
TAKE CARE.
UM...
YES?
I COULD SWEAR I SAW YOUR SON ON TV JUST NOW...
SIGH...
DID YOU?
WHY DID I SAY THAT?
I SOUND LIKE SUCH A FOOL...

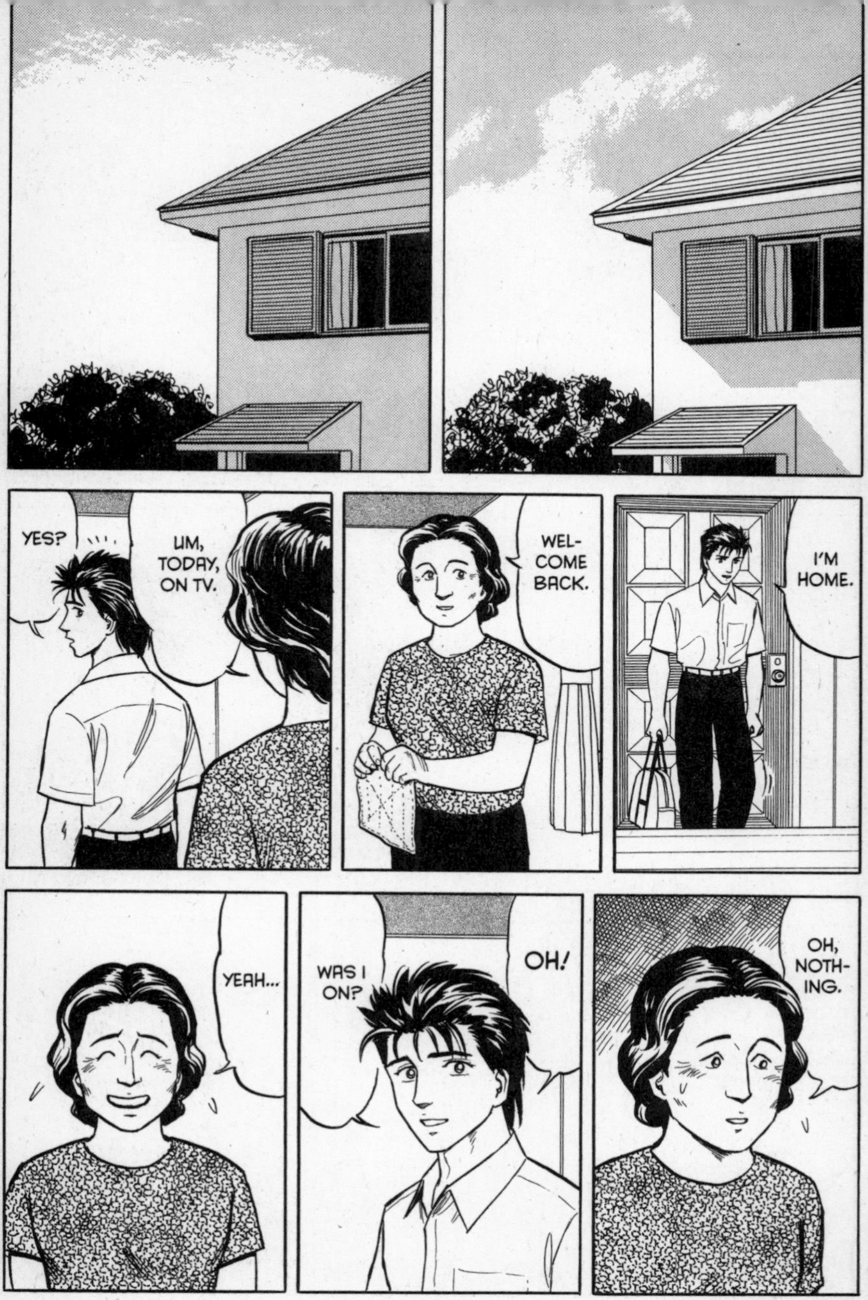
I'M HOME.
WEL-COME BACK.
UM, TODAY, ON TV.
YES?
OH, NOTH-ING.
OH!
WAS I ON?
YEAH...

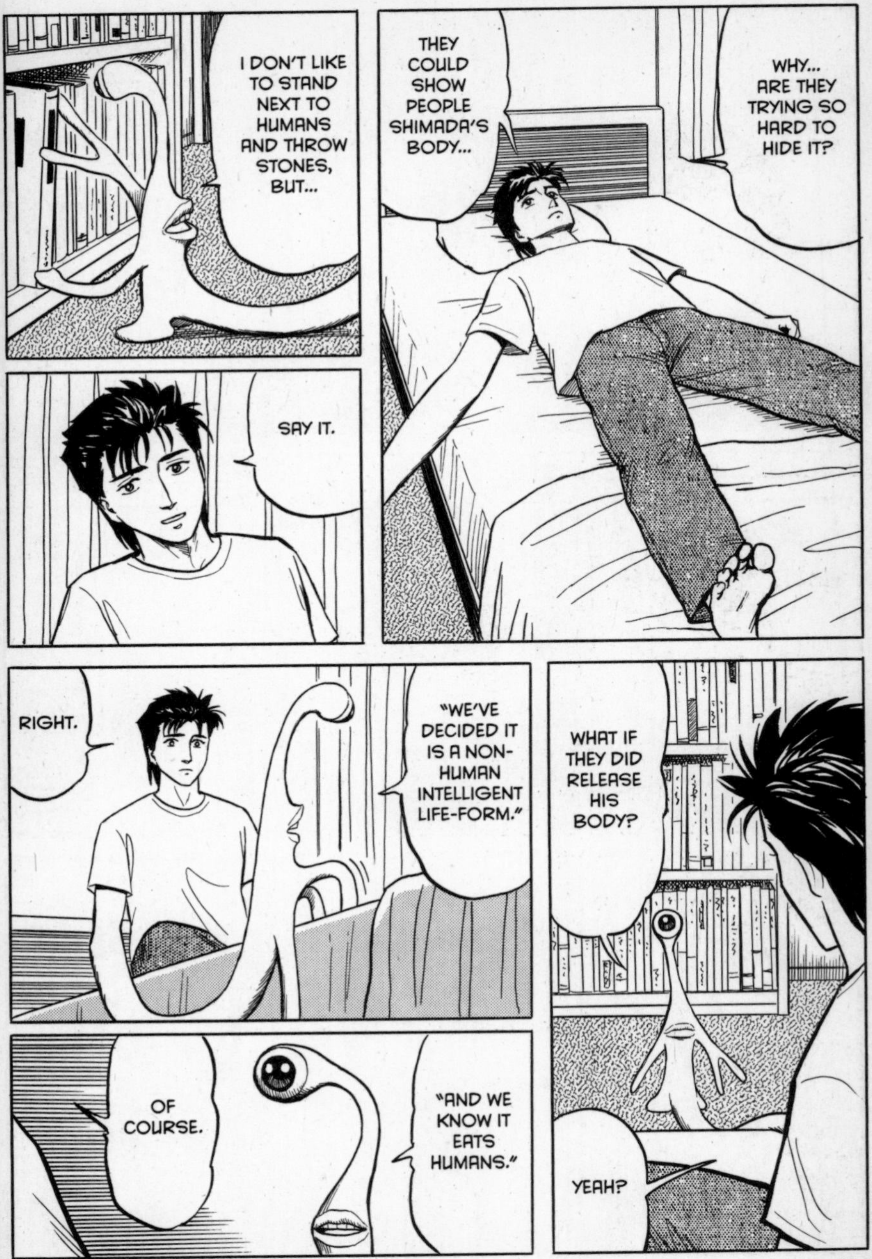
WHY... ARE THEY TRYING SO HARD TO HIDE IT?
THEY COULD SHOW PEOPLE SHIMADA'S BODY...
I DON'T LIKE TO STAND NEXT TO HUMANS AND THROW STONES, BUT...
SAY IT.
WHAT IF THEY DID RELEASE HIS BODY?
YEAH?
"WE'VE DECIDED IT IS A NON-HUMAN INTELLIGENT LIFE-FORM."
RIGHT.
"AND WE KNOW IT EATS HUMANS."
OF COURSE.

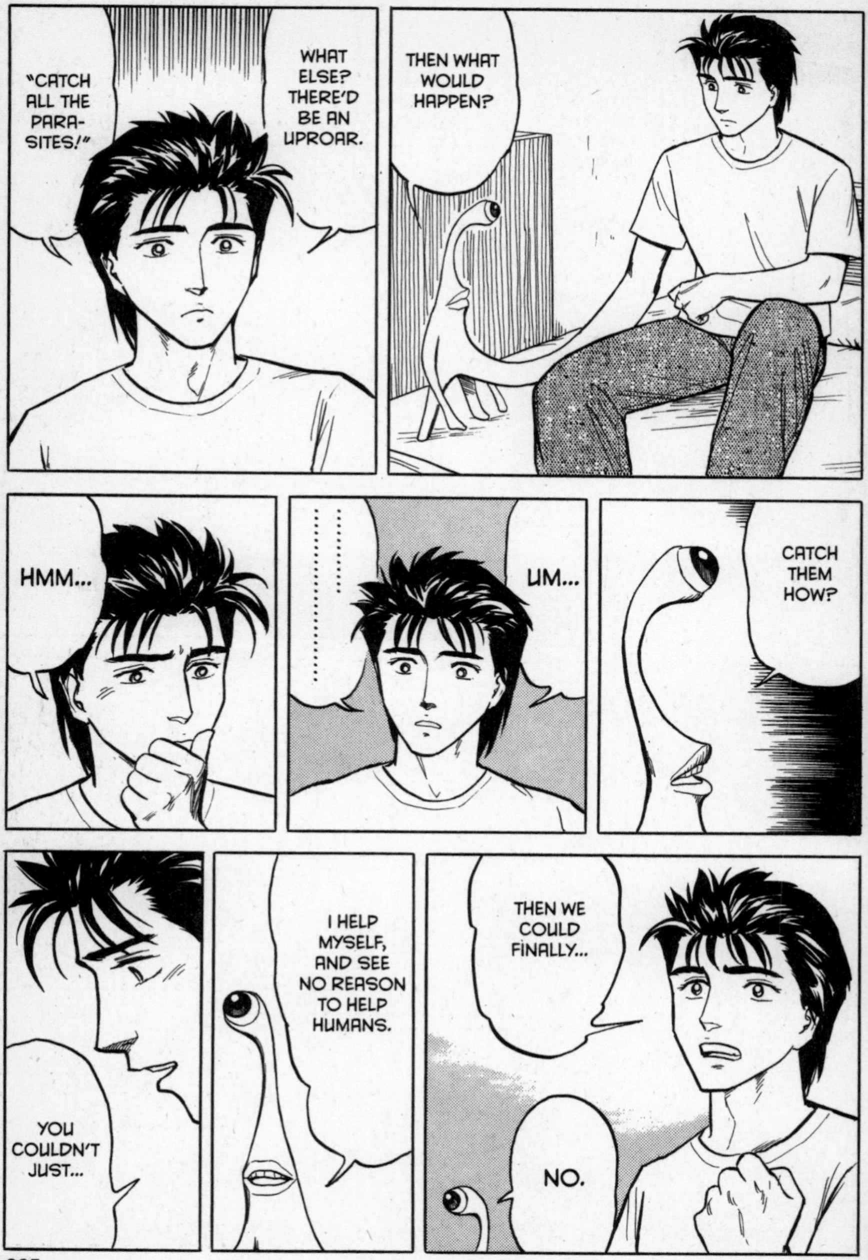
THEN WHAT WOULD HAPPEN?
WHAT ELSE? THERE'D BE AN UPROAR.
"CATCH ALL THE PARASITES!"
CATCH THEM HOW?
UM...
......
HMM...
THEN WE COULD FINALLY...
NO.
I HELP MYSELF, AND SEE NO REASON TO HELP HUMANS.
YOU COULDN'T JUST...

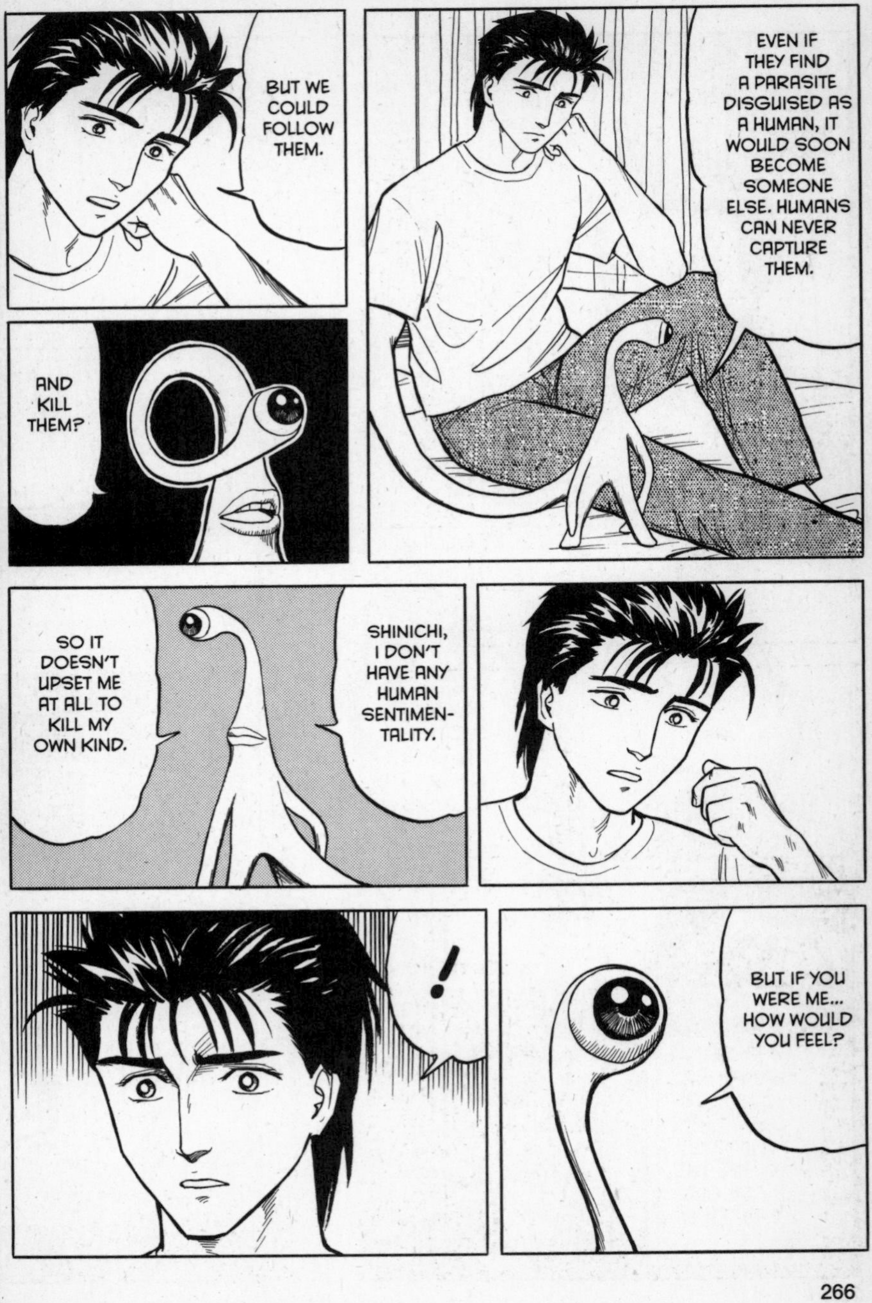
EVEN IF THEY FIND A PARASITE DISGUISED AS A HUMAN, IT WOULD SOON BECOME SOMEONE ELSE. HUMANS CAN NEVER CAPTURE THEM.
BUT WE COULD FOLLOW THEM.
AND KILL THEM?
SHINICHI, I DON'T HAVE ANY HUMAN SENTIMEN-TALITY.
SO IT DOESN'T UPSET ME AT ALL TO KILL MY OWN KIND.
BUT IF YOU WERE ME... HOW WOULD YOU FEEL?
!

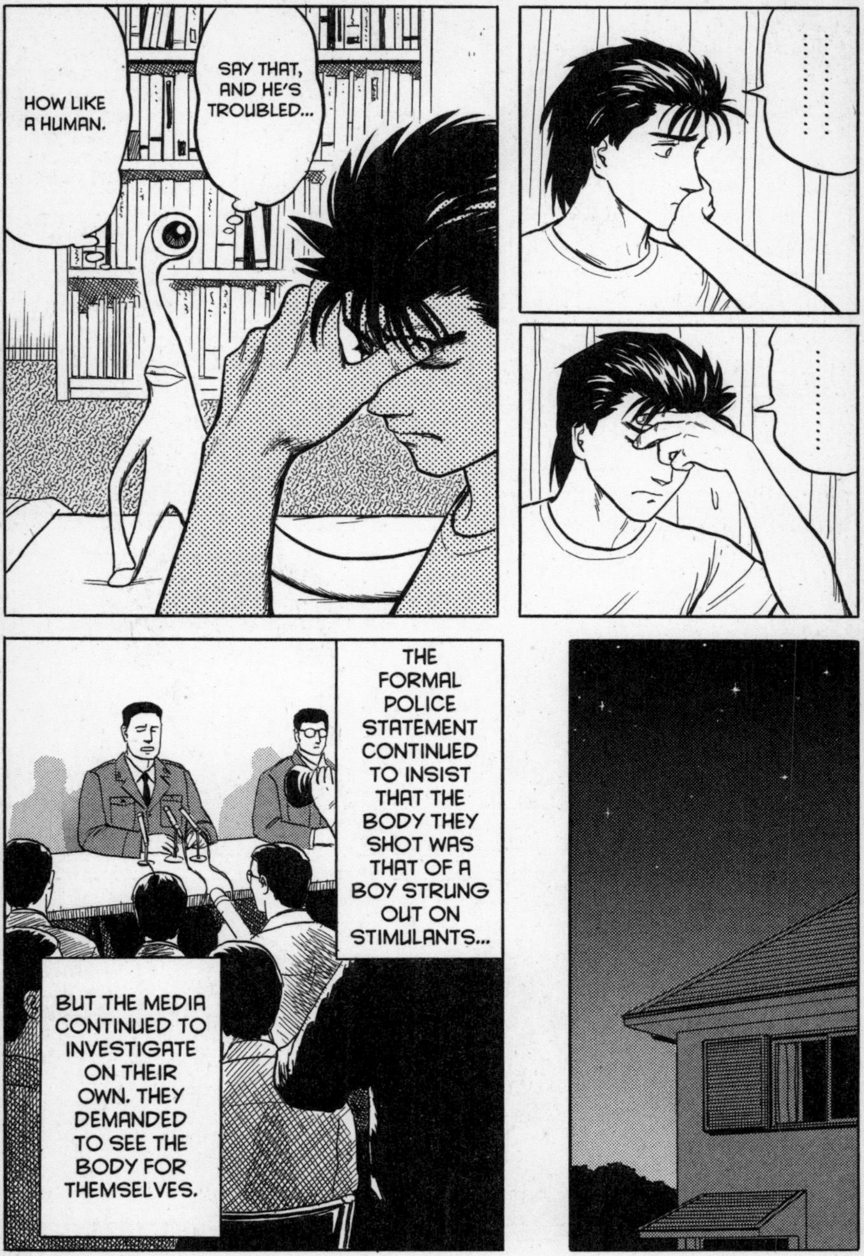

......
......
SAY THAT, AND HE'S TROUBLED...
HOW LIKE A HUMAN.
THE FORMAL POLICE STATEMENT CONTINUED TO INSIST THAT THE BODY THEY SHOT WAS THAT OF A BOY STRUNG OUT ON STIMULANTS...
BUT THE MEDIA CONTINUED TO INVESTIGATE ON THEIR OWN. THEY DEMANDED TO SEE THE BODY FOR THEMSELVES.

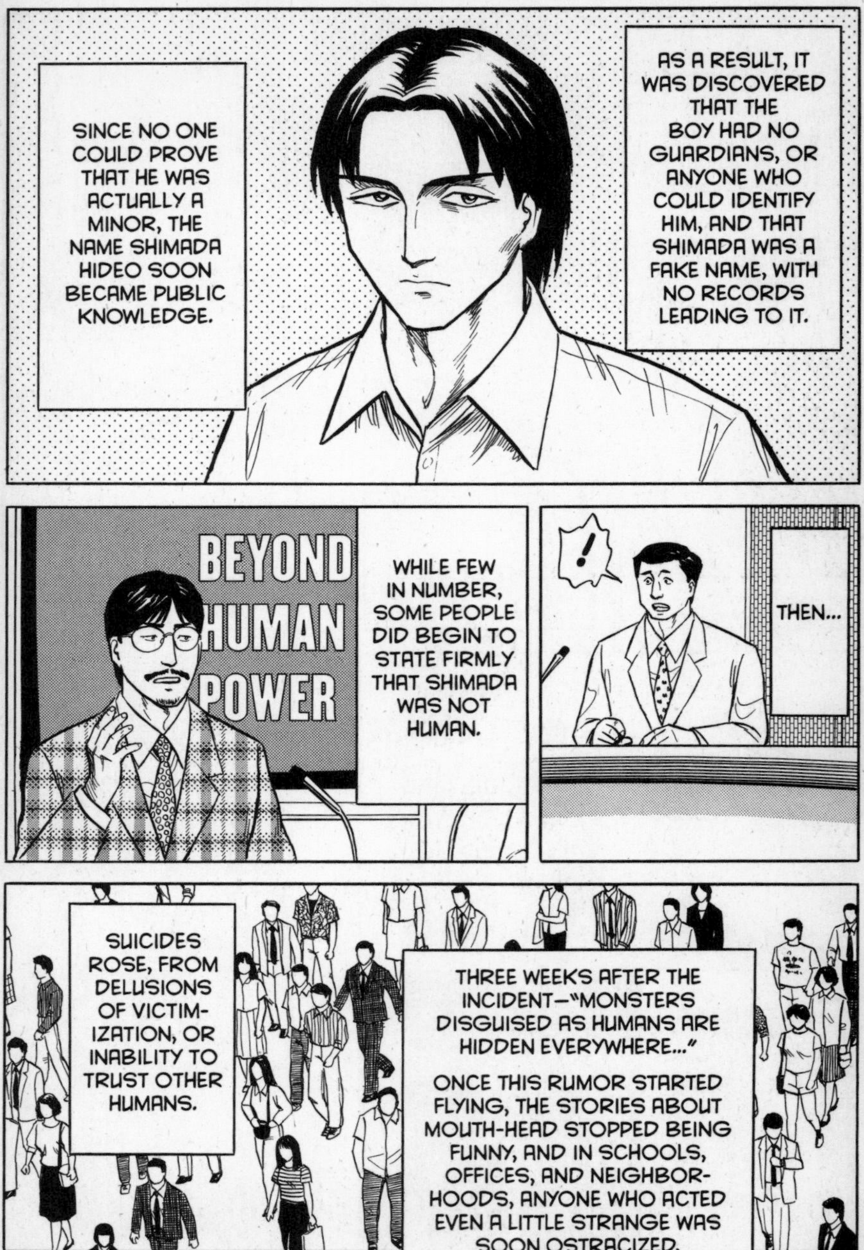
SINCE NO ONE COULD PROVE THAT HE WAS ACTUALLY A MINOR, THE NAME SHIMADA HIDEO SOON BECAME PUBLIC KNOWLEDGE.
AS A RESULT, IT WAS DISCOVERED THAT THE BOY HAD NO GUARDIANS, OR ANYONE WHO COULD IDENTIFY HIM, AND THAT SHIMADA WAS A FAKE NAME, WITH NO RECORDS LEADING TO IT.
BEYOND HUMAN POWER
WHILE FEW IN NUMBER, SOME PEOPLE DID BEGIN TO STATE FIRMLY THAT SHIMADA WAS NOT HUMAN.
!
THEN...
SUICIDES ROSE, FROM DELUSIONS OF VICTIM-IZATION, OR INABILITY TO TRUST OTHER HUMANS.
THREE WEEKS AFTER THE INCIDENT—"MONSTERS DISGUISED AS HUMANS ARE HIDDEN EVERYWHERE..."
ONCE THIS RUMOR STARTED FLYING, THE STORIES ABOUT MOUTH-HEAD STOPPED BEING FUNNY, AND IN SCHOOLS, OFFICES, AND NEIGHBOR-HOODS, ANYONE WHO ACTED EVEN A LITTLE STRANGE WAS SOON OSTRACIZED, OR BULLIED.

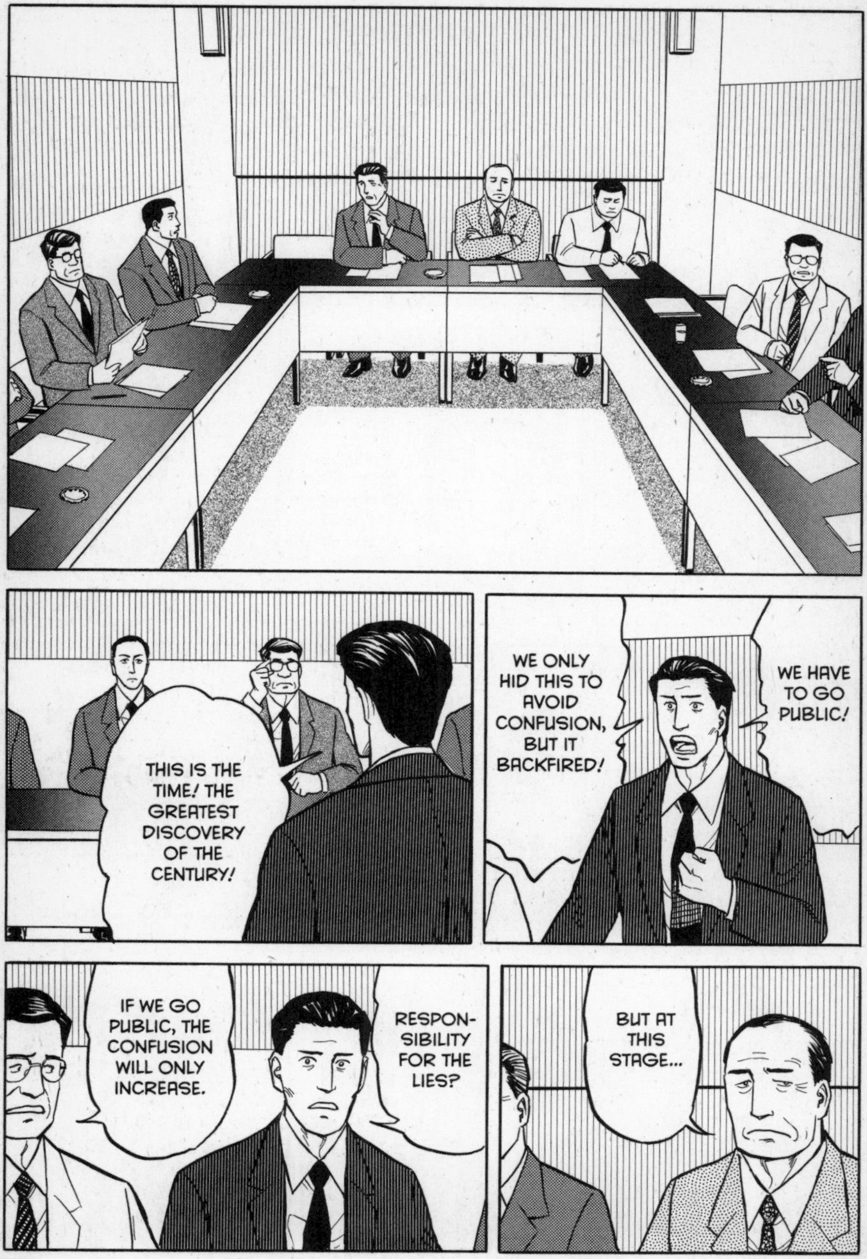
WE HAVE TO GO PUBLIC!
WE ONLY HID THIS TO AVOID CONFUSION, BUT IT BACKFIRED!
THIS IS THE TIME! THE GREATEST DISCOVERY OF THE CENTURY!
BUT AT THIS STAGE...
RESPON-SIBILITY FOR THE LIES?
IF WE GO PUBLIC, THE CONFUSION WILL ONLY INCREASE.

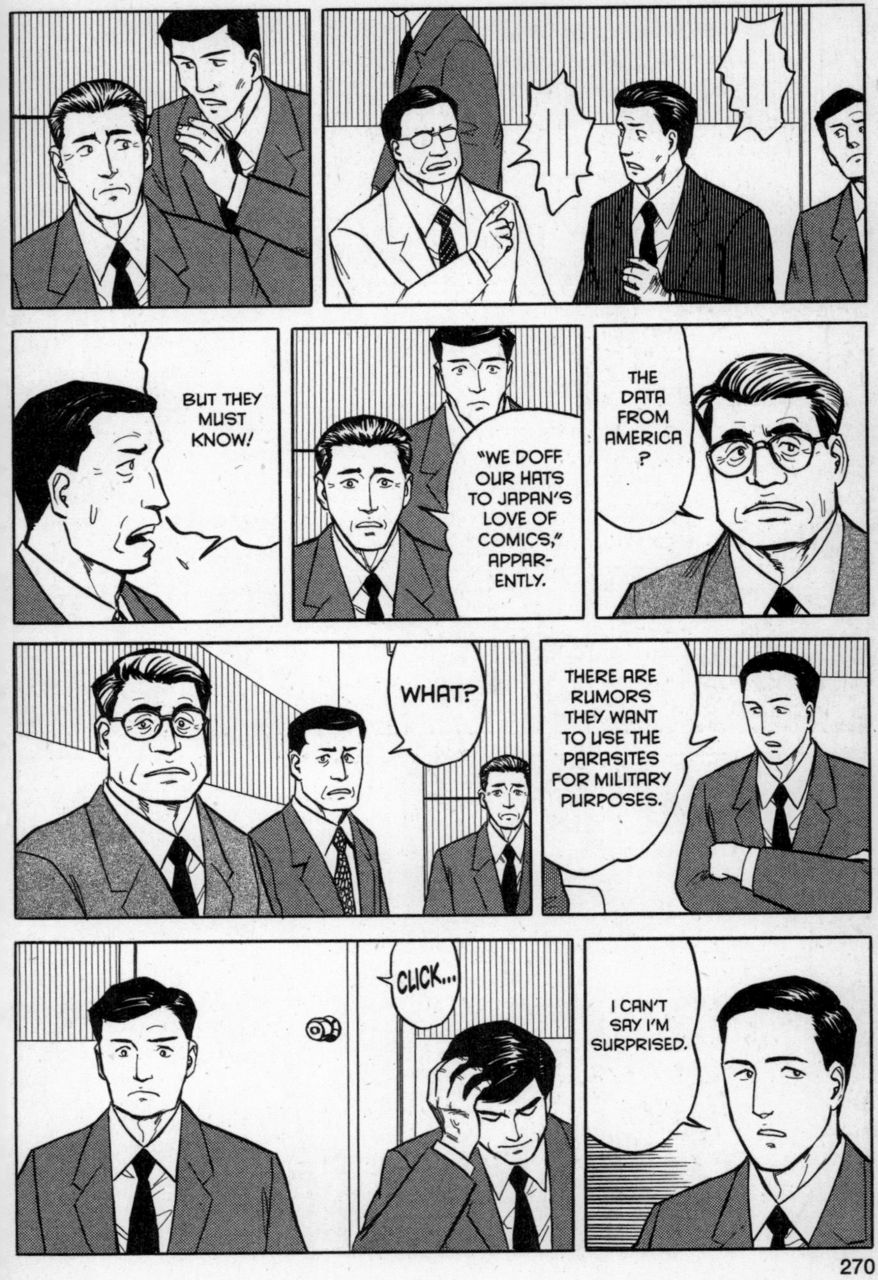
THE DATA FROM AMERICA?
"WE DOFF OUR HATS TO JAPAN'S LOVE OF COMICS," APPARENTLY.
BUT THEY MUST KNOW!
THERE ARE RUMORS THEY WANT TO USE THE PARASITES FOR MILITARY PURPOSES.
WHAT?
I CAN'T SAY I'M SURPRISED.
CLICK...

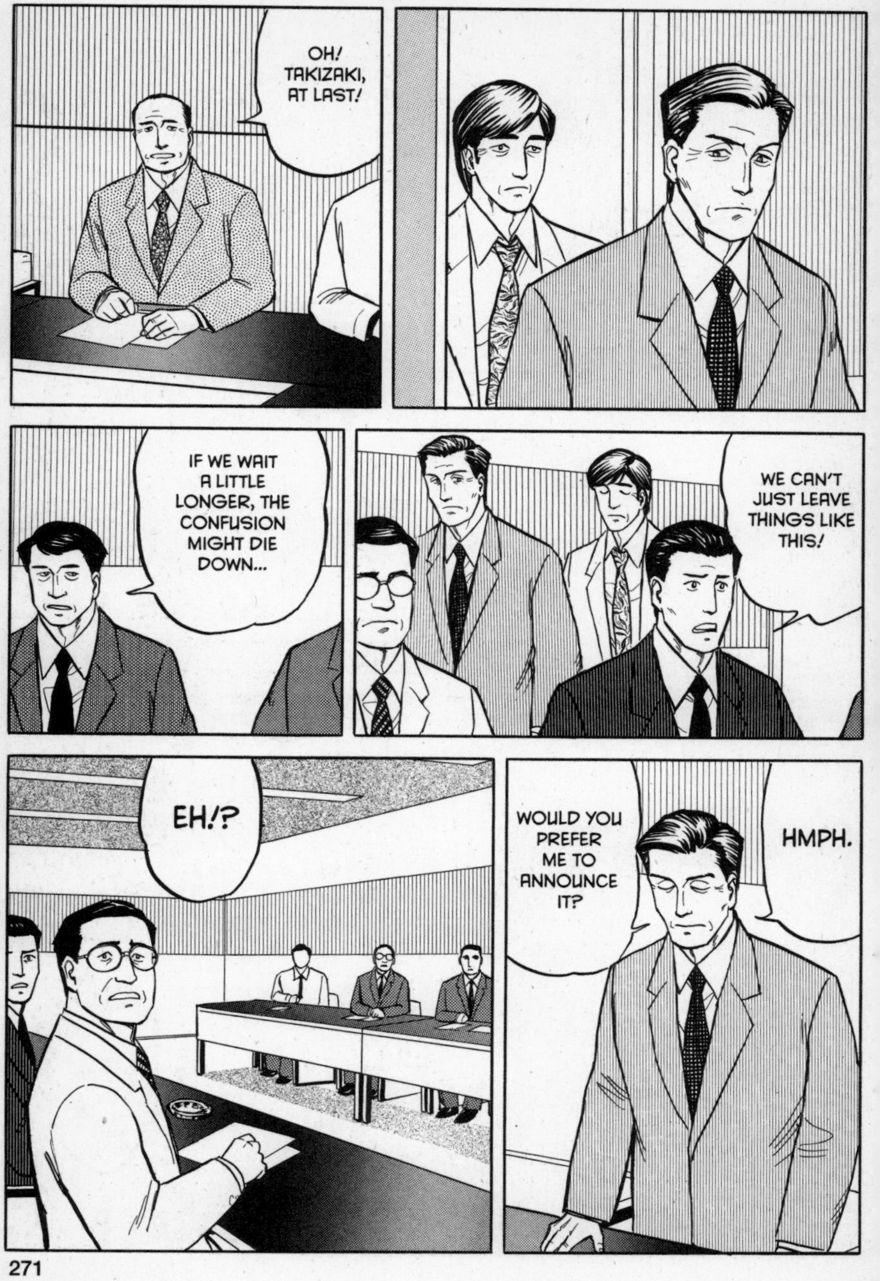
OH! TAKIZAKI, AT LAST!
WE CAN'T JUST LEAVE THINGS LIKE THIS!
IF WE WAIT A LITTLE LONGER, THE CONFUSION MIGHT DIE DOWN...
HMPH.
WOULD YOU PREFER ME TO ANNOUNCE IT?
EH!?

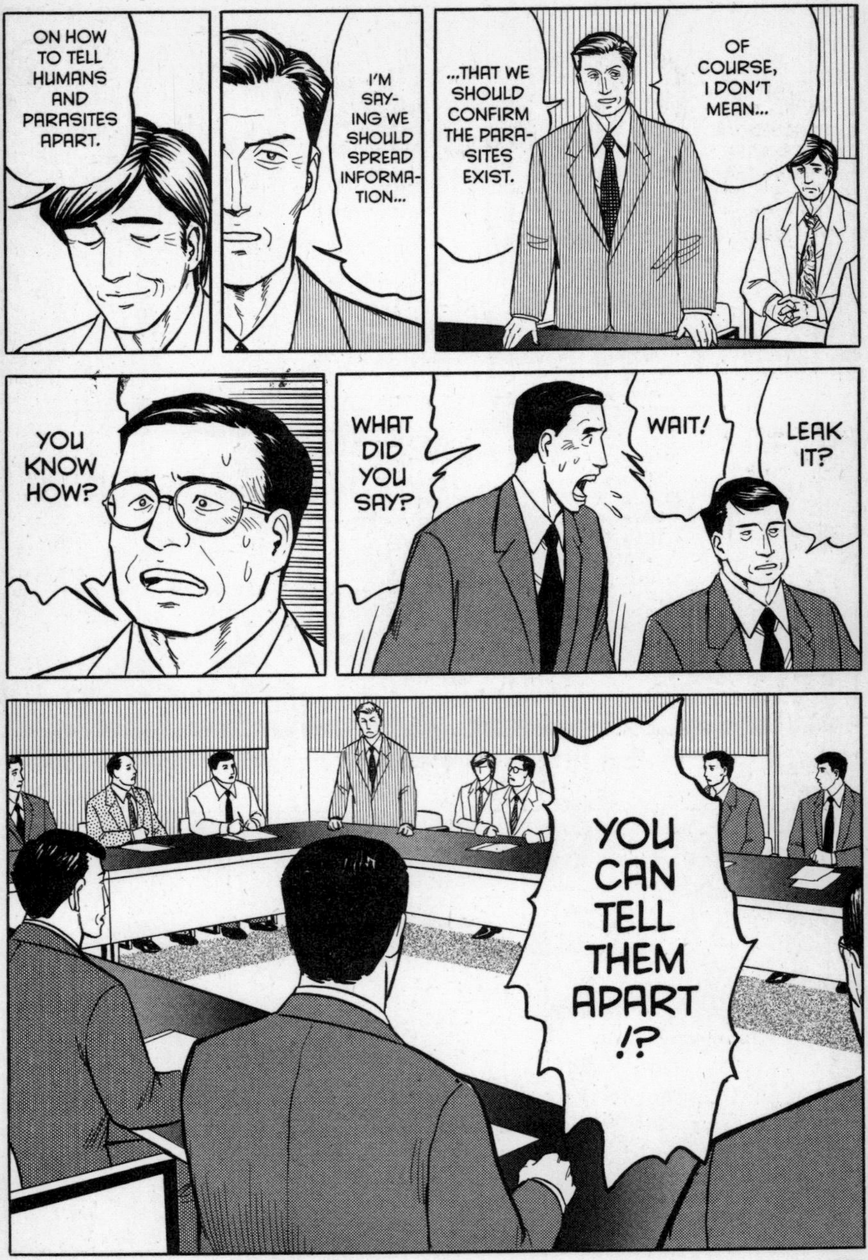
OF COURSE, I DON'T MEAN...
...THAT WE SHOULD CONFIRM THE PARASITES EXIST.
I'M SAYING WE SHOULD SPREAD INFORMATION...
ON HOW TO TELL HUMANS AND PARASITES APART.
LEAK IT?
WAIT!
WHAT DID YOU SAY?
YOU KNOW HOW?
YOU CAN TELL THEM APART!?

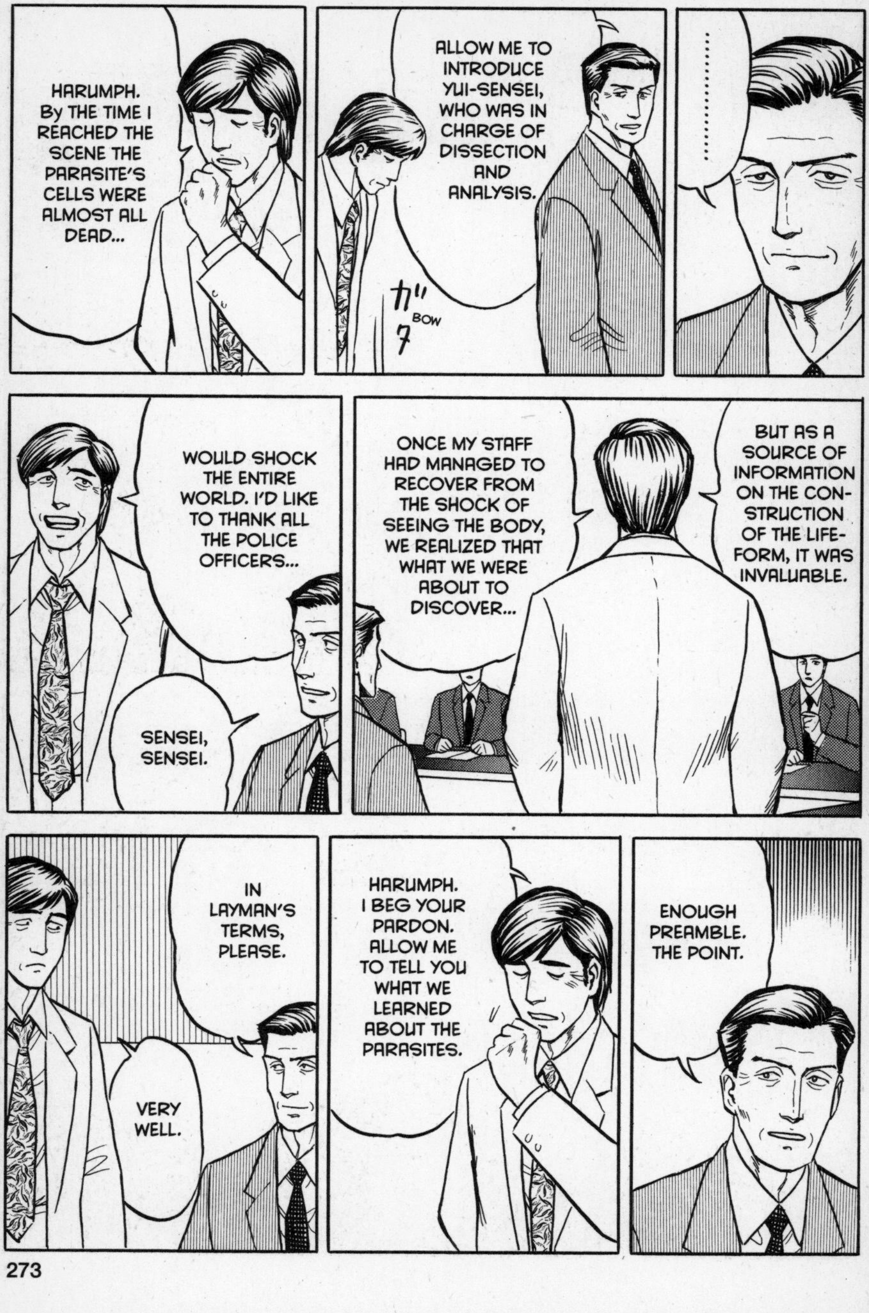
......
ALLOW ME TO INTRODUCE YUI-SENSEI, WHO WAS IN CHARGE OF DISSECTION AND ANALYSIS.
BOW
HARUMPH. By THE TIME I REACHED THE SCENE THE PARASITE'S CELLS WERE ALMOST ALL DEAD...
BUT AS A SOURCE OF INFORMATION ON THE CONSTRUCTION OF THE LIFE-FORM, IT WAS INVALUABLE.
ONCE MY STAFF HAD MANAGED TO RECOVER FROM THE SHOCK OF SEEING THE BODY, WE REALIZED THAT WHAT WE WERE ABOUT TO DISCOVER...
WOULD SHOCK THE ENTIRE WORLD. I'D LIKE TO THANK ALL THE POLICE OFFICERS...
SENSEI, SENSEI.
ENOUGH PREAMBLE. THE POINT.
HARUMPH. I BEG YOUR PARDON. ALLOW ME TO TELL YOU WHAT WE LEARNED ABOUT THE PARASITES.
IN LAYMAN'S TERMS, PLEASE.
VERY WELL.

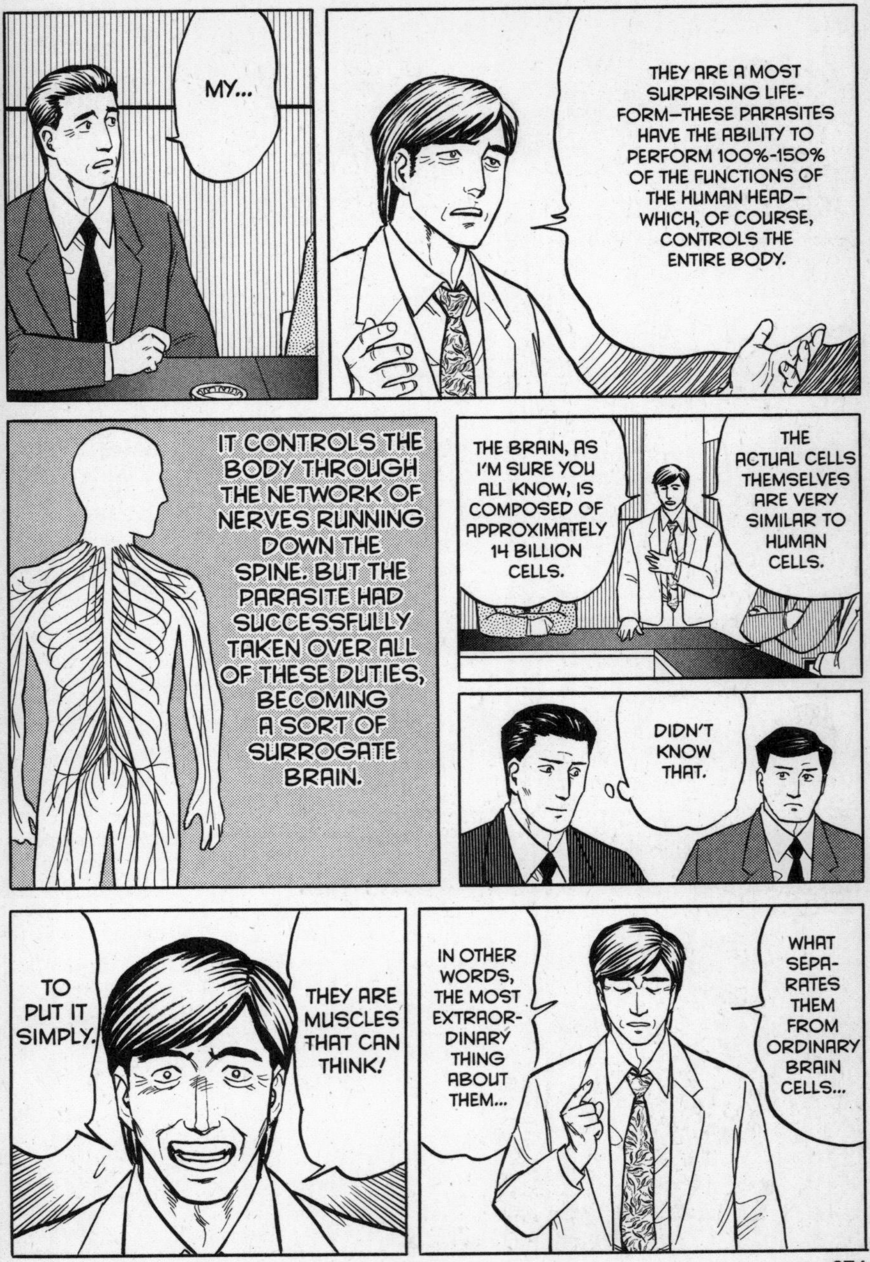
MY...
THEY ARE A MOST SURPRISING LIFE-FORM—THESE PARASITES HAVE THE ABILITY TO PERFORM 100%-150% OF THE FUNCTIONS OF THE HUMAN HEAD—WHICH, OF COURSE, CONTROLS THE ENTIRE BODY.
IT CONTROLS THE BODY THROUGH THE NETWORK OF NERVES RUNNING DOWN THE SPINE. BUT THE PARASITE HAD SUCCESSFULLY TAKEN OVER ALL OF THESE DUTIES, BECOMING A SORT OF SURROGATE BRAIN.
THE BRAIN, AS I'M SURE YOU ALL KNOW, IS COMPOSED OF APPROXIMATELY 14 BILLION CELLS.
THE ACTUAL CELLS THEMSELVES ARE VERY SIMILAR TO HUMAN CELLS.
DIDN'T KNOW THAT.
TO PUT IT SIMPLY.
THEY ARE MUSCLES THAT CAN THINK!
IN OTHER WORDS, THE MOST EXTRAORDINARY THING ABOUT THEM...
WHAT SEPARATES THEM FROM ORDINARY BRAIN CELLS...

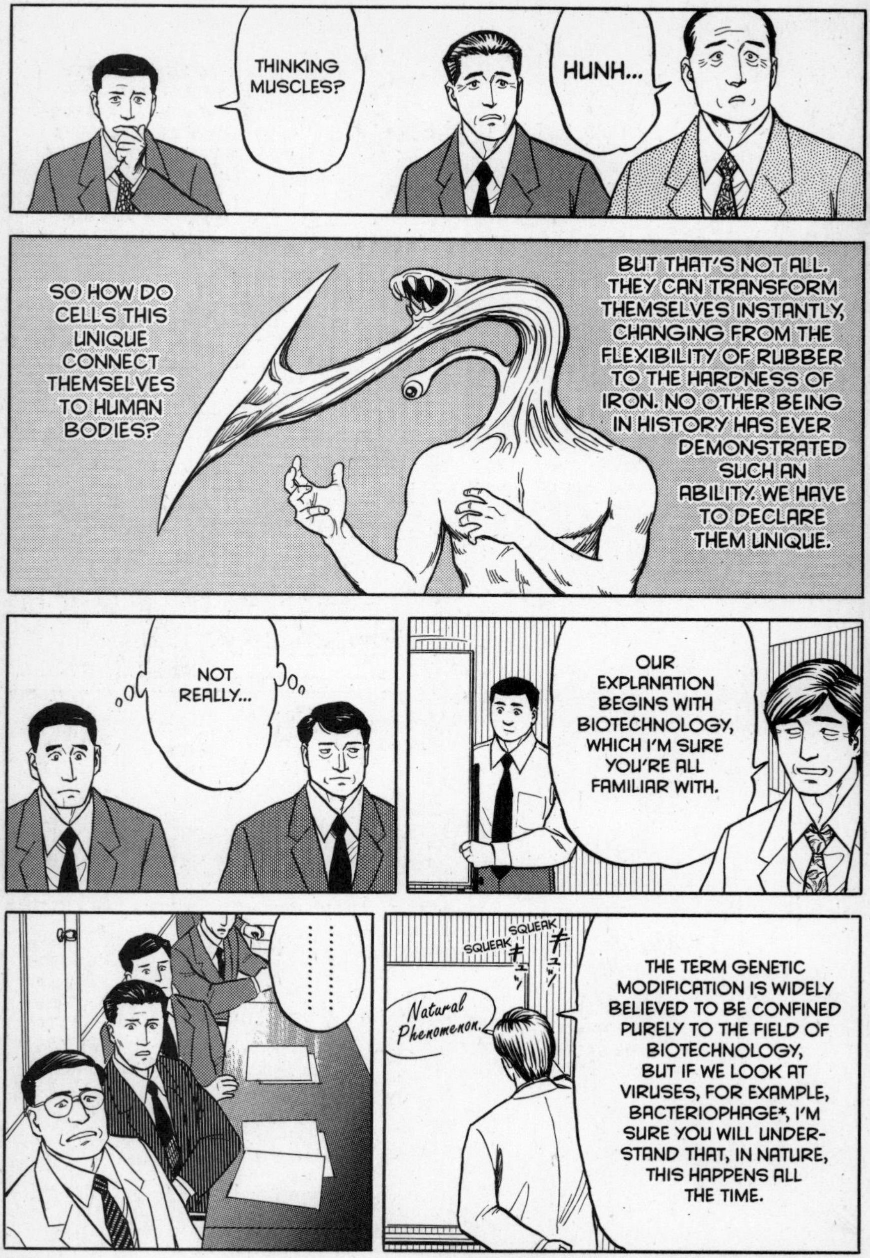
HUNH...
THINKING MUSCLES?
BUT THAT'S NOT ALL. THEY CAN TRANSFORM THEMSELVES INSTANTLY, CHANGING FROM THE FLEXIBILITY OF RUBBER TO THE HARDNESS OF IRON. NO OTHER BEING IN HISTORY HAS EVER DEMONSTRATED SUCH AN ABILITY. WE HAVE TO DECLARE THEM UNIQUE.
SO HOW DO CELLS THIS UNIQUE CONNECT THEMSELVES TO HUMAN BODIES?
OUR EXPLANATION BEGINS WITH BIOTECHNOLOGY, WHICH I'M SURE YOU'RE ALL FAMILIAR WITH.
NOT REALLY...
SQUEAK SQUEAK
Natural Phenomenon.
THE TERM GENETIC MODIFICATION IS WIDELY BELIEVED TO BE CONFINED PURELY TO THE FIELD OF BIOTECHNOLOGY, BUT IF WE LOOK AT VIRUSES, FOR EXAMPLE, BACTERIOPHAGE*, I'M SURE YOU WILL UNDERSTAND THAT, IN NATURE, THIS HAPPENS ALL THE TIME.
....

* BACTERIOPHAGE—A TYPE OF VIRUS THAT INFECTS BACTERIA, AND CAUSES THE CELLS TO DISSOLVE.

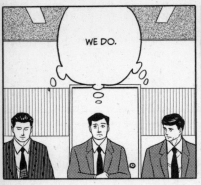

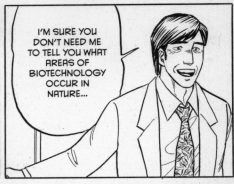

I'M SURE YOU DON'T NEED ME TO TELL YOU WHAT AREAS OF BIOTECHNOLOGY OCCUR IN NATURE...
WE DO.
BUT THIS CREATURE IS ONLY FOLLOWING ITS INSTINCTS, WHICH MAKES IT ALL THE MORE IMPRESSIVE.
I SUPPOSE THE EASIEST WAY TO DESCRIBE IT IS "CELL FUSION."
I KNOW! IT'S HARD TO BELIEVE!
INSTANTA-NEOUS CELL FUSION!
HMM...
UNH-HUNH...
SQUEAK
TO SIMPLIFY STILL FURTHER, THE CELL WALL CHANGES LIKE POLYETHYLENE-GLYCOL, BUT THE SPEED!
SENSEI... UM, SENSEI?
WE'LL HAVE TIME FOR THE DETAILS IN A MORE ACADEMIC VENUE. FOR NOW, HOW CAN WE IDENTIFY THE PARASITES?
OH! YES!

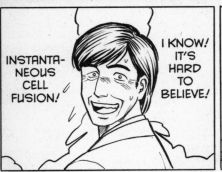

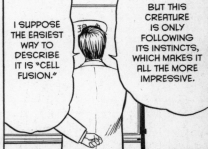

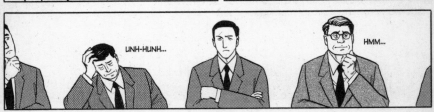

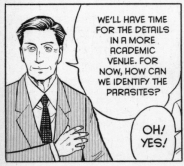

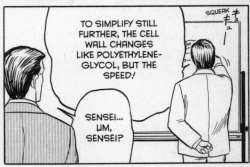

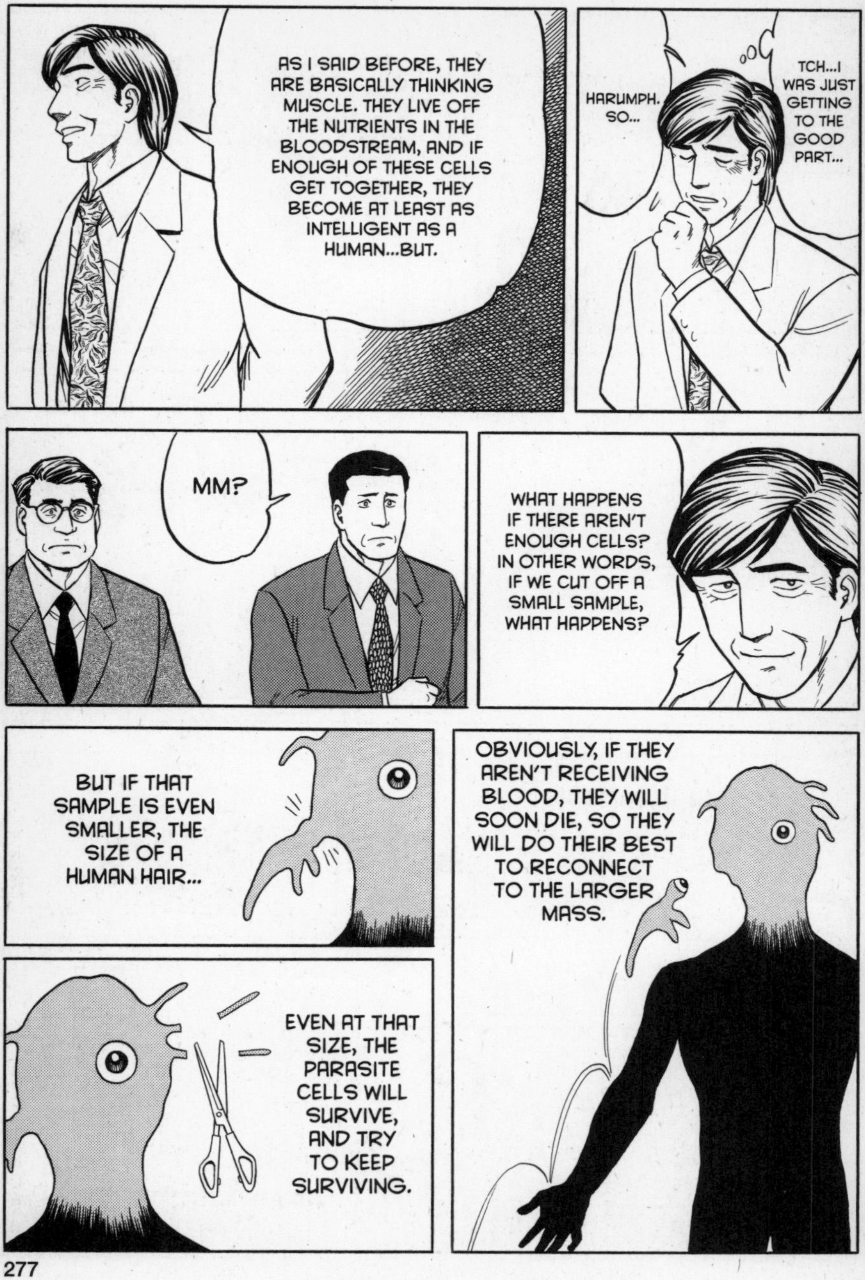
TCH...I WAS JUST GETTING TO THE GOOD PART...
HARUMPH. SO...
AS I SAID BEFORE, THEY ARE BASICALLY THINKING MUSCLE. THEY LIVE OFF THE NUTRIENTS IN THE BLOODSTREAM, AND IF ENOUGH OF THESE CELLS GET TOGETHER, THEY BECOME AT LEAST AS INTELLIGENT AS A HUMAN...BUT.
WHAT HAPPENS IF THERE AREN'T ENOUGH CELLS? IN OTHER WORDS, IF WE CUT OFF A SMALL SAMPLE, WHAT HAPPENS?
MM?
OBVIOUSLY, IF THEY AREN'T RECEIVING BLOOD, THEY WILL SOON DIE, SO THEY WILL DO THEIR BEST TO RECONNECT TO THE LARGER MASS.
BUT IF THAT SAMPLE IS EVEN SMALLER, THE SIZE OF A HUMAN HAIR...
EVEN AT THAT SIZE, THE PARASITE CELLS WILL SURVIVE, AND TRY TO KEEP SURVIVING.

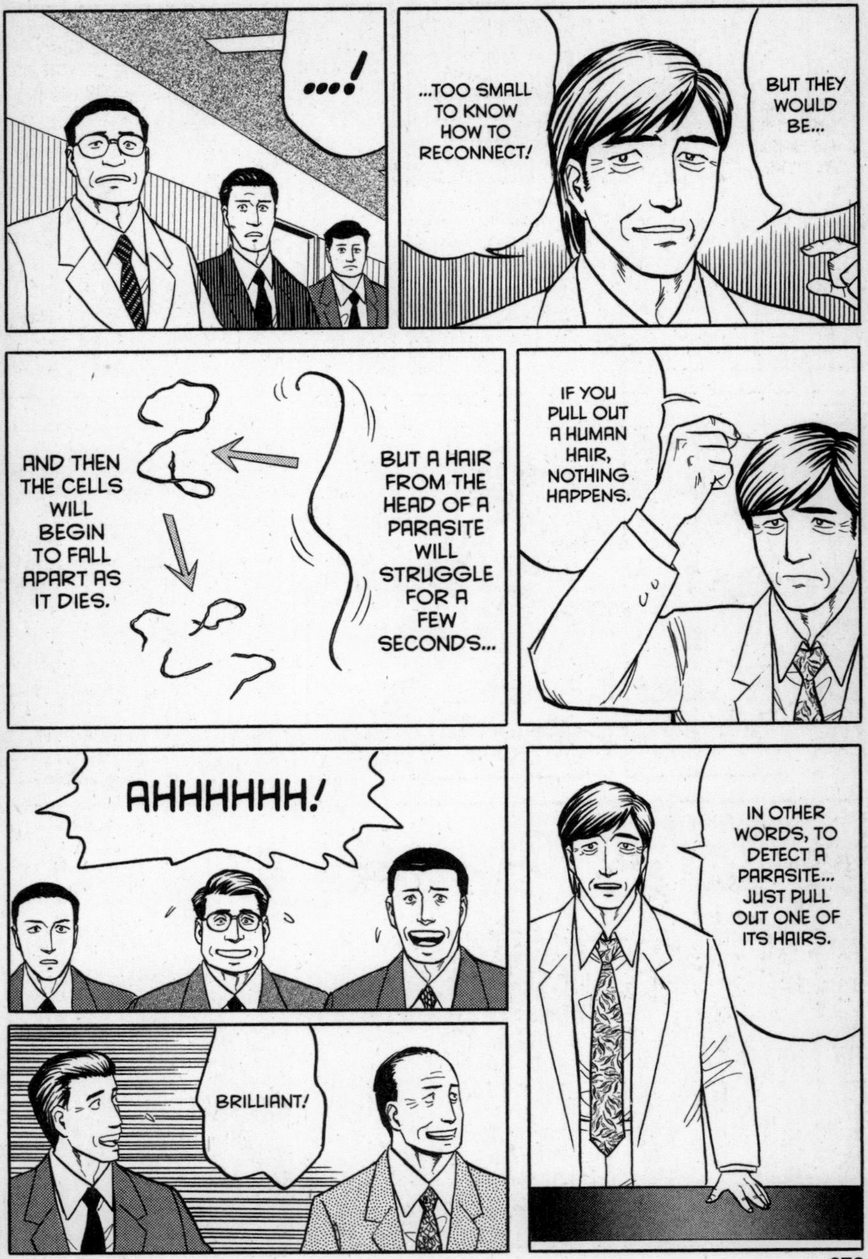
BUT THEY WOULD BE...
...TOO SMALL TO KNOW HOW TO RECONNECT!
...!
IF YOU PULL OUT A HUMAN HAIR, NOTHING HAPPENS.
BUT A HAIR FROM THE HEAD OF A PARASITE WILL STRUGGLE FOR A FEW SECONDS...
AND THEN THE CELLS WILL BEGIN TO FALL APART AS IT DIES.
IN OTHER WORDS, TO DETECT A PARASITE... JUST PULL OUT ONE OF ITS HAIRS.
AHHHHHH!
BRILLIANT!

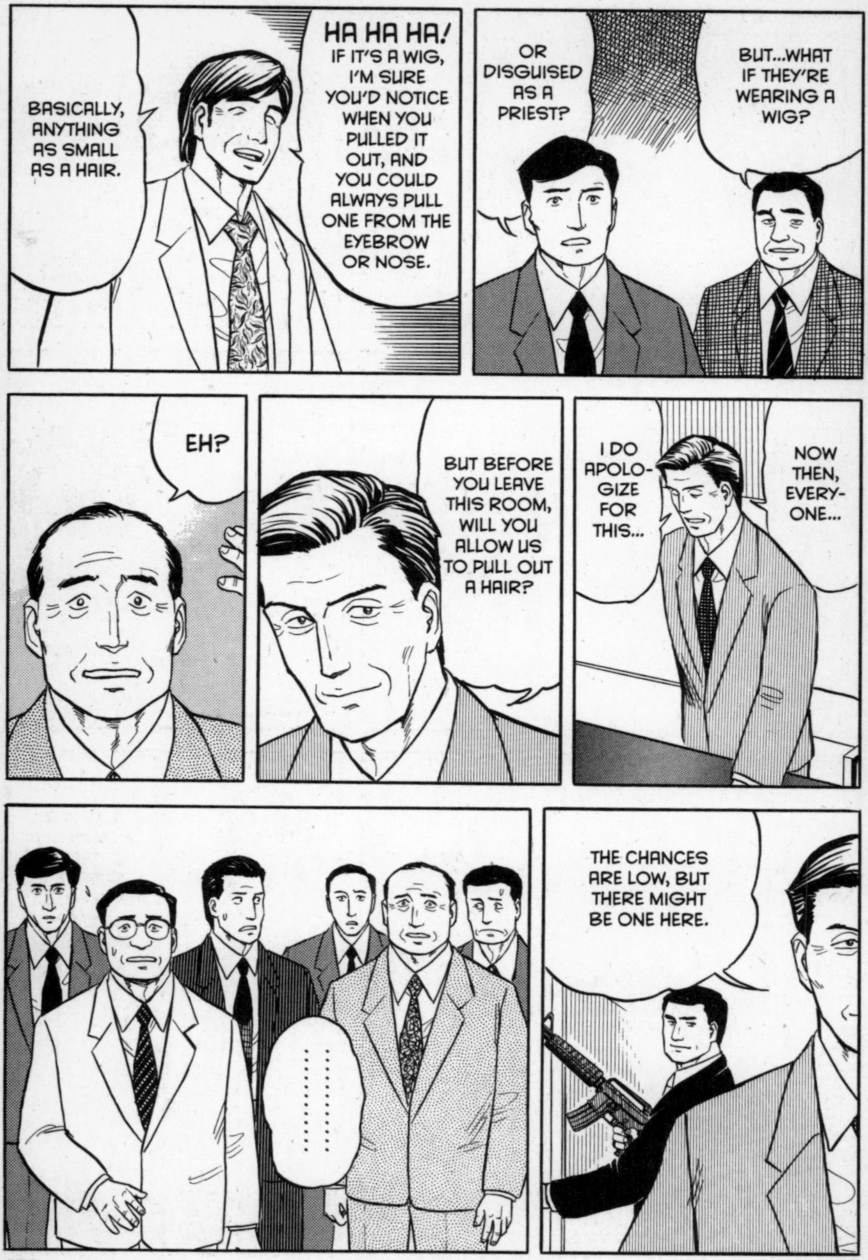

BUT...WHAT IF THEY'RE WEARING A WIG?
OR DISGUISED AS A PRIEST?
HA HA HA! IF IT'S A WIG, I'M SURE YOU'D NOTICE WHEN YOU PULLED IT OUT, AND YOU COULD ALWAYS PULL ONE FROM THE EYEBROW OR NOSE.
BASICALLY, ANYTHING AS SMALL AS A HAIR.
NOW THEN, EVERY-ONE...
I DO APOLO-GIZE FOR THIS...
BUT BEFORE YOU LEAVE THIS ROOM, WILL YOU ALLOW US TO PULL OUT A HAIR?
EH?
THE CHANCES ARE LOW, BUT THERE MIGHT BE ONE HERE.
......

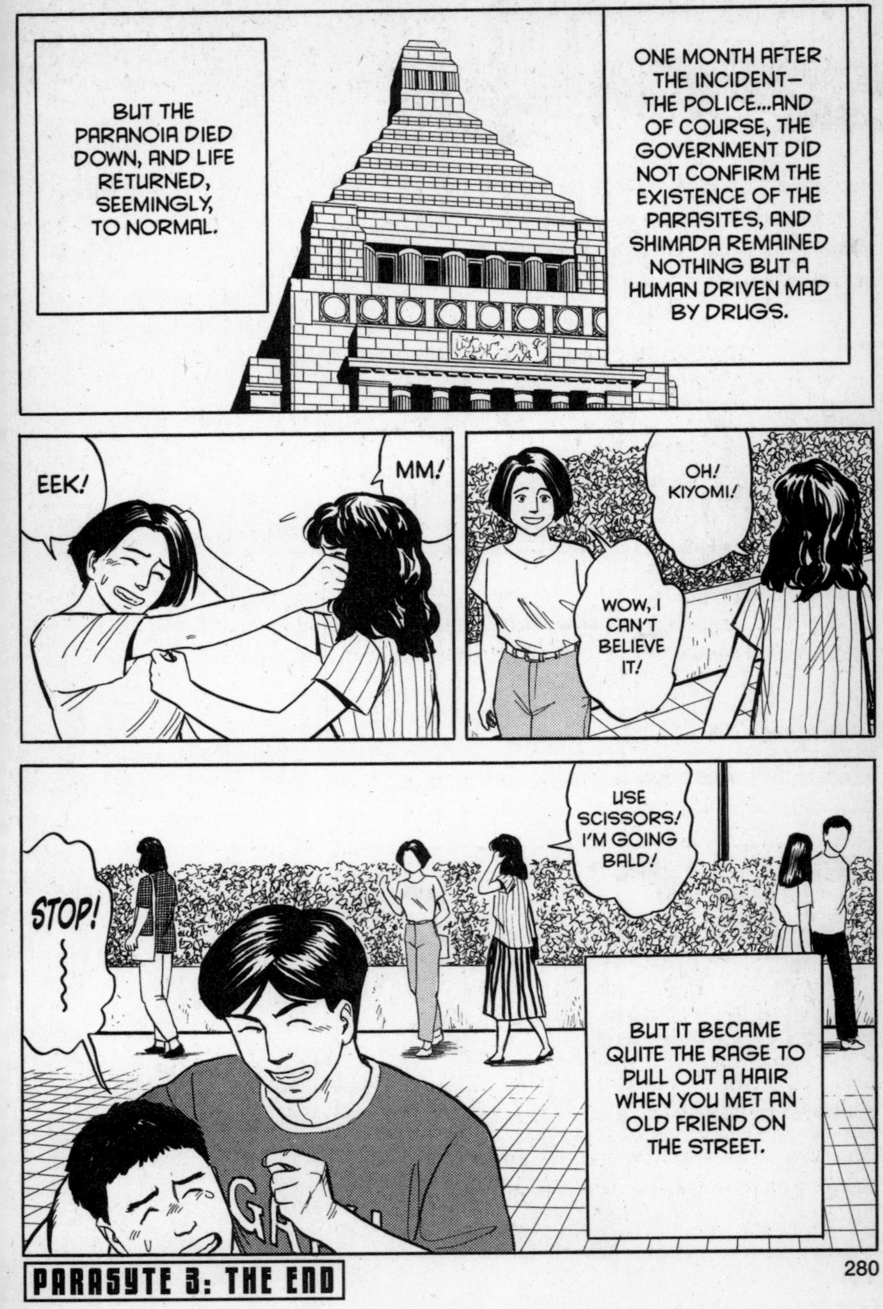
ONE MONTH AFTER THE INCIDENT— THE POLICE...AND OF COURSE, THE GOVERNMENT DID NOT CONFIRM THE EXISTENCE OF THE PARASITES, AND SHIMADA REMAINED NOTHING BUT A HUMAN DRIVEN MAD BY DRUGS.
BUT THE PARANOIA DIED DOWN, AND LIFE RETURNED, SEEMINGLY, TO NORMAL.
OH! KIYOMI!
WOW, I CAN'T BELIEVE IT!
MM!
EEK!
USE SCISSORS! I'M GOING BALD!
BUT IT BECAME QUITE THE RAGE TO PULL OUT A HAIR WHEN YOU MET AN OLD FRIEND ON THE STREET.
STOP!

TRANSLATION NOTES

Japanese is a tricky language for most Westerners, and translation is often more an art than a science. For your edification and reading pleasure, here are notes on some of the places where we could have gone in a different direction or where a Japanese cultural reference is used.

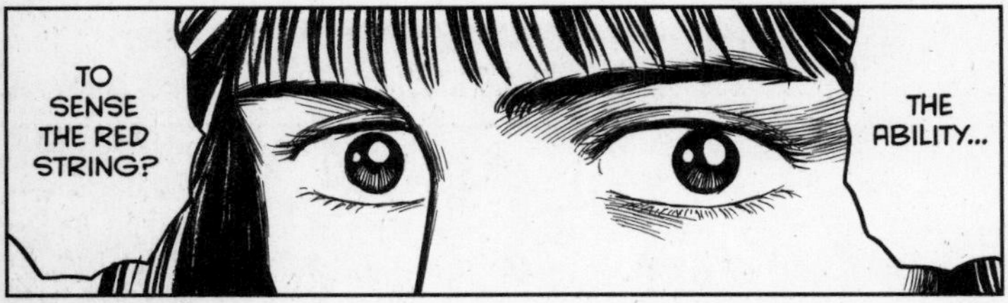
THE ABILITY...
TO SENSE THE RED STRING?

Red string, page 56

A popular superstition in Japan states that those who are destined to become lovers are connected to each other by a red string tied to their pinkies.

Signs, page 75

Kizashi can means signs, omens, or symptoms.

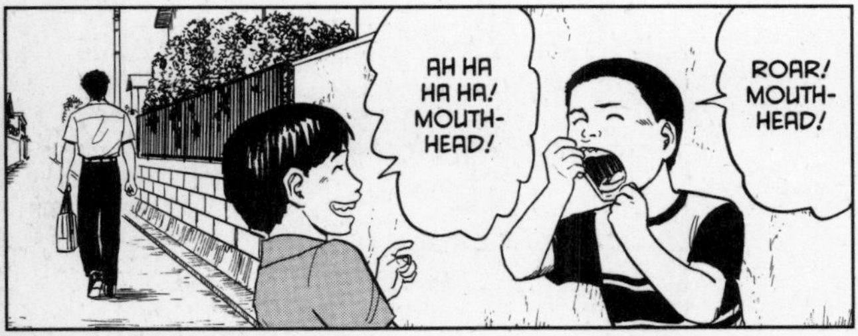
ROAR! MOUTH-HEAD!
AH HA HA HA! MOUTH-HEAD!

Mouth-head, page 83

The literal Japanese name is *kuchi dake atama*, or “only mouth head” implying that the head consists only of a giant mouth.

Split-Mouth Woman and Man-Faced Dog, page 90

Both of these are famous urban legends in Japan. Split-Mouth Woman, or *kuchi sake onna*, has a mouth that goes all the way to her ears. Except according to Wikipedia it was actually in 1979 that she was first spotted. A woman wearing a mask asks strangers if she is beautiful. If they say "No," she kills them on the spot, if they say "Yes," she follows them home and kills them there. But if they say "Average" or "Okay," they won't be killed. The legend caused quite a panic at the time and cropped up again in 2000, and in Korea in 2004. Man-Faced Dog is not nearly as interesting; the rumors went around and died down, and there appear to be many different possible sources. But these were both well-known horror stories spread mainly among children and picked up by the mass media once the stories had reached fever pitch.

TV show, page 90

This show is a "wideshow," following a format that is very, very common in Japan. A group of minor celebrities sit around discussing topics of the day, intercut with overwrought videos.

Youkai, page 92

Unlike the other creatures mentioned on this show, *youkai* are from traditional Japanese folklore.

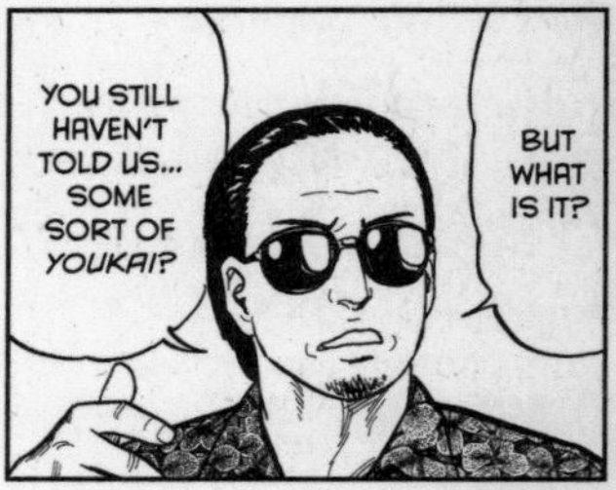
BUT WHAT IS IT?
YOU STILL HAVEN'T TOLD US... SOME SORT OF *YOUKAI*?

Sesame Street, page 93

Sesame Street actually airs in Japan. This translation did not change the reference.

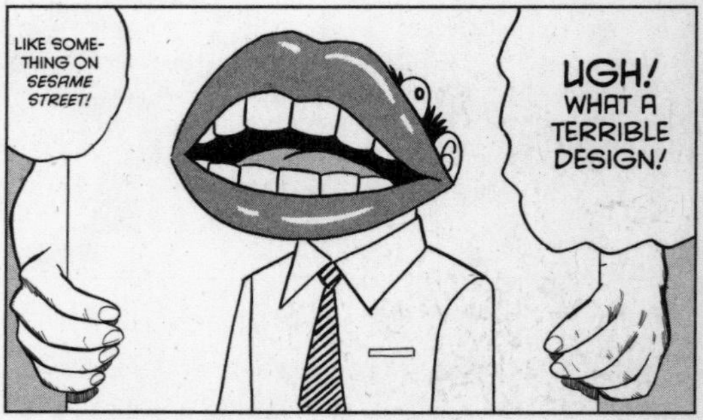
UGH! WHAT A TERRIBLE DESIGN!
LIKE SOME-THING ON *SESAME STREET!*

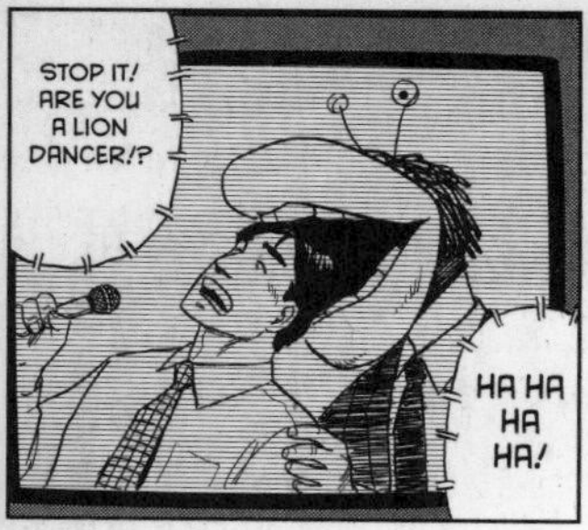
HA HA
HA
HA!
STOP IT!
ARE YOU
A LION
DANCER!?

Lion dance, page 136

The Chinese lion dance may be more famous, but the tradition spread to Japan and evolved in its own direction. Like the lion dance early in Miike's *The Great Youkai War*, the dance often ends with the dragon biting someone's head.

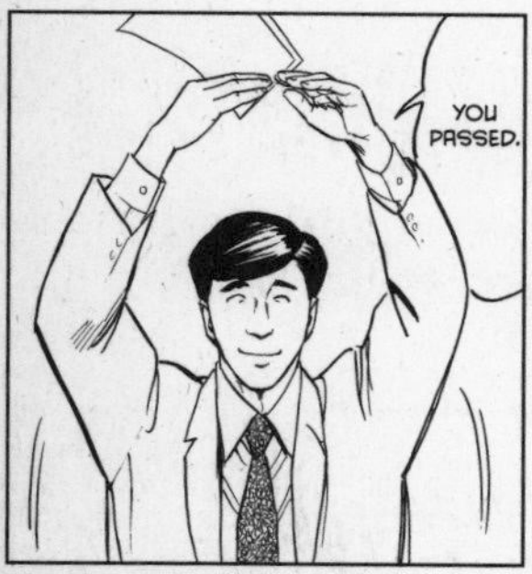
YOU
PASSED.

Pass, page 144

Obviously, this refers to his high school entrance exams. Why does the teacher have his arms in a circle? The circle is often used for yes, while an X is used for no.

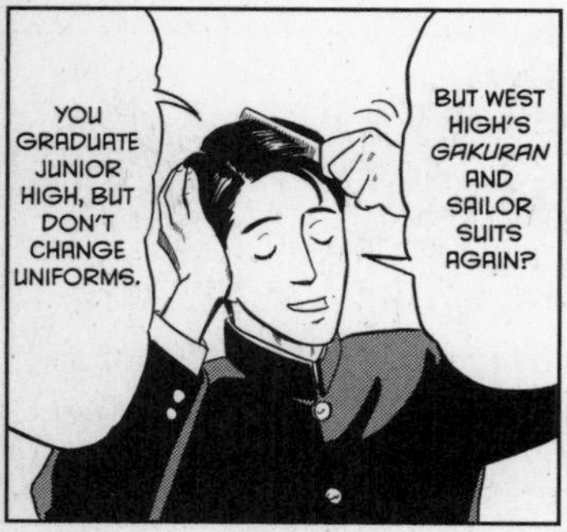
BUT WEST
HIGH'S
GAKURAN
AND
SAILOR
SUITS
AGAIN?
YOU
GRADUATE
JUNIOR
HIGH, BUT
DON'T
CHANGE
UNIFORMS.

Gakuran, page 145

Gakuran is the term for the style of the boys' uniforms, with the choke clasp at the neck.

TOMARE!

STOP

YOU'RE GOING THE WRONG WAY!

MANGA IS A COMPLETELY DIFFERENT TYPE OF READING EXPERIENCE.

TO START AT THE *BEGINNING*, GO TO THE *END*!

THAT'S RIGHT!

AUTHENTIC MANGA IS READ THE TRADITIONAL JAPANESE WAY—FROM RIGHT TO LEFT, EXACTLY THE *OPPOSITE* OF HOW AMERICAN BOOKS ARE READ. IT'S EASY TO FOLLOW: JUST GO TO THE OTHER END OF THE BOOK, AND READ EACH PAGE—AND EACH PANEL—FROM RIGHT SIDE TO LEFT SIDE, STARTING AT THE TOP RIGHT. NOW YOU'RE EXPERIENCING MANGA AS IT WAS MEANT TO BE.